OTHER BOOKS BY CRAIG CLAIBORNE

THE BEST OF
CRAIG CLAIBORNE

THE BEST OF
CRAIG CLAIBORNE

BASED ON <u>THE</u> NEW <u>NEW YORK TIMES</u> COOKBOOK

1,000 RECIPES FROM
HIS <u>NEW YORK TIMES</u> FOOD COLUMNS
AND FOUR OF HIS CLASSIC COOKBOOKS

CRAIG CLAIBORNE WITH PIERRE FRANEY

EDITED BY JOAN WHITMAN
INTRODUCTION BY PAUL PRUDHOMME
ILLUSTRATIONS BY ED LAM

TIMES T BOOKS

RANDOM HOUSE

Library of Congress Cataloging-in-Publication Data

Claiborne, Craig.
    The best of Craig Claiborne / by Craig Claiborne. — 1st ed.
         p.   cm.
    Based on his The New New York Times Cookbook.
    Includes index.
    ISBN 0-8129-3089-4
    1. Cookery, International. 2. Cookery, American. I. Claiborne,
Craig. Craig Claiborne's new New York times cookbook. II. Title.
III. Title: Best of.
TX725.A1C5582   1999
    641.59—dc21   99-12087
                                                                        CIP

Random House website address: www.atrandom.com

Art direction by Naomi Osnos

Book design by Maura Fadden Rosenthal/M-space

Printed in the United States of America on acid-free paper

9 8 7 6 5 4 3 2

First Edition

FOR PIERRE FRANEY

FOREWORD

The best of Craig Claiborne is the best, indeed.

From the late 1950s through the late eighties, as food editor of *The New York Times,* Craig changed and shaped the way we thought about food and led us to an appreciation of cuisines of all nations.

With the late Pierre Franey, former chef of the acclaimed Pavillon restaurant in New York, he introduced us to the best chefs in America and Europe, as well as to accomplished amateur cooks who went on to become best-selling cookbook authors.

In his kitchen in East Hampton, New York, Craig interviewed the chefs, helped them prepare their celebrated dishes, and took copious notes. He and Pierre (we know them by their first names) then reproduced these dishes for home cooks, as they did with many of those they had enjoyed in restaurants. They also developed hundreds of their own recipes, using seasonal ingredients.

As they shared them with their readers, we developed more sophisticated tastes and joined in their celebration of fine dining and just plain good food.

The one thousand recipes in this collection reflect the great diversity of Craig's interests—from the ethereal coulibiac of salmon to an equally delicious but more down-to-earth tapioca pudding, from many-flavored eggplant to chili con carne with cubed meat.

Join in the celebration and add to your repertoire, because these foolproof recipes will become your best, too.

—Joan Whitman

INTRODUCTION

What an honor it is to be asked to provide the introduction to Craig Claiborne's latest cookbook, for it's a small way of repaying the incalculable debt I owe him. I honestly believe that neither my career, nor for that matter the recent history of American food, would have occurred without three people: James Beard, Julia Child, and Craig Claiborne.

These three had a tremendous influence on the development of great cooking and the appreciation of fine food in this country. Craig's contribution has been enormous, for through his columns and books, often in collaboration with his great partner Pierre Franey, he's placed these concepts before the vast public not involved in the food business. Of course fine food had been enjoyed for centuries—royalty and the mega-rich often employed specialty chefs who brought fame to the castles' kitchens for the richness and variety of their dishes—but it seems to me it was in the middle years of this century that the widespread interest in great food, the passion for taste, really took off.

And I firmly believe that Craig's work is one of the reasons for this phenomenon. He's worked tirelessly to transcribe recipes from the world's master chefs, he's written intelligently and enthusiastically about food, and he's most generously encouraged the careers of cooks he admired. I am humble yet proud to say that I was one of those lucky ones, for not only has Craig been a great influence on my work, but he very kindly wrote about me and my cooking. His confidence and support have added immeasurably to my determination to achieve in this field, and his sending literally thousands of customers to my restaurant almost guaranteed its success.

I mentioned Craig's ardor for great food. I remember one particular article of his, which made news internationally, about a wonderful dinner he had in Paris, where the main course was comprised of an exquisite bird of some kind, and from his impassioned account of the meal I could almost savor the aroma and flavors. I shouldn't have been surprised, and wouldn't have been perhaps, had I been a little more sophisticated, but I remember being thoroughly amazed to discover that we Louisianians are not the only people who go crazy over food! That was a very important revelation for me.

One thing that greatly impressed me about Craig, especially in later years as he has gotten older and travel became difficult for him, is the fact that he continued to participate in food events. He was always generous with his time and effort for the sake of charitable organizations and advancing the profession.

He was generous in other ways as well. Until 1997, my restaurant,

K-Paul's Louisiana Kitchen, was almost like a rural Louisiana road-house, with great food and simple surroundings, because that's exactly the way K, my late wife, and I wanted it to be, so the food and service would be the center of attention. Craig must have misunderstood our mission, though, for during a phone call in which he told me that some friends had eaten there and raved about the food and service, I realized that the conversation was going in a different direction from our usual exchanges. He asked about how we were doing at the restaurant and, without being intrusive, inquired about our finances. What he ended up saying was "If you don't have enough money to renovate the restaurant, I'll lend you some!" I can only hope that I managed to say something appropriate, because I was almost speechless from amazement at his kindness.

Over the decades of his career, Craig has helped a lot of people. He is known for his knowledge of the food business, his caring for and generosity to its practitioners, his devotion to top quality, and his warmth, sincerity, and character. So when I say "Thank you" to Craig, I really mean "Thank you, Craig, for all you've done for American cooking."

I hope everyone will enjoy these recipes *The New York Times* has collected for you. I only got one more thing to say, and that's

Good cooking,

Good eating,

Good loving!

We love you guys!

—Paul Prudhomme,
July 1999

PREFACE

If one of the major attributes of this book is a considerable diversity in flavor and taste—and it is most assuredly international in scope—it is due to an incalculable extent to a peculiar fact of geography. It could not have happened anywhere in the world other than New York. It is not chauvinistic to say that where food is concerned, New York is and has been for more than a century the focal point of the globe. That is not to say that Paris does not have a greater wealth in the world's restaurants, for that it does.

But New York offers the broadest possible ethnic diversity, and it is preeminent as a gastronomic crossroad. A few years ago the great chefs of France and the world discovered that an occasional visit to New York would enhance their reputations. Some of them came for a day or a week en route to cooking demonstrations or other engagements in California, China, and Japan.

It has been my great good fortune that many of them were generous enough to drive out to Long Island, where they shared with readers of *The New York Times* their "secrets," the dishes for which they were much praised in the confines of their own kitchens and restaurants— Paul Bocuse of Lyons, Alain Chapel of Mionnay, Jean Troisgros of Roanne, Gaston Lenotre of Paris, and many others. During their stays in my home, they produced such dishes as an elaborately good mousse of chicken livers, an extraordinary salad with greens and herbs and quickly sautéed chicken breasts, delectable desserts, pâtés, terrines, main courses by the hundreds.

At other times, the finest chefs of New York have come into my home to pass a few hours, a day, or an evening confecting their most desirable creations that have titillated the public palate over the years. One of the most agreeable reminiscences of my life, in fact, was an interview that occured one February day. Seppi Renggli, the celebrated chef of New York's Four Seasons restaurant, was scheduled to come to prepare a several-course dinner for the vicarious delectation and delight of those who read *The New York Times* food columns.

Seppi, handsome, soft-spoken, and dedicated, had arisen in his New Jersey home at 5 A.M. to reach my house at an appointed hour. He had stopped by his restaurant to obtain a few supplies and by the time his car turned into my driveway, snowflakes were coming down with a vengence. A veritable tempest had been building and an hour or so after his arrival, the radio announced that the expressway back to New York was closed. So were all other highways. The power in my home failed and Seppi proceeded to cook (the gas stove worked) by lamp and candlelight an unforgettable dinner for eight. Meanwhile, my roadway had become impassable because of the snowfall. Thus the two of us sat before a roaring fire, sipping a fine Bordeaux, raising a glass now and then to toast our absent friends.

In addition to the great chefs, there are included here the recipes of scores of great, lesser sung, amateur chefs, many of them from foreign shores: Thailand, Japan, China, and so on. There are classic and traditional dishes that have been adapted in the most authentic manner possible to the resources of America.

Finally, and most important, are the immeasurable contributions of the late Pierre Franey. Pierre and I worked together for more than twenty years. He was for many years chef of Le Pavillon when it was considered, almost without challenge, the greatest French restaurant in America. We worked side by side day after day and often on weekends to provide the readers of *The Times* food columns with the greatest assortment, the most varied collection of recipes that it has been within our power to produce. It is certainly not all foie gras and truffles. There is an abundance of recipes that use leftovers, ground meats, stuffed vegetables, and many of the less expensive viands.

Thus this volume is a compilation of the best recipes that have appeared in *The New York Times* food pages—Sunday and daily. They include the contributions from hundreds of interviews with fine cooks and chefs, plus the recipes that were developed by Pierre Franey and myself.

CONTENTS

APPETIZERS   1

Dips for crudités or pita; caviar; hot vegetable first courses; fish and shellfish, from baked clams to sushi; Chinese dim sum; pâtés.

EGGS AND LUNCHEON DISHES   51

From a basic omelet to individual corn and salmon soufflés, as well as old-fashioned stuffed eggs; quiches and more substantial vegetable and meat pies; filled crêpes and cream puffs; pizza and tacos.

SOUPS   105

Cold and hot chicken, vegetable, fish, and meat soups; hearty bean soups; main-course chowders.

POULTRY   169

Roast and sautéed chicken, with recipes from India, Morocco, Mexico, Vietnam, and China; curries; turkey scaloppine; charcoal-grilled duck, roast goose, pheasant, and my favorite squabs.

MEATS   261

Roasts, steaks, and ground meat dishes, including croquettes and tamale pie; veal and lamb shanks; ham, venison, and rabbit recipes.

FISH AND SHELLFISH   367

Simple baked or steamed fillets; stuffed whole fish; bluefish, catfish, cod, mackerel, salmon, shad, tuna, and the famous blackened redfish, as well as striped bass in phyllo pastry; poached, deviled, stir-fried, and broiled crab; elegant lobsters, shrimp, oysters, mussels, and scallops.

STEWS AND CASSEROLES   461

Those sought-after dishes that can be cooked ahead—many of which will serve a crowd: ragouts, gumbos, curries, and classics like cassoulet, paella, and Brunswick stew.

PASTA   515

Homemade pasta serves as a basis for fresh vegetable, fish, seafood, and meat sauces; also unusual lasagne dishes with decidedly different flavors.

VEGETABLES   561

Stuffed artichokes, cabbage, chayotes, eggplant, mushrooms, onions, peppers, tomatoes, and zucchini—just a few of my favorite things.

RICE, POTATOES, AND BEANS   625

Variations on a perfect batch of rice; polenta and grits; puréed, sautéed, and baked potatoes stuffed with shrimp, pork, or oysters; flageolets, cannellini, lentils, and other beans.

SALADS   657

Dressings for vegetable, fish, bean, and meat salads, as well as elegant lobster and duck salads, and chicken salad for a crowd.

BREADS   717

French dough with variations; whole wheat, rye, and corn breads; croissants, bagels, and other rolls and biscuits; holiday breads, pita, pooris, and specialty breads.

SAUCES AND STOCKS   763

Mayonnaise, hollandaise, butter sauces, tomato sauces (including salsa); barbecue marinades, relishes, chutney, and stocks.

DESSERTS   805

Puddings (my favorite), soufflés, pastries, fruit mélanges, cookies, cakes, pies, tarts, ice cream, and sorbets.

APPETIZERS

Generally speaking, I find nothing more barbarous and unconvivial than dining buffet-style when that implies eating off one's lap, one's plate balanced precariously on both knees and the napkin tucked in some unseemly place to prevent its falling. There are two occasions when I find a buffet to have a redeeming virtue—a picnic and when an hors d'oeuvre table is at the heart of it.

The French, of course, have no monopoly on appetizers. When it comes to such food, there is, in fact, no civilized society on earth that does not accord a special place to that assortment of dishes known as appetizers or hors d'oeuvres. What would the Italian table be without its antipasti, the Greeks without mezedaki, the Spanish without their entremeses, the Russians without zakuska tables, the Chinese without dim sum, and the Germans without vorspeise? Or the Swedes without cocktail tilltugg and the Mexicans without antojitos?

HUMMUS BI TAHINI (CHICKPEA SPREAD)

1. Combine the sesame seed paste, water, olive oil, lemon juice, and garlic in the container of a food processor or electric blender. Blend until smooth and light colored.
2. Add the chickpeas, cumin, and coriander. Blend to a purée. Fold in the scallions and add salt and pepper to taste. Serve with warm pita bread.

Yield: 20 or more servings.

½ cup sesame seed paste (not sesame oil), available in specialty food shops

⅓ cup water

¼ cup olive oil

6 tablespoons lemon juice

4 garlic cloves, peeled

3½ cups (two 15-ounce cans) well-drained chickpeas (garbanzos)

½ teaspoon ground cumin

1 teaspoon ground coriander seeds

5 scallions, trimmed and chopped

Salt and freshly ground pepper to taste

Bagna Caôda (Anchovy and Garlic Sauce for Crudités)

1 cup olive oil

¼ pound butter

Two 2-ounce cans anchovy fillets

20 garlic cloves, peeled and thinly sliced (about ½ cup)

1 small white truffle, available in Italian specialty food stores, optional

¼ cup heavy cream

Assorted raw vegetables

The Italian bagna caôda is one of the most savory, delectable, and unlikely appetizers in the world. It is a sort of fondue in the original and proper sense of the word (meaning melted), containing anchovies that melt in a bath of olive oil and butter and in keen liaison with twenty thinly sliced garlic cloves. Twenty is an arbitrary number. Frequently there are more. I had always assumed that bagna caôda meant "hot bath." But I have learned that it has another meaning entirely.

Teresa Candler, an authority on Italian cooking, told me that *bagna* is a dialectical Piedmont word for gravy or a thickened sauce. It started out as a peasant dish eaten by farmers during harvest time; the point was that it could be cooked at home in an earthenware casserole, then taken to the vineyard, where it could be kept over an open fire.

1. Combine the olive oil, butter, anchovies, and garlic in a saucepan. Cook over very low heat for about 1 hour. The sauce must barely simmer as it cooks.

2. Thinly slice the truffle, if used, and add it to the saucepan. Add the cream and simmer about 5 minutes longer. Serve with assorted vegetables cut into bite-size cubes and lengths.

Yield: 4 servings.

TARAMOSALATA (A CARP ROE SPREAD)

1. Place the English muffin in a small bowl and add water to cover. Let stand until thoroughly saturated with water; then squeeze the muffin to extract most of the excess moisture. Put the squeezed muffin in the container of a food processor or electric blender.

2. Add the tarama, garlic, lemon juice, olive oil, and water and blend to a mayonnaise consistency. Spoon the taramosalata into a bowl and fold in the scallions.

Yield: 20 or more servings.

1 English muffin, preferably onion-flavored

10 tablespoons tarama, available in specialty food shops

1 garlic clove, finely minced

5 tablespoons lemon juice, more or less to taste

⅔ cup olive oil

2 tablespoons water

½ cup chopped scallions

GUACAMOLE

1. Cut the avocado in half and peel it. Discard the pit. Scoop the pulp into a mixing bowl and add the lime juice.

2. Put the tomato cubes in a small bowl and add the salt. Toss and refrigerate until ready to use.

3. Put half the minced onion, all the chilies, and half the coriander into a mortar and grind to a paste. Or do this in a food processor.

4. Using a knife and fork, cut the avocado flesh back and forth until smooth but coarse. The texture must not be too smooth. Add the onion mixture and salt to taste. Blend.

5. When ready to serve, add the remaining chopped onion and coriander. Drain the tomato and add it. Mix well.

Yield: 4 to 6 servings.

1 large ripe avocado

Juice of ½ lime

¾ cup seeded and cubed ripe tomato

Salt to taste

½ cup finely minced onion

1 or 2 fresh or canned serrano chilies, trimmed at the ends

¼ cup finely chopped fresh coriander

TAPENADE

One 2-ounce can anchovies, undrained

3 tablespoons drained capers

Juice of 1 lemon

1 tablespoon Dijon mustard

3 dried figs, stems removed

¾ to 1 cup olive oil

2 tablespoons cold water

¼ cup finely chopped, pitted ripe olives, preferably Greek or Italian olives packed in brine

1. Empty the anchovies and the oil in which they were packed into the container of a food processor or electric blender.

2. Add the capers, lemon juice, mustard, and figs and start blending. Gradually add the olive oil while blending. Add ¾ cup and, if desired, continue adding more oil. The tapenade should have the consistency of a thin mayonnaise. Add the cold water. Serve in a bowl, sprinkled with chopped olives, as a dip.

Yield: About 1½ cups.

EGGS IN TAPENADE

1½ cups tapenade (see recipe above)

8 to 10 hard-cooked eggs

8 to 10 capers

Parsley for garnish

Spoon the tapenade over the bottom of a serving dish. Cut the eggs in half and arrange them cut side down. Garnish with capers and parsley sprigs.

Yield: 8 or more servings.

Eggplant Caviar

This is a variation of an old-fashioned and delectable Russian favorite—eggplant caviar. The complementary seasonings include onion, garlic, scallions, tomatoes, and lemon juice. A touch of sugar is also added to produce a slight sweet-and-sour effect.

1. Preheat the oven to 400 degrees.

2. Place the eggplants on a sheet of heavy-duty aluminum foil and bake for 1 hour, or until the eggplants collapse. Let cool. Remove the pulp. There should be about 3 cups.

3. Add the onion, scallions, garlic, green pepper, tomatoes, olive oil, sugar, lemon juice, salt, and pepper. Serve with toast.

Yield: 4 servings.

2 eggplants, about 1 pound each

¼ cup finely minced onion

¼ cup finely minced scallions

1 teaspoon finely minced garlic

¼ cup finely chopped sweet green pepper

1 cup cored, peeled, and finely diced tomatoes

¼ cup olive oil

1 teaspoon sugar

1 tablespoon lemon juice, or more to taste

Salt and freshly ground pepper to taste

MELITZANOSALATA
(EGGPLANT AND SESAME SPREAD)

2 eggplants, about
1 pound each

½ cup sesame seed paste
(not sesame oil),
available in specialty
food shops

6 tablespoons lemon
juice

½ cup olive oil

⅓ cup water

3 garlic cloves, finely
minced

Salt and freshly ground
pepper to taste

¾ teaspoon dried oregano

½ cup chopped scallions

1 cup peeled, seeded, and
cubed tomato

¼ cup finely chopped
parsley

1. Place the unpeeled eggplants over a gas flame, turning them as they cook and adjusting the flame as necessary. Cook until the eggplants are somewhat charred. The skin will no doubt burst during the cooking. When ready, the eggplants should be cooked through the center. Or, prick the eggplants in several places and place on a baking dish in an oven preheated to about 375 degrees, for about 1 hour. Let the eggplants stand until they are cool enough to handle.

2. Peel the eggplants and put the inner pulp in a mixing bowl.

3. Put the sesame seed paste, lemon juice, olive oil, water, and garlic in the container of a food processor or electric blender and blend until a white paste is obtained. Add the eggplant pulp, salt, pepper, and oregano and blend until smooth. Spoon the mixture into a bowl and, just before serving, fold in the remaining ingredients. Serve with pita bread.

Yield: 20 or more servings.

CROSTINI (TOAST WITH LIVER SPREAD)

1. Heat the ¼ cup olive oil in a wide saucepan and add the onion and garlic. Cook briefly until wilted and add the sage and chicken livers. Sprinkle with salt and pepper. Cook over high heat, turning the pieces. Do not overcook. The livers should remain a trifle pink in the center.

2. Scrape the mixture into the container of a food processor or the bowl of an electric mixer. Add the anchovy fillets and prosciutto and process coarsely but thoroughly. The texture should not be too fine. Let cool briefly.

3. Brush the pieces of toast with oil and smear the chicken liver mixture on top. Serve warm.

Yield: 12 or more crostini.

¼ cup olive oil

¾ cup finely chopped onion

1 garlic clove, finely chopped

3 small fresh sage leaves, or ½ teaspoon dried sage

¾ pound chicken livers, picked over and cut in half

  Salt and freshly ground pepper to taste

4 anchovy fillets

2 ounces thinly sliced proscuitto

12 to 16 hot, freshly made toast points or rounds

  Olive oil for brushing toast

CAVIAR AND POTATOES MARCEL DRAGON

12 to 14 small, red
   potatoes, 1 pound
   or less

 4 to 5 cups rock salt
   Oil for deep frying

½ cup sour cream,
   approximately

   One 14-ounce tin fresh
   caviar or less

Blessed, indeed, is the house that finds itself the recipient of fresh black caviar. No matter how small the amount, it can be served in festive ways. This recipe for bite-size potato halves topped with sour cream and caviar is from James Nassikas, proprietor of the elegant Stanford Court Hotel in San Francisco. Mr. Nassikas had his chef, Marcel Dragon, prepare this simple but marvelous fare on request for special occasions. The potatoes are baked, split in half, the pulp scooped out, the potato shells deep-fried. The crisp shells are then refilled with potato, dabbed with sour cream, and served with a spoonful of caviar on top. For those less fortunate, we offer a relatively inexpensive red caviar pie.

1. Preheat the oven to 450 degrees.

2. Wash and dry the potatoes. Arrange them on a bed of rock salt and place in the oven. Bake for 30 to 35 minutes, or until tender.

3. Remove the potatoes and slice them in half.

4. Scoop out the center pulp with a melon-ball cutter or small spoon; reserve both the pulp and skins. Mash the pulp slightly and keep it warm.

5. Heat the oil for deep frying to 375 degrees. Drop the potato shells into the oil and cook quickly until they are golden brown and crisp. Drain well.

6. Fill the shells with the mashed potato. Top with a spoonful or so of sour cream. Then add a teaspoon or more of caviar to the top. Serve on a bed of hot rock salt, if desired.

Yield: 24 to 28 pieces.

EGGS WITH CAVIAR PAUL STEINDLER

Paul Steindler, a chef and longtime friend, served an elegant egg and scallion dish topped with caviar.

1. Place the eggs in a saucepan and add cold water to cover. Bring to the boil and simmer for about 6 minutes. (When the eggs are cooked this briefly, the whites should remain firm and the center of the yolk a bit runny. But if the eggs do become firm throughout, it does not matter.) Drain the eggs and run under cold water until chilled.

2. Using a heavy knife with a serrated blade, crack around the top of each egg in a neat circle. Remove and discard the tops.

3. Spoon out the inside of each egg into a mixing bowl. Using a fork, mash the whites and yolks together coarsely. Set the hollowed-out eggshells aside.

4. Trim the scallions and chop them. Add them to the eggs and blend.

5. Make layers of crushed ice in a bordered dish and sprinkle each layer with salt. Make indentations over the surface to hold the eggshells.

6. Using a spoon, fill each reserved eggshell about one third full with the egg and scallion mixture. Serve the remaining egg and scallion mixture separately as refills. Arrange the eggs over the ice.

7. Using a pastry bag, pipe equal amounts of sour cream into the shells. Add a rounded heaping spoonful of caviar to each shell. Serve the remaining sour cream and caviar separately as refills.

8. Garnish the dish with lemon halves and small, tight clusters of parsley.

Yield: 6 servings.

12	eggs at room temperature
2	scallions, green part and all
	Crushed ice
	Salt
¾	cup sour cream
½	to 1 pound fresh caviar
	Lemon halves for garnish
	Parsley for garnish

RED CAVIAR PIE

6 large hard-cooked eggs, peeled

¼ pound butter at room temperature

½ cup finely chopped onion

Tabasco sauce to taste

½ cup sour cream

4 ounces red caviar (salmon roe)

Buttered toast wedges

1. Put half the eggs through a sieve. Chop the remainder on a flat surface until fine and blend the two together. Add the butter, onion, and Tabasco. Blend well and shape into a flat round cake. Chill until set.

2. Make a built-up rim of sour cream around the upper rim of the pie. Make a shallower, flat layer of sour cream in the center. Spoon the red caviar over the flat layer. Cut the pie into wedges and serve with buttered toast.

Yield: 6 to 8 servings.

CHEESE CRUSTS

2 teaspoons butter

1 tablespoon flour

½ cup milk

Salt and freshly ground pepper to taste

1 egg, lightly beaten

½ pound grated Gruyère cheese, about 2½ cups

¼ teaspoon grated nutmeg

Pinch of cayenne

2 tablespoons dry white wine

¾ teaspoon finely chopped garlic

12 slices French bread, cut on the bias

1. Melt the butter in a small saucepan and stir in the flour, using a wire whisk. Add the milk, stirring rapidly with the whisk. Add the salt and pepper and let cool.

2. Preheat the oven to 400 degrees.

3. Spoon the white sauce into a mixing bowl and add the egg, cheese, nutmeg, cayenne, wine, and garlic. Blend well with a fork.

4. Toast the bread lightly on both sides and spoon equal amounts of the cheese mixture on one side. Smooth it over. Place the toast on a baking sheet and bake for 10 minutes.

Yield: 4 to 6 servings.

PEPPERS AND ANCHOVIES, ITALIAN STYLE

1. Core and seed the peppers and cut them lengthwise into ½-inch strips. There should be about 4 cups.

2. Heat the olive oil in a heavy skillet and add the peppers. Cook, stirring and shaking the skillet, for about 2 minutes.

3. Drain and chop the anchovies and add them to the peppers. Add the capers, oregano, salt, pepper, and garlic, stirring and shaking the skillet, about 2 minutes. Sprinkle with wine vinegar and remove from the heat. Serve hot or cold sprinkled with parsley. Serve with lemon.

Yield: 6 to 8 servings.

1 pound sweet green or red peppers

3 tablespoons olive oil

One 2-ounce can flat anchovies

2 tablespoons drained capers

1 teaspoon dried oregano

Salt and freshly ground pepper to taste

1 teaspoon finely chopped garlic

1 tablespoon red wine vinegar

1 tablespoon finely chopped fresh parsley

Lemon wedges

CHERRY TOMATOES WITH SARDINE MAYONNAISE

1. Cut off a small round from the top of each tomato. Using a very small spoon, scoop out some of the inside. Salt each tomato and set aside.

2. Put the yolk in a bowl and add the vinegar, mustard, salt, pepper, and Tabasco sauce.

3. Beat with a wire whisk or an electric mixer. Gradually add the oil, beating constantly. Continue beating until the mixture is thickened.

4. Chop the sardines and stir them in. Stir in the horseradish, if desired.

5. Fill the tomatoes with the sardine mayonnaise and garnish each with a parsley leaf. Leftover mayonnaise will keep for several days in the refrigerator.

Yield: 24 stuffed tomatoes.

24 cherry tomatoes

Salt

1 egg yolk

1 tablespoon wine vinegar

1 tablespoon Dijon mustard

Salt and freshly ground pepper to taste

Tabasco sauce to taste

1 cup peanut, vegetable, or corn oil

2 to 4 sardines

1 tablespoon grated horseradish, optional

Italian parsley leaves for garnish

Céleri Rémoulade (Celery Root with Mustard Mayonnaise)

2   medium celery root
1   tablespoon Dijon mustard
1   tablespoon red wine vinegar
    Salt and freshly ground pepper to taste
¾   cup freshly made mayonnaise

Celery root, which also goes by the names celeriac and knob celery, is not simply the base or root of stalk celery, the common variety of celery used in almost all American kitchens. It is another, separate vegetable, a root vegetable like turnips. It looks like a brownish globe and ranges in size from a goose egg to a cantaloupe. To use it, the brown outside skin must be pared away. When combined with mustard and mayonnaise, it makes a marvelous first course. It's also delicious combined with potatoes in puréed potatoes.

1. Peel the celery root, trimming off all the dark spots. Slice the celery as thin as possible using a food processor, hand slicer, mandoline, or even a sharp knife. There should be about 3 cups.

2. Stack the slices and cut them into the finest julienne strips. Place in a mixing bowl and add the remaining ingredients. Toss with the hands until thoroughly blended.

Yield: 6 servings.

Mushrooms à la Grecque

2   pounds mushrooms, the smaller the better
½   cup olive oil
1   tablespoon finely minced garlic
½   cup red wine vinegar
1   tablespoon coriander seeds
1   bay leaf
½   teaspoon dried thyme
½   teaspoon freshly ground black pepper

The following is one of the great appetizers called à la grecque. It is an uncommonly good cold dish, thanks in large part to the presence and flavor of coriander seeds.

1. Unless the mushrooms are quite small, cut them in half or quarter them.

2. Heat the olive oil in a large skillet and add the garlic. Do not brown the garlic.

3. When the oil is quite hot but not smoking, add the vinegar, coriander, bay leaf, thyme, and pepper. Cover and cook, shaking the skillet, for about 1 minute.

4. Add the mushrooms and cover. Cook over high heat for about 7 minutes. Uncover occasionally and stir so that the mushrooms cook evenly. Remove from the heat.

5. Transfer the mixture to one or two glass jars. There will be about 1½ pints. Let cool to room temperature. Refrigerate for several days before serving.

Yield: 24 servings.

BREADED MUSHROOMS WITH HERBS

1. Rinse and drain the mushrooms. Dredge them in flour.

2. Blend the eggs, olive oil, salt, pepper, and water. Beat well. Blend the crumbs, oregano, marjoram, pepper flakes, and thyme. Dip the mushrooms in the egg mixture, then in the crumbs. Dip a second time in egg and in crumbs.

3. Heat the oil to 360 degrees in a heavy skillet. Add the mushrooms and cook, stirring and turning with a slotted spoon, for 4 to 6 minutes, or until nicely browned all over. Drain well. Serve with anchovy mayonnaise and lemon wedges.

Yield: 6 servings.

1 pound mushrooms, the larger the better

½ cup flour

2 eggs

1 tablespoon olive oil

Salt and freshly ground pepper to taste

¼ cup water

2 cups fresh bread crumbs

¼ teaspoon crushed dried oregano

¼ teaspoon crushed dried marjoram

¼ teaspoon crushed red pepper flakes

¼ teaspoon dried thyme

Peanut, vegetable, or corn oil for deep frying

Anchovy mayonnaise (see recipe page 772)

Lemon wedges

MUSHROOMS WITH SNAIL BUTTER AUX TROIS TONNEAUX

THE STUFFED MUSHROOMS:

24 large, fresh mushrooms, about 1 pound

½ cup dry white wine

Juice of 1 lemon

Salt and freshly ground pepper to taste

2 tablespoons butter

1 tablespoon olive oil

2 tablespoons finely chopped shallots

1½ tablespoons flour

¾ cup milk

½ cup bread crumbs

⅛ teaspoon grated nutmeg

1 tablespoon finely chopped parsley

THE SNAIL BUTTER:

3 tablespoons butter

1 tablespoon finely chopped garlic

1 tablespoon finely chopped fresh parsley

Many years ago, when I was a student at a hotel school in Switzerland, a favorite diversion was an occasional visit with a friend to a restaurant in Lausanne called Aux Trois Tonneaux. A short while ago that same friend forwarded a recipe from Aux Trois Tonneaux: It was for stuffed mushrooms with snail butter. It is unusual and good.

1. Rinse and drain the mushrooms well. Remove and reserve the stems.

2. Put the caps in a skillet and add the wine, half of the lemon juice, the salt, and pepper. Bring to the boil. Cover and cook, stirring occasionally, for about 5 minutes. Remove from the heat and drain the caps. Discard the liquid.

3. Chop the mushroom stems. There should be about 1¼ cups.

4. Heat 1 tablespoon of the butter and the olive oil in a saucepan and add the shallots, chopped mushroom stems, remaining lemon juice, and salt and pepper to taste. Cook until wilted and the moisture has evaporated.

5. Melt the remaining tablespoon of butter in a small saucepan and add the flour, stirring to blend. When blended, add the milk, stirring rapidly with a wire whisk. Add the chopped mushroom mixture, bread crumbs, nutmeg, and salt and pepper to taste. Stir in the parsley. Let cool slightly.

6. Spoon equal portions of the mixture into the mushroom caps and mound it up, smoothing it over with a spatula. Continue until all the caps are filled and all the filling is used. Arrange the filled caps in a baking dish.

7. Preheat the oven to 400 degrees.

8. Bake the filled caps for about 5 minutes, or until piping hot throughout.

9. To make the snail butter, heat the butter with the garlic and parsley. When it is bubbling, pour the mixture over the mushrooms and serve hot.

Yield: 4 to 8 servings.

Spanakopetes (Spinach in Phyllo Pastry Triangles)

1. Preheat the oven to 350 degrees.

2. Pull off and discard any tough stems and blemished leaves from the spinach. Wash and drain well. If packaged spinach is used, rinse once and drain. Chop the spinach coarsely. Heat the olive oil in a skillet and add the spinach. Cook until wilted. Drain well.

3. Add the butter to the skillet and cook the onions, garlic, and scallions until wilted, stirring often. When the mixture starts to brown, transfer it to a mixing bowl. Add the spinach, feta cheese, Parmesan, dill, and parsley to the onion mixture. Beat the egg and yolk together lightly and add to the spinach mixture. Add very little salt. Add pepper to taste. Stir in the pine nuts, if desired.

4. Use one sheet of phyllo pastry for each two spinach triangles. Brush a marble or Formica surface with butter. Spread out one square of phyllo and, using a sharp knife, cut it lengthwise in half. Set one rectangle aside and keep it covered with a damp cloth. Keep all the sheets of phyllo covered when not using them or they will dry rapidly.

5. Brush one rectangle generously with melted butter. Fold half of the rectangle over to make a smaller rectangle. Add 2 tablespoons of the spinach mixture to the bottom of the rectangle. Fold one corner of the rectangle over the spinach filling in a triangle. Fold this filled triangle over itself toward the top. Continue folding up until a complete, self-contained triangle is produced. Brush this all over with butter and set aside. Continue making triangles until all the spinach filling is used.

6. Arrange the triangles on a baking sheet and bake about 20 minutes, or until puffed and golden brown.

Yield: 16 spinach triangles.

1 pound fresh spinach
1½ tablespoons olive oil
2 tablespoons butter
2 cups chopped onions
1 teaspoon finely chopped garlic
1 cup chopped scallions
1 cup crumbled or chopped feta cheese, about ¼ pound
¼ cup grated Parmesan cheese
¼ cup finely chopped fresh dill
⅓ cup finely chopped parsley
1 egg
1 egg yolk
Salt and freshly ground pepper to taste
¼ cup pine nuts, optional
8 sheets phyllo pastry
4 tablespoons butter, melted

BAKED STUFFED CLAMS

36 to 48 littleneck clams

6 shallots, peeled

4 garlic cloves, finely minced

½ cup loosely packed fresh basil

½ cup loosely packed fresh parsley

1 small tomato, about ⅓ pound, cored and quartered

4 fresh mushrooms, sliced

¾ cup freshly grated Parmesan cheese

½ cup fresh bread crumbs

2 slices lean bacon, cut into pieces

Salt and freshly ground pepper

½ teaspoon red pepper flakes, more or less to taste, optional

1 tablespoon finely chopped chives, optional

¼ cup olive oil

½ cup dry white wine

For the nonexpert and would-be clam shucker, there are two things to remember that facilitate opening the bivalves. Clams are tightly closed because of the powerful (but delicious and tender) muscle that joins the two shells together. If the clams are well chilled before they are to be opened, the muscle tends to relax. The clams can be chilled for several hours in the refrigerator or briefly in the freezer. It is also imperative that the clam knife be sharp. Avoid those guillontinelike clam-shucking gadgets. They mangle clams and are quite frankly an abomination.

1. Preheat the oven to 400 degrees.

2. Open the clams or have them opened, discarding the top shell and loosening the clam on the bottom half shell.

3. Combine the shallots, garlic, basil, parsley, tomato, mushrooms, ½ cup of grated cheese, bread crumbs, bacon, salt, and pepper to taste. Do not add much salt because the clams are salty. Grind the ingredients or blend them in a food processor to a medium fine purée. Fold in the red pepper flakes and chives, if desired.

4. Spoon the mixture over the clams and smooth it over. Arrange the clams on a baking dish and sprinkle with the remaining cheese. Sprinkle with the oil and wine. Bake for 20 minutes, or until golden brown and piping hot. Run briefly under the broiler for a deeper glaze.

Yield: 6 to 8 servings.

CLAMS ON THE HALF SHELL WITH FRESH SALSA

Open the clams and discard half the shells. Leave the remaining clams on the half shell. Arrange them on a serving platter. Combine the remaining ingredients and spoon equal portions of the tomato mixture on each clam. Serve on the half shell.

Yield: 6 servings.

36 littleneck clams, the smaller the better

1 cup cubed firm, ripe, unpeeled tomatoes

2 tablespoons finely chopped onion

1 garlic clove, finely minced

½ cup finely chopped scallions

1 green chili, finely chopped

1 jalapeño pepper, finely chopped

¼ cup fresh lime juice

¼ cup olive oil

Salt and freshly ground pepper to taste

½ cup chopped fresh coriander

OYSTERS WITH MIGNONETTE SAUCE

¼ cup red wine vinegar
2 tablespoons finely chopped shallots
½ teaspoon freshly ground pepper, preferably white
1 dozen oysters

One of the simplest of all sauces for oysters on the half shell is the one known as mignonette. It consists of vinegar, chopped shallots, and ground pepper. The name derives from a kind of white peppercorn that is known as mignonette.

Combine the vinegar, shallots, and pepper and serve with oysters on the half shell. About 1 teaspoon of mignonette sauce should be spooned over each oyster.

Yield: 2 servings.

OYSTERS CASINO

Rock salt
¼ pound butter
½ cup chopped green or red sweet pepper
Salt and freshly ground pepper to taste
1 tablespoon finely chopped parsley
1 tablespoon finely chopped chives
Juice of ½ lemon
Grated rind of lemon
12 oysters on the half shell
4 bacon strips
6 teaspoons fresh bread crumbs

1. Preheat the oven to 500 degrees.
2. Pour rock salt into two rimmed, heatproof dishes large enough to hold 6 oysters on the half shell in one layer. Place the dishes in the oven for at least 5 minutes to heat the salt.
3. Blend the butter, green pepper, salt, and pepper. Add the parsley, chives, lemon juice, and lemon rind and blend well. Spoon equal parts of this mixture onto each of the 12 oysters.
4. Cut the bacon strips into rectangles, each large enough to cover 1 oyster. Cover the butter topping with bacon and sprinkle each serving with ½ teaspoon of bread crumbs.
5. Arrange the oysters on the rock salt and place in the oven. Bake for 10 minutes, or until bacon is crisp and oysters are heated through.

Yield: 2 servings.

OYSTERS ROCKEFELLER

The origin of oysters Rockefeller is generally credited to Antoine's Restaurant in New Orleans. It is said to be the creation of Jules Alciatore, the grandson of the restaurant's founder. He once told an interviewer that he had called the dish, which is made with great quantities of butter, oysters Rockefeller because they are so rich.

36	oysters
2	pounds fresh spinach
1	cup finely chopped scallions
½	cup finely chopped celery
½	cup finely chopped parsley
1	garlic clove, finely minced
	One 2-ounce can anchovies, drained
¼	pound butter
1	tablespoon flour
½	cup heavy cream
	Tabasco sauce to taste
1	or 2 tablespoons Pernod, Ricard, or other anise-flavored liqueur
⅓	cup grated Parmesan cheese

1. Preheat the oven to 450 degrees.

2. Open the oysters, leaving them on the half shell and reserving the oyster liquor.

3. Pick over the spinach and remove any tough stems and blemished leaves. Rinse well and put in a saucepan. Cover and cook, stirring, until the spinach is wilted. Cook briefly and drain well. Squeeze to remove excess moisture. Blend or put through a food grinder. There should be about 2 cups.

4. Put the scallions, celery, and parsley into the container of a food processor or an electric blender and blend. There should be about 1 cup finely blended.

5. Chop the garlic and anchovies together.

6. Heat 4 tablespoons of the butter in a skillet and add the scallion and celery mixture. Stir about 1 minute and add the anchovy mixture. Cook, stirring, for about 1 minute and add the spinach. Stir to blend.

7. Heat the remaining 4 tablespoons of butter in a saucepan and add the flour. Blend, stirring with a wire whisk, and add the oyster liquor, stirring vigorously with the whisk. Stir in the cream. Season with Tabasco. Do not add salt. Add the spinach mixture and Pernod. Let cool.

8. Spoon equal portions of the mixture on top of the oysters and smooth over the tops. Sprinkle with Parmesan. Bake for about 25 minutes, or until piping hot.

Yield: 6 servings.

Note: The same spinach topping is equally good (some think it is better) with clams on the half shell.

MUSSELS IN BROTH

24 large, meaty mussels
¼ cup olive oil
4 garlic cloves, thinly sliced
½ teaspoon hot red pepper flakes
⅓ cup finely chopped parsley
   Crisp Italian bread

1. Rinse the mussels and drain well. Place in a kettle and cover. Steam until the mussels open. Discard any mussels that don't open.

2. Meanwhile, heat the oil in a casserole and add the garlic. Cook until the garlic starts to brown. Pour in the mussels and their liquid and toss. Sprinkle with pepper flakes and parsley and serve over sliced, crusty bread in soup bowls.

Yield: 4 servings.

MUSSELS WITH CAPER MAYONNAISE

2 quarts well-scrubbed mussels, about 3½ pounds
¼ cup dry white wine
1 bay leaf
   Freshly ground pepper to taste
3 fresh parsley sprigs
½ cup freshly made mayonnaise
3 tablespoons drained capers
1 teaspoon finely chopped garlic
1 tablespoon finely chopped dill
   Fresh dill sprigs for garnish

1. Put the mussels in a kettle and add the wine, bay leaf, and pepper. Do not add salt. Cover and cook for 5 minutes or longer, until the mussels open. Discard any mussels that don't open.

2. Let the mussels cool. Remove the mussels from the shells (the liquid may be used for a small portion of soup). Combine the mussels with as much mayonnaise as it takes to bind them together. Add the capers, garlic, and chopped dill and toss to blend. Serve at room temperature. Garnish with fresh dill sprigs.

Yield: 6 to 8 servings.

SHRIMP SEVICHE

1. Cover the shrimp with cold water. Add salt to taste, pepper flakes, and allspice. Bring to the boil and simmer for 30 seconds. Remove from the heat and let cool. Shell and devein the shrimp.

2. Put the shrimp in a bowl and add salt to taste and the remaining ingredients. Cover and refrigerate for several hours. Serve at room temperature.

Yield: 6 servings.

1¼ pounds fresh shrimp in the shell

Salt

¼ teaspoon red pepper flakes

4 whole allspice

½ cup finely chopped onion

⅓ cup olive oil

½ cup lime juice

¼ cup chopped fresh coriander

½ lime, squeezed and cut into tiny cubes

2 long hot green or red chilies, cored, seeded, and chopped

1 teaspoon finely chopped garlic

1 teaspoon crushed oregano

COLD SHRIMP À LA GRECQUE

2 pounds fresh shrimp, shelled and deveined

¼ cup olive oil

2 teaspoons finely chopped garlic

1 bay leaf

1 cup dry white wine

Juice of 2 lemons

¼ cup finely chopped dill

1 small dried hot red chili

Salt and freshly ground pepper to taste

Almost every national cuisine embraces specific flavors that are endlessly repeated in various combinations. Chinese cookery, for example, relies heavily on soy sauce, fresh ginger, and garlic. French cooking would seem impoverished without dry red and white wines, shallots, thyme, bay leaves, and heavy cream. Two of the staples of Greek cookery are lemons and olive oil. French chefs put these to good use in an assortment of inspired appetizers and call them à la grecque, or Greek-style.

1. Rinse the shrimp and drain. Pat dry.

2. Heat the oil in a large skillet and add the garlic. Cook briefly without browning. Add the bay leaf and wine. Bring to the simmer and add the shrimp. Add half the lemon juice, the dill, and red pepper. Add salt and pepper and bring to the simmer. Cover and simmer for 5 minutes. Remove from the heat and let cool. Refrigerate.

3. When ready to serve, sprinkle with the remaining lemon juice.

Yield: 8 or more servings.

SHRIMP WITH A TARRAGON AND ANCHOVY MAYONNAISE

1½ pounds fresh shrimp, about 36

12 whole allspice

1 dried hot red pepper

Salt

1 cup freshly made mayonnaise

2 teaspoons fresh lemon juice, or more to taste

6 anchovies, finely chopped

1 tablespoon chopped fresh tarragon

1. Place the shrimp in a saucepan and add cold water to cover. Add the allspice, hot red pepper, and salt to taste. Bring to the boil and simmer for 1 minute. Remove the shrimp from the heat and let cool. Drain, shell, and devein the shrimp.

2. Combine the mayonnaise with the lemon juice, chopped anchovies, and tarragon. Cut the shrimp in half and add them. Chill and serve cold with crusty French bread.

Yield: 6 or more servings.

SHRIMP WITH MUSTARD AND DILL SAUCE

1. Combine the shrimp, bay leaf, allspice, parsley, celery, water, salt, and peppercorns in a saucepan.
2. Bring to the boil and turn off the heat. Let the shrimp cool in the cooking liquid. Chill.
3. Shell and devein the shrimp. Combine the mayonnaise, mustard, and dill and spoon over the shrimp.

Yield: 6 or more servings.

2 pounds shrimp in the shell
1 bay leaf
12 whole allspice
6 parsley sprigs
1 celery rib with leaves, quartered
  Water to cover
  Salt to taste
10 peppercorns, crushed
1 cup freshly made mayonnaise
1 tablespoon Dijon mustard
¼ cup finely chopped fresh dill

RAW SCALLOPS IN SOY MARINADE

In a small mixing bowl combine the soy sauce, lime juice, horseradish, pepper flakes, oil, coriander, and garlic. Blend well. Add the scallops and stir to blend. Chill or serve immediately.

Yield: 6 or more servings.

6 tablespoons soy sauce
3 tablespoons fresh lime juice
1½ tablespoons grated horseradish, preferably fresh
¼ teaspoon hot red pepper flakes
2 teaspoons olive oil
1 tablespoon chopped fresh coriander
1 teaspoon finely chopped garlic
1 pint (1 pound) fresh raw scallops, preferably bay scallops

MARINATED SEAFOOD COCKTAIL, MEXICAN STYLE

24 littleneck clams

½ pound shrimp, peeled and deveined

Salt to taste

1 bay leaf

1 dried hot red pepper

20 small mussels, well scrubbed

3 tablespoons dry white wine

½ cup cubed ripe tomatoes

½ cup finely chopped onion

1 tablespoon finely minced garlic

1½ cups cubed avocado

¼ cup fresh lime juice

1 cup tomato juice

2 teaspoons crushed coriander seeds

¼ teaspoon hot red pepper flakes

2 teaspoons chopped fresh coriander or parsley

1. Open and save the clams and their liquid. There should be about 1 cup of liquid.

2. Place the shrimp in a saucepan and add water to cover, salt, bay leaf, and hot red pepper. Bring to the boil. Remove from the heat and let cool. Drain the shrimp and cut into cubes. Set aside.

3. Put the mussels in a saucepan with the wine. Cover closely and bring to the boil. Cook 4 or 5 minutes, until the mussels open. Discard any mussels that don't open. Drain. Remove the mussels from the shells.

4. Put the clams and their liquid in a mixing bowl. Add the shrimp, mussels, tomatoes, onion, garlic, avocado, lime juice, tomato juice, coriander seeds, pepper flakes, and chopped coriander. Cover and refrigerate for several hours, or until ready to serve.

Yield: 8 or more servings.

CAJUN POPCORN (BATTER-FRIED CRAWFISH)

This is a recipe, one of several, given to me by my friend of many years, Paul Prudhomme, the finest Creole and Cajun chef. One taste of these and you can't stop popping the tiny deep-fried crawfish into your mouth. That shrimp-shaped critter, incidentally, is always referred to as crawfish in the South. Crayfish to a Southern ear sounds pretentious, as though you are putting on airs.

1. Blend the eggs and milk; beat well.
2. In a large bowl, combine the corn flour, all-purpose flour, sugar, salt, 1 teaspoon of the garlic, the onion, white and black pepper, cayenne, thyme, and bay leaf. Blend well. Gradually add the milk mixture, stirring well with a whisk. Let stand for 1 hour at room temperature.
3. Combine the 1 tablespoon finely chopped garlic with the mayonnaise and Tabasco to taste.
4. Heat 1 inch of oil in a cast-iron skillet, or use a deep-fat fryer. It is important that the oil be heated to a temperature as close to 370 degrees as possible. Coat a few pieces of seafood with batter and drop them into the hot fat. Cook, stirring occasionally, until golden brown all over, about 2 minutes.
5. As the coated seafood is cooked, drain well on paper towels. Continue with the remaining seafood.
6. Serve with the garlic mayonnaise on the side.

Yield: 4 to 8 servings.

Note: Corn flour is available at many health-food stores. If not available, increase the all-purpose flour to 1 cup.

2 eggs, well beaten
1¼ cups milk
½ cup corn flour (see note)
½ cup all-purpose flour
1 teaspoon sugar
Salt to taste
1 teaspoon plus 1 tablespoon finely chopped garlic
1 teaspoon finely chopped onion
1 teaspoon finely ground white pepper
⅛ teaspoon finely ground black pepper
½ teaspoon cayenne
¼ teaspoon dried thyme
⅛ teaspoon pulverized bay leaf
1 cup freshly made mayonnaise
Tabasco sauce
Oil for deep-frying
2 pounds crawfish tails, peeled, or very small shrimp, peeled and deveined

BROILED SNAPPERS WITH HERBS

16 very small snappers (baby bluefish), cleaned but with head and tail left on, gills removed

16 small fresh oregano sprigs or mint leaves

1 tablespoon soy sauce

8 lime slices, cut in half

1 teaspoon peanut oil

Lime wedges

1. Preheat the broiler.
2. Stuff each snapper with a small sprig of fresh oregano. Arrange the fish in one layer in a lightly oiled baking dish. Brush lightly with soy sauce and stuff half a lime slice in each gill flap. Brush with oil.
3. Broil for 3 to 5 minutes. Serve with lime wedges.

Yield: 4 servings.

RAW FISH WITH GREEN PEPPERCORNS

1½ pounds skinless, boneless fillet of very fresh fish such as tuna, striped bass, sea trout, and so on

Salt and freshly ground pepper to taste

2 tablespoons fresh lime juice

1 tablespoon green peppercorns (if possible, use the peppercorns packed in brine rather than those packed in vinegar or dry)

Lime slices for garnish

Parsley sprigs for garnish

1. Place the fillet on a flat surface and cut it on the diagonal into very thin slices like smoked salmon. As the slices are cut, arrange them neatly in one layer and slightly overlapping on a chilled platter.
2. Sprinkle with salt and pepper. Sprinkle with lime juice. Crush the peppercorns and smear them over the fish. Garnish with lime slices and parsley sprigs.

Yield: 8 to 12 servings.

MATJES HERRING
WITH DILL AND SOUR CREAM

Drain the fillets and cut them into 1-inch pieces. Arrange them neatly on a dish and sprinkle with chopped dill and onion. Garnish with bay leaves. Serve with sour cream on the side.

Yield: 12 servings for a buffet.

8 matjes herring fillets, available in tins where fine Swedish foods are sold

¼ cup chopped fresh dill

½ cup finely chopped onion

2 bay leaves for garnish
Sour cream

HERRING TIDBITS WITH LEEKS AND ONION

1. Drain the tidbits and arrange them on a dish in a neat pattern.
2. Blend the leeks and onion. Spoon the mixture to one side of the tidbits. Spoon the sour cream down the other side.

Yield: 12 servings for a buffet.

36 herring tidbits, available in jars

⅓ cup finely chopped leeks, green part and all

⅓ cup finely chopped onion

1 cup sour cream

GRAVLAX (SALT- AND SUGAR-CURED SALMON)

2 bunches fresh dill

One 3½- to 4-pound section of fresh salmon, preferably cut from the center of the fish

¼ cup kosher salt

¼ cup sugar

1 teaspoon coarsely ground white peppercorns

Mustard-dill sauce (see following recipe)

1. Cut off and discard any very tough stems from the dill. Rinse the dill and pat it dry.

2. Bone the salmon section or have it boned. There should be two fillets of equal size and weight. Do not rinse the fish but pat it dry with paper toweling.

3. Combine the salt, sugar, and pepper. Rub this mixture into the pink flesh of the salmon.

4. Spread one third of the dill over the bottom of a flat dish. Add one of the salmon pieces, skin side down. Cover this with another third of the dill. Add the remaining piece of salmon, placing it sandwich-fashion over the dill, skin side up. Cover with the remaining dill and place a plate on top. Add a sizable weight and let stand in a very cool place or in the refrigerator for 48 hours. Turn the "sandwich" every 12 hours, always covering with the plate and weighting it down. Serve thinly sliced on the bias, like smoked salmon, with mustard-dill sauce.

Yield: 12 to 20 servings.

MUSTARD-DILL SAUCE

½ cup Dijon mustard

2 teaspoons dry mustard

6 tablespoons sugar

¼ cup white vinegar

⅔ cup vegetable oil

½ cup chopped fresh dill

Salt

Combine the prepared mustard, dry mustard, and sugar in a mixing bowl. Using a wire whisk, stir in the vinegar. Gradually add the oil, stirring rapidly with the whisk. Add the dill and salt. Taste and correct the flavors by gradually adding more sugar, vinegar, or salt.

Yield: About 1½ cups.

BRANDADE DE MORUE (MOUSSE OF SALT COD)

Salt cod, one of the great preserved fish of all times, is highly prized in Europe, particularly by the inhabitants of the Mediterranean countries. It goes by the name of *bacalao* in Spain and *baccalá* in Italy. The French term is *morue*. This mousse of salt cod from the south of France is delectable and easily made in the food processor.

1. Place the cod in a basin and add cold water to cover. Let soak, changing the water occasionally, for about 12 hours.

2. When ready to cook, preheat the oven to 375 degrees.

3. Place the potatoes in the oven and bake for 45 minutes to 1 hour, or until tender.

4. Drain the soaked cod and place it in a deep skillet. Add cold water to cover, ½ cup of the milk, bay leaf, and the onion stuck with cloves. Bring to the boil and simmer for about 3 minutes. Drain. If the cod is not boneless, carefully remove any skin and bones.

5. Gently heat the remaining milk, oil, and cream in separate saucepans.

6. Split the potatoes in half. Scoop the hot flesh into the container of a food processor. Start blending and add the cod and garlic. Gradually add the hot milk, oil, and cream. Beat in the salt, pepper, nutmeg, and cayenne and stir in the truffle, if desired.

7. Serve warm with triangles of French bread fried in olive oil, or with sliced French bread.

Yield: 12 to 20 servings.

1½ pounds dried salt cod, preferably boneless

1 pound potatoes, about 2

2 cups milk

1 bay leaf

½ onion stuck with 2 cloves

1 cup olive oil

1 cup heavy cream

1½ tablespoons finely chopped garlic

Salt and freshly ground pepper to taste

¼ teaspoon grated nutmeg

⅛ teaspoon cayenne

1 truffle cut into ¼-inch cubes, optional

SUSHI

The giddy proliferation of Japanese restaurants in America has been very much a part of this nation's much-heralded gastronomic revolution. Americans have developed a strong affinity for foods of extraordinary variety and flavor. And it is not stretching a point to propose that Japanese cooking was the world's first cuisine minceur.

Sushi, that gastronomic wonder of raw fish served on rice, is a prime example. The kinds of fish and shellfish that can be eaten as sushi are virtually endless. Tuna, one of the favorite fish, is seasonal, but sea bass, striped bass, fresh mackerel, and even bluefish are all excellent. Salmon roe, sometimes called red caviar and available in jars, is delicious as a topping for sushi rice. Thinly sliced raw clams, even the large chowder clams sliced razor-thin along the meaty section, are delectable. Sea urchins, that delicacy so prized in Mediterranean regions, offer an incredibly good roe best eaten raw. Although raw shrimp are a great delicacy in Japan, they are not recommended to be served as sushi in this country unless they are caught live and out of the freshest waters. The vast majority of shrimp sold in America have been frozen. The important thing is that each morsel for sushi be of the freshest quality.

HOW TO SHAPE PLAIN SUSHI

Prepare the fish or seafood and the rice to be used in making sushi. Follow the recipe for sushi rice carefully. Have ready a small bowl of prepared wasabi (Japanese horseradish), and a small bowl of cold water to which has been added a teaspoon of rice vinegar.

Take a thin slice of fish fillet or a piece of seafood in one hand. Dip the index finger of the other hand into the wasabi and smear a little of it into the center of the fish. Wet the palm and fingers with the vinegar water and take up about 1½ tablespoons of sushi rice. Shape it into a ball, using one hand. Apply it to the wasabi-smeared fish and shape it into an oval so that it just fits the fish. Serve with sushi dip.

Although tuna is the most basic, traditional fish for making sushi, it is by no means the sum of it. Almost any fresh-caught, firm-fleshed, saltwater fish may be used, including sea bass, striped bass, mackerel, and so on.

The fillets must be free of bones and skin. Place a slab of the fish on a cutting board and, using a very sharp slicing knife, cut the fillet, preferably on the bias, into ¼-inch-thick slices.

Open the clams and remove the body. Cut away any digestive organs, leaving the firm, meaty muscle of the shellfish. Cut the muscle into thin slices and add salt. Massage well and rinse under cold running water. These slices may be butterflied to make them larger. Score the slices gently with a knife without cutting through the meat.

SEAWEED-WRAPPED SUSHI (DOTÉ)

There are several ways to wrap foods in seaweed to be served as sushi. One of the most common is to shape about 1½ tablespoons of sushi rice into an oval, apply a dab of wasabi to the top, and encircle the rice with a rectangle of laver or nori (seaweed; see directions for preparing below), leaving an open space at the top for other small ingredients such as tiny scallops, slivers of raw fish, salmon roe, sea-urchin roe, and so on. At times a sprinkle of lemon juice is added.

Another common technique is to place a rectangle of seaweed flat on a rectangular shaping mat made with thin bamboo reeds. This device is called a *makisushi* and is available where Japanese cooking utensils are sold. Put 2 or 3 tablespoons of sushi rice in the center and, using the fingers, spread it out neatly over the seaweed, but leave a margin top and bottom. Add a dab of wasabi to the center, left to right, and add a thin strip of tuna or other fish or seafood across the center. Add a strip of cucumber if desired. Or use strips of broiled eel and Japanese pickles in place of the tuna and cucumber.

Fold the bamboo mat over in such a manner that the filling is enclosed in seaweed. Cut the sushi roll into sections of any desired length and serve with a sushi dip on the side.

DRIED SEAWEED (LAVER OR NORI) FOR SUSHI

To prepare the seaweed for sushi, pass it quickly on both sides over heat such as a gas flame or a hot grill. Cut it to any desired size, and shape around sushi rice plus other ingredients.

Combine all the ingredients in a saucepan and heat, stirring, until the sugar is dissolved. Remove from the heat.

Yield: About 1½ cups.

SUSHI VINEGAR

  1 cup rice vinegar
1¼ cups sugar
 ¼ cup salt

Sushi is traditionally served with a small saucer or bowl of light soy sauce with wasabi (Japanese horseradish) on the side. The wasabi is added to the soy sauce as desired.

SUSHI DIP

SUSHI RICE

1. Place the rice in a kettle and add cold water to cover. Stir rapidly with the hands and drain. Return the rice to the kettle and rinse again, stirring. Drain. Repeat once more. Drain finally in a sieve and let stand for 1 hour.

2. Measure the rice once more. It should measure 3½ to 4 cups. Put it in a saucepan. Add an equal quantity of cold water. Add the kelp and bring to the boil. As soon as the water boils, remove and discard the kelp. Cover the saucepan and cook the rice over high heat (the lid may rock from the steam) for about 6 minutes, or until the rice is tender. Sprinkle with the mirin and cover with a cloth, then with the lid. Let stand for 20 minutes.

3. Empty the piping hot rice into a bowl, preferably wide and made of wood, and gradually add the vinegar, turning the rice with a wooden spoon so that the vinegar is evenly distributed. Traditionally the rice should be fanned to cool it quickly as the vinegar is stirred in. Smooth the rice into a thin layer and let it stand until thoroughly cooled.

Yield: About 6 cups.

  3 cups rice (about 1½ pounds), preferably Japanese or Italian (such as arborio)

  1 piece dried kelp (seaweed), about 3 inches square, available in Japanese markets

1½ teaspoons mirin (sweet sake), available in Japanese markets

 ½ cup sushi vinegar (see recipe above)

MEAT-FILLED PHYLLO ROLLS

1 tablespoon butter

½ cup finely chopped onion

1 tablespoon water

½ pound ground round steak

2 tablespoons dry white wine

6 tablespoons tomato paste

  Salt and freshly ground pepper

1 tablespoon Parmesan cheese

1 small egg, beaten

6 sheets phyllo pastry

4 to 6 tablespoons butter, melted

1. Heat the butter in a small skillet and add the onion and water. Cook, stirring often, until the liquid evaporates.

2. Add the meat and stir to break up the lumps that may form. Cook until the meat is light brown, stirring often. Add the wine and cook until it comes to the boil. Add the tomato paste, salt, and pepper to taste. Cover and cook slowly for about 15 minutes. Uncover and remove from heat. Let cool slightly. Add the Parmesan and beaten egg and blend well. Let cool.

3. Roll the 6 pastry sheets over themselves into a long, neat, sausage-shaped bundle. Cut the bundle crosswise into 4 pieces of equal width (approximately 4 inches wide). Remember as you work with one strip of dough to keep the others covered with a damp cloth so that they won't dry out. Unroll one piece and keep the remainder covered. Spread out this strip on a flat surface.

4. Brush the strip with melted butter. Spoon about 2 teaspoons of meat filling toward one end of the strip. Start rolling the strip from that end. Roll the strip over itself to enclose the meat filling. Fold the two outer edges partly toward the center. Continue to roll the strip until all of it is used. Continue until all the strips and filling are used. As the rolls are made, arrange them on a baking sheet.

5. Meanwhile, preheat the oven to 350 degrees.

6. Before baking, brush the tops of each roll with butter. Place the baking sheet in the oven and bake for 15 to 20 minutes, or until golden brown.

Yield: About 24 pieces.

Carpaccio (Sliced raw beef with shallot mayonnaise)

1. Place each slice of meat, one at a time, between 2 sheets of plastic wrap and pound with a flat mallet or the bottom of a clean, heavy skillet until the slices are approximately ⅛ inch thick. As the slices are prepared, arrange two on each of 6 chilled appetizer plates. Chill until ready to serve.

2. Wrap the chopped shallots in cheesecloth and run under cold water. Squeeze to extract most of the moisture. Add the shallots to the mayonnaise.

3. To serve, spread a little more than 1 tablespoon of the shallot mayonnaise over each slice. Garnish with lemon wedges. Serve with a peppermill on the side.

Yield: 6 servings.

1½ pounds boneless shell steak, cut into twelve ¼-inch-thick slices
2 tablespoons finely chopped shallots
1 cup freshly made mayonnaise
12 seedless lemon wedges or lemon halves
Freshly ground pepper

Sautéed Brains

1. The calf's brain consists of a pair of lobes. Place them in a mixing bowl and add cold water to cover. Let them stand for several hours, changing the cold water frequently.

2. Drain and pick over the brains to remove the outer membranes, blood, and other extraneous matter. Place the brains in a saucepan and add cold water to about ½ inch above the brains. Add the peppercorns, salt to taste, vinegar, bay leaf, and thyme. Bring to the boil and simmer for 3 minutes, no longer. Remove from the heat and drain. Run brains under cold water until chilled. They are now ready to cook when patted dry. If the brains are not to be cooked until later, leave them covered with cold water.

3. Season enough flour with salt and pepper to coat the brains lightly. Cut the brains into slices about ¼ inch thick. Dredge in flour. Heat the butter in a skillet and brown the slices on both sides. Add more butter if necessary. Transfer the brains to a serving dish.

4. Combine the olive oil, lemon juice, water, dill, parsley, oregano, and capers in a saucepan and bring to the boil. Pour the sauce over the brains and serve lukewarm.

Yield: 6 or more servings.

1 pair calf's brains, about 1 pound
12 peppercorns
Salt
2 tablespoons wine vinegar
1 bay leaf
2 sprigs fresh thyme, or ½ teaspoon dried
Freshly ground pepper
Flour for dredging
3 tablespoons butter
3 tablespoons olive oil
3 tablespoons lemon juice
3 tablespoons water
1½ tablespoons finely chopped fresh dill
2 tablespoons finely chopped fresh parsley
½ teaspoon dried oregano
1 tablespoon capers

SESAME CHICKEN WINGS

12 chicken wings
1 tablespoon salted black beans
1 tablespoon water
1 tablespoon peanut, vegetable, or corn oil
2 garlic cloves, crushed
2 slices fresh ginger, cut into very fine shreds
3 tablespoons dark soy sauce
1½ tablespoons dry sherry
¼ teaspoon freshly ground pepper
1 tablespoon toasted sesame seeds
2 tablespoons chopped scallions, green part and all

1. Cut off and discard the small wing tips. Cut between and reserve the main wing bones and the second wing joint.

2. Crush the beans and add 1 tablespoon of water. Let stand.

3. Heat the oil in a wok or skillet and add the garlic and ginger. Stir briefly and add the chicken wings. Cook, stirring, until lightly browned, about 3 minutes. Add the soy sauce and sherry and cook, stirring, about 30 seconds longer. Add the soaked black beans.

4. Cover closely and let simmer for 8 to 10 minutes. Uncover, turn the heat to high, and continue cooking, stirring, until the liquid is almost evaporated and the chicken pieces are glazed with sauce.

5. Remove from the heat and add the pepper. Toss. Just before serving, toss in the sesame seeds and scallions. This dish can be made in advance and reheated.

Yield: 8 or more servings.

BEEHIVE DUMPLINGS

On a visit to China, I never did get to taste the highly praised dim sum, those varied Chinese appetizers, at the Pan Hsi restaurant. My guide took me for suckling pig instead. But when a group of chefs from that restaurant came to the United States for a series of banquets, I invited them to come into my kitchen to demonstrate the making of dumplings, all marvelously inventive. The rabbit dumplings, particularly, are enchanting to behold and they are easy to make.

4 salted duck eggs, available in Asian groceries and supermarkets

¾ cup plus 1 tablespoon wheat starch, available in Asian groceries and supermarkets

½ cup plus 2 tablespoons rapidly boiling water

Beehive stuffing (see following recipe)

Oil for deep frying

1. Crack the eggs and separate the whites from the yolks. Put the yolks in a small mixing bowl. (The whites may be discarded or saved for another purpose.) Set the bowl in a steamer and place it over boiling water. Cover and let steam for 30 minutes. Remove from the heat and let cool.

2. Put the wheat starch in a small mixing bowl.

3. Add the ½ cup plus 2 tablespoons boiling water to the wheat starch, stirring rapidly with chopsticks. Turn the dough out onto a flat surface and knead for about 30 seconds. The dough must be quite thick and a trifle—but only a trifle—sticky.

4. Put the cooked yolks through a sieve. Combine the yolks with the dough, kneading rapidly but thoroughly for about 30 seconds. Roll the dough into a long sausage shape. Bring up the ends to the center. Press down and knead. Again, roll the dough into a sausage shape, bring up the ends, knead, and so on for about 1 minute.

5. Now shape the dough again into a long sausage shape about 1 inch thick. Cut the dough into 16 pieces.

6. Using the fingers, shape each piece into a slightly curved cup. Fill the cups with about 1 teaspoon of the beehive stuffing. Bring the edges together and seal with the fingers to make a football shape with pointed ends.

7. Heat the oil for deep frying. Add the dumplings and cook until crisp and golden all over, about 5 minutes.

Yield: 16 dumplings.

BEEHIVE STUFFING

¾ cup finely diced lean pork

4 tablespoons cornstarch

⅓ cup finely chopped peeled and deveined shrimp, about 7 ounces

2 cups peanut, vegetable, or corn oil

½ cup finely chopped black Chinese mushrooms that have been soaked in warm water, drained, and squeezed to extract most of their liquid

1 tablespoon dry sherry

1 teaspoon light soy sauce

1 teaspoon sugar

1 teaspoon salt

5 tablespoons chicken broth

1. Combine the pork, 1 tablespoon of the cornstarch, and the shrimp and blend well.

2. Heat the oil in a wok and, when it is quite hot, add the shrimp mixture, stirring. Cook, stirring, for about 15 seconds, or until the mixture loses its raw color. Pour and scrape the mixture into a strainer.

3. Return about 2 tablespoons of the oil to the wok. Return the drained shrimp mixture to the wok. Add the mushrooms and cook for about 10 seconds. Add the sherry, soy sauce, sugar, and salt, stirring.

4. Blend the remaining 3 tablespoons cornstarch and broth and add it gradually, stirring. Add 1 tablespoon oil and stir. Remove from the heat.

Yield: Enough stuffing for 16 or more dumplings.

Note: The amount of stuffing indicated here will be in excess of that used in the recipe for beehive dumplings. Leftover stuffing may be reheated and served with rice.

Rabbit-Shaped Dim Sum

1. Put the wheat starch in a small mixing bowl.

2. Add the boiling water, stirring rapidly with chopsticks. Turn the dough out onto a flat surface and knead briefly. The dough must be quite thick and a trifle—but only a trifle—sticky. Set aside briefly.

3. To make the filling, put the pork fat in a sieve and place the sieve in a pan of boiling water. Let stand for about 10 seconds. Drain well. Run under cold water to chill. Drain thoroughly on paper toweling.

4. In a bowl, combine the shrimp, water chestnuts, sugar, salt, pepper, sesame oil, and the pork fat. Blend well with the fingers.

5. Using the palms of the hands, roll the dough out into a long sausage shape about 1 inch thick. Cut the dough into 1-inch lengths. This should produce about 20 pieces.

6. Place each piece on a small, flat surface and roll it into a ball. Using a large, smooth cleaver, flatten each piece into a circle as perfectly as possible. If the circle of dough tears, it may be gathered up and rolled again.

7. Fill each circle with about 1 teaspoon of filling. Gather up the edges of the dough. Twirl the dough around with the fingers of the left hand while pressing the top of the dough with the fingers of the right hand. There will be excess dough at the point where the dough is sealed. Twirl this excess dough out into a thin, smooth pencil shape with a pointed end about 1 inch long.

8. Using a pair of scissors, cut through the "pencil" lengthwise. Bend the split ends back over the dumpling to resemble a pair of rabbit ears.

9. Press the dumpling slightly inward at the base of the ears. This will fashion an indentation for the eyes and at the same time will fashion the rabbit's nose so that it protrudes slightly.

10. Add one tiny cube of cooked ham on either side of the nose to make a pink-eyed rabbit.

11. Arrange the dumplings in a bamboo or metal steamer. Cover. Place the steamer over boiling water and steam for 8 minutes.

Yield: 20 dumplings.

THE DOUGH:

¾ cup plus 1 tablespoon wheat starch, available in Asian groceries and supermarkets

½ cup plus 2 tablespoons rapidly boiling water

THE FILLING:

¾ cup finely chopped unsalted pork fat

¾ cup finely chopped peeled and deveined shrimp

⅓ cup finely diced water chestnuts

½ teaspoon sugar

¼ teaspoon salt

⅛ teaspoon freshly ground white pepper

¼ teaspoon sesame oil

20 very small pieces cooked ham

Phoenix Rolls

⅓ cup finely chopped peeled and deveined shrimp, about 7 ounces

1 cup finely diced lean raw pork

2 eggs

Salt to taste

1 teaspoon dry sherry

1½ tablespoons cornstarch

1 teaspoon peanut, vegetable, or corn oil

¼ teaspoon sesame oil

2 tablespoons finely chopped black Chinese mushrooms that have been soaked in warm water, drained, and squeezed to extract most of their liquid

2 tablespoons finely chopped cooked ham

2 hard-cooked eggs, peeled and each cut into three wedges

½ cup wheat starch, available in Asian groceries and supermarkets

Oil for deep frying

1. Combine the shrimp, pork, 1 of the eggs, and the salt in a mixing bowl. Blend well with the hands, stirring and beating vigorously for about 2 minutes.

2. Add the sherry and cornstarch and blend well. Add 1 teaspoon of the oil and the sesame oil and blend well.

3. Add the chopped mushrooms and ham and blend well.

4. Put half the mixture on a flat surface. Flatten it with the hands into a rectangle measuring about 4½ × 7 inches. Arrange three egg wedges lengthwise near the bottom of the rectangle, ends touching.

5. Using a knife, lift up one side of the rectangle and fold it over the eggs. Roll the mixture over itself to form a thick sausage shape, sealing the ends with the fingers.

6. Repeat with the remaining mixture and egg wedges.

7. Place the rolls in a bamboo or metal steamer. Cover and place the steamer over boiling water and steam for 20 minutes.

8. Remove from the heat and let cool.

9. When thoroughly cool, coat the rolls all over with the remaining raw egg, which has been well beaten.

10. Coat the rolls all over with wheat starch.

11. Heat the oil for deep frying. Add the rolls and cook until golden brown all over, about 5 minutes.

12. Drain and let cool. Serve cut into ¼-inch-thick slices.

Yield: About 50 dumplings.

SHRIMP IN BAMBOO SHAPE

1. Peel and devein the shrimp, but leave the last tail segment intact. Rinse the shrimp and pat dry.

2. Give each shrimp a slight gash crosswise at the top.

3. Sprinkle the shrimp with 1 teaspoon of the salt and the ½ teaspoon of sesame oil and rub them with the mixture.

4. Dip the shrimp, one at a time, into the cornstarch. Arrange on a platter.

5. Put ½ cup of the leftover cornstarch in a bowl. Add the eggs and remaining ¼ teaspoon salt. Mix well with the fingers.

6. Heat the oil in a wok until it is hot and almost but not quite smoking. Dip the shrimp into the egg-cornstarch mixture. Lift them one at a time and slide them into the hot oil. Cook, turning the shrimp, until golden brown, about 2 minutes. Cook a few at a time, draining and setting aside after browning.

7. Return the shrimp to the hot oil and deep-fry a second time, for about 1 minute longer.

Yield: 24 shrimp.

¼ pound fresh shrimp, about 24

1¼ teaspoons salt

½ teaspoon sesame oil

1 cup cornstarch

3 eggs

3 cups peanut, vegetable, or corn oil

ESCARGOTS BOURGUIGNONNE

24 snail shells

One 7½-ounce can imported snails (24 snails), undrained

2 tablespoons dry white wine

1 shallot, thinly sliced

1 garlic clove, thinly sliced

1 parsley sprig

6 thin carrot rounds

¼ teaspoon thyme

¼ bay leaf

Salt and freshly ground pepper to taste

Snail butter (see following recipe)

Someone has claimed that snails, those elegant, fine-textured delicacies that grow on vine leaves, are merely a good excuse for gastronomes to eat lots of garlic without apology. That may be stretching things a bit, but snails do belong to that category of foods more or less neutral—like macaroni and potatoes—whose character relies on the flavors and seasonings with which they are linked.

1. Wash the shells in hot water and drain well. Cool.

2. Empty the snails and their liquid into a saucepan and add all the remaining ingredients except the snail butter. Bring to the boil, cover, and simmer for 10 minutes. Let cool and drain.

3. Spoon about ½ teaspoon of the snail butter into each of the shells. Add one snail to each shell, pushing it in with the fingers. Spoon equal portions of the remaining snail butter into the hole, filling it and smoothing off the butter at the opening. This may be done in advance and the snails refrigerated or frozen.

4. When ready to cook, preheat the oven to 500 degrees.

5. Arrange the snails on 4 traditional snail dishes. Bake for 5 minutes, or until sizzling hot. Serve piping hot with French bread.

Yield: 4 servings.

SNAIL BUTTER

12 tablespoons butter, at room temperature

2 tablespoons fine fresh bread crumbs

4 tablespoons finely chopped fresh parsley

1 tablespoon finely chopped shallots

1 tablespoon finely chopped garlic

Salt and freshly ground pepper to taste

Cream together all the ingredients and use for stuffing snails.

Yield: Sufficient butter for 24 snails.

COUNTRY PÂTÉ

1. Preheat the oven to 375 degrees.
2. Put the pork liver, pork butt, onion, and garlic through a meat grinder, using the fine blade of the grinder. Grind into a mixing bowl.
3. Add the thyme, flour, saltpeter, salt, pepper, wine, eggs, and nutmeg. Mix well with the hands until thoroughly blended and no lumps remain.
4. Select a 10- or 12-cup rectangular pâté mold. (One that measures 14 × 3¾ × 3½ inches is suitable.) Line the bottom and sides of the mold with the fatback slices, letting them hang generously over the sides of the mold. Spoon the mixture into the mold and smooth it over. Fold the fatback overhanging over the filling to completely enclose it.
5. Set the mold in a large basin and pour boiling water around it. Bake for 2 hours. The pâté is done when the internal temperature registers 160 degrees on a meat thermometer. Remove from the water bath. Cover with foil and weight the pâté with one or two heavy objects. Let stand until cool and then refrigerate.
6. When ready to serve, unmold the pâté and slice.

Yield: 18 or more servings.

3 pounds pork liver

2 pounds boneless pork butt, both lean and fat

2 cups coarsely chopped onion

1 garlic clove, chopped

1 teaspoon chopped fresh thyme, or ½ teaspoon dried

1 cup flour

½ teaspoon saltpeter, available in drugstores

2 teaspoons salt

½ teaspoon freshly ground pepper

½ cup dry white wine

4 eggs, lightly beaten

¼ teaspoon grated nutmeg

12 or more slices very thinly sliced unsalted fatback

QUICK PÂTÉ

¼ pound salt pork, cut into small rectangles about ½ inch wide and ⅛ inch thick

1 pound ground pork

½ cup rendered chicken fat, preferably homemade, although bottled chicken fat can be used

¾ pound chicken livers

¼ cup thinly sliced shallots

1 small garlic clove, finely minced

½ bay leaf

¼ teaspoon dried thyme

⅛ teaspoon grated nutmeg

1 clove, crushed

Pinch of ground allspice

Salt and freshly ground pepper to taste

Pinch of cayenne

¼ cup dry white wine

1. Put the salt pork in a saucepan and add cold water to cover. Bring to the boil and drain.

2. Put the salt pork pieces in a heavy skillet and cook until rendered of fat, stirring occasionally. When slightly browned, add the ground pork, stirring to break up lumps.

3. Heat the chicken fat separately in a skillet and add the chicken livers and cook, turning the livers occasionally, until they lose their raw look. Add the chicken livers and chicken fat to the pork. Cover and cook for about 2 minutes.

4. Add the shallots, garlic, bay leaf, thyme, nutmeg, clove, allspice, salt, and pepper to taste. Use very little salt. The salt pork adds its own salt. Add the cayenne and white wine. Cover and cook for 10 minutes. Remove from the heat and let stand until warm.

5. Put half the mixture in the container of a food processor. Process for several minutes, or until as fine as the pâté can become. Repeat with the rest of the mixture.

6. If desired, spoon the pâté into a small crock. Serve with buttered toast.

Yield: 6 to 8 servings.

SALMON PÂTÉ

1. Place the fish in the container of a food processor or blender. Add about ¼ cup of cream and blend. Gradually add more cream until the desired consistency is reached, taking care the mixture does not become too liquid. Stop the blending at intervals and scrape down the sides of the container with a plastic spatula. When properly blended, the mass should be mousselike, holding its shape when picked up with the spatula.

2. Spoon and scrape the mixture into a bowl and add the lemon juice, capers, dill, salt, and pepper. Spoon the pâté into a serving dish such as a small soufflé mold. Cover and chill well, preferably overnight. Garnish, if desired, with chopped dill. Serve with lightly buttered toast.

Yield: 4 to 6 servings.

Note: This pâté is particularly good if made with the leftover morsels of a poached whole salmon, the bits that cling around the main bones of the fish, near and in the head of the fish. These morsels are rich and gelatinous.

2 cups cooked, boneless, skinless salmon (see note)

¼ to ½ cup heavy cream

2 tablespoons lemon juice, more or less to taste

2 tablespoons capers

1 tablespoon chopped fresh dill

Salt and freshly ground pepper to taste

CHICKEN AND VEAL PÂTÉ

1   pound skinless, boneless chicken breast, cut into 1-inch cubes

¾   pound chicken livers

1   tablespoon butter plus butter for greasing the pan

1½   cups finely chopped onions

1   teaspoon finely minced garlic

¼   teaspoon finely minced fresh or dried thyme

1¼   cups finely diced, sweet green or red pepper

½   pound spinach, trimmed and cleaned, about 6 cups loosely packed

1   cup plus 2 tablespoons fine fresh bread crumbs

1½   pounds ground veal

1   egg, lightly beaten

⅛   teaspoon grated nutmeg

Salt and freshly ground pepper to taste

1. Put the chicken breast into the container of a food processor and blend it to a coarse grind. Or put it through the medium blade of a meat grinder. Set aside.

2. Put the chicken livers into the container of a food processor or blender and process to a fine purée. Set aside.

3. Melt the 1 tablespoon of butter in a heavy skillet and add the onions, garlic, thyme, and diced pepper. Cook, stirring often, until the mixture is wilted.

4. Coarsely chop the spinach and add it. Cook, stirring, until it is wilted. Spoon and scrape the mixture into a mixing bowl. Let cool briefly.

5. Add the liver purée, chicken, 1 cup of the bread crumbs, veal, egg, and nutmeg. Add salt and pepper to taste. Blend thoroughly.

6. Preheat the oven to 400 degrees.

7. Lightly butter a loaf pan (9 × 5 × 2¾ inches). Spoon in the mixture, smooth over the top, and sprinkle with the remaining bread crumbs.

8. Cover the loaf pan closely with aluminum foil. Place the loaf pan in a larger pan and pour an inch or so of water around it. Bring the water to the boil on top of the stove. Place the pans in the oven and bake for 1 hour and 15 minutes. Remove from the oven and let cool. Chill thoroughly before unmolding.

Yield: 10 or more servings.

Eggs and Luncheon Dishes

OMELETTE NATURE (BASIC OMELET)

A properly prepared omelet is a joy to the eye and an absolute pleasure to the palate. It is infinite in the number of flavors with which it can be made, ranging from all manner of vegetables to jams or jellies. We are of the school that much prefers the savory omelet to the sweet.

3 eggs, well beaten
  Salt and freshly ground
  pepper to taste
1½ teaspoons butter

1. Combine the eggs, salt, and pepper in a mixing bowl.

2. Place an 8- or 9-inch well-cured metal or nonstick omelet pan on the stove and heat well. Add the butter and, when melted, add the egg mixture and start cooking, shaking the skillet and simultaneously stirring rapidly with a fork, holding the tines parallel to the bottom of the skillet. Try not to scrape the bottom.

3. Cook to the desired degree of doneness. Ideally, the omelet must remain runny in the center, yet firm on the bottom. Remember that the omelet will continue to cook until the moment it is turned out of the pan and that it cooks quickly.

4. When the omelet is properly done, lift the handle of the skillet with the left hand. Knock the omelet pan on the surface of the stove so that the omelet jumps to the bottom curve of the pan. Use the fork and quickly fold the omelet from the top down. Let the omelet stand as briefly as possible over high heat until it browns on the bottom. Turn it out neatly onto a hot serving plate, seam side down.

Yield: 1 serving.

OMELET AUX FINES HERBES

Before making the omelet, blend 1 teaspoon chopped parsley, 1 teaspoon chopped chives, and 1 teaspoon chopped fresh tarragon, or ½ teaspoon dried. Add these mixed herbs to the eggs along with the salt and pepper.

CHEESE OMELET

Grate enough cheese, preferably Gruyère, to make ¼ cup. One tablespoon of grated Parmesan cheese may also be added. Prepare the basic omelet. Before turning the omelet out, add the grated cheese to the center of the omelet. Fold it down and turn it out onto a plate.

FILLED OMELET

Prepare the basic omelet, but in step 4, when the omelet is ready to be folded, add a spoonful or so of any desired filling (see following pages) and then fold. Turn out as indicated.

Classically, if one wants to garnish a filled omelet, one makes a slight gash on the top of the omelet once it is turned out. Spoon into the gash a bit of the filling used for the interior of the omelet.

SHRIMP IN PAPRIKA AND SOUR CREAM SAUCE

1. Peel and devein the shrimp. Cut them into ½-inch cubes.
2. Melt the butter in a small skillet and add the shallots. Cook briefly and add the sherry. Cook until the wine has almost evaporated. Add the shrimp, salt, pepper, and paprika. Cook, stirring, for about 1 minute.
3. Add the sour cream and cook just until the cream is piping hot without boiling. Stir in the dill. Use as a filling for omelets.

Yield: 4 servings.

½ pound raw shrimp in the shell

1 tablespoon butter

2 tablespoons finely chopped shallots

2 tablespoons dry sherry

Salt and freshly ground pepper to taste

1 tablespoon paprika, preferably mild Hungarian

½ cup sour cream

1 tablespoon finely chopped fresh dill

CHICKEN LIVERS IN MADEIRA WINE SAUCE

½ pound chicken livers
4 tablespoons corn oil
  Salt and freshly ground pepper
2 tablespoons butter
2 tablespoons finely chopped shallots
¼ cup Madeira wine

1. Pick over the livers. Cut away and discard any connective tissue. Cut the livers in half.

2. Heat the oil in a skillet and add the livers, salt, and pepper. Cook for about 1 minute and drain well. Pour off all fat from the skillet and wipe it out well with paper toweling. Transfer the livers to a very small saucepan.

3. Melt 1 tablespoon of the butter in the skillet and add the shallots. Cook, stirring, until they are wilted. Add the Madeira and cook until the wine is reduced by half. Pour this over the livers. Heat the livers in the sauce and swirl in the remaining tablespoon of butter. Use as a filling for omelets.

Yield: 4 servings.

SAUCE PROVENÇALE

2 tablespoons olive oil
1 cup thinly sliced, halved onions
1 cup thinly sliced cored and seeded green pepper
1 tablespoon finely minced garlic
1 cup drained imported canned tomatoes
¼ teaspoon dried thyme
1 bay leaf
  Salt and freshly ground pepper to taste

1. Heat the oil in a small skillet and add the onions, green pepper, and garlic. Cook, stirring often, for about 2 minutes.

2. Add the tomatoes, thyme, bay leaf, salt, and pepper. Cook, stirring, for about 1 minute. Cover closely and cook for about 5 minutes longer. Uncover and cook until the tomato sauce is thickened, 1 minute or less. Use as a filling for omelets.

Yield: 4 servings.

HOT CHILI SAUCE WITH AVOCADO

Combine all the ingredients in a mixing bowl and use as a filling for omelets.

Yield: 4 servings.

½ cup finely chopped fresh or bottled jalapeño peppers

½ cup seeded, finely diced tomatoes

½ cup finely diced red onion

½ cup diced avocado

4 tablespoons finely chopped fresh coriander

2 tablespoons freshly squeezed lime juice

Salt and freshly ground pepper to taste

2 teaspoons olive oil

OMELETTE PAVILLON

7 tablespoons butter

3 tablespoons flour

1 cup fresh or canned chicken broth

½ cup heavy cream

3 tablespoons finely chopped onion

2 cups peeled, seeded, chopped tomatoes

2 fresh thyme sprigs, or ½ teaspoon dried

1 bay leaf

   Salt and freshly ground pepper to taste

1 cup finely cubed cooked breast of chicken

1 egg yolk

¼ cup grated Gruyère or Fontina cheese

10 eggs

3 tablespoons grated Parmesan cheese

1. Heat 2 tablespoons of the butter in a saucepan and add the flour. Stir with a wire whisk until blended. Add the chicken broth and cook, stirring vigorously with the whisk. Add the cream and bring to the boil. Simmer for about 10 minutes.

2. Meanwhile, heat 1 tablespoon of the butter in a saucepan and add the onion. Cook, stirring, until wilted and add the tomatoes, thyme, bay leaf, salt, and pepper. Simmer, stirring occasionally, for about 10 minutes.

3. Heat another tablespoon of the butter and add the chicken. Cook, stirring, for about 30 seconds. Add 3 tablespoons of the cream sauce. Bring to the boil and remove from the heat. Set aside.

4. To the remaining cream sauce, add the egg yolk and stir to blend. Add salt and pepper to taste and the grated cheese. Heat, stirring, just until the cheese melts. Set aside.

5. Beat the eggs with salt and pepper. Add 6 tablespoons of the tomato sauce. Heat the remaining 3 tablespoons of butter in an omelet pan or a nonstick skillet and, when it is hot, add the eggs. Cook, stirring, until the omelet is set on the bottom but moist and runny in the center. Spoon creamed chicken down the center of the omelet and add the remaining tomato sauce. Quickly turn the omelet out into a baking dish.

6. Spoon the remaining cream sauce over the omelet and sprinkle with grated Parmesan cheese. Run the dish under the broiler until golden brown.

Yield: 4 to 6 servings.

FRITTATA

1. Heat the oil in a heavy skillet. Add the potatoes and spread them out to brown. When they are crisp on the bottom, turn and brown the other side. Transfer with a slotted spoon to paper towels to drain.

2. Add the onion, green pepper, and zucchini to the oil in the skillet. Cook, stirring, until the vegetables have wilted, about 5 minutes. Transfer with a slotted spoon to a bowl. Discard the oil.

3. Beat the eggs lightly with a fork. Add the potatoes, vegetables, salt, and pepper. Mix well to combine.

4. Heat the butter in the skillet over very low heat. Pour in the egg mixture and spread it out with a fork. Cook for about 15 minutes, until the eggs have set but the top is still runny.

5. Run the frittata under the broiler for about 1 minute, just until the top has set.

6. Loosen the frittata with a spatula and slide it out onto a plate. Cut into wedges to serve.

Yield: 4 to 6 servings.

3 tablespoons vegetable oil

2½ cups peeled and cubed (¼ inch) potatoes

1 onion, very thinly sliced

1 green pepper, cut into thin strips

1 small zucchini, thinly sliced

8 eggs
Salt and freshly ground pepper to taste

2 tablespoons butter

CHEESE SOUFFLÉ

¼ pound Gruyère or Swiss cheese, cut into ¼-inch slices

8 large eggs

6 tablespoons butter

5 tablespoons flour

2 cups milk

Salt and freshly ground pepper to taste

⅛ teaspoon grated nutmeg

Pinch of cayenne

2 tablespoons cornstarch

3 tablespoons water

¼ cup grated Parmesan cheese

2 tablespoons grated Gruyère or Swiss cheese

1. Preheat the oven to 400 degrees.

2. Stack the cheese slices on a flat surface. Using a sharp knife, cut into ¼-inch strips. Cut the strips into ¼-inch cubes. There should be about 1 cup. Set aside.

3. Separate the eggs, placing the yolks in one bowl and the whites in another.

4. Use 2 tablespoons of the butter and butter all around the inside rim and bottom of a 2-quart soufflé dish. Place the dish in the freezer until ready to use.

5. Melt the remaining butter in a saucepan and add the flour, stirring with a wire whisk. When blended, add the milk, stirring rapidly with the whisk. Add the salt, pepper, nutmeg, and cayenne. Cook for 30 seconds, stirring.

6. Blend the cornstarch and water and add this to the bubbling sauce, stirring. Cook for about 2 minutes. Add yolks, stirring vigorously. Cook, stirring, for about 1 minute.

7. Spoon and scrape the mixture into a large mixing bowl. Add the cubed Gruyère or Swiss cheese and the Parmesan cheese. Blend well.

8. Beat the egg whites until stiff. Add half the whites to the soufflé mixture and beat them in thoroughly. Add the remaining whites and fold them in quickly but gently with a rubber spatula.

9. Spoon and scrape the mixture into the soufflé dish. Sprinkle with the grated Gruyère and place in the oven.

10. Bake for 15 minutes. Reduce the oven heat to 375 degrees and bake for 15 minutes longer.

Yield: 4 to 6 servings.

CORN AND SALMON SOUFFLÉ

1. Preheat the oven to 375 degrees. Generously butter two 1-quart soufflé dishes or one 8-cup soufflé dish. Refrigerate or place briefly in the freezer.

2. Cut and scrape the kernels from the cob. There should be about 1 cup. Set aside.

3. Coarsely flake the salmon. Set aside.

4. Melt the 3 tablespoons of butter in a saucepan and add the flour, stirring with a wire whisk. When blended, add the milk, stirring rapidly with the whisk. When blended and smooth, add the salt and pepper. Add the corn and cook, stirring frequently, for about 3 minutes. Remove from heat and add ¾ cup of the cheese.

5. Blend the cornstarch and water and add it. Cook briefly, stirring with the whisk.

6. Add the egg yolks, stirring them in briskly with the whisk. Add the salt, pepper, nutmeg, and cayenne. Heat briefly but do not boil. Remove from the heat and let cool briefly.

7. Beat the whites until stiff and fold them in.

8. Fill the soufflé dishes half full with the mixture. Add a layer of the salmon. Cover with the remaining mixture. Sprinkle with the remaining cheese and bake for 25 to 35 minutes, or until well risen and nicely browned on top.

Yield: 4 to 8 servings.

4 ears of corn, shucked

1 cup cooked, skinless, boneless salmon, fresh or canned

3 tablespoons butter

3 tablespoons flour

1 cup milk

Salt and freshly ground pepper to taste

1 cup grated Gruyère or Cheddar cheese

1 tablespoon cornstarch

2 tablespoons water

6 eggs, separated

¼ teaspoon grated nutmeg

⅛ teaspoon cayenne

ALSATIAN MEAT PIE

Alsatian pastry for one 10-inch pie (see following recipe)

1 pound lean leg or shoulder of veal, ground, or use an equal quantity of ground lean pork

⅛ pound ground lean pork (in addition to the above meat)

Salt and freshly ground pepper to taste

⅛ teaspoon grated nutmeg

2 teaspoons butter

1½ tablespoons finely chopped shallots

⅓ cup finely chopped onion

¾ cup finely chopped mushrooms

1 whole egg

1 egg yolk

1 cup heavy cream

To many cooks, a quiche is a quiche lorraine, but quiche is really the generic name for a host of nonsweet pies. One of the finest we know is this Alsatian meat pie made with veal or pork. It is a tasty appetizer or luncheon dish and was a specialty of Pierre Franey's Uncle Louis, a native of Alsace.

1. Line a 10-inch quiche pan with a removable bottom with the pastry and chill it.

2. Preheat the oven to 375 degrees.

3. Sprinkle the veal and pork with the salt, pepper, and nutmeg.

4. Heat the butter in a skillet and add the shallots and onion. Cook, stirring, until wilted and add the mushrooms. Cook for 5 minutes, stirring frequently. Add the meat, stirring and breaking up lumps of meat with the side of a large metal spoon. Cook until most of the liquid is given up.

5. Beat the egg and yolk with a fork until well blended and add the cream and salt and pepper to taste. Blend well and add the mixture to the meat. Stir well.

6. Pour the mixture into the prepared pie shell and bake for 15 minutes. Reduce the oven heat to 350 degrees. Bake for 30 to 35 minutes longer, or until the custard is set. Remove from the oven and let stand. Serve lukewarm or at room temperature.

Yield: 8 servings.

1. Put the flour in a mixing bowl and place it in the freezer. Place the butter in the freezer and let both stand for half an hour or longer.

2. Remove the flour and butter from the freezer and cut the butter into bits, adding it to the flour. Add the salt. Using the fingers or a pastry blender, cut the butter into the flour until the mixture is like coarse cornmeal. Gradually add the oil, stirring with a two-pronged fork. When blended, add the milk gradually, working the pastry with the hands until it forms a dough. Knead briefly and gather the dough into a ball. Wrap it in wax paper and chill for at least 30 minutes.

3. Remove the dough from the refrigerator and place it on a lightly floured surface. Roll it out into a rectangle measuring about 12 × 6 inches. Fold a third of the dough over toward the center. Fold the other side of the dough over toward the center, thus making a three-layer package of dough. Cover and refrigerate for about half an hour.

4. Roll out the dough once more on a lightly floured surface, sprinkling the surface with additional flour as necessary. Roll it into another rectangle. Fold the dough into thirds as before, cover, and chill. The dough is now ready to be rolled into a circle for fitting into a 10-inch metal quiche pan.

Yield: Pastry for a 10-inch quiche.

ALSATIAN PASTRY

2½ cups flour
¼ pound butter
   Salt to taste
6 tablespoons well-chilled corn oil
6 tablespoons cold milk, approximately

ZUCCHINI AND HAM QUICHE

Pastry to line a 10-inch quiche tin (see following recipe)

2 tablespoons butter

¼ cup finely chopped onion

1 small garlic clove, finely minced

Salt and freshly ground pepper to taste

1¼ pounds zucchini, trimmed and thinly sliced, about 5 cups

¼ pound sliced boiled ham, finely diced, about ¾ cup

4 large eggs

¾ cup milk

½ cup heavy cream

¼ cup grated Parmesan cheese

1. Preheat the oven to 350 degrees.
2. Roll out the pastry. Line a 10-inch quiche tin with the pastry and then with foil. Add dried beans to weight the bottom down. Place in the oven and bake for 20 minutes. Remove the foil and beans from the pastry.
3. Heat the butter in a skillet and add the onion and garlic. Cook, stirring, until wilted. Add the salt, pepper, and zucchini and cook, stirring gently and shaking the pan occasionally, for about 5 minutes. Add the ham, stirring gently to blend, and remove from the heat.
4. Break the eggs into a mixing bowl. Beat well and add the milk, cream, salt, and pepper to taste. Scrape into the zucchini mixture.
5. Increase oven heat to 375 degrees.
6. Pour the zucchini and custard mixture into the pastry. Sprinkle with cheese. Place the quiche on a baking sheet and bake for 30 minutes.
7. Reduce the oven heat to 350 degrees. Bake for 15 minutes longer.

Yield: 6 to 8 servings.

PASTRY DOUGH

2 cups flour

½ teaspoon salt

½ cup solid white shortening

3 tablespoons butter

3 to 4 tablespoons ice water

1. Put the flour and salt into the container of a food processor or a mixing bowl.
2. Add the shortening and butter and process while gradually adding the water. Add only enough water so that the dough comes clean from the sides of the container and can be handled. Shape into a flat rectangle and wrap in plastic wrap or wax paper. Chill for 1 hour or longer.

Yield: Pastry for a 10-inch quiche.

MEXICAN QUICHE WITH CHILIES AND CHEESE

1. Preheat the oven to 425 degrees.

2. Roll out the pastry and line a quiche or pie tin with the pastry. Line the shell with foil and add enough dried beans to weight the bottom down. Place the shell in the oven and bake for 10 minutes.

3. Remove the foil and dried beans. Return the shell to the oven and bake for 2 minutes longer.

4. Remove the shell and reduce the oven heat to 350 degrees.

5. Heat the butter in a small skillet and add the shallots. Cook briefly and add the chilies. Stir and remove from the heat. Let cool.

6. Scrape the chili mixture into the prebaked pie shell. Sprinkle evenly with the cheese.

7. Blend the egg yolks lightly with the cream. Add the salt and pour the custard over the cheese. Place the pie on a baking sheet and bake for 35 minutes, or until the custard is set.

Yield: 6 to 8 servings.

Pastry for a 10-inch quiche (see preceding recipe)

2 tablespoons butter

1 tablespoon finely chopped shallots

One 4-ounce can chopped green chilies

2 cups grated Gruyère, Cheddar, or Swiss cheese

4 large or 6 small egg yolks, about ⅓ cup

1½ cups heavy cream

Salt to taste

HAM-STUFFED EGGS

4 hard-cooked eggs (see following instructions)

1 ounce boiled ham

1 tablespoon imported mustard, such as Dijon or Düsseldorf

1 tablespoon butter at room temperature

¼ teaspoon Worcestershire sauce

2 teaspoons mayonnaise

Salt and freshly ground pepper to taste

1 tablespoon finely chopped chives

Cutouts of black or green olives, pimientos, pickles, and so on

There is an argument to the effect that the most interesting dishes to work with in any cuisine are those whose character can be changed at will. One of the great foods for summer feasting—cold stuffed eggs—fits that definition precisely. The fillings are virtually without end. Cold cubed chicken, ham, turkey, veal, and poached fish can be used, garnished with anchovies, olives, pimientos, and other kindred edibles. The sweet herbs are virtuous: parsley, chives, tarragon, chervil, even rosemary. The egg yolks, sieved or blended, are generally bound with mayonnaise and/or butter. Add a bit of salt and pepper and your creativity can take it from there.

1. Split the eggs in half. Put the yolks in a sieve and press through with the fingers.

2. Cut the ham into very fine dice and chop it. Combine the sieved yolks and ham in a mixing bowl. Add the mustard and butter. Stir to blend.

3. Add the remaining ingredients except the cutouts and blend thoroughly. Equip a pastry bag with a star tube (No. 4). Fill the bag with the ham mixture and pipe it into the egg hollows. Garnish the top of each egg with a small slice of black or green olive or other cutout.

Yield: 8 stuffed egg halves.

HARD-COOKED EGGS

Place any given number of eggs in a saucepan and add warm water to cover. Add a little salt, if desired, to facilitate later peeling. Bring slowly to the boil and simmer gently for about 12 minutes. Cool immediately under cold running water. Drain and peel.

MUSHROOM-STUFFED EGGS

The stuffed eggs of our childhood were, more often than not, deviled, which is to say flavored with mustard, Worcestershire sauce, and a dash or two of Tabasco, perhaps.

We still have a fancy for those deviled eggs, but our taste overall is a bit more sophisticated now. So we created a few luncheon dishes based on eggs stuffed with a mushroom filling, topped with a sauce of one sort or another, and then baked. The flavors included a dandy provençale sauce, made with tomatoes and mushrooms, plus, of course, a touch of garlic.

We might note that the basic recipe for eggs stuffed with mushrooms is delicious served cold and unsauced.

1. Slice the mushrooms and chop them as fine as possible. This can be done in a food processor after slicing.

2. Melt the butter in a small skillet and add the onion and shallots. Cook, stirring, until they are wilted. Add the mushrooms and lemon juice. Cook, stirring, for about 1 minute.

3. Add the cream and continue cooking for about 2 minutes. There should be about ½ cup of the mushroom mixture.

4. Put the egg yolks through a fine sieve into a mixing bowl. Set the white aside.

5. Add the mushroom mixture, mustard, parsley, salt, and pepper to the sieved egg yolks. Blend well. Stuff each egg half with an equal portion of the stuffing and set aside.

6. Serve the stuffed eggs hot, topped with a sauce and baked according to the following recipe. Or serve them cold, each simply garnished with a rolled anchovy fillet, half a stuffed olive, or a small morsel of sardine.

Yield: 16 stuffed egg halves.

¼ pound mushrooms

2 tablespoons butter

2 tablespoons finely chopped onion

2 tablespoons finely chopped shallots

Juice of ½ lemon

2 tablespoons heavy cream

8 hard-cooked eggs, peeled and split in half

2 tablespoons Dijon mustard

3 tablespoons finely chopped parsley

Salt and freshly ground pepper to taste

BAKED STUFFED EGGS
WITH TOMATO SAUCE

16 mushroom-stuffed,
    hard-cooked egg halves
    (see preceding recipe)

 3 tablespoons butter

½ cup finely chopped
    onion

½ teaspoon finely minced
    garlic

 1 tablespoon cornstarch
    or arrowroot

¼ pound mushrooms,
    thinly sliced, about
    1½ cups

 1 cup imported canned
    tomatoes

½ cup fresh or canned
    chicken broth

    Salt and freshly ground
    pepper to taste

 2 tablespoons finely
    chopped parsley

½ bay leaf

 2 fresh thyme sprigs, or
    ½ teaspoon dried

1. Prepare the stuffed eggs.

2. Preheat the oven to 400 degrees.

3. Use 1 tablespoon of the butter to grease 4 individual ramekins,
    each large enough to hold 4 stuffed egg halves. Arrange 4 stuffed
    egg halves, stuffed side up, in each ramekin. Set aside.

4. Melt the remaining 2 tablespoons of butter in a saucepan and add
    the onion and garlic. Cook, stirring, until they are wilted. Sprinkle
    with cornstarch and stir to blend. Add the mushrooms and cook
    until they are wilted.

5. Add the tomatoes and broth, stirring. Bring to the boil and add
    the salt, pepper, parsley, bay leaf, and thyme. Simmer for about
    10 minutes.

6. Place the ramekins in the oven and bake the stuffed eggs for
    5 minutes.

7. Spoon equal portions of the sauce over the stuffed eggs and serve
    hot.

Yield: 4 servings.

NEW ORLEANS OYSTER LOAF

One of my fondest memories of childhood came about on my first visit to New Orleans (the saying was that when a good Mississippian died, his soul went to New Orleans forever). It was then that I ate a New Orleans oyster loaf. It consisted of Italian bread sliced through the center and filled with crisp, cornmeal-covered oysters, deep-fried, with mayonnaise smeared on the oysters and Tabasco (mother's milk, it was laughingly referred to) sprinkled on according to taste.

1. Preheat the oven to 400 degrees.
2. Split the loaf in half lengthwise. Wrap it in foil and bake for about 10 minutes.
3. Preheat the broiler. Brush each half of the bread on the split sides with melted butter and toast until golden on the split sides.
4. Pile the oysters on one half of the bread. Spoon the mayonnaise on top and add a few dashes of Tabasco sauce. Cover with the second half of the bread. Cut the loaf in half crosswise and serve.

Yield: 2 servings.

1 loaf crusty French or Italian bread, preferably 10 or 12 inches long

2 to 4 tablespoons butter, melted

24 oysters fried in cornmeal (see recipe page 436)

2 to 4 tablespoons mayonnaise

Tabasco sauce to taste

CRABMEAT SALAD

1 egg yolk
  Salt and freshly ground
  pepper to taste
1 tablespoon Dijon
  mustard
1 teaspoon vinegar
¼ teaspoon
  Worcestershire sauce
  Dash of Tabasco sauce
1 cup peanut oil
3 tablespoons water
¾ cup flaked crabmeat,
  picked over to remove
  any trace of shell or
  cartilage

1. Put the yolk, salt, pepper, mustard, vinegar, Worcestershire, and Tabasco in a mixing bowl. Start beating with a wire whisk.
2. Gradually add the oil, beating vigorously until all the oil is added. Thin the sauce a bit with the water.
3. Add the crabmeat and stir to combine.

Yield: 2 to 4 servings.

AVOCADO WITH CRABMEAT

⅓ cup sour cream
⅓ cup freshly made
  mayonnaise
3 tablespoons lemon
  juice
¼ teaspoon paprika
  Salt and freshly ground
  pepper to taste
¾ pound fresh crabmeat,
  preferably lump or
  backfin, picked over to
  remove all trace of
  shell and cartilage
2 or 3 ripe, unblemished
  avocados, split in half
  and seeded

1. Combine the sour cream and mayonnaise in a mixing bowl. Stir in the lemon juice, paprika, salt, and pepper.
2. Fold in the crabmeat, stirring as little as possible so as not to break up the lumps. Fill the avocado halves with the mixture and serve.

Yield: 4 to 6 servings.

MUSHROOMS STUFFED WITH CRABMEAT

1. Preheat the oven to 400 degrees.

2. Remove the stems and reserve the caps from the mushrooms. Chop the stems. There should be about 1 cup.

3. Melt 1 tablespoon of the butter in a saucepan and add the flour, stirring with a wire whisk. When blended, add the milk, stirring rapidly with the whisk. When blended and smooth, add the salt and pepper.

4. In another saucepan, heat the remaining 2 tablespoons of butter and add the scallions and chopped mushroom stems. Cook, stirring, for 4 minutes. Add the crabmeat, stir to blend, and add the Cognac. Add the white sauce and salt and pepper to taste. Blend. Add the egg yolk and Tabasco sauce.

5. Place the mushrooms, hollow side down, in a buttered baking dish. Brush with half of the melted butter and place in the oven for 10 minutes. Remove. Let cool.

6. Stuff the cavity of each mushroom with the crab mixture, heaping it up and smoothing it over. Arrange the mushrooms in the baking dish and sprinkle with Parmesan cheese and the remaining melted butter. Place in the oven and bake for 20 minutes.

Yield: 6 servings.

1 pound mushrooms, preferably large ones
3 tablespoons butter
1 tablespoon flour
½ cup milk
  Salt and freshly ground pepper to taste
½ cup finely chopped scallions
⅓ pound crabmeat
1 tablespoon Cognac
1 egg yolk
  Tabasco sauce to taste
3 tablespoons butter, melted
¼ cup grated Parmesan cheese

Seviche of Scallops with Avocado

1½ pounds fresh bay scallops

5 tablespoons lime juice

½ squeezed lime

Salt and freshly ground pepper to taste

1 tablespoon finely chopped fresh hot green or red pepper, or 1 or 2 canned serrano chilies added according to taste

¼ teaspoon dried oregano

1½ cups cubed, ripe but firm, unblemished avocado

2 tablespoons finely chopped fresh coriander

1. Even if the scallops are small, cut them in half against the grain. Place them in a bowl and add 4 tablespoons of lime juice. Stir.

2. Cut the lime shell into tiny pieces and add them. Add salt and pepper and stir. Cover and refrigerate for at least 12 hours.

3. Add the remaining ingredients. Stir well and serve with crisp leaves of romaine lettuce.

Yield: 6 or more servings.

RATATOUILLE PIE

We have written often about the virtues of ratatouille, not the least of which is that it improves on standing. When we found ourselves with an impressive amount of yesterday's ratatouille, it occurred to us that the mélange of eggplant, tomatoes, zucchini, and so on would make a fine filling for a vegetable pie. We used the ratatouille in layers with sliced Fontina and Parmesan cheeses, and the result was of such goodness it occurred to us that the pie could well be an end in itself. That is to say, why wait for leftovers?

1. Preheat the oven to 425 degrees.

2. Peel the eggplant and cut it into 1½-inch cubes. There should be about 4½ cups.

3. Cut each zucchini in half lengthwise. Cut each half crosswise into ¾-inch pieces.

4. Cut the onion into ½-inch cubes.

5. Cut the green peppers into 1½-inch cubes.

6. Cut the tomatoes into 2-inch cubes. There should be about 2½ cups.

7. Heat the oil in a casserole and add the eggplant. Cook, stirring occasionally, for about 5 minutes. Add the onion, zucchini, and green pepper. Stir to blend the ingredients.

8. Add the garlic, thyme, bay leaf, salt, and pepper. Cook for about 4 minutes, stirring.

9. Add the tomatoes and parsley and stir. Cook for about 5 minutes longer.

10. Place the casserole in the oven and bake for 30 minutes. Stir in the olives and bake for 10 minutes longer.

11. Let the ratatouille stand until thoroughly cold.

12. When ready to bake the pie, reheat the oven to 425 degrees.

13. Line a 10-inch pie plate with half of the pastry, letting 1 inch of the pastry hang over the side. Add about one third of the ratatouille mixture, a layer of Fontina, and a layer of Parmesan cheese and so on. Continue making layers until all of the ratatouille mixture and cheese are used.

14. Brush the overlapping rim of the pastry with a little of the egg blended with the water. Cover with a second layer of pastry. Seal by pressing the edges together. Flute, if desired, or use the tines of a fork to make a pattern all around.

1 eggplant, about 1¾ pounds

2 small zucchini, about 1¼ pounds, trimmed

1 large onion, peeled

2 green peppers, cored and seeded

1 pound ripe tomatoes, cored and peeled

¼ cup olive oil

2 tablespoons finely chopped garlic

1 teaspoon finely chopped fresh thyme, or ½ teaspoon dried

1 bay leaf

Salt and freshly ground pepper to taste

1 cup coarsely chopped parsley

½ cup pitted black olives

1 recipe for pie pastry (see following recipe)

2 cups grated Fontina cheese, preferably imported

¾ cup freshly grated Parmesan cheese

1 egg yolk

2 teaspoons water

15. Use a small biscuit cutter to make a hole in the center of the top pastry. This will allow the steam to escape. Brush the top all over with the egg yolk mixture.

16. Bake the pie for 30 minutes. Reduce the oven temperature to 375 degrees and bake for 15 to 20 minutes longer, or until golden brown on top.

Yield: 6 servings.

PIE PASTRY

1¾ cups flour
½ teaspoon salt
12 tablespoons butter
 2 tablespoons chilled, solid white shortening
 2 to 3 tablespoons ice water

1. Put the flour and salt into the container of a food processor.

2. Cut the butter into small pieces and add it. Add the shortening in small bits.

3. Pulse the machine on and off until the mixture resembles coarse cornmeal. Start processing while gradually dribbling in the water. Add just enough water so that the dough can be gathered into a mass. Do not overblend.

4. Turn the dough out onto a lightly floured board and shape into a ball. Pat the dough into a large flat round biscuit shape.

5. Dust the dough on both sides with flour. Wrap in plastic wrap and chill for 1 hour. Roll out on a lightly floured board.

Yield: Pastry for a 2-crust pie.

SPINACH PIE

1. Preheat the oven to 400 degrees.

2. Pick over the spinach to remove any tough stems. Bring enough water to the boil to cover the spinach when it is added. Add the spinach and cook, stirring down, until spinach is wilted. Do not overcook.

3. Drain the spinach. Run under cold water to chill. Gather the spinach into a ball and squeeze to extract as much liquid as possible.

4. Line a 10-inch quiche tin with slightly more than half of the pastry rolled into a circle. Prick the bottom with the tines of a fork. Line the pastry with wax paper and scatter dried beans or peas to prevent the pie from buckling as it bakes.

5. Roll out the remaining pastry into a circle. If desired, cut the pastry into fancy shapes. In any event, brush the pastry lightly with a blend of egg yolk and water. Arrange the pastry ring or cutouts on a baking sheet.

6. Place the pie tin and the baking sheet in the oven. Bake the pie shell for 8 minutes and remove it from the oven. Remove the wax paper and beans. Brush the bottom of the pie shell lightly with egg yolk blended with water. Return the pie shell to the oven and continue baking for 8 to 10 minutes, until golden brown. Remove from the oven and let cool.

7. Meanwhile, continue baking the pastry ring or cutouts for a total of 8 to 10 minutes, or until golden brown. Remove from the oven and let stand until thoroughly cool.

8. Coarsely chop the spinach and put it in a mixing bowl. Add enough mayonnaise to bind the spinach, the mustard, scallions, salt, pepper, cheese, and chopped egg. Blend well. Chill.

9. Spoon the spinach mixture into the pie shell. Cover with the pastry ring or with the cutouts. Serve as a light luncheon course.

Yield: 6 servings.

1¼ pounds fresh, unblemished spinach leaves

1 recipe for pie pastry (see preceding recipe)

1 egg yolk

2 tablespoons water

¾ to 1 cup freshly made mayonnaise

2 teaspoons Dijon mustard

½ cup finely chopped scallions, green part and all

Salt and freshly ground pepper to taste

⅓ pound Swiss cheese, grated, or crumbled feta cheese, optional

1 hard-cooked egg, peeled and chopped, optional

LEEK TART

Pastry for a 9- or
10-inch pie (see recipe
page 74)
4 to 8 trimmed leeks,
  about 1 pound
3 eggs
1 egg yolk
1 cup heavy cream
2 tablespoons butter
Salt and freshly ground
pepper to taste

1. Preheat the oven to 400 degrees.

2. Line a pie or quiche pan with the pastry. Cover it with wax paper and add dried beans to weight down the bottom.

3. Bake the pastry for 10 minutes. Remove the wax paper and beans. Bake for 5 minutes longer.

4. Meanwhile, split the leeks in half and rinse thoroughly between the leaves to remove all trace of sand and dirt. Drain well.

5. Finely chop the leeks crosswise. There should be about 5 cups. Set aside.

6. Combine the eggs, egg yolk, and ½ cup of the cream. Set aside.

7. Melt the butter in a skillet and add the leeks. Sprinkle with salt and pepper and cook, stirring often, for about 5 minutes.

8. Add the remaining ½ cup of cream and simmer for about 5 minutes. Remove from the heat. Add the cooked leeks to the egg and cream mixture and blend well.

9. Pour the custard mixture into the baked pie shell.

10. Reduce the oven temperature to 350 degrees; bake the tart for 40 minutes. Serve hot, lukewarm, or at room temperature.

Yield: 8 servings.

SPANAKOPITTA (GREEK-STYLE SPINACH PIE)

1. Preheat the oven to 350 degrees.

2. Pick over the spinach to remove and discard all blemished leaves and tough stems. Rinse the spinach in several changes of cold water to remove all traces of sand. Steam the spinach briefly over boiling water just until the leaves are wilted. Let cool. Coarsely chop the spinach.

3. Heat 1 tablespoon of the oil in a skillet and add the scallions. Cook, stirring, until the scallions are wilted.

4. In a mixing bowl, combine the spinach, scallions, parsley, cheese, eggs, salt, and pepper. Add 1 tablespoon of the oil and blend thoroughly.

5. Select a baking pan measuring approximately 13 × 9 inches. Or use a round pan of similar size. Cover the pan with one layer of phyllo pastry, letting the edges of the pastry hang over the sides. Brush the pastry generously with oil. Continue adding 4 more layers, brushing each layer with oil as it is added. Spoon the spinach mixture into the center and smooth it over. Cover with another layer of phyllo, brush with oil, and continue adding 4 more layers, brushing oil between each layer. Use a sharp knife or scissors to trim off the overhanging edges of pastry. Bake the pie for 40 to 50 minutes, or until it is piping hot throughout and golden brown on top.

Yield: 18 or more servings.

3 pounds fresh spinach

¾ cup olive oil, approximately

2 bunches scallions, trimmed and chopped

¼ cup chopped parsley

½ pound feta cheese, crumbled

6 eggs, lightly beaten
Salt and freshly ground pepper to taste

10 sheets phyllo pastry

BASIC CRÊPES

1 egg
½ cup flour
Salt to taste
½ cup plus 2 tablespoons milk
2 tablespoons butter

Crêpes are, without question, one of the finest creations of Western cuisine, admirable on many counts. Primary among these is the contrast between their texture and flavor and whatever they are allied with—sweet crêpes with the likes of a Grand Marnier sauce or savory crêpes to be filled with countless foods in cream and other sauces. There are many ways to fold crêpes. They may be folded in quarters to make a fan shape. They may be rolled cigar shape with the filling in the center. And they may be folded into a lily shape, with the top open slightly and the bottom pointed.

1. Put the egg, flour, and salt into a mixing bowl and start beating and blending with a wire whisk. Add the milk, stirring.

2. Melt 1 tablespoon of the butter in a 7- or 8-inch crêpe or nonstick pan. When it is melted, pour the butter into the crêpe batter.

3. Line a mixing bowl with a sieve and pour the batter into the sieve. Strain the batter, pushing any solids through with a rubber spatula.

4. Melt the remaining tablespoon of butter and use this to brush the pan each time, or as necessary, before making a crêpe.

5. Brush the pan lightly and place it on the stove. When the pan is hot but not burning, add 2 tablespoons of the batter (it is preferable if you use a small ladle with a 2-tablespoon capacity), and swirl it around neatly to completely cover the bottom of the pan. Cook over moderately high heat for 30 to 40 seconds, or until lightly browned on the bottom. Turn the crêpe and cook the second side for about 15 seconds. Turn the crêpe out onto a sheet of wax paper.

6. Continue making crêpes, brushing the pan lightly as necessary to prevent sticking, until all the batter is used. As the crêpes are made, turn them out, edges slightly overlapping, onto the wax paper.

Yield: 8 or 9 crêpes.

CRÊPES FILLED WITH LOBSTER NEWBURG

1. Cut the lobster into bite-size cubes. There should be about 1½ cups.

2. Melt 2 tablespoons of the butter in a saucepan and add the shallots and paprika. Cook briefly, stirring. Sprinkle with flour, stirring with a wire whisk.

3. Add the milk, stirring rapidly with the whisk. Add the cream and any liquid that has accumulated around the lobster. Add the salt and pepper. Add the Madeira and egg yolk, stirring rapidly with the whisk. Stir in the cayenne.

4. Melt the remaining tablespoon of butter and add the cubed lobster, shaking the skillet and stirring just until the lobster pieces are heated through.

5. Put the sauce through a strainer.

6. Pour half of the sauce over the lobster pieces and stir to blend.

7. Use equal, small portions of the lobster in the sauce to fill each of 8 crêpes. About 2 tablespoons of filling will suffice for each crêpe.

8. Fold the crêpe over. Spoon the remaining sauce without the lobster meat over the filled crêpes.

Yield: 4 servings.

½ pound cooked lobster meat

3 tablespoons butter

2 tablespoons finely chopped shallots

1 tablespoon paprika

1 tablespoon flour

1 cup milk

½ cup heavy cream

Salt and freshly ground pepper to taste

1 tablespoon Madeira

1 egg yolk

Pinch of cayenne

8 crêpes (see preceding recipe)

CRÊPES FILLED WITH CURRIED SHRIMP

1 pound raw shrimp in the shell

3 tablespoons butter

¼ cup finely chopped onion

1 teaspoon finely minced garlic

2 tablespoons flour

2 tablespoons curry powder

⅓ cup milk

1 cup plain yogurt

Salt and freshly ground pepper to taste

8 crêpes (see recipe page 78)

2 tablespoons finely chopped fresh coriander, optional

1. Shell and devein the shrimp. Cut the shrimp into bite-size pieces. There should be about 1½ cups.

2. Melt 1 tablespoon of the butter in a saucepan and add the onion and garlic. Cook, stirring, until the onion is wilted. Add the flour and curry powder and stir.

3. Add the milk, stirring rapidly with the whisk. Add the yogurt, salt, and pepper and bring to the boil, stirring with the whisk.

4. Melt 1 tablespoon of butter in a skillet and add the shrimp. Cook, stirring, for about 1 minute or less, just until the shrimp lose their raw look throughout. Pour and scrape the sauce over the shrimp. Stir to blend.

5. Lay out 2 crêpes on each of 4 plates. Spoon equal portions of the shrimp curry on each crêpe, leaving enough left over to be spooned on top as garnish. Roll the crêpes.

6. Melt the remaining 1 tablespoon of butter and brush the tops of the crêpes with butter. Spoon the reserved curried shrimp on top. Sprinkle with chopped coriander and serve.

Yield: 4 servings.

MEXICAN-STYLE CHICKEN WITH CRÊPES

1. Place the chicken in a saucepan and add chicken broth to cover and salt. Bring to the boil and simmer for 10 to 15 minutes. Do not overcook. Let the chicken cool in the cooking liquid.

2. Drain the tomatillos and put them into the container of a food processor or blender.

3. Remove and discard the stems, seeds, and veins from the chilies. Add them to the tomatillos. Add the garlic and blend until finely puréed.

4. Heat the oil in a skillet and cook the onion until wilted. Add the tomatillo mixture, sugar, and salt. Cook, stirring often, for 6 or 7 minutes. Add more sugar and salt to taste. Just before using, stir in the coriander.

5. Prepare the crêpes and have them ready.

6. When ready to serve, preheat the oven to 400 degrees.

7. Shred the chicken, discarding all cartilage.

8. To assemble, lightly oil a baking dish large enough to hold the stuffed, rolled crêpes compactly. Place the crêpes, one at a time, on a flat surface and spoon in a layer of green tomatillo sauce. Add a portion of chicken and more sauce. Roll. Arrange the filled crêpes close together in the dish. Spoon any remaining sauce over the crêpes.

9. Place in the oven and bake for 8 to 10 minutes, or until piping hot. Serve with the sour cream spooned over each serving.

Yield: 4 to 8 servings.

THE CHICKEN:

1 pound skinned and boned chicken breasts

Fresh or canned chicken broth to cover

Salt to taste

THE SAUCE:

Two 12-ounce cans tomatillos, available in Mexican and Spanish grocery stores

2 small green hot chilies, or use canned drained serrano or jalapeño peppers

1 garlic clove, finely minced

3 tablespoons peanut, vegetable, or corn oil

½ cup finely chopped onion

½ teaspoon sugar

Salt to taste

1 tablespoon finely chopped fresh coriander

THE ASSEMBLY:

Eight 7-inch crêpes (see recipe page 78) or tortillas

¾ cup sour cream

MANICOTTI WITH RICOTTA CHEESE

¼ cup grated Parmesan cheese

Crêpe batter (see recipe page 78)

2 cups ricotta cheese

2 egg yolks

2 tablespoon finely chopped parsley

Salt to taste

⅛ teaspoon grated nutmeg

1 cup plus 2 tablespoons grated Parmesan cheese

Freshly ground pepper to taste

2 cups tomato sauce, preferably homemade

2 tablespoons butter, melted

1. Add the ¼ cup Parmesan cheese to the crêpe batter. Cook the crêpes and lay them on a flat surface.

2. Blend the ricotta, yolks, parsley, salt, nutmeg, 1 cup of Parmesan cheese, and pepper. Blend well. Spoon equal portions of the filling down the center of each crêpe and roll it.

3. Spoon about 3 tablespoons of tomato sauce over the bottom of a baking dish (a rectangular dish measuring 8 × 14 inches would be appropriate). Arrange the filled crêpes in the dish.

4. Spoon the remaining sauce over the crêpes and sprinkle with the remaining 2 tablespoons of cheese. Pour the melted butter over all.

5. When ready to bake, preheat the oven to 400 degrees. Bake for about 20 minutes.

Yield: 4 to 8 servings.

BLINI WITH SMOKED SALMON AND RED CAVIAR

1. Place the blini on a flat surface and arrange slices of smoked salmon down the center. Roll the blini.
2. Blend the sour cream with salt. Spoon a dollop of sour cream over the blini and top with spoonfuls of red caviar. Garnish with dill or parsley.

Yield: 4 servings.

8 blini (see following recipe)
½ pound thinly sliced smoked salmon
1½ cups sour cream
Salt to taste
4 to 8 ounces red caviar
Sprigs of dill or parsley for garnish

1. Scoop the flour into a mixing bowl and add the egg yolk. Dissolve the yeast in the milk and add it, stirring with a wire whisk. Add the salt. Set in a warm place and let stand for about 2 hours, covered with a towel.
2. When ready to cook, add the cream and chopped dill. Beat the egg white and fold it in. Cook in a crêpe pan as with ordinary crêpes.

Yield: 8 blini.

BLINI

¾ cup flour
1 egg, separated
2 teaspoons granular yeast
¾ cup milk
Salt to taste
2 tablespoons heavy cream
2 tablespoons chopped fresh dill

PROFITEROLES WITH TARRAGON-FLAVORED CHICKEN HASH

2 tablespoons butter

2 tablespoons flour

½ cup fresh or canned chicken broth

½ cup heavy cream

Salt and freshly ground pepper to taste

Pinch of grated nutmeg

Pinch of cayenne

2 teaspoons chopped fresh tarragon, or 1 teaspoon dried

1½ cups cubed leftover chicken

24 profiteroles (see following recipe)

1. Melt the butter in a saucepan and add the flour, stirring with a wire whisk. When blended, add the broth, stirring rapidly with the whisk. When thickened and smooth, stir in the cream.

2. Add the salt, pepper, nutmeg, cayenne, and tarragon. Let simmer, stirring, for about 2 minutes.

3. Stir in the chicken and bring to the boil.

4. Slice off the tops of all the cream puffs (profiteroles). Spoon an equal portion of the mixture into the bottom of each cream puff. Replace the tops and serve.

Yield: 24 filled cream puffs.

PROFITEROLES WITH CURRIED SHRIMP FILLING

¾ pound fresh shrimp, shelled and deveined

1 tablespoon butter

3 tablespoons finely chopped onion

1 tablespoon curry powder

1 cup heavy cream

3 tablespoons finely chopped chutney

Salt and freshly ground pepper to taste

24 cream puffs (see following recipe)

1. Cut the shrimp into ½-inch or slightly smaller pieces. There should be about 1¼ cups. Set aside.

2. Melt the butter in a saucepan and add the onion. Cook, stirring, until wilted. Add the curry powder and stir to blend.

3. Add the cream and chutney and cook down to about ½ cup. Add the salt, pepper, and shrimp, and cook, stirring, for 1 or 2 minutes, or until the shrimp lose their raw look throughout.

4. Slice off the tops of all the cream puffs. Spoon an equal portion of the mixture into the bottom of each cream puff. Replace the tops and serve.

Yield: 24 filled cream puffs.

1. Preheat the oven to 425 degrees.

2. Lightly but thoroughly butter a jelly roll pan. Sprinkle the pan with flour and shake it around until the pan is well coated. Shake and tap out any excess flour.

3. Put the water in a saucepan and add the ¼ pound of butter and the salt. Bring to the boil and add the flour all at once, stirring vigorously and thoroughly in a circular motion until a ball is formed and the mixture pulls away from the sides of the saucepan.

4. Add 1 egg, beating thoroughly and rapidly with the spoon until it is well blended with the mixture. Add another egg, beat, and so on. When all the eggs are added, fit a pastry bag with a round-tipped, No. 6 pastry tube. Spoon the mixture into the bag. Holding the pastry bag straight up with the tip close to the floured surface of the jelly roll pan, squeeze the bag to make mounds of pastry at intervals all over the pan. There should be about 24 mounds.

5. The mounds may have pointed tips on top. To flatten these, wet a clean tea towel and squeeze it well. Open it up, fold it over in thirds. Hold it stretched directly over the mounds, quickly patting down just enough to rid the mounds of the pointed tips. Do not squash the mounds.

6. Place the pan in the oven and bake for 30 minutes, or until the cream puffs are golden brown and cooked throughout. Remove and let cool.

Yield: 24 cream puffs.

PROFITEROLES (CREAM PUFFS)

¼ pound butter plus additional butter for greasing the pan

1 cup flour plus additional flour for flouring the pan

1 cup water

Salt to taste

4 large eggs

HOW TO FILL AND BAKE A PIROG

Brioche dough (see
following recipe)
Filling of choice
1 egg yolk
2 teaspoons water
Melted butter, optional

There are many excellent dishes that can be attributed to the kitchens of Russia. Some of the best known, of course, are borscht, blini, beef stroganoff, and chicken Kiev. But one of our favorites is a baked filled pastry known as a pirog. It is prepared with an outer crust of brioche and stuffed with fillings ranging from salmon and dill to meat and mushrooms.

In Russia, pirogi are usually served at lunch with a cup of consommé. It is our feeling, however, that a well-made pirog makes an elegant main dish for lunch or a light supper.

1. Prepare the brioche pastry the day before as indicated in the recipe. Put the dough in the refrigerator and let stand until it is to be rolled out.

2. Lightly flour a flat surface, preferably cold marble. Roll the dough into a rectangle, measuring about 16 × 24 inches. Add the filling, placing it dead center. Do not let the filling get closer than 4 inches from the edge of the rectangle.

3. Fold one long side of the pastry over the filling.

4. Blend the egg yolk with water. Brush the top and exposed parts of the dough (including the inside portion of the unfolded portion of dough) with the egg wash. Fold over the second fold of dough to completely and compactly enclose the filling. Cut off 2 or 3 inches of the bottom and top ends of the dough to use for decoration. Neatly and carefully fold over the bottom and top of the dough to enclose the ends of the filling compactly.

5. Turn the filled pastry over onto a baking sheet. Brush the top with more egg wash.

6. Roll out the cut-off pieces of dough and cut them into strips about ¼ inch wide. Place these strips of dough crosswise at parallel intervals over the dough as decoration. Cut a hole about ½ inch in diameter in the direct center of the pastry top. Set the dough in a warm place for about 30 minutes.

7. Meanwhile, preheat the oven to 375 degrees.

8. Place the pirog in the oven and bake for 20 minutes. Reduce the oven temperature to 325 degrees and continue baking for 25 minutes longer.

9. Let stand for at least 15 minutes before slicing. Serve, if desired, with melted butter to be spooned on top of the slices.

Yield: 6 to 8 servings.

1. Put the milk in a saucepan and heat it gradually to lukewarm. Remove from the heat. If the milk has become too hot, let it cool to lukewarm.

2. Sprinkle the milk with sugar and yeast and stir to dissolve. Cover with a towel. Let stand for about 5 minutes and place the mixture in a warm place (the natural warmth of a turned-off oven is good for this) for about 5 minutes. It should ferment during the period and increase in volume.

3. Place 4 cups of the flour in the bowl of an electric mixer fitted with a dough hook, or use a mixing bowl and a wooden spoon. Make a well in the center and pour in the yeast mixture, egg yolks, and ¼ pound of the butter. With the dough hook or wooden spoon, gradually work in the flour until well blended. Then beat vigorously until the dough is quite smooth and can be shaped into a ball.

4. Turn the dough out onto a lightly floured board and knead it until it is smooth and satiny, 10 to 15 minutes. As you work the dough, continue to add flour to the kneading surface as necessary to prevent sticking, but take care not to add an excess or the finished product will be tough.

5. Lightly butter a clean mixing bowl and add the ball of dough. Cover with a clean towel and let stand in a warm place for about 1 hour, or until double in bulk. Punch down the dough. Turn it out once more onto a lightly floured board. Knead it for about 1 minute and return it to a clean bowl. Cover closely with plastic wrap and refrigerate overnight.

6. The next morning, punch down the dough again and continue to refrigerate, covered, until ready to use.

Yield: Enough for 1 large pirog.

BRIOCHE DOUGH

¾ **cup milk**

¼ **teaspoon sugar**

3 **packages granular yeast**

4 **to 4½ cups flour**

12 **egg yolks**

¼ **pound butter, at room temperature, plus butter for greasing the bowl**

SALMON FILLING FOR PIROGI

4 cups poached fresh salmon, or use canned salmon

¼ pound butter

¼ cup finely chopped shallots

½ pound mushrooms, sliced, about 3 cups

Salt and freshly ground pepper to taste

¼ cup dry white wine

¼ cup stock from the poached salmon

½ cup finely chopped fresh dill

4 hard-cooked eggs, peeled and chopped, about 2 cups

4 cups cooked rice

¼ cup lemon juice

1. Put the salmon in a large mixing bowl.

2. Melt half the butter in a saucepan and add the shallots. Cook until the shallots are wilted, and add the mushrooms and salt and pepper. Cook, stirring, until mushrooms give up their liquid.

3. Add the wine and stock and bring to the boil. Cook the liquid down by about half. Add half the dill.

4. To the salmon, add the chopped eggs, rice, and mushroom mixture with its liquid. Melt the remaining butter and add it. Add the remaining dill and lemon juice. Blend well.

Yield: About 10 cups.

MEAT AND MUSHROOM FILLING FOR PIROGI

1. Put the meat in a mixing bowl and set aside.

2. Melt the butter in a fairly deep skillet and add the onion and garlic. Cook, stirring, until the onion is wilted. Add the mushrooms and cook until the mushrooms give up their liquid. Sprinkle with the salt and pepper. Sprinkle with flour and stir to distribute it evenly.

3. Add the meat and stir, chopping down with the side of a heavy metal spoon to break up any lumps. Add the broth and continue cooking, stirring, until the meat loses its raw look. Add the lemon juice, a generous grinding of black pepper, the chopped eggs, rice, and dill. Blend well.

Yield: About 10 cups.

1¾ pounds lean ground sirloin

6 tablespoons butter

½ cup finely chopped onion

1 tablespoon finely minced garlic

¾ pound mushrooms, thinly sliced, about 5 cups

Salt and freshly ground pepper to taste

2 tablespoons flour

¼ cup chicken broth

⅓ cup lemon juice

4 hard-cooked eggs, peeled and chopped, about 2 cups

4 cups cooked rice

½ cup finely chopped fresh dill

Beef Piroshki

Sour cream pastry (see following recipe)

2 tablespoons butter

3 cups finely chopped onion

1 pound ground beef

Salt and freshly ground pepper to taste

3 hard-cooked eggs, peeled and finely chopped

¼ cup finely chopped fresh dill

1 egg, lightly beaten

3 tablespoons water

Piroshki, in our minds best made with a rich, sour cream pastry, are really miniature versions of pirogi. They are usually served with a soup, such as a rich clear beef broth, borscht, cabbage, or sauerkraut soup.

1. Prepare the pastry and chill it.

2. Preheat the oven to 400 degrees.

3. Melt the butter in a skillet and add the onion. Cook, stirring, until the onion is wilted.

4. Add the beef and, using a heavy metal kitchen spoon, stir and chop down to break up any lumps in the meat. Cook until the meat loses its raw look. Add salt and pepper.

5. Add the chopped egg and dill. Stir to blend. There should be about 4 cups. Remove to a mixing bowl and let cool.

6. Roll out the pastry as thin as possible (less than ⅛ inch thick). Using a cookie cutter, cut the dough into rounds. We used a 4-inch cookie cutter to produce 30 rounds. The dough will shrink after cutting. You may roll out the circles or rounds to make them larger or you may stretch them carefully by hand. Beat the egg with the water. Brush the top of each pastry with the egg mixture.

7. Use about 2 tablespoons of the filling for each circle of dough. Shape the filling into an oval and place it on half of the circle of dough. Fold the other half of the circle of dough over to enclose the filling. Press the edges of the dough with the fingers or the tines of a fork to seal. Brush the tops with egg mixture to seal.

8. Arrange the filled pieces on a lightly greased baking sheet and bake for 25 minutes.

Yield: 30 piroshki.

1. Put 3¼ cups of the flour, the salt, the baking powder, butter, eggs, and sour cream into the container of a food processor. Process until thoroughly blended.

2. If a food processor is not used, put the flour, salt, and baking powder in a mixing bowl. Add the butter and cut it in with two knives or a pastry blender until the mixture looks like coarse corn- meal. Using a fork, add the eggs and sour cream and thoroughly blend.

3. Scrape the mixture out onto a lightly floured board and knead as briefly as possible, using as little flour as possible to make a smooth and workable dough.

4. Shape the dough into a flat cake and wrap it in plastic wrap. Chill until ready to use.

Yield: 2 pounds of dough.

SOUR CREAM PASTRY

3½ cups flour

   Salt to taste

1 teaspoon baking powder

¼ pound butter, chilled and cut into small pieces

2 eggs

1 cup sour cream

MUSHROOM PIROSHKI

Sour cream pastry (see preceding recipe)

2 tablespoons butter

2 cups finely chopped onion

¾ pound mushrooms, finely chopped, about 3½ cups

Salt and freshly ground pepper to taste

¼ cup sour cream

2 tablespoons finely chopped fresh dill

1 hard-cooked egg, peeled and finely chopped

1 cup cooked rice

1 egg, lightly beaten

3 tablespoons water

1. Prepare the pastry and chill it.

2. Preheat the oven to 400 degrees.

3. Melt the butter in a skillet and add the onion. Cook, stirring, until the onion is wilted.

4. Add the mushrooms and cook, stirring often, until they give up their liquid. Cook until most but not all of the liquid evaporates. Add salt and pepper and stir.

5. Add the sour cream, dill, chopped egg, and rice. Blend well. There should be about 4 cups. Remove to a mixing bowl and let cool.

6. Roll out the pastry as thin as possible (less than ⅛ inch thick). Using a cookie cutter, cut the dough into rounds. We used a 4-inch cookie cutter to produce 30 rounds. The dough will shrink after cutting. You may roll out the circles or round to make them larger or you may stretch them carefully by hand. Beat the egg with the water. Brush the top of each pastry round with the egg mixture.

7. Use 2 tablespoons of the filling for each circle of dough. Shape the filling into an oval and place it on half of the circle of dough. Fold the other half of the circle of dough over to enclose the filling. Press the edges of the dough with the fingers or the tines of a fork to seal. Brush the tops with egg mixture to seal.

8. Arrange the filled pieces on a lightly greased baking sheet, and bake for 25 minutes.

Yield: 30 piroshki.

Pissaladière (A Provençale Pizza)

1. Put the flour, 4 tablespoons of the olive oil, and the yeast into the container of a food processor and blend. Gradually add the water and continue processing until the dough can be gathered into a ball. Rub the outside of the dough with 1 teaspoon oil. Put the ball of dough into a mixing bowl and cover. Let stand for 30 minutes in a warm but not hot place.

2. Meanwhile, peel the onions and cut them in half. Thinly slice each onion half. There should be about 10 cups.

3. Heat 1 tablespoon of the oil in a large heavy Dutch oven or casserole and add the sliced onions, garlic, thyme, cloves, and bay leaf. Cook, stirring often, for 20 to 30 minutes, or until the onions are nicely browned or light amber colored.

4. Pat the dough into a flat shape. Rub 1 tablespoon of oil all over the surface of a round 14-inch pizza pan. Place the dough in the center of the pan and pat it out with the fingers and knuckles all the way to the rim. Build up the rim slightly with the fingers. Cover and let stand in a warm place for 30 minutes.

5. Preheat the oven to 450 degrees.

6. Spoon the onion mixture into the center of the dough-lined pan. Spread it out to the rim. Arrange the anchovy fillets in a crossed pattern over the onions. Dot with the olives. Spoon the remaining tablespoon of oil over the onions.

7. Put the pissaladière in the oven and bake for 30 minutes.

Yield: 4 to 8 servings.

1½ cups flour
7 tablespoons plus 1 teaspoon olive oil
2½ teaspoons granular yeast
½ cup lukewarm water
2 or 3 large onions
2 teaspoons finely chopped garlic
½ teaspoon dried thyme
2 whole cloves
1 bay leaf
12 flat anchovy fillets
12 pitted imported black olives, preferably oil-cured

Pizza with Everything

Pizza dough (see
following recipe)
¼ cup olive oil plus oil
for greasing a pizza pan
2 cups marinara sauce
(see recipe page 787)
1 cup thinly sliced
mushrooms
1 cup thinly sliced
sausages, such as
Italian sausages or
salami or Polish
sausages
2 cups coarsely grated
mozzarella cheese
¼ cup freshly grated
Parmesan cheese
Hot red pepper flakes

1. There are two recommended ways of cooking pizza at home. It may be prepared and cooked in a 14-inch pizza pan or it may be baked on a baking stone. If it is to be baked in a pizza pan, preheat the oven to 475 degrees; if it is to be baked on a stone, preheat the oven to 500 degrees and put the stone in the oven.

2. Divide the dough in half. Flatten each half with the hands into a circle. Start punching it all around with the back of a clenched fist to shape it into a larger circle 12 or 13 inches in diameter. Keep the surface floured lightly but enough so that the dough does not stick.

3. If pizza pans are used, rub the surface of each with 1 tablespoon of oil. If a baking stone is used, you will place the pizza circle on the wooden paddle. You should bake 1 pizza first and continue to make the second after the first is baked.

4. Arrange 1 circle of dough on each pan or on the wooden paddle. Add half of the marinara sauce to the center of each circle of pastry and smooth it almost, but not quite, to the edge. Scatter half of the mushrooms, half of the sausage slices, half of the mozzarella, and half of the Parmesan over the sauce. Sprinkle each pizza with 2 tablespoons of olive oil.

5. If a pizza pan is used, place it in the oven for 14 minutes, or until the pizza is well done. If the baking stone is used, slide the pizza off onto the stone and bake for 14 minutes, or until the pizza is well done. Repeat with the second pizza. Serve with red pepper flakes on the side.

Yield: Two 14-inch pizzas.

PIZZA DOUGH

1½ envelopes granular
yeast
1½ cups lukewarm water
2 tablespoons olive oil
4 cups flour
Pinch of salt

1. Put the yeast, water, and oil into the container of a food processor.

2. Add the flour and salt and process until the mixture becomes a soft but firm and kneadable mixture.

3. If a food processor is not used, soak the yeast in the water and oil. Put the flour and salt into a mixing bowl. Add the yeast liquid and blend by hand.

4. Turn the dough out onto a lightly floured board and knead briefly. Shape into a ball. Place the ball in a mixing bowl and cover. Let stand until double in bulk, 45 minutes to 1 hour. It is now ready to be used for pizza or calzoni.

Yield: Enough dough for 2 pizzas or 4 large calzoni.

CALZONI (A CHEESE-FILLED YEAST PASTRY)

Although we've admired many variations of calzoni, we encountered the finest and most inspired we have ever eaten during a visit to Chez Panisse, the excellent restaurant in Berkeley, California, run by Alice Waters, one of the finest cooks in this country. Her version of the dish was pizza dough filled with goat cheese and chopped prosciutto, seasoned to perfection and baked until crisp and golden on the outside. We cannot claim to have entirely duplicated her calzoni, but we have made an earnest effort and are particularly proud of the result.

1. Prepare the pizza dough and divide it into 4 portions. Shape into balls. Keep covered with a cloth.

2. Preheat the oven to 400 degrees.

3. Combine the goat cheese, mozzarella, ricotta, prosciutto, Parmesan, rosemary, basil, parsley, pepper, and 1 egg in a mixing bowl. Blend well.

4. Roll out each ball of pizza dough on a lightly floured surface into a circle 8½ to 9 inches in diameter.

5. Spoon an equal portion of the filling onto half of each circle, leaving a margin for sealing. Beat the remaining egg with the water. Rub a small amount of the egg mixture around the margin. Fold over the unfilled half and press around the margin with the fingers or a fork to seal.

6. As the calzoni are filled and sealed, arrange them on a baking sheet. Cut a 1-inch slit in the top of each to allow steam to escape. Brush the calzoni all over with the egg mixture.

7. Bake the calzoni for 30 minutes.

Yield: 4 servings.

Pizza dough (see preceding recipe)

½ pound goat cheese

¼ pound mozzarella cheese, cut into small cubes

¼ cup ricotta cheese

½ cup cubed prosciutto, about 2 ounces

¼ cup grated Parmesan cheese

¼ teaspoon chopped fresh rosemary

4 fresh basil leaves, chopped, about 1 tablespoon

2 tablespoons finely chopped parsley

Freshly ground pepper to taste

2 eggs, lightly beaten

1 tablespoon water

EMPANADITAS FRITAS (MEAT-FILLED TURNOVERS)

Pastry for deep-fried
turnovers (see
following recipe)

3 tablespoons olive oil

½ cup finely chopped
onion

2 teaspoons finely
chopped garlic

¾ cup finely chopped
green pepper

¾ pound ground top
sirloin

1 teaspoon ground cumin

½ teaspoon hot red
pepper flakes

Salt and freshly ground
pepper to taste

¾ cup peeled, seeded, and
chopped tomatoes

12 stuffed olives, finely
chopped, about ¼ cup

¼ cup raisins or currants

⅓ cup pine nuts

2 hard-cooked eggs,
peeled and chopped

2 tablespoons finely
chopped parsley

2 tablespoons finely
chopped fresh
coriander, optional

Corn, peanut, or
vegetable oil for deep
frying

1. Prepare the pastry and let stand, covered, while preparing the filling.

2. Heat the olive oil in a skillet and add the onion, garlic, and green pepper. Cook, stirring, until wilted. Add the beef and cook, stirring and chopping down with the sides of a metal spoon to break up any lumps. Cook until the meat has lost its raw look.

3. Add the cumin, pepper flakes, salt, pepper, tomatoes, olives, and raisins. Cook, stirring, until most of the liquid has evaporated.

4. Add the pine nuts, eggs, parsley, and coriander. Blend well. Let cool. The chilling may be hastened if the filling is spooned onto a platter and placed briefly in the freezer. Stir occasionally. By all means do not freeze.

5. Roll out the pastry on a lightly floured board to a thickness of ⅛ inch or less.

6. Use a cutter 6 inches in diameter, such as the rim of an emptied can of tomatoes or coffee, and cut out circles.

7. Gather together the scraps of dough and form a ball quickly. Roll this dough out to the same thickness and cut it into 6-inch circles.

8. Fill half of each circle of dough with about 2 tablespoons of filling, leaving a slight margin for sealing when the dough is folded. Moisten all around the edges of the circle of dough. Fold the unfilled half of dough over to enclose the filling. Press around the edges with the tines of a fork to seal well.

9. Heat the oil to 360 degrees. Add the empanaditas, four to six at a time without crowding. Cook, turning the empanaditas in the hot oil until nicely browned and cooked through, for about 8 minutes. Drain well on paper towels. Serve hot.

Yield: 20 empanaditas.

1. Put the flour and salt into the container of a food processor.
2. Heat the lard, oil, and water in a saucepan just until the lard is melted.
3. Start processing while gradually adding the lard mixture.
4. Remove the dough and shape it into a ball. Set it on a lightly floured board and cover with a cloth. Let stand for about 15 minutes before rolling out.

Yield: Enough pastry for twenty 6-inch circles of dough.

PASTRY FOR DEEP-FRIED TURNOVERS

4 cups flour
Salt to taste
¼ cup lard
¼ olive oil
1⅓ cups water

Chiles con Queso (Chili and cheese fondue, California-style)

1 pound Monterey Jack or Cheddar cheese
2 tablespoons butter
1 teaspoon finely chopped garlic
¾ cup cored, cubed unpeeled tomato
½ cup milk
2 teaspoons cornstarch
1 tablespoon water
1 to 4 tablespoons chopped canned chilies
Salt to taste

1. Grate the cheese on the coarse grater. There should be about 4 cups.

2. Heat the butter in a chafing dish or electric cooker and add the garlic. Cook briefly and add the tomato. Stir and add the cheese and milk.

3. Bring gradually to the boil, stirring. Blend the cornstarch and water and stir it in. Add the chilies and salt. Serve hot with tostadas, corn chips, fried tortillas, or French bread.

Yield: 6 to 8 servings.

Green Chili Gordas

12 dried tortillas
3 peeled Anaheim chilies, fresh or canned
⅔ cup hot milk
1 tablespoon melted lard or oil
¾ teaspoon salt
Lard or oil for frying
1 medium-size onion, peeled and finely chopped
1½ cups sour cream, thinned with a little milk and salted

1. If the tortillas are not completely dry, spread them out on a baking sheet and put them into a low oven for about ½ hour. Remove and cool. When they are cool, break them into small pieces and blend until fine but not pulverized. Transfer to a bowl.

2. Remove and discard some of the seeds from the chilies and blend the chilies with the hot milk until smooth. Add, together with the melted lard and salt, to the ground tortillas and knead the mixture well. Add more milk if dough is not pliable enough. Set the dough aside for about 1 hour or longer, well covered.

3. Divide the dough into 12 equal portions and roll into balls about 1½ inches in diameter. Flatten to form 2-inch cakes about ⅜ inch thick.

4. Heat ¼ inch oil or lard in a frying pan and fry the cakes gently for 3 to 5 minutes on both sides (take care that the fat is not too hot, or it will make a crust on the outside instantaneously and the inside of the dough will not be heated through properly).

5. Drain well on paper towels. (They will hold in a 350-degree oven for about 20 minutes if necessary.) Garnish with the chopped onion and sour cream and serve immediately.

Yield: 12 gordas.

MUSHROOM TACOS

One of the anecdotes that has always amused us about Diana Kennedy, who sets a splendid and authentic Mexican table, was her search for epazote, a much-used herb in Mexican cooking. For a long time she shopped all the local markets in New York where Spanish and Mexican herbs are sold, with no success. One day, while jogging in Riverside Park, she found epazote growing wild and in abundance at her feet. It is a tall, greenish plant with pointed leaves and gives a distinctive, pungent flavor to Diana's mushroom tacos.

1. Heat the 3 tablespoons oil to smoking in a saucepan, lower flame, and cook the onion and garlic gently until soft but not brown.

2. Add the remaining ingredients, except tortillas and oil for frying, and cook the mixture, uncovered, over a fairly high flame, stirring from time to time, until the mushrooms are soft, 15 to 20 minutes. The mixture should be fairly dry. Set aside to cool a little.

3. Put a little of the mixture across one side of the tortilla—not in the center—and roll it up fairly tightly. Fasten with a toothpick.

4. Heat the oil or lard—there should be no more than ¼ inch in the frying pan or it will seep into the tacos—and fry them, turning them over and removing the toothpicks. They should be just crisp, but not hard. Drain on paper towels and serve immediately. They become leathery if left heating through in the oven after you have made them. This is pan-to-mouth food and should be eaten as soon as your fingers can hold them. They can be served just as they are or with a little sour cream.

Yield: 12 tacos.

3 tablespoons peanut oil

1 small onion, finely chopped

2 garlic cloves, peeled and chopped

2 medium-size fresh tomatoes, peeled and chopped, or 1½ cups canned peeled tomatoes, drained

3 fresh hot serrano chili peppers, finely chopped

1 pound fresh mushrooms, finely sliced

3 sprigs epazote or parsley

1 teaspoon salt

12 tortillas

Oil or melted lard for frying

CHILES RELLENOS (STUFFED CHILIES)

4 fresh poblano chilies

1 cup bay leaf tea (see following recipe)

½ cup white wine vinegar

2 garlic cloves, thinly sliced

1 cup peeled, diced potato

½ cup peeled, trimmed, diced carrot

⅓ cup diced raw jícama, optional

2 tablespoons mayonnaise

Salt to taste

⅓ cup heavy cream

½ cup grated white Cheddar cheese

1. Put the chilies over a gas flame or heat them over charcoal, turning often, until the outsides are well burned or charred, 5 to 7 minutes. Dampen a cloth and wrap it around the chilies and let them cool.

2. Remove the chilies and peel. Make a lengthwise slit down one side. Leave the stems intact. Remove and discard the seeds and veins.

3. Blend the bay leaf tea, vinegar, and garlic in a small mixing bowl. Add the chilies and let stand at least 30 minutes. Drain, reserving the liquid.

4. Meanwhile, put the potatoes in a small saucepan and the diced carrot in another saucepan. Add cold water to cover. Bring to the boil. Let the diced carrot simmer about 3 minutes, or until crisp-tender. Let the potatoes cook about 5 minutes, or until crisp-tender. Drain both.

5. Add the potatoes and carrots to the reserved liquid. Let stand briefly.

6. Drain the vegetables. Put them in a mixing bowl and add the jícama and mayonnaise. Add salt to taste.

7. Whip the cream until it is almost but not quite stiff. Fold 2 tablespoons into the vegetables.

8. Spoon equal portions of the vegetable mixture into each of the chilies. Spoon an equal portion of the remaining whipped cream on top of each stuffed chili. Sprinkle with cheese and serve.

Yield: 4 servings.

BAY LEAF TEA

4 large bay leaves

2 cups water

1. Combine the bay leaves and water in a saucepan and bring to the boil. Let cook over high heat 10 to 15 minutes, or until the water is reduced to 1 cup.

2. Strain, discarding the leaves.

Yield: About 1 cup.

WELSH RABBIT

We subscribe to the story that a Welshman went hunting and returned home empty-handed. His wife concocted a dish with melted cheese and dubbed it "rabbit." Thus, Welsh rabbit, not rarebit.

1. Grate the cheese and set it aside.

2. Put the mustard, paprika, cayenne, and nutmeg in a small mixing bowl. Add the beer, a few drops at a time, stirring with a fork to make a paste. Continue adding and stirring until all the ingredients are well blended.

3. Melt the butter in a saucepan and add the beer mixture. Set the saucepan in a skillet and pour boiling water around the saucepan to a depth of about ½ inch. Let the water simmer until the beer mixture becomes quite hot.

4. Add the cheese and stir with a wooden spoon until the cheese melts. Add the egg, stirring constantly over the bottom of the saucepan, making sure all areas are covered. Add the salt and Worcestershire sauce. Continue "cooking" and stirring until the rabbit is thickened and smooth. The cheese mixture must not boil at any time or the egg will "scramble" or curdle.

5. When the rabbit is piping hot, it will thicken. Serve over dry toast with a peppermill on the side.

Yield: 2 servings.

½ pound very sharp Cheddar cheese
1 teaspoon dry mustard
1 teaspoon paprika
⅛ teaspoon cayenne
 Freshly grated nutmeg to taste
½ cup beer
1 tablespoon butter
1 egg, lightly beaten
 Salt to taste
1 teaspoon Worcestershire sauce
4 slices dry toast

GOLDEN BUCK

½ pound yellow Cheddar
   cheese
4 eggs, beaten
2 tablespoons butter
½ cup dark beer
¼ cup heavy cream
   Dash of Tabasco sauce
2 teaspoons Worcester-
   shire sauce
¼ teaspoon freshly
   ground pepper
   Salt to taste
   Buttered toast points

1. Cut the cheese into ½-inch cubes and put it in a heavy, small casserole. Add the eggs, butter, beer, cream, Tabasco, Worcestershire, pepper, and salt.

2. Place the casserole over moderate heat and cook, stirring constantly, until the cheese has melted and the mixture is piping hot. Do not boil or the eggs will curdle.

3. Serve over buttered toast points.

Yield: 2 to 4 servings.

CHEESE FONDUE

3 pounds Gruyère cheese
1 garlic clove
2½ cups dry white wine
¼ cup kirsch
4 teaspoons cornstarch
   Salt, optional
1 loaf French bread
   Freshly ground pepper

1. Grate or shred the cheese or cut into small cubes.

2. Rub the inside of a fondue pot (see note) with the clove of garlic. Add the wine and heat without boiling. This is probably best done at the stove, using a Flame Tamer or other heatproof pad to prevent sticking on the bottom.

3. Add the cheese and stir with a wooden spoon without stopping until the mixture is runny. Blend the kirsch and cornstarch and add it to the mixture, stirring. The cornstarch should bind the mixture and make it smooth. If desired, add a touch of salt to the fondue. The saltiness of Gruyère varies. When the fondue is boiling and smooth, it may be transferred to a fondue cooker with a flame for serving at table.

4. Cut the French bread into 1-inch cubes. Serve with fondue forks, first spearing a cube of bread and dipping it into the hot fondue. Serve with a peppermill on the side. Add more kirsch to taste.

Yield: 6 to 8 servings.

Note: Prior to using an earthenware fondue pot or casserole, rub the inside and outside unglazed surface with a clove of garlic. Preheat the oven to 400 degrees. Fill the pot with water and place in the oven. Let simmer for about 1 hour. Fondue pots can be used over direct flame but it is chancy. There is less danger of breakage if the pot is placed over a heatproof pad to insure equal distribution of heat.

Soups

CHICKEN AND TOMATO BROTH WITH SOUR CREAM AND HERBS

1. Combine the chicken broth and tomato juice in a saucepan and bring to the boil. Add the Tabasco, salt, pepper, and lemon juice. Bring to a simmer without boiling.

2. Spoon equal amounts of parsley, scallions, green chilies, and other herbs, if desired, into the bottom of each of 6 to 8 soup bowls. Pour equal portions of the soup into each bowl.

3. Beat the sour cream with salt to taste and spoon equal portions of sour cream atop each serving. Serve immediately with Parmesan toast.

Yield: 6 to 8 servings.

3 cups fresh or canned chicken broth

3 cups tomato juice

A touch of Tabasco sauce

Salt and freshly ground pepper to taste

Juice of ½ lemon, or more to taste

½ cup chopped parsley or coriander

½ cup chopped scallions

¼ cup chopped, canned (or fresh) mild green chilies, optional

1 cup sour cream

Parmesan toast (see following recipe)

Preheat the oven to 450 degrees. Place the butter in a mixing bowl and work it with a plastic spatula or wire whisk until it is smooth and spreadable. Add the cheese and Tabasco and beat until thoroughly blended. Spread equal portions of the butter on one side of each slice of bread. Arrange the slices, buttered side up, on a baking sheet. Bake for 10 minutes, or until the bread is golden. The bread should brown on both sides without turning. Watch carefully to guard against burning or overbrowning. Let cool and cut each slice into two rectangles or triangles.

Yield: 6 to 12 servings.

PARMESAN TOAST

¼ pound butter at room temperature

¾ cup freshly grated Parmesan cheese

⅛ teaspoon Tabasco sauce

12 very thin slices bread

CRÈME SENEGALESE (CURRIED CREAM OF CHICKEN SOUP)

2 tablespoons butter

½ cup chopped onion

1 tablespoon curry powder

1 cup chopped leeks

1 garlic clove, finely minced

½ cup diced banana

1½ cups peeled, cored, and diced apples

1 cup peeled, chopped tomatoes

1 cup peeled, cubed potatoes

Salt and freshly ground pepper to taste

4 drops Tabasco sauce, or more to taste

3½ cups rich chicken broth (see recipe page 800)

1 cup heavy cream

½ cup finely diced, cooked chicken breast

Although we have had a fair amount of success tracking down the origins of recipes and their names, we have had some difficulty with the curried cream soup dubbed Senegalese. Although the name derives from Senegal, the former French West African territory, we have been unable to find it in any French reference work. We suspect that it may even be an American creation. Whatever its origins, the soup is a delight served well chilled.

1. Melt the butter in a heavy casserole and add the onion. Cook, stirring, for about 1 minute. Add the curry powder and stir to coat the onion.

2. Add the leeks, garlic, bananas, apples, tomatoes, potatoes, salt, pepper, and Tabasco. Stir well.

3. Add the chicken broth and simmer for 20 minutes.

4. Pour half of the mixture at a time into the container of a food processor or blender and blend well. When the soup is well blended, pour it into a bowl and chill thoroughly. When ready to serve, add the heavy cream and chicken and mix well. Serve thoroughly chilled.

Yield: 4 to 8 servings.

Avgolemono Soup with Orzo

1. Bring the chicken broth to the boiling point. Add the orzo and cook until the orzo is tender, about 15 minutes. Add the salt.

2. Beat the eggs until frothy. Add the lemon juice to the beaten eggs and continue beating until the mixture thickens and is tripled or quadrupled in volume.

3. Continue beating while slowly adding 2 cups of hot chicken broth to the egg mixture. Return this mixture to the simmering chicken broth. Turn off the heat and serve immediately. Do not let the soup continue to cook after the egg mixture is added or it is apt to curdle.

Yield: 8 servings.

8 cups rich chicken broth (see recipe page 800)
½ cup orzo
Salt to taste
3 eggs
½ cup lemon juice

Mulligatawny Soup

1. Combine the chicken, broth, salt, pepper, carrots, whole onion, celery, mushrooms, and parsley in a saucepan. Bring to the boil and cook for 10 minutes. Skim to remove the surface foam, partly cover, and continue to cook for 1 hour or longer, until the chicken is tender. Strain the broth. Reserve half of a chicken breast, remove the bone, and cut the chicken into very thin slices. The rest of the chicken may be refrigerated for another use.

2. Melt the butter and add the chopped onion. Cook, stirring, for about 5 minutes. Do not let the onion brown. Stir in the flour and curry powder. Gradually add the strained broth, while stirring, and bring to the boil, skimming as needed. Simmer for 10 minutes. Adjust the seasoning if necessary. Stir in the cream and rice and return to the boil. Serve in hot cups or soup bowls and garnish each serving with julienne strips of chicken.

Yield: 4 to 6 servings.

One 5-pound stewing chicken, cut into serving pieces
4 cups fresh or canned chicken broth
Salt and freshly ground pepper to taste
1 carrot, scraped and sliced
1 whole onion
2 celery ribs with leaves
¼ pound mushrooms
3 parsley sprigs
3 tablespoons butter
½ cup finely chopped onion
1½ tablespoons flour
1 tablespoon curry powder, or more to taste
½ cup heavy cream
¼ cup cooked rice

CHICKEN GUMBO

One 3½-pound chicken, cut into serving pieces

½ cup flour

Salt and freshly ground pepper to taste

2 tablespoons sweet paprika

3 tablespoons bacon fat

4 cups boiling chicken broth

2 tablespoons butter

1 cup finely chopped onion

¾ cup chopped green pepper

3 ears sweet corn, or 1½ cups frozen corn kernels (do not defrost before using)

2 cups canned tomatoes, preferably Italian plum tomatoes

¼ cup uncooked rice

½ teaspoon hot red pepper flakes

One 10-ounce package frozen cut okra

1. Dredge the chicken pieces in the flour seasoned with salt, pepper, and paprika. Shake the pieces to remove excess flour. Heat the bacon fat in a large skillet and brown the chicken on all sides. As it is browned, transfer the pieces to a deep saucepan or kettle. Add the chicken broth and cover. Cook for 20 to 30 minutes, or until the chicken is tender.

2. Meanwhile, melt the butter in a saucepan and add the onion. Cook, stirring, until wilted and add the green pepper. Cook, stirring, for about 2 minutes. When the chicken has cooked for 20 minutes, or until tender, add the pepper-and-onion mixture. Continue cooking for about 10 minutes. Remove the chicken pieces and let cool.

3. Drop the shucked corn into boiling water to cover. When the water returns to a boil, cover and remove from the heat. Let stand for 5 minutes. Drain and let cool. When cool enough to handle, cut the kernels from the cob. There should be about 1½ cups. Set it aside.

4. Add the tomatoes, rice, and hot pepper flakes to the kettle. Simmer for about 5 minutes, stirring frequently. Add the okra and cook for 10 minutes longer, or until the rice is tender without being mushy. Meanwhile, skin and bone the chicken pieces. Shred the chicken and add it to the kettle. Add the corn. Bring to the boil and serve very hot.

Yield: 6 to 8 servings.

PHO GA (RICE-NOODLE SOUP WITH CHICKEN)

One of the great dishes of summer is, curiously enough, a hot soup of Vietnamese origin—elegant, humble, and eminently delicious. It is essentially a summer dish in that its goodness is based, as with so many Vietnamese dishes, on fresh herbs.

1. Place the chicken in a kettle and add the chicken broth to cover. Do not add salt. Bring to the boil and simmer for about 20 minutes. Turn off the heat and let the chicken stand for 30 minutes or so.

2. Meanwhile, rinse the mint, basil, and coriander leaves separately. Pat dry and arrange in separate bowls. Put the scallions in a bowl. Pour boiling water over the bean sprouts. Drain immediately. Rinse under cold water and drain. Arrange in a bowl. Cut the cucumber into thin slices. Stack the slices and cut them into thin strips. Place in another bowl. Peel the onion and slice it thin, top to bottom rather than crosswise into rings. Arrange the onion slices in a bowl and toss in the vinegar. Cut the limes top to bottom and off center to avoid the seedy portion. Each lime should produce 4 seedless wedges. Arrange in a bowl or add them to the mint bowl. Cut the chilies into ⅛-inch slices crosswise. Arrange in another bowl. Add the nuoc mam to another bowl or to a pitcher.

3. Skin the chicken and remove the meat from the bones. Tear the meat into bite-size pieces. Strain the broth into a saucepan and bring it to the boil. Do not add salt. The nuoc mam will add the salty flavor. Add a little of the broth to the chicken meat to keep it moist.

4. Place the noodles in a large bowl and add boiling water to cover. If the water from the tap is steaming, that is hot enough. Let the noodles stand briefly and drain. Add more very hot water; let stand briefly and drain. Continue adding hot water and draining about seven times, or until noodles are thoroughly tender without being mushy. They overcook easily.

5. When ready to serve, arrange all the bowls of seasonings in the center of the dining table. Heat the chicken meat. Drain the noodles and add equal portions to each of four to six hot soup bowls, the deeper the better to help retain the heat. Top with equal amounts of chicken. Ladle the boiling broth over all.

6. Let each participant at the table add seasonings, including lime juice, cucumber, nuoc mam, and so on, according to taste.

Yield: 4 to 6 servings.

Note: Bottled fish sauce and rice noodles are available in Asian groceries and supermarkets.

One 3½-pound chicken

Fresh or canned chicken broth to cover

16 to 20 fresh mint leaves

16 to 20 fresh basil leaves

16 to 20 fresh coriander leaves

1 cup chopped scallions

2 cups fresh bean sprouts

One 4-inch length of trimmed, peeled, cucumber, optional

1 small red onion

1 tablespoon red wine vinegar

1 or 2 limes

1 or 2 long, hot green or red chilies

1 cup nuoc mam sauce (see recipe page 759), or pure nuoc mam or Chinese fish sauce straight from the bottle (see note)

1 pound rice noodles, preferably Vietnamese or Thai (see note)

4 to 6 raw eggs, optional

Freshly ground pepper

KENTUCKY BURGOO

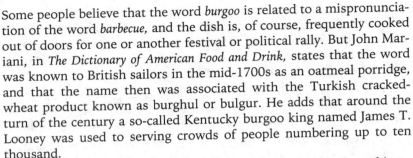

1 fowl (4½ to 5 pounds)

1 quart fresh or canned beef broth

6 large ripe tomatoes, cut up

2 medium-size onions, whole and unpeeled

2 teaspoons curry powder

1 tablespoon freshly ground pepper

1 tablespoon coarse salt

1½ cups 100-proof bourbon

2 chicken breasts, skinned, boned, and cut into large pieces

1 cup diced country ham trimmings, optional

2 cups corn kernels, fresh or frozen and thawed

1 cup diced raw potatoes

2 cups shelled fresh lima beans

2½ cups okra, trimmed of stems and cut in half

1 tablespoon filé powder, optional

Some people believe that the word *burgoo* is related to a mispronunciation of the word *barbecue*, and the dish is, of course, frequently cooked out of doors for one or another festival or political rally. But John Mariani, in *The Dictionary of American Food and Drink*, states that the word was known to British sailors in the mid-1700s as an oatmeal porridge, and that the name then was associated with the Turkish cracked-wheat product known as burghul or bulgur. He adds that around the turn of the century a so-called Kentucky burgoo king named James T. Looney was used to serving crowds of people numbering up to ten thousand.

This is the recipe of a friend of mine who told me that in making a burgoo, which is first cousin to a Louisiana gumbo, "It is customary to begin with chicken, then add to the kettle something that happens to run by—a squirrel, possum, or rabbit." He added that nothing ran by when he made this version, so he added ham for depth of flavor.

1. Place the whole, cleaned fowl in a large stockpot with 3 quarts of water and the beef broth. Bring to the boil, reduce to a simmer, and skim off foam as it rises to the surface. When the broth is clear, add the tomatoes, onions, curry powder, pepper, and salt. Simmer gently but steadily, partly covered, for 2 hours.

2. Add 1 cup of the bourbon and simmer gently but steadily, partly covered, for 4 more hours.

3. Remove all the chicken. Trim off and discard skin and bones. Reserve the meat in large pieces.

4. Strain the soup, removing the onion skin and rubbing any remaining tomato and onion solids through a sieve into the broth. Cool completely, then skim fat from the surface.

5. Return the soup to a rinsed pot. Add the remaining ½ cup bourbon, the reserved cooked chicken, raw breast meat, ham, and all the vegetables. Simmer gently but steadily, partly covered, for 30 minutes. Adjust the seasonings. If you are using filé powder, add it to the hot soup as soon as it is removed from the heat. If filé has been added, the soup should not be reheated because it will become gummy, so do not add filé to any more burgoo than you expect to serve at one time.

6. Traditionally, burgoo is ladled into the mugs from which mint juleps are drunk, but any mugs or bowls can, of course, be substituted. Eat with spoons.

Yield: Sixteen 1-cup servings.

TURKEY SOUP

1. Pick over the carcass and reserve any tender morsels of meat. Use this for the cup of meat indicated, adding more meat as necessary.

2. Place the carcass in a kettle and set the meat aside. Add any jellied gravy that may have accumulated on the turkey platter or dish. Add the water to the kettle. Add the leftover giblet gravy, if there is any. Add the onion, bay leaf, salt, pepper, cloves, parsley, thyme, carrots, and celery. Bring to the boil and simmer for 1 hour, skimming the surface as necessary.

3. Strain the soup through a sieve lined with a clean kitchen towel or a double thickness of cheesecloth. Discard all the solids except the carrots and celery.

4. Pour about 2 cups of the soup into a saucepan and add the vermicelli. Cook until just tender. Add this to the soup. Cut the carrots and celery into ½-inch cubes and add them. Add the 1 cup of cubed turkey meat. Bring to the boil. Serve piping hot.

Yield: About 14 cups.

1 turkey carcass

1 cup cubed turkey meat, for garnish

16 cups water

Leftover giblet gravy, if any

1 cup coarsely chopped onion

1 bay leaf

Salt and freshly ground pepper to taste

2 whole cloves

4 fresh parsley sprigs

2 fresh thyme sprigs, or ½ teaspoon dried

3 whole carrots, trimmed and scraped

3 whole celery ribs, trimmed and scraped

½ cup broken vermicelli, capellini, or spaghettini

SHCHI (SAUERKRAUT AND BEEF SOUP)

2 pounds sauerkraut

10 cups beef broth (see following recipe)

1 tablespoon plus 1 teaspoon sugar

2 tablespoons tomato paste

4 tablespoons butter

2 cups chopped onion

⅓ cup chopped celery

1 cup chopped carrots

1 cup chopped parsnip, optional

½ bay leaf

Salt

1 tablespoon lemon juice

This rich, hearty soup, pronounced "shkee," was served to us by Maria Robbins, who was born in the Ukraine and maintains that it is a more common "everyday" dish in Russia than borscht. It is traditionally served with piroshki (see following recipe).

1. Drain the sauerkraut. Rinse it in cold water and squeeze to extract most of the moisture. Put the sauerkraut in a Dutch oven or heavy casserole and add ½ cup of the broth, 1 tablespoon of the sugar, and the tomato paste. Stir and cover. Cook for about 45 minutes. Add a little more broth if the sauerkraut starts to become dry.

2. Heat the butter in a skillet and add the onion. Cook, stirring, until wilted. Add the celery, carrots, and parsnip, if desired. Add this to the sauerkraut. Cover and let cook for about 10 minutes. Add the remaining broth, the bay leaf, remaining teaspoon of sugar, the salt, and lemon juice. Cover and cook for 1 hour. Serve hot with piroshki.

Yield: 4 to 6 servings.

BEEF BROTH

2 pounds chuck

4 marrow bones

2 carrots, scraped and quartered

1 onion, peeled and stuck with 4 cloves

1 parsnip, trimmed and quartered

3 celery ribs, trimmed and quartered

5 quarts water

Salt

12 peppercorns

Combine all the ingredients in a kettle and bring to the boil. Simmer 3 to 4 hours. Skim the surface frequently to remove foam and scum. Strain and reserve the broth for the soup and the beef for the piroshki. Discard the vegetables. Skim the surface to remove excess fat.

Yield: About 3 quarts.

Note: Leftover beef broth can be frozen.

1. To prepare the dough, put the milk in a saucepan and bring just to the boil. Remove from the heat and add the 4 tablespoons butter. Let stand until the butter melts and the mixture is just warm.

2. Combine the yeast with the water and ¼ teaspoon of the sugar. Stir to dissolve the yeast.

3. Measure out 4 cups of flour into a large bowl and add the remaining sugar and the salt. Stir. Make a well in the center and add 2 eggs, warm milk-and-butter mixture, and the yeast. Start combining the flour with the center liquid ingredients, working rapidly and beating with a wooden spoon until well blended. Scoop out onto a floured board and start kneading. Add more flour, up to 1 more cup, until the dough is smooth and no longer sticky. Add the flour about ¼ cup at a time. Gather the dough into a ball. Rub a warm bowl with butter and add the ball of dough.

4. Cover the dough with plastic wrap and let rise in a warm place until double in bulk, about 1½ hours. Punch down and let rise again, about 1 hour.

5. Meanwhile, to make the filling, grind the beef, using the fine blade of a food grinder. There should be about 4 cups.

6. Heat the oil in a skillet and add the onion. Cook until golden brown and add the beef. Blend well, adding salt and pepper to taste.

7. Heat the butter in another skillet and add the mushrooms, salt, and pepper to taste. A good deal of liquid will come from the mushrooms. Cook this down briefly. The mixture should not be very dry. Add this to the meat mixture. Blend well.

8. Preheat the oven to 350 degrees.

9. Turn the dough out onto a lightly floured board when it is ready. Knead it briefly and divide it into 4 pieces. Work one part at a time and keep the remainder covered. Roll out one piece at a time into a long, snakelike rope. Cut this off into 1½-inch lengths. Roll each piece into a ball and flatten with the fingers, turning it around and around into a 3-inch circle. Add to each circle 1 level teaspoon of the filling. Fold the dough over to enclose the meat. Press around the edges to seal, tucking the pointed edges under. Place on a baking sheet. Continue making piroshki until all the dough and filling are used. Brush with remaining beaten egg and bake 25 minutes. Serve hot with the soup. These are also good cold and can be reheated.

Yield: About 45 piroshki.

PIROSHKI (MEAT-FILLED DUMPLINGS)

THE DOUGH:

1½ cups milk

4 tablespoons butter

1 envelope granular yeast

⅓ cup warm water

3 tablespoons sugar

4 to 5 cups unbleached flour

1 tablespoon salt, or to taste

3 eggs, slightly beaten

THE FILLING:

2 pounds chuck, used for the beef broth (see preceding recipe)

⅓ cup oil

2 cups finely chopped onion

Salt and freshly ground pepper

4 tablespoons butter

1 pound fresh mushrooms, cut into very fine dice or chopped

POZOLE

THE SOUP:

2 ancho chilies

2 pasilla chilies

2 whole chicken breasts with bone and skin, about 2 pounds

1½ pounds boneless pork loin, cut into 1-inch cubes

2 quarts pork broth (see note), or water

1 whole onion, peeled

2 whole large garlic cloves, peeled

1 bay leaf

2 sprigs fresh thyme, or ½ teaspoon dried

Salt to taste

1¾ cups water

1 tablespoon peanut, vegetable, or corn oil

Two 16-ounce cans whole hominy, available where Spanish and Puerto Rican foods are sold

THE GARNISHES:

Toasted tortillas or corn chips

1 small head iceberg lettuce, shredded and coarsely chopped

8 radishes, thinly sliced

3 tablespoons crushed oregano leaves

Hot powdered pepper or cayenne

12 lemon or lime wedges

Coarsely chopped fresh coriander, optional

1 avocado, peeled and cubed, optional

We have a special enthusiasm for this Mexican soup and have made abbreviated versions of it in our own kitchen. This one, however, is superior. It is the recipe of Margarita de Rozenzweig-Diaz, who says it is best made with two kinds of dried chilies. It is one of those dishes where garnishes play an essential role and it is, of course, a meal in itself.

1. Place the ancho and pasilla chilies in a bowl and add water to cover. Soak several hours, turning occasionally, until slightly softened.

2. Put the chicken and pork in a kettle and add pork broth to cover. Add the whole onion, 1 clove of garlic, bay leaf, thyme, and salt. Bring to the boil and simmer, skimming the surface to remove the scum and foam. Cook for 30 minutes, or until pork is tender.

3. Meanwhile, drain the chilies. Remove and discard the stems. Split the chilies in half and remove and discard the seeds. Slice away and discard the inside veins. Put the chilies in a saucepan and add 1½ cups cold water. Bring to the boil and cook, stirring down occasionally, until the chilies are tender. Pour the chilies and their cooking liquid into the container of a food processor or blender. Add the remaining 1 clove of garlic. Blend to a fine purée. Heat the oil in a saucepan and add the purée, stirring. Add salt to taste. Rinse out the processor container with the remaining ¼ cup of water and add it to the saucepan. Cook briefly, stirring.

4. When the pork and chicken have cooked for 30 minutes, remove the chicken and let the remaining ingredients continue to simmer. When the chicken is cool enough to handle, pull away and discard the skin and bones. Cut the meat into 2-inch pieces.

5. Discard the thyme, bay leaf, garlic, and onion from the soup. Add the chicken and the puréed chili mixture. Drain 1 can of hominy and add it. Do not drain the remaining can of hominy, but add the hominy and liquid to the soup. Continue cooking for 30 minutes, skimming the surface to remove the scum and fat.

6. Serve boiling hot in very hot bowls. Serve with toasted tortillas on the side. Serve the remaining garnishes to be added to the soup according to each guest's whim and appetite.

Yield: 4 to 6 servings.

Note: Place neck bones of pork in a kettle of water to cover and add salt to taste. Simmer for 1 hour and strain.

OXTAIL SOUP

1. Put the oxtails in a kettle and add cold water to cover. Bring to the boil and simmer for about 1 minute. Drain. Run the oxtails under cold water until chilled.

2. Return the oxtails to a clean kettle and add the water, peppercorns, bay leaf, thyme, parsley, salt, and pepper. Bring to the boil and simmer over low heat for 2½ hours.

3. Cut the carrots into 1½-inch lengths. Cut each piece lengthwise into quarters. There should be about 1½ cups.

4. Cut the turnips into pieces of a size to match that of the carrots. There should be about 1½ cups.

5. Add all the vegetables to the kettle and cook for about 1 hour longer.

Yield: 6 to 8 servings.

2 well-trimmed oxtails, about 1½ pounds each, and each cut into 8 crosswise sections

12 cups water

6 whole black peppercorns

1 bay leaf

½ teaspoon dried thyme

6 fresh parsley sprigs

Salt and freshly ground pepper to taste

2 small carrots, trimmed and scraped

3 turnips, peeled

12 small white onions, peeled, about 1 cup

4 cups coarsely chopped cabbage, about ½ pound

1 cup trimmed, chopped celery

2 cups chopped leeks

OXTAIL SOUP WITH PAPRIKA AND SOUR CREAM

3 pounds meaty oxtail, cut into 2-inch lengths

3 quarts water

Salt to taste

1 pound green or red sweet peppers (see note)

4 tablespoons butter

4 cups thinly sliced onion

2 tablespoons sweet or hot paprika

2 garlic cloves, finely minced

5 tablespoons flour

Freshly ground pepper

2 cups sour cream

1. Trim excess fat from the pieces of oxtail. Place the pieces in a kettle and add water to cover. Bring to the boil and simmer for about 3 minutes. Drain and run under cold running water. Return the pieces to a clean kettle and add 3 quarts of water and the salt. Bring to the boil and simmer for 1 hour.

2. Core and seed the peppers. Cut them in half and cut the halves into thin strips. There should be about 5 cups. Heat the butter in a kettle and add the onions and peppers and cook briefly until wilted. Sprinkle with paprika, garlic, and flour, stirring. Gradually add about half the oxtail broth, stirring rapidly to prevent lumping. Return this mixture to the remaining broth and oxtail in the kettle. Add salt and pepper to taste. Bring to the boil and simmer for about 2½ hours. The total cooking time should be about 3½ hours, or until oxtail meat is tender and almost falling from the bone.

3. Beat the sour cream with a little salt to make it smooth and seasoned. Serve the hot soup in individual bowls with the sour cream on the side to be added according to taste.

Yield: 8 to 12 servings.

Note: If your taste runs to the piquant side, a few hot Hungarian or other peppers may be used to replace part of the sweet peppers in this recipe.

PHILADELPHIA PEPPER POT

1. Heat the butter in a deep kettle or casserole and, when it is hot but not brown, add the chopped onion, whole onion with cloves, celery, carrot, and green or red pepper. Cook, stirring, for about 10 minutes. Do not brown. Sprinkle with flour and stir to coat the vegetables evenly. Add the chicken broth, stirring constantly to prevent lumping. Add the veal bones, tripe, garlic, dried hot red pepper, bay leaf, marjoram, basil, thyme, salt, and pepper. Bring to the boil and simmer covered for 1½ to 2 hours, or until tripe is tender.

2. Remove the whole onion with cloves, the veal bones (pull off any meat, shred it, and return it to the pot), and bay leaf. Add the potatoes and cook until potatoes are tender. Add the heavy cream and bring to the boil. Serve piping hot in hot soup bowls with crusty French or Italian bread. More ground pepper may be added before serving.

Yield: 6 to 8 servings.

4 tablespoons butter

1 cup finely chopped onion

1 whole onion stuck with 2 cloves

½ cup finely chopped celery

½ cup finely chopped carrot

½ cup chopped sweet green or red pepper (or use hot fresh pepper if desired)

3½ tablespoons flour

5 cups fresh or canned chicken broth

1½ pounds veal bones

2 pounds honeycomb tripe, cut into bite-size pieces

1 whole garlic clove

1 dried hot red pepper, or more to taste

1 bay leaf

1 teaspoon dried marjoram

1 teaspoon dried basil

½ teaspoon dried thyme
   Salt and freshly ground pepper to taste

2 cups peeled and cubed potatoes

1 cup heavy cream

VEGETABLE SOUP

3 pounds raw, meaty short ribs of beef, or an equal weight of shin bone with meat

3 quarts water

Salt

1¼ pounds raw green or Savoy cabbage, chopped into 1-inch pieces

2 cups cubed, peeled white turnips

2 cups cubed carrots

2 cups chopped leeks, optional

1 cup chopped onion

2 cups finely chopped celery with leaves

Freshly ground pepper to taste

4 potatoes, about 1 pound, peeled and cut into ½-inch cubes

1. Place the ribs of beef or shin bone in a kettle and add cold water to cover. Bring to the boil and simmer for about 3 minutes. Drain and run under cold water. Return the bones to a clean kettle and add the 3 quarts of water and salt to taste. Bring to the boil and simmer for 30 minutes, skimming the surface as necessary to remove the foam and scum.

2. Add the cabbage, turnips, carrots, leeks, onion, and celery. Sprinkle with pepper to taste and return to the boil. Simmer for 1 hour and 30 minutes. Add the potatoes and cook for 1 hour longer, skimming the surface as necessary. Remove the short ribs of beef or shin. Carve off the meat and cut it into 1-inch cubes. Return meat to the kettle. Discard the bones. Serve the soup piping hot in hot bowls.

Yield: 8 to 12 servings.

Note: One cup of dried "no soaking necessary" pea beans may be added to the soup at the same time as the cabbage and turnips. Grated Parmesan cheese may be served on the side if desired.

MINESTRONE

1. Unless the package of beans specifies no soaking, put them in a bowl and add water to cover about 2 inches above the top of the beans. Soak overnight.

2. Drain the beans. Put them in a kettle and add 4 cups of water. Bring to the boil, covered, and simmer for 50 minutes to 1 hour, or until the beans are tender. Drain and save 2 cups of the liquid.

3. Heat the oil in a kettle and add the onion. Cook, stirring, until the onion is wilted. Add the garlic and stir. Add the leeks, cabbage, carrots, zucchini, and tomatoes and cook, stirring occasionally, for about 10 minutes. Add the salt, pepper, parsley, basil, rosemary, cloves, the reserved bean liquid, and the broth.

4. Put half the beans into the container of a food processor or food mill. Purée the beans. Add them to the soup. Add the remaining cooked beans.

5. Bring to the boil and simmer for 25 minutes. Add the macaroni and cook for 15 minutes longer, or until the macaroni is tender.

Yield: 10 servings.

1 cup dried white beans, such as white kidney beans

4 cups water

3 tablespoons olive or corn oil

2 cups finely chopped onion

2 tablespoons minced garlic

1½ cups finely shredded leeks

3 cups finely shredded cabbage

¾ pound carrots, finely diced, about 2 cups

2 zucchini, about ½ pound, quartered and sliced crosswise, about 2 cups

2 tomatoes, about ¾ pound, peeled and cut into 1-inch cubes, about 2 cups

Salt and freshly ground pepper to taste

½ cup finely chopped parsley

¼ cup finely chopped basil

1 teaspoon finely chopped fresh rosemary

⅛ teaspoon ground cloves

4 cups beef or vegetable broth

¾ cup small macaroni, preferably ditalini

YOGURT AND BARLEY SOUP

1 quart plain yogurt
7 cups water
⅓ cup barley
2 tablespoons butter
½ cup finely chopped onion
6 eggs
2 tablespoons flour
Salt and freshly ground white pepper to taste
2 tablespoons finely chopped chives
1 tablespoon finely chopped fresh mint
1 tablespoon finely chopped fresh coriander

1. Place a sieve in a mixing bowl. Line the sieve with cheesecloth that has been soaked in cold water and wrung out. Add the yogurt and let it drain for 1 hour.

2. Meanwhile, combine 3 cups of the water and the barley in a saucepan and bring to the boil. Cover closely and let simmer for 1 hour, or until the barley is tender. Drain.

3. In a mixing bowl, combine the remaining 4 cups of water and the drained yogurt. Blend well.

4. Melt the butter in a saucepan. Add the onion and cook, stirring, until it is wilted. Do not let the onion brown.

5. In a large casserole, combine the eggs and flour, stirring rapidly with a wire whisk until the mixture is smooth. The flour should not be lumpy.

6. Add the yogurt mixture and cook over very low heat for about 5 minutes, stirring rapidly with the whisk. Let simmer gently but do not boil. When the soup has thickened slightly, remove it from the heat. Add the barley and onion and stir. Add the salt, pepper, chives, mint, and coriander. Serve very hot or well chilled.

Yield: 10 to 12 servings.

LAMB AND WHITE BEAN SOUP

1. Soak the beans or not, according to the package directions.
2. Melt the butter in a kettle and add the onion, garlic, and lamb shanks. Cook, stirring the onion and turning the shanks, for about 5 minutes.
3. Drain the beans and add them to the kettle. Add the water, tomatoes, bay leaf, parsley sprigs, thyme, cloves, peppercorns, and salt. Bring to the boil and simmer for 2 hours.
4. Remove the lamb shanks, bay leaf, and parsley and thyme sprigs.
5. Remove the skin from the shanks. Remove the meat from the bones and shred it or cut it into small bite-size pieces. Return the meat to the soup. Reheat and serve sprinkled with chopped parsley.

Yield: 8 or more servings.

1 pound dried Great Northern beans

2 tablespoons butter

1 cup coarsely chopped onion

1 garlic clove, finely minced

2 lamb shanks, about 1 pound each

10 cups water

1½ cups peeled and diced tomatoes

1 bay leaf

6 fresh parsley sprigs tied in a bundle

3 fresh thyme sprigs tied in a bundle, or ½ teaspoon dried

2 whole cloves

20 whole black peppercorns

Salt to taste

¼ cup finely chopped parsley

LAMB AND BARLEY SOUP

4 pounds meaty neck bones of lamb, cut into 2-inch pieces

20 cups water

Salt to taste

20 peppercorns, crushed

½ cup barley

2 cups finely diced carrots

2 cups diced leeks

1 cup finely diced rutabaga

2 cups finely diced celery

2 cups chopped onion

1 tablespoon finely minced garlic

¾ cup finely chopped parsley

1. Place the bones in a kettle and add cold water to cover. Bring to the boil and simmer for about 1 minute. Drain well and run under cold running water until chilled. Drain. Return to a clean kettle. Add the 20 cups of water, the salt, and peppercorns and bring to the boil. Simmer for 2 hours.

2. Add the barley and vegetables, including the ¾ cup parsley, and cook for 1 hour longer. Remove the neck bones. Pull off the meat and cut into bite-size morsels. Discard the bones. Return the meat to the kettle and add salt and pepper to taste. If desired, sprinkle with more chopped parsley before serving.

Yield: 8 to 12 servings.

LA RIBOLLITA (A TUSCAN BEAN SOUP)

Ribollita means "twice-cooked" (actually, twice-boiled), and is a kind of minestrone. It was served to us, well chilled, on a scorching hot day at the distinguished Sabatini restaurant in Milan. One rarely thinks of bean soup as something to serve cold, but this one is delicious. And our version is cooked only once.

1. Heat the 2 tablespoons of olive oil in a kettle and add the onion, celery, and minced garlic. Cook briefly, stirring, and add the leeks, zucchini, carrot, cabbage, tomatoes, rosemary, red pepper, and salt.

2. Cook for about 5 minutes and add the beans, broth, and water. Bring to the boil. Cover and simmer for 1½ hours.

3. Purée half the soup at a time and then combine the two mixtures. The soup may be served hot at this point with grated Parmesan cheese on the side.

4. To serve the soup cold, let it cool, then refrigerate it. Prepare the dry toast and, when it is crisp, rub the toast on both sides with the whole clove of garlic. Brush liberally with olive oil. Serve the toast in the soup with a trace more olive oil poured over. Serve with grated Parmesan cheese.

Yield: 12 or more servings.

2 tablespoons olive oil

1 cup finely chopped onion

½ cup finely chopped celery

1 garlic clove, finely minced

3 cups chopped leeks

½ pound zucchini, trimmed, unpeeled, and cut into ½-inch cubes, about 2 cups

½ cup finely diced carrot

½ pound cabbage, coarsely chopped

2 cups chopped fresh or canned tomatoes

1 teaspoon finely chopped fresh rosemary

1 dried hot red pepper

Salt to taste

1 pound dried white pea beans, Navy beans, or Michigan beans (use the no-soaking variety)

4 cups beef broth

6 cups water

Freshly grated Parmesan cheese

Dry toast, 1 or 2 pieces per serving, made from crusty French or Italian loaves

1 whole garlic clove, peeled

Olive oil

Cuban Black Bean Soup

1 pound dried black beans, preferably black turtle beans

12 cups water

Salt to taste

¼ pound lean salt pork, cut into ¼-inch cubes

2 cups finely chopped onion

1 tablespoon finely chopped garlic

1 cup chopped sweet green pepper

½ teaspoon dried oregano

½ cup finely chopped cooked, smoked ham, preferably a country ham

1 cup crushed fresh or canned tomatoes

2 tablespoons chopped fresh coriander

1 to 2 cups fresh or canned beef broth

1 teaspoon cumin

Wine vinegar

1. Place the beans in a bowl and add cold water to cover to a depth of 1 inch above the top of the beans. Soak overnight. Drain.

2. Place the beans in a kettle and add the 12 cups of water. Add the salt. Bring to the boil. As the beans cook, heat the salt pork in a skillet and, when it is rendered of fat, add the onion, garlic, and green pepper and cook until onion is wilted. Add the oregano, ham, tomatoes, and coriander. Cook briefly. This mixture is known as a sofrito.

3. Spoon and scrape the sofrito into the beans and continue cooking 1½ to 2 hours, or until the beans are thoroughly tender. If they become too dry, add beef broth. When ready to serve, add the cumin and dilute with beef broth to the desired consistency. Serve piping hot with vinegar on the side to be added according to individual taste. Chopped hard-boiled egg white is sometimes served as a garnish. And, if the vinegar is omitted, lemon slices stuck with one clove each also may be used as a garnish.

Yield: 10 or more servings.

PURÉE OF SPLIT PEA SOUP

1. Core the tomatoes and cut them into 1-inch cubes. There should be about 2 cups. Heat 2 tablespoons of the butter in a kettle and add the onion. Cook until wilted, stirring, and add the tomatoes. Cook for about 5 minutes and add the ham hock, split peas, chicken broth, water, salt, and pepper. Cook for about 2 hours.

2. Meanwhile, peel the turnip, if used, and carrot. Slice each very thin. Cut the slices into very thin strips to resemble matchsticks about 1 inch long. There should be about ⅔ cup each. Drop the carrot sticks into boiling salted water and cook for about 5 minutes. Add the turnip and cook for 5 to 10 minutes, until crisp-tender. Drain well.

3. Remove the ham hock from the soup and put the soup into the container of a food processor or blender. Blend the soup, one portion at a time, and return it to a kettle. Add the cream and bring to the boil. Add the strips of carrot and turnip and swirl in the remaining 1 tablespoon of butter.

Yield: 10 to 14 servings.

1½ pounds tomatoes

3 tablespoons butter

1 cup coarsely chopped onion

One 2-pound ham hock

1 pound yellow split peas

4 cups fresh or canned chicken broth

4 cups water

Salt and freshly ground pepper to taste

1 white turnip, about ¼ pound, optional

1 carrot

1 cup heavy cream

LENTIL SOUP

2 tablespoons butter

¼ pound slice of smoked ham, fat left on, cut into quarters

¼ cup coarsely chopped onion

½ pound dried lentils

5 cups fresh or canned chicken broth

2 cups water

½ bay leaf

1 fresh thyme sprig, or ¼ teaspoon dried

Salt and freshly ground pepper to taste

1. Heat 1 tablespoon of the butter in a small kettle or deep saucepan and add the ham and onion. Cook briefly until the onion wilts. Add the lentils and 4 cups of the chicken broth. Add the remaining ingredients and simmer for 30 to 40 minutes. Remove ½ cup of the soup with lentils and set aside. Discard the bay leaf. Remove the ham pieces and set aside.

2. Put the soup through a food mill to eliminate the coarse lentil hulls. Return the soup to the stove and bring to the boil. Add the remaining cup of chicken broth and the reserved soup with lentils. Finely dice the ham and add it to the soup. Return the soup to the boil and swirl in the remaining 1 tablespoon butter.

Yield: 4 to 6 servings.

PURÉE OF FLAGEOLETS SOUP

1 pound dried flageolets

12 cups water

Salt to taste

1 carrot, scraped but left whole

1 onion stuck with 2 whole cloves

1 bay leaf

2 garlic cloves, finely minced

2 fresh thyme sprigs, or ½ teaspoon dried

1 cup half-and-half

2 tablespoons butter

Freshly ground pepper to taste

Bread croutons

1. Put the beans in a bowl and add cold water to cover to a depth of 1 inch above the top of the beans. Soak overnight.

2. Drain the beans and put them in a kettle. Add the water, salt, carrot, onion, bay leaf, garlic, and thyme. Bring to the boil and simmer for about 1¼ hours, or until the beans are tender.

3. Remove and reserve 1 cup of the beans to be used as garnish.

4. Put the remaining bean mixture through a food mill or purée in a food processor. Return the puréed mixture to the kettle and add the half-and-half and reserved flageolets. Bring to the boil and swirl in the butter. Add salt and pepper to taste. Serve hot with croutons on each serving.

Yield: 10 or more servings.

BEAN SOUP WITH BASIL SAUCE

1. Place the beans in a kettle and add the water. Bring to the boil and simmer for 30 minutes. Peel the potatoes and cut them into ½-inch cubes. There should be about 3½ cups. Add them to the kettle. Trim the green beans and cut them into ½-inch lengths. There should be about 2 cups. Add them to the kettle. Shell the fresh lima beans, if used. There should be about 1 cup of beans. Add them to the kettle. If frozen lima beans are used, do not add them at this point. Add salt and pepper to taste. Cover and simmer for 50 minutes.

2. Peel and core the tomatoes and cut them into ½-inch cubes. Add them to the kettle. Trim and discard the ends of the zucchini and cut them into ½-inch cubes. Add them to the kettle. If frozen lima beans are used, add them. Cover and cook for 30 minutes longer.

3. Meanwhile, blend to a paste the basil and garlic. Stir in the oil gradually. This is the pistou. When ready to serve, add the pasta to the soup and simmer for about 1 minute. Stir in the pistou and serve piping hot in hot bowls.

Yield: 8 or more servings.

THE SOUP:

¾ cup dried pea beans

3 quarts water

2 potatoes, about 1¼ pounds

½ pound green beans

1½ pounds lima beans in the shell, or one 10-ounce package frozen

Salt and freshly ground pepper to taste

2 ripe tomatoes, about 1¼ pounds, or 2 cups chopped canned imported tomatoes

3 or 4 small zucchini, about 1 pound

¼ cup broken small pasta, preferably capellini or vermicelli

THE PISTOU:

10 or 12 fresh basil leaves

2 to 4 fresh garlic cloves, peeled

3 tablespoons olive oil

CALDO VERDE

⅓ pound dried white lima beans

6 tablespoons olive oil

3 cups thin wedges of onion

8 cups boiling water

Salt to taste

¾ pound beef, cut into ¾-inch or smaller cubes

¾ pound bratwurst, kielbasa (Polish sausage), or krainer sausage cut into ½-inch rounds

2 cups chopped tomatoes

1 pound greens of the cabbage family such as collard greens, broccoli leaves, mustard greens, or, as a last resort, green cabbage

Freshly ground pepper to taste

1. Place the beans in a bowl and add cold water to cover to a depth of about 2 inches above the beans. Let stand overnight.

2. Drain the beans. Remove and discard the tough skin on each bean. Heat the oil in a kettle and add the onions. Cook, stirring often, until the onions are golden brown. Add half the boiling water and the salt. At the boil, add the beef, sausages, tomatoes, and beans. Simmer for 1 hour, skimming the surface as necessary to remove the scum and foam.

3. Remove any tough stems from the greens. Finely shred the leaves (chiffonade). Add the remaining boiling water and the greens to the kettle and simmer 1½ hours longer. Add salt and pepper to taste.

Yield: 6 or more servings.

MISOSHIRU (JAPANESE BEAN SOUP)

1. Pour the dashi into a saucepan and add the bean paste, stirring constantly. Taste the soup. If it is not strong enough, stir in a little more bean paste. If it is too strong, thin it with more dashi.

2. When ready to serve, strain the soup into another saucepan. Add the mushrooms, bring to the boil, and pour equal quantities into 3 soup bowls. Garnish each serving with chopped scallions.

Yield: 3 servings.

Note: Many ingredients can be added to this soup, including bean curd cut into cubes and shrimp or eel. Very small cherrystone clams, cooked just until they open, are also excellent served in the shell.

3 cups dashi (see recipe page 802)

⅓ cup miso (bean paste), available in Japanese food outlets

½ cup thinly sliced fresh mushrooms (see note)

2 or 3 tablespoons chopped scallion for garnish

COLD AVOCADO SOUP

4 ripe, unblemished
  avocados

3 cups fresh or canned
  chicken broth

1 cup sour cream

  Salt and freshly ground
  pepper, preferably
  white pepper, to taste

Peel and pit the avocados and cut each into pieces. Put the flesh into the container of a blender or food processor. Add a little chicken broth to aid the processing. When very smooth, pour and scrape the avocado into a bowl. Add the chicken broth, sour cream, salt, and pepper and blend well. For an even smoother soup, strain the soup through a fine sieve. Chill thoroughly.

Yield: 8 or more servings.

BORSCHT

2 tablespoons butter

1 cup finely chopped
  onion

1 garlic clove, finely
  minced

1½ cups finely shredded
  cabbage

6 to 8 medium-size
  beets, about
  1½ pounds, trimmed
  and peeled

2 cups cored, peeled, and
  chopped tomatoes

¼ cup red wine vinegar

1 teaspoon sugar

  Salt and freshly ground
  pepper to taste

5 cups fresh or canned
  beef broth

  Boiled potatoes

  Sour cream

1. Heat the butter in a large, deep saucepan or a small kettle and add the finely chopped onion. Cook, stirring, until the onion is wilted and add the garlic and cabbage. Continue cooking, stirring the cabbage until it is wilted.

2. Grate or shred the beets and add them to the cabbage. Add the tomatoes, vinegar, sugar, salt, pepper, and beef broth. Bring to the boil and simmer for about 1 hour. Serve with boiled potatoes and sour cream beaten lightly with salt to taste on the side.

Yield: 4 to 6 servings.

BEET AND YOGURT SOUP

1. Wash the beets well and put them in a saucepan. Add the orange juice. If necessary, add water to cover the beets. Simmer slowly until tender (this may take up to 2 hours if beets are old). Drain and reserve both the beets and the cooking liquid. Reserve the beets for another use, such as salad.

2. Put the gelatin in a small bowl and add ½ cup of the beet liquid. Stir. Add this to the remaining beet liquid. Add the tomato liquid, onion, coriander, salt, and pepper. Refrigerate until the soup sets.

3. Pour and scrape the mixture into the container of a food processor or blender. Add the yogurt and blend thoroughly. Taste the soup. Add more salt if desired. Refrigerate until ready to serve. Serve in chilled soup bowls and garnish with a dab of sour cream and a tarragon sprig.

Yield: 6 servings.

Note: To make tomato liquid, put red, ripe, cored, and peeled tomatoes through a food mill.

1 pound beets, unpeeled
2 cups orange juice
1 envelope gelatin
2 cups fresh tomato liquid (see note)
2 tablespoons freshly grated onion
1 teaspoon chopped fresh coriander
Salt and freshly ground pepper to taste
1 cup yogurt
Sour cream for garnish
Tarragon sprigs for garnish

CABBAGE SOUP WITH PORK MEATBALLS

THE SOUP:

2 pounds meaty pork bones

One 3-pound head firm, unblemished green cabbage

¼ pound lean salt pork, cut into ¼-inch cubes

1 cup finely chopped onion

2 garlic cloves, finely minced

12 cups water

1 bay leaf

Salt and freshly ground pepper to taste

THE MEATBALLS:

½ pound ground pork

6 tablespoons bread crumbs

1 egg, lightly beaten

2 tablespoons heavy cream

1 tablespoon finely grated onion

1 tablespoon finely chopped parsley

1 teaspoon caraway seeds, crushed

Salt and freshly ground pepper to taste

1. Place the bones in a kettle and add cold water to cover. Bring to the boil and drain. Run under cold running water. Drain again. Set aside.

2. Remove the core from the cabbage. Discard very large and blemished outer leaves. Shred and finely chop the cabbage. There should be about 8 cups. Set aside.

3. Meanwhile, heat the salt pork in a heavy soup kettle and, when rendered of fat and crisp, add the onion. Cook until wilted, for about 5 minutes, and add the garlic. Add the cabbage and pork bones and 12 cups of water. Add the bay leaf, salt, and pepper. Bring to the boil and simmer, partly covered, for about 1½ hours. Skim the surface often to remove excess fat.

4. As the soup cooks, prepare the pork balls. Place the pork in a mixing bowl and add the remaining ingredients. Blend well with the hands. Shape into 24 balls. Add the pork balls to the soup and continue to simmer, partly covered, for about 15 minutes.

Yield: 6 to 8 servings.

CREAM OF CARROT SOUP

1. Trim off the ends of the carrots. Pare the carrots and potatoes with a swivel-bladed vegetable scraper. Cut the carrots into rounds. Cube the potatoes. Set aside.

2. Heat the butter in a kettle and add the onion. Cook briefly, stirring. Add the carrots, potatoes, and chicken broth and bring to the boil. Add the thyme and bay leaf. Bring to the boil and simmer for 30 to 40 minutes, or until the carrots and potatoes are tender.

3. Put the mixture through a food mill and let it chill. Put it in the container of a food processor or blender and blend. This may have to be done in two stages. If the soup is to be served hot, put it in a saucepan, bring to the boil, and add the remaining ingredients. When the soup returns to the boil, serve it piping hot. Or pour it into a bowl, add remaining ingredients, and chill thoroughly. Serve very cold.

Yield: 6 to 8 servings.

1 pound (8 to 10) carrots

1 pound (3 to 5) potatoes

2 tablespoons butter

½ cup coarsely chopped onion

6 cups fresh or canned chicken broth

2 fresh thyme sprigs, or ½ teaspoon dried

1 bay leaf

1 cup heavy cream

⅛ teaspoon Tabasco sauce, or to taste

½ teaspoon Worcestershire sauce

½ teaspoon sugar

Salt and freshly ground pepper to taste

1 cup cold milk

CRÈME DUBARRY (CREAM OF CAULIFLOWER SOUP)

1 large or 2 small
cauliflowers, about
3 pounds untrimmed

3 cups fresh or canned
chicken broth

½ cup raw rice

Salt and freshly ground
pepper to taste

3 cups milk

¼ teaspoon freshly
ground nutmeg, or to
taste

⅛ teaspoon cayenne, or
to taste

½ cup heavy cream

No one knows at what point in history or under what French chef's auspices cauliflower and the Comtesse DuBarry, mistress to Louis XV, became eternally associated. But on any menu, a dish bearing the name DuBarry indicates the invariable presence of cauliflower.

1. Trim the cauliflower of leaves and carve out and discard the center core. Cut or break the cauliflower into large florets. Place them in a kettle and add cold water to cover. Do not add salt. Cover with a lid and bring to the boil. Simmer for about 2 minutes, no longer. Drain immediately. Set aside about 3 pieces of cauliflower for garnish when the soup is cooked. Break them into smaller pieces. Place the remaining cauliflower in a saucepan and add the chicken stock. Add the rice, salt, and pepper to taste. Simmer for 30 minutes.

2. Pour the cauliflower with broth into the container of a food processor or blender. This will probably have to be done in two or three steps. Blend until smooth and, as the cauliflower is blended, return it to the saucepan. Add the milk, salt, pepper, nutmeg, and cayenne. Bring to the boil and add the cream.

3. Spoon the piping hot soup into hot cream soup dishes and sprinkle the top of each serving with a few pieces of garnish.

Yield: 6 to 8 servings.

CELERY ROOT AND CELERY SOUP

1. Heat the butter in a kettle or large saucepan and add the garlic and onion. Cook until the onion is wilted. Sprinkle with flour and stir to blend. Add the celery root, rib celery, chicken broth, water, and salt. Bring to the boil and simmer for about 45 minutes.

2. Purée the mixture in a food processor or blender and return it to the kettle or saucepan. Add the cream, salt, and pepper and serve hot.

Yield: 9 to 10 cups.

2 tablespoons butter

1 garlic clove, finely minced

1 cup coarsely chopped onion

¼ cup flour

4 cups cubed celery root, about 1¼ pounds

8 cups celery rib cut into 1-inch lengths

4 cups fresh or canned chicken broth

4 cups water

Salt to taste

½ cup heavy cream

Freshly ground pepper to taste

COCK-A-LEEKIE

1. Truss the chicken and put it in a kettle with the neck and giblets. Add the water, salt, peppercorns, bay leaf, parsley, and carrot. Bring to the boil and simmer, skimming the surface often to remove scum and foam, for about 20 minutes.

2. Add the leeks, onion, and rice and continue simmering for 20 minutes longer. Remove and discard the parsley and bay leaf. Remove the chicken and giblets.

3. Serve the soup as a first course. Serve the chicken later, carved, as a main course. You can, of course, serve the cut-up chicken in bowls with the soup.

Yield: 4 to 6 servings.

One 3-pound chicken with giblets

8 cups water, or to cover

Salt to taste

10 peppercorns, crushed

1 bay leaf

2 parsley sprigs

1 carrot, trimmed, scraped, and quartered

4 cups finely shredded leeks (before shredding, cut the leeks into 3-inch lengths)

¼ cup chopped onion

3 tablespoons rice

Leek and Potato Soup

4 leeks
1¼ pounds Idaho potatoes
3 tablespoons butter
4 cups fresh or canned chicken broth
4 cups water
  Salt and freshly ground pepper to taste
½ cup milk or heavy cream
2 tablespoons butter

There are probably few foods and especially soups in this country that have been written about at greater length than vichyssoise. The reason is that it is one of the few "French" dishes to have been created in America.

It is common knowledge that Louis Diat, while chef of the Ritz Hotel in New York, concocted a peasant soup of his childhood, a hot potage made with leeks and potatoes. He puréed it, added heavy cream, topped it with chives, and served it cold. The date of this invention is generally given as 1910. But according to an old edition of *Vanity Fair,* the soup was presented at the opening of the hotel's roof garden. That event took place in June 1917.

1. Trim off the root ends at the very base of the leeks. Cut off the tops of the leeks crosswise at the center. Remove the bruised outside leaves. Split lengthwise, inserting a knife about 1 inch from the base. Give it a ¼-inch turn and make another lengthwise cut. This allows the leaves to be opened up. Drop the leeks into a basin of cold water and let stand until ready to use.

2. Shake the leeks to make certain they are cleaned of inner dirt or sand. Cut them into fine, crosswise slices, about 3 cups. Peel the potatoes. Cut them into thin slices. Cut the slices into small squares. There should be about 4 cups. Soak the potatoes in cold water as they stand.

3. Melt the butter in a small kettle or large saucepan and add the leeks. Cook for about 5 minutes, stirring often. Do not brown. Add the chicken broth, water, salt, and pepper. Drain the potatoes and add them to the soup. Bring to the boil and simmer for about 45 minutes. Add the milk and, if desired, more salt and pepper. Swirl in the butter.

Yield: 8 to 10 servings.

VICHYSSOISE

Prepare the Leek and Potato Soup (see preceding recipe) and purée it in a food processor or blender, or put through a food mill. Chill thoroughly. Add more milk, if desired, and serve garnished with chopped chives.

MUSHROOM SOUP

1. Place the dried mushrooms in a bowl and add boiling water to cover. Let stand until thoroughly softened.

2. Melt the butter in a saucepan and add the onion. Cook until wilted and add the fresh mushrooms. Stir and cook until wilted. Sprinkle with flour, salt, and pepper to taste. Stir to coat the mushrooms and add the broth.

3. Drain the dried mushrooms and measure the soaking liquid. Add enough water to make 2 cups. Add this and the dried mushrooms to the saucepan. Simmer all together for 15 minutes.

4. Purée the mushrooms, using a food processor or blender. Return to the heat and bring to the boil. Add the sour cream, if desired. Serve piping hot or chill and serve cold.

Yield: 8 to 12 servings.

2 ounces dried mushrooms

2 tablespoons butter

1 cup finely chopped onion

1 pound fresh mushrooms, sliced, about 5 cups

¼ cup flour

Salt and freshly ground pepper to taste

2 cups fresh or canned beef broth

1 cup sour cream, optional

ONION SOUP

3 pounds onions

4 tablespoons butter

1 garlic clove, finely minced

   Salt and freshly ground pepper to taste

2 tablespoons flour

10 cups water

1 cup dry white wine

1 bay leaf

1 fresh thyme sprig, or ½ teaspoon dried

12 very thin (¼-inch) slices French bread

2 cups grated Gruyère or Swiss cheese

6 tablespoons grated Parmesan cheese

1. Preheat the oven to 400 degrees.

2. Peel the onions and cut them in half. Slice each half wafer-thin. There should be about 12 cups. In a large, heavy, ovenproof casserole or deep skillet, heat the butter and add the onions and garlic. Cook, stirring, until the onions are wilted and start to brown, about 10 minutes. Sprinkle with salt and pepper. Put the casserole in the oven and bake for 15 minutes.

3. Remove the casserole from the oven and sprinkle the onion mixture with flour, stirring to coat onion pieces evenly. Add the water and wine and cook over high heat, scraping around the bottom and sides to dissolve the browned particles. Add the bay leaf and thyme and simmer for 30 minutes, stirring frequently.

4. Meanwhile, put the bread slices on a baking sheet and bake until brown and crisp.

5. Increase the oven heat to 450 degrees.

6. Fill six individual ovenproof soup tureens, or one large tureen, with the soup. If individual tureens are used, place 2 slices of toast atop the soup. If a large tureen is used, cover with the toast, overlapping. Sprinkle the toast with the Gruyère, then the Parmesan. Place the tureens on a baking sheet or jelly roll pan to catch any drippings. Bake for about 10 minutes, or until the soup is piping hot, bubbling, and brown on top.

Yield: 6 servings.

YELLOW BELL PEPPER AND
SERRANO CHILI SOUP

All my life I have had a fondness for dishes made with sweet green peppers. I considered it a blessing when peppers of various colors came on the market. One of my favorite soups, given to me by a friend in Dallas, is made with sweet yellow peppers (the red version may be substituted) combined with serrano chilies.

1. Place the peppers over a gas flame or under a preheated broiler. Turn often until the peppers are charred all over. Remove and let cool.

2. Heat the oil in a kettle or casserole and add the onion, celery, and carrots. Cook, stirring, over moderately high heat until the onions are wilted and the vegetables start to brown.

3. Add the thyme, peppercorns, and bay leaf and stir. Add the chicken broth and cook about for 20 minutes, or until reduced to about 2½ cups.

4. Blend the butter and flour and add to the boiling liquid, stirring rapidly with a wire whisk. Simmer the mixture over low heat, stirring occasionally, for about 5 minutes.

5. Add 3 cups of the cream and continue cooking over relatively high heat for about 20 minutes. Place a sieve, preferably a chinois, over a bowl. Pour the mixture into the sieve, pressing the solids with a wooden spoon or spatula to extract as much liquid as possible. There should be about 3¼ cups. Pour this mixture into a saucepan and bring to the simmer.

6. Meanwhile, peel the peppers and remove and discard the cores and seeds. Cut the peppers into strips. Put the strips in the container of a blender or food processor. Blend thoroughly. There should be about 1 cup. Add the puréed peppers to the soup mixture.

7. Combine the serrano chilies with the water and salt in a saucepan and bring to the boil. Let cook for about 6 minutes.

8. Drain the chilies. Run them immediately under cold water and drain. Cut away and discard the stems. Cut the chilies in half and remove the seeds.

9. Put the chilies in the container of a blender or food processor and add the fresh coriander. Add ¼ cup of the cream soup and blend as thoroughly as possible.

10. Put the remaining ⅓ cup cream in a bowl and beat until it stands in peaks. Add the chili-and-coriander mixture, folding it into the cream. Add salt to taste and ½ teaspoon lemon juice. Set aside.

1 pound sweet peppers, preferably yellow

1 tablespoon corn, peanut, or vegetable oil

1 cup coarsely chopped onion

½ cup coarsely chopped celery

¾ cup coarsely chopped carrots

3 fresh thyme sprigs, or ½ teaspoon dried

1 teaspoon black peppercorns

1 small bay leaf

3 cups fresh or canned chicken broth

1 tablespoon butter, at room temperature

2 tablespoons flour

3⅓ cups heavy cream

5 serrano chilies (about 1 ounce)

1 cup water

Salt to taste

12 fresh coriander sprigs

1½ teaspoons lemon juice

11. Add the remaining 1 teaspoon lemon juice and salt to taste to the cream soup. There should be about 4 cups of soup.

12. Pour equal portions of the soup into 4 to 6 soup bowls. Top each serving with a spoonful of the reserved cream-and-coriander mixture.

Yield: 4 to 6 servings.

PUMPKIN SOUP

2½ pounds new pumpkin with skin and seeds

3 tablespoons butter

1 cup finely chopped onion

1 cup water

1 cup fresh or canned chicken broth

　Salt and freshly ground pepper to taste

1 cup milk

1 cup heavy cream

¼ teaspoon freshly grated nutmeg

⅛ teaspoon cayenne

½ cup rice

1 cup water

1. Scrape away the seeds and inside fibers of the pumpkin. Cut or pare away the outside skin of the pumpkin. Cut the pumpkin into 1½-inch cubes. There should be about 6 cups.

2. Heat the butter in a kettle and add the onion. Cook briefly. Add the pumpkin. Add the water and chicken broth, salt and pepper. Bring to the boil and cook until tender, about 20 minutes. Using a food processor, food mill, or blender, purée the pumpkin mixture, liquid and all. Return the mixture to a clean kettle.

3. Add the milk and cream, nutmeg, cayenne, and salt and pepper to taste. Meanwhile, combine the rice and water in a saucepan. Bring to the boil and simmer for about 2 minutes. Drain well. Add the rice to the soup and continue to simmer until the rice is tender. Serve hot.

Yield: 8 or more servings.

CREAM OF SPINACH SOUP

1. Pick over the spinach to remove any tough stems. Rinse the spinach well in several changes of cold water to remove any traces of sand. Bring the 3 cups of water to the boil and add the salt. Add the spinach, stirring it down to wilt. Cook for about 3 minutes and drain in a colander. Run under cold water and drain. Squeeze between the hands to extract excess moisture. There should be slightly more than ½ cup. Chop the spinach fine or blend it, stirring down as necessary with a spatula. Do not add liquid.

2. Melt the butter and add the flour, stirring with a wire whisk. When blended, add the broth, stirring rapidly with the whisk. Simmer for about 30 minutes, stirring frequently.

3. Blend the cream and yolks. Remove the soup from the heat and stir in the yolk and cream mixture. Add the spinach and bring the soup almost but not quite to the boil, stirring vigorously. Add the remaining ingredients. Serve piping hot or let cool, then refrigerate and serve cold.

Yield: 6 to 8 servings.

1½ pounds fresh spinach
3 cups water
  Salt to taste
3 tablespoons butter
4 tablespoons flour
6 cups fresh or canned chicken broth
½ cup heavy cream
4 egg yolks
⅛ teaspoon freshly grated nutmeg, or to taste
  Cayenne
2 tablespoons fresh lime or lemon juice

CURRIED TOMATO SOUP

3 pounds tomatoes, cored but not peeled

4 tablespoons butter

½ pound onions, diced, about 1¾ cups

1 small garlic clove, finely minced

2 to 3 tablespoons curry powder

3 cups fresh or canned chicken broth

1 bay leaf

1 small dried hot red pepper, optional

Salt to taste

½ cup sour cream

1. Cut the tomatoes into eighths. There should be about 6 cups.

2. Melt the butter and add the onions and garlic. Cook, stirring, until the onion is wilted. Sprinkle with the curry powder and stir. Cook for about 5 minutes without browning. Add the tomatoes, broth, bay leaf, and red pepper.

3. Bring to the boil and simmer, uncovered, for 20 to 30 minutes. Remove the bay leaf and hot pepper.

4. Pour half or less of the mixture into the container of a food processor. (If a blender is used, it will be necessary to blend even smaller portions at a time.) Process or blend thoroughly. Continue processing until all the soup is blended and smooth. As it is processed pour it into a large bowl. Add salt to taste.

5. Stir in the sour cream. Serve hot or very cold.

Yield: 12 or more servings.

CHILLED TOMATO SOUP WITH MINT

2 pounds ripe tomatoes

3 tablespoons butter

½ cup finely chopped onion

1 garlic clove, finely minced

4 whole allspice, crushed

3 tablespoons flour

3 cups fresh or canned chicken broth

½ cup sour cream

1 tablespoon chopped fresh mint (see note)

Sour cream for garnish, optional

1. Core the tomatoes and cut them into eighths. Melt the butter in a saucepan and add the onion, garlic, and allspice. Cook briefly and add the flour, stirring. Add the tomatoes and broth and stir constantly. Bring to the boil and let simmer for about 20 minutes. Strain through a food mill. Let cool, then chill thoroughly.

2. Put the soup in a mixing bowl and add the sour cream, stirring with a wire whisk to blend. Add the mint and garnish, if desired, with sour cream.

Yield: 6 to 8 servings.

Note: Small cubes of seedless cucumber are also delicious in this soup. If added, the mint is optional.

CUCUMBER, TOMATO, AND AVOCADO SOUP

1. Melt the butter in a deep saucepan or kettle and add the onion. Cook, stirring, until wilted and sprinkle with flour. Add the tomatoes, stirring rapidly with a whisk. Add the cucumbers, salt, and pepper. When blended, stir in the broth. Simmer for 25 minutes.

2. Pour the mixture, a few ladlesful at a time, into the container of a food processor or blender. Blend well. Strain the soup into a bowl if it is to be served cold and chill. If it is to be served hot, return it to the stove and heat thoroughly.

3. Peel the avocado and remove the pulp. Chop the flesh and add it to the soup, stirring rapidly with a whisk. Stir in the cream. Serve very cold or piping hot.

Yield: 8 servings.

4 tablespoons butter

1 cup chopped onion

4 tablespoons flour

4 cups peeled, cubed tomatoes, preferably fresh although canned may be used

4 cups peeled, cubed cucumbers

Salt and freshly ground pepper to taste

4 cups fresh or canned chicken broth

1 ripe, unblemished avocado

1 cup heavy cream

GAZPACHO

2 large ripe tomatoes,
  cored, peeled, and
  quartered

1 green pepper, cored,
  seeded, and quartered

1 medium-size onion,
  peeled and quartered

1 small garlic clove,
  optional

  One 2-ounce jar
  pimientos

1 cucumber, peeled and
  cut into cubes

3 cups tomato juice

⅓ cup red wine vinegar

¼ cup olive oil

¾ cup fresh or canned
  chicken broth

  Tabasco sauce to taste

  Salt and freshly ground
  pepper to taste

  Garlic croutons (see
  following recipe)

Put the tomatoes, pepper, onion, garlic, pimiento, and cucumber in the container of a food processor or blender. Blend. Add tomato juice and blend again. Pour the mixture into a bowl and add the vinegar, oil, broth, Tabasco, salt, and pepper. Blend well and cover. Refrigerate for several hours before serving. Serve well-chilled, sprinkled with croutons.

Yield: 8 to 12 servings.

GARLIC CROUTONS

2 garlic cloves

4 tablespoons butter

1½ cups cubed bread

Peel the garlic and crush each clove slightly. Heat the butter in a heavy skillet and, when it is hot, add the garlic and bread cubes. Cook, stirring and shaking the skillet, until the cubes are golden brown all over. Drain the cubes and discard the garlic.

Yield: 1½ cups.

Gazpacho Mexican Style

Combine all the ingredients in a mixing bowl except the garlic croutons. Quantities of various ingredients may be increased according to taste. Serve sprinkled with garlic croutons.

Yield: 4 to 6 servings.

2 pounds ripe tomatoes, cored and finely chopped

2 tablespoons red wine vinegar

2 tablespoons chopped red onion

2 tablespoons chopped scallions

2 tablespoons chopped long green hot or mild chilies

2 garlic cloves, finely minced

1 cup diced cucumber

2 tablespoons chopped coriander

2 tablespoons chopped fresh basil

¼ cup olive oil

Salt and freshly ground pepper

Garlic croutons (see preceding recipe)

WHITE GAZPACHO, ESTREMADURA STYLE

1 egg
4 slices day-old bread
7 tablespoons olive oil
2 garlic cloves, peeled and cut in half
1 green pepper, seeded and cut into thin strips
2 small or 1 large very fresh cucumber, peeled and cut into cubes
Salt and freshly ground pepper to taste
¼ teaspoon sugar
2 tablespoons red wine vinegar
2 tablespoons white tarragon vinegar
3 cups chilled vegetable broth (see recipe page 802)
½ cup cold water
Finely chopped cucumber and green pepper and toasted bread croutons for garnish

The gazpacho that most Americans know, a zesty blend of tomatoes, chopped peppers, cucumbers, garlic, and oil, hails from Seville. What few people in this country are aware of are the gazpachos of other regions that contain neither a speck nor a smidgen of tomatoes. These are the white gazpachos. The palate-beguiling version here was served to me in the home of Dr. Luis Casas, a Spanish physician, and his American-born wife, Penelope. Penny has subsequently written what I consider the finest and most comprehensive book on Spanish food ever published in English.

1. Break the egg into the container of a food processor or blender. Beat until light colored.

2. Soak the bread in cold water. Squeeze to extract most of the moisture.

3. With the motor of the food processor running, add the oil to the egg, pouring it in in a thin stream. Add the bread, garlic, green pepper, cucumber, salt, pepper, sugar, and the vinegars. Blend until no large pieces remain.

4. Beat in 1 cup of the broth. Hold a sieve over a bowl and pour in the soup. Strain, forcing the solid pieces through the sieve with the back of a wooden spoon. Discard the solids that will not pass through.

5. Stir in the remaining broth and the water. Add more seasonings as desired.

6. Cover and refrigerate overnight. Serve very cold, garnished with finely chopped cucumber and green pepper and toasted bread croutons.

Yield: 6 servings.

GOLDEN GAZPACHO WITH CHILIES AND SHRIMP

1. Combine the chilies, chicken broth, saffron, and lime juice in the container of a food processor or, preferably, a blender. Blend thoroughly. Pour the mixture into a small mixing bowl and let stand for a minimum of 10 minutes.

2. Drop the tomatoes into a basin of boiling water and let stand 12 seconds. Drain immediately. Peel the tomatoes, cut them crosswise in half, and remove the seeds. Cut the tomato flesh into a very small dice. There should be about 2 cups.

3. Combine the tomatoes, yellow pepper, cantaloupe, papaya, mango, cucumber, jícama, and scallions in a mixing bowl. Add the chili-and-broth mixture and stir to blend. There should be about 4 cups. Refrigerate at least 1 hour. Season with salt.

4. Cut each shrimp crosswise in half. There should be about 1¼ cups. Roll the shrimp in chopped coriander.

5. Spoon equal portions of the soup into four to six chilled soup bowls. Garnish each bowl with equal portions of the shrimp.

Yield: 4 to 6 servings.

1½ teaspoons finely chopped fresh chilies, preferably serrano, stems and seeds removed

¾ cup fresh or canned chicken broth

¼ teaspoon saffron threads

2 tablespoons freshly squeezed lime juice

2 pounds yellow tomatoes (about 6)

3 tablespoons finely chopped sweet yellow pepper

5 tablespoons finely chopped peeled cantaloupe

5 tablespoons chopped, peeled, and seeded papaya

5 tablespoons chopped, peeled, and seeded mango

½ cup peeled, seeded, and finely diced cucumber

5 tablespoons peeled, finely diced jícama, optional

2 tablespoons finely chopped scallions

Salt to taste

1 pound cooked, peeled small shrimp

1 tablespoon finely chopped fresh coriander

WATERCRESS SOUP

2 firm, bright green
  bunches of watercress
6 cups fresh or canned
  chicken broth
¼ pound butter
6 tablespoons flour
3 cups freshly cubed
  white bread
3 egg yolks
⅛ teaspoon grated
  nutmeg

1. Cut the watercress bunches in half and rinse well under cold running water. Drain well. Bring a large quantity of water to the boil and add the watercress. Stir and bring to the boil. Simmer for about 3 minutes and drain in a colander. Run under cold water. Drain and squeeze between the hands to extract most of the moisture. Put the watercress in the container of a food processor or blender and add ½ cup of broth. Blend, stirring down as necessary.

2. Melt 4 tablespoons of the butter in a saucepan and add the flour, stirring with a wire whisk. When blended, add the remaining broth and simmer for 30 minutes.

3. Heat the remaining 4 tablespoons of butter in a skillet and add the bread cubes. Toss the cubes until golden brown all over. Set aside.

4. In a mixing bowl, blend the puréed watercress with the egg yolks and nutmeg. Add about ¼ cup of the boiling soup to the mixture, stirring. Add this to the soup, stirring constantly. Bring to the boil. Do not cook or the soup will curdle. Serve the hot soup in bowls, garnishing each serving with the bread croutons.

Yield: 6 to 8 servings.

COLD ZUCCHINI SOUP

5 or 6 small- to medium-
  size zucchini
1 large onion, peeled and
  thinly sliced, about
  1 cup
1½ teaspoons curry
  powder
3 cups fresh or canned
  chicken broth
1½ cups half-and-half
  Salt and freshly ground
  pepper to taste
  Finely chopped chives

1. Rinse the zucchini and pat dry. Trim off the ends. Cut one zucchini in two crosswise and thinly slice one half. Stack the slices and cut them into very thin matchlike strips. There should be about 1 cup. Place in a saucepan and add cold water to cover. Boil 3 to 4 minutes and drain. Set aside.

2. Cut the remaining zucchini half and the other zucchini into 1-inch lengths. Cut each length into quarters. Place the pieces of quartered zucchini in a kettle or saucepan and add the onion slices. Sprinkle with curry powder and stir to coat the pieces. Add the chicken broth and bring to the boil. Cover and simmer for about 45 minutes.

3. Spoon and scrape the mixture into the container of a blender or food processor and blend to a fine purée. There should be about 4 cups. Add the half-and-half, salt, and pepper to taste. Add the reserved zucchini strips. Chill thoroughly. Serve sprinkled with chopped chives.

Yield: 6 to 8 servings.

MANHATTAN CLAM CHOWDER

1. Wash the clams well. If razor clams are used, they may be placed in a basin of cold water to which about ½ cup of cornmeal is added. Let stand about 1 hour to disgorge excess sand. Drain well and rinse thoroughly. Drain again. Place the clams in a kettle and add the water. Simmer until the shells open.

2. Meanwhile, chop the bacon and put it in a kettle. Cook until the bacon is rendered of its fat. Add the carrots, celery, onions, and green pepper. Cook for about 5 minutes, stirring often. Add the garlic, thyme, and bay leaf.

3. When the clams open, strain them but reserve both the clams and their liquid. Discard any clams that don't open. Add 10 cups of liquid to the bacon mixture. (If there are not 10 cups, add enough water to make 10 cups.) Add the tomatoes. Cook for 15 minutes. Remove the clams from the shells and discard the shells. Chop the clams on a flat surface or put them through a meat grinder, using the small blade. Add them to the kettle and add the potatoes. Add salt and pepper and cook for about 1 hour.

Yield: 8 to 10 servings.

24	chowder clams or razor clams
4	cups water
4	slices bacon
2	cups finely diced carrots
1½	cups celery cubes
2	cups chopped onions
¾	cup chopped green pepper
1	garlic clove, finely chopped
1	teaspoon thyme
1	bay leaf
1	cup fresh or canned tomatoes
4	cups cubed potatoes
	Salt and freshly ground pepper to taste

NEW ENGLAND CLAM CHOWDER

24 large cherrystone clams

 1 quart water

 2 ounces lean salt pork

2½ cups finely chopped
   onions

 ¼ cup flour

 4 large potatoes, about
   1½ pounds, peeled

 1 quart milk

 1 cup heavy cream

   Salt and freshly ground
   pepper to taste

 4 tablespoons butter,
   optional

1. Wash the clams well to remove all trace of sand. Put them in a kettle and add the water. Cover and bring to the boil. Cook until the clams open. Discard any clams that don't open. When the clams are cool enough to handle, remove them, one at a time. Cut out the flesh and discard the shells. Reserve all the juices that flow from the clams plus the kettle liquid. There should be about 6 cups. Put the clams on a flat surface and coarsely chop the clam meat. Or use a food processor to chop them. Do not overblend. The clams must retain a coarse texture.

2. Cut the salt pork into thin slices. Place on a flat surface and cut into small cubes. Heat the salt pork in a kettle and add the onions. Cook, stirring, for about 5 minutes, or until the onions wilt. Add the flour and stir briskly to blend. Add the 6 cups of liquid (if there is not enough to make 6 cups, add enough water to make this quantity), stirring. Add the chopped clams.

3. Cut the potatoes lengthwise into ½-inch slices. Stack the slices and cut them into ½-inch strips. Cut the strips into ½-inch cubes. There should be about 4 cups. Cover with cold water and let stand until ready to add.

4. When the clams have cooked for 30 minutes, drain the potatoes and add them. Continue cooking for 30 minutes longer. Add the milk and cream and bring just to the boil. Do not boil or the chowder will curdle. Add the salt and pepper. When ready to serve, add the butter, if desired, and swirl it in. Serve piping hot with buttered toast or, if you prefer, oyster crackers.

Yield: 12 servings.

CLAM SOUP

1. Soak the soft-shell clams for several hours in several changes of cold, salted water. Wash thoroughly.

2. Heat the oil in a kettle and add the shallots and garlic. Cook for about 30 seconds, stirring, and add the clams and crushed red peppers. Add the basil and wine and cover. Cook for 5 minutes and add the tomatoes, water, parsley, and oregano. Stir. Add salt and pepper and cook for 20 minutes.

Yield: 8 servings.

4 quarts soft-shell clams
  Salt
½ cup olive oil
6 shallots, peeled and thinly sliced
4 garlic cloves, thinly sliced
3 dried hot red peppers, crushed
10 fresh basil sprigs
1 cup dry white wine
2¼ cups canned tomatoes, preferably Italian plum tomatoes
1 cup water
½ cup coarsely chopped parsley
1 teaspoon dried oregano
  Freshly ground pepper to taste

FISH SOUP WITH MUSSELS AND CLAMS

1¾ pounds boneless cod,
      sea bass, or other
      white-flesh fish

¾ pound bones from a
      nonoily fish such as
      cod or sea bass

6 cups water

1 cup dry white wine

1 quart well-scrubbed
      mussels

4 tablespoons olive oil

1 cup finely minced leeks

1 cup finely chopped
      onion

1 cup finely minced
      celery

3 garlic cloves, finely
      chopped

2 fresh thyme sprigs, or
      1 teaspoon dried

1 bay leaf

   Salt and freshly ground
      pepper to taste

1 tablespoon saffron
      stems

4 cups canned tomatoes,
      preferably Italian plum
      tomatoes

   One 6-ounce can
      tomato paste

   Hot red pepper flakes
      to taste

24 well-scrubbed
      littleneck clams, the
      smaller the better

2 tablespoons Ricard,
      Pernod, or other anise-
      flavored liqueur

1. Cut the fish into 1-inch cubes and set aside. Place the bones in a kettle and add the water, wine, and mussels. Bring to the boil and simmer until the mussels open. Discard any mussels that don't open. Drain, but reserve both the broth and the mussels. There should be about 8 cups of broth. Remove the mussels from the shells. Pull off and discard the stringlike band that is a part of each mussel. Set the prepared mussels aside.

2. Heat the oil in a kettle and add the leeks, onion, celery, garlic, thyme, bay leaf, salt, pepper, and saffron. Cook, stirring, for about 5 minutes and add the tomatoes and tomato paste. Add the hot red pepper flakes and simmer for 30 minutes, stirring occasionally. Add the cubed fish and stir to blend. Add the broth to the fish mixture and bring to the boil. Add the clams and simmer until they open. Discard any clams that don't open. Add the Ricard and mussels and serve piping hot.

Yield: 8 to 12 servings.

BILLI BI

This cream of mussel soup is, to my mind, one of the greatest soups ever created. It was served at Maxim's in Paris and was for many years the favorite dish of William B. Leeds, an American tin magnate. Mr. Leeds spent much time in Paris, dined more often than not at Maxim's, and invariably began his meal with the soup. He became so thoroughly associated with the dish it was renamed in his honor on the menu.

7	quarts cleaned mussels
4	tablespoons finely chopped shallots
8	tablespoons finely chopped onion
4	tablespoons finely chopped parsley
¼	teaspoon chopped fresh thyme, or ½ teaspoon dried
1	bay leaf
	Salt and freshly ground pepper
1	cup dry white wine
4	tablespoons butter, cut into small cubes, plus 2 tablespoons
2	tablespoons flour
1½	cups heavy cream
2	egg yolks
	Finely chopped parsley for garnish

1. The mussels must be well cleaned and tested to see if they are alive. To do this, take the top shell in one hand, the bottom in the other, and pull the shells gently in opposite directions. If they remain firmly together, they are alive. If they open, they will probably be full of silt and should be discarded.

2. Place the mussels in a deep kettle and add the shallots, onion, 4 tablespoons chopped parsley, thyme, bay leaf, salt, pepper, wine, and 4 tablespoons of butter cut into cubes. Cover and bring to the boil. Simmer for about 10 minutes, shaking and tossing the mussels in the kettle to redistribute them. Cook mussels only until they have opened. Discard any mussels that don't open.

3. Remove the mussels from the shells and discard the shells. Keep the mussels warm.

4. Strain the cooking liquid from the kettle into a saucepan and reduce it over high heat for about 5 minutes.

5. Make a beurre manié by blending the flour and remaining 2 tablespoons of butter. Add it bit by bit to the soup, stirring. Blend the cream and yolks and add it to the soup, stirring. Make certain the soup does not boil more than a second or two or it may curdle. Put the mussels in the soup just to heat through. Serve sprinkled with chopped parsley.

Yield: 6 to 8 servings.

Oyster and Corn Chowder

2 tablespoons unsalted butter

½ cup grated onion

1 large garlic clove, peeled and chopped fine

4 scallions, white and light green, finely chopped

1½ cups milk

1 cup heavy cream

Salt to taste

¼ teaspoon freshly ground pepper

About 1 cup oyster liquor

1 dozen fairly large oysters, cut into halves (see note)

2 cups fresh corn kernels (cut from 4 ears of corn)

1 tablespoon freshly chopped chives

1. Melt the butter in a heavy saucepan and add the grated onion, garlic, and scallions. Cook over medium heat for 1 minute.
2. Add the milk and cream and bring to the boil.
3. Add the salt, pepper, oyster liquor, oysters, and corn kernels. Bring to the boil. Remove from the heat and let sit for 5 minutes.
4. Serve sprinkled with chives.

Yield: 6 servings.

Note: Use freshly shucked oysters; canned oysters tend to curdle the milk mixture.

OYSTER STEW

1. Combine the milk, bay leaf, celery, onion, and thyme in a saucepan. Bring just to the boil but do not boil. Pour the oysters into a deep skillet large enough to hold the stew. Sprinkle with salt and bring to the boil. Cook just until the oysters curl. Strain the milk over the oysters and stir. Discard the solids. Do not boil.

2. Beat the cream with the egg yolk and add Tabasco, celery salt, salt, and pepper. Add this to the stew. Bring just to the boil and swirl in the butter. Add the Worcestershire and serve piping hot with buttered toast or oyster crackers.

Yield: 4 servings.

3 cups milk

1 bay leaf

1 celery rib with leaves

1 small onion, peeled and quartered

2 fresh thyme sprigs, or ½ teaspoon dried

12 to 24 oysters, 1 to 2 cups, depending on size and whether you want several or few oysters in each serving

Salt to taste

¾ cup heavy cream

1 egg yolk

Tabasco sauce to taste

½ teaspoon celery salt

Freshly ground pepper to taste

2 tablespoons butter

½ teaspoon Worcestershire sauce, optional

FISH SOUP

3 tablespoons olive oil

1 cup chopped onion

1 teaspoon finely minced garlic

½ tablespoon loosely packed saffron stems

¼ cup flour

2 cups fish stock or water

2 cups peeled, chopped tomatoes, fresh or canned

1 cup dry white wine

1¼ pounds fillet of white-fleshed, nonoily fish such as sea trout or sea bass

1 pint scrubbed, well-cleaned mussels or very small littleneck clams

½ teaspoon dried thyme

1 cup heavy cream

Salt and freshly ground pepper to taste

Tabasco sauce to taste

For those who fancy fish and seafood (and pity those who don't), there is nothing more gratifying to the senses of taste and well-being than a piping hot fish soup. We are fortunate to live in a community where fresh fish and shellfish are found in abundance, and we are constantly improvising our own soups, as well as enjoying those of many other nationalities. We urge you, by the way, to make your own fish stock, a recipe for which appears on page 801. In a pinch, a combination of water and bottled clam juice, or plain water, can be substituted, but the soup will not have the flavor that the stock gives it.

1. Heat the oil in a kettle and add the onion, garlic, and saffron. Stir in the flour, using a wire whisk. Add the fish stock, tomatoes, and wine, stirring rapidly with the whisk. When blended, cook, stirring frequently, for about half an hour.

2. Cut the fish into 1½-inch cubes (there should be about 3 cups). Add the fish and cook for about 5 minutes, or until the fish flakes easily. Add the remaining ingredients and simmer for about 5 minutes longer.

Yield: 8 servings.

BOURRIDE

One of our all-time favorite fish soups is called bourride. Unlike the famed bouillabaisse of Marseilles and environs, it does not contain shellfish. Another distinctive feature is its use of aïoli, a Mediterranean specialty and a sort of garlic mayonnaise. Part of this aïoli is stirred into the soup; the remainder is served on the side to be added at will.

1. Heat the oil in a kettle and add the onion. Cook, stirring, until the onion is wilted. Add the celery, leeks, minced garlic, saffron, bay leaf, wine, potatoes, fish stock, salt, pepper, and cayenne. Bring to the boil and simmer for 30 minutes.

2. While the soup cooks, prepare the aïoli.

3. Cut the fish fillets into 2-inch cubes and arrange them in one layer in a large casserole.

4. Put the soup through a food mill, pressing to purée the vegetables. Pour the soup over the fish and cover. Bring to the boil and simmer for about 3 minutes.

5. Meanwhile, rub the outside of the French bread with the whole clove of garlic. Cut the bread into 12 or 14 very thin slices, ¼ inch or less thick. Arrange the slices in a baking dish and place under the broiler. Brown on both sides.

6. When the fish is done, use a slotted spoon and transfer the pieces to a heated round or oval serving dish.

7. Spoon half the prepared aïoli into a serving dish. Spoon the remaining aïoli into a saucepan. While stirring the aïoli vigorously with a wire whisk, add the hot soup. Heat thoroughly, but do not boil or the soup will curdle.

8. Arrange the toast over the fish and pour the hot soup over all. Serve the soup with the remaining aïoli on the side.

Yield: 8 servings.

2 tablespoons olive oil

¾ cup finely chopped onion

1 cup finely chopped celery

1 cup finely chopped leeks

1 garlic clove, finely minced

1 teaspoon loosely packed saffron stems

1 bay leaf

1 cup dry white wine

¾ pound small potatoes, peeled and cut into ¼-inch rounds (there should be about 2 cups)

4 cups fish stock (see recipe page 801)

Salt and freshly ground pepper to taste

⅛ teaspoon cayenne

2 cups aïoli (see following recipe)

2 pounds white-fleshed fish fillets from nonoily fish such as sea trout or sea bass

1 loaf French bread

1 whole garlic clove, peeled

AÏOLI (A GARLIC MAYONNAISE)

3 egg yolks

Salt and freshly ground pepper to taste

1 tablespoon Dijon mustard

1 tablespoon finely minced garlic, or more according to taste

1 tablespoon white wine vinegar

2 cups olive oil

Tabasco sauce, optional

1. Put the yolks in a mixing bowl and add the salt, pepper, mustard, garlic, and vinegar.

2. Start beating with a wire whisk or an electric beater and gradually add the oil. When the mixture starts to thicken, the oil may be added in ever increasing quantities. Continue beating until all the oil is used. Add Tabasco sauce to taste. If a thinner mayonnaise is desired, beat in a teaspoon of cold water.

Yield: About 2 cups.

Nag's Head Fisherman's Soup

1. Heat the oil in a kettle and add the onions, sweet peppers, carrots, and the hot pepper. Cook, stirring, for about 5 minutes. Add the potatoes and cook for about 1 minute. Add the tomatoes, salt, and pepper. Add the fish stock and bring to the boil.

2. Combine the saffron with the water and add it to the stock. Add the fennel seeds, turmeric, orange peel, and sugar. Simmer for about 10 minutes. Add the scallops, fish, shrimp, and clams and cook for about 10 minutes, or until the clams open. Discard any clams that don't open. If desired, the clams may be steamed separately and added to the soup, layered with the other ingredients. Add salt and pepper to taste. Remove the fish, cut into pieces, and return to the soup. Serve piping hot.

Yield: 6 servings.

½ cup olive oil

2 cups finely chopped onions

1½ cups chopped sweet green or red peppers

1 cup cubed carrots

1 small hot green or red pepper, chopped, optional

1½ pounds potatoes, peeled and cut into ¼-inch slices

2 pounds ripe tomatoes, cored and cut into ½-inch cubes, or 4 cups imported canned tomatoes, chopped

Salt and freshly ground pepper to taste

7 cups fish stock (see recipe page 801)

2 teaspoons loosely packed saffron stems

1 tablespoon water

1 teaspoon fennel seeds, crushed

½ teaspoon turmeric

1 thin slice orange peel, white pulp removed

1 teaspoon sugar

1½ pounds fresh scallops, cut in half or quartered if large

1 cleaned 2-pound saltwater fish, such as weakfish

1¼ pounds raw shrimp, the smaller the better, shelled and deveined

24 littleneck clams, well scrubbed

Fresh Corn and Grouper Chowder

4 to 8 ears of corn, shucked

2 potatoes (about ¾ pound)

3 tablespoons cubed salt pork

1½ cups finely chopped onions

1½ cups fish stock (see recipe page 801)

¼ pound nonoily, white-fleshed fish, such as grouper, striped bass, flounder, etc.

Salt and freshly ground pepper to taste

Tabasco sauce to taste

3 cups milk

2 tablespoons butter

1. Drop the corn into boiling water and cover. When the water returns to the boil, remove from the heat. Let stand for 5 minutes and drain.

2. When the corn is cool enough to handle, cut and scrape the kernels from the cob. There should be about 2 cups.

3. Peel the potatoes and cut them into ½-inch cubes. Drop into cold water and let stand until ready to use.

4. Place the salt pork in a saucepan or small kettle over low heat. When it is rendered of its fat, add the onions and cook until wilted. Drain the potatoes and add them and the 1½ cups stock and bring to the boil. Simmer until the potatoes are tender, 5 minutes or longer.

5. Cut the fish into ½-inch cubes and add it to the stock. Add salt, pepper, and Tabasco sauce. Cook for about 5 minutes and add the milk. Bring to the boil and add the corn. Add the butter and swirl it in. Serve piping hot.

Yield: 4 to 6 servings.

CIOPPINO

There is a fish soup indigenous to California that is as much a part of American culture as Boston clam chowder in the East or oyster gumbo in the South. At its best—and the best we've ever sampled was in Dinah Shore's kitchen—cioppino is delectable. When Dinah invited us to dine in her home, we accepted with unusual alacrity. In addition to being a well-known singer, she was justly celebrated as one of the finest cooks in Beverly Hills.

1. Heat the oil and butter in a kettle and add the onions, leek, and garlic. Cook, stirring often, until the vegetables are lightly browned. Add the green peppers and continue cooking, stirring, until the peppers wilt. Add the tomatoes and tomato sauce. Add the salt, pepper, bay leaf, oregano, thyme, basil, and about ¼ teaspoon red pepper flakes. Add the fish stock and cook slowly for about 2 hours, stirring often to prevent burning. More fish stock may be added if desired. Add the clam juice and wine and continue cooking about 10 minutes. The soup may be made in advance to this point.

2. Twenty minutes or so before serving, return the soup to the boil and add the striped bass or other fish. Cook for about 5 minutes and add the scallops and shrimp. Simmer for about 8 minutes and add the clams, oysters, lobster tail, and crab. Cook, stirring gently, for about 5 minutes, or until the clams open. Discard any clams that don't open. Serve in very hot soup bowls with red pepper flakes on the side.

Yield: 10 servings.

2 tablespoons olive oil
2 tablespoons butter
3 cups chopped onions
1 leek, trimmed, washed well, and finely chopped
2 to 4 garlic cloves, finely chopped
2 green peppers, cored, seeded, and cut into thin strips
4 cups chopped imported peeled tomatoes
1 cup fresh or canned tomato sauce
  Salt and freshly ground pepper to taste
1 bay leaf
1 teaspoon dried oregano
1 teaspoon dried thyme
1 tablespoon dried basil
  Red pepper flakes
2 cups fish stock (see recipe page 801)
1 cup fresh or bottled clam juice
1 cup dry white wine
1 pound firm-fleshed fish such as striped bass, red snapper, rock cod, or sea bass, cut into bite-size pieces
½ pound fresh scallops, preferably bay scallops
1 pound raw shrimp, shelled and deveined
1 dozen well-washed small clams in the shell
¼ cup shucked oysters with their liquor
½ pound lobster tail, cooked in the shell, optional
1 hard-shell crab, cooked in the shell and cracked, optional

HOT AND SOUR FISH SOUP

3 to 4 pounds very fresh
  fish bones, preferably
  with head but with
  gills removed
  Water
  One 1½-inch length
  fresh ginger
4 scallions
20 sprigs of fresh
  coriander
3 to 4 tablespoons white
  vinegar
⅛ to ¼ teaspoon ground
  white pepper
½ teaspoon sesame oil
  Salt
½ pound skinless,
  boneless nonoily fish,
  such as flounder, fluke,
  sole, striped bass, etc.

There are some recipes for which fresh coriander is a *sine qua non,* and among them is this irresistible hot and sour fish soup.

1. Place the fish bones in a kettle and let cold running water flow over them to remove all traces of blood. When the water runs clear, drain and add enough cold water to barely cover the bones. Do not add salt. Bring to the boil and let simmer over very gentle heat for about 20 minutes. Strain. Reserve the broth and discard the bones. Add 6 to 7 cups of the broth to a saucepan and bring to the boil.

2. Meanwhile, scrape the ginger. Cut the ginger into the thinnest possible slices. Stack the slices and cut them into the finest possible shreds. Set aside. Add the scrapings to the soup. Trim the scallions and cut into 2-inch lengths. Cut the lengths into very fine shreds. Set aside. Pluck or cut off the coriander leaves from the stems. Set leaves aside. Crush the stems and add to the soup.

3. Strain the soup into another saucepan and add the shredded ginger, scallions, coriander leaves, vinegar, white pepper, sesame oil, and salt. Stir to blend the flavors, but do not cook. Cut the fish into ½-inch cubes and add it to the soup. Bring just to the boil and simmer just until the fish loses its raw look. Spoon into individual soup bowls and serve piping hot.

Yield: 6 servings.

JAPANESE FISH AND MUSHROOM SOUP

Put the dashi in a saucepan and add the salt and soy sauce. Add the mushrooms and bring to the boil. Arrange 1 shrimp in each of three soup bowls and add a few shreds of lemon peel. Pour equal quantities of boiling hot soup into the bowls and serve immediately.

Yield: 3 servings.

3 cups fish stock or dashi (see recipes pages 801 and 802)

Salt to taste

½ teaspoon light soy sauce

12 thin slices fresh mushroom

3 shrimp (see following instructions for shrimp to garnish Japanese soups)

Grated lemon peel

SHRIMP TO GARNISH JAPANESE SOUPS

If the shrimp are whole, tear off the head. In any event, peel the shrimp, leaving the last tail section intact. Butterfly the shrimp without cutting through. Score each shrimp on the underside at ½-inch intervals. Sprinkle with salt and dip lightly in cornstarch. Drop the shrimp into rapidly boiling water and cook for 30 to 40 seconds, until just heated through. Drain and drop immediately into ice water. Drain and pat dry. Use one shrimp in each serving of piping hot soup.

THAI SHRIMP SOUP

1¼ pounds raw, unshelled shrimp, about 40

10 cups water

1 medium-size onion, unpeeled and cut in half

Salt to taste

5 lime leaves, soaked overnight in cold water (see note)

2 tablespoons dried lemongrass, soaked overnight in cold water (see note)

½ pound mushrooms, preferably very small button mushrooms

2 tablespoons shrimp paste with bean oil (see note)

2 tablespoons Thai chili in oil (see note)

6 tablespoons lemon juice

5 tablespoons fish sauce (see note)

6 or more fresh coriander sprigs

1. Peel the shrimp but leave the last tail segment intact. Save the shells. Set the shrimp aside.

2. Combine the shells, water, and onion in a saucepan. Bring to the boil and cook, uncovered, for about 15 minutes. Strain the liquid. Discard the solids.

3. Pour the strained liquid into a kettle. Add salt to taste.

4. Drain the lime leaves and lemongrass and add to the kettle. Simmer for 15 minutes.

5. If small mushrooms are used, leave them whole. Otherwise, slice or quarter them and add them to the kettle.

6. Blend the shrimp paste, chili in oil, and lemon juice in a small bowl. Add it to the soup. Add the fish sauce and shrimp. Bring to the boil and simmer for about 2 minutes.

7. Add the fresh coriander and simmer about 1 minute longer. Serve hot.

Yield: 6 to 8 servings.

Note: All the foreign ingredients necessary for this soup can be found in Asian groceries and supermarkets. Fish sauce, which is essence of anchovy, is called nuoc mam or nam pla.

POULTRY

ROAST CHICKEN WITH ROSEMARY AND GARLIC

1. Preheat the oven to 425 degrees.

2. Sprinkle the chicken inside and out with salt and pepper. Stuff it with the rosemary and garlic. Truss the chicken.

3. Place the chicken in a shallow, not too large roasting pan and rub it with the butter. Put the chicken on its side. Scatter the onion, neck, liver, gizzard, and heart around the chicken.

4. Place the chicken in the oven and roast for about 15 minutes, basting occasionally. Turn the chicken to the opposite side; continue roasting, basting often.

5. Roast for 15 minutes and turn the chicken onto its back. Continue roasting and basting for 15 minutes.

6. Pour off the fat from the roasting pan. Add the water and return the chicken, on its back, to the oven. Roast for 10 minutes longer, basting often. Remove from the oven and let the chicken stand for 10 minutes before carving. Serve with the pan liquid.

Yield: 2 to 4 servings.

One 3½-pound chicken with giblets

Salt and freshly ground pepper to taste

2 fresh rosemary sprigs

2 garlic cloves, unpeeled

2 tablespoons butter

1 onion (about ¼ pound), peeled

¾ cup water

ROAST CHICKEN WITH MUSTARD SAUCE

Two 3½-pound chickens

3 tablespoons butter

Salt and freshly ground pepper to taste

1 cup water

½ cup heavy cream

4 tablespoons Dijon mustard

1. Preheat the oven to 400 degrees.
2. Rub the chickens all over with butter. Sprinkle them inside and out with salt and pepper. Truss. Arrange the chickens on their sides in a shallow roasting pan.
3. Roast the chickens for about 20 minutes then turn them on the other side. Baste often. Continue roasting for about 20 minutes and turn the chickens on their backs. Roast for 20 minutes, or until cavity juices run clear when the chickens are lifted so that the juices flow into the pan. Continue roasting, if necessary, until done.
4. Remove the chickens and keep warm. Pour off the fat from the pan and add the water, stirring to dissolve the brown particles that cling to the pan. Pour this liquid into a saucepan and cook to reduce by half.
5. Add the cream and cook briefly. Add the mustard and cook, stirring, for about 30 seconds.
6. Serve the chicken sliced with the mustard sauce.

Yield: 8 to 12 servings.

BARBECUED CHICKEN

Barbecues were a focal point of my early nourishment. When I was young, hundreds of guests would arrive on special occasions for barbecues that consisted of long trenches, filled with hot coals, that were specially dug on my father's property. Wire was laid over these trenches to hold hundreds of pounds of chicken and ribs of pork. These were then basted for hours until the meat shredded at a touch.

1 chicken (about 2½ pounds)

Salt and freshly ground pepper to taste

1 tablespoon oil or, preferably, softened lard

Country barbecue sauce (see recipe page 794)

1. Prepare a charcoal grill and have it ready. The coals must be white-hot but not overly plentiful, or the food will cook too fast. Arrange the grill 6 to 8 inches above the coals.

2. Split the chicken in half for grilling. Place it skin side up on a flat surface and flatten it lightly with a flat mallet. This will help it lie flat on the grill. Sprinkle the chicken with salt and pepper. Sprinkle with oil or rub with lard.

3. Place the chicken skin side down on the grill and cook until browned, about 10 minutes. Brush the top with barbecue sauce and turn. Brush the skin side with sauce. Continue grilling and turning, brushing often with sauce, until the chicken is thoroughly cooked, 30 minutes or less.

4. Give the chicken a final brushing with the sauce and remove to a serving dish.

Yield: 2 to 4 servings.

CHICKEN COOKED IN A CLAY POT

One 3½-pound chicken
1 tablespoon finely ground black pepper
1 small onion, peeled
½ cup tightly packed fresh parsley or dill
1 bay leaf
1 tablespoon butter, at room temperature
4 to 8 small carrots, trimmed, peeled, and cut in half crosswise
8 small to medium fresh mushrooms
¼ teaspoon crushed hot red pepper flakes
½ cup canned tomatoes

For a long time I was a bit wary of buying and using a clay pot. When I learned that they had been sold in the millions, I bought one out of curiosity. I must say that it does a spectacularly good job of "roasting" chicken with vegetables and herbs. This is a remarkably easy dish to prepare and you need not watch the pot as it bakes.

1. Place a clay pot in a basin of cold water and let it soak for at least 10 minutes. Drain well.

2. Sprinkle the inside of the chicken with half the ground pepper. Stuff the cavity with the onion, parsley or dill, and bay leaf.

3. Sprinkle the outside of the chicken with the remaining ground pepper. Rub the breast and legs of the chicken with butter.

4. Arrange the chicken breast side up in the bottom of the clay pot. Arrange the carrot pieces and mushrooms all around the chicken. Sprinkle with hot red pepper. Place pieces of tomato on top of the vegetables.

5. Cover the pot with the lid. Place in the oven and bake at 450 degrees for 1 hour and 30 minutes.

6. Carve the chicken and serve it with its natural juices.

Yield: 4 servings.

CIRCASSIAN CHICKEN
(CHICKEN IN WALNUT SAUCE)

This is an incredible Turkish dish made with a sauce containing an ample amount of walnuts. Circassia is that region on the Black Sea noted for its walnuts. This makes a fine buffet dish.

1. Combine the chicken, broth, onion, carrots, parsley, peppercorns, bay leaf, thyme, and parsnip, if used, in a saucepan. Bring to the boil and partly cover. Cook for about 40 minutes. Let the chicken cool in the broth.

2. Remove the chicken and, if it is trussed, remove the strings. Strain the broth and reserve 1¼ cups.

3. Pull the meat of the chicken off the bones. Shred it. There should be about 3 cups. Discard the skin and bones.

4. Blend the walnuts, bread crumbs, garlic, and cayenne in the container of a food processor or blender, gradually adding 1¼ cups reserved chicken broth.

5. Mix half the walnut sauce with the chicken and arrange it on a serving dish. Smooth it over in a mound. Spoon the remaining sauce over the mound, smoothing this layer over.

6. Combine the oil and paprika in a small skillet and cook briefly without browning. Use a very fine strainer and strain the paprika oil over the chicken dish.

Yield: 6 servings.

One 3-pound chicken, preferably trussed

8 cups fresh or canned chicken broth

1 medium-size onion, peeled and stuck with 2 cloves

2 small carrots, peeled and trimmed

2 fresh parsley sprigs

6 crushed peppercorns

1 bay leaf

2 fresh thyme sprigs, or ¼ teaspoon dried

1 small parsnip, peeled and cut in half, optional

2 cups shelled walnuts

1 cup fresh bread crumbs

2 garlic cloves, finely minced

⅛ teaspoon cayenne

2 tablespoons olive oil

1 tablespoon paprika

Gaylord's Tandoori Chicken

Two 2½-pound chickens

2 cups plain yogurt

½ teaspoon ground cumin

½ teaspoon freshly ground pepper

¼ teaspoon grated nutmeg

¼ teaspoon ground cloves

½ teaspoon ground coriander

1 teaspoon grated fresh ginger, or ½ teaspoon ground

1 garlic clove, finely minced

⅛ to ¼ teaspoon cayenne

Salt to taste

½ teaspoon ground cardamom

½ cup chopped white onion

2 tablespoons milk

½ teaspoon loosely packed saffron stems, or ⅛ teaspoon powdered saffron

1. Cut off and discard the small wing tips of each chicken. Using the fingers, pull off and discard the skin of the chickens.

2. Using a sharp knife, make brief gashes across the grain on both sides of the chicken breasts and legs.

3. In the container of a food processor, combine the yogurt, cumin, black pepper, nutmeg, cloves, coriander, ginger, garlic, cayenne, salt, cardamom, and onion. Process to a fine liquid.

4. Pour the mixture into a mixing bowl and add the chickens. Turn the chickens to coat all over. Cover and refrigerate for at least 24 hours.

5. Remove the chickens from the yogurt mixture at least 1 hour before cooking. Discard the marinade.

6. Preheat the oven to 500 degrees. Heat a charcoal grill.

7. Heat the milk in a small saucepan and add the saffron. Remove from the heat and let stand for 10 minutes.

8. Spoon the saffron mixture evenly over the chickens.

9. Line a baking sheet with heavy-duty aluminum foil. Place the chickens on it breast side up.

10. Place the chickens in the oven and bake for 20 minutes.

11. Cut the chickens into serving pieces. Put them on the grill and cook briefly on both sides.

Yield: 4 to 8 servings.

Note: These chickens can be cooked entirely on a charcoal grill. To grill them, split the chickens as for broiling. After marinating, place on the grill breast side down. Grill on one side. Turn and continue grilling on the second side until the chickens are thoroughly cooked.

SMOTHERED CHICKEN, CREOLE STYLE

One dish that was very much a part of my Mississippi childhood was dubbed smothered chicken. I suppose it could be regarded as soul food, basic, easy to prepare; in my books, it belongs in the "comfort" category, a food that gives solace to the spirit.

In its most basic form, it consists of cooking a chicken that has been split down the back and opened up, as for broiling. You cook it skin side down in a black iron skillet with a plate on top. The plate is weighted down and it is this method that contributes the name *smothered*. The chicken is turned over and continues to cook in a flour-thickened gravy until it is exceptionally tender, the meat almost falling from the bones.

1. A black iron skillet is essential for the authentic preparation of this dish. Sprinkle the chicken on both sides with salt and pepper. Select a skillet large enough to hold the chicken comfortably when it is opened up, as for broiling. Fold the chicken wings under to hold them secure.

2. Melt the butter in the skillet and add the chicken, skin side down. Cover the chicken firmly with a plate that will fit comfortably inside the skillet. Add several weights, approximately 5 pounds, to the top of the plate. Cook over low heat until the skin side of the chicken is nicely browned, about 25 minutes.

3. Remove the chicken to a warm platter. Add the onion, celery, green peppers, and garlic to the skillet and cook, stirring, until the onion is wilted.

4. Sprinkle with flour and stir to blend. Add the tomatoes, bay leaf, salt, and pepper, stirring rapidly with a whisk. Bring to the boil.

5. Return the chicken, skin side up, to the sauce. Cover with the plate and weights and continue cooking over low heat for 45 minutes longer. Remove the chicken to a warm platter and cook down the sauce briefly, stirring. Pour the sauce over the chicken and sprinkle with parsley.

Yield: 4 servings.

---

1 chicken (3½ pounds), butterflied (split down the backbone, breast left intact and unsplit)

Salt and freshly ground pepper to taste

2 tablespoons butter

1 cup finely chopped onion

1 cup finely chopped celery

1 cup finely chopped sweet green peppers

1½ teaspoons finely minced garlic

2 tablespoons flour

1¾ cups crushed or chopped imported canned tomatoes

1 bay leaf

2 tablespoons finely chopped parsley

MOROCCAN CHICKEN
WITH LEMON AND OLIVES

Two 2½-pound chickens

2 preserved lemons (see following instructions)

2 teaspoons finely chopped garlic

2 teaspoons ground ginger

¾ teaspoon finely ground pepper

¼ teaspoon powdered saffron

½ cup peanut, vegetable, or corn oil

4 cups water

¾ cup grated onion (see note)

8 fresh coriander stalks tied with a string

Salt to taste

24 imported black olives, about 1 cup

1. Wipe the inner cavity of the chicken carefully.

2. Rinse the preserved lemons with cold water. Drain. Remove the pulp from the skins of the lemons. Reserve the skins. Put the pulp in the container of a blender or food processor. Add the garlic, ginger, pepper, and saffron and start blending. Gradually add the oil. Spoon the mixture into a large mixing bowl.

3. Add the chickens to the bowl and rub them inside and out with the mixture. Add the livers. Cover and let stand overnight in the refrigerator.

4. Transfer the chickens, breast side down, to a kettle in which they will fit neatly and in one layer. Add the livers and the marinating mixture. To the bowl in which the chickens marinated, add the water, stirring to blend with remaining remnants of marinade in the bowl. Add this to the chickens. Add the onion and the coriander. Add the salt. Bring the cooking liquid to a boil. Partly cover and simmer for about 30 minutes. Uncover, turn the chickens breast side up, and continue cooking for about 15 minutes.

5. Remove the chickens and livers. Place the chickens breast side up in a baking dish. Set aside.

6. Chop and mash the livers to a paste. Add the liver paste to the cooking liquid. Quarter the reserved lemon peel and add the pieces. Add the olives. Cook down the liquid to 4 cups.

7. Place the baking dish containing the chickens in a 500-degree oven to brown. Serve the chicken carved into pieces with the sauce on the side.

Yield: 12 servings.

Note: To grate onions for Moroccan cooking, peel about 1 pound of onions. Cut them into quarters. Blend thoroughly in a food processor, using a regular blade. Place a sieve over a bowl and add the onions. Let drain.

6 to 10 lemons
Kosher salt

1. Set each lemon on the flat stem end. Using a sharp knife, cut straight down through the center of each lemon to about ½ inch of the base. Leave each sliced lemon on its base, but give it a quarter turn. Slice down once more to within ½ inch of the base. Continue until all the lemons are prepared.

2. Make a ¼-inch layer of salt in a sterile quart Mason jar.

3. Pack the inside of each lemon with salt. As each lemon is prepared, add it to the jar, pushing down. Make a layer of lemons, then a layer of salt, pressing down lightly on the lemons to make sure they are snug. They will, of course, give up much of their juices as they are pressed. Continue until the jar is packed full. Press down until the juices rise to cover the lemons. Make certain that a little air space is left when the jar is sealed. Let stand in a not too warm place for at least two weeks, until the lemons are firm but tender.

Note: Always rinse the lemons before using. After the jar is opened, refrigerate. These lemons may also be used with baked fish dishes, in salads, and in marinades.

CAPILLOTADE (A FRENCH CHICKEN HASH)

One 3-pound chicken, simmered in chicken broth until done

½ pound fresh mushrooms

4 tablespoons butter

¼ cup finely chopped onion

Salt and freshly ground pepper to taste

½ cup dry white wine

¼ cup flour

1 cup heavy cream

⅛ teaspoon freshly grated nutmeg

Pinch of cayenne

1 egg yolk

3 tablespoons grated Gruyère

1. Preheat the oven to 425 degrees.

2. Remove the flesh from the chicken bones. Pull off the skin. Add both skin and bones to the broth in which the chicken cooked and continue cooking for 20 minutes or longer.

3. Cut the chicken into bite-size pieces. There should be about 2 cups.

4. Finely chop the mushrooms. There should be about 2 cups.

5. Heat 1 tablespoon of butter in a skillet and add the onion. Cook until wilted. Add the mushrooms, salt, and pepper. Cook for about 2 minutes and add the wine. Cook over high heat until reduced by half. Add the chicken and stir to blend. Cook for about 4 minutes and set aside.

6. Heat the remaining 3 tablespoons of butter in a 1-quart saucepan. Add the flour and stir to blend with a wire whisk. Add 2 cups of the simmering stock, stirring rapidly with the whisk. Strain and reserve remaining stock for another use. Add the cream, nutmeg, and cayenne. Add about two thirds of this to the chicken mixture. Simmer for about 5 minutes.

7. To the remaining sauce add the egg yolk and stir. Bring just to the boil, stirring rapidly, but do not cook further.

8. Pour the chicken mixture into an oval baking dish and spoon the remaining sauce over all. Sprinkle with cheese and bake until browned in the oven, for about 10 minutes.

Yield: 8 to 10 servings.

CHICKEN AU POIVRE

1. Sprinkle the chicken breasts with the salt and pepper.

2. Melt the butter in a skillet large enough to hold the pieces in one layer. Add the onion, carrots, and garlic and cook, stirring, for about 10 minutes without browning. Sprinkle with the flour and stir to blend. Arrange the chicken pieces, boned side down, in the skillet and sprinkle with thyme, bay leaf, parsley, celery, and leeks, if used. Cover closely and let cook for 5 minutes. Add the vermouth, cream, and broth and cover once more. Simmer for 20 minutes.

3. Remove the chicken pieces to a platter and keep warm. Spoon and scrape the sauce into the container of a food processor or blender and blend to a fine purée. Return this sauce to a saucepan and add salt to taste. Add the mustard, stirring, and remove from the heat. Sprinkle with chives and pour the sauce over the chicken. Serve hot.

Yield: 8 servings.

8 skinless, boneless chicken breast halves, the larger the better

Salt to taste

1 tablespoon coarsely ground pepper

6 tablespoons butter

1 cup thinly sliced onion

1 cup thinly sliced carrots

1 garlic clove, crushed

2 tablespoons flour

½ teaspoon dried thyme

1 bay leaf

3 tablespoons finely chopped parsley

½ cup coarsely chopped celery

½ cup coarsely chopped leeks, optional

1 cup dry vermouth

½ cup heavy cream

1 cup fresh or canned chicken broth

1 tablespoon Dijon mustard

1 tablespoon chopped chives

CHICKEN BREASTS WITH SWEET PEPPER STRIPS

4 skinless, boneless chicken breast halves, about 2 pounds

Salt and freshly ground pepper to taste

3 tablespoons butter

½ teaspoon finely minced garlic

½ pound sweet red or green peppers, cored, seeded, and cut into thin strips, about 2 cups

½ cup dry white wine

1 tablespoon finely chopped parsley

1. Sprinkle the chicken with the salt and a generous grinding of pepper.

2. Heat 2 tablespoons of the butter in a skillet and add the chicken pieces skinned side down. Cook for about 4 minutes, or until golden brown on one side. Turn and continue cooking for about 4 minutes.

3. Add the garlic and pepper strips. Cook for about 4 minutes. Add the wine. Cover and cook about 4 minutes longer.

4. Remove the chicken pieces to a warm serving dish.

5. Add the remaining tablespoon of butter to the peppers and stir. Pour the peppers and sauce over the chicken. Sprinkle with parsley.

Yield: 4 servings.

CURRIED STUFFED CHICKEN BREASTS

1. If possible, buy the breasts already boned but with the skin left on. Otherwise, using a paring knife and the fingers, remove and discard the bone or use it for soup. Set the boned chicken breasts aside.

2. Put the raisins in a small bowl and add warm water to cover. Set aside so the raisins will swell.

3. Preheat the oven to 425 degrees.

4. Melt 1 tablespoon of the butter in a skillet and add the onion, celery, garlic, and bay leaf. Cook, stirring often, until the onion is wilted. Add the apple and stir. Cook for about 1 minute, stirring occasionally.

5. Squeeze the raisins to extract the liquid and add them. Add the chutney. Stir and remove from the heat. Let cool.

6. Place the chicken breasts skin side down on a flat surface. Pat lightly with a flat mallet or the bottom of a small, heavy skillet. Sprinkle with salt and pepper.

7. Spoon equal portions of the filling in the center of each breast. Bring up the edges of the breast, folding the edges over to enclose the filling and make a package.

8. Melt the remaining 2 tablespoons of butter in a shallow, flame-proof baking dish. Transfer the chicken breasts to the dish and brush the tops with the butter. Sprinkle with salt and pepper and place them seam side down.

9. Place the dish on top of the stove and cook for about 1 minute. Place the dish in the oven and bake for 10 minutes. Baste once as they bake.

10. Blend the cream and curry powder and pour this over the chicken breasts. Bake 10 minutes longer, basting occasionally.

Yield: 4 servings.

2 large whole chicken breasts, about 2 pounds each, split in half

3 tablespoons seedless golden raisins

3 tablespoons butter

½ cup finely chopped onion

½ cup finely chopped celery

¼ teaspoon finely minced garlic

1 bay leaf

1 cup peeled, cored, and cubed apple

3 tablespoons chutney

Salt and freshly ground pepper to taste

½ cup heavy cream

1 teaspoon curry powder

CHICKEN KIEV

¼ to ½ **pound butter**

1 to 2 **tablespoons chopped chives**

Salt to taste

3 **whole or 6 halved skinless, boneless chicken breasts**

Salt and freshly ground pepper to taste

2 **large eggs**

¼ **cup water**

½ **cup flour**

3 **cups fresh bread crumbs**

Oil for deep frying

1. Cream the butter with the chives. If unsalted butter is used, beat in salt to taste. Chill briefly. If the chicken breast pieces are small, use the lesser amounts of butter and chives. If quite large, use the greater amounts.

2. Place the chicken breasts between sheets of plastic wrap and pound lightly with a flat mallet to make them larger. Sprinkle with salt and pepper.

3. Put 1½ to 3 tablespoons of filling in the center of each chicken breast. Fold the edges over to enclose the filling. Place the stuffed chicken breasts briefly in the freezer before breading them.

4. Beat the eggs with the water in a flat container. Dip the stuffed chicken breasts first in flour to coat well, then in the egg mixture, coating all over. Finally, roll them in bread crumbs.

5. Cook in deep fat until golden brown and cooked through, 10 minutes, more or less, depending on the size of the stuffed pieces.

Yield: 6 servings.

LEMON CHICKEN

One of the most popular recipes we have ever printed was the lemon chicken devised by chef Lee Lum of the once popular but now closed Pearl's restaurant in Manhattan.

1. Trim off any fat and membranous fibers surrounding the chicken pieces.

2. Combine the soy sauce, vodka, sesame oil, salt, and egg white in a bowl. Add the chicken breasts and set aside.

3. When ready to cook, combine the sugar, cornstarch, vinegar, lemon rind, and lemon juice in a saucepan. Bring to the boil, stirring. Add the chicken broth and return to the boil.

4. Cut the carrot into 2-inch lengths. Cut the lengths into thin slices. Cut the slices into fine slivers. Cut the scallion into thin slivers.

5. Add the carrot, scallion, green pepper, and pineapple chunks to the sauce. Bring to the boil and set aside.

6. Heat the oil for deep frying. Dip the chicken pieces into the water chestnut powder and shake off any excess. Cook the chicken pieces in the oil for about 10 minutes, or until the coating is crisp and the chicken is cooked through.

7. Place each piece of chicken on a flat surface. Using a sharp knife, cut it crosswise into 1- or 2-inch lengths. Arrange the pieces on a platter. Heat the sauce, add the lemon extract, if desired, and pour it over the chicken. Serve immediately.

Yield: 6 servings.

3 skinless, boneless chicken breasts

2 tablespoons light soy sauce

1 tablespoon vodka

½ teaspoon sesame oil

1 teaspoon salt

1 egg white, lightly beaten

¾ cup sugar

1 tablespoon cornstarch

½ cup white vinegar

Grated rind of 1 lemon

Juice of 1 lemon

¼ cup chicken broth

1 carrot, trimmed and scraped

1 scallion, trimmed

¼ cup thin julienne strips of green pepper

¼ cup drained pineapple chunks, cut in half

Peanut oil for deep frying

¾ cup water chestnut powder

1 tablespoon lemon extract

CHICKEN BREASTS PORTUGAISE

5 tablespoons butter or chicken fat

2 medium-size onions, thinly sliced

3 cups thin strips of cored, seeded green peppers (or use sweet red peppers, if available, to give color)

Salt and freshly ground pepper to taste

3 cups thinly sliced mushrooms

2 tablespoons finely minced garlic

2 cups whole canned tomatoes, preferably Italian plum tomatoes

4 whole chicken breasts, skinned and boned and split in half

2 shallots, finely chopped

⅓ cup dry white wine

⅓ cup fresh or canned chicken broth

Saffron rice (see recipe page 627) optional

Finely chopped parsley for garnish

1. Preheat the oven to 400 degrees.

2. Heat 1 tablespoon of the butter (or use chicken fat) in a saucepan and add the onion, green or red peppers, salt, and pepper. Cook, stirring, for about 3 minutes, until crisp-tender. Add the mushrooms and cook, stirring, for about 1 minute. Add the garlic, cook for 1 minute, then add the tomatoes. Add salt and pepper to taste and cover. Bake for 20 minutes. Remove the saucepan to the top of the stove and uncover. Cook, stirring occasionally, for about 10 minutes.

3. Melt 2 tablespoons of the butter (or more if you think it necessary) in one large or two small heavy skillets. Add the chicken, skinned side down, and cook over moderate heat until that side is a gentle brown, 3 to 5 minutes. Turn the pieces. Cook for 8 to 10 minutes longer, until the other side is lightly browned. Do not overcook. Transfer the chicken to a warm platter and cover to keep warm.

4. Add the shallots to the skillet and stir. Pour in the white wine and stir to dissolve any brown particles that may cling to the bottom of the skillet. Let the wine reduce almost completely and add the chicken broth. Let this cook until it is almost totally reduced. Add the tomato sauce and bring to a boil. Swirl in the remaining 2 tablespoons of butter, shaking the skillet. Return the chicken to the skillet and spoon the sauce over. Serve, if desired, with saffron rice on the side. Sprinkle with parsley.

Yield: 8 servings.

CHICKEN BREASTS STUFFED WITH SPINACH AND RICOTTA

1. Preheat the oven to 375 degrees.

2. Skin and bone the chicken breasts or have them skinned, boned, and halved.

3. Using the fingers, make a pocket on the underside or boned side of the chicken breasts for stuffing. Salt and pepper the breasts.

4. Heat 2 tablespoons of the butter in a skillet and add the onion. Cook until wilted.

5. Rinse the spinach well and cook, covered in the water that clings to the leaves, stirring so that it cooks evenly, about 1 minute. Drain the cooked spinach and, when cool enough to handle, squeeze to extract excess moisture. Chop fine.

6. Add the spinach to the onion in the skillet. Add the ham, ricotta, egg yolk, Parmesan, nutmeg, sausage, garlic, and basil. Blend thoroughly.

7. Stuff the 8 pieces of chicken breast with 2 or 3 tablespoons of the mixture. Fold the ends of the chicken to enclose the filling. It is not necessary to tie the pieces. Arrange the pieces close together in a baking dish, stuffed side down.

8. Melt the remaining 4 tablespoons of butter and dribble it over the chicken. Sprinkle with the sherry. Do not cover, but bake for 45 minutes to 1 hour, basting often. Serve hot with hot tomato sauce.

Yield: 8 servings.

4 large whole chicken breasts, the larger the better

Salt and freshly ground pepper to taste

6 tablespoons butter

¼ cup finely chopped onion

1 pound fresh spinach

1 cup ground cooked ham

1 cup ricotta cheese

1 egg yolk

½ cup freshly grated Parmesan cheese

¼ teaspoon grated nutmeg

¼ pound ground sausage

1 garlic clove, finely minced

1 teaspoon dried basil

¼ cup dry sherry

Tomato sauce with herbs (see recipe page 784)

BATTER-FRIED CHICKEN PIECES

2 large whole skinless, boneless chicken breasts, about 1¼ pounds

Salt and freshly ground pepper to taste

¼ cup peanut, vegetable, or corn oil

¼ cup lemon juice

4 tablespoons finely chopped parsley

Fritter batter (see following recipe)

Oil for deep frying

Lemon wedges for garnish

Fresh tomato sauce (see recipe page 784)

The success of deep frying depends on the temperature of the oil and on the batter. A good fritter batter is one of the simplest things to make and its uses are countless. This batter-fried chicken is delectable when served with lemon wedges and a fresh tomato sauce. It is excellent as a luncheon or supper dish.

1. Place the chicken breasts on a flat surface. Split each whole breast in half. Slice the meat on the bias into about 18 pieces.

2. Put the pieces of chicken in a bowl and add the salt and pepper, ¼ cup oil, the lemon juice, and parsley. Let stand for 20 minutes.

3. Remove the chicken pieces from the marinade, one piece at a time, and add them to a small bowl containing the fritter batter. Manipulate the pieces in the batter so that they are well coated.

4. Heat the oil for deep frying and, when it is quite hot, or 365 degrees, add the batter-coated chicken pieces, one at a time. Do not crowd them in the oil. Cook, turning the pieces occasionally, for about 2 minutes, or until each piece starts to float. Remove with a slotted spoon and drain on paper towels.

5. Add the remaining chicken pieces to the oil and cook until done. When drained, sprinkle with salt to taste. Garnish with lemon wedges and serve with tomato sauce.

Yield: 4 servings.

FRITTER BATTER

1½ cups flour

3 tablespoons peanut, vegetable, or corn oil

1 teaspoon salt

2 large eggs

½ cup water

Sift the flour into a mixing bowl. Add the oil and salt. Add the eggs and stir with a wire whisk. Add the water gradually, beating with the whisk.

Yield: About 2 cups.

GRILLED MEXICAN CHICKEN

1. There will, of course, be 6 chicken breast halves. Cut each half crosswise into 4 pieces. This will yield 24 cubes.

2. Place the chicken in a dish and add the remaining ingredients except the salsa cruda. Turn the cubes occasionally so that they are well seasoned. Let stand until ready to cook.

3. Arrange the pieces on 4 to 6 skewers. If wooden skewers are used, it is best if they are soaked for an hour or so in water. Cover the tips with foil to prevent burning.

4. Prepare a charcoal fire in a grill. When the coals and grill are properly hot, brush the grill lightly with oil. Arrange the skewered chicken on the grill and cook, turning as necessary, until done, 20 minutes or longer. Serve with salsa cruda and, if desired, with mushroom rice with turmeric (see recipe page 630).

Yield: 4 to 6 servings.

3 chicken breasts, split in half and boned, but preferably with the skin left on

1 teaspoon dried oregano

Salt and freshly ground pepper to taste

2 tablespoons lime juice

2 tablespoons peanut, vegetable, or corn oil

2 tablespoons finely chopped parsley

Salsa cruda (see recipe page 789)

SESAME CHICKEN WITH ASPARAGUS RING

3 to 4 whole chicken breasts

3 tablespoons sesame paste (see note)

2 tablespoons light soy sauce

¼ teaspoon chili oil (see note)

¼ cup plus ⅓ cup corn oil

¼ cup water

¼ cup Sichuan peppercorns (see note)

Salt to taste

1 pound asparagus

4 thin slices fresh ginger

Freshly ground pepper to taste

½ tablespoon dry sherry

¼ teaspoon sugar

¾ cup loosely packed fresh coriander leaves

1. Place the chicken breasts in a kettle and add water to cover. Bring to the boil and simmer for 10 to 15 minutes, depending on size. Turn off the heat and let stand until cool.

2. Drain the chicken and pull the skin and meat from the bones. Shred the skin and meat. There should be about 5 cups.

3. Combine the sesame paste, soy sauce, chili oil, ¼ cup corn oil, and water.

4. Place the peppercorns in a small skillet and cook briefly, shaking the skillet until the peppercorns give off a pleasant roasted aroma. Pour out onto a flat surface and crush lightly. Hold a sieve over the sauce and add the peppercorns to the sieve. Sift the fine, loose particles into the sauce. Reserve the coarse pieces for another use.

5. Scrape the asparagus with a swivel-bladed vegetable knife. Cut the stalks and tips on the bias into 2-inch lengths.

6. Heat the remaining ⅓ cup of corn oil in a wok or skillet and add the ginger. When it is quite hot but not smoking, add the asparagus pieces and immediately add the pepper, sherry, and sugar. Cook, stirring constantly, for about 30 seconds. Cover for about 15 seconds. Uncover and cook, stirring, for about 15 seconds longer. Take care not to overcook. Scoop out the asparagus.

7. When ready to serve, make a border of asparagus around an oval or round serving dish.

8. Add the coriander leaves to the sesame sauce and stir. Pour this over the chicken and toss to blend. Spoon the chicken into the center of the asparagus. Garnish with sprigs of fresh coriander. Serve at room temperature.

Yield: 8 to 12 servings.

Note: These ingredients are widely available in Asian grocery stores.

Chicken Soong (Cubed Chicken in Lettuce Leaves)

1. Core the lettuce and separate it into leaves. Pile on a platter and set aside.

2. Place the chicken breast on a flat surface and, holding a sharp kitchen knife almost parallel to the cutting surface, cut the breast into the thinnest possible slices. Stack the slices and cut into shreds. Cut the shreds into tiny cubes. There should be about 2 cups. Place the chicken meat in a mixing bowl and add the egg white, salt, and 1 tablespoon of the cornstarch. Blend well with the fingers. Refrigerate for 30 minutes.

3. Core the chilies. Split them in half and shred them. Cut the shreds into small cubes. There should be about ½ cup.

4. Thinly slice the water chestnuts. Cut the slices into small cubes. There should be about ½ cup. Combine the chopped chilies, water chestnuts, celery, carrots, and ginger. Set aside.

5. In another bowl, combine the garlic and scallion and set aside.

6. Combine the sherry, soy sauce, chili paste with garlic, and sugar and set aside.

7. Combine the remaining 1 tablespoon of cornstarch and the water and stir to blend. Set aside.

8. Heat the peanut oil in a wok or skillet and, when it is hot, add the chicken, stirring constantly to separate the cubes. Cook for about 1½ minutes and drain. Set aside.

9. Return 2 tablespoons of the oil to the wok and add the celery-and–water chestnut mixture. Cook, stirring, for about 30 seconds and add the scallion and garlic. Cook, stirring, for about 10 seconds and add the chicken. Cook, stirring, for about 30 seconds, or until the chicken is piping hot. Add the sherry-and–soy sauce mixture and the sesame oil. Stir the cornstarch mixture until smooth and add it quickly. Stir rapidly for about 30 seconds and transfer to a hot platter.

10. Serve the chicken with the lettuce on the side. Let the guests help themselves, adding a spoonful or so of the chicken mixture to a lettuce leaf, folding it before eating.

Yield: 6 to 12 servings.

Note: These ingredients are widely available in Asian grocery stores.

- 1 head iceberg lettuce
- 1 large boneless chicken breast, about 1 pound
- 1 egg white
- ½ teaspoon salt
- 2 tablespoons cornstarch
- 2 long green chilies, hot or mild
- 10 or 12 water chestnuts
- ½ cup finely diced celery
- 3 tablespoons finely diced carrots
- 1 teaspoon chopped fresh ginger
- 2 teaspoons or more finely chopped garlic
- 3 tablespoons finely chopped scallions
- 2 tablespoons dry sherry
- ½ tablespoon soy sauce
- ½ tablespoon chili paste with garlic (see note)
- 1 teaspoon sugar
- 1 tablespoon water
- 2 cups peanut, vegetable, or corn oil
- ½ teaspoon sesame oil (see note)

SHREDDED CHICKEN WITH BEAN SPROUTS

2 or 3 large chicken breasts, about 2 pounds

Salt to taste

3½ tablespoons dry sherry

2 egg whites

3 tablespoons cornstarch

3 cups plus 1½ tablespoons peanut, vegetable, or corn oil

⅓ pound bean sprouts, about 3 cups

2 tablespoons water

⅛ teaspoon sugar

½ teaspoon sesame oil

⅓ cup fresh or canned chicken broth

2 tablespoons chopped scallions

1 teaspoon chopped fresh ginger

1 teaspoon white vinegar

1. Skin and bone the chicken breasts. Place on a flat surface and, using a sharp knife, cut them against the grain into thin slices. Cut the slices into very thin shreds. There should be about 2 cups. If desired, the chicken may be partly frozen to facilitate the slicing and shredding.

2. Place the chicken in a mixing bowl and add the salt, 1½ tablespoons sherry, and the egg whites. Stir in a circular motion until the whites become a bit bubbly. Add 2 tablespoons of cornstarch and 1½ tablespoons of oil. Stir to blend well. Refrigerate, preferably overnight, or for at least 1 hour.

3. Ideally, the tips of the bean sprouts should be plucked, leaving only the firm white center portion. This is tedious, however, and is not necessary. Set aside.

4. Combine the remaining 2 tablespoons of wine, the remaining 1 tablespoon of cornstarch mixed with the water, salt, sugar, sesame oil, and chicken broth. Stir to blend. Set aside.

5. Heat the remaining 3 cups of oil in a wok or skillet and add the chicken mixture. Cook over high heat, stirring constantly and vigorously to separate the shreds, for about 1 minute. Drain almost completely, leaving about 1 tablespoon of oil in the wok.

6. Add the scallions and ginger, stir for a second, and add the bean sprouts. Cook, stirring vigorously, for about 15 seconds. Add the chicken, sesame oil mixture, and vinegar and cook, stirring, until piping hot and lightly thickened. Serve hot.

Yield: 4 to 8 servings.

CHICKEN BURGERS

Do not be put off by the pedestrian name of this dish. It is a variation of chicken cutlet pojarkski without the sour cream.

1. Trim the breasts to remove all nerve fibers, cartilage, and so on. Cut the chicken into cubes.

2. Put the prepared breast meat into the container of a food processor and process until fairly but not totally smooth.

3. Scrape the chicken into a mixing bowl. Add the salt, pepper, parsley, bread crumbs, cumin, and broth or water. Blend well with the hands.

4. Divide the mixture equally into 12 portions. Using dampened hands, pat the portions into flat round patties. Chill until ready to cook.

5. These patties are excellent when cooked on a preheated charcoal grill, about 4 minutes to a side. Or cook them in a little butter in a heavy skillet, 4 to 5 minutes to a side. Or cook them in a little butter in a heavy skillet, 4 to 5 minutes to a side. Serve with a little melted butter poured over.

Yield: 6 servings.

2 pounds skinless, boneless chicken breasts

Salt and freshly ground pepper to taste

½ cup finely chopped parsley

1 cup fine fresh bread crumbs

1 teaspoon ground cumin

¼ cup chicken broth or water

4 tablespoons butter, approximately

CHICKEN PATTIES WITH TARRAGON

3 whole skinless,
  boneless chicken
  breasts, about
  1½ pounds

½ cup bread crumbs

⅛ teaspoon grated
  nutmeg

  Pinch of cayenne

  Salt and freshly ground
  pepper to taste

2 teaspoons plus
  1 tablespoon chopped
  fresh tarragon

½ cup heavy cream

4 tablespoons peanut,
  vegetable, or corn oil

2 cups fresh tomato
  sauce (see recipe
  page 784)

1. Trim off all fat, cartilage, and membranes from the chicken. Cut the chicken into 1-inch cubes. Put the cubes into the container of a food processor. Process until the meat is coarse-fine. Do not over-process it or it will be like pulp.

2. Put the ground chicken into a mixing bowl and add the bread crumbs, nutmeg, cayenne, salt, and pepper, 2 teaspoons of the tarragon, and the cream. Blend well by beating with a wooden spoon. Chill the mixture.

3. Shape the mixture into 12 patties.

4. Heat the oil in a skillet and add the patties. Cook until golden brown on one side, about 3 minutes. Turn and cook on the other side, for about 3 minutes.

5. Serve the patties with fresh tomato sauce and the remaining chopped fresh tarragon sprinkled over.

Yield: 6 servings.

French chefs have a much more "elegant" way of cutting up chickens for sautéed dishes than you're likely to get from any butcher. It produces ten separate pieces, including four that contain breast meat.

1. Place the chicken on its back and cut off the wing tips.

2. Place the fingers where the thigh and leg are joined, either left or right. Pull the thigh and leg away from the body and, using a sharp knife, carefully cut through and sever the thigh, cutting the joint where the thigh is joined to the body. Repeat this to remove the second thigh and leg. Cut through the joint where thigh and leg meet to make two pieces.

3. Hold the main wing bone with one hand and, using a small knife, cut through the joint that joins the wing bone to the body. While pulling the wing bone away from the body with the fingers, slice toward the rear of the chicken, cutting away a small strip of breast meat, 3 or 4 inches long. Leave most of the breast intact. If desired, cut off but reserve the "second," or middle wing joint. Repeat this on the other side.

4. Turn the breast section on its side. With a sharp knife, cut through both sides, cutting away the back bones and leaving the almost whole breast intact with bones.

5. Place the breast skin side up. Split it in half crosswise.

6. All the pieces are now ready to be sautéed. There are the two legs, two thighs, two wings with small strips of breast meat, two breast pieces, and two second wing joints. The wing tips may be discarded.

CHICKEN SAUTÉ WITH ROSEMARY

**Two 2½-pound
chickens, cut into
serving pieces**

**Salt and freshly ground
pepper to taste**

4 tablespoons butter

**2 teaspoons finely
chopped fresh
rosemary leaves, or
1 teaspoon dried**

**2 tablespoons finely
chopped shallots**

¼ cup dry white wine

1 cup chicken broth

1. Sprinkle the chicken pieces with the salt and pepper.

2. Melt 3 tablespoons of the butter in one or two heavy skillets and,
    when it is melted, add the chicken pieces skin side down. Cook for
    15 minutes, or until golden brown on one side.

3. Turn the pieces and add the chopped rosemary. Cook for 10 to 15
    minutes longer, turning the pieces occasionally. Add the shallots
    and cook briefly.

4. Remove the chicken pieces and arrange them neatly on a serving
    dish, piling them up as necessary. Keep warm.

5. Meanwhile, pour off the fat from the skillet and add the wine.
    Cook, stirring to dissolve the brown particles that cling to the
    bottom and sides of the skillet. When the wine is almost reduced,
    add the chicken broth and stir to blend well. Continue to cook
    and, when the sauce is reduced to about ¾ cup, swirl in the
    remaining 1 tablespoon of butter. Pour the sauce over the chicken
    and serve immediately.

Yield: 6 to 8 servings.

CHICKEN WITH PARSLEY COATING

1. Preheat the oven to 450 degrees.

2. Sprinkle the chicken pieces with salt and pepper. Spoon the oil into a skillet in which the chicken pieces will fit in one layer. Put the chicken pieces in the skillet and rub all over in the oil. Arrange the chicken pieces skin side down in the skillet.

3. Combine the bread crumbs, shallots, garlic, and 3 tablespoons of the parsley.

4. Put the skillet on the stove and, when the chicken starts to sizzle, put the skillet in the oven and bake for 20 minutes. Sprinkle with half of the bread crumb mixture. Return the chicken to the oven and continue baking for 5 minutes longer.

5. Turn the chicken pieces in the skillet. Sprinkle with the remaining bread crumb mixture. Return the dish to the oven and bake for 15 minutes longer.

6. Melt the butter in a skillet and heat, swirling it around, until it is hazelnut brown. Do not burn. Pour this over the chicken. Sprinkle the chicken with the remaining 1 tablespoon of parsley.

Yield: 4 servings.

One 2½-pound chicken, cut into serving pieces

Salt and freshly ground pepper to taste

2 tablespoons corn, peanut, or vegetable oil

1 cup fine fresh bread crumbs

3 tablespoons finely chopped shallots

½ teaspoon finely minced garlic

4 tablespoons finely chopped parsley

2 tablespoons butter

SAUTÉ OF CHICKEN ANTIBOISE

One 3-pound chicken, cut into serving pieces

Salt and freshly ground pepper to taste

2 tablespoons plus 1 teaspoon olive oil

12 to 18 cherry tomatoes

12 stuffed green olives

12 pitted ripe olives, preferably imported olives, such as Italian or Greek

2 tablespoons finely chopped onion

1 tablespoon finely chopped shallots

1 teaspoon finely minced garlic

1 bay leaf

2 fresh thyme sprigs, or ½ teaspoon dried

½ cup dry white wine

½ cup fresh or canned chicken broth

2 tablespoons finely chopped parsley

½ teaspoon hot red pepper flakes, optional

The name antiboise derives, of course, from the resort town of Antibes on the southern coast of France. Dishes bearing the name are similar to those bearing South of France–related names such as niçoise, provençale, and so on. They invariably contain tomatoes and, generally, other ingredients characteristic of the region, such as garlic, olives, and olive oil.

1. Sprinkle the chicken pieces all over with salt and pepper.

2. Heat 2 tablespoons of the oil in a heavy skillet and add the chicken, skin side down. Cook for about 5 minutes over fairly high heat until nicely browned on the skin side. Turn the pieces and reduce the heat to moderate. Continue cooking to brown evenly all over, about 15 minutes, turning the pieces as necessary.

3. Transfer the pieces to a warm platter and cover with foil. Place in a warm place while finishing the sauce.

4. Add the cherry tomatoes and olives to the skillet and cook, stirring gently, to heat through. Spoon out the tomatoes and olives and add them to the chicken.

5. Pour out most of the oil from the skillet, but leave a shallow coating of oil. Add the onion, shallots, garlic, bay leaf, and thyme and cook, stirring, for about 1 minute. Add the wine and cook over high heat until it is reduced by about half, stirring with a wooden spoon to dissolve the brown particles that cling to the bottom and sides of the skillet.

6. Add the chicken broth and sprinkle with the parsley. Add the hot pepper flakes, if used. Cook down until the sauce is somewhat thickened, about 10 minutes.

7. Sprinkle the remaining oil over the sauce and stir briefly to blend. Add salt and pepper to taste.

8. Uncover the chicken and add any juices that may have accumulated to the sauce. Add the chicken mixture and reheat briefly. Serve the chicken with the sauce spooned over.

Yield: 4 to 6 servings.

Sautéed Chicken with Watercress

1. Trim off and discard ½ inch or so from the watercress stems.

2. Drop the watercress sprigs into boiling salted water to cover. Use more salt than you normally would; it helps keep the sprigs green. When the water returns to the boil, cook for about 3 minutes, no longer. Drain quickly and run under cold running water to chill. Drain well and pat dry with paper towels. Put the watercress in the container of a food processor or blender and blend. Do not overblend and make a purée of the watercress. Tiny pieces should be identifiable. Set aside. There should be about ¾ cup.

3. Sprinkle the chicken pieces all over with salt and pepper to taste.

4. Heat 2 tablespoons of the butter in a heavy skillet and add the chicken, skin side down. Cook for about 5 minutes over fairly high heat until nicely browned on the skin side. Turn the pieces and reduce the heat to moderate. Continue cooking to brown evenly all over, about 15 minutes, turning the pieces as necessary.

5. Transfer the pieces to a warm serving platter and cover with foil. Place in a warm place while finishing the sauce.

6. Pour out most of the oil from the skillet, but leave a shallow coating of oil. Add the shallots to the skillet and cook, stirring, for about 1 minute. Add the wine and cook over high heat until it is reduced by about half, stirring with a wooden spoon to dissolve the brown particles that cling to the bottom and sides of the skillet.

7. Add the heavy cream and cook over high heat, stirring, for about 5 minutes. Add the watercress, salt, and pepper to taste, stirring.

8. Uncover the chicken and add any juices that may have accumulated to the sauce. Stir. Swirl in the remaining butter. Add the chicken and heat as briefly as possible. Serve the chicken with the sauce spooned over.

Yield: 4 to 6 servings.

2 bunches crisp, unblemished watercress

Salt to taste

One 3-pound chicken, cut into serving pieces

Freshly ground pepper to taste

3 tablespoons butter

2 tablespoons finely chopped shallots

½ cup dry white wine

1 cup heavy cream

SAUTÉED CHICKEN WITH TWO VINEGARS

2 chickens, about
   2½ pounds each, cut
   into serving pieces

   Salt and freshly ground
   pepper to taste

4 tablespoons butter

6 whole, peeled garlic
   cloves

6 whole, unpeeled garlic
   cloves

½ cup red wine vinegar

¾ cup dry white wine

1 cup fresh or canned
   chicken broth

3 tablespoons tomato
   paste

1 pound ripe tomatoes,
   peeled, seeded, and cut
   into 1-inch cubes,
   about 2 cups

2 tablespoons tarragon
   wine vinegar

3 tablespoons chopped
   fresh tarragon, or
   1 tablespoon dried

There are many dishes, mostly imported, that enjoy a tremendous vogue in America. We have adopted such foods as boeuf bourguignonne, steak tartare, quiche lorraine, beef Wellington (for which we hold no high regard), and salmon with sorrel sauce. One of the most recent of these dining diversions is a chicken sauté served in a sauce lightly laced with vinegar.

One man who played no small part in this vogue is Paul Bocuse, almost indisputably the most famous chef in the world. He has done more to "propagandize" French cooking than anyone else of his generation. When he spent a day in our kitchen, assisted by Pierre Franey and Jacques Pepin, two of America's best-known chefs, we came into an original source for the chicken sauté, which was served at Bocuse's restaurant in Lyons.

1. Preheat the oven to 400 degrees.

2. Sprinkle the chicken pieces with salt and pepper.

3. Heat equal amounts of the butter in two heavy skillets and add the chicken pieces, skin side down. Brown on one side, for 6 to 8 minutes, and turn. Add equal amounts of peeled and unpeeled garlic to both skillets. Cook the chicken, turning the pieces often, for about 10 minutes. Using a slotted spoon, transfer the chicken from one skillet to the other. Pour off and discard the fat from the first skillet. Place the skillet containing all the chicken in the oven, uncovered. Let bake for 10 minutes. Remove from the oven and cover.

4. Meanwhile, add the red wine vinegar to the first skillet, stirring to dissolve the brown particles that cling to the bottom and sides of the pan. Cook over high heat until reduced by half and add the wine and chicken broth. Add the tomato paste and stir to dissolve.

5. Cook for about 15 minutes and add the tomatoes and tarragon wine vinegar. Bring to the boil over high heat and cook for 10 minutes. Add the tarragon and cook for about 3 minutes.

6. Pour off the fat from the skillet containing all the chicken. Pour the tomato and tarragon sauce over the chicken and stir to blend. Bring to the boil, stirring, making sure the chicken pieces are well coated.

Yield: 6 servings.

CHICKEN CHASSEUR

Chicken chasseur is the French way of saying chicken hunter's-style. The term actually means that mushrooms are included and the original recipe, of course, was for wild mushrooms picked up on the way to the chase.

1. Sprinkle the chicken with salt and a generous grinding of pepper.

2. Heat the oil in a heavy skillet large enough to hold the chicken pieces in one layer. Add the chicken pieces skin side down and cook for about 5 minutes, or until golden brown on one side.

3. Turn the pieces and cook until browned on the other side, about 5 minutes. Carefully pour off the fat from the skillet. Add the mushrooms and stir. Add the shallots and garlic and stir. Cook for about 5 minutes and add the tarragon and bay leaf. Cook until the liquid in the skillet has evaporated.

4. Add the ½ cup wine and cook until the wine has almost evaporated. Add the tomatoes and water. Cover and cook for about 10 minutes.

5. Blend the arrowroot and the remaining 1 tablespoon of wine and stir it into the sauce. Cover and continue cooking for about 5 minutes. Serve sprinkled with chopped tarragon.

Yield: 4 servings.

One 2½-pound chicken, cut into serving pieces

Salt and freshly ground pepper to taste

2 tablespoons peanut, vegetable, or corn oil

¾ pound mushrooms, cut into thin slices, about 4 cups

2 tablespoons finely minced shallots

1 teaspoon finely minced garlic

1 teaspoon dried tarragon

1 bay leaf

½ cup plus 1 tablespoon dry white wine

1 cup chopped tomatoes

¼ cup water

½ teaspoon arrowroot or cornstarch

2 teaspoons finely chopped fresh tarragon or parsley

CHICKEN WITH PROSCIUTTO AND MUSHROOMS

Two 3½-pound chickens, cut into serving pieces

Salt and freshly ground pepper to taste

Flour for dredging

Oil for shallow frying

¾ cup dried Italian mushrooms

4 tablespoons butter

2 garlic cloves, finely minced

⅓ cup finely chopped onion

¼ cup chopped shallots

¼ pound prosciutto, cut into fine julienne strips

1 tablespoon chopped fresh tarragon, or 2 teaspoons dried

3 tablespoons lemon juice

¾ cup dry white wine

1. Sprinkle the chicken pieces with the salt and pepper and dredge lightly in the flour.

2. Heat the oil to a depth of about ⅓ inch in one or two large, heavy skillets. Cook the chicken pieces, turning often, until golden brown all over. Drain.

3. Place the mushrooms in a saucepan and add water to barely cover. Bring to the boil. Simmer for 1 minute and set aside.

4. Heat 2 tablespoons of the butter in a skillet and add the garlic, onion, and shallots. Cook, stirring, until wilted and add the prosciutto. Cook briefly and sprinkle with tarragon. Cook for about 3 minutes and add the browned chicken pieces.

5. Drain the mushrooms but reserve the cooking liquid. Add the mushrooms, lemon juice, and white wine to the chicken. Add a little of the reserved mushroom cooking liquid and stir. Boil gently for about 5 minutes and add the remaining butter. When it melts, stir to blend and serve.

Yield: 8 servings.

CHICKEN AND SAUSAGE WITH OLIVE AND ANCHOVY SAUCE

1. Cut the sausage links into 3-inch pieces. Cook them in a heavy skillet, turning until browned all over. Remove, drain, and put them in a casserole with a tight-fitting cover. Discard the fat.

2. Sprinkle the chicken pieces with salt and pepper. In another skillet, heat the olive oil and brown the chicken pieces lightly on all sides. Add the chicken to the sausage.

3. Meanwhile, put the celery in a saucepan and add water to cover and salt to taste. Bring to the boil and simmer for about 5 minutes, or until crisp-tender. Drain but reserve both the celery and the cooking liquid.

4. To the fat remaining in the skillet after the chicken is cooked, add the onion and mushrooms. Cook, stirring, until wilted. Add the anchovies, olives, and capers. Add the drained celery, wine, and tomato sauce and simmer for about 10 minutes. Add this to the chicken and sausage. Add salt and pepper to taste and cover closely. Simmer on top of stove for about 30 minutes, or until the chicken is tender. As the dish cooks, if it becomes too dry, add a little of the reserved celery liquid or a bit more tomato sauce.

Yield: 6 to 8 servings.

1½ pounds sweet or hot Italian sausage links

One 3-pound chicken, cut into serving pieces

Salt and freshly ground pepper to taste

3 tablespoons olive oil

1 cup chopped celery

1 cup chopped onion

½ pound mushrooms, sliced

8 flat fillets of anchovies

½ cup imported ripe olives, preferably in brine and from Italy or Greece

1 tablespoon drained capers

¼ cup dry white wine

¼ cup tomato sauce or tomato paste

CHICKEN CACCIATORE

One 3-pound chicken, cut into serving pieces

⅓ cup plus 1 tablespoon olive oil

3 tablespoons finely chopped onion

¼ cup flour

4 tablespoons butter

2 teaspoons finely minced garlic

Salt and freshly ground pepper to taste

¼ cup dry white wine

1¾ cups fresh or canned chicken broth

1 cup marinara sauce (see recipe page 787)

1. Carefully remove the bones from the chicken pieces or have this done by the butcher. Cut each breast half in two, crosswise.

2. Heat 1 tablespoon of the oil and cook the onion, stirring, until lightly brown. Set aside.

3. Heat the remaining ⅓ cup of oil in a heavy skillet or casserole.

4. Dredge the pieces of chicken lightly in the flour and shake off any excess. Add the pieces skin side down to the skillet and cook until golden on one side, about 3 minutes. Turn the pieces and cook on the second side, about 3 minutes.

5. Pour off the fat from the skillet and add the butter and garlic to the chicken. Add the onion, salt, pepper. Stir to blend. Add the wine and cook for about 1 minute.

6. Add the chicken broth and marinara sauce. Bring to the boil and cover closely. Let cook, covered, over high heat for about 15 minutes, or until tender. Serve with portions of polenta, if desired.

Yield: 4 servings.

CHICKEN PARMESAN

2 broiling or frying chickens, cut into serving pieces

½ cup olive oil

1 teaspoon dried, crumbled oregano

Salt and freshly ground pepper to taste

1 teaspoon finely chopped garlic

6 tablespoons grated Parmesan cheese

1 cup dry white wine

1 pound noodles, cooked to the desired tenderness and drained

1. Combine the chicken, oil, oregano, salt, pepper, garlic, and 4 tablespoons of the grated cheese in a baking pan. The pan must be large enough to hold the chicken pieces in one layer in a not too crowded fashion. Blend well and let stand, covered, until ready to cook.

2. Preheat the oven to 350 degrees.

3. Separate the pieces of chicken in the pan, arranging them skin side up. Leave the marinade in the pan. Sprinkle the chicken with wine. Sprinkle with remaining cheese and place in the oven.

4. Bake for 1 hour, or until the chicken is tender. If desired, run the chicken under the broiler for a second or so to crisp the skin. Spoon some of the pan drippings over the chicken. Pour the remaining drippings over the drained noodles and toss. Serve the chicken with the noodles.

Yield: 4 to 6 servings.

SOUTHERN FRIED CHICKEN

There are many ways to prepare Southern fried chicken, but this is my favorite. It is my family's recipe for the dish and has a crisp, crunchy crust because the chicken pieces are soaked in milk before coating with flour.

1. Put the chicken pieces in a bowl and add milk to cover. Add the Tabasco sauce and stir. Refrigerate for 1 hour or longer.

2. Combine the flour, salt, and pepper (the flavor of pepper is important) in a flat baking dish. Blend well. Remove the chicken pieces, two or three at a time, and dip them into the flour mixture, turning to coat well.

3. Heat the lard and butter in a skillet, preferably a black iron skillet, large enough to hold the chicken pieces in one layer without touching. Heat the fat over high heat. Add the chicken pieces skin side down and cook until golden brown on one side. Turn the pieces and reduce the heat to medium low. Continue cooking until golden brown and cooked through. The total cooking time should be 20 to 30 minutes. As the pieces are cooked, transfer them to absorbent paper towels to drain.

Yield: 4 servings.

1 chicken, 2½ to 3 pounds, cut into serving pieces

Milk to cover

¼ teaspoon Tabasco sauce

1 cup flour

1½ to 2 teaspoons salt

2 teaspoons freshly ground pepper

1 pound lard, or corn oil for frying

¼ pound butter

CHICKEN PAPRIKASH

One 3-pound chicken, cut into serving pieces

Salt and freshly ground pepper to taste

2 tablespoons butter

1 cup thinly sliced onions

1 tablespoon finely minced garlic

1 tablespoon sweet paprika

½ cup fresh or canned chicken broth

1 cup sour cream

1 tablespoon flour

It is ruefully true that in many American households paprika is considered nothing more than an element of color to enliven a cheese sauce. And it's no wonder, for the innocuous powder that stores often pass off as paprika has little more character than chalk. In its finer forms, however, paprika is a distinctive and much prized spice. There are three types—sweet, mild, and hot—each with a pronounced flavor. The best is imported from Hungary and, logically enough, is called Hungarian or rose paprika. It is available in the gourmet sections of most high-quality supermarkets and in fine specialty food shops, as well as in Hungarian grocery stores.

1. Sprinkle the chicken with salt and pepper.

2. Melt the butter in a heavy skillet and add the chicken pieces, skin side down. Cook over moderately high heat for about 5 minutes and turn the pieces. Continue cooking for about 5 minutes until brown on the second side.

3. Sprinkle the onions and garlic around the chicken pieces. Sprinkle with paprika and stir. Add the chicken broth and cover. Simmer for 10 minutes or longer, until the chicken is cooked.

4. Remove the chicken to a warm serving dish.

5. Blend the sour cream and flour and stir it into the sauce. Cook, stirring, for about 1 minute. Pour the sauce over the chicken.

Yield: 4 servings.

CHICKEN SAUTÉ WITH LEMON

Two 1¾-pound chickens, cut into serving pieces

Salt and freshly ground pepper to taste

3 tablespoons butter

¼ cup finely chopped shallots

10 thin lemon slices

½ cup dry white wine

1. Sprinkle the chicken pieces with the salt and pepper.

2. Melt the butter in a skillet and brown the chicken skin side down. When golden, turn the pieces and brown on the other side.

3. Sprinkle with shallots and arrange the lemon slices over the chicken. Cover and cook for 5 minutes. Pour off the fat and add the wine. Cover and cook for 15 minutes, or until tender. Serve with the pan gravy.

Yield: 4 to 6 servings.

CHICKEN AND SPANISH RICE CASSEROLE

A basic chicken and Spanish rice casserole is a traditionally American dish. This is our version, made a bit more elaborate and flavorful in its seasonings and in the use of cubed zucchini as well as green peppers.

1. Sprinkle the chicken pieces with salt and a generous grinding of pepper.

2. Heat the oil in a deep heavy skillet or casserole and add the chicken pieces skin side down. Cook over high heat until golden brown on one side. Turn and cook until golden brown on the other side.

3. Add the onion and garlic and stir to blend. When the onion wilts, scatter the green peppers and zucchini over all. Add the tomatoes, rice, chicken broth, bay leaf, and thyme. Add pepper to taste. Cover closely and cook for 20 minutes. Uncover and cook for 5 minutes longer.

Yield: 4 servings.

One 2½-pound chicken, cut into serving pieces

Salt and freshly ground pepper to taste

2 tablespoons olive oil

1 cup finely chopped onion

2 teaspoons finely minced garlic

1¼ cups cubed green peppers

1½ cups cubed zucchini

2 cups fresh or canned cubed tomatoes

1 cup rice

1 cup fresh or canned chicken broth

1 bay leaf

½ teaspoon dried thyme

CHICKEN ARRABBIATO

1 ounce, or slightly less,
   dried imported
   mushrooms, preferably
   Italian

   One 3-pound chicken,
   cut into serving pieces

   Salt and freshly ground
   pepper to taste

2 cups imported canned
   tomatoes

3 tablespoons olive oil

8 thin slices of hard
   salami, cut into very
   fine, matchlike strips

1 teaspoon finely
   chopped garlic

½ cup dry white wine

1 teaspoon hot red
   pepper flakes

   Chopped parsley for
   garnish

If you like spicy foods, as I do, your palate will be enchanted with this devilishly hot dish of chicken with garlic, salami, and hot red pepper flakes, called *arrabbiato,* which means enraged.

1. Put the mushrooms in a mixing bowl and add warm water to cover. Let stand for an hour or so to soften.

2. Sprinkle the chicken pieces with the salt and pepper.

3. Put the tomatoes in a saucepan and cook down, stirring often, until reduced to 1 cup.

4. Meanwhile, heat the oil in a large heavy skillet and, when it is quite hot, add the chicken skin side down. Cook for 8 to 10 minutes on each side, turning often. Add the strips of salami. Cook to heat through, stirring.

5. Remove the chicken pieces and salami strips to a platter and keep warm.

6. Pour off the fat from the skillet and add the garlic. Cook briefly and add the wine. Cook to reduce by half and add the cooked down tomatoes.

7. Drain the mushrooms but reserve ½ cup of the soaking liquid. Squeeze the mushrooms and add them and the reserved soaking liquid to the sauce. Add the red pepper flakes and salt and pepper to taste. Return the chicken to the sauce and reheat. Serve sprinkled with chopped parsley.

Yield: 4 servings.

CHICKEN POT PIE

This can be one of the great dishes of the world. We are not speaking of the basic and hearty pie of New England and Pennsylvania Dutch territory made with boiled birds. No offense intended, but that is wine from a lesser bottle. What we do speak of is the elegant, when perfectly made, chicken pot pie of England.

1. For the pastry, put the flour in a mixing bowl and add the butter, lard, and salt to taste. Using a pastry blender, work the mixture until it looks like coarse cornmeal. Add the water a little at a time, working the dough lightly with the fingers. Add just enough water to have it hold together. Shape into a ball and wrap in wax paper. Refrigerate for at least half an hour.

2. To make the filling, melt 3 tablespoons butter in a skillet and add the chicken, skin side down. Sprinkle with salt and pepper. Cook over low heat without browning for about 5 minutes, turning once. Scatter the carrots, celery, and white onions over.

3. Heat the remaining 2 tablespoons of butter in another skillet and add the mushrooms. Cook, stirring, until they give up their liquid. Continue cooking until most of the liquid evaporates. Add the mushrooms to the chicken.

4. In a cheesecloth square tie together the parsley, cloves, and thyme. Add it to the chicken. Cook, stirring frequently, for about 10 minutes. Do not burn.

5. Sprinkle with the flour, stirring to distribute it evenly. Add the wine and broth. Add the Tabasco sauce and cover. Simmer for half an hour.

6. Preheat the oven to 400 degrees.

7. Meanwhile, cut the bacon into 2-inch lengths. Cook the pieces until crisp and brown. Drain.

8. Strain the chicken and pour the cooking liquid into a saucepan. Discard the cheesecloth bag. Arrange the chicken and vegetables in a baking dish (we used a 16 × 10½ × 2-inch oval dish). Cut the eggs into sixths and arrange them over the chicken and vegetables. Scatter the bacon bits over the chicken and vegetables.

9. Skim off and discard the fat from the cooking liquid. Bring the liquid to the boil and add the heavy cream. Bring the sauce to the boil. Simmer for about 20 minutes. Add the Worcestershire sauce and salt and pepper to taste. Pour the sauce over the chicken mixture.

10. Roll out the pastry. Cut a round or oval just large enough to fit

THE PASTRY:

2 cups flour

8 tablespoons butter

4 tablespoons lard or vegetable shortening
Salt

2 to 3 tablespoons cold water

THE FILLING:

5 tablespoons butter

Two 2½-pound chickens, cut into serving pieces

Salt and freshly ground pepper to taste

½ cup coarsely chopped carrots

½ cup coarsely chopped celery

1 cup small white onions, peeled

½ pound mushrooms, thinly sliced

3 fresh parsley sprigs

2 whole cloves

3 fresh thyme sprigs, or ½ teaspoon dried

4 tablespoons flour

1 cup dry white wine

4 cups fresh or canned chicken broth

A few drops of Tabasco sauce

5 strips bacon

3 hard-cooked eggs, peeled

1 cup heavy cream

1 teaspoon Worcestershire sauce

1 egg, beaten

the baking dish. Arrange it over the chicken mixture and cut out a small hole in the center to allow steam to escape. Brush with the beaten egg. Bake for 30 minutes.

Yield: 6 to 8 servings.

MURGHI MASSALA (CHICKEN CURRY)

One 3-pound chicken, cut into serving pieces

⅔ cup peanut, vegetable, or corn oil

1 large onion, coarsely grated, about 1½ cups

One 4-inch piece cinnamon stick

2 whole, unhusked cardamom seeds, or ½ teaspoon ground

1 tablespoon finely minced garlic

2¼ cups water

1 cup yogurt

⅓ cup matchstick-size pieces of fresh ginger

1 teaspoon turmeric

2 teaspoons sweet paprika

1 teaspoon ground ginger

½ teaspoon ground cumin

1 teaspoon ground coriander

Salt to taste

½ cup heavy cream

1. Pull off and discard the skin of the chicken or use the skin for soup. It is easy to skin the chicken, using the fingers and a dry clean towel for tugging.

2. Heat the oil in a large heavy kettle and add the onion. Cook, stirring, for about 5 minutes, until the onion is dry but not brown. Add the cinnamon and cardamom seeds and continue cooking, stirring, until the onion is golden brown. Add the garlic and ¼ cup water.

3. Add the yogurt and cook briskly, stirring, for about 5 minutes. Add the ginger pieces, turmeric, paprika, powdered ginger, cumin, coriander, and 1 cup of water.

4. Cook, stirring, for about 5 minutes and add the chicken pieces. Add the salt. Cook for 20 minutes, stirring frequently.

5. Add the remaining cup of water and cook for about 10 minutes, stirring often. Add the cream and bring to the boil. Cook for about 2 minutes.

Yield: 4 to 6 servings.

CHICKEN FRICASSEE FOR A CROWD

1. Select one or two large heavy casseroles or Dutch ovens of sufficient size to contain the chicken and the sauce. One casserole with a capacity of about 14 quarts (3½ gallons) is ideal. Or use two casseroles, each with approximately half that capacity.

2. Sprinkle the chicken with the salt and pepper.

3. Melt the butter in one casserole or half the butter in each of two casseroles. Add the chicken pieces to the one casserole or half of the chicken to each of the two casseroles.

4. Add the onions, garlic, cloves, nutmeg, bay leaves, and cayenne.

5. Cook, stirring the chicken occasionally, without browning, for about 5 minutes, or until the chicken loses its raw look.

6. Sprinkle with flour and stir to coat the pieces evenly. Add the wine and stir. Add the chicken broth, stirring.

7. Dilute half of the mustard with a little of the cooking liquid and add it. Add the mushrooms and stir.

8. Cook, uncovered, for about 20 minutes, stirring occasionally. Skim the fat from the surface as it cooks.

9. Add the cream and continue cooking, uncovered, about 5 minutes longer.

10. Dilute the remaining mustard with a little of the hot sauce and add it. Add the lemon juice. Skim off any remaining fat, and serve with rice.

Yield: 25 servings.

6 chickens, about 3½ pounds each, cut into serving pieces

Salt and freshly ground pepper to taste

4 tablespoons butter

2 cups finely chopped onions

1 tablespoon finely minced garlic

2 whole cloves

⅛ teaspoon grated nutmeg

2 bay leaves

⅛ teaspoon cayenne

½ cup flour

1 cup dry white wine

3 cups fresh or canned chicken broth

6 tablespoons imported mustard, preferably of an extra-strong variety

1¼ pounds mushrooms, quartered if large or left whole if small

1 cup heavy cream

2 tablespoons lemon juice

ANYTHING CURRY

3 tablespoons butter

1 cup finely chopped onion

1 teaspoon finely chopped garlic

½ cup finely minced celery, optional

1 cup peeled and cubed tart apple

¼ cup flour

1 to 2 tablespoons curry powder

¾ teaspoon dry mustard

1 bay leaf

2½ cups fresh or canned chicken broth

3 cups cooked chicken or meat cut into bite-sized pieces

½ cup milk or cream

3 tablespoons finely chopped mango chutney (see recipe page 798)

Over the years I must have made at least a thousand curry-flavored dishes. It occurred to me that there could be a universal recipe for a basic curry sauce to which almost any cooked food might be added—chicken or any leftover meat. This is the delectable result. You will find a seductive relish to serve with the curry on page 797 in this book. It is of Indian inspiration—yogurt with scallions and tomatoes. There is also a fine homemade chutney recipe.

1. Melt the butter in a saucepan and add the onion, garlic, celery, and apple. Cook, stirring often, for about 5 minutes.

2. Blend the flour, curry powder, and mustard and sprinkle it over the vegetables, stirring. Add the bay leaf.

3. Add the chicken broth, stirring rapidly with a wire whisk. When the mixture has thickened, let it simmer for 15 minutes. Stir often from the bottom to prevent sticking.

4. Add the chicken or meat, milk, and chutney and simmer for 4 or 5 minutes longer. Serve with rice.

Yield: 6 servings.

HAITIAN-STYLE CHICKEN (A KIND OF ESCABECHE)

1. Rinse and drain the chicken pieces well. Rub the pieces all over with half a cut lemon or lime. Place in a mixing bowl. Add the vinegar, garlic, pepper, salt, and hot pepper.

2. Cut the onions into ¼-inch slices and break the slices into rings. Add them. Add the parsley and let stand for an hour or so, turning the chicken in the marinade from time to time.

3. Heat the oil in a large heavy skillet and cook the chicken, a few pieces at a time, until browned on all sides. As the pieces are cooked, transfer them to a Dutch oven large enough to hold them all. When the pieces are transferred, add the marinade to the skillet and stir to dissolve all brown particles that cling to the bottom and sides of the skillet. Cook for about 5 minutes. Add the wine, chicken broth, and tomato paste. Add the salt.

4. Pour this over the chicken and partly cover. Cook, moving the pieces of chicken around occasionally, for about 45 minutes, or until very tender. Serve the chicken, hot or cold, with the sauce.

Yield: 8 to 12 servings.

Three 2½-pound chickens, quartered

½ lemon or lime

¾ cup tarragon vinegar

2 garlic cloves, finely chopped

½ teaspoon freshly ground pepper

Salt to taste

½ long fresh, hot red or green pepper, chopped or cut into rings

2 onions, about ¾ pound total weight

½ cup coarsely chopped, loosely packed parsley

¼ cup peanut or corn oil

½ cup dry white wine

½ cup fresh or canned chicken broth

1 teaspoon tomato paste

JOE LUPPI'S SMOKED CHICKEN

One 3-pound chicken, cut into serving pieces
1 tablespoon sesame oil
1 teaspoon lemon juice
2 tablespoons melted butter or peanut oil
1 teaspoon coarsely ground Sichuan peppercorns

A friend of ours, Joseph Luppi, a passionately devoted cook who lives in our vicinity, makes a splendid smoked chicken with Sichuan peppercorns and lemon juice. He insists that apple or hickory chips are essential for a good flavor, and he's absolutely right.

1. Prepare the smoker by heating apple or hickory chips as indicated in the manufacturer's instructions.
2. Arrange the chicken pieces on two or more smoker shelves. Let the chicken smoke for about 1½ hours.
3. Preheat the oven to 450 degrees.
4. Put the chicken in a bowl and add the sesame oil, lemon juice, butter or oil, and peppercorns. Mix to coat the chicken thoroughly.
5. Arrange the chicken pieces skin side down on a flat baking dish in one layer. Bake for 10 minutes. Turn the pieces, baste with the pan juices, and continue cooking for 10 minutes.

Yield: 4 servings.

BAKED CHICKEN LEGS WITH HERBS

1. Preheat the oven to 425 degrees.

2. Sprinkle the chicken pieces with the salt and pepper. Melt the butter in a baking dish large enough to hold the legs in one layer. Add the chicken legs and turn them in the butter until well coated. Arrange the pieces skin side down in one layer. Place the chicken legs in the oven and bake for 30 minutes.

3. Meanwhile, combine the bread crumbs, shallots, garlic, parsley, thyme, and rosemary.

4. Turn the chicken pieces skin side up and sprinkle with the bread crumb mixture. Bake for 30 minutes longer. Pour the wine around (not over) the chicken pieces. Bake for 5 minutes longer and serve.

Yield: 8 or more servings.

16 chicken legs with thighs attached, about 1 pound each

Salt and freshly ground pepper to taste

8 tablespoons butter

1½ cups fresh bread crumbs

2 tablespoons finely chopped shallots

2 teaspoons finely chopped garlic

4 tablespoons chopped parsley

1 teaspoon chopped thyme

2 teaspoons chopped fresh rosemary

½ cup dry white wine

CURRIED CHICKEN WINGS

18 to 24 chicken wings

3   tablespoons curry
    powder

¾   cup finely chopped
    onion

1   tablespoon finely
    minced garlic

2   apples, cored, peeled,
    and cut into small
    cubes (about 2 cups)

1   banana, peeled and cut
    into small cubes

1½ cups water

1   cup plain yogurt

1   cup drained tomatoes

1   bay leaf

    Salt and freshly ground
    pepper to taste

We have always treasured the writing of Janet Flanner, who for many years wrote a letter from Paris, signed Genét, for *The New Yorker*. We were delighted to read in an interview that she shared one of our passions. "My favorite dish is chicken wings," she declared. "It's the most refined part of the creature." We can only add bravo and contribute several refined uses for that part of the creature.

1. Cut off and discard the small wing tips of the chicken wings. Leave the main wing bone and second wing bone attached and intact.

2. Heat a large heavy skillet and, without adding fat, cook the chicken wings, stirring often, to brown. The chicken will brown in its own natural fat. Sprinkle the pieces with curry powder and stir. Cook, stirring often, for about 10 minutes.

3. Add the onion, garlic, apples, and banana. Stir and add the water, yogurt, tomatoes, bay leaf, salt, and pepper. Cover and cook for 45 minutes to 1 hour.

Yield: 6 to 8 servings.

CHICKEN WINGS WITH OYSTER SAUCE

The primary ingredients of oyster sauce, used in many Chinese recipes, are shucked oysters, soy sauce, salt, and seasonings, such as garlic, ginger, sugar, and leeks. The sauce is simmered a long time and is generally thickened with cornstarch. Tightly capped, it will keep indefinitely if it is refrigerated.

1. Cut off and discard the small wing tips of the chicken pieces. Cut the main wing bone from the second joint and reserve both. Set aside.

2. Put the pieces in a bowl and add 2 teaspoons of the cornstarch, 1 tablespoon of the oil, the dark soy sauce, and sugar. Blend well.

3. Heat the remaining 2 tablespoons of oil in a wok or skillet and add the chicken mixture. Cook, stirring, for about 5 minutes, taking care that the sauce does not burn.

4. Add the chicken broth and cover. Cook for about 10 minutes, or until the chicken pieces are cooked. Remove the chicken and set aside.

5. Cook down the liquid in the wok and add the ginger and scallion. Cook, stirring, and add the oyster sauce and 2 tablespoons of water.

6. Blend the remaining cornstarch with 1 tablespoon of water and stir this in. Add the sherry. Return the chicken wings to the pan and stir over high heat to coat with the sauce.

Yield: 4 servings.

8 chicken wings

3 teaspoons cornstarch

3 tablespoons peanut, vegetable, or corn oil

1 tablespoon dark soy sauce

1 teaspoon sugar

¼ cup fresh or canned chicken broth

1 tablespoon finely chopped fresh ginger

⅓ cup chopped scallion, green part and all

2 tablespoons oyster sauce

3 tablespoons water

1 tablespoon dry sherry

OVEN-BAKED CHICKEN WINGS WITH HONEY

18 chicken wings
    Salt and freshly ground
    pepper to taste
2   tablespoons vegetable
    oil
½   cup soy sauce
2   tablespoons ketchup
1   cup honey
½   garlic clove, chopped

1. Preheat the oven to 375 degrees.
2. Cut off and discard the wing tips of the chicken wings. Cut the remaining wings in two parts and sprinkle with salt and pepper.
3. Combine the remaining ingredients and pour over chicken wings in a greased baking dish. Bake for 1 hour, until well done and the sauce is caramelized. If chicken starts to burn, reduce the heat and cover with foil.

Yield: 6 servings.

OVEN-BARBECUED CHICKEN WINGS

24 chicken wings (about
    5 pounds)
    Salt to taste
2   teaspoons freshly
    ground black pepper
3   teaspoons paprika
½   cup corn, peanut, or
    vegetable oil
1   cup ketchup
¼   cup honey
6   tablespoons white
    vinegar
2   tablespoons Worcester-
    shire sauce
1   teaspoon Tabasco
    sauce
1   tablespoon Dijon
    mustard
1   tablespoon finely
    minced garlic
4   tablespoons butter
1   bay leaf

1. Preheat the oven to 400 degrees.
2. Fold the small tips of the chicken wings under the main wing bones. Arrange the wings in one layer in a baking dish so that they bake comfortably close together without crowding.
3. Sprinkle with salt, pepper, and 2 teaspoons of the paprika. Pour ¼ cup of the oil over all, and turn the wings in the mixture so that they are evenly coated. Rearrange them in one layer with the small wing side down.
4. Place in the oven and bake for 15 minutes.
5. Meanwhile, combine the ketchup, the remaining ¼ cup oil, the honey, vinegar, Worcestershire, Tabasco, mustard, garlic, butter, bay leaf, and remaining 1 teaspoon paprika. Bring to the boil.
6. Brush the wings lightly with the sauce and turn them on the other side. Brush this side with sauce and continue cooking for 15 minutes.
7. Brush the wings with the sauce again. Turn the pieces and brush the other side again. Continue baking for 15 minutes.
8. Continue turning, brushing, and baking the chicken for 15 minutes longer, for a total cooking time of about 1 hour.

Yield: 6 or more servings.

CHICKEN OR TURKEY CROQUETTES

It has long been our contention that some of the best dishes in the world are those that bear the unseemly and unpalatable label "leftovers." Two cases in point are roast turkey and roast beef. We like them piping hot from the oven, but how much more delectable we find them the day after, thinly carved and tucked between slices of a decent loaf of bread, the slices smeared with freshly made mayonnaise. That and a pickle. Omar the tentmaker probably never knew his "paradise enow." Our enthusiasm for leftovers is evidenced by this heartily endorsed recipe for chicken or turkey metamorphosed into croquettes to be served with a fresh mushroom sauce.

1. Prepare the chicken or turkey and set aside. The chopped pieces should be no more than ¼ inch in diameter.

2. Melt the butter in a saucepan and add the onion, stirring to wilt. Sprinkle with flour and stir with a wire whisk until blended. Add the broth, stirring rapidly with a whisk. Stir in the chicken. Add the salt and pepper, nutmeg, and Tabasco. Remove the sauce from the heat and add the yolks, stirring vigorously with the whisk. Cook briefly, stirring, and remove from the heat.

3. Spoon the mixture into a dish (one measuring 8 × 8 × 2 inches is convenient) and smooth it over. Cover with a piece of buttered wax paper and refrigerate, preferably overnight.

4. Remove the paper and, using the fingers, divide the mixture into 12 to 14 portions. Shape into balls and roll lightly in flour. The portions may be shaped finally into balls or cylinders. When smooth on the surface and neatly coated with flour, dredge in the whole egg combined with the 3 tablespoons water, and then in bread crumbs. Arrange on a rack and chill until ready to cook.

5. Heat the oil and, when it is hot, add the balls or cylinders, a few at a time. Cook for 2 or 3 minutes, or until golden and cooked through. Serve hot with mushroom sauce.

Yield: 6 to 8 servings.

3½ cups coarsely chopped cooked chicken or turkey meat, including skin

2 tablespoons butter

3 tablespoons finely minced onion

3 tablespoons flour

1½ cups fresh or canned chicken broth

Salt and freshly ground pepper to taste

¼ teaspoon freshly grated nutmeg

3 drops Tabasco sauce

3 egg yolks

Flour for dredging

1 egg, lightly beaten

3 tablespoons water

1½ cups fine, fresh bread crumbs

Peanut, vegetable, or corn oil for deep frying

Mushroom sauce (see recipe page 781)

PON PON CHICKEN

2 cups shredded cooked chicken

Lettuce leaves

1 tablespoon chopped scallion

1 teaspoon or more chopped garlic

1½ teaspoons finely chopped fresh ginger

3 tablespoons well-stirred sesame paste (see note)

1½ tablespoons soy sauce, preferably dark soy sauce

1 tablespoon white vinegar, preferably rice vinegar

1 teaspoon sugar

Salt to taste

1 tablespoon chili paste with garlic (see note)

1 tablespoon sesame oil (see note)

Place the chicken on the lettuce leaves on a serving dish. Blend the remaining ingredients and pour the sauce over the chicken. Serve at room temperature.

Yield: 6 to 12 servings with other Chinese dishes

Note: These ingredients are widely available in Asian grocery stores.

Sesame Chicken with Garlic Sauce

1. Bone the thighs or have them boned. Slice the thighs into 4 or 6 squares of approximately the same size. Place the pieces in a bowl and add the egg yolk, 1 tablespoon soy sauce, and minced garlic. Let stand.

2. Sift the flour, cornstarch, and baking powder into a bowl. Stir in the water, eggs, 2 teaspoons oil, and sesame seeds.

3. To prepare the sauce, heat 1 tablespoon of oil and add the garlic and ginger. Cook briefly and add the chicken broth, sugar, soy sauce, and ground pepper. Simmer for about 5 minutes.

4. Coat the chicken in batter.

5. Heat 4 cups of oil in a wok or skillet and add the batter-coated chicken pieces, one at a time. Do not add all the chicken pieces at once. Cook, stirring to separate the pieces, for about 1 minute, or until golden brown. Drain each batch as they cook. Pour out the oil after cooking the chicken pieces. Return the chicken pieces to the wok.

6. Add the garlic sauce and blend well. Stir in the chopped scallions and sesame seeds and heat through.

Yield: 4 servings.

THE CHICKEN:

6 chicken thighs

1 egg yolk

1 tablespoon soy sauce

1 garlic clove, finely minced

THE BATTER:

1 cup plus 2 tablespoons flour

3 tablespoons cornstarch

1¼ teaspoons baking powder

¾ cup cold water

2 eggs, lightly beaten

2 teaspoons peanut, vegetable, or corn oil

1 tablespoon sesame seeds

THE GARLIC SAUCE:

1 tablespoon peanut, vegetable, or corn oil

4 garlic cloves, finely minced

1 teaspoon finely chopped fresh ginger

½ cup fresh or canned chicken broth

1½ teaspoons sugar

2 tablespoons dark soy sauce

¼ teaspoon freshly ground pepper

4 cups peanut, vegetable, or corn oil

¾ cup chopped scallions, green part and all

1 tablespoon sesame seeds

INDONESIAN-STYLE CHICKEN

10 to 12 chicken thighs
   Salt and freshly ground pepper to taste
½ teaspoon ground mace
4 tablespoons butter
1 large onion, finely chopped, about 3 cups
1 garlic clove, crushed
1 tablespoon lemon juice
1 tablespoon dark brown sugar
1½ teaspoons ground cumin (djinten) (see note)
½ teaspoons ground coriander (ketumbar) (see note)
2 teaspoons bottled imported meat seasoning (bumboe sesate) (see note)
½ to 1 teaspoon imported hot chili paste (sambal oelek) (see note)
½ cup ketjap manis (see recipe page 795)
2 ounces dried grated coconut (klapper) (see note)
1½ cups hot water

1. Preheat the oven to 325 degrees.
2. Skin the chicken thighs and place them in a bowl. Sprinkle with the salt, pepper, and mace and rub to coat well. Heat the butter in a skillet and brown the chicken pieces lightly. Transfer the chicken pieces to a baking dish.
3. Meanwhile, combine the onion, garlic, lemon juice, sugar, cumin, coriander, meat seasoning, hot chili paste, and ketjap manis.
4. Add the onion-and-spice mixture to the skillet in which the chicken cooked. Cook, stirring, for 8 to 10 minutes.
5. Combine the grated coconut and water and let stand briefly, kneading with the hands. Squeeze the mixture through cheesecloth or a potato ricer. Add 1 cup of the coconut milk to the onion-and-spice mixture and stir to blend. Discard the coconut. Bring to the boil. Pour over the chicken and bake, uncovered, until the chicken is tender, 20 to 30 minutes. Turn the chicken pieces once as they cook.

Yield: 5 to 6 servings.

Note: These are Indonesian names of the various spices, which are available at outlets that sell imported spices.

YAKITORI (JAPANESE SKEWERED CHICKEN)

Yakitori could be described as the Japanese equivalent of hamburger, but in its variety and nature it is infinitely more sophisticated. There seems to be almost universal sides-taking in Tokyo as to the superiority of one fin bec's choice of yakitori restaurant over that of another. *Yaki* means "grilled"; *tori* means "birds." And the bird of choice is usually chicken, cut into boneless cubes and arranged on skewers before grilling.

Bone the light and dark meat of a chicken, setting aside the heart, liver, gizzard, and so on. Cut the light and dark meat into bite-size cubes. Arrange the cubes on skewers. If desired, arrange 1- or 2-inch lengths of scallions alternately on some skewers with the chicken pieces.

Trim and cut away the tough, muscular parts of the gizzards, if used. Arrange the tender gizzard pieces on skewers. Arrange the liver and heart on skewers. Grill the unseasoned chicken pieces, brushing as necessary with yakitori-no-tare (see following recipe). Cook, turning often, until the chicken pieces are done. Remove from the heat, sprinkle with lemon, and serve hot.

YAKITORI-NO-TARE (SAUCE FOR YAKITORI)

Chicken bones, optional
½ cup sake
½ cup mirin (sweet sake), available in Japanese markets
⅓ cup or slightly more coarsely cracked rock sugar (see Note)
1 cup dark soy sauce (see note)
2 to 3 tablespoons honey

1. If chicken bones are used, cook the mover a charcoal fire, turning often and without burning. Crack them and put them in a saucepan. Add the sake, mirin, rock sugar, and soy sauce. Bring to the boil and cook for 3 minutes.

2. Stir in the honey and boil 2 minutes longer. Strain before using. Use to brush chicken on skewers as it is grilled.

Yield: About 2½ cups.

Note: Rock sugar and dark soy sauce are available in Asian food shops.

CHICKEN LIVERS EN BROCHETTE

¾ pound chicken livers

¼ cup soy sauce

4 teaspoons sweet sherry
   wine

1 tablespoon sugar

1 garlic clove, finely
   minced

⅛ teaspoon crushed red
   pepper flakes

10 or more bacon strips

1. Pick over the chicken livers and trim them to remove veins and connecting tissues. Cut the livers in half. Place them in a mixing bowl. Add the soy sauce, sherry, sugar, garlic, and pepper flakes. Let stand until ready to cook.

2. Cut the bacon in half crosswise. Wrap 1 chicken liver half in half a bacon strip and arrange on four to six skewers. If wooden skewers are used, it is best if they are soaked for an hour or so in cold water. Cover the tips with foil to prevent burning.

3. Prepare a charcoal fire in a grill. When the coals and grill are properly hot, brush the grill lightly with oil. Arrange the skewered chicken livers on the grill and cook, turning as necessary, for 10 minutes or longer, according to the desired degree of doneness.

Yield: 4 to 6 servings.

CHICKEN LIVERS IN MADEIRA SAUCE

½ pound chicken livers

2 tablespoons butter

2 tablespoons chopped
   shallots

2 tablespoons Madeira

½ cup brown sauce or
   canned beef gravy

   Salt and freshly ground
   pepper to taste

¼ cup peanut, vegetable,
   or corn oil

1. Pick over the livers to remove any tough veins. Cut each liver in half. Set aside.

2. Heat 1 tablespoon butter in a saucepan and add the shallots, Madeira, brown sauce, salt, and pepper. Simmer for 15 minutes. Add the remaining 1 tablespoon of butter and swirl it around until blended.

3. Heat the oil in a skillet and, when it is very hot, add the livers. Cook, turning the livers quickly, for about 1 minute. Drain in a sieve and add the livers to the Madeira sauce. Serve piping hot.

Yield: 4 servings.

Cornish Hens à la Diable

French chefs and many serious home cooks often lament the fact that here they are unable to find the small poussins or young chickens that are so widely available in the markets of France. Poussins differ from just any young chickens in that they have reached maturity and developed flavor, yet they generally weigh only about one pound or slightly more. On rare occasions, one can buy these little chickens in rural areas where poultry farms exist. An excellent substitute for the small birds, however, are Rock Cornish game hens. They are a delicacy and remarkably easy to prepare. One unstuffed bird, roasted or grilled, will serve one. When filled with a meat stuffing, one bird will suffice for two servings.

1. Preheat the broiler to high. If the oven has a separate temperature control, set the oven temperature to 450 degrees.

2. Place the split hens on a flat surface and pound lightly with a flat mallet. Sprinkle the hens on all sides with the salt, pepper, and oil.

3. Combine the mustard and wine in a small bowl and set aside.

4. Arrange the halves neatly in one layer, skin side down, on a baking sheet and place under the broiler about 3 inches from the source of heat. Broil for 8 or 9 minutes and turn the halves.

5. Return to the broiler and broil for about 3 minutes. Remove the halves and brush the skin side with the mustard and wine mixture. Turn the halves and brush the second side with the mustard mixture. Brush with the pan drippings and sprinkle with the bread crumbs.

6. If the oven and broiler have dual heat controls, turn off the broiler and set the oven temperature at 450 degrees. Put the hens in the oven and bake for 15 minutes. Serve with sauce diable.

Yield: 4 servings.

4 Cornish hens, about 1¼ pounds each, split in half for broiling

Salt and freshly ground pepper to taste

¼ cup peanut, vegetable, or corn oil

2 tablespoons Dijon mustard

1 tablespoon dry white wine

½ cup fine fresh bread crumbs

Sauce diable (see recipe page 780)

CORNISH HENS STUFFED WITH PROSCIUTTO AND GIBLETS

2 Cornish hens with giblets, about 2 pounds each

2 ounces prosciutto

½ bay leaf

1 garlic clove, finely chopped

½ teaspoon chopped fresh thyme, or ¼ teaspoon dried thyme

Salt and freshly ground pepper to taste

1 tablespoon peanut, vegetable, or corn oil

1. Preheat the oven to 375 degrees.

2. Remove the livers and hearts from the hens and chop them fine.

3. Chop the prosciutto and bay leaf. Combine the chopped livers, hearts, proscuitto, bay leaf, garlic, thyme, salt, and pepper. Blend well.

4. Stuff the hens with equal portions of the mixture.

5. Arrange them in a shallow baking dish and sprinkle with salt and pepper and rub with oil. Scatter the necks and gizzards around the hens. Arrange the hens on their sides and place in the oven.

6. Bake for 20 minutes and turn the hens on their other side. Bake for 20 minutes and turn the hens on their backs and baste. Return to the oven and continue cooking, basting occasionally, for about 20 minutes. Total cooking time should be about 1 hour. Remove from the oven and serve hot or cold with the stuffing.

Yield: 4 servings.

ROAST TURKEY

1. Preheat the oven to 450 degrees.
2. Stuff with any desired stuffing (see following recipes) and truss the turkey. Place it in a shallow roasting pan. Brush the turkey with oil and sprinkle with salt.
3. Roast the turkey for about 50 minutes, until it is nicely browned. Turn the pan in the oven occasionally to brown evenly. When browned, cover loosely with a sheet of aluminum foil. Continue roasting, basting at intervals. After 2 hours, reduce the oven heat to 375 degrees. Continue roasting for about 1 hour longer, or until the turkey is done (a thermometer inserted in the dressing should register about 160 degrees).
4. Remove the turkey and pour off any fat that may have accumulated. Add about ½ cup of water to the roasting pan and stir to dissolve the brown particles clinging to the bottom and sides of the pan. Add this to the giblet gravy, if desired (see recipe page 230). Let the turkey rest for 20 to 30 minutes. Remove the trussing strings. Carve the turkey and serve with dressing and gravy.

Yield: 12 to 20 servings.

One 12- to 16-pound turkey
4 tablespoons peanut, vegetable, or corn oil
Salt to taste

1. Melt 4 tablespoons of the butter and add the onions, green pepper, and celery. Cook, stirring, until vegetables are crisp-tender. Set aside.
2. Place the corn bread and toast in a mixing bowl and add the hard-cooked eggs and the celery mixture. Add a generous amount of pepper, the chicken broth, eggs, salt, and the remaining butter. Stir to blend well.

Yield: Enough for a 12- to 16-pound turkey.

CORN BREAD STUFFING

¼ pound butter
2 cups finely chopped onions
1 cup finely chopped green pepper
1½ cups freshly chopped heart of celery
4 cups finely crumbled Southern corn bread (see recipe page 733)
3 cups crumbled toast
2 hard-cooked eggs, coarsely chopped
Freshly ground pepper to taste
½ cup fresh or canned chicken broth
3 raw eggs
Salt to taste

GROUND PORK AND CHESTNUT STUFFING

2 pounds ground boneless shoulder of pork

Salt and freshly ground pepper to taste

1 large bay leaf

¼ teaspoon dried thyme

2 cups finely chopped onion

1 teaspoon finely chopped garlic

1 cup dry white wine

12 breakfast sausages in links, about ¾ pound

1 turkey liver

3 cups peeled, cooked whole chestnuts (canned may be used)

½ cup finely chopped parsley

1. Put the meat in a deep saucepan or small casserole. Cook, stirring with the side of a heavy metal spoon to break up lumps, until meat loses its red color.

2. Add the salt, pepper, bay leaf, and thyme. Cook for about 5 minutes, stirring. Add the onion and garlic and stir to blend. Cover and cook for about 15 minutes. Add the wine. Stir. Cover and cook for 15 minutes longer.

3. Meanwhile, twist each link sausage at midpoint to make 24 miniature sausages. Fry these in a skillet, turning and shaking the skillet so that they brown evenly. Cook until done. Drain on absorbent paper towels.

4. Spoon and scrape the ground pork mixture into a mixing bowl. Drain the sausages and add them.

5. Put the turkey liver on a flat surface. Chop it and add it to the stuffing. Add the chestnuts, parsley, salt, and pepper and blend well.

Yield: Enough for a 12- to 16-pound turkey.

1. Place the turkey liver in the container of a food processor or blender. Cut away and discard the tough fibrous membrane from the gizzard and add the gizzard to the container. Rinse the heart well to remove blood and add the heart. Blend thoroughly.

2. Cook the bacon in a large skillet and, when it is rendered of fat, add the sausage meat. Cook until both are rendered of fat. Add the chopped onions and garlic and cook until the onions are wilted. Add the puréed liver mixture and sage. Cook until the liver mixture loses its red color. Add the butter, bread crumbs, eggs, parsley, salt, and pepper. Cool.

Yield: Enough for a 12- to 16-pound turkey.

SAUSAGE STUFFING

Turkey liver, gizzard, and heart

½ pound sliced bacon, cut into small squares

½ pound sausage meat

2 cups finely chopped onions

3 garlic cloves, finely minced

1 teaspoon rubbed sage

4 tablespoons butter

4 cups fresh bread crumbs

3 hard-cooked eggs, coarsely chopped

½ cup chopped parsley

Salt and freshly ground pepper to taste

GIBLET GRAVY

1 turkey neck
1 turkey gizzard
1 turkey heart
1 turkey liver
  Salt to taste
1 tablespoon peanut,
  vegetable, or corn oil
  Freshly ground pepper
  to taste
1¼ cups finely chopped
  onions
½ cup finely chopped
  carrots
¾ cup finely chopped
  celery
1 garlic clove, coarsely
  chopped
3 tablespoons flour
1 bay leaf
2 sprigs fresh thyme, or
  1 teaspoon dried
3 cups chicken broth
2 sprigs parsley
1 tablespoon tomato
  paste
1 tablespoon butter

1. Cut the neck into 1-inch lengths and set aside.

2. Cut away and discard the tough casing from the tender part of the gizzard. Place the gizzard pieces in a saucepan. Cut the heart in half and add it. Add the liver and cold water to cover. Add the salt and bring to the boil. Simmer for 30 minutes. Remove from the heat and drain. Set aside.

3. Meanwhile, heat the oil in a saucepan and add the neck and salt and pepper to taste. Cook, stirring frequently, over medium heat until the neck is golden brown, about 20 minutes. Add ¾ cup of the onion, the carrots, celery, and garlic and stir. Sprinkle with flour and stir until the neck pieces are evenly coated. Add the bay leaf, thyme, broth, parsley, and tomato paste. Stir until the sauce reaches the boil. Continue cooking for about 1½ hours. Strain the sauce. Discard all solids.

4. Slice the giblets and cut them into slivers. Cut the slivers into fine dice.

5. In a saucepan, heat the 1 tablespoon of butter and add the remaining ½ cup of chopped onion. Add the chopped giblet mixture and cook, stirring occasionally, for about 5 minutes. Add the strained sauce and bring to the boil. Simmer for about 5 minutes and add salt and pepper to taste.

Yield: About 3 cups.

TURKEY SCALOPPINE IN BATTER WITH LEMON

One dish on Italian menus consists of thinly sliced turkey breast, cut and cooked to resemble scaloppine of veal. In fact, the resemblance is so close that if one were blindfolded and offered a bite of both the veal and the turkey, it would be difficult to tell the difference. But where cost is concerned the difference is vast. If you have an accommodating butcher, he may be willing to slice the turkey for you. If not, you can do it easily with a sharp slicing knife.

Preferably, you should buy a breast or half a breast that is skinless and boneless. A 1½-pound skinless, boneless turkey breast will yield 12 scaloppine of nice size. When cutting the breast, slice it on the bias, trying to cut pieces of about the same size and weight. Before cooking, place each slice between sheets of plastic wrap and, using a flat mallet, flatten them lightly and uniformly. Do not break the flesh.

4 turkey scaloppine
Salt and freshly ground pepper to taste
1 egg
2 tablespoons milk
¼ cup flour
5 tablespoons butter
4 thin slices lemon
Juice of 1 lemon
Chopped parsley for garnish

1. Sprinkle the scaloppine with salt and pepper.

2. Put the egg in a flat, shallow dish and beat it lightly. Add the milk and beat until well blended.

3. Put the flour plus a little salt and pepper in another shallow dish.

4. Dip the scaloppine first in flour to coat well, then in the beaten egg.

5. Select a skillet wide enough to accommodate two scaloppine at a time.

6. Melt 4 tablespoons of the butter in the skillet and add the scaloppine. Cook for about 1 minute, or until golden brown on one side. Turn and cook the other side. Transfer them to a warm serving dish.

7. Repeat with the remaining scaloppine.

8. Garnish with the lemon slices.

9. To the skillet add the lemon juice and remaining 1 tablespoon of butter. When the butter is melted, pour the sauce over the meat. Sprinkle with parsley and serve.

Yield: 4 servings.

BREADED TURKEY SCALOPPINE WITH ANCHOVY

4 turkey scaloppine
  Salt and freshly ground
  pepper to taste
1 egg
2 tablespoons water
4 tablespoons plus
  1 teaspoon peanut,
  vegetable, or corn oil
¼ cup flour
2 cups bread crumbs
4 slices lemon
4 rolled anchovy fillets
  Finely chopped parsley
  for garnish
4 tablespoons butter

1. Sprinkle the scaloppine with salt and pepper to taste.

2. Put the egg in a flat, shallow dish and beat it lightly. Add the water, 1 teaspoon of the oil, the salt, and pepper and beat until well blended.

3. Put the flour in another shallow dish and the bread crumbs in a third.

4. Dip each scaloppine first in flour, then in beaten egg, and finally in bread crumbs to coat on both sides. Place the scaloppine on a flat surface and pat lightly with the flat side of a knife to make the crumbs adhere.

5. Heat 2 tablespoons of the oil in a heavy skillet and add one scaloppine. Cook for about 1 minute, or until golden brown on one side. Turn and cook on the other side for 1 minute. Remove to a warm platter.

6. Continue cooking scaloppine until all are done, adding more oil to the skillet, about a tablespoon at a time as necessary. About 4 tablespoons of oil should be enough to cook them all.

7. To serve, place one lemon slice in the center of each scaloppine. Place one anchovy fillet in the center of the lemon slice. Sprinkle with parsley.

8. Melt the butter in a skillet, shaking it until it is hot and foamy. When the butter starts to turn brown, pour it over the scaloppine and serve.

Yield: 4 servings.

TURKEY SCALOPPINE
WITH GARLIC AND BAY LEAVES

1. Sprinkle the scaloppine with the salt and pepper. Dip them on both sides in the flour.

2. Select a skillet wide enough to accommodate two scaloppine at a time.

3. Melt 3 tablespoons of the butter in the skillet and, when it is hot, add the scaloppine. Scatter the garlic and bay leaves over and around the scaloppine.

4. Cook the scaloppine for about 1 minute, or until golden brown on one side. Turn and cook on the other side for about 1 minute. Transfer them to a warm serving dish.

5. Cook the remaining scaloppine, adding a bit more butter as necessary.

6. Add the wine to the skillet and cook until it has almost evaporated. Add the broth and cook briefly. Add salt and pepper to taste. Cook down briefly and pour the sauce over the scaloppine.

Yield: 4 servings.

4 turkey scaloppine
Salt and freshly ground pepper to taste
¼ cup flour
5 tablespoons butter, approximately
4 garlic cloves, peeled and cut in half lengthwise
2 bay leaves, split in half
¼ cup dry white wine
¼ cup chicken broth

Roast Duck

Three 5- to 6-pound ducks

Salt and freshly ground pepper to taste

6 celery stalks, trimmed

¼ cup peanut, corn, or vegetable oil

2 medium-size onions, peeled

1½ cups water

2 tablespoons butter

1. Preheat the oven to 450 degrees.

2. Remove the necks and giblets from each duck's cavity and set aside. Pat the ducks dry inside and out. Sprinkle the ducks inside and out with the salt and pepper, and insert 2 celery stalks inside each duck.

3. Truss the ducks with string. Arrange the ducks breast side up in one or two shallow roasting pans. The ducks should not be touching. Rub the oil over the ducks so that they are evenly coated. Scatter the necks, gizzards, hearts, and onions around the ducks. Place in the oven and bake for 1 hour.

4. Pour off the fat from each pan. (The fatness of ducks varies; if a great deal of fat accumulates in the pan before the hour is up, pour it off.) Leave the ducks in the pans and continue roasting for 30 minutes. Pour off any fat that has accumulated around the ducks.

5. Lift the ducks, one at a time, and let the juices in their cavities flow back into the pan or pans.

6. Cut and pull off the trussing strings. Transfer the ducks to a large platter and cover loosely with foil.

7. Pour or spoon off any fat from the roasting pans and combine the remaining juices in one pan. Add the water to the pan. Bring to the boil, stirring with a spoon to dissolve the brown particles that cling to the bottom and sides of the pan. Let the sauce cook down over high heat for about 4 minutes, stirring constantly.

8. Strain through a fine sieve, pressing to extract as much liquid from the solids as possible. There should be about 1½ cups of liquid.

9. Skim off any fat that rises to the surface. Set the sauce aside in a saucepan.

10. When ready to serve, return the ducks to the oven, preheated to 400 degrees, for 10 minutes. Carve the ducks (or simply split in two and serve half a duck per person). Heat the sauce and, at the last minute, melt the butter in a skillet, swirling it around and over the heat until it is browned a light hazelnut color. Pour the butter into the sauce and stir. Serve the sauce separately.

Yield: 6 servings.

CANARD À L'ORANGE
(ROAST DUCK WITH ORANGES)

1. Preheat the oven to 375 degrees.

2. Using a swivel-bladed vegetable peeler, peel off the zest of one orange. Discard any of the white pulp that may cling to it. Cut the zest into very fine shreds (julienne). Drop the shreds into boiling water and let simmer for about 30 seconds. Drain and set aside.

3. Completely peel all the oranges and carefully section them, cutting between the membranous intersections around each section.

4. Truss the duck with string and sprinkle it inside and out with the salt and pepper. Chop the neck into 1- or 2-inch lengths. Cut away the tough outer membrane of the gizzard. Sprinkle the pieces of neck and gizzard with salt and pepper.

5. Place the duck on its back in a roasting pan. Surround it with the neck and gizzard. Place in the oven and bake for 30 minutes.

6. Remove the pan and pour or spoon off the accumulated fat. Turn the duck on its side and return to the oven. Bake for 30 minutes.

7. Remove the pan and spoon or pour off the fat. Take care not to pour off the nonfat liquid in the pan.

8. Increase the oven heat to 400 degrees. Turn the duck breast side down and return to the oven. Bake for 30 minutes.

9. Turn the duck on its other side and bake for 30 minutes.

10. Remove the pan from the oven. Remove and discard the trussing string from the duck. Transfer the duck, back side down, to another roasting pan. Return to the oven for 10 minutes longer.

11. Meanwhile, place the original roasting pan on top of the stove and add the chicken broth, stirring to dissolve the brown particles that cling to the bottom of the pan. Bring to the boil. Strain into a pan.

12. Blend the sugar and vinegar in a very small saucepan and cook, watching carefully, until large bubbles form on the surface. Continue cooking until the syrup is slightly caramelized. Add the sauce from the roasting pan. Bring to the boil.

13. Blend the cornstarch and water and stir it into the sauce.

14. Just before serving, add the zest and Grand Marnier to the sauce. Drain the orange sections and add them. Cook, stirring gently, just until sections are thoroughly hot. Do not break them in cooking and do not overcook or they will become mushy.

15. Serve the duck cut into quarters or carved. Pour a little of the sauce over the duck and serve the remainder separately.

Yield: 4 servings.

---

4 whole seedless oranges

One 4- to 5-pound duckling

Salt and freshly ground pepper to taste

¾ cup fresh or canned chicken broth

¼ cup sugar

¼ cup red wine vinegar

1 teaspoon cornstarch

1 tablespoon water

2 tablespoons Grand Marnier

DUCK IN RED WINE SAUCE

2 oven-ready ducks, 5 to
  6 pounds each
  Salt and freshly ground
  pepper to taste
1 tablespoon butter
⅓ cup coarsely chopped
  shallots
¾ cup coarsely chopped
  onion
½ bay leaf
½ garlic clove
2 parsley sprigs
¼ cup flour
1 bottle (3 cups) dry red
  wine, preferably
  Burgundy
1 cup fresh or canned
  chicken broth

1. Preheat the oven to 450 degrees.

2. Remove and discard the inner fat from the ducks. Sprinkle the ducks inside and out with the salt and pepper.

3. Arrange the ducks back side down in a roasting pan (a rack is not necessary) and bake for 30 minutes. Remove the ducks and pour off the fat from the pan. Return the ducks to the oven and bake for 30 minutes longer. The ducks should now be fairly crisp and free of skin fat. If they are not, return to the oven for 10 minutes or so.

4. Remove the ducks from the oven and, when they are cool enough to handle, carve them as follows: Carve away and separate the legs and thighs. Carve on either side of the breast bone, carving the breast halves in whole pieces and leaving the main wing bone attached. Cut off and reserve the second joint and wing tip from the wing bone. Trim off and discard any excess fat but leave the skin intact.

5. As the ducks are carved, arrange the pieces, skin side up, in one layer in a heavy casserole. Cover with a round of wax paper, then with the casserole lid, and set aside.

6. Chop the neck and carcass and other reserved bones of the ducks. Set aside. Discard any excess fat.

7. Heat the butter in a deep, heavy saucepan and add the shallots, onion, bay leaf, garlic, and parsley. Cook, stirring frequently, until the vegetables start to take on color. Add the chopped duck bones and cook, stirring often, for about 10 minutes. Sprinkle the vegetables and bones with flour and stir until the bones are well coated. Add the wine and broth and stir well. Bring to the boil and add salt and pepper to taste. Cook, uncovered, for about 1 hour. Strain the sauce over the duck pieces. Press to extract juices from the solids. Discard the solids.

8. Cover the casserole and simmer gently for about 30 minutes. Serve, if desired, with steamed wild rice (see recipe page 634).

Yield: About 8 servings.

CHARCOAL-GRILLED DUCK

In this method of grilling duck, the breast is cut away in two neat, flat pieces without skin or bone. The legs and thighs are left more or less intact with skin on and bones in. The legs and thighs are cooked first because they require the longest cooking, about 30 minutes.

1. Place the duck back side down on a flat surface. Rub a sharp knife such as a boning knife along the breast bone, cutting through the skin and down to the bone. Carefully run the knife between the skin and the meat, pulling the skin with the fingers to expose the smooth breast meat. Cut off and discard the skin. Now, carefully run the knife between the breast meat and the carcass, using the fingers as necessary. Remove the two pieces of breast meat.

2. Cut or carve off the two thighs, leaving the legs attached. Use the carcass for another purpose such as soup. Place the legs and thighs on a flat surface, skin side down, and carefully cut away the excessive peripheral skin fat that borders the thighs.

3. Sever the bone joint between the legs and thighs. This will facilitate cooking, but do not cut the legs and thighs in two.

4. Chop together the bay leaf, salt, pepper, and thyme, chopping until the bay leaf is quite fine. Rub this mixture on the legs and thighs and over the breast and giblets. Brush all with the oil.

5. Arrange the breast pieces, ends touching, in a flat dish. Cover with giblets and neatly arrange the legs and thighs skin side up over all.

6. Prepare a charcoal grill and have it ready. The coals must be white hot but not too plentiful or the meat will cook too fast. Arrange the grill that will hold the duck about 6 inches above the bed of coals. Arrange the giblets on a skewer and add them to the grill.

7. Place the legs and thighs skin side down on the grill. Grill the legs and thighs, turning as often as necessary, until the skin is crisp and the flesh is cooked. If necessary, brush the food with a little more oil as it cooks. Grill the giblets until done, turning as often as necessary. About 5 minutes before these foods are done, add the breast meat and cook for 1 or 2 minutes to a side, until done. Ideally, the breast meat should be served a bit rare.

8. Transfer the pieces to a serving platter. Slice the breast meat on the bias and cut the legs and thighs in half where they join.

9. Melt the butter and cook the shallots for about 30 seconds. Add the vinegar and cook until almost evaporated. Pour over the duck pieces. Sprinkle with chopped parsley and serve immediately.

Yield: 2 to 4 servings.

1 whole, cleaned, 4½- to 5-pound duck with giblets
½ bay leaf
  Salt and freshly ground pepper to taste
¼ teaspoon dried thyme
1 tablespoon peanut, vegetable, or corn oil
1 tablespoon butter
1 teaspoon minced shallots
1 tablespoon raspberry vinegar
1 teaspoon finely chopped parsley

VIETNAMESE GRILLED LEMON DUCK

One 4½- to 5½-pound
duck, cut into quarters

4 scallions, trimmed and
finely chopped

1 teaspoon grated fresh
ginger

2 teaspoons powdered
turmeric

2 tablespoons dark soy
sauce

1 teaspoon sugar

Salt and freshly ground
pepper to taste

½ teaspoon grated lemon
rind

Lemon wedges

Nuoc mam sauce (see
recipe page 795)

1. Quarter the duck or have it quartered. If the backbone is removed it will lie flatter on the grill. It will also cook more evenly if the wing tip and second wing bone are removed. Use a sharp knife and trim away all peripheral and excess fat.

2. Combine the scallions, ginger, turmeric, soy sauce, sugar, salt, pepper, and lemon rind. Rub the mixture into the duck. Let stand for 4 hours or so, turning the duck in the marinade.

3. Meanwhile, prepare a charcoal fire. When the fire is ready, place the duck fat side down. Cook about 1 hour, turning the duck frequently and as necessary until it is evenly cooked and the skin is crisp. Serve with lemon wedges. Serve individual small bowls of nuoc mam sauce on the side as a dip for the duck.

Yield: 4 servings.

RED-COOKED DUCK

Red-cooked foods in Chinese cuisine are simmered in dark soy sauce with seasonings, which gives them a reddish-brown color. Duck cooked this way is delicious as is, or it can be used in the many flavor duck salad (see recipe page 711).

1. Preheat the oven to 400 degrees.

2. Cut away and discard the peripheral fat and skin from the duck. That is to say, the fat from the cavity, the excess skin around the neck and cavity opening, and so on.

3. Brush the duck all over with 1 tablespoon of the dark soy sauce. Place on a rack breast side up and roast for 30 minutes.

4. Meanwhile, in a kettle combine the remaining dark soy sauce, the light soy sauce, cold water, sherry, rock sugar, ginger, whole scallions, star anise, and tangerine peel. Set aside.

5. Remove the duck from the roasting pan and add it breast side down to the sauce. Bring the sauce to the boil, cover, lower the heat, and simmer for 30 minutes.

6. Turn the duck in the sauce. Cover and return to the boil. Simmer for 30 minutes. Carve the duck and serve hot or cold.

Yield: 2 to 4 servings.

Note: The sauce in which the duck is cooked may be kept indefinitely if it is strained and reheated, adding more ingredients as necessary to maintain the volume and flavor. You may cook more duck or other poultry, beef, or pork in the sauce as you desire. Keep the strained sauce tightly covered and refrigerated until ready to use.

One 5- to 6-pound duck
1 tablespoon plus ½ cup dark soy sauce
¼ cup light soy sauce
4 cups cold water
¼ cup dry sherry
2 ounces (about ¼ cup when cracked) Chinese rock sugar
2 slices fresh ginger
2 whole scallions
1 whole star anise
1 piece dried tangerine or orange peel

BRAISED DUCK WITH LEEKS

One 5-pound duck,
preferably with head
left on, available in
Chinese poultry
markets

6 tablespoons dark soy
sauce

6 cups peanut, vegetable,
or corn oil

6 tablespoons dry sherry

6 cups water

1 tablespoon plus
1 teaspoon salt

2 tablespoons plus
1 teaspoon sugar

6 leeks

1. Remove and discard any cavity fat from the duck. Cut off the wing tips but leave the main wing bone and second joint intact.

2. Slice the skin of the duck from head to tail. Using a sharp cleaver, hack the duck's backbone from head to tail to open up the inside of the duck.

3. Open up the duck's inside, placing it skin side down on a flat surface. Trim and pull away the dark pulpy matter, veins, and so on. Rinse the duck and drain. Pat dry.

4. Place the duck skin side up and, using a small trussing needle, skewer the skin of the tail section together neatly and firmly. Brush the duck skin all over with 3 tablespoons dark soy sauce. If the head is still on, loop a long, heavy string around the neck to facilitate turning it in hot oil.

5. Heat the oil in a wok or other utensil large enough to hold the duck with the body flattened. Add the duck skin side down and cook over high heat for about 3 minutes. Turn, spooning oil over the head so that it cooks, too. Cook for 3 minutes longer and remove. Pour out the oil and wipe out the wok. Reserve the oil. Return the duck to the wok skin side up. Add the sherry. Turn the duck skin side down and add 2 tablespoons of dark soy sauce and 6 cups of water. Add 1 tablespoon of the salt and 2 tablespoons of the sugar. Cover and cook over low heat for about 45 minutes. Turn the duck and cook 1 hour. (The duck may be cooked to this point and left to stand.)

6. Meanwhile, trim off the end of the leeks. Cut off the tops of the leeks but leave leeks 7 or 8 inches long. Split leeks in half and rinse well under cold water. A spoonful of salt added to the water helps in cleaning. Drain the leeks.

7. Heat reserved oil for deep-fat frying in a wok or kettle and add the leeks. Cook for about 4 minutes. Remove and drain.

8. About half an hour before serving, reheat the duck and add the leeks. Cover and cook for 15 minutes.

9. Remove the duck to a platter skin side up and remove the string from the neck. Cover the duck with the leeks. Add the remaining tablespoon of dark soy sauce, the remaining teaspoon of salt, and the remaining teaspoon of sugar to the sauce and boil down until syrupy. Pour it over the duck and serve hot.

Yield: 8 servings with other Chinese dishes.

SLICED DUCK WITH YOUNG GINGERROOT

1. Using a sharp knife, carefully remove and discard the skin from the duck. Bone the duck, or have your butcher bone it, reserving the bones, if desired, for soup. To facilitate slicing, the duck meat may be partly frozen. In any event, cut the duck meat into very thin slices, about 3 cups. To this, add ½ teaspoon of the salt and 4 teaspoons of the cornstarch and blend well.

2. Prepare the water chestnuts, sweet pepper, and scallions and set aside.

3. Rinse off the ginger and thinly slice. There should be about ⅔ cup. Set aside.

4. Scrape the asparagus spears, if used, leaving the tips intact. Drop the spears into boiling water for about 50 seconds. Drain and immediately run under cold water to crisp. Drain thoroughly.

5. Heat 2 cups of the oil in a wok or skillet and add the asparagus. Cook for about 45 seconds and drain completely. Reserve the oil. Add ½ cup of the chicken broth to the wok and the asparagus. Cook for about 10 seconds and sprinkle with the remaining salt. Drain and transfer to a platter.

6. Combine the sherry, the remaining cornstarch blended with the water, the soy sauce, vinegar, sesame oil, and the remaining ¼ cup of chicken broth. Set aside.

7. Heat the remaining oil, including reserved oil, in a wok or skillet and add the water chestnuts. Cook for about 10 seconds and add the duck, stirring and tossing constantly. Cook for about 30 seconds. Add the sweet red pepper and ginger pieces and cook, stirring, for about 10 seconds. Drain completely.

8. To the wok add 2 teaspoons of hot pepper oil and add the scallions and fresh ginger. Add the duck mixture and the vinegar mixture, stirring rapidly. Cook until piping hot and until the duck pieces are thoroughly coated. Serve on the platter with the asparagus spears as a garnish.

Yield: 4 to 8 servings.

One 4- to 5-pound duck, the smaller the better

1 teaspoon salt

1 tablespoon plus 4 teaspoons cornstarch

6 water chestnuts, sliced, about 1½ cups

1 sweet red pepper, cored, seeded, and cut into ½-inch cubes, about ½ cup

2 scallions, trimmed and cut into ½-inch lengths, about ½ cup

5 pieces bottled young gingerroot in syrup, available in 1-pound jars in Chinese markets

15 whole fresh asparagus spears for garnish, optional

4 cups peanut, vegetable, or corn oil

¾ cup fresh or canned chicken broth

2 tablespoons dry sherry

2 tablespoons water

2 tablespoons soy sauce

½ teaspoon white vinegar

½ teaspoon sesame oil

1 tablespoon finely chopped fresh ginger

2 teaspoons hot pepper or chili oil, available in bottles in Chinese markets

Roast Muscovy Duck

One 4-pound Muscovy
duck

Salt and freshly ground
pepper to taste

1 teaspoon peanut oil

⅓ cup coarsely chopped
celery

⅓ cup coarsely chopped
onion

½ cup coarsely chopped
carrot

½ bay leaf

½ teaspoon dried thyme

1 garlic clove, peeled and
crushed

⅓ cup dry white wine

½ cup chicken broth

2 tablespoons butter

There are some foods that are not readily available in supermarkets throughout the country, though they have enormous appeal in areas where they can be found. This is increasingly true of the Muscovy duck.

These ducks arrive at markets in late fall and are available throughout the winter, frequently at local poultry farms. Unlike most domestically raised birds, they should not be cooked until they are well done. They should be cooked to a rare or medium-rare state. Otherwise, the meat tends to become dry.

The choicest part of the Muscovy duck, which has a gamier flavor than regular duckling, is the breast. When the duck is done, transfer it to a carving board and neatly carve away half of its breast. Place the breast half skin side up on the board and cut it slightly on the bias, as with London broil. The thighs may be carved off the bone into thin slices. The thighs and legs tend to be a trifle tough.

1. Preheat the oven to 475 degrees.

2. Cut off and reserve the wing tips and second wing joint of the duck. Leave the main wing bone intact. Remove the fat from inside the duck and rub it all over the duck.

3. Sprinkle the duck inside and out with the salt and pepper. Brush the duck with the oil.

4. Arrange the duck breast side up in a roasting pan. Add the cut-off wing bones, gizzard, and cavity fat. Bake for 30 minutes and pour off the fat from the roasting pan. Return the duck to the oven and scatter the celery, onion, carrot, bay leaf, thyme, and garlic around the duck. Bake for 15 minutes longer if you wish the duck to be medium rare.

5. Transfer the duck to a warm platter. Pour off the fat from the roasting pan, leaving the vegetables in the pan. Place the pan on the stove and cook the vegetables briefly, stirring. Add the wine and boil for 1 minute.

6. Add the broth and accumulated cavity drippings from the duck and cook, stirring, for about 5 minutes. Strain the broth and solids, pushing the solids with the back of a spoon to extract as much liquid as possible.

7. Melt the butter in a small saucepan, swirling it around until it takes on a nice hazelnut color. Do not burn. Pour the butter over the duck. Carve and serve with the hot pan sauce.

Yield: 2 to 4 servings.

Roast Goose with Fruit Stuffing

1. Preheat the oven to 400 degrees.

2. Fill the cavity of the goose with the stuffing. Truss the goose and sprinkle it all over with the salt and pepper.

3. Place the goose breast side up in a shallow roasting pan. Place it in the oven and bake for 1 hour, basting occasionally.

4. Pour off the fat from the roasting pan and scatter the onion, celery, carrots, garlic, and bay leaf around the goose. Add the neck and cook for 1 hour. Baste often. At the end of 2 hours of cooking time, or before if the goose becomes too brown, cover with foil.

5. Continue roasting for 1 hour, a total of 3 hours. Remove the goose to a warm platter. Pour off the fat from the roasting pan and add the cup of water, stirring to dissolve the brown particles on the bottom and around the sides of the pan. Strain the pan liquid and serve as a sauce.

6. Remove and discard the trussing string from the goose. Carve the goose and serve.

Yield: 10 or more servings.

One 19-pound goose

Fruit stuffing (see following recipe)

Salt and freshly ground pepper to taste

1 cup coarsely chopped onion

1 cup coarsely chopped celery

¾ cup coarsely chopped carrots

1 whole garlic clove, unpeeled

1 bay leaf

1 cup water

FRUIT STUFFING FOR GOOSE

Goose gizzard, liver, and heart

3 tablespoons butter

2 cups finely chopped celery

2½ cups finely chopped onions

1 garlic clove, finely chopped

1 cup dry white wine

1 tablespoon chopped sage

¼ teaspoon chopped thyme

1 bay leaf

1 cup finely chopped parsley

One 12-ounce package pitted prunes, chopped

6 cups thin wedges peeled, seeded apples

2 cups coarse fresh bread crumbs

Salt and freshly ground pepper to taste

2 egg yolks, lightly beaten

1. Trim off and discard the tough outer coating of the gizzard. Pick over the liver and remove the veins. Put the gizzard, liver, and heart pieces into the container of a food processor or blender and blend thoroughly.

2. Heat the butter in a large heavy skillet and add the celery and onions. Cook until wilted and add the puréed liver mixture. Stir and add the garlic, wine, sage, thyme, bay leaf, and parsley. Cook, stirring, for about 5 minutes. Add the remaining ingredients and blend well with the hands.

PRESERVED GOOSE

One of the glories of the French table is a dish that has received little notice in America. Except for some rare and special occasions, it is almost nonexistent in the nation's French restaurants. Confit d'oie, or preserved goose, is a delicacy of consummate goodness that is easily, if a trifle expensively, made. The goose is cut into large pieces, seasoned, and marinated overnight. The following morning it is cooked in a boiling bath of goose fat and lard. The goose is then cooled and stored for up to a year.

Those Americans who may be conversant with the dish know it best as the classic ingredient for some of the traditional cassoulets of France. It is an essential taste that is often missing in cassoulets in this country, but one that is well worth the effort.

But preserved goose, sliced and cooked until it is crisp and golden brown and served with thin sliced potatoes cooked in hot goose fat, is paradise enough.

One 12- to 14-pound oven-ready goose
Salt and freshly ground pepper to taste
1 bay leaf
½ teaspoon dried thyme
½ teaspoon saltpeter, available in drugstores
3 pounds lard (see note)

1. Cut off and discard the wing tips of the goose. Cut off and reserve the second wing joints. Cut or pull way any solid goose fat and reserve it.

2. Carefully cut partway through the thigh and leg joints of the goose, leaving each leg and thigh attached.

3. Carefully bone away the breast of the goose in two sections, left and right, but leaving the main wing bone attached and unboned. Reserve the gizzard.

4. Use the bony carcass of the goose for making soup. Cut off and reserve any additional pieces or scraps of goose skin.

5. Sprinkle the goose pieces—the leg and thigh pieces, the breast halves, and the second wing joints—with the salt and pepper, using a fairly generous amount of salt. Rub it in on all sides.

6. Place the bay leaf on a flat surface. Using a sharp heavy knife, finely chop it. Add the thyme and chop it. Add the saltpeter. Rub the mixture into the goose pieces on all sides. Pack the pieces into a mixing bowl or other utensil. Cover closely and refrigerate for 24 hours.

7. Heat one or two large, heavy, deep skillets, flameproof casseroles, or Dutch ovens and add the breast and thigh pieces skin side down in one layer. Add the second wing joints, gizzard, and the reserved goose fat and the skin. Add the lard and bring to a boil. The goose will be cooked in fat without any additional liquid. The goose pieces must be totally immersed in fat when the fat melts. Cover and cook for 2 hours.

8. Using a two-pronged fork, carefully remove the goose pieces (thighs with legs, breast halves, and second wing joints). Reserve the cooking fat.

9. Arrange equal portions of the goose pieces in two earthenware terrines or casseroles. The pieces should be arranged as compactly as possible.

10. Strain enough of the cooking fat over both terrines so that the goose parts are completely submerged in fat. If the goose pieces are not completely covered, it will be necessary to add more lard and pour it over. Let stand until thoroughly cool. Refrigerate. Cover closely. Properly refrigerated or stored in a cold, dry place, preserved goose should keep for weeks and even months.

Yield: 1 preserved goose.

Note: It is a minor point, but it would be preferable if all goose fat rather than lard were used for cooking the goose. For example, if you were cooking three geese (roasting or whatever) during the winter season, the extra fat in each goose could be reserved and frozen until ready to make the confit d'oie.

ROAST CAPON WITH NUT STUFFING

1. Preheat the oven to 425 degrees.

2. Remove the inner fat from the cavity of the capon. Set aside with the liver, neck, gizzard, and heart.

3. Place the pecans or walnuts on a baking dish and bake until crisp. Take care not to burn them. Remove and let cool.

4. Cut or chop the mushrooms into very small dice.

5. Cut both the capon liver and chicken livers into small pieces.

6. Heat the butter and add the finely chopped onion. Cook until wilted and add the minced garlic and mushrooms. Cook briefly, stirring, until the mushrooms give up their liquid. Continue cooking until the liquid evaporates. Add the chopped livers, chopped thyme, parsley, salt, and pepper.

7. Cook until the liver changes color. Add the sausage meat, stirring to break up the sausage with the side of a spoon. Add the eggs and bread crumbs and blend well. Crumble the nuts and add them. Cool.

8. Stuff the capon both in the cavity and in the neck and truss.

9. Rub the roasting pan with reserved capon fat and add the capon breast side up. Scatter the coarsely chopped onion, celery, carrots, garlic clove, bay leaf, and thyme sprigs around it. Add the capon neck, gizzard, and heart. Do not add liquid. Sprinkle the capon with salt and pepper to taste.

10. Place the pan, uncovered, in the oven and bake for 45 minutes, basting often. Cover loosely with a large sheet of aluminum foil. Reduce the oven heat to 400 degrees and continue cooking for 45 minutes, basting often.

11. Reduce the oven heat to 375 degrees. Remove the foil or let it remain, depending on the brownness of the bird. Continue roasting and basting for about 1 hour longer. The total cooking time is approximately 20 minutes per pound. When the capon has cooked for about 2 hours, carefully pour off all the fat from the roasting pan. Add the chicken broth. Continue cooking until done.

12. Remove the capon and strain the liquid from the pan into a saucepan. Reduce slightly and serve hot with the carved capon.

Yield: 8 to 12 servings.

One 8- to 10-pound capon, cleaned weight

1 cup pecans or walnuts

½ pound fresh mushrooms

½ pound chicken livers

2 tablespoons butter

1 cup finely chopped onion

2 garlic cloves, finely minced

2 teaspoons chopped fresh thyme, or 1 teaspoon dried

½ cup coarsely chopped parsley

Salt and freshly ground pepper to taste

1 pound sausage meat

2 eggs

2 cups bread crumbs

¾ cup coarsely chopped onion

¾ cup coarsely chopped celery

½ cup coarsely chopped carrots

1 whole garlic clove

½ bay leaf

2 fresh thyme sprigs, or ½ teaspoon dried

1 cup fresh or canned chicken broth

QUAIL IN ESCABECHE

12 quail or 3 Cornish hens
6 tablespoons olive oil
  (see note)
2 medium-size onions,
  coarsely chopped
12 garlic cloves, peeled
2 tablespoons finely
  chopped shallots
4 carrots, scraped and
  cut into ⅛-inch rounds
1 peeled potato, cooked
  in water for about
  5 minutes and drained
5 bay leaves
3 fresh parsley sprigs
2 teaspoon dried thyme
  Salt to taste
20 whole black
  peppercorns
½ celery stalk with leaves
  Pinch of saffron
¾ cup red wine vinegar
3 cups dry white wine
¾ cup chicken broth,
  skimmed of all fat
1 lemon, thinly sliced
2 tablespoons finely
  chopped parsley

1. Truss the quail or have them trussed. If Cornish hens are used, cut them in half or have them split.

2. Heat the oil in a large shallow casserole. Add the birds and cook over moderate heat until well browned on all sides. Transfer the birds to a platter.

3. To the casserole add the onions, garlic, shallots, and carrots. Quarter the potato and add it. Cook, stirring, until the onions are wilted.

4. Add the bay leaves, parsley sprigs, thyme, salt, peppercorns, celery, and saffron. Stir.

5. Add the vinegar, wine, and broth. (Use only ½ cup vinegar if the Cornish hens are used.)

6. Return the birds to the casserole. Cover and simmer for 45 minutes. Transfer the birds to a platter.

7. Cook down the liquid in the casserole for about 5 minutes. When ready, there should be enough liquid to cover the birds.

8. Pour the sauce into a deep casserole, preferably made of earthenware. Add the birds. Ideally, they should be covered with sauce.

9. Cover the casserole and refrigerate for 3 or 4 days. Place the birds and the marinade in a shallow serving dish. Garnish with lemon slices and chopped parsley.

Yield: 6 servings.

Note: In Spain it is customary to prepare the oil before cooking the quail. This is done by heating the oil with a piece of lemon rind until the rind blackens. The oil is cooled immediately by adding a peeled raw potato to it.

CHARCOAL-GRILLED STUFFED QUAIL

The following is a recipe demonstrated for me by a young master chef from Chapel Hill, North Carolina—Bill Neal, owner and chief cook of the Crook's Corner Restaurant. I would label it nouveau Southern. It is excellent.

1. Preheat a charcoal grill until white ash forms on top of the coals.

2. Split each quail neatly along the backbone. Set aside.

3. Put the bacon or salt pork and garlic on a flat surface and chop until almost a paste. Put the mixture in a mixing bowl and add the bread crumbs, carrot, celery, basil, parsley, thyme, salt, and pepper. Blend thoroughly with the fingers.

4. By hand, carefully separate a portion of the breast meat from the bone to form a small pocket. Push equal portions of the stuffing into the cavities. Push any additional stuffing under the skin of the birds, without breaking the skin. Brush the birds all over with bacon fat or oil.

5. Place the quail skin side down on the grill and cook until nicely browned on one side, 4 to 5 minutes. Turn and press the outer portions together to give the bodies more of their original shape. Let cook for 4 to 5 minutes on the second side, or until the desired doneness.

Yield: 4 to 8 servings.

8 cleaned quail (¼ pound each)

⅛ pound streaky bacon or salt pork, cut into small cubes (about ½ cup)

1 tablespoon finely chopped garlic

2½ tablespoons fine dry bread crumbs

2½ tablespoons finely diced carrot

2½ tablespoons finely diced celery

1 tablespoon finely chopped fresh basil

1 tablespoon finely chopped parsley

½ teaspoon finely chopped fresh thyme, or ¼ teaspoon dried

Salt and freshly ground pepper to taste

2 tablespoons bacon fat or corn oil

ROAST PHEASANT WITH SOUR CREAM SAUCE

1 plucked, cleaned, ready-to-cook pheasant, about 2½ pounds

Salt and freshly ground pepper to taste

2 tablespoons butter

⅓ cup finely chopped onion

½ cup dry white wine

½ cup heavy cream

½ cup sour cream

1. Preheat the oven to 425 degrees.

2. Truss the pheasant and sprinkle it with the salt and pepper. Arrange it on one side in a roasting pan. Split the gizzard in half. Put the gizzard and heart around the bird. Place in the oven and bake for 15 minutes, basting occasionally. Turn the bird to the other side and continue baking and basting with the butter for about 15 minutes.

3. Turn the pheasant on its back and reduce the oven heat to 400 degrees. Continue roasting and basting for about 10 minutes. Add the liver and continue roasting and basting for about 10 minutes longer.

4. Transfer the pheasant to a serving dish. Pour the fat from the pan. Add the onion and stir until wilted. Add the wine and stir to dissolve the brown particles that cling to the bottom and sides of the pan. Let most of the wine evaporate and add the heavy cream. Cook, stirring, until the cream is reduced by half. Turn off the heat and stir in the sour cream. Bring to the boil, stirring until smooth. Pour any liquid that has accumulated in the cavity of the bird into the sauce. Add salt and pepper to taste. Strain the sauce, using a fine sieve.

5. Untruss and carve the pheasant and serve with the sauce.

Yield: 4 servings.

PHEASANT IN WINE SAUCE

1. Cut the pheasant as follows: Separate the legs from the thighs; split the breasts in half; bone the breast halves, but leave the main wing bone attached. Reserve all the bones.

2. Heat the oil in a heavy skillet and add the reserved bones. Cook, stirring frequently, until golden brown on all sides, about 30 minutes. Pour off the fat.

3. Add the chopped carrot, onion, celery, mushrooms, juniper berries, bay leaves, and shallots. Cook, stirring often, for about 15 minutes. Add half the wine, the chicken broth, water, salt, and pepper. Cover and cook for 1 hour.

4. In another heavy skillet, heat 4 tablespoons of the butter and add the meaty pheasant pieces skin side down. Cook, turning as necessary, until golden brown all over. Pour the Cognac over the pheasant pieces and ignite it.

5. Strain the bone and wine sauce, pushing the solids with the back of a wooden spoon to extract as much liquid as possible. Discard the solids. Add the sauce to the pheasant pieces. Add the remaining wine and partly cover. Simmer for about 45 minutes if the pheasant are young and tender. Cook longer if necessary.

6. If desired, remove the pheasant and strain the sauce again. Bring the sauce to the boil. Blend the remaining 2 tablespoons of butter with the flour and add it gradually to the sauce, stirring constantly. Return the pheasant to the sauce and serve hot.

Yield: 8 to 12 servings.

- 4 pheasant, 1¾ to 2 pound each
- 2 tablespoons peanut, vegetable, or corn oil
- ½ cup chopped carrot
- ¾ cup chopped onion
- ½ cup chopped celery
- 1 cup chopped mushrooms
- 12 juniper berries, crushed
- 2 bay leaves
- 4 shallots, thinly sliced
- 3 cups dry Burgundy wine
- 2 cups fresh or canned chicken broth
- 4 cups water
- Salt and freshly ground pepper
- 6 tablespoons butter
- ½ cup Cognac
- 2 tablespoons flour

SQUAB WITH ENDIVES

16 firm, unblemished
   endives, about
   3 pounds

 6 tablespoons butter

   Salt and freshly ground
   pepper to taste

¼ cup sugar

 4 fresh cleaned squabs,
   about 1 pound each

½ cup water

Squabs, small pigeons that have never flown, are one of our favorite foods. They have a slightly gamier taste than other domestic fowl, and it is customary in most European countries to serve them slightly underdone. The squab served on a bed of endives is the creation of Alain Senderens, a distinguished restaurant owner and chef in Paris.

1. Trim off the ends of the endives and separate the leaves.

2. Bring enough water to the boil to cover the endive leaves when they are added. Add the endives, cover, and cook exactly 4 minutes. Drain well.

3. Melt 4 tablespoons of the butter in a large, heavy skillet and, when it is very hot, add the endives. Sprinkle with the salt, pepper, and sugar. Cook over high heat, stirring and shaking the skillet so that the leaves cook evenly all over. The liquid will start to evaporate and the vegetable will become amber colored. Cook for about 20 minutes, or until the endives are caramel colored all over. Do not burn. Drain in a colander.

4. Meanwhile, preheat the oven to 525 degrees.

5. Cut off the wing tips and the second wing joints of each squab. Set these pieces aside.

6. Melt the remaining 2 tablespoons of butter in a heavy skillet large enough to hold the squabs in one layer without crowding.

7. Add the squabs and brown them on all sides, turning them often so that they brown evenly. Add the wing tips and second wing joints. Place in the oven and reduce the oven temperature to 425 degrees. Bake for 25 to 30 minutes. The squabs will be slightly undercooked. Transfer the squabs to a warm platter. Pour off the fat from the skillet. Set the skillet aside.

8. Spoon equal portions of the endives on each of four hot plates.

9. Carefully carve away the breast and leg meat from each side of the carcasses. Save the carcasses. Arrange 2 squab halves on each bed of endive.

10. Chop the carcasses into small pieces with a heavy cleaver. Add these pieces to the skillet and cook over moderately high heat until well browned. Add the water and cook down to about ¼ cup. Pour the liquid over the squabs and serve.

Yield: 4 servings.

Squab with Mushrooms and Tomatoes

1. Soak the mushrooms in cold water to cover for 1 hour or longer.
2. Sprinkle the squab halves with the salt and pepper. Set aside and reserve the squab livers.
3. Heat all but 2 tablespoons of the oil in a large heavy skillet and add the squab split side down. Brown over high heat, turning, and add the garlic, onion, and rosemary. Add the wine, tomatoes, and salt and pepper to taste. Squeeze the black mushrooms to extract most of the moisture and add them.
4. In another skillet, heat the remaining 2 tablespoons of oil and cook the fresh mushrooms until wilted. Add them to the squab and cook for 5 minutes.
5. Blend the tomato paste with the water and add it. Cover closely and cook for 30 minutes. Add the squab livers and continue cooking for about half an hour. Serve with hot polenta.

Yield: 8 servings.

8 or 10 pieces dried black mushrooms, preferably imported Italian mushrooms

4 fresh, cleaned squabs, split in half

Salt and freshly ground pepper to taste

½ cup olive oil

1 garlic clove, thinly sliced

1 cup finely chopped onion

1 teaspoon dried rosemary

½ cup dry red wine

2 cups crushed fresh or canned tomatoes

1 cup thinly sliced mushrooms

¼ cup tomato paste

⅓ cup water

STUFFED SQUAB DERBY

8 squabs, each about ¾ pound cleaned weight

5 tablespoons butter

8 squab livers, each cut in half

2 cups cooked rice

1¼ ounces pure foie gras, available in tins in fine specialty food markets

1 tablespoon chopped truffles

Salt and freshly ground pepper to taste

3 tablespoons Cognac

1½ cups brown sauce for squab (see following recipe)

8 truffle slices

What would you command if you were allowed one last great meal on this earth? We have our answer. The menu would move blissfully from caviar with vodka to, in due course, a fine fat squab stuffed with truffles and foie gras. It would end with an elegant grapefruit ice. Now, preferences in food are highly subjective and there may be those who would question our choice of squab. But to our minds, squab is one of the most sumptuous of birds and for the last go-round at table we would not willingly accept a substitute.

1. The squabs should be cleaned and ready for roasting, but reserve the necks, feet, and gizzards for the brown sauce. Reserve the livers for the stuffing.

2. Preheat the oven to 425 degrees.

3. Heat 1 tablespoon of the butter in a small skillet and add the livers. Cook over high heat, shaking the skillet and stirring, about 1 minute. The livers must cook quickly or they will be tough. Add the livers to the rice.

4. Cube the foie gras. Add the foie gras and chopped truffles to the rice and stir to blend well.

5. Sprinkle the inside of the squabs with the salt and pepper and stuff them with the rice mixture. Truss the squabs. Sprinkle with salt and pepper.

6. Melt 3 tablespoons of butter in a heavy roasting pan large enough to hold the squabs. Turn the squabs in the butter until coated on all sides. Place the squabs on their sides and bake for 15 minutes. Baste often. Turn onto their other sides and bake for 15 minutes, basting frequently. Place squabs on their backs and continue roasting and basting for another 10 to 15 minutes. Remove to a warm platter and cover with foil.

7. Skim off all fat from the roasting pan, leaving the squab drippings. Add 2 tablespoons Cognac and ignite it. Pour in the brown sauce and stir to blend. Put the sauce through a fine sieve and bring it to the boil. Swirl in the remaining tablespoon of butter. Add the remaining Cognac and serve piping hot with the squab. Garnish each squab with a truffle slice before serving.

Yield: 8 servings.

1. Heat the oil in a small heavy saucepan and add the necks, feet, and gizzards. Sprinkle with the salt and pepper. Cook, stirring frequently, until the parts are nicely browned all over. Drain.

2. Return the squab pieces to the saucepan and add the celery, onion, carrots, thyme, parsley, and bay leaf. Continue cooking, stirring occasionally, for about 5 minutes.

3. Sprinkle with the flour and stir until all the pieces are well coated. Cook, stirring occasionally, for about 5 minutes. Add the remaining ingredients and stir rapidly until blended. Bring to the boil and simmer, uncovered, for 1½ hours. Put the sauce through a fine sieve, pressing the solids with the back of a wooden spoon to extract as much of the liquid as possible. Discard the solids. Put the sauce in a small saucepan and simmer, uncovered, for about 30 minutes longer.

Yield: 1½ cups.

Note: If the squabs have been trimmed, bony chicken pieces such as necks may be substituted.

BROWN SAUCE FOR SQUAB

1 tablespoon oil

Necks, feet, and gizzards from 8 squabs (see note)

Salt and freshly ground pepper to taste

¼ cup chopped celery

½ cup chopped onion

½ cup chopped carrots

3 sprigs fresh thyme, or ½ teaspoon dried

3 parsley sprigs

½ bay leaf

2 tablespoons flour

½ cup dry white wine

1 cup fresh or canned chicken broth

1 cup water

1 tablespoon tomato paste

B'steeya or Pastilla (Moroccan Squab or Poultry Pie)

THE SQUAB OR GAME HENS:

- 5 squabs or 4 Cornish hens
  Salt and freshly ground pepper to taste
- 2 tablespoons butter
- 2 cups chopped onion
- 1 large garlic clove, unpeeled but crushed
- 1½ teaspoons turmeric
- ½ teaspoon saffron stems
- 5 small slices fresh ginger
- 1 teaspoon crushed coriander seeds
- 1 small hot dried red pepper
- 6 fresh parsley sprigs
- 12 peppercorns, crushed
- 2 cinnamon sticks, each about 2 inches long
- 4 cups water

THE FILLING:

- 1 cup blanched almonds
- 2 tablespoons peanut, vegetable, or corn oil
- 1½ tablespoons confectioners' sugar
- ½ teaspoon ground cinnamon

THE EGG MIXTURE:

- 8 large eggs
- ¼ cup lemon juice
- 2 tablespoons butter

THE FINAL ASSEMBLY:

- 18 to 24 squares (see note) phyllo pastry
- 1 cup clarified butter (see following instructions)
- 3 tablespoons confectioners' sugar

One of the great main courses of the world is this buttery, fragile-crusted pigeon pie that comes out of Morocco. It is a curious dish but infinitely gratifying. Curious, because it contains, in addition to shredded cooked flesh of squab (Cornish hens make an admirable substitute), ground almonds, confectioners' sugar, and cinnamon.

I first tasted the dish in 1942 when I was stationed as a third-class petty officer aboard the U.S.S. *Augusta* in the harbor of Casablanca. I timidly requested to stay with the admiral in charge of the amphibious forces and, a day or so after the cease-fire, I found myself in a place of pure enchantment. I fell in love with Morocco and, naturally, Moroccan cooking.

Years later, we recreated the dish in our kitchen. Although the recipe may seem long, it isn't complicated. And it is well worth the effort.

1. Rub the squabs or Cornish hens inside and out with the salt and pepper. Heat the butter in a large casserole or Dutch oven and brown the squabs lightly on all sides, turning as necessary. Do not burn the butter. Scatter the onion around the birds and cook until wilted. Add the garlic, turmeric, saffron, ginger, coriander, hot red pepper, parsley, peppercorns, cinnamon sticks, and water. Bring to the boil. Simmer, covered, for 45 minutes to 1 hour. When ready, the birds should be quite tender.

2. Remove the birds to a platter and let cool. Let the cooking liquid reduce over high heat to about half the volume. Let this cool.

3. As the birds cook, brown the almonds in a skillet containing the oil. Cook, shaking the skillet and stirring, until the nuts are evenly browned. Drain on absorbent paper towels and let cool. Chop or blend them coarsely with a rolling pin. Blend them with the sugar and cinnamon and set aside.

4. Remove the flesh from the birds. Discard the skin and bones. Shred the flesh and set aside.

5. Put the eggs in a mixing bowl and add the lemon juice and about ¾ cup of the reduced liquid. Discard the remaining liquid. Beat the eggs with a whisk until thoroughly blended.

6. Heat about 2 tablespoons of butter in a large skillet and add the egg mixture. Stir with a rubber spatula, scraping the bottom and sides as for making scrambled eggs. Continue cooking until the eggs are fairly firm but not dry. Some of the liquid may separate. Ignore it. Remove from the heat and let cool.

7. Preheat the oven to 475 degrees. Generously butter a 10 × 10-inch or slightly larger cake pan.

8. Lay out the 18 squares of phyllo pastry on a flat surface. At this point it is best to work as a team of two, with one person brushing clarified butter on the pastry, the other transferring the leaves as they are prepared. Work quickly.

9. Brush the pastry copiously with melted butter. Transfer it quickly to the buttered pan. It should be situated symmetrically. Press the center down gently inside the pan. Butter another sheet and repeat. Continue until a total of 10 generously buttered pastry layers are piled on top of each other.

10. Add a light layer of the shredded squab or Cornish hens to the pastry-lined pan. Add the scrambled egg mixture, leaving the liquid, if any, in the skillet. Add the remaining squab, smoothing it over to the edges of the pastry. Sprinkle all but ¼ cup of the almond mixture over the squab. Dribble a little butter on top.

11. Butter 4 more sheets of pastry and cover the top of the pie as before. Bring up the edges and corners of the pastry, folding them inward to enclose the filling. Butter 4 more sheets of pastry and arrange these buttered side up. Quickly and with great care, tuck and fold these under the entire pie, lifting the pie up with the fingers so that, when ready, it nestles neatly inside the cake pan.

12. Place the pie in the oven and bake for 20 minutes, brushing the top occasionally with more butter. When nicely browned on top, cover loosely with foil and continue baking for about 20 minutes longer.

13. Or, preferably, when the pie has baked the first 20 minutes and is nicely browned, place a rimmed but otherwise flat pan, like a pizza pan, over the pie. Hold it over a basin to catch any drippings. Invert quickly, turning the pie out. Now, invert a similar rimmed but otherwise flat pan over the pie and turn it over once more. This way the pie has its original crust side up. Return it to the oven. Cover loosely with a sheet of aluminum foil and continue baking until the sides are nicely browned, about 20 minutes.

14. Immediately sprinkle the top of the pie with confectioners' sugar and the remaining ¼ cup of the almond mixture.

15. Serve the pie hot.

Yield: 6 servings.

Note: To make this pie, use a minimum of 18 pastry sheets. A few additional sheets of pastry will not matter. Note, too, that there will probably be leftover butter, which can be reserved for another use.

CLARIFIED BUTTER

Place ¾ pound of butter (the quantity is arbitrary) in a 1-quart measuring cup and let it stand on an asbestos pad over very low heat, or place it in a 200-degree oven until melted. Do not disturb the liquid. Let cool, then refrigerate. The clarified butter will harden between two soft, somewhat liquid or foamy layers. Scrape off the top layer. Invert the cup so the clarified butter comes out in one solid piece (you may have to encourage this with a fork or knife). Wipe off the clarified butter with paper towels. This butter will keep for weeks in the refrigerator. Melt the butter before each use.

MEATS

HIGH-TEMPERATURE RIB ROAST OF BEEF

To judge from the correspondence we receive, this recipe for roasting beef marked some sort of record in popularity. The technique of roasting the beef at a high temperature and then turning off the oven was developed by Ann Seranne, a good friend and an innovative genius in the kitchen. One word of caution: This method should be attempted only with a well-insulated oven.

One 2- to 4-rib roast of beef, short ribs removed, 4½ to 12 pounds

Flour

Salt and freshly ground pepper to taste

1. Remove the roast from the refrigerator 2½ to 4 hours before cooking. Preheat the oven to 500 degrees.

2. Place the roast in an open shallow roasting pan, fat side up. Sprinkle with a little flour and rub the flour into the fat lightly. Season with the salt and pepper. Put the roast in the preheated oven and roast according to the chart below, timing exactly. When cooking time is finished, turn off the oven. Do not open the door at any time.

3. Leave the roast in the oven until the oven is lukewarm, or for about 2 hours. Roast will have a crunchy brown outside and an internal heat that will be suitable for serving for as long as 4 hours.

Yield: 2 servings per rib.

Note: To make thin pan gravy, remove excess fat from the meat drippings, leaving any meat pieces in the pan. Stir in ½ to 1 cup beef stock or broth. Bring to the boil, scraping the bottom of the pan to loosen the meat pieces. Simmer for 1 minute and season to taste.

ROASTING CHART

Ribs	Weight Without Short Ribs	Roast at 500 Degrees
2	4½ to 5 pounds	25 to 30 minutes
3	8 to 9 pounds	40 to 45 minutes
4	11 to 12 pounds	55 to 60 minutes

This works out to be about 15 minutes per rib, or approximately 5 minutes cooking time per pound of trimmed, ready-to-cook roast.

ROAST RIBS OF BEEF

One 6-pound standing rib roast with ribs (but with the ends of ribs and chine bone removed)

Salt to taste

¼ cup cold water

1. Preheat the oven to 500 degrees.

2. A very light layer of fat may be trimmed from the roast but leave a layer of fat at least ¼ inch thick. Arrange the roast fat side up in a shallow baking dish and sprinkle with salt. Pour the water around the meat. Place in the oven and bake for 15 minutes.

3. Reduce the oven heat to 400 degrees and continue baking for 25 minutes. Reduce the oven heat to 350 degrees and bake for 15 minutes for rare beef, 30 minutes for medium rare, longer for well done. Carefully transfer the roast to a serving dish rib side down. Cover loosely with foil to keep warm.

4. Pour off all the fat from the roasting pan, but save about ½ cup for preparing Yorkshire pudding. To make a light "juice" for the beef, add about ½ cup of cold water to the pan and stir to dissolve the brown particles that cling to the bottom and sides of the pan. Serve the beef sliced with Yorkshire pudding and grated horseradish.

Yield: 6 to 8 servings.

YORKSHIRE PUDDING

1 cup flour

1 cup milk

⅛ teaspoon grated nutmeg

4 large eggs, about ¾ cup when measured

½ cup beef drippings

1. Preheat the oven to 425 degrees.

2. Combine the flour, milk, and nutmeg in a mixing bowl. Put the eggs in another bowl and beat until frothy. Add this to the milk and stir.

3. Pour the beef drippings into a heatproof baking dish and place on the stove over moderate heat. When quite hot and almost smoking, add the batter. Smooth it over with a rubber spatula. Place the pudding in the oven and bake for about 15 minutes. Turn the baking dish as the cooking proceeds for even cooking.

Yield: 8 or more servings.

BOILED RIBS OF BEEF

Don't be put off by the idea of boiling a rib roast of beef. It is an absolutely triumphant dish that we were served at Savini's in Rome.

1. Place the beef in a large kettle and add cold water to cover. Bring to the boil and simmer for about 2 minutes. Drain thoroughly and run briefly under cold water. Let stand at room temperature until ready to cook.

2. Meanwhile, quarter the carrots lengthwise and cut them into 2-inch lengths. Set aside. Cut the turnips into eighths. Set aside. Peel the potatoes and add cold water to cover. Set aside. Trim the ends of the zucchini. Cut them into convenient serving pieces. Trim the green beans and cut them into 2-inch lengths.

3. Place the ribs of beef in a kettle and add beef broth to cover. If necessary, add water to make certain the beef is covered. Add salt to taste. Bring to the boil and simmer for 1 hour.

4. Add the carrots and potatoes and cook for 15 minutes. Add the zucchini, turnips, and green beans and cook for 15 minutes longer.

5. Remove the meat and cover with foil. Let it rest for 15 minutes. Stand the rib roast on one end and carve like roast beef. Serve with the cooked vegetables. Serve with salsa verde and coarse salt on the side.

Yield: 8 to 10 servings.

One 9½-pound ready-to-cook rib roast of beef (4-rib roast)

4 large carrots, trimmed and scraped

2 turnips, about 1½ pounds, trimmed and peeled

8 to 12 small red potatoes

1 pound zucchini

½ pound green beans

Beef broth to cover

Salt to taste

Salsa verde (see following recipe)

Coarse salt for garnish

Combine all the ingredients in the container of a food processor or blender and blend. Do not overblend. This sauce must retain a coarse consistency. Serve with boiled meats, poultry, fish, and so on.

Yield: About 2 cups.

SALSA VERDE

3 tablespoons coarsely chopped chives

1 cup chopped parsley

¼ cup coarsely chopped onion

6 small cornichons

2 tablespoons drained capers

3 anchovy fillets

1 garlic clove, chopped

24 small cocktail onions, drained

¼ cup red wine vinegar

1¼ cups olive oil

Salt and freshly ground pepper to taste

STEAKS AU POIVRE PAVILLON

1 teaspoon black peppercorns

4 shell steaks with bone

1 tablespoon peanut, vegetable, or corn oil

¼ cup finely chopped shallots

2 tablespoons Cognac

½ cup dry red wine

2 tablespoons butter

2 tablespoons finely chopped parsley

1. Put the peppercorns on a flat surface and, using the bottom of a clean heavy skillet, crush the peppercorns until they are coarse-fine.

2. Dip the steaks on both sides in the peppercorns, pressing the pepper into the meat.

3. Heat the oil in a large heavy skillet and add the steaks. Cook over moderately high heat until the steaks are seared on one side, about 5 minutes. Turn and cook on the other side until seared, about 3 minutes. Or grill over hot coals for 2 or 3 minutes a side for rare meat.

4. Transfer the steaks to a warm serving dish. Pour off the fat from the skillet. Add the shallots and cook briefly, stirring. Add the Cognac and stir. Add the wine and cook down for about 1 minute. Remove the skillet from the heat and swirl in the butter. Pour the sauce over the meat. Sprinkle with parsley and serve.

Yield: 4 servings.

SHELL STEAKS WITH ANCHOVIES

THE STEAKS AND GARNISH:

4 shell steaks, about ¾ pound each

Salt and freshly ground pepper to taste

12 flat anchovy fillets

8 pimiento-stuffed green olives

16 fresh tarragon leaves, optional

THE ANCHOVY BUTTER:

3 tablespoons butter, at room temperature

1 tablespoon finely chopped anchovies, or anchovy paste

1 teaspoon lemon juice

1. Sprinkle the steaks on all sides with salt and pepper to taste. Preferably, grill them for about 4 minutes to a side for rare meat, 5 minutes to a side for medium rare, and so on up to 7 or 8 minutes to a side for well done. Or cook the steaks to the desired degree of doneness in a little butter in a hot skillet.

2. Place the anchovy fillets on a flat surface and split each in half lengthwise. Arrange 6 of the anchovy halves in a lattice pattern over the steaks. Split the stuffed olives down the center crosswise. Arrange 4 olive pieces, sliced side up, in a symmetrical pattern inside the lattice. Garnish, if desired, with fresh tarragon leaves.

3. Melt the 3 tablespoons butter in a small saucepan and add the chopped anchovies and lemon juice. Spoon about 2 teaspoons of the anchovy butter on top of each steak and serve.

Yield: 4 servings.

SLICED STEAK PERSILLADE

1. Place the steak on a flat surface and cut it into thin strips that measure about 2 inches long and ½ inch wide. Sprinkle the pieces with the salt and pepper. Have ready two warm skillets.

2. Heat one skillet and add 2 tablespoons butter. Add about half the meat (the pieces should not be crowded in the skillet or the inside juices will run). The meat should also cook over very high heat. Turn the pieces of meat so that they cook quickly and evenly for a total of 2 to 3 minutes. Transfer the cooked pieces to the second warmed skillet.

3. Add 2 more tablespoons of butter to the skillet in which the meat cooked. When very hot, add the second batch of steak and cook quickly as before. When the second batch is cooked, combine the two batches.

4. Add the shallots and, if necessary, more salt and pepper. Sprinkle with 4 tablespoons of parsley. Toss quickly in the very hot skillet and serve hot. Before serving, sprinkle with the remaining tablespoon of parsley.

Yield: 4 to 6 servings.

1¾ pounds boneless shell steak, trimmed of excess outside fat

Salt and freshly ground pepper to taste

4 tablespoons butter

2 tablespoons finely chopped shallots

5 tablespoons chopped parsley

SLICED FILLET OF BEEF WITH SHALLOTS

1. Sprinkle the pieces of beef with salt and pepper.

2. Melt 2 tablespoons of the butter in a heavy skillet and add the beef slices. Cook for about 30 seconds to a side, or until quickly browned on both sides. As the pieces cook, transfer them to a warm platter.

3. Add the remaining butter and the shallots to the skillet. Cook for about 30 seconds, swirling the shallots in the skillet. Add the vinegar. Bring to the boil. Pour this over the meat.

4. Serve sprinkled with finely chopped parsley.

Yield: 4 to 6 servings.

16 thin slices of fillet of beef, such as filets mignons, about 1½ pounds

Salt and freshly ground pepper to taste

4 tablespoons butter

4 tablespoons finely chopped shallots

1 tablespoon red wine vinegar

Finely chopped parsley

BEEF BROCHETTES

1¼ pounds sirloin steak in one piece

Sixteen 1-inch squares of cored, seeded green pepper

2 tablespoons peanut, vegetable, or corn oil

Salt and freshly ground pepper to taste

Sauce bérnaise (see recipe page 772)

1. Heat the grill.
2. Cut the steak into cubes of about 1½ inches. There should be 48 pieces.
3. Arrange the pieces of beef on skewers, starting with one piece of green pepper. Add four pieces of beef, another green pepper, four of beef, another pepper piece, four more pieces of beef, and finally a piece of pepper.
4. Repeat with three more skewers.
5. Place the skewered foods in a flat dish and brush all over with oil.
6. Place the brochettes on the grill and cook for 3 to 4 minutes on one side. Sprinkle all over with salt and pepper and turn the brochettes to cook on the other side, 3 to 4 minutes. Serve immediately with béarnaise sauce.

Yield: 4 servings.

Beef Fajitas

This is, to my taste, one of the greatest Tex-Mex dishes. I first sampled it at a backyard outing on a visit to San Antonio. The name of the dish is pronounced fah-HEAT-ahs and consists of well-trimmed skirt steak, grilled quickly, and placed in the center of the flour tortillas. The meat is topped with a well-seasoned guacamole, a layer of salsa, and the fiery hot garnish known as *pico de gallo*, or "rooster's beak." To balance this fiery dish, serve a small portion of pinto beans cooked with tomatoes and fresh coriander on the side. Altogether it is glorious combination of flavors.

1. Preheat a charcoal fire.

2. The skirt steak should be as free of surface fat as possible. Place each steak on a flat surface and, using a sharp knife, carefully trim away most of the fat. Trim well on all sides.

3. Cut each piece crosswise into 3- or 4-inch pieces, each about 6 inches long.

4. Place each piece of meat on the flat surface and, holding a sharp slicing knife parallel to the cutting surface, cut each piece of meat, sandwich-style, into two thin rectangles. Count on four or five slices per person.

5. Blend the garlic, lime juice, water, salt, and pepper in a flat plate. Make layers of the meat slices, brushing a little of the sauce between each layer.

6. Brush the top of the grill with a little oil. Add the meat slices and cook about 2 minutes on each side, turning once. Meanwhile, heat a nonstick skillet and cook each flour tortilla briefly to heat through. The tortillas must remain soft.

7. To serve, arrange equal portions of the meat on each of six preheated plates. Place a basket of tortillas and bowls of guacamole, salsa, and pico de gallo on the table for guests to help themselves. Serve individual bowls of the hot beans on the side.

Yield: 6 servings.

3 skirt steaks (about 3 pounds)

1 tablespoon finely minced garlic

1½ tablespoons freshly squeezed lime juice

1 tablespoon water

Salt and freshly ground pepper to taste

12 flour tortillas

Guacamole (see recipe page 5)

Salsa (see recipe page 788)

Pico de gallo (see recipe page 789)

Pinto beans (see recipe page 652)

BEEF GOULASH

2 pounds lean, boneless shell steak, fillet, or sirloin

Salt and freshly ground pepper to taste

1 tablespoon paprika

2 tablespoons peanut, vegetable, or corn oil

1 tablespoon butter

½ cup finely chopped onion

2 tablespoons flour

½ cup red wine

¼ cup crushed, canned, unsalted tomatoes

1 cup yogurt

½ teaspoon thyme

1. Cut the meat into strips about 2 inches long and ¼ inch wide. Sprinkle the strips with salt, a generous grinding of pepper, and paprika.

2. Heat the oil in a large heavy skillet and add half the meat, cooking and stirring over high heat until meat is browned, about 3 minutes. Using a slotted spoon, transfer the meat to another skillet.

3. Add the remaining beef and cook rapidly over high heat until browned. Transfer this meat to the other skillet.

4. Pour off any fat remaining in the skillet. Add the butter and onion to the skillet and cook until the onion wilts. Sprinkle with flour and stir. Add the wine and tomatoes, stirring. Cook for about 4 minutes.

5. Add the yogurt, stirring rapidly. Add any juices that have accumulated around the meat. Add the thyme. Cook for about 5 minutes, stirring constantly.

6. Place a strainer over the meat and strain the sauce, stirring with a wooden spoon or spatula to push through as much of the solids in the sauce as possible.

7. Heat thoroughly and serve with noodles or rice.

Yield: 4 servings.

DEVILED SHORT RIBS OF BEEF

1. Preheat the oven to 375 degrees.

2. Put the ribs of beef in a mixing bowl.

3. Blend the flour, paprika, salt, and pepper and spoon it over the ribs. Toss the ribs to coat well.

4. Select a baking dish large enough to hold the ribs in one layer without crowding. Add the oil. Add the ribs of beef and rub them all over with oil. Arrange the pieces neatly in the pan without letting them touch. Place in the oven and bake for about 1 hour, turning the pan in the oven occasionally so that the ribs cook evenly. Turn the pieces.

5. Reduce the oven temperature to 350 degrees. Continue baking the ribs for 20 to 30 minutes.

6. Pour off the fat from the baking pan.

7. Blend the mustard, wine, and Worcestershire sauce in a mixing bowl. Use the mixture to brush the meaty part of the ribs all over. As they are brushed, use the fingers to sprinkle them liberally with the bread crumbs. Do not dip them in the crumbs or the crumbs in the bowl will become soggy.

8. As the ribs are crumbed, arrange them on a rack placed in a baking pan. Put the pan in the oven and continue baking for 30 minutes.

Yield: 4 to 6 servings.

4 pounds short ribs of beef, the meatier the better, cut into 3- or 4-inch lengths

1 cup flour

1 teaspoon paprika

Salt to taste

1 teaspoon freshly ground pepper

2 tablespoons corn, peanut, or vegetable oil

3 tablespoons imported mustard, the stronger the better

1 tablespoon dry white wine

1 teaspoon Worcestershire sauce

1½ cups fine fresh bread crumbs

BRAISED SHORT RIBS OF BEEF WITH CARAWAY

4 pounds short ribs of beef, the meatier the better, cut into 3- or 4-inch lengths

¼ cup flour

Salt and freshly ground black pepper to taste

2 tablespoons corn, peanut, or vegetable oil

1 cup finely chopped onion

1 cup finely chopped carrot

½ cup finely chopped celery

2 garlic cloves, peeled and left whole

2 tablespoons crushed caraway seeds

1 bay leaf

3 fresh thyme sprigs, or ½ teaspoon dried

½ cup dry white wine

1½ cups imported canned tomatoes

3 tablespoons tomato paste

2 cups fresh or canned chicken broth

6 parsley sprigs

1. Sprinkle the ribs with the flour and salt and pepper.

2. Heat the oil in a casserole or Dutch oven large enough to hold the ribs without crowding. When it is hot, add the ribs and cook, turning occasionally so that they brown quite well and evenly on all sides, about 10 minutes.

3. Add the onion, carrot, celery, garlic, caraway seeds, bay leaf, and thyme. Cook for about 3 minutes. Pour off all the fat. Add the wine and cook briefly, stirring the ribs around. Add the tomatoes, tomato paste, broth, parsley, and salt and pepper to taste. Cover closely and bring to the boil. Cook for 1 hour and 45 minutes to 2 hours, or until the rib meat is extremely tender.

4. Transfer the ribs to a platter. Pour the sauce into a bowl. Skim off and discard as much surface fat as possible.

5. Return the ribs to the casserole and pour the sauce over them. Bring to the boil and serve.

Yield 6 to 8 servings.

FRENCH POT ROAST WITH RED WINE SAUCE

1. Place the beef in a mixing bowl. Combine the vinegar, 1½ cups each chopped onions and carrots, 1 cup of the celery, the leeks, if used, garlic, and parsley in a saucepan. Tie the sage, rosemary, marjoram, and coriander seeds in a cheesecloth bag and add the bag. Bring to the boil, stirring. Pour the vinegar mixture over the meat and add enough wine to barely cover the meat. Sprinkle with salt and pepper to taste. Cover closely and refrigerate overnight or longer, for up to 3 days.

2. Remove the meat and pat it dry. Strain and reserve 3 cups of the liquid. Discard the remaining liquid and vegetables.

3. Heat the oil in a heavy Dutch oven or casserole. Sprinkle the beef with salt and pepper. Add it to the Dutch oven or casserole and brown well on all sides. Transfer the meat to a warm place.

4. Add the remaining ¾ cup each of chopped onion and carrots and remaining ½ cup of celery. Cook, stirring, until the onions are wilted. Sprinkle with the flour and stir to blend thoroughly. Add the reserved marinade and beef broth, stirring with a wire whisk. When the mixture is thickened, add the meat. Cover closely and cook over low heat for about 3 hours, or until the roast is thoroughly tender.

5. Remove the meat and keep it warm. Cook the sauce down to the desired consistency. Slice the meat and serve with the sauce.

Yield: 6 to 10 servings.

One 5- to 6-pound round roast of beef
½ cup red wine vinegar
2¼ cups chopped onions
2¼ cups chopped carrots
1½ cups chopped celery
2 cups chopped leeks, optional
2 garlic cloves, crushed
3 parsley sprigs
1 teaspoon each of leaf sage, dried rosemary, marjoram, and coriander seeds
4 to 5 cups dry red wine
Salt and freshly ground pepper
2 tablespoons vegetable oil
½ cup flour
2 cups fresh or canned beef broth

New England Boiled Dinner

One 6½-pound corned beef

6 quarts water

5 or 6 carrots, about 1 pound

8 to 12 small white turnips or 1 rutabaga, about ¾ pound

8 small, whole white onions, about ¾ pound

1 or 2 young heads of cabbage, about 4 pounds

10 potatoes, about 1¾ pounds

10 young beets, about 1 pound

Salt

4 tablespoons butter

Horseradish, preferably freshly grated

Mustard

1. Place the corned beef in a large kettle or Dutch oven and add the water. The water should cover the top of the beef by about 2 inches. Cover and cook for about 2 hours, or until the corned beef is almost tender. Do not add salt.

2. Meanwhile, trim the carrots and cut them in half crosswise. Cut each half into quarters. Set aside. Peel the turnips and set aside. Peel the onions and set aside. If two cabbages are used, quarter them. If one head is used, cut it into eighths. Pull away any tough outer leaves and cut away part of the core of each section. Set aside. Peel the potatoes and drop them into cold water to prevent discoloration. Set aside. Peel the beets and set aside.

3. After approximately 2 hours, when the meat is almost tender, add all the vegetables except the beets. Taste the cooking liquid. It should not need salt. If it does, add it to taste. Cook until vegetables are tender.

4. Put the beets in a saucepan and add water to cover and salt to taste and cook until tender.

5. Remove the meat and slice it thin. Arrange the drained vegetables symmetrically on a hot platter. Melt the butter and pour it over the vegetables. Serve with horseradish and mustard on the side.

Yield: About 10 servings.

CORNED BEEF AND CABBAGE

1. Place the corned beef in a kettle and add the water, carrot, and onions.

2. If the leek is used, trim the end. Split the leek down the center almost but not through the root end. Insert the bay leaf, parsley, and thyme in the center and tie with a string. Add it to the kettle. Otherwise omit the leek and simply add the other ingredients to the kettle. Add the peppercorns.

3. Bring to the boil and simmer for 2 to 2½ hours. The cooking time of corned beef varies greatly because of the unpredictable quality of the meat. Cook until fork-tender. Approximately 15 minutes before the beef is tender, core the cabbage, and peel the potatoes. Cut the cabbage into eighths. Add cabbage and potatoes to the kettle and cook for 15 minutes, or until the vegetables are tender. As the vegetables cook, prepare the parsley sauce, which is made with 1 cup of the corned beef cooking liquid.

4. Serve the corned beef sliced with the cabbage wedges and potatoes. Serve with parsley sauce and mustard.

Yield: 6 to 8 servings.

One 3-pound slab of corned beef

16 cups water

1 whole carrot, scraped

2 whole onions, peeled and stuck with 4 cloves

1 leek, optional

1 bay leaf

2 fresh parsley sprigs

2 fresh thyme sprigs, or ½ teaspoon dried

12 peppercorns, crushed

One 2½-pound cabbage

1½ pounds small potatoes, preferably the red-skinned variety

Mustard

Parsley sauce (see following recipe)

PARSLEY SAUCE

1. Melt the butter in a saucepan and add the flour, stirring with a wire whisk. When blended, add the broth, stirring rapidly with the whisk. When blended and smooth, add the milk, salt, and pepper. Simmer for about 5 minutes.

2. Add the parsley and stir to blend. Add lemon juice and serve piping hot.

Yield: About 1¾ cups.

2 tablespoons butter

3 tablespoons flour

1 cup broth from the corned beef

½ cup milk

Salt and freshly ground pepper to taste

1½ cups finely chopped parsley

Juice of ½ lemon

Sauerbraten

One 4½-pound bottom round roast of beef

¾ cup red wine vinegar

¾ cup red wine

2 cups water

½ cup carrot rounds

1 small onion, sliced and broken into rings

6 crushed black peppercorns

6 juniper berries

¾ cup coarsely chopped leeks, optional

1 bay leaf

3 fresh thyme springs, or ½ teaspoon dried

3 parsley sprigs

2 tablespoons peanut, vegetable, or corn oil

¾ cup finely diced carrots

¾ cup finely diced onion

½ teaspoon finely minced garlic

2 tablespoons flour

½ cup water

2 whole cloves

One 1-inch piece cinnamon stick

½ cup chopped ginger cookies, or 1 teaspoon ground ginger plus 2 teaspoons sugar

1. If there is any fat on the meat, trim it away. Place the meat in a bowl.

2. Combine the wine vinegar, wine, water, carrots, onion rings, peppercorns, juniper berries, leeks, bay leaf, thyme, and parsley in a saucepan. Bring to the boil. Remove from the heat and let cool.

3. Pour the marinade over the beef. Cover and refrigerate for 1 to 3 days.

4. Strain the beef and vegetables. Discard the vegetables. Place the beef in one bowl, the marinade in another.

5. Heat the oil in a deep casserole large enough to hold the meat comfortably. Add the meat and cook, turning occasionally, until well browned on all sides. This will take about 10 minutes.

6. Transfer the beef to another dish. Pour off the fat from the casserole. Add the diced carrots and onion to the casserole and cook, stirring, until the onion wilts. Add the garlic and stir.

7. Sprinkle with flour and stir to blend. Add the reserved marinade, water, cloves, and cinnamon stick. Bring to the boil.

8. Return the meat to the casserole. Cover closely and cook over gentle heat for about 2 hours, or until the meat is quite tender.

9. Remove the meat to a dish and keep covered.

10. There are two ways to complete this sauce: one with ginger cookies and the other with the addition of ground ginger. If you are to finish it with cookies, finely grind them in a food processor or blender. Do not reduce the sauce. Add the ground ginger cookies and 1 teaspoon sugar or more to taste. Cook down for about 10 minutes.

11. If you are using ground ginger, cook down the sauce until it is reduced to 2½ cups. Add the ginger and 1 teaspoon of sugar or more to taste. Bring to the boil.

12. Serve the meat sliced with the sauce.

Yield: 10 servings.

BRAISED BRISKET OF BEEF

It is not an original thought to say that some of the greatest dishes on earth are the simplest and with a "peasant" origin. One of these is a simple braised brisket of beef, the chief attribute of which is a sweet, sugarlike flavor that comes from chopped onion.

1. Have the butcher trim and slice away almost all the fat from the top and bottom of the beef.

2. Sprinkle the beef with salt and a generous grinding of pepper.

3. Heat the oil in a heavy casserole large enough to accommodate the brisket without crowding.

4. Add the brisket and brown on one side for about 10 minutes. Turn the meat and brown on the second side for about 10 minutes.

5. Pour off the fat from the casserole and add the onions, carrots, garlic, bay leaf, parsley, thyme, cloves, and peppercorns. No liquid is added at this point.

6. Cover closely and cook over low heat for 15 minutes. Add 1 cup of wine, the tomatoes, and water. Cover and cook for 45 minutes. Uncover and turn the meat. Cover and cook for about 45 minutes.

7. Uncover and turn the meat a third time. Cover and cook for 45 minutes longer. Total cooking time after browning is 2½ hours.

8. Remove the brisket. Skim off all traces of fat from the surface of the sauce. Cook the sauce down for about 5 minutes.

9. Blend the arrowroot with 1 tablespoon of wine and stir it into the boiling sauce. Serve the brisket sliced with the sauce. An excellent accompaniment for this is braised carrots and onions.

Yield: 10 servings.

One 4½-pound brisket of beef

Salt and freshly ground pepper to taste

2 tablespoons peanut, vegetable, or corn oil

2 cups finely chopped onions

1 cup finely chopped carrots

3 garlic cloves, peeled and left whole

1 bay leaf

6 parsley sprigs

2 thyme sprigs, or ½ teaspoon dried

4 whole cloves

6 crushed peppercorns

1 cup plus 1 tablespoon dry white wine

1 cup chopped, canned tomatoes

1 cup water

1 tablespoon arrowroot or cornstarch

CROQUETTES

1 pound cooked meat, such as ham, veal, lamb, beef, pork, chicken, or seafood, such as shrimp, crab, and fish

4 tablespoons butter

3 tablespoons flour

1¼ cups milk

1 cup finely chopped celery

¾ cup finely chopped onion

½ teaspoon finely minced garlic

⅛ teaspoon grated nutmeg

Salt and freshly ground pepper to taste

3 egg yolks

1 egg

1 teaspoon oil

¼ cup water

Flour for dredging

Fresh bread crumbs for breading

Fat for deep frying

Sauce suprême (see following recipe)

Leftovers pose an undeniable challenge. What can a cook do when guests and family are fed to the teeth with sandwiches made from yesterday's roast beef, ham, chicken, fish, seafood, lamb, or veal? The answer is simple: Chop the meat for croquettes. We offer here a foundation recipe for leftovers that could be called the "anything croquettes."

1. If cooked solid meat such as ham, veal, lamb, beef, pork, or shrimp is to be used, chop it. It is best to chop this with a heavy knife on a flat surface. Or it may be chopped in a food processor but it should not be too fine. As a last resort, it could be ground in a meat grinder. If crabmeat or fish is to be used, shred it. There should be about 3½ cups.

2. Melt 2 tablespoons of the butter in a saucepan and add the flour, stirring with a wire whisk. When blended, add the milk, stirring rapidly with the whisk. Stir constantly until thickened.

3. Heat the remaining butter in a skillet and add the celery, onion, and garlic. Cook, stirring, until the vegetables are wilted. Add the chopped or shredded food. Stir until heated through.

4. Add the white sauce and stir to blend. Add the nutmeg, salt, and pepper. Add the egg yolks, stirring briskly. Heat thoroughly but do not cook. Remove from the heat.

5. Spoon and scrape the mixture into a flat dish to facilitate cooling. Chill.

6. Divide the mixture into 18 portions. Shape each portion by hand into any desired shape, pyramidal, round, oval, and so on.

7. Beat the egg in a shallow, wide vessel with the teaspoon of oil, the water, and salt and pepper to taste.

8. Dredge the croquettes first in flour, then in egg, and finally in bread crumbs. Coat well.

9. Heat the fat for deep frying. Add the croquettes a few at a time and cook, turning in the fat, for 2 or 3 minutes, or until golden brown all over. Drain on absorbent paper towels.

10. Serve hot with sauce suprême.

Yield: 6 to 8 servings.

SAUCE SUPRÊME (CREAM SAUCE)

1. Melt the butter in a saucepan and add the flour, stirring with a wire whisk. Add the broth, stirring rapidly with the whisk. When the mixture is thickened and smooth, add the cream. Continue cooking for about 5 minutes.

2. Add the salt and pepper. Add the lemon juice. Strain the sauce if desired.

Yield: About 2 cups.

Note: Use beef broth for beef croquettes; chicken may be used for chicken, ham, veal, pork, and so on; use fish stock for fish or seafood croquettes.

2 tablespoons butter
3 tablespoons flour
1½ cups rich broth (see note)
½ cup heavy cream
Salt and freshly ground pepper to taste
Juice of ½ lemon

BEEF HASH BONNE FEMME

1. Peel the potatoes and cut them into quarters. Put them in a casserole with boiling salted water to cover and simmer for 20 minutes, or until tender. Do not let them become mushy.

2. Preheat the oven to 400 degrees.

3. Meanwhile, grind the meat or chop it fine. There should be about 4 cups loosely packed.

4. When the potatoes are cooked, drain and put them through a food mill or ricer. Whip in 2 tablespoons of the butter. Beat in the milk and add salt to taste.

5. Heat the remaining 2 tablespoons of butter and add the onion. Cook, stirring, for about 3 minutes and add the garlic, meat, salt, pepper, and nutmeg. Cook, stirring, for about 5 minutes. Fold in the potatoes and parsley. Add the eggs and blend well.

6. Butter a 6-cup charlotte mold or another mold of equal capacity. Sprinkle with bread crumbs, shaking them around to coat the bottom and sides evenly. Shake the excess crumbs out and reserve them.

7. Spoon in the meat and potato mixture and smooth it on top. Sprinkle with reserved bread crumbs and cover with a buttered round of wax paper. Place the mold in a slightly larger utensil and pour boiling water around it. Set this in the oven and bake for 45 minutes. Remove from the oven and let the mold stand in the water bath for 10 minutes.

8. Remove the mold and wipe the bottom. Invert it onto a round plate. Serve with tomato sauce spooned over and around it.

Yield: 4 to 6 servings.

6 potatoes, about 1¼ pounds
Salt
1 pound leftover boiled beef brisket, shin of beef, or leftover pork or veal
4 tablespoons butter
½ cup milk
1 cup finely chopped onion
1 garlic clove, finely minced
Freshly ground pepper
¼ teaspoon grated nutmeg
¼ cup finely chopped parsley
3 eggs, lightly beaten
½ cup bread crumbs, preferably made from golden brown toast

Meat Loaf with Parsley

2 pounds twice-ground veal, beef, or pork, or a combination of all three

1 tablespoon butter

1 cup chopped onion

1 tablespoon finely chopped garlic

½ teaspoon chopped fresh thyme

2 cups thinly sliced mushrooms

1 cup finely chopped parsley

2 eggs, lightly beaten

⅛ teaspoon freshly grated nutmeg

¼ teaspoon ground allspice

⅛ teaspoon ground cloves

⅛ teaspoon cayenne

1¼ cups fresh, unsalted bread crumbs

Salt and freshly ground pepper to taste

1 bay leaf

How many times have I said that if someone gave me a whole cow or a fillet of beef I would probably grind it all and turn it into a meat loaf, a meatball, or chili con carne? I am absolutely addicted to ground meat because of the endless variety of flavors with which it can be transformed. The important thing about this recipe is the uncommon amount of parsley—that plus the fine flavor of mushrooms.

1. Preheat the oven to 375 degrees.

2. Put the meat into a mixing bowl.

3. Heat the butter in a skillet and add the onion. Cook until wilted and add the garlic.

4. Add the thyme and mushrooms. Cook until the mushrooms give up their liquid. Cook until the liquid has evaporated.

5. Put the mushroom mixture into the container of a food processor or blender and blend to a purée. Add to the meat.

6. Add the parsley, eggs, nutmeg, allspice, cloves, cayenne, bread crumbs, salt, and pepper. Mix the meat and other ingredients with the hands.

7. Spoon and scrape the meat mixture into a standard loaf pan. Pack it down and smooth it over with the hands.

8. Place the bay leaf in the center of the loaf and press down gently to make it adhere to the meat.

9. Set the loaf pan in a basin of water. Bring the water to the boil on top of the stove. Place the pan in the oven and bake for 1 hour.

Yield: 8 servings.

MEAT AND SPINACH LOAF

1. Preheat the oven to 350 degrees.

2. If the spinach is in bulk, pick it over to remove any tough stems. Rinse the spinach well in cold water, drain, place in a saucepan, and cover. It is not necessary to add liquid; the spinach will cook in the water clinging to the leaves. Cook for about 2 minutes, stirring once or twice. Transfer to a colander and douse with cold water to chill. Drain and press with the hands to extract most of the moisture. Chop the spinach.

3. Put the meat in a mixing bowl and add the chopped spinach, bread crumbs, salt, pepper, and nutmeg.

4. Put the celery, parsley, and milk in the container of a food processor or blender. Blend well and add to the meat mixture. Add the garlic.

5. Heat the butter in a small skillet and cook the onion until wilted. Add it to the meat mixture. Add the eggs and blend well with the hands. Shape and fit into an oval or round baking dish, or place in a loaf pan. Cover with the bacon and bake for 1¼ to 1½ hours. Pour off the fat and let the loaf stand for 20 minutes before slicing. Serve, if desired, with tomato sauce.

Yield: 6 to 8 servings.

---

1 pound fresh spinach

1¼ pounds ground beef, veal, or pork, or a combination of all

½ cup fresh bread crumbs

Salt to taste

1½ teaspoons freshly ground pepper

¼ teaspoon grated nutmeg

½ cup coarsely chopped celery

½ cup loosely packed parsley

¼ cup milk

1 garlic clove, finely minced

1 tablespoon butter

½ cup finely chopped onion

2 eggs, lightly beaten

3 slices bacon

Meat Loaf with Ginger and Garlic

1 pound ground lean
  pork

1 pound ground lean
  beef

2 tablespoons peanut,
  vegetable, or corn oil

1 cup finely chopped
  onion

1 tablespoon finely
  minced garlic

½ cup finely chopped,
  drained water
  chestnuts

½ cup finely chopped
  parsley

2 tablespoons finely
  chopped fresh ginger

¾ cup finely chopped
  scallions

1 cup fine fresh bread
  crumbs

2 tablespoons soy sauce

⅓ cup dry sherry

1 egg, lightly beaten
  Salt and freshly ground
  pepper to taste

1. Preheat the oven to 400 degrees.

2. Combine the pork and beef in a mixing bowl

3. Heat the oil in a saucepan and add the onion and garlic. Cook, stirring, until the onion is wilted. Let cool briefly.

4. To the combined meats add the onion and garlic mixture, water chestnuts, parsley, ginger, scallions, bread crumbs, soy sauce, wine, egg, salt, and pepper. Blend well with the hands.

5. Pack the mixture into a loaf pan measuring about 9 × 5 × 3 inches. Set the pan in a larger pan of water. Bring to the boil on top of the stove. Place both pans in the oven and bake for 1 hour (internal temperature should be 160 degrees). Let stand about 15 minutes before slicing.

Yield: 8 or more servings.

STEAK TARTARE

1. The fresher the beef, the redder it will remain. After the meat is ground, it is best to serve it as expeditiously as possible. If the butcher grinds it, have him grind it twice. Or grind it at home using a meat grinder or a food processor. Take care not to over-grind the meat and make it mushy if a food processor is used.

2. Place 4 mounds of meat of equal weight in the center of 4 chilled plates. Make an indentation in the center of each mound and add 1 yolk. Or embed half a clean eggshell in the center of each mound and add the yolk to that.

3. Surround the meat with equal portions of onion, parsley, anchovy halves, capers, chopped chives, and lemon half. Serve the Cognac, Worcestershire sauce, mustard, and Tabasco sauce in bottles or separate containers on the side. All the quantities to be added to the meat are, of course, arbitrary, and optional.

4. Blend the ingredients together as desired. Serve with buttered toast.

Yield: 4 servings.

1 pound top sirloin, or top round

4 egg yolks

½ cup finely chopped onion

4 teaspoons chopped parsley

6 flat anchovies, split in half lengthwise

¼ cup capers

8 teaspoons finely chopped chives

4 lemon halves

4 teaspoons Cognac

2 teaspoons Worcester-shire sauce

4 teaspoons Dijon mustard

Tabasco sauce to taste

CHILI CON CARNE WITH CUBED MEAT

5 pounds lean chuck roast

½ cup olive oil

½ cup flour

½ cup chili powder, more or less to taste

2 teaspoons cumin seeds

2 teaspoons dried oregano

6 to 10 garlic cloves, finely minced

4 cups fresh or canned beef broth

Salt and freshly ground pepper

To our mind, no matter how Texans and assorted citizens of the West and Southwest may boast otherwise, there is no such thing as "the one real, authentic recipe" for chili con carne. Part of the fun is in composing your own version and we must admit to a keen fancy for almost all honestly conceived chilies.

Our personal favorite came to us from a friend, Margaret Field, who lives in San Antonio. "Meat for chili," Mrs. Field told us, "must always be cut in cubes. When you add cumin and oregano, you should always rub them between the palms of the hands, because that brings out the flavor. The chili should also be made at least twenty-four hours in advance." Mrs. Field's chili contains neither tomatoes nor beans, although pinto beans may be served on the side.

The second chili recipe is our own version with ground meat. To our taste, it is enhanced by the addition of chili paste with garlic, which is available in Asian markets.

We happen to have a passion for a choice of things to be added to chili—among them a raw tomato sauce served cold, chopped lettuce, sour cream, grated Cheddar cheese, chopped fresh coriander, and hot pepper flakes.

1. Trim the meat and cut it into 1-inch cubes. Heat the oil in a deep kettle and add the cubed meat. Cook, stirring, just until the meat loses its red color.

2. Sift together the flour and chili powder and sprinkle the meat with it, stirring constantly so that the pieces are evenly coated.

3. Place the cumin and oregano in the palm of one hand. Rub the spices between the palms, sprinkling over the meat. Add the garlic and stir. Add the broth, stirring the meat constantly. Add the salt and pepper and bring to the boil. Partly cover and simmer for 3 to 4 hours, or until the meat almost falls apart. If necessary, add more broth as the meat cooks. This chili should not be soupy, however. Serve with pinto beans (see recipe page 652), if desired.

Yield: 8 to 12 servings.

CHILI CON CARNE WITH GROUND MEAT

1. Put the suet in a large deep casserole or Dutch oven. Cook until rendered of fat. Scrape out solids. Pour off all but 3 tablespoons of fat. Or use bacon fat or oil.

2. Add the onions and green peppers. Cook until the onions are wilted.

3. Add the meat. Using a heavy metal spoon, cook, chopping down with the spoon to break up lumps in the meat.

4. Add the garlic and pepper and stir to blend. Add the chili powder, oregano, cumin, and celery salt. Stir and add the vinegar. Add the tomatoes with tomato paste, water, salt, pepper, and, if desired, chili paste with garlic. Bring to the boil, stirring to break up tomatoes. Cook over low heat for about 30 minutes.

Yield: 8 servings.

¼ pound beef suet from the kidney, or use bacon fat or oil

3 cups chopped onions

1½ cups finely chopped green peppers

3 pounds ground beef

3 tablespoons finely chopped garlic

¾ teaspoon freshly ground pepper

6 tablespoons chili powder

1 tablespoon crushed dried oregano

1 teaspoon ground cumin

1 teaspoon celery salt

1 tablespoon red wine vinegar

One 35-ounce can tomatoes with tomato paste and basil leaf

1 cup water

Salt and freshly ground pepper to taste

1 tablespoon chili paste with garlic, optional

MEATBALLS STROGANOFF

1 pound ground round steak

1 egg, lightly beaten

⅓ cup fine, fresh bread crumbs

¼ cup milk

¼ teaspoon grated nutmeg

Salt and freshly ground pepper to taste

3 tablespoons paprika

4 tablespoons butter

¼ pound mushrooms, thinly sliced

⅓ cup finely chopped onion

¼ cup dry sherry

2 tablespoons brown sauce, or canned beef gravy

¼ cup heavy cream

1 cup sour cream

¼ cup finely chopped parsley

1. Place the meat in a mixing bowl and add the egg. Soak the crumbs in milk and add this to the meat. Add the nutmeg, salt, and pepper and mix well with the hands. Shape the mixture into balls about 1½ inches in diameter. There should be 38 to 40 meatballs.

2. Sprinkle a pan with the paprika and roll the meatballs in it. Heat the butter in a heavy skillet and cook the meatballs, turning gently, until they are nicely browned, about 5 minutes. Sprinkle the mushrooms and onion between and around the meatballs and shake the skillet to distribute the ingredients evenly. Cook for about 1 minute and partly cover. Simmer for about 5 minutes and add the wine and brown sauce. Stir in the heavy cream. Partly cover and cook over low heat for about 15 minutes. Stir in the sour cream and bring just to the boil without cooking. Sprinkle with parsley and serve piping hot with fine buttered noodles as an accompaniment.

Yield: 4 to 6 servings.

ITALIAN MEATBALLS

1. To make the meatballs, put the beef into a mixing bowl. Add the prosciutto and blend.

2. Combine the bread crumbs and milk in another bowl and blend well. Let stand a minute or so and add to the beef. Add the garlic, cheese, eggs, nutmeg, and parsley. Add a little salt (the prosciutto is salty) and pepper.

3. Blend the mixture well. Shape into about 36 meatballs, each about 1½ inches in diameter.

4. To prepare the sauce, heat the oil or pancetta in a skillet and add the onion, carrot, celery, and zucchini. Cook, stirring often, until the onion starts to brown.

5. Put the tomatoes into the container of a food processor or blender. Blend. There should be about 3 cups. Add this to the cooked vegetables. Cook for about 10 minutes. Add the salt and pepper to taste and the basil.

6. When ready to cook the meatballs, heat the tablespoon of olive oil in a skillet and add the balls a few at a time. Do not crowd them. Brown them all over, turning often so that they cook evenly. When one batch is cooked, remove it and cook another until all the balls are browned.

7. Add the meatballs to the sauce and simmer for about 15 minutes, turning the balls in the sauce occasionally.

Yield: 4 to 6 servings.

THE MEATBALLS:

1¼ pounds ground beef

¼ pound prosciutto, finely chopped, about ¾ cup

1 cup fresh bread crumbs

½ cup milk

½ teaspoon finely minced garlic

3 tablespoons freshly grated Parmesan cheese

2 eggs, lightly beaten

⅛ teaspoon grated nutmeg

¼ cup finely chopped parsley

Salt and freshly ground pepper to taste

1 tablespoon olive oil

THE SAUCE:

¼ cup olive oil or finely diced pancetta

¼ cup finely chopped onion

¼ cup finely diced carrot

¼ cup chopped celery

½ cup finely diced, unpeeled zucchini

1½ pounds fresh tomatoes, peeled and cored, or use 3 cups canned tomatoes

Salt and freshly ground pepper to taste

1 tablespoon chopped fresh basil

TAMALE PIE

THE BEEF:

2 pounds very lean beef, preferably top sirloin

2 cups fresh or canned beef broth

3 cups water

2 garlic cloves, peeled but left whole

THE CORNMEAL MUSH:

2 cups cornmeal

Salt

5 cups cold beef broth or water

1½ tablespoons lard or vegetable oil

THE FILLING:

2 tablespoons bacon fat or oil

1 cup finely chopped onion

3 tablespoons finely minced garlic

1 cup finely chopped sweet green or red pepper

3 tablespoons chili powder

1 teaspoon ground cumin

½ teaspoon dried oregano

½ teaspoon ground coriander

Salt and freshly ground pepper to taste

2 cups canned tomatoes

1 cup whole kernel corn, fresh, or canned

2 tablespoons chopped hot canned chilies

1 tablespoon butter

1. Put the meat in a large saucepan or small kettle. Add the broth, water, and whole garlic. Bring to the boil and simmer for 2 hours, or until quite tender. Drain but reserve about ¼ cup of the cooking liquid. Shred the meat. If the meat is not tender enough, chop it in a food processor.

2. Put the cornmeal in a heavy saucepan and add the salt, broth, and lard. Bring to the boil, stirring constantly with a wire whisk. Cook until thickened. Continue cooking, stirring, for about 5 minutes. Set aside. The mush should be slightly cooled, but do not let it get cold or it will not be manageable.

3. Preheat the oven to 400 degrees.

4. To make the filling, heat the bacon fat or oil in a saucepan and add the onion, garlic, and chopped pepper. Cook, stirring, until the vegetables are wilted. Add the shredded meat, chili powder, cumin, oregano, coriander, salt and pepper to taste, tomatoes, corn, and hot chilies. Add the reserved ¼ cup of broth. Stir.

5. Butter a 10-cup baking dish.

6. Add enough of the mush to coat the bottom and sides of the dish. Leave enough mush to cover the top. Spread the mush in the dish as neatly as possible over and around the bottom and sides. Add the filling. Smooth it over. Add the remaining mush and smooth it over. Dot the top with butter. Place the dish in the oven and bake for 45 minutes, or until piping hot throughout and nicely browned on top.

Yield: 8 servings.

BEEF AND KIDNEY PIE

1. Cut the beef into small rounds about ½ inch thick and 3 inches in diameter. If fillet is used, cut the fillet ends into 2- or 3-inch lengths. Set aside.

2. Cut the kidneys into rounds about ½ inch thick. Set aside.

3. Heat 2 tablespoons of the butter in a heavy casserole and add the shallots, onion, and garlic. Cook, stirring, until the onion is wilted. Add the mushrooms, salt, and pepper. Cook for about 5 minutes. Sprinkle with flour and tarragon and stir to blend. Add the wine and stir rapidly until thickened and smooth. Add the tomatoes and broth and bring to the boil, stirring. Continue cooking while browning the meat and kidneys.

4. Sprinkle the beef and kidneys with salt and pepper. Heat remaining 2 tablespoons of butter in a skillet large enough to hold the beef without crowding. Add the beef in one layer and cook over high heat for about 2 minutes. Turn and brown quickly on the other side. As the meat is browned on both sides, transfer the pieces temporarily to a side dish and keep warm. When all the beef is cooked, add the pieces and the accumulated juices to the tomato and mushroom stew. Continue cooking.

5. When the beef is cooked, start adding the kidney pieces to the skillet, cooking them in similar fashion until quickly browned on both sides. As the pieces cook, transfer them to the side dish. Add the water to the skillet and stir to dissolve the brown particles that cling to the bottom and sides of the skillet. Add this to the stew.

6. Drain the kidneys and discard the kidney juices. Add the kidneys to the stew. Add the bay leaf. Cover and cook for about 30 minutes longer. As the stew cooks, skim off and discard the fat and scum that accumulates on the surface. Let cool and add the Worcestershire sauce.

7. Preheat the oven to 375 degrees.

8. Spoon the stew into an oval, round, or rectangular baking dish. It should almost but not quite fill the dish. Arrange the egg wedges yolk side down symmetrically over the stew. Brush around the outer rim and sides of the baking dish with the yolk beaten with a little water.

9. Roll out the dough to fit the baking dish, leaving a 1- or 2-inch margin. Neatly fit the pastry over the dish, letting the overlapping margin hang down. Press gently around the pastry to seal it against the yolk mixture. Trim off the bottom of the pastry. Cut

2 pounds very tender prime beef, preferably fillet, or use top sirloin, in one piece

2 veal or beef kidneys, about 1½ pounds

4 tablespoons butter

3 tablespoons finely chopped shallots

½ cup chopped onion

1 garlic clove, finely minced

6 cups thinly sliced mushrooms, about 1 pound

Salt and freshly ground pepper to taste

¼ cup flour

1 teaspoon dried tarragon

2 cups dry white wine

1 cup chopped fresh or canned imported tomatoes

1¾ cups fresh or canned beef broth

½ cup water

1 bay leaf

1 tablespoon Worcestershire sauce

4 hard-cooked eggs, peeled and quartered

1 egg yolk

Pie pastry (see recipe page 884)

small slits or one round on top of the dough to allow steam to escape. You may gather scraps of dough together and roll out to make a pattern on top of the pie. Brush spots where cutouts will be applied with the yolk mixture before adding. Brush the top and sides of the dough with the yolk mixture all around to aid browning.

10. Place the dish on a baking sheet, which will facilitate turning the dish in the oven for even browning. Place in the oven and bake until piping hot and the pastry is nicely browned. The cooking time for this dish is about 45 minutes if fillet of beef and veal kidney are used; about 1 hour or longer if a lesser cut of beef and beef kidney are used.

Yield: 8 or more servings.

JAPANESE SKEWERED BEEF AND SHRIMP

1. The flank steak can be sliced more easily if it is first frozen. Remove from the freezer ½ hour before slicing. Cut the flank steak against the grain into ¼-inch-thick slices.

2. Blend the soy sauce, half the sake, and the mirin in a mixing bowl. Add the beef and let stand briefly.

3. Peel the shrimp but leave the last tail segment intact. Put them in a bowl and add the remaining sake and salt.

4. Use six skewers and arrange one shrimp, then two green pieces of scallion, another shrimp, and two more green pieces of scallion. Spear the shrimp and scallion pieces down the center and push them close together.

5. Similarly, thread pieces of beef on each of six skewers, alternating them with three pieces of white scallion. Adjust the quantities of skewered beef so that all the meat is used.

6. Preheat the broiler to high. Arrange the skewered foods on a rack and place about 2 inches from the source of heat. Broil for 3 or 4 minutes to a side until lightly browned. Brush with marinade as the skewered foods are cooked. The foods may also be grilled, basting often.

Yield: 6 servings.

Note: Mirin is a sweet sake, widely available in wine and spirit shops in metropolitan areas. As a substitute for mirin, blend 1 cup of dry sherry with ½ cup of sugar. Boil briefly until sugar dissolves. Let cool.

¾ pound flank steak

½ cup soy sauce

½ cup sake

¼ cup mirin, or use sugared sherry (see note)

12 large shrimp, about ½ pound

½ teaspoon salt

24 pieces of scallion, green part only, each cut into 1½-inch lengths

18 pieces of scallion, white part only, each cut into 1½-inch lengths

THAI BEEF WITH CHINESE VEGETABLES

1 pound lean round steak

2 tablespoons corn oil

2 tablespoons coarsely chopped garlic

3 or more tablespoons bottled oyster sauce (see note)

3 cups Chinese broccoli, Chinese cabbage, or other Chinese vegetable, cut on the bias into large bite-size pieces

1 teaspoon fish sauce (see note)

1. Cut the meat into thin, bite-size pieces. This is facilitated if the meat is partly frozen.

2. Heat the oil in a wok or skillet and cook the garlic until it is nicely browned, a bit darker than golden. Add the beef and stir-fry quickly until the meat is cooked through. Add the oyster sauce, stirring. Add the Chinese vegetable and cook, stirring, for about 1 minute. Cover and cook for about 1 minute. Uncover, add the fish sauce, and continue cooking for about 2 minutes.

Yield: 4 to 6 servings

Note: Unfamiliar ingredients are available in Asian stores.

HUNAN BEEF

Keen observers of Chinese food served in America have often noted that the dominant number of beef dishes specify flank steak. "What in the name of heavens happens to the rest of the beef?" We took the occasion of a visit to our kitchen by one of New York's finest Chinese chefs to find out.

The chef was Wen Dah Tai, better known as Uncle Tai, and he told us over a cup of tea that the remainder of a cow was in no sense wasted or ignored in the Chinese kitchen. The fillet is always cut into neat cubes and used in high-class banquet dishes; the shin of beef, the juiciest part, goes into a cold appetizer, five-flavored beef; and the rest of the animal goes into casserole dishes.

We also learned that hot Hunanese cooking is not only a professional outlet, it is a predilection for the chef. It is empirically true that spicy food pleases the body and appetite in hot, humid, climates, and Hunan is such a place. East Hampton must be too, judging by our predilection.

1. Place the flank steak on a flat surface and, holding a sharp knife parallel to the beef, slice it in half widthwise. Cut each half into very thin strips, about ¼ inch each. There should be about 4 cups loosely packed.

2. Place the beef in a mixing bowl and add ⅔ cup water blended with the baking soda. Refrigerate overnight or for at least 1 hour. When ready to cook, rinse the beef thoroughly under cold running water. Drain thoroughly and pat dry.

3. To the meat add the salt, 1 tablespoon of the sherry, and the egg white. Stir in a circular motion until the white is bubbly. Add 1½ tablespoons of cornstarch and 2 tablespoons of oil. Stir to blend.

4. Combine the scallions, dried orange peel, fresh ginger, and fresh red pepper, if used. Set aside.

5. Combine the remaining 2 tablespoons of sherry, the soy sauce, sugar, the remaining 2 tablespoons of cornstarch blended with the remaining 3 tablespoons of water, the sesame oil, and chicken broth. Stir to blend.

6. Heat the remaining 4 cups of oil in a wok or skillet and, when it is almost smoking, add the beef. Cook for about 45 seconds, stirring constantly, and scoop it out. Drain the meat well, but leave the oil in the wok, continuously heating. Return the meat to the wok and cook over high heat for about 15 seconds, stirring. Drain once more. Return the meat a third time to the hot oil and cook, stir-

Ingredients

1½ pounds flank steak

⅔ cup plus 3 tablespoons water

½ teaspoon baking soda

¼ teaspoon salt

3 tablespoons dry sherry

1 egg white

3½ tablespoons cornstarch

4 cups plus 2 tablespoons peanut, vegetable, or corn oil

2 scallions, cut into ½-inch lengths, about ⅓ cup

3 tablespoons dried orange peel (see note)

3 thin slices fresh ginger, cut into ½-inch cubes

1 long, thin, fresh, hot red pepper, chopped, optional

3 tablespoons soy sauce

2 tablespoons sugar

1 teaspoon sesame oil

¼ cup chicken broth

10 dried small hot red pepper pods

ring. Drain the meat. The purpose of this is to make the meat crisp on the outside but retain its juiciness within.

7. Drain the wok completely. Return 2 tablespoons of the oil to the wok and add the hot pepper pods, stirring over high heat until brown and almost blackened, about 30 seconds. Remove. Add the scallion mixture and stir. Add the beef and cook, stirring constantly, for about 10 seconds. Add the wine mixture, stirring, and cook for about 15 seconds, until piping hot and the meat is well coated.

Yield: 4 to 8 servings.

Note: Dried orange peel is available in many Asian grocery and spice stores. It may be made at home, however, by peeling an orange, eliminating as much of the white pithy part as possible. The peel is cut into pieces, placed on a baking sheet, and baked in a 200-degree oven until dried. It may be stored for months in a tight container.

SMOKED TONGUE WITH MADEIRA SAUCE

One 3½-pound smoked tongue

1 onion stuck with 3 cloves

1 bay leaf

3 sprigs fresh thyme, or ½ teaspoon dried

2 cups sauce madère (see recipe page 777)

1. Place the tongue in a bowl and add cold water to cover. Let stand overnight. Drain.

2. Place the tongue in a kettle and add cold water to cover. Add the onion, bay leaf, and thyme. Bring to the boil and simmer for about 2½ hours, or until quite tender.

3. Drain the tongue and cut off the bulky throat section. Peel off and discard the tough outer skin.

4. Preheat the oven to 400 degrees.

5. Place the tongue in a baking dish and pour about 1 cup of sauce madère over it. Place in the oven for about 10 minutes to glaze it. Thinly slice the tongue and serve the remaining sauce on the side.

Yield: 8 servings.

BRAISED OXTAIL

To many palates, oxtails are one of the finer, more gratifying delicacies of the table. One of the additional virtues is that they are relatively inexpensive. Oxtail soup is probably the best known dish in which these meaty bones appear, and while this soup is excellent for early spring menus, there are other dishes that are equally appealing, including braised or deviled oxtail.

1. Sprinkle the pieces of oxtail with salt and pepper.

2. Heat the oil in a heavy casserole or Dutch oven and add the oxtails. Brown on all sides, about 10 minutes. Pour off all the fat from the casserole.

3. Add the onion, carrot, celery, bay leaf, and thyme. Stir to distribute the vegetables. Cook, stirring, for about 2 minutes.

4. Sprinkle all the ingredients with flour and stir to distribute the flour evenly. Add the wine and stir. Add the boiling water, tomatoes, and parsley sprigs and bring to the boil. Cover closely and cook for 2 hours.

5. Meanwhile, cut the carrots into 1½-inch lengths. Cut each length into quarters. Put the pieces in a saucepan with cold water to cover. Bring to the boil and simmer for about 5 minutes. Drain.

6. Cut the mushrooms into quarters, halves, or slices, depending on size. There should be about 3 cups.

7. Melt the butter in a skillet and add the mushrooms. Cook, shaking the skillet and tossing, until the mushrooms give up their liquid. Cook until this liquid evaporates. Add the carrots and toss. Cook for about 5 minutes.

8. Transfer the pieces of oxtail to another casserole. Hold a sieve over the pieces and pour and scrape the sauce with the solids into the sieve. Press the solids with a spatula to extract any juices. Discard the solids. Add the ½ cup of water to the casserole. Bring to the boil.

9. Add the carrot-and-mushroom combination to the casserole. Cover and cook for 30 minutes.

Yield: 4 to 6 servings.

---

2 well-trimmed oxtails, about 1½ pounds each and each cut into 8 crosswise pieces

Salt and freshly ground pepper to taste

2 tablespoons peanut, vegetable, or corn oil

1 cup coarsely chopped onion

½ cup coarsely chopped carrot

½ cup coarsely chopped celery

1 bay leaf

½ teaspoon dried thyme

¼ cup flour

1 cup dry white wine

2 cups boiling water

1 cup chopped tomatoes

4 fresh parsley sprigs

4 carrots, trimmed and scraped, about ¾ pound

½ pound mushrooms

1 tablespoon butter

½ cup water

DEVILED OXTAIL

2 well-trimmed oxtails, about 3 pounds total

8 cups water

½ cup coarsely chopped onion

½ cup coarsely chopped carrot

1 garlic clove, finely minced

¼ cup coarsely chopped celery

1 bay leaf

½ teaspoon dried thyme

6 fresh parsley sprigs

6 whole black peppercorns

Salt to taste

3 or 4 tablespoons Dijon mustard

2 or 3 cups fine fresh bread crumbs

4 tablespoons butter

1. Cut each oxtail, or have the butcher cut each, into 8 pieces. Put the pieces in a kettle and add the water, onion, carrot, garlic, celery, bay leaf, thyme, parsley, peppercorns, and salt. Bring to the boil and simmer for 2½ hours, or until the meat is fork tender.

2. Drain the oxtails. The liquid may be reserved for a soup.

3. Preheat the oven to 450 degrees.

4. When the oxtails are lukewarm, brush the pieces all over generously with mustard. Dredge the pieces in bread crumbs until they are well coated. Pat the pieces to help the crumbs adhere. Put the pieces in one layer in a baking dish.

5. Melt the butter in a saucepan. Pour the butter evenly over the pieces.

6. Put the baking dish in the oven and bake for 15 minutes. Carefully turn the pieces and bake for 15 minutes longer, or until the oxtails are golden brown.

Yield: 4 to 6 servings.

TRIPES À LA MODE DE CAEN (BAKED TRIPE WITH CALVADOS)

There are some quotations about food that are so exquisitely related to a subject at hand we find them irresistible. This is certainly true of a few lines pertaining to tripe that we discovered years ago in the *Wise Encyclopedia of Cookery*.

"Tripe," David B. Wise noted, "like certain alluring vices, is enjoyed by society's two extremes, the topmost and the lowermost strata, while the multitudinous middle classes of the world look upon it with genteel disdain and noses tilted. Patricians relished tripe in Babylon's gardens, plebeians have always welcomed it as something good and cheap, always the peasant cook has taught the prince how to eat it."

To that we say amen. We are so inordinately fond of the food that we cannot understand the general lack of enthusiasm that greets it. It is curious that tripe is looked upon far more favorably in European kitchens than in those of the United States.

1. Preheat the oven to 350 degrees.

2. Put the tripe and calf's foot pieces in a kettle and add cold water to cover. Bring to the boil and cook for 5 minutes. Drain well.

3. Place the onion, leeks, celery, garlic, bay leaves, thyme, cloves, parsley sprigs, and peppercorns in a square of cheesecloth. Bring up the ends of the cloth and tie with string to make a bundle.

4. Put the tripe, calf's foot pieces, carrots, the cheesecloth bundle, 8 cups of the chicken broth, the 2 cups of water, the wine, and salt in a kettle and bring to the boil. Cover closely and place in the oven. Bake for 5 hours.

5. Skim off and discard most of the fat from the surface of the tripe. Remove and discard the cheesecloth bundle.

6. Remove the carrots and cut them into ¼-inch rounds. Add to the tripe.

7. Remove the calf's foot pieces. Cut away the gelatinous skin and discard the bones. Shred the skin and add it to the tripe. Add the remaining 1 cup of chicken broth. Bring to the boil. Add the Calvados. Return to the boil and serve.

Yield: 10 or more servings.

6 pounds fresh beef tripe, trimmed of all fat and cut into 2-inch squares, about 12 cups

1 calf's foot, about 1½ pounds, cut into 2-inch pieces

2 cups coarsely chopped onion

2 cups coarsely chopped leeks

1 cup finely chopped celery

4 garlic cloves, left whole

2 bay leaves

1 teaspoon dried thyme

2 whole cloves

6 fresh parsley sprigs

1 teaspoon crushed black peppercorns

4 whole carrots, trimmed and scraped

9 cups fresh or canned chicken broth

2 cups water

2 cups dry white wine

Salt to taste

¼ cup Calvados

TRIPE LYONNAISE

1½ pounds honeycomb tripe

4 cups water

Salt to taste

10 peppercorns

1 carrot, scraped and cut into 2-inch lengths

3 fresh parsley sprigs

1 bay leaf

1 small onion, stuck with 3 whole cloves

1 celery rib, cut into quarters

2 fresh thyme sprigs, or ½ teaspoon dried

1 hot red pepper

2 tablespoons butter

1 large or 2 medium-size onions, peeled and sliced as thin as possible, about 2 cups

1 small garlic clove, peeled but left whole

2 tablespoons red wine vinegar, or more to taste

Chopped parsley for garnish

Assorted mustards

1. Put the tripe in a kettle and add the water, salt, peppercorns, carrot, parsley, bay leaf, onion stuck with cloves, celery, thyme, and red pepper. Cover and cook for about 5 hours. Let cool.

2. Drain the tripe and cut it into thin, bite-size strips (there should be about 2 cups).

3. Heat the butter in a skillet and add the tripe. Cook, stirring briefly, and add the sliced onions. Cook over moderately high heat until the onions start to brown, stirring gently and shaking the skillet. Add the garlic, turn the heat to low, and cook, stirring frequently, for about 10 minutes longer. Remove the garlic.

4. Add the vinegar and serve sprinkled with chopped parsley. Serve mustard on the side, letting guests help themselves.

Yield: 4 to 6 servings.

BRAISED VEAL ROAST WITH ROSEMARY

1. Sprinkle the veal with salt and pepper.
2. Melt the butter in a heavy casserole in which the veal fits snugly but without crowding. Add the veal and brown on all sides over moderate heat for about 15 minutes, turning often.
3. Add the carrots, onion, garlic, and rosemary. Stir the vegetables around in the bottom. Add the wine, tomatoes, and parsley. Cover closely and cook over low heat for about 1¼ hours. Turn the meat.
4. Uncover and cook for about 15 minutes longer.

Yield: 4 to 6 servings.

One 2½-pound veal roast, tied

Salt and freshly ground pepper to taste

2 tablespoons butter

¾ cup finely cubed carrots

¾ cup finely diced onion

1 whole garlic clove, peeled

2 fresh rosemary sprigs, or 2 teaspoons dried

½ cup dry white wine

1 cup diced fresh or canned tomatoes

2 parsley sprigs

PAILLARDE OF VEAL

This is a soaringly good dish that is quickly cooked over charcoal and seasoned with salt, pepper, and lemon.

1. Put the veal steaks between sheets of plastic wrap and pound them as thin as possible, without breaking the flesh. The steaks should be about ⅛ inch thick after pounding.
2. Ideally, the meat should be cooked over hot charcoal. You can also cook it in a very hot, heavy skillet. In either case, brush each side of the veal with ½ teaspoon of the oil. Cook the veal for about 30 seconds on each side. If you wish to make a grilled pattern, give the meat a half turn on each side.
3. Sprinkle the meat with salt and a generous grinding of pepper and serve with lemon wedges.

Yield: 4 servings.

Note: You can also use veal chops for this dish with the bone left intact. Pound, or have the butcher pound, the meat of the chop as thin as possible without breaking the flesh.

4 skinless, boneless, lean veal steaks, cut from the leg or loin (see note)

4 teaspoons peanut, vegetable, or corn oil

Salt and freshly ground pepper to taste

4 lemon wedges

VEAL SAUTÉ IN TOMATO SAUCE

4 pounds veal shoulder
  and/or breast, boned
  and cut into 2-inch
  cubes

Salt and freshly ground
pepper to taste

4 tablespoons oil

2 cups finely chopped
  onions

1 tablespoon finely
  chopped garlic

1 teaspoon stem saffron,
  optional

¼ cup flour

¼ cup dry white wine

3½ cups peeled, chopped
  tomatoes or the
  contents of a 28-ounce
  can whole peeled
  tomatoes

1 cup fresh or canned
  chicken broth

2 teaspoons dried
  rosemary

1. Preheat the oven to 375 degrees.

2. Sprinkle the veal with the salt and pepper. Heat the oil in a heavy, large casserole or Dutch oven and add the meat. Cook, stirring frequently, for about 20 minutes. In the beginning the meat will give up liquid. This will evaporate as the meat cooks. Continue until the meat is browned all over.

3. Add the onions, garlic, saffron, if desired, and cook, stirring occasionally, for about 5 minutes. Sprinkle with flour and stir until the pieces of meat are evenly coated. Add the wine, tomatoes, and chicken broth. Sprinkle with salt and pepper to taste. Add the dried rosemary. Cover and bake for 1 hour.

Yield: 6 to 8 servings.

BREAST OF VEAL
WITH WATERCRESS STUFFING

There is, we are convinced, a definite hierarchy or pecking order for foods. Ground meat dishes—which rank high on our list of preferences—belong to the baser and lesser order of things. Veal—and again, this is highly subjective—ranks among the most aristocratic.

The trouble with veal is cost. The reason for the elevated price is natural. It simply requires more careful nurturing and coddling to produce the finest grade of veal, compared with the finest piece of beef or pork.

The most expensive part of the veal is the loin, from which come the rack, the saddle, and the chops. The least expensive is the breast of veal and for this particular cut we have a special liking. It is juicy, meaty, and flavorful.

1. Wipe the meat well with a damp cloth.

2. Rinse the watercress well and drop it into boiling water. Let stand for about 10 seconds. Drain well and, when cool enough to handle, squeeze it to extract excess moisture. Chop it and set aside.

3. Put the pork in a deep saucepan and add the 2 cups of chopped onions and the finely minced garlic. Cook, stirring, for about 5 minutes and add the mushrooms, chopped thyme, and chopped bay leaf. Cook, stirring occasionally, for about 15 minutes. Add the chopped watercress and stir to blend well. Remove from the heat. Stir in the bread crumbs and add the beaten eggs, salt, and pepper. Stir and let cool.

4. Meanwhile, preheat the oven to 400 degrees.

5. Stuff the veal with the watercress mixture and sew up the pocket all around to enclose the filling. Sprinkle the meat on all sides with salt and pepper to taste.

6. Melt the butter in a heavy skillet or roasting pan and add the veal skin side down and bone side up. Bake for 15 minutes and turn the meat skin side up. Bake for 15 minutes longer.

7. Scatter the celery, green peppers, coarsely chopped onion, coarsely chopped garlic, whole bay leaf, thyme sprigs, and tomatoes around, but not on top of, the meat. Cover closely with foil and bake for 1 hour.

8. Reduce the oven temperature to 350 degrees. Uncover the meat and bake for 30 minutes longer. Let stand for about 10 minutes before slicing. Serve with vegetables in sauce surrounding the roast.

Yield: 12 or more servings.

One 8- to 9-pound breast of veal with a pocket for stuffing

2 bunches fresh watercress, trimmed, about ½ pound

1 pound ground pork

2 cups finely chopped onions

2 garlic cloves, finely minced

½ pound mushrooms, finely chopped

2 fresh thyme sprigs, finely chopped, or ½ teaspoon dried

1 bay leaf, chopped

1½ cups fresh bread crumbs

3 eggs, lightly beaten

Salt and freshly ground pepper to taste

3 tablespoons butter

4 to 6 celery stalks, cut into ½-inch cubes

2 green peppers, cored and cut into ¾-inch pieces

1 large onion, coarsely chopped

2 garlic cloves, coarsely chopped

1 whole bay leaf

2 fresh thyme sprigs, or 1 teaspoon dried

4 cups canned imported Italian tomatoes

SAUTÉED VEAL CHOPS WITH VINEGAR GLAZE

4 loin veal chops, about
½ pound each

Salt and freshly ground
pepper to taste

2 tablespoons butter

4 whole garlic cloves,
peeled

2 bay leaves

4 fresh thyme sprigs, or
½ teaspoon dried

1 tablespoon red wine
vinegar

½ cup fresh or canned
chicken broth

Sprinkle the chops on both sides with the salt and pepper. Heat the butter in a skillet and add the chops. Brown on both sides, turning once. They should cook about 5 minutes to a side. Add the garlic, bay leaves, and thyme and cook for about 3 minutes. Pour the vinegar around the chops and turn the heat to high. Add the broth, cover closely, and cook for about 20 minutes.

Yield: 4 servings.

VEAL À LA OSKAR

1. Sprinkle the chops on both sides with the salt and pepper. Skewer the tail of each chop to hold it neatly in place.

2. Scrape the sides of the asparagus spears but leave the tips intact. Put in a skillet with cold water to cover and salt to taste. Bring to the boil and simmer for about 3 minutes, or until crisp-tender. Drain.

3. Heat 2 tablespoons of the butter in a heavy skillet large enough to hold the chops in one layer. Brown on one side, for about 10 minutes. Turn and brown on the other side, for about 10 minutes.

4. Melt a teaspoon of butter in a small skillet and add the shrimp. Cook briefly just to heat through.

5. Arrange the chops on a serving platter and garnish each with 2 asparagus spears. Spoon béarnaise sauce over the asparagus and garnish the top of each serving with 1 shrimp.

Yield: 4 servings.

4 loin veal chops, about 2½ pounds

Salt and freshly ground pepper to taste

8 asparagus spears

2 tablespoons plus 1 teaspoon butter

4 cooked, peeled shrimp

¾ cup béarnaise sauce (see recipe page 772)

BREADED VEAL SCALOPPINE

4 slices veal scaloppine
   Salt and freshly ground
   pepper to taste
2 tablespoons flour
1 large egg, beaten
2 tablespoons water
1½ cups bread crumbs
3 tablespoons oil, plus
   more as necessary
1 tablespoon butter, plus
   more as necessary
4 tablespoons brown
   sauce, or canned brown
   beef gravy, optional
4 tablespoons beurre
   noisette (see following
   recipe), optional
   Parsley sprigs for
   garnish

One of the fundamental principles of any traditional cooking is that almost every dish is a variation on another dish. Perhaps the finest and most basic illustration of this can be found in a plain, unadorned, breaded veal cutlet or scaloppine. With a bit of hot butter and a garnish of lemon, it can be delectable as is. But over the years, chefs have dramatically altered this basic recipe by simply adding other foods—capers, chopped eggs, anchovies, cheese, mushrooms, and so on. Veal, of course, is one of the most versatile of foods and adapts well to scores of flavors and seasonings.

1. Pound the meat with a flat mallet to make it thin. Sprinkle with the salt and pepper. Dredge first in the flour, then in the beaten egg mixed with water, and finally in bread crumbs. As each piece is breaded, transfer to a flat surface and pound lightly with the flat side of a heavy kitchen knife to help crumbs adhere.

2. Heat the oil and butter in a heavy skillet and cook the meat until brown on one side. If the skillet is not large enough to hold them in one layer, this will have to be repeated two or more times. When the veal is brown on one side, turn and cook to brown on the other side. Cook until cooked through. Total cooking time for each slice should be from 3 to 5 minutes, depending on the thickness of the meat and the degree of heat. If necessary, add a little more oil and butter to the skillet until all the pieces are cooked.

3. Place one slice of veal on each of four serving dishes. Surround each serving with 1 tablespoon of hot brown sauce and pour over each serving 1 tablespoon of sizzling beurre noisette. Garnish each serving with a sprig of parsley.

Yield: 4 servings.

BEURRE NOISETTE
(HAZELNUT BUTTER)

Put any given amount of butter in a small skillet. Cook over moderate heat, shaking the skillet so that the butter browns evenly. At first the butter will foam. This will subside. When the butter becomes hazelnut brown, remove it immediately from the heat and spoon over the scaloppine.

SCALOPPINE WITH MUSHROOMS

1. Pound the scaloppine on a flat surface with a flat mallet. Do not break the tissues. Set aside.

2. Slice the mushrooms thin. There should be about 5 cups. Set aside.

3. Heat the olive oil in a large skillet. When it is hot and almost smoking, add the mushrooms. Cook over moderately high heat until the mushrooms give up their liquid. Cook until the liquid evaporates and the mushrooms are browned. Set aside.

4. Heat the peanut oil in a heavy skillet. Dredge the scaloppine in flour seasoned with pepper. Cook the scaloppine, a few at a time, on both sides until lightly browned, for about 45 seconds on each side. As they are cooked, transfer them to a warm platter.

5. Pour off the oil from the skillet in which the scaloppine cooked. Add the butter and, when it is hot, add the mushrooms. Cook briefly, shaking the skillet and turning the mushrooms. Add the shallots and cook briefly, stirring. Add the wine and cook, stirring to dissolve the brown particles that cling to the bottom of the skillet. Pour the mushrooms over the veal and serve sprinkled with chopped parsley.

Yield: 4 to 6 servings.

12 slices veal scaloppine, about 1¼ pounds
¾ pound mushrooms
2 tablespoons olive oil
¼ cup peanut, vegetable, or corn oil
¼ cup flour
Freshly ground pepper to taste
2 tablespoons butter
⅓ cup finely chopped shallots
⅓ cup dry white wine
¼ cup finely chopped parsley

Veal Scaloppine with Mustard Seeds

8 slices veal scaloppine, about ¾ pound

1 tablespoon Dijon mustard

2 teaspoons mustard seeds

2 tablespoons butter

¼ cup water

½ to ¾ cup fresh tomato sauce (see recipe page 784)

One of the greatest of all French chefs is the celebrated Jean Troisgros. It was he who introduced me to this uncommonly delicious and hastily made preparation.

1. Put each piece of scaloppine between sheets of plastic wrap and pound lightly with a flat mallet. Do not break the flesh. Brush both sides of the scaloppine with the mustard. Sprinkle both sides with mustard seeds.

2. Heat the butter in a skillet and, when it is quite hot but not brown, add the scaloppine. Cook for 20 or 30 seconds over high heat. Turn. Cook for 10 or 15 seconds over high heat and transfer to a warm platter. This may need to be done in several batches.

3. When all the veal is cooked and transferred to the platter, add the water and swirl it around. When it boils rapidly, pour and scrape the pan sauce over the veal. Serve with hot, fresh tomato sauce.

Yield: 4 servings.

Veal Piccata with Lemon

½ pound veal scaloppine, cut into ¼-inch-thick slices

Flour for dredging

Salt and freshly ground pepper to taste

2 tablespoons butter

2 tablespoons olive oil

2 tablespoons dry white wine

2 tablespoons lemon juice

2 thin lemon slices

2 teaspoons finely chopped parsley

1. Unless the scaloppine are very small, cut them into pieces measuring about 3 x 3 inches. Place them between sheets of wax paper and pound lightly to flatten, using the bottom of a heavy skillet or a flat mallet.

2. Blend the flour with the salt and pepper. Dip the meat into the flour to coat lightly. Using a large heavy skillet, heat the butter and oil and, when it is very hot but not brown, add the meat in one layer. Cook over relatively high heat until golden brown on one side. Turn and cook until golden brown on the other.

3. Carefully pour off the fat from the skillet, holding the meat back with a spoon or lid. Return the skillet to the heat and add the wine. Cook briefly until it starts to evaporate, stirring to dissolve any brown particles in the skillet. Add the lemon juice and turn the meat in the thin sauce thus created. Transfer the meat to two plates and garnish each with a lemon slice and parsley.

Yield: 2 servings.

VEAL AND ARTICHOKES

1. Pull away all the tough outer leaves from the artichokes. Carve away the stem from each artichoke and carve away the leaves around the base of each artichoke. Cut each artichoke bottom in half crosswise. Cut away the fuzzy choke from the center of each. Place the cut side of each bottom half on a flat surface and cut into thin slices. As each half is sliced, sprinkle with a little lemon juice and toss the slices so that they are lightly coated with lemon. This will prevent discoloration.

2. Use a large heavy skillet and add peanut oil. Add the whole cloves of garlic and cook until browned. Discard the garlic.

3. Add the sliced artichokes to the skillet and cook, stirring, for about 5 minutes. Add the chopped garlic. Cook for about 1 minute and add the wine. Cook for about 1 minute; then simmer for about 5 minutes.

4. Meanwhile, stack the veal slices. Cut the veal into very thin ¼-inch strips. Put the flour in a shallow dish and toss the veal strips in the flour.

5. Use a clean wide skillet and add the olive oil.

6. Shake the excess flour from the veal strips.

7. When the olive oil is very hot, add the veal. Cook quickly over high heat, stirring. Sprinkle with salt and the rosemary. Continue stirring for about 4 minutes, or until the veal is lightly browned.

8. Add the artichokes and continue cooking for about 2 minutes longer. Serve with hot polenta, if desired.

Yield: 4 to 6 servings.

6 small artichokes, about 3½ pounds

Juice of 1 lemon

¾ cup peanut, vegetable, or corn oil

3 whole garlic cloves, peeled

2 teaspoons coarsely chopped garlic

½ cup dry white wine

1 pound thinly sliced veal, preferably from the leg

2 tablespoons flour

½ cup olive oil

Salt to taste

½ teaspoon dried rosemary leaves

OISEAUX SANS TÊTES (VEAL ROLLS STUFFED WITH SAUSAGE AND HERBS)

12 thin slices veal, about
1½ pounds, cut as for
scaloppine

1 teaspoon plus
3 tablespoons butter

1 cup finely chopped
onion

1½ teaspoons finely
minced garlic

¾ pound lean bulk
sausage meat

¼ cup finely chopped
parsley

1 egg, lightly beaten

Salt and freshly ground
pepper to taste

¼ cup flour

2 tablespoons finely
chopped shallots

1 bay leaf

½ teaspoon dried thyme

¾ cup finely diced carrot

¾ cup finely diced celery

½ cup dry white wine

1 cup crushed tomatoes

1. Put each slice of veal between sheets of plastic wrap and pound with a flat mallet without breaking the tissues. Set aside.

2. Melt 1 teaspoon of the butter in a saucepan and add ½ cup of the onion and ½ teaspoon of the garlic. Cook, stirring, until the mixture is wilted.

3. Spoon and scrape the mixture into a mixing bowl and add the sausage meat, parsley, egg, salt, and pepper. Blend well.

4. Lay out the pieces of veal in one layer on a flat surface. Sprinkle with salt and pepper. Spoon an equal portion of the filling on each slice. Wrap the meat around the filling, folding and tucking in the ends in envelope fashion. Tie each roll neatly in two places with string. Sprinkle with salt and pepper. Dredge the rolls all over in flour and shake off any excess.

5. Select a heavy skillet large enough to hold the rolls in one layer without crowding them. Melt the remaining 3 tablespoons of butter and, when it is quite hot but not browned, add the rolls. Cook, turning occasionally, until they are nicely browned all over, 3 or 4 minutes.

6. Transfer the rolls to a warm platter.

7. Add the shallots, the remaining ½ cup of onion, the remaining teaspoon of garlic, bay leaf, thyme, carrot, and celery. Cook, stirring, for about 2 minutes. Add the wine and stir to dissolve the brown particles that cling to the bottom and sides of the skillet. Add the tomatoes and cook, stirring occasionally, for about 5 minutes.

8. Return the veal rolls to the skillet and turn to coat them with sauce. Cover closely and simmer for 30 minutes. Remove the strings and serve.

Yield: 6 servings.

VEAL ROLLS STUFFED WITH PROSCIUTTO AND CHEESE

1. Put the slices of veal between sheets of plastic wrap and pound with a flat mallet without breaking the tissues. Set aside.

2. Combine the prosciutto and pork in a mixing bowl.

3. Melt 1 tablespoon of the butter in a small skillet and cook the onion, stirring, until it is wilted. Add this to the mixing bowl. Add the garlic, bread crumbs, nutmeg, pepper, lemon rind, egg, and cheese. Blend well.

4. Lay out the pieces of veal in one layer on a flat surface. Sprinkle with salt and pepper. Spoon an equal portion of the filling on each slice. Wrap the meat around the filling, folding and tucking the ends in envelope fashion. Tie each roll neatly in two places with string. Sprinkle with salt and pepper. Dredge the rolls all over in flour and shake off any excess.

5. Select a heavy skillet large enough to hold the rolls in one layer without crowding them. Melt the remaining 3 tablespoons of butter and, when it is quite hot but not browned, add the veal rolls. Cook, turning occasionally, until they are nicely browned all over, 3 or 4 minutes. Reduce the heat and continue cooking over moderately low heat for about 15 minutes.

6. Add the wine and stir to dissolve the brown particles that cling to the bottom and sides of the pan. Add the chicken broth. Bring to the boil and let cook over high heat for about 5 minutes. Remove the strings and serve the veal rolls with the sauce spooned over.

Yield: 6 servings.

12 thin slices veal, about 1½ pounds, cut as for scaloppine

¼ cup chopped prosciutto or cooked ham

½ pound ground lean pork

1 teaspoon plus 3 tablespoons butter

½ cup finely chopped onion

½ teaspoon finely minced garlic

½ cup fine fresh bread crumbs

⅛ teaspoon grated nutmeg

Freshly ground pepper to taste

½ teaspoon grated lemon rind

1 egg, lightly beaten

¼ cup freshly grated Parmesan cheese

Salt to taste

¼ cup flour

½ cup dry white wine

1 cup fresh or canned chicken broth

BEEF ROLLS STUFFED WITH PORK AND DILL PICKLES

12 thin slices top round of beef, about 1½ pounds, cut as for scaloppine

12 teaspoons Dijon mustard

½ pound ground lean pork

12 tablespoons plus ½ cup finely chopped onion

Salt and freshly ground pepper to taste

3 dill pickles, quartered

3 tablespoons corn, peanut, or vegetable oil

½ cup thinly sliced carrot

½ cup finely chopped celery

1 tablespoon paprika

½ cup dry white wine

1 cup fresh or canned chicken broth

2 teaspoons cornstarch or arrowroot

1 tablespoon cold water

½ cup sour cream

1. Put the slices of beef between sheets of plastic wrap and pound with a flat mallet without breaking the tissues.

2. Lay out the pieces of beef in one layer on a flat surface. Spread the top of each with 1 teaspoon of mustard. Spoon an equal portion of the pork in the center of each piece. Flatten the pork over the center, leaving the margin uncovered. Sprinkle 1 tablespoon of the chopped onion over each portion of pork. Sprinkle with salt and pepper and cover with 1 strip of pickle. Wrap the meat around the filling, folding and tucking in the ends in envelope fashion. Tie each roll neatly in two places with string. Sprinkle with salt and pepper.

3. Select a skillet large enough to hold the meat rolls in one layer without crowding them. Heat the oil and, when it is quite hot but not smoking, add the rolls. Cook, turning occasionally, 3 to 5 minutes, or until nicely browned all over.

4. Transfer the rolls to a warm platter and pour off all the fat from the skillet. Return the skillet to the heat. Add the remaining ½ cup chopped onion, carrot, and celery and cook, stirring, until the onion is wilted. Sprinkle with paprika and stir. Add the wine and stir to dissolve the brown particles that cling to the bottom and sides of the skillet. Return the meat rolls to the skillet and add the chicken broth.

5. Cover and cook for 5 minutes. Transfer the meat rolls to a warm platter. Remove the strings.

6. Cook down the pan liquid with vegetables until reduced to about 2 cups. Blend the cornstarch or arrowroot with water and stir it into the sauce. Cook, stirring, for about 10 seconds. Remove from the heat.

7. Stir in the sour cream. Strain the sauce, pushing with a wooden spoon to extract as much liquid from the solids as possible. Serve the meat rolls with the sauce spooned over.

Yield: 6 servings.

VEAL, CHICKEN, AND
WILD MUSHROOM MEAT LOAF

1. Put the mushrooms in a bowl and add warm water to cover. Let stand for 30 minutes or longer. Drain thoroughly, but reserve ¼ cup of the liquid.

2. Preheat the oven to 400 degrees.

3. Have the chicken breast ground by the butcher or grind it in a food processor. Put it in a bowl and add the veal.

4. Melt the butter in a saucepan and add the onion and garlic. Cook, stirring, until wilted. Add the mushrooms and cook, stirring, for about 1 minute. Let cool briefly.

5. Add the mushroom mixture and egg to the meat. Blend. Add the bread crumbs, parsley, nutmeg, cream, the reserved ¼ cup of mushroom liquid, salt and pepper to taste. Mix thoroughly.

6. Pack the mixture into a loaf pan measuring about 9 x 5 x 3 inches. Set the pan in a larger pan of water. Bring to the boil on top of the stove. Place both pans in the oven and bake for 1 hour (internal temperature should be 160 degrees). Let stand for about 15 minutes before slicing.

Yield: 8 or more servings.

1 cup dried imported mushrooms

1 pound skinless, boneless chicken breast

1 pound ground veal

2 tablespoons butter

½ cup finely chopped onion

½ teaspoon finely minced garlic

1 egg, lightly beaten

1 cup fine fresh bread crumbs

⅓ cup finely chopped parsley

¼ teaspoon ground nutmeg

¼ cup heavy cream

Salt and freshly ground pepper to taste

OSSOBUCO MILANESE

3 veal shanks, each
  sawed into 3 pieces
  2 inches thick

⅓ cup flour

2 teaspoons salt

½ teaspoon freshly
  ground pepper

3 tablespoons olive oil

3 tablespoons butter

½ teaspoon ground sage

1 teaspoon rosemary

1 medium-size onion,
  finely chopped

3 garlic cloves

2 small carrots, diced

1 celery rib, diced

1¼ cups dry white wine

1¼ cups fresh or canned
   chicken broth

2 tablespoons tomato
  paste

1½ tablespoons chopped
   parsley

1 tablespoon grated
  lemon peel

It may be a cliché, the thought that the nearer the bone, the sweeter the meat, but it is the absolute reason why dishes made with shanks of meat are rich in flavor. One of the most admired dishes in the cooking of Italy is ossobuco, veal shanks perfumed with herbs and, classically, grated lemon peel.

The braised shank of veal is a creation that we adapted from a dish sampled at the fashionable El Toula restaurant in Rome. The recipe calls for a purée of white truffles, which is a nice conceit but not essential to the success of the dish.

1. Dredge the meat in the flour seasoned with 1 teaspoon of the salt and the pepper. Heat the oil and butter together in a large skillet. Using medium heat, cook the meat on all sides until golden brown. If necessary, add a little more oil or butter.

2. Arrange the meat in a Dutch oven, standing each piece on its side so the marrow in the bones does not fall out as the meat cooks. Sprinkle the veal with the sage and rosemary. Add the onion, 1 clove of minced garlic, the carrots, and celery. Sprinkle the vegetables with the remaining 1 teaspoon of salt. Cover the Dutch oven closely and cook for 10 minutes. Remove the cover and add the wine, chicken broth, and tomato paste. Cover and simmer the dish on top of the stove for 2 hours.

3. Mince the remaining 2 cloves of garlic and combine with the parsley and lemon peel. Sprinkle the mixture, called gremolada, over the veal and serve immediately.

Yield: 6 to 8 servings.

BRAISED VEAL SHANK

1. Sprinkle the veal with salt and pepper to taste. Heat the butter in a casserole and brown the meat all over until golden, about 5 minutes. Scatter around it the carrot rounds, onion, celery, and garlic and cook for about 5 minutes. Add the wine, chicken broth, tomatoes, parsley, bay leaf, thyme, salt, and pepper. Cover closely and cook for about 2 hours, or until fork tender.

2. Transfer the meat to a warm platter and cover with foil to keep warm.

3. Strain the sauce through a sieve, pushing through as much liquid from the solids as possible, using a heavy metal or wooden spoon. Discard the solids. Let the sauce simmer slowly for about 10 minutes and add the truffle purée, if desired. Simmer briefly. Blend the cornstarch with wine and stir it in. Simmer for about 30 seconds and remove from the heat.

4. Meanwhile, prepare the vegetables for garnish. Put the onions in a saucepan and add cold water to cover and salt to taste. Simmer for about 10 minutes and add the carrots. Simmer for 5 minutes longer. Drain.

5. As the onions cook, put the potatoes in another saucepan and add cold water to cover and salt to taste. Bring to the boil and simmer for 1 minute. Drain.

6. Heat the butter in a large casserole and add the onions, carrots, potatoes, and peas. Sprinkle with salt and pepper to taste. Cover and cook for about 5 minutes. Add ½ cup of the sauce and cover. Cook for about 10 minutes longer, or until tender. Serve the meat carved with the vegetables. Serve the sauce separately.

Yield: 8 to 12 servings.

THE VEAL:

One 3½- to 4-pound veal shank, taken from the leg

Salt and freshly ground pepper to taste

2 tablespoons butter

½ cup carrot rounds

½ cup coarsely chopped onion

½ cup chopped celery

1 garlic clove, cut into quarters

1 cup dry white wine

1 cup fresh or canned chicken broth

½ cup chopped tomatoes

4 fresh parsley sprigs

1 bay leaf

2 fresh thyme sprigs

2 tablespoons white truffle purée, available in cans where fine Italian foods are sold, optional

1 teaspoon cornstarch

2 teaspoons dry white wine

THE VEGETABLE GARNISH:

8 small white onions, peeled, about ¾ pound

Salt

2 large carrots, trimmed, scraped, and quartered

1 large potato, peeled and cut into 10 wedges

2 tablespoons butter

1 cup freshly shelled peas

Freshly ground pepper

VEAL SHANK WITH FRESH BASIL

One 3-pound veal shank taken from the hind leg

2 garlic cloves, peeled and cut lengthwise into 4 pieces

Salt and freshly ground pepper to taste

2 tablespoons olive oil

1 cup coarsely chopped onion

1 cup coarsely chopped celery

2 large carrots, scraped, quartered, and cut into 2-inch lengths

2 garlic cloves, finely minced

1 tablespoon finely chopped fresh basil

½ cup dry white wine

½ cup fresh or canned chicken broth

1. Preheat the oven to 425 degrees.

2. Wipe the shank with a damp, clean cloth. Pierce the meaty part of the shank in eight places and insert the garlic slivers. Sprinkle the shank with the salt and pepper.

3. Place the shank in an ovenproof casserole and pour the oil over the shank. Turn the shank in the oil to coat completely. Place in the oven and bake for 15 minutes. Turn the shank and continue cooking.

4. When the shank has cooked 15 minutes longer, or a total of 30 minutes, reduce the oven temperature to 350 degrees.

5. Remove the shank from the oven and pour off the fat from the pan. Return the shank to the pan and add the onion, celery, carrots, minced garlic, and basil. Return the shank with vegetables to the oven and bake for 30 minutes. Add the wine and broth and cover the pan closely with foil. Return to the oven and bake for 1 hour longer. Total baking time is 2 hours.

6. Place the pan on the stove and remove the foil. Bring the pan juices to the boil and reduce slightly, stirring occasionally, about 4 minutes. Serve, sliced, with buttered noodles.

Yield: 3 to 4 servings.

CALF'S LIVER SAUTÉ WITH AVOCADO

1. If there are any membranes or nerves in the liver, cut them away and discard. Put each liver slice on a flat surface and cut it into ¼-inch-wide strips (julienne).

2. Peel the avocados and cut them in half. Remove and discard the pits. Cut the avocados into thin wedges. Cut each wedge crosswise in half. Add the lemon juice and toss to prevent discoloration.

3. Melt 3 tablespoons of the butter in a large heavy skillet and add the liver strips, stirring quickly over high heat to cook evenly. Add the shallots and bay leaf and cook for 2 minutes or less.

4. Have ready another large skillet and in this melt the remaining tablespoon of butter.

5. Using a slotted spoon, transfer the drained strips of liver to the second skillet. Cook briefly and add the avocados. Let cook gently as you complete the dish.

6. Let any pan liquid from the first skillet cook down for about 1 minute and add the Cognac. Add the crème fraîche and cook down over high heat for about 2 minutes. Add salt and pepper to taste.

7. Strain the cream sauce over the liver and avocado. Add the mustard and stir. Heat thoroughly and serve hot.

Yield: 4 to 6 servings.

1½ pounds thinly sliced calf's liver

2 avocados

Juice of ½ lemon

4 tablespoons butter

2 tablespoons finely chopped shallots

1 bay leaf

1 tablespoon Cognac

1 cup crème fraîche

Salt and freshly ground pepper to taste

1 tablespoon Dijon mustard

SAUTÉED CALF'S LIVER WITH BACON

8 slices bacon

8 thin slices calf's liver, about 1¼ pounds

Salt and freshly ground pepper to taste

¼ cup flour

2 tablespoons vegetable, peanut, or corn oil

3 tablespoons butter

1 tablespoon Worcestershire sauce

1. Arrange the bacon slices in one layer in a skillet. Cook, turning as often as necessary, until browned and crisp. Drain on paper towels. Pour off all but about 1 teaspoon of the bacon fat.

2. Sprinkle the liver with salt and pepper on both sides. Dredge lightly in flour, shaking to remove excess.

3. Add the oil to the skillet and, when hot, add as many slices of liver as the skillet will hold in one layer. Cook over high heat for 1 minute or longer until nicely browned. The cooking time will vary, depending on the thickness of the slices. Turn and cook for 1 minute or longer to the desired degree of doneness. Continue until all the slices are cooked. Transfer the liver to a warm platter and keep warm.

4. Pour off any fat that is left in the pan. Wipe out the pan with a clean cloth or paper towels. Add the butter to the skillet and cook over high heat until butter is hazelnut brown.

5. Garnish the liver with the bacon. Spoon the Worcestershire sauce over and around the liver. Pour the hazelnut butter over all and serve immediately.

Yield: 4 servings.

SAUTÉED CALF'S LIVER WITH VINEGAR GLAZE

1 pound calf's liver, sliced (see note)

½ cup flour

Salt and freshly ground pepper to taste

4 tablespoons butter

¼ cup finely chopped parsley

¼ cup sherry wine or red wine vinegar

1. The liver may be cut into 4 to 8 slices according to taste. We prefer it sliced thin. Blend the flour with the salt and pepper and dredge the liver slices on all sides with the mixture.

2. Heat half the butter in a heavy skillet and add the liver. Cook on one side, for 2 minutes or according to taste. Turn the liver and cook that side for 2 minutes more. Transfer the liver to a heated platter and sprinkle with the parsley.

3. Add the remaining butter to the skillet. Let it brown briefly. Pour this over the liver. Add the vinegar to the skillet and bring to the boil, swirling it around in the skillet. Pour this over the liver.

Yield: 4 servings.

Note: If you can persuade your butcher to remove the nerves or veins in each slice of liver, so much the better. Or this may be done at home with a small, sharp knife or scissors.

BREADED SWEETBREADS

There is no more reason why sweetbreads are the basis for some of the most elegant dishes in the world than there is in why people climb mountains or take to the air in ascension balloons. Sweetbread dishes are simply a natural thread in the fabric of fine dining, and have been for centuries. They, along with brains, are the choicest part of the calf to people of taste and discernment.

Sweetbreads should always be soaked, to rid them of residual blood, and weighted, which gives them a firmer, more appetizing texture.

1. Soak the sweetbreads in cold water in the refrigerator for several hours, changing the water frequently. Drain.

2. Put the sweetbreads in a saucepan and add cold water to cover and salt to taste. Bring to the boil and simmer for 5 minutes, no longer. Drain and cover with cold water. When the sweetbreads are cool, drain them. Place them on a wire rack. Cover with another rack and weight them down. For this we have used everything from meat pounders to saucepans filled with stones. Weight the sweetbreads for about 2 hours.

3. Pick over the sweetbreads and remove any odd membranes, filaments, or tendons. Cut the sweetbreads into 8 flat pieces. Dredge the pieces on all sides in flour.

4. Beat the egg and stir in the water, 1 teaspoon of oil, salt, and pepper to taste. Dip the sweetbreads first in the egg mixture, then in the bread crumbs. When well coated, tap lightly to help the crumbs adhere. In a large skillet, heat 1 tablespoon of the butter and the remaining 2 tablespoons of oil. Add the sweetbreads. Cook until golden on one side. Turn and cook until golden on the other side.

5. Remove the sweetbreads to a warm platter. Wipe out the skillet and add the remaining 2 tablespoons of butter. Cook until the foam subsides and the butter is hazelnut brown. Pour the butter over the sweetbreads. Garnish with lemon slices and serve immediately.

Yield: 4 servings.

1 pound sweetbreads
  Salt
½ cup flour
1 egg
2 tablespoons water
2 tablespoons plus
  1 teaspoon peanut,
  vegetable, or corn oil
  Freshly ground pepper
1¼ cups fresh bread
  crumbs
3 tablespoons butter
  Lemon slices for
  garnish

CURRIED SWEETBREADS WITH MUSHROOMS

3½ pounds sweetbreads

4 tablespoons butter

1 cup finely chopped onion

3 tablespoons curry powder

1 cup finely chopped apple

½ cup finely chopped banana

2 tablespoons tomato paste

2 cups fresh or canned chicken broth

Salt to taste

½ pound mushrooms, quartered if small, or cut into eighths if large (3½ to 4 cups)

Freshly ground pepper

½ cup dry white wine

1. Put the sweetbreads in a bowl and add cold water to cover. Soak overnight or for several hours in the refrigerator, changing the water occasionally. Drain.

2. Put the sweetbreads in a large saucepan and add cold water to cover. Bring to the boil and simmer for 5 minutes. Drain immediately. Run under cold water and let stand in the water until thoroughly chilled. Drain. Put the sweetbreads on a rack in a flat pan and cover with another flat pan of the same size. Cover with a heavy weight and let stand for several hours. Cut the sweetbreads into 1-inch cubes, cutting, trimming, or pulling off and discarding connecting tissues and so forth as necessary. Set aside.

3. Heat 2 tablespoons of the butter in a saucepan or skillet and add the onion. Cook until wilted and sprinkle with curry powder. Cook briefly, stirring, and add the apple and banana. Add the tomato paste, stirring, and add the chicken broth. Continue stirring until well blended. Add the salt. Pour the sauce into the container of a food processor or blender and blend until smooth. Set aside.

4. Meanwhile, heat the remaining butter in a large, heavy skillet or casserole and add the sweetbreads. Cook, stirring and shaking the skillet, for about 5 minutes. Add the mushrooms and salt and pepper to taste. Cook, stirring often, for about 10 minutes and add the wine. Cook until most of the wine has evaporated. Add the sauce. Cook, stirring occasionally, for 15 or 20 minutes. Serve with rice, in puff pastry shells, or on toast.

Yield: 6 to 8 servings.

BRAINS IN BEER BATTER

1. Prepare the batter.
2. Cut the brains into 24 cubes of equal size. Place in a bowl and add lemon juice, parsley, 2 tablespoons oil, salt, and pepper.
3. Heat the oil for deep frying. Dip the pieces of brains, one at a time, in the beer batter and then put in the hot fat. Cook, turning and submerging the pieces in the oil as necessary, until golden brown all over. Drain on absorbent paper towels.

Yield: 4 to 6 servings.

Beer batter (see recipe page 447)

2 sets precooked calf's brains, about 1 pound (see following recipe)

Juice of ½ lemon

2 tablespoons chopped parsley

2 tablespoons peanut, vegetable, or corn oil

Salt and freshly ground pepper to taste

Oil for deep frying

PRECOOKED CALF'S BRAINS

1. A calf's brain consists of a pair of lobes. Place in a mixing bowl and add cold water to cover. Let stand for several hours, changing the cold water frequently.
2. Drain and pick over the brains to remove the outer membranes, blood, and other extraneous matter. Place the brains in a saucepan and add cold water to cover to a depth of about ½ inch above the brains. Add the peppercorns, salt to taste, vinegar, bay leaf, and thyme. Bring to the boil and simmer for about 3 minutes. Let cool in the cooking liquid. They are now ready to be drained and given a final preparation as for brains in beer batter.

2 sets calf's brains (about 1 pound)

12 peppercorns
Salt

2 tablespoons vinegar

1 bay leaf

2 fresh thyme sprigs, or ½ teaspoon dried

VEAL KIDNEYS IN RED WINE SAUCE

3 tablespoons coarsely chopped shallots

1 cup dry red wine

½ bay leaf

2 fresh thyme sprigs, or ½ teaspoon dried

½ teaspoon crushed peppercorns

2 parsley sprigs

4 teaspoons red wine vinegar

1 10¾-ounce can brown beef gravy

Salt and freshly ground pepper to taste

3 veal kidneys, about 1¾ pounds

3 tablespoons butter

½ pound fresh mushrooms, thinly sliced

½ cup heavy cream

1. Combine the shallots, wine, bay leaf, thyme, peppercorns, parsley, and 1 teaspoon of the wine vinegar in a saucepan. Bring to the boil and cook for about 5 minutes over high heat to reduce. Add the brown beef gravy and simmer for 15 minutes. Add salt and pepper and the remaining vinegar.

2. Meanwhile, split the kidneys in half and cut away the white center core. Thinly slice the kidneys crosswise and sprinkle with salt and pepper to taste. Heat 2 tablespoons of butter in a skillet and, when it is very hot and starts to brown, add the kidneys. Cook, shaking the skillet and stirring, over high heat for 2 to 3 minutes, no longer. Turn the kidneys into a colander and let stand for 10 to 15 minutes to drain thoroughly. Do not wash the skillet.

3. To the skillet in which the kidneys cooked add 1 tablespoon of butter and the mushrooms. Cook over high heat until the mushrooms give up their juices and then until the liquid evaporates.

4. Add the drained kidneys to the mushrooms. Strain the sauce over all and bring to the boil. Add the heavy cream and, when it reaches the boil, swirl in the remaining butter. Add salt and pepper to taste and serve piping hot.

Yield: 4 to 6 servings.

HIGH-TEMPERATURE ROAST LEG OF LAMB

Inspired by the immensely popular technique for roasting beef developed by Ann Seranne, Dorothy Moore attempted a similar "foolproof" recipe for cooking a whole leg of lamb. The technique is simple—roasting at a high temperature and then turning off the oven—and the results are admirable. As with the beef, this should not be attempted unless the oven is well insulated.

1. It is recommended that you have the butcher remove and set aside the hip bone of the lamb. This is the upper bone that is attached to the main (straight) leg bone. This can also be done in the home kitchen. Using a sharp knife, cut away a very thin layer of top fat. Do not cut away all the fat, however. Leave a thin coating.

2. Place the lamb, fat side up, in a shallow roasting pan. Make several gashes in the fat and near the bone of the lamb. Insert slivers of garlic in the gashes. Rub the lamb all over with salt, pepper, bay leaf, thyme, and rosemary leaves. Add the vermouth and olive oil. The lamb may be covered closely and refrigerated at this point for several hours or overnight. Remember, however, it is best to let the lamb return to room temperature before putting it in the oven.

3. Preheat the oven to 500 degrees.

4. If you wish the lamb to be rare, place it in the oven and bake for 15 minutes. Turn off the oven. Do not open the door at any time until the lamb is ready to be carved and served. Let stand in the oven for 3 hours. If you wish the lamb to be medium-well done, let it bake for 20 minutes. Turn off the oven and, without opening the door, let stand for 3½ hours. If you wish the lamb to be well done, let it bake for 25 minutes and let it stand in the oven for 3¾ hours.

5. Strain the pan liquid. Strain off most of the surface fat from the drippings. Reheat and serve the natural sauce with the lamb when carved.

Yield: 8 or more servings.

1 small leg of lamb, about 6 pounds

2 garlic cloves, cut into slivers

Salt and freshly ground pepper to taste

1 bay leaf, broken

3 fresh thyme sprigs, chopped, or ½ teaspoon dried

½ teaspoon rosemary leaves

2 tablespoons dry vermouth

2 tablespoons olive oil

LEG OF LAMB WITH FLAGEOLETS

1 pound dried flageolets

2 pounds onions, thinly sliced

2 tablespoons butter

2 pounds potatoes, unpeeled and thinly sliced

2 tablespoons salt

¼ teaspoon freshly ground pepper

1 cup fresh or canned beef broth

1 bay leaf

One 6- to 7-pound leg of lamb

1 teaspoon dried rosemary

1. Cover beans with cold water. Refrigerate, covered, overnight.

2. Drain the beans. Into a 6-quart saucepan pour 2 quarts of water. Bring to the boil and add the beans. Cover and simmer for 45 minutes, or until tender. Drain.

3. Preheat the oven to 325 degrees.

4. Sauté the onions in hot butter until golden.

5. In a baking dish (one measuring 13 x 10 x 4 inches is ideal), layer half of the potatoes, onions, beans, salt, and pepper. Repeat layering. Heat the broth with bay leaf to boiling. Pour over the vegetables.

6. Rub the lamb with rosemary. Place on top of the vegetables. Bake uncovered for 2 to 2½ hours, or until rare or medium-well done.

Yield: 8 servings.

BRAISED LAMB WITH BASIL AND GARLIC STUFFING

1. When the lamb is boned, ask the butcher to reserve the bones and crack them.

2. Combine the bacon, garlic, parsley, and basil in a food processor or use a blender. Blend the ingredients to a fine purée.

3. Sprinkle the lamb inside with salt and pepper. Spread the bacon mixture inside the lamb to fill it. If some of the stuffing oozes out, no matter. Sew up the lamb, tucking in torn pieces as necessary. Sprinkle the lamb all over with salt and pepper. Rub the lamb with any excess bacon and herb mixture.

4. Place the lamb, fat side down, in a heavy casserole and arrange the bones around it. The lamb and bones should fit snugly inside the casserole. Brown the lamb on all sides and sprinkle onion and carrots around it. Cover and cook for about 5 minutes.

5. Carefully pour off and discard all fat that has accumulated. Add the wine, tomatoes, salt, and pepper. Cover and bring to the boil. Cook over moderate heat for about 2 hours.

6. Remove the lamb and strain the sauce into a saucepan. Bring to the boil and skim the surface as necessary to remove as much fat as possible. Cook the sauce down until it is properly concentrated and saucelike. Slice the meat and spoon a little of the sauce over each serving.

Yield: 8 to 12 servings

One 5-pound leg of lamb, boned

¼ pound bacon or salt pork

6 garlic cloves, finely minced

3 fresh parsley sprigs

10 fresh basil leaves

Salt and freshly ground pepper to taste

1 cup coarsely chopped onion

½ cup coarsely chopped carrots

¾ cup dry white wine

2 cups chopped, peeled, fresh or canned tomatoes

ROAST LEG OF LAMB WITH ORZO

One 5- to 6-pound leg of lamb

Salt and freshly ground pepper to taste

2 garlic cloves, peeled and cut in half

1½ cups thinly sliced onions

4 tablespoons butter

4 cups canned plum tomatoes

1 cup water

5 cups rich chicken broth (see recipe page 800)

2 cups orzo

Freshly grated Parmesan cheese

1. Preheat the oven to 400 degrees.

2. Cut away most of the surface fat from the lamb. Rub the lamb all over with the salt, pepper, and garlic cloves.

3. Place the lamb in a shallow roasting pan (one that measures about 12 x 15 inches is ideal). Scatter the slices of onion around it. Melt the butter and pour it over the meat.

4. Place the lamb in the oven and bake for about 20 minutes, or until browned.

5. Lower the oven temperature to 350 degrees. Add the tomatoes and water and cook, basting often, for about 1½ hours, or until cooked to the desired degree of doneness.

6. Remove the lamb to a heated platter and cover loosely with foil.

7. Add the chicken broth and orzo to the roasting pan and stir. Continue baking until the orzo is tender and most of the liquid has been absorbed, 15 to 20 minutes.

8. Carve the lamb and serve with orzo. Serve grated Parmesan cheese to sprinkle over the orzo.

Yield: 6 to 8 servings.

BUTTERFLIED LAMB WITH ROSEMARY

1. Trim off most of the surface fat and tough outer coating of the lamb. Place the lamb in a shallow pan that will hold it snugly.

2. Combine the oil, lemon juice, rosemary, salt, pepper, and bay leaf. Blend well and rub the mixture all over the lamb. Cover and let stand for 2 hours or longer, unrefrigerated but in a cool place. Turn the meat occasionally as it stands.

3. Prepare a charcoal fire or preheat the broiler. Place the lamb on the fire or under the broiler, as far from the broiler heat as the rack allows. Grill or broil the meat to the desired degree of doneness. Turn the meat several times as it cooks. Cooking time will depend on the distance of the meat from the heat, the intensity of the heat, and whether the grill is covered. It should vary from about 20 minutes for rare meat to 40 minutes for medium well done. Let stand for 20 minutes, covered with foil. Serve sliced with any drippings that accumulate around the lamb as it stands.

Yield: 8 servings.

Note: If you wish to bone the lamb yourself, select an 8- to 9-pound leg of lamb with bone in.

One 5½- to 6-pound boned leg of lamb in one piece (see note)

¼ cup olive oil

1 tablespoon lemon juice

1 tablespoon dried rosemary

Salt and coarsely ground pepper to taste

1 bay leaf

GRILLED BONELESS LEG OF LAMB, INDIAN STYLE

One 8- to 9-pound leg of lamb, boned

2 medium-size onions

1 piece fresh ginger, about 3 inches long and 1 inch wide

5 to 7 garlic cloves, peeled and coarsely chopped

⅔ cup lemon juice

1 tablespoon ground coriander

1 teaspoon ground cumin

1 teaspoon garam masala (see recipe page 793)

1 teaspoon ground turmeric

¼ teaspoon ground mace

¼ teaspoon grated nutmeg

¼ teaspoon ground cinnamon

¼ teaspoon ground cloves

1 cup olive oil

2½ teaspoons salt

¼ teaspoon freshly ground pepper

Cayenne to taste

Coloring (see note)

12 radishes for garnish

1. Have the butcher "butterfly" the meat, or do it at home. Cut the meat, leaving it in one piece, so that it will lie flat on a grill.

2. Chop 1 onion and put it into the container of a food processor or blender. Add the ginger, garlic, and ¼ cup lemon juice. Blend to a smooth paste.

3. Pour the mixture into a stainless steel or enamel dish large enough to hold the meat. Add the remaining spices, oil, salt, pepper, cayenne, and coloring and blend well.

4. Carefully cut off all fat and tissue from the lamb and use a sharp pointed knife to pierce the flesh at many spots on both sides. Add the meat to the dish and rub in the paste of herbs and spices. Cover and place in the refrigerator. Let stand for 24 hours, turning it occasionally.

5. Grill the meat over charcoal, under the broiler, or on an electric grill. In India the meat is generally cooked until well done. Ideally, it should be quite dark on the outside and slightly pink within, with no juices flowing.

6. As the meat cooks, slice the remaining onion into very thin rounds and drop into ice water. Cover and refrigerate. Clean the radishes and make radish roses if desired. Drop into ice water and refrigerate.

7. When ready to serve, transfer the meat to a warm platter. Garnish with the drained onion slices and radishes.

Yield: 10 to 12 servings

Note: Ideally, the coloring for this dish is an Indian food coloring in powdered form. A good substitute is about 12 drops of red food coloring, 15 drops of yellow food coloring, and 1 tablespoon of mild paprika.

PAN-ROASTED LAMB

1. Cut the lamb or have it cut into 1½-inch cubes.
2. Place the lamb in a bowl and add the remaining ingredients. Set aside until ready to cook, for 1 hour or longer.
3. Preheat the oven to 350 degrees.
4. Spoon the lamb into a shallow roasting pan. A recommended size is 16 x 9½ x 2½ inches. Smooth the lamb over and place the pan in the oven, uncovered. Bake for 1 hour and 15 minutes without stirring. The lamb should be quite tender and the pan juices will be quite liquid. Serve with rice.

Yield: 12 servings.

One 4¼-pound lean, skinless, boneless leg of lamb (about 7 pounds before boning)

2 tablespoons finely chopped fresh ginger

3 hot green chilies, chopped, with seeds

1 tablespoon finely chopped garlic

1½ tablespoons chopped fresh coriander

Juice of 1 lemon

Salt to taste

1 teaspoon freshly ground pepper

1 tablespoon peanut, vegetable, or corn oil

LEG OF LAMB, PERSIAN STYLE

One 6- to 7-pound leg of lamb
1 cup plain yogurt
¼ cup olive oil
½ cup grated onion
Salt and freshly ground pepper to taste

One of the many fine dishes we sampled in the home of Jennifer Manocherian was an excellent roast lamb with yogurt, the meat having been marinated for many hours in yogurt with seasonings. Mrs. Manocherian has rather a solid background in cooking. Her mother was Ann Roe Robbins, who for many years directed one of the best cooking schools in Manhattan, and her husband, Fred, who was born in Teheran, came from a family where fine food was a tradition.

1. Place the lamb in a large plastic bag and add the yogurt, olive oil, onion, salt, and pepper. Seal tightly and, using the hands, maneuver the marinade all over the meat. Refrigerate overnight or leave at room temperature for several hours. Leave the lamb in the bag but turn it occasionally to redistribute the marinade.

2. Preheat the oven to 500 degrees.

3. Remove the lamb from the bag and place it in a roasting pan large enough to hold it amply. Pour and squeeze the marinade over the meat and bake, uncovered, until the meat is very brown on top, 30 to 40 minutes. As the meat bakes, add ½ cup or so of water to the roasting pan to prevent sticking. There should be about ¼ inch of liquid on the bottom of the pan at all times. When the meat is brown on top, turn it and bake for about 15 minutes on that side. Cover tightly with the lid and reduce the heat to 375 degrees. Bake from 1 to 1½ hours, or until almost fork tender. Serve with the natural pan juices, skimmed of most of the fat.

Yield: 8 to 12 servings.

ROAST RACK OF LAMB WITH GREEN PEPPERCORNS

1. Preheat the oven to 500 or 525 degrees.

2. Have the butcher hack away the chine bone of each rack. Take care that all the scraps of meat and bone are reserved. Cut the chine bones into 2-inch pieces and set aside. There is a top coating of fat on top of each rack. At one side of each rack there is a small, cartilage-like half-moon-shaped shoulder blade between the meat and the top coating of fat. Have this removed.

3. Using a sharp knife, make deep diamond-shaped scorings down to the bottom of the top layer of fat. Neatly trim the bottom of each rib about 1 inch from the bottom. Sprinkle the racks with the salt and pepper and cover the French-style ends of the chops with aluminum foil to prevent burning.

4. Scatter the scraps of meat and bones over the bottom of a shallow roasting pan large enough to hold the racks in one layer. Scatter the thyme and garlic cloves over the scraps. Arrange the racks, fat side up, in the baking dish.

5. Put the lamb in the oven and bake for 20 minutes. Turn the racks and continue roasting for about 15 minutes.

6. Transfer the racks to a warm platter. Put the roasting pan on top of the stove and heat the pan liquids. Add the water. Let simmer for 10 minutes.

7. Meanwhile, remove the garlic cloves and remove the outer coatings. Chop the garlic to a fine purée and set aside.

8. Beat the whites until stiff. Add the parsley, green peppercorns, and mustard. Blend well.

9. Discard the foil from the lamb racks. Smear half the beaten white mixture on top of each rack. Sprinkle each rack with an equal amount of the bread crumbs. Pat the crumbs lightly to make them adhere.

10. Melt the butter in a small saucepan. Dribble the butter on top of the racks.

11. Return the lamb to the oven and bake 5 minutes or less, until the top of the lamb coating starts to brown. Place the lamb briefly under the broiler to give a nice brown glaze.

12. Strain the pain juices from the roasting pan into a saucepan. Add the reserved chopped garlic. Stir and reheat briefly.

13. Carve the lamb, slicing between each two ribs, and serve with the pan juices.

Yield: 4 to 6 servings.

2 untrimmed 7- or 8-rib racks of lamb, about 2½ pounds each

Salt and freshly ground pepper to taste

10 small fresh thyme sprigs, broken into small pieces, or 1 teaspoon dried

10 whole, unpeeled garlic cloves

2 cups water

2 egg whites

¼ cup finely chopped parsley

2 tablespoons drained green peppercorns

2 tablespoons strong Dijon mustard

2 tablespoons fine fresh bread crumbs

3 tablespoons butter

CROWN ROAST OF LAMB
WITH GROUND LAMB AND PINE NUTS

1 ready-to-cook crown
roast of lamb, 3 to
4 pounds

Salt and freshly ground
pepper to taste

1 tablespoon olive oil

1½ cups finely chopped
onions

1 tablespoon finely
chopped garlic

¼ pound mushrooms,
finely chopped, about
1½ cups

⅓ cup pine nuts

1 pound ground lamb

½ teaspoon finely
chopped dried
rosemary

½ cup finely chopped
parsley

1 cup plus 1 tablespoon
fine fresh bread crumbs

1 egg, lightly beaten

¼ cup coarsely chopped
onion

¼ cup coarsely chopped
carrot

¼ cup coarsely chopped
celery

1 bay leaf

2 fresh thyme sprigs, or
½ teaspoon dried

1 cup fresh or canned
chicken broth

1. Preheat the oven to 425 degrees.

2. Sprinkle the lamb inside and out with the salt and pepper.

3. Heat the oil in a small skillet and add the finely chopped onions and garlic. Cook, stirring, until the onions are wilted. Add the mushrooms and cook, stirring, until the mushrooms give up their liquid. Cook until the liquid evaporates.

4. Meanwhile, put the pine nuts in a small skillet and cook, shaking the skillet, until they are lightly browned. Add the ground lamb, stirring and chopping down with the side of a heavy metal kitchen spoon to break up the lumps. Cook until the meat loses its raw look. Add salt and pepper to taste. Transfer the mixture to a mixing bowl.

5. Add the rosemary, parsley, 1 cup of the bread crumbs, and the egg. Add the mushroom mixture and a generous grinding of pepper. Blend well.

6. Place the crown roast on a sheet of aluminum foil. Fill the center with the stuffing, smoothing it over in a rounded fashion with a spatula. Sprinkle with the remaining tablespoon of bread crumbs.

7. Lift up the foil, keeping the roast neatly intact, and transfer it to a shallow roasting pan. Keep the stuffed lamb as neatly intact as possible. If there are any lamb bones, scatter them around the roast.

8. Scatter the coarsely chopped onion, carrot, celery, bay leaf, and thyme around the roast. Place in the oven and bake for 1 hour.

9. Transfer the stuffed lamb to a serving dish. Remove and discard the foil.

10. Add the chicken broth to the baking pan with the bones. Bring to the boil, stirring. Strain the sauce around the lamb. Carve the lamb, serving two to four ribs, plus a generous helping of the stuffing, for each portion.

Yield: 6 or more servings.

If the butcher will not prepare a crown roast of lamb, here is how to go about it. Buy two racks of lamb, about seven ribs each. Have them neatly trimmed, removing almost all the surface fat. Cut and pull away the skin, but leave the single thin layer of fat beneath the skin. The ribs should measure about 4 inches in length. Using a sharp knife, make a slight slit between each rib and the meaty end.

Place the ribs together, matching the ribs and meat of the joining racks. Using a heavy needle and string, tie the ends of the racks neatly together. If there are any spare lamb bones, save them for the roasting process.

ROAST STUFFED SHOULDER OF LAMB

1 boned shoulder of
  lamb, about 3½ pounds
  Salt and freshly ground
  pepper to taste
½ pound fresh
  mushrooms
1 tablespoon butter
1 cup finely minced
  onion
1 tablespoon finely
  minced shallots
1 garlic clove, finely
  minced
  Juice of ½ lemon
1 cup fine fresh bread
  crumbs
2 tablespoons finely
  chopped parsley
¼ teaspoon fresh or dried
  thyme
1 tablespoon peanut,
  vegetable, or corn oil
1 onion, peeled
1 carrot, trimmed,
  peeled, and split in half
  lengthwise
½ cup fresh or canned
  chicken broth

1. Preheat the oven to 400 degrees.

2. Spread the boned shoulder of lamb fat side up on a flat surface. Sprinkle with the salt and pepper.

3. Chop the mushrooms or process them in a food processor. They must be finely chopped but not pasty. There should be about 2 cups.

4. Heat the butter in a skillet and add the onion, shallots, and garlic. Cook briefly, stirring, until wilted and add the chopped mushrooms, salt, pepper, and lemon juice. Cook for about 5 minutes, stirring, and add the bread crumbs. Stir and remove from the heat. Spoon and scrape into a mixing bowl. Add the parsley and thyme.

5. Spread the filling onto and over the opened-up shoulder of lamb. Carefully roll the meat like a jelly roll to enclose the filling. This will be a bit tricky for the filling will spill out. Push it back in as neatly as possible. Tie the roast in several places with string.

6. Brush the roast with oil and place it fat side up in a small roasting pan. Surround it with the onion and carrot halves. Place in the oven and bake for 1 hour to 1 hour and 15 minutes.

7. Remove the roast and place the pan over moderate heat. Add the chicken broth and bring to the boil. Discard the onion and carrot. Untie the roast and slice it. Serve with the pan gravy.

Yield: 8 or more servings.

BREAST OF LAMB À LA FRANÇAISE

1. Preheat the oven to 450 degrees.

2. Have most of the fat trimmed from the top of the lamb breast. The breast should preferably be in one or two pieces and not cut into ribs.

3. Place the pieces of lamb meaty side down on a baking dish and sprinkle with salt and pepper. Place the lamb in the oven and bake for 30 minutes. Turn and bake for 15 or 20 minutes. Turn again and pour off the fat that has accumulated.

4. Combine the remaining ingredients and blend well. The lamb should be meaty side up. Sprinkle it with the bread crumb mixture and continue baking for 15 to 20 minutes. The crumbs should be appetizingly brown. Cut the lamb into pieces.

Yield: 4 servings.

2 to 2½ pounds breast of lamb with bones, or lamb riblets

Salt and freshly ground pepper to taste

1 cup fresh bread crumbs

1 tablespoon finely chopped shallots

1 tablespoon finely chopped parsley

1 garlic clove, minced

½ teaspoon chopped rosemary

Shish Kebab

1½ pounds lamb, veal, or
    beef cut into
    approximately thirty
    1-inch pieces
  2 tablespoons olive oil
  1 tablespoon red wine
    vinegar
  2 tablespoons lemon juice
  2 teaspoons finely
    minced garlic
  2 tablespoons finely
    grated onion
  ¼ teaspoon dried thyme
12 medium-size
    mushroom caps
    Thirty 1-inch cubes
    of onion
    Thirty 1-inch cubes of
    green pepper

One of the most memorable meals of my life was eaten in the home of Neset Eren, the wife of the then Turkish ambassador to the United Nations. It was a many-course affair, which included, of course, shish kebab. This is an adaptation of Mrs. Eren's skewered specialty.

1. Put the meat in a bowl and add the oil, vinegar, lemon juice, garlic, onion, and thyme. Let stand for at least 4 hours.
2. When ready to serve, heat a charcoal or other grill.
3. If using wooden skewers, soak them in water to prevent burning. Skewer one mushroom cap and push it down the skewer. Add one cube of meat and one of green pepper. Alternate the meat, onion, and green pepper cubes, using five pieces of meat and five pieces each of the vegetables. Add one more mushroom cap. Continue preparing kebabs, making a total of six in all. Reserve the marinade.
4. Grill the prepared kebabs, turning as often as necessary so that the meat cooks evenly. Baste often with the marinade. The total cooking time is 15 to 20 minutes, depending on the heat, the distance of the skewers from the source of heat, and the desired degree of doneness.

Yield: 6 servings.

Lamb Brochettes with Tarragon

½ leg of lamb, 3½ to
    4 pounds
  1 cup dry red wine
    Salt and freshly ground
    pepper to taste
  1 tablespoon dried
    tarragon
  2 tablespoons red wine
    vinegar
  2 tablespoons olive oil
  2 teaspoons finely
    minced garlic
12 to 16 mushroom caps
    Melted butter
    Fresh lemon juice

1. Bone the leg of lamb or have it boned. Have all the fat and skin removed. Cut the meat into 1½-inch cubes. There should be about 2¼ pounds of meat. Put the meat in a mixing bowl.
2. Add the wine, salt, pepper, tarragon, vinegar, oil, and garlic. Stir. Let stand for 4 hours. Drain.
3. If using wooden skewers, soak them in water to prevent burning. Arrange 1 mushroom cap on each of 6 or 8 skewers. Arrange equal portions of meat on each of the skewers. Add 1 more mushroom cap.
4. Preheat a charcoal grill.
5. Place the brochettes on the grill and cook, turning often, for about 10 minutes. Serve with melted butter and a squeeze of lemon juice sprinkled over.

Yield: 6 to 8 servings.

Julie Sahni's Sookha Keema (Dry-Cooked, Spicy Ground Meat)

1. Heat the oil in a heavy skillet and add the onion. Cook, stirring, for about 10 minutes, or until the onion is caramel colored. Do not burn.

2. Add the garlic, ginger, and green chilies. Cook, stirring, for about 2 minutes longer.

3. Add the lamb and, using the side of a heavy metal spoon, chop and stir the meat to break up any lumps. When the meat loses its raw, red look, sprinkle the mixture with the turmeric and salt. Stir briefly and add the water. Reduce the heat and cover. Cook for about 25 minutes. Stir often to prevent burning.

4. Remove from the heat and stir in the garam masala, lemon juice, and coriander. Serve.

Yield: 4 servings.

Note: Garam masala is a basic blend of Indian spices and varies from Indian cook to Indian cook. Our version appears on page 793. It is also available in bottles and tins from specialty food shops.

2 tablespoons peanut, vegetable, or corn oil

⅔ cup finely chopped onion

4 teaspoons finely minced garlic

1½ tablespoons chopped fresh ginger

1 teaspoon finely chopped fresh hot green chilies, seeded

1 pound ground lean lamb or beef

½ teaspoon turmeric

Salt to taste

¼ cup hot water

2 teaspoons garam masala (see note)

2 teaspoons lemon juice

2 tablespoons chopped fresh coriander

Indian Keema with Peas

¾ cup finely chopped onion

1 tablespoon finely chopped fresh ginger

1 teaspoon finely minced garlic

1 tablespoon peanut, vegetable, or corn oil

1 tablespoon curry powder

¼ teaspoon ground cinnamon

½ teaspoon ground turmeric

¼ teaspoon ground coriander seeds

¼ teaspoon ground cumin

1 pound ground meat, such as lamb, beef, or veal

1 cup chopped fresh or canned tomatoes

1 tablespoon lime juice

1 teaspoon sugar

Salt and freshly ground pepper to taste

¼ teaspoon crushed hot red pepper flakes, optional

1 cup peas

1. Combine the onion, ginger, garlic, and oil in the container of a food processor or blender. Blend to a fine purée.

2. Spoon and scrape the mixture into a small skillet and cook, stirring often, until the mixture almost starts to brown, but do not brown. Add the curry powder, cinnamon, turmeric, coriander, and cumin and stir to blend.

3. Add the meat and cook, stirring and chopping down with the side of a heavy metal spoon to break up any lumps.

4. When the meat has lost its raw look, add the tomatoes, lime juice, and sugar. Add salt, pepper, and hot red pepper, if desired. Cover closely and let simmer for 30 minutes.

5. Add the peas and continue cooking until the peas are tender, 5 to 10 minutes. Serve with cucumber, tomato, scallion, and yogurt relish (see recipe page 797); carrots and yogurt (see recipe page 796); or yogurt and onion relish (see recipe page 796).

Yield: 4 servings.

CASSEROLE OF LAMB AND EGGPLANT

1. Preheat the oven to 425 degrees.

2. If the eggplant is not young and tender, peel it. Otherwise, leave the skin intact.

3. Cut the eggplant into 1-inch-thick lengthwise slices. Cut the slices into strips 1 inch wide. Cut the strips into 1-inch cubes. There should be about 6 cups.

4. Heat the oil in a casserole and add the onion and garlic. Cook, stirring, until the onion is wilted. Add the lamb, chopping down with the side of a heavy metal spoon to break up lumps. Add the eggplant and cook, stirring often, for about 5 minutes.

5. Add the pepper, cinnamon, bay leaf, hot red pepper, and tomatoes. Cook, stirring, for 5 minutes.

6. Spoon and scrape the mixture into a casserole or baking dish. Sprinkle with a mixture of crumbs and cheese. Place in the oven and bake for 15 minutes.

Yield: 4 to 6 servings.

---

1 large eggplant, about 1½ pounds

¼ cup olive oil

1 cup finely minced onion

1 teaspoon finely minced garlic

1½ pounds ground lamb
Freshly ground pepper to taste

½ teaspoon ground cinnamon

1 bay leaf

1 dried hot red pepper

4 cups tomatoes with tomato paste

1 cup bread crumbs

½ cup freshly grated Parmesan or Gruyère cheese

Lamb Shanks with Mint

2 lamb shanks, about
   1¼ pounds each

   Salt and freshly ground
   pepper to taste

1 cup coarsely chopped
   onion

2 bay leaves

2 garlic cloves, coarsely
   chopped

1 fresh thyme sprig, or
   ¼ teaspoon dried

1 tablespoon crumbled
   dried mint leaves

2 cups cored and cubed
   ripe tomatoes

1 cup fresh or canned
   chicken broth

Shanks, whether they be lamb, veal, or pork, have a tenderness, a gelatinous texture that makes them, to some palates, far superior to the more luxurious cuts of meat such as tenderloins, fillets, and the like. Shanks, too, are exceptionally easy to cook. Other than an occasional basting, they require little attention once they are placed in the oven.

1. Preheat the oven to 425 degrees.

2. Sprinkle the shanks with the salt and pepper. Place in a baking dish. If a few spare lamb bones are available, scatter them around the shanks. Place in the oven and bake for 25 minutes. Turn the shanks and continue baking.

3. When the shanks have cooked 5 minutes longer, or a total of half an hour, reduce the oven temperature to 350 degrees.

4. Pour off all the fat from the pan. Scatter the onion, bay leaves, garlic, thyme, and mint around the shanks. Return to the oven and bake for 15 minutes.

5. Scatter the tomatoes over the lamb and add the broth. Cover the pan closely with foil. Continue baking for 1 hour and 15 minutes longer. Total baking time is 2 hours.

Yield: 2 servings.

BRAISED LAMB SHANKS, GREEK STYLE

1. Preheat the oven to 400 degrees.

2. There will probably be a meaty flap attached to each shank. Attach this neatly onto the shank with string. Sprinkle the shanks with salt and pepper to taste. Arrange close together in one layer in a large baking dish. Place in the oven and bake for 30 minutes. Turn the shanks and bake for 15 minutes longer.

3. Scatter the onion, garlic, oregano, peppers, tomatoes, eggplant, zucchini, and mint sprigs over the top of the shanks. Sprinkle with salt and pepper to taste. Continue baking for 30 minutes.

4. Reduce the heat to 350 degrees. Continue baking for 15 minutes or longer, until the shanks are fork-tender.

Yield: 6 servings.

6 meaty lamb shanks,
about 6¼ pounds

Salt and freshly ground
pepper to taste

1 large onion, halved
and thinly sliced, about
2 cups

2 garlic cloves, finely
minced

2 teaspoons dried
oregano

2 green peppers, cored,
seeded, and cut into
2-inch cubes

½ pound fresh tomatoes,
cored and cut into
large cubes, about
3 cups

1 eggplant, about
1 pound, trimmed and
cut into 1½-inch cubes

3 zucchini, about
¾ pound, halved and
cut into 1-inch lengths

3 fresh mint sprigs

CHINESE LAMB WITH SCALLIONS

1¼ pounds very lean lamb, cut from the leg in one piece

¼ teaspoon salt

2 small egg whites

2½ tablespoons cornstarch

4 cups plus 3½ tablespoons peanut, vegetable, or corn oil

30 scallions

3 large garlic cloves

2 tablespoons dry sherry

2 tablespoons water

3 tablespoons soy sauce

½ teaspoon sugar

1 tablespoon red wine vinegar

½ teaspoon sesame oil

⅓ cup fresh or canned chicken broth

1. Place the lamb on a flat surface and, using a sharp knife, cut it against the grain into ¼-inch-thick slices. If desired, the lamb may be partly frozen to facilitate slicing.

2. Place the slices in a mixing bowl and add the salt and egg whites. Stir in a circular motion until the whites become a bit bubbly. Stir in 1½ tablespoons of the cornstarch and 1½ of the tablespoons oil. Refrigerate, preferably overnight, or for at least 1 hour.

3. Trim the scallions at the white tips, but otherwise leave them whole. Flatten them by pounding lightly with the flat side of a cleaver or heavy knife. Cut the scallions on the diagonal into 1-inch lengths. There should be about 4 cups. Set aside.

4. Coarsely chop the garlic. Set aside.

5. Combine the sherry, the remaining 1 tablespoon of cornstarch blended with the water, the soy sauce, sugar, vinegar, sesame oil, and chicken broth. Stir to blend and set aside.

6. Heat the 4 cups of oil in a wok or skillet and, when it is almost smoking, add the lamb, stirring to separate the slices. Cook, stirring constantly, for a total of 45 seconds, no longer, and drain the meat. Drain the wok completely.

7. Heat the remaining 2 tablespoons of oil in the wok and, when it is very hot, add the scallions and garlic and cook, stirring and tossing, for about 30 seconds. Add the lamb, stirring, and the vinegar mixture. Cook, tossing and stirring, until piping hot and slightly thickened. Serve hot.

Yield: 4 to 8 servings.

HUNAN LAMB

This is perhaps the most delectable dish of many prepared in our kitchen by Chef Tsung Ting Wang, one of the most successful Chinese chefs in the United States when he was with the Shun Lee Palace and Shun Lee Dynasty restaurants. It is a spicy, long-cooked casserole dish, which makes it ideal in Chinese menu planning. With a cold appetizer, a hot soup, and one or two stir-fry dishes, it could be the center of an outstanding Chinese meal.

1. Cut the lamb into 2-inch cubes.

2. Bring to the boil enough water to cover the lamb. Add the lamb and cook for about 3 minutes, stirring occasionally. Drain quickly and run under cold water until thoroughly chilled throughout. Drain.

3. Heat the oil in a wok or skillet and add the garlic. Cook for about 10 seconds and add the chili peppers and ginger. Cook over high heat until the garlic and chili peppers are dark brown. Add the scallions and cook, stirring, for about 20 seconds. Add the lamb and cook, stirring, for about 1 minute. Add the rock sugar, chili paste with garlic, soy sauce, and salt and stir to blend. Transfer the mixture to a casserole and pour in the beer.

4. Cover the casserole and cook until the lamb is tender, 45 minutes to an hour.

Yield: 6 to 12 servings.

3 pounds lean leg of lamb

½ cup peanut oil

12 garlic cloves, crushed

12 hot dried red chili peppers

One 1-inch cube fresh ginger, thinly sliced

2 scallions, cut into 2-inch lengths

½ pound rock sugar (available in Chinese groceries and at times in supermarkets)

2 tablespoons chili paste with garlic (available in bottles in Chinese groceries)

¼ cup dark soy sauce

2 teaspoons salt

2¼ cups (1½ bottles) beer

ROAST PORK WITH GARLIC

3 large garlic cloves

One 5- to 6-pound center cut pork roast

Salt and freshly ground pepper to taste

1 tablespoon peanut, vegetable, or corn oil

1 small onion, peeled and quartered

1 teaspoon thyme

1 cup fresh or canned chicken broth

1. Preheat the oven to 400 degrees.

2. Cut each clove of garlic into 8 slivers. Make little holes near the bone end of the meat and in the fat. Insert the garlic slivers in the holes. Sprinkle the roast with the salt and pepper and rub all over with the oil. Arrange the roast fat side down in a roasting pan. Add the onion and sprinkle with thyme. Bake for 30 minutes and turn the roast fat side up. Baste well with the pan drippings. Bake for 45 minutes.

3. Pour off the fat from the roasting pan and add the chicken broth, stirring to dissolve the brown particles that cling to the bottom and sides of the pan. Return the roast to the oven and reduce the oven heat to 375 degrees. Continue roasting for about 45 minutes longer.

4. Serve the pan juices separately with the carved roast.

Yield: 6 to 8 servings.

INDONESIAN PORK ROAST WITH COCONUT

One reference work has observed that if Robinson Crusoe had been cast on that island without benefit of chests, casks, ropes, food, gunpowder, and other necessities of life, he could have managed a happy existence if he had access to a coconut tree. Its fruit would have provided him with milk and nutrition. And, culinary lore has it, the roots of the tree can be ground and used like tea or coffee. Besides, half a coconut shell could have given him one of the nicer amenities of life, a cup from which to sip.

Those with better facilities than Crusoe had can enjoy coconut in an Indonesian creation made with pork and a sweetened soy sauce (the Indonesian word for this special bottled sauce is ketjap manis) plus coconut milk. The coconut milk that is used in cooking is not, by the way, that clear liquid that drains from the coconut when it is cracked. This genuine coconut milk or coconut cream is made by blending grated coconut with water and squeezing to extract the liquid.

1. Sprinkle the pork with salt and pepper.

2. Heat the oil in a heavy Dutch oven or casserole and add the pork. Cook, turning often, until nicely browned all over, about 30 minutes.

3. Pour off most of the oil from the Dutch oven.

4. Combine the onion, garlic, ginger, and sambal oelek in the container of a blender or food processor. Or use a mortar and pestle. Grind as fine as possible. Add this to the fat remaining in the Dutch oven. Cook, stirring, briefly.

5. Add the ketjap manis and coconut milk. Cover and bring to the boil. Simmer slowly until quite tender, about 1½ hours. Serve sliced with fluffy rice.

Yield: 6 servings.

Note: Ketjap manis and sambal oelek are widely available in food specialty shops that deal in fine imported products.

One 2½-pound lean, boneless pork roast

Salt and freshly ground pepper to taste

2 tablespoons peanut, vegetable, or corn oil

½ cup finely chopped onion

2 tablespoons finely minced garlic

1 tablespoon finely minced fresh ginger

2 teaspoons sambal oelek (see note), or ½ teaspoon hot red pepper flakes

¾ cup ketjap manis (see note), or use an equal amount of soy sauce plus 1 tablespoon sugar

¾ cup coconut milk (see instructions for making coconut milk, page 800)

BRAISED PORK WITH SAUERKRAUT

THE BRAISED PORK:

3½ pounds boneless pork, cut into 2-inch cubes

   Salt and freshly ground pepper to taste

1 cup chopped onion

2 tablespoons paprika

2 garlic cloves, finely minced

1 bay leaf

½ cup fresh or canned chicken broth

THE SAUERKRAUT:

3 pounds sauerkraut

1 tablespoon oil

1 cup finely chopped onions

1 garlic clove, finely minced

1 pound tomatoes, peeled and cut into 1-inch cubes, about 2 cups

   Salt and freshly ground pepper to taste

1 teaspoon crushed caraway seeds

¾ cup Alsatian, Rhine, or Moselle wine

¾ cup fresh or canned chicken broth

1. Preheat the oven to 400 degrees.

2. Sprinkle the pork with the salt and pepper. Arrange in one layer in a large roasting pan and place in the oven. Bake uncovered for 30 minutes.

3. Add the chopped onion, paprika, garlic, and bay leaf to the pork and stir. Bake uncovered for 15 minutes. Add the ½ cup chicken broth and bake for 30 minutes.

4. Reduce the oven heat to 350 degrees and bake the pork until fork-tender, 20 to 30 minutes.

5. As the pork bakes, cook the sauerkraut.

6. Drain the sauerkraut well, pressing with the hands to remove excess liquid. Use as is or, if you prefer a blander dish, rinse under cold water and drain well, pressing to remove more liquid.

7. Heat the oil in a saucepan and add the onion and garlic. Cook, stirring often, until the onion is browned lightly. Add the tomatoes, salt, and pepper.

8. Add the sauerkraut, caraway seeds, wine, and broth. Cover and cook for about 45 minutes.

9. Make a layer of the hot sauerkraut on a serving dish and spoon the sauce from the pork over it. Spoon the cubes of pork on top and serve immediately. Serve with plain boiled potatoes.

Yield: 6 to 8 servings.

CHINESE ROAST PORK

Leslie Newman is one of the most dedicated and talented home cooks we have ever encountered. There are very few cuisines about which she cannot speak with authority, including Indian, Creole, Thai, French, Tex-Mex, and Chinese, and which serve as the focal point for her ambitious New Year's buffets for 200 guests. In real, hardworking life, Mrs. Newman turns out scripts for such epics as *Superman*, *Superman II*, and *Superman III*. Her husband, David, is a film director and also worked on the *Superman* scripts. Mrs. Newman makes dishes such as this Chinese roast pork and the following bean curd in spicy meat sauce in several batches when she is cooking for a large gathering.

1. Put the pork strips in a mixing bowl.

2. Combine the remaining ingredients and pour over the pork, turning the pieces until the meat is coated.

3. Preheat the oven to 450 degrees.

4. Place a rack on top of a roasting pan. The rack should be about 2 inches above the bottom of the pan. Arrange the pieces of meat parallel to each other but without the sides touching. Bake for 30 minutes, basting, then turn each piece of meat and bake for 15 minutes longer. Continue baking and turning the pieces often, basting, for about 15 minutes longer.

Yield: 8 to 12 servings.

2¼ pounds lean pork loin, cut into six lengthwise strips

1 tablespoon bourbon, Cognac, or rum

½ cup sugar

6 tablespoons light soy sauce

1 tablespoon sesame paste

2 tablespoons bean sauce, available in Asian markets

1 cup honey

1 teaspoon five-spice powder, commercially prepared or homemade (see following recipe)

Blend all the ingredients in a spice mill to a fine powder.

Yield: About 3 tablespoons.

FIVE-SPICE POWDER

60 whole black peppercorns

4 whole star anise

2 teaspoons fennel seeds

1 teaspoon ground cinnamon

12 whole cloves

BEAN CURD IN SPICY MEAT SAUCE

4 tablespoons corn, peanut, or vegetable oil

1⅓ cups diced sweet red pepper

1⅓ cups diced sweet green pepper

2 pounds ground pork, preferably not too lean

½ cup brown bean sauce, available in Asian markets

4 teaspoons bottled chili paste with garlic

4 teaspoons sugar

4 tablespoons dry sherry

2 cups plus 3 tablespoons chicken broth

4 tablespoons cornstarch

12 squares bean curd, each cut into 16 pieces

1 cup finely chopped scallions, green and white parts combined

1 teaspoon ground roasted Sichuan peppercorns (see note)

1½ teaspoons sesame oil

Hot chili oil, optional

1. Heat half of the oil in a wok and, when it is hot but not quite smoking, add half the red and green peppers. Cook, stirring and pressing them against the side of the wok so that they blacken a bit without burning. Using a slotted spoon, remove them while they are still crisp and set aside. Leave the oil in the wok.

2. To the wok add half the pork and cook over high heat, stirring and chopping down to break up any lumps. Cook only until the pork loses its raw look.

3. Add half the bean sauce, half the chili paste with garlic, half the sugar, and 1 tablespoon of the sherry, blending thoroughly. Add 1 cup of the chicken broth and bring to the simmer.

4. Blend half the cornstarch with 1 tablespoon of the sherry and 1½ tablespoons chicken broth.

5. Stir this into the simmering meat sauce. When thickened, spoon and scrape the sauce into a large mixing bowl.

6. Wipe out the wok. Repeat the procedure using the remaining oil, peppers, pork, bean sauce, chili paste with garlic, sugar, sherry, chicken broth, and cornstarch. Add the second batch of peppers to the first and let cool. Add the second batch of meat sauce to the first batch and let cool. Refrigerate overnight or until ready to use. Refrigerate the peppers separately.

7. When ready to serve, return the meat sauce to room temperature. Return the sauce to large saucepans or casseroles and bring to the boil.

8. Carefully add the bean curd pieces to the meat sauce. Stir and heat gently so as not to break up the bean curd pieces more than necessary. Add the cooked red and green pepper. Heat briefly.

9. Add the scallions, peppercorns, and sesame oil. Stir gently and serve. Serve with hot chili oil on the side, if desired, to be added by those who enjoy very spicy foods.

Yield: 20 to 25 servings.

Note: Place the peppercorns in a heavy skillet and cook over moderately low heat for about 3 minutes. Grind to a powder using a coffee or spice grinder.

BROCHETTES OF PORK WITH ROSEMARY

1. Cut the pork into 1½-inch cubes and put the meat in a mixing bowl.
2. Add the wine, garlic, rosemary, parsley, lemon rind, salt, pepper, olive oil, and vinegar. Blend well and marinate for 2 to 4 hours.
3. Drain the meat. Arrange equal portions of meat on each of 6 to 8 skewers. If using wooden skewers, soak in water to prevent burning.
4. Preheat a charcoal grill.
5. Place the brochettes on the grill and cook, turning the pieces often, for 15 to 20 minutes, or until the pork is thoroughly cooked but not dry.

Yield: 6 to 8 servings.

1¼ pounds lean, boneless pork

1 cup dry white wine

1 tablespoon finely minced garlic

1 tablespoon dried rosemary leaves

2 tablespoons finely chopped parsley

1 teaspoon grated lemon rind

Salt and freshly ground pepper to taste

2 tablespoons olive oil

2 tablespoons white wine vinegar

BARBECUED SPARERIBS

1. Preheat the oven to 325 degrees.
2. Place the spareribs meaty side up in a large shallow baking pan and bake for 1 hour and 30 minutes.
3. Meanwhile, combine the ketchup, soy sauce, chili powder, honey, garlic, vinegar, and ginger in a saucepan. Bring to the boil. Squeeze the juice from the lemon half into the sauce. Cut the squeezed-out shell into quarters and add it to the sauce. Bring to the boil.
4. Pour off the fat from the spareribs. Brush them on top with the sauce. Turn the spareribs and brush the other side with the sauce.
5. Return the spareribs to the oven and bake for 15 minutes, basting occasionally with more sauce. Turn the ribs and baste well. Bake for about 10 minutes longer. Serve hot or cold.

Yield: 6 servings.

1 rack of spareribs, about 3½ pounds

1 cup ketchup

¼ cup soy sauce

1 tablespoon chili powder

3 tablespoons honey

2 teaspoons finely minced garlic

1 tablespoon red wine vinegar

1 tablespoon finely grated fresh ginger

½ lemon

SWEET AND SOUR PORK

1 pound lean pork, cut
   into 1-inch cubes

1 tablespoon dark soy
   sauce

1 tablespoon dry sherry

1 cup plus 2 tablespoons
   cornstarch

½ carrot, trimmed and
   scraped

1 scallion, trimmed

1 small sweet green or,
   preferably, red pepper,
   cored and seeded

4 thin slices peeled
   ginger

4 garlic cloves, peeled
   and lightly crushed

⅓ cup canned pineapple
   chunks, drained

1 tablespoon corn or
   peanut oil, plus enough
   for deep frying

½ cup thinly sliced
   mushrooms

1¼ cups water

1 tablespoon light soy
   sauce

½ cup sugar

⅓ cup red wine vinegar

12 drops red food coloring

More than any other people, the Chinese are masters of the art of sweet and sour cookery. This recipe for pork had its genesis during the days when I collaborated with Virginia Lee on a Chinese cookbook.

1. Pat each pork cube very lightly with the back of a knife or a flat mallet. Put the cubes in a mixing bowl and add the dark soy sauce and sherry.

2. Pour 1 cup of the cornstarch onto a sheet of wax paper. Dredge the cubes of pork, a few at a time, in the cornstarch. Work the cornstarch into the pork; the cubes must be liberally coated. Set the cubes aside and discard the leftover cornstarch.

3. Cut the carrot into 24 rounds. Put the rounds in a bowl.

4. Cut the scallion into 2-inch lengths. Cut the lengths into thin (julienne) slivers. Add these to the carrots.

5. Cut the pepper into 1-inch cubes. Add them to the bowl. Add the ginger, garlic, and pineapple.

6. Heat the 1 tablespoon of oil in a small skillet and add the mushrooms. Cook, stirring, until they give up their liquid. Cook until the liquid has evaporated. Add the vegetable and pineapple mixture. Cook, stirring often, for about 5 minutes. Set aside.

7. Meanwhile, combine 1 cup of the water, the light soy sauce, sugar, and vinegar in a saucepan and bring to the boil, stirring until the sugar is dissolved.

8. Combine the 2 tablespoons of cornstarch with ¼ cup of water and stir this into the sugar syrup until thickened. Add the red food coloring.

9. Pour the sauce over the vegetable mixture and bring to the boil.

10. Heat the oil for deep frying and, when it is almost smoking, add the cubes of pork. Cook over high heat, stirring to prevent the pieces from sticking together, for about 4 minutes, or until the pieces are golden brown and crisp.

11. Drain the pork and put it on a platter. Heat the sauce and pour it over the pork.

Yield: 4 servings.

PORK CHOPS WITH MUSTARD AND GREEN PEPPERCORNS

1. Sprinkle the chops on both sides with the salt and pepper. Blend the flour and paprika and dredge the chops with the mixture. Heat the oil in a heavy skillet and brown the chops for about 5 minutes to a side.

2. Pour off the fat from the skillet and sprinkle the chops with the carrots, onion, and garlic. Add the bay leaf and thyme. Add the wine and chicken broth and cover. Cook over low heat for about 1 hour. Remove the chops.

3. Stir the mustard into the pan drippings. Bring to the boil but do not boil. Add the peppercorns, capers, and parsley. Serve hot over the chops.

Yield: 8 servings.

8 center-cut pork chops, about ½ pound each

Salt and freshly ground pepper to taste

½ cup flour

1 teaspoon paprika

1 tablespoon peanut, vegetable, or corn oil

⅔ cup finely diced carrots

⅔ cup finely diced onion

1 garlic clove, finely chopped

1 bay leaf

1 fresh thyme sprig, or ½ teaspoon dried

1 cup dry white wine

1 cup fresh or canned chicken broth

1 tablespoon Dijon mustard

1 tablespoon green peppercorns

2 tablespoons capers

1 tablespoon finely chopped parsley

HERB-STUFFED PORK CHOPS

4   loin center-cut pork chops, each about 1 inch thick

¼   cup shelled pistachio nuts, optional

¼   pound ground pork

¼   cup finely chopped onion

1   cup thinly sliced mushrooms

1   small garlic clove, peeled

3   tablespoons parsley

½   teaspoon dried marjoram or sage

¼   cup fine fresh bread crumbs

1   raw chicken liver

    Salt and freshly ground pepper to taste

1   egg, beaten

    Flour for dredging

1   tablespoon butter

1   cup fresh or canned chicken broth

1. Preheat the oven to 350 degrees.

2. Open the chops for stuffing "butterfly" fashion. To do this, use a sharp knife and slice the chops through the center down to the bone, top to bottom. Open them up and, using a flat mallet, pound the opened-up flaps to flatten lightly. Do not break the meat, however, in pounding.

3. Drop the pistachios, if used, into boiling water. Let stand a few seconds and drain. Rub off the skins. Set the pistachio meats aside.

4. Cook the ground pork in a saucepan, stirring, until it loses its red color. Add the onion and mushrooms and cook, stirring. Chop the garlic with the parsley and marjoram and add to the pork mixture. Stir in the bread crumbs. Chop the chicken liver and add it, stirring. Add the salt and pepper and the pistachios. Cook briefly and remove from the heat. Let cool. Add the egg and blend well.

5. Sprinkle the opened-up chops with salt and pepper to taste. Add equal amounts of the filling to the chops and bring the flaps together to enclose the stuffing. Skewer the ends of each chop with toothpicks or sew with string.

6. Dredge the chops on all sides in flour seasoned with salt and pepper. Heat the butter in a large heavy skillet and brown the chops well on one side, for 5 minutes or longer. Turn and brown on the other side. Cover loosely with aluminum foil.

7. Place the skillet in the oven and bake for 1 hour. Remove the chops briefly and add half the chicken broth to the skillet, stirring it into the brown particles on the bottom of the skillet. Return the chops to the skillet. Cover with foil and bake for 15 minutes longer. Turn the chops in the pan glaze, then transfer them to a hot serving dish. Add the remaining broth to the skillet and cook, stirring, to dissolve the brown particles remaining. Strain this over the chops.

Yield: 4 servings.

PORK CUTLETS STUFFED WITH CHEESE AND HAM

1. The pork cutlets should be trimmed of all fat. Place them, one at a time, on a flat surface and pound them with a flat mallet or the back of a heavy skillet. Sprinkle one side with salt and pepper.

2. Finely chop the prosciutto. Cut the cheese into ¼-inch cubes. Blend the prosciutto and cheese. Divide the mixture into 8 equal portions and shape each into a ball.

3. Place 1 ball of prosciutto and cheese in the center of each flattened piece of pork. Fold up the bottom of each pork cutlet to partly enclose the filling. Bring the two outside edges over, envelope-fashion. Finally, fold over the top to totally enclose the filling. Press down the seams to seal.

4. Dredge each package in flour. Beat the eggs with water and drop the packages in this. Finally, dredge all over with bread crumbs.

5. Add oil to a depth of about 1 inch in a large heavy skillet. When hot, add the packages and cook until brown, turning as necessary until cooked through, about 6 minutes. Drain on paper towels. Serve with lemon wedges.

Yield: 4 to 8 servings.

8 lean, boneless pork cutlets taken from the loin, about 1½ pounds trimmed weight

Salt and freshly ground pepper to taste

¼ pound thinly sliced prosciutto

¼ pound fontina or Gruyère cheese

⅓ cup flour

2 eggs

2 tablespoons water

1½ cups bread crumbs

Oil for deep frying

Lemon wedges

VIETNAMESE GRILLED PORK PATTIES IN LETTUCE LEAVES

THE PORK:

2 pounds ground pork

2 garlic cloves, finely chopped

1 teaspoon grated fresh ginger

1 tablespoon dry sherry

2 tablespoons light soy sauce

2 tablespoons peanut, vegetable, or corn oil

1 teaspoon sugar

Salt to taste

THE WRAPPING AND GARNISHES:

24 large Boston lettuce leaves, well rinsed and patted dry

1 cup loosely packed fresh coriander

1 cup loosely packed fresh mint leaves

1 cup chopped scallions

2 cups raw rice cooked without salt until tender and cooled to room temperature

Nuoc mam sauce (see page 795)

1. Combine all the ingredients for the ground pork in a bowl and blend well with the fingers. Place the bowl briefly in the refrigerator. Do not freeze. The chilling will facilitate shaping the patties.

2. Meanwhile, prepare a charcoal fire.

3. With the fingers and palms, shape the pork into 2-inch balls. Make them all approximately the same size. Maneuver each ball into a miniature football shape, approximately 3 inches long. Chill until ready to use.

4. Run a skewer lengthwise through each patty and grill, turning frequently, until browned and cooked through. Serve immediately. The technique for eating the patties is as follows: Open a lettuce leaf and add a sprig of coriander, 1 or 2 mint leaves, chopped scallion, and a small spoonful of rice. Add the hot pork patty and wrap the leaf around. Using the fingers, dip the "package" into the nuoc mam sauce and eat with the fingers.

Yield: 4 to 8 servings.

ALBONDIGAS (MEXICAN MEATBALLS IN TOMATO AND CHILI SAUCE)

1. Place the pork in a mixing bowl. Beat the egg, and add the oregano and cumin. Stir and add this mixture to the pork. Add salt and pepper.

2. Trim off the ends of the zucchini. Cut the zucchini into thin slices. Stack the slices and cut them into strips. Cut the strips into fine cubes. There should be about ¾ cup. Add the zucchini, onion, and garlic to the meat. Blend well with the hands. Using lightly oiled fingers and palms, shape the mixture into 18 meatballs.

3. Combine the tomatoes and chilies in the container of a blender. Blend thoroughly.

4. Heat the oil in a Dutch oven or casserole. Add the tomato mixture. Add salt and pepper to taste and cook, stirring, for about 5 minutes. Add the chicken broth and bring to the boil. Add the meatballs one at a time and bring to the boil. Cover closely and simmer for about 45 minutes. Serve sprinkled with chopped coriander. Serve with hot rice.

Yield: 4 servings.

1 pound twice-ground pork

1 egg

1 teaspoon dried oregano

½ teaspoon ground cumin

Salt and freshly ground pepper to taste

1 small zucchini

3 tablespoons finely chopped onion

2 garlic cloves, finely minced

3 cups drained imported canned tomatoes

2 or 3 chipotle chilies, available in tins in Mexican and Spanish stores

2 tablespoons peanut, vegetable, or corn oil

½ cup fresh or canned chicken broth

¼ cup finely chopped fresh coriander

LION'S HEAD (CHINESE MEATBALLS)

8 dried black mushrooms

1¼ pounds ground pork

20 water chestnuts, finely diced

1 teaspoon finely minced fresh ginger

3 scallions, chopped

1 teaspoon finely minced garlic

Grated rind of 1 orange

¼ teaspoon sesame oil

1 tablespoon dry sherry

1 tablespoon light soy sauce

1 teaspoon salt

1 tablespoon cornstarch

Peanut, vegetable, or corn oil for deep frying

Steamed spinach or broccoli, optional

1. Place the mushrooms in a mixing bowl and add hot water to cover. Let stand for 20 minutes or longer until softened.

2. Place the pork in a mixing bowl. Drain the mushrooms and squeeze dry. Chop them. Add them to the pork. Add the water chestnuts, ginger, scallions, garlic, grated orange rind, sesame oil, sherry, soy sauce, salt, and cornstarch. Mix well and shape into 8 to 12 balls.

3. Heat the oil for deep frying and add the meatballs. Deep-fry until crisp and golden on the outside. Drain well. Place the meatballs in a steamer and steam for 20 to 25 minutes. Serve on a bed of spinach or broccoli.

Yield: 8 servings.

DEVILED PIGS' FEET

1. Place the pigs' feet in a kettle and add water to cover, the salt, bay leaf, onion, parsley, peppercorns, carrots, and celery. Bring to the boil and simmer for about 3 hours, or until the pigs' feet are quite tender. Let stand until cool.

2. Preheat the oven to 400 degrees.

3. Remove the pigs' feet. Blend the mustard with wine, salt, and pepper to taste. Brush the pigs' feet with this. Roll the pigs' feet in fresh bread crumbs and arrange them on a rack. Dribble 2 tablespoons of oil over each pigs' foot. Bake for 30 minutes, or until crisp and golden brown. Serve with mustard on the side.

Yield: 4 servings.

4 pigs' feet, preferably large ones

Salt to taste

1 bay leaf

1 small onion, peeled and stuck with 2 cloves

2 parsley sprigs

12 crushed peppercorns

2 carrots, trimmed and scraped

3 celery ribs, rinsed and quartered

3 tablespoons Dijon mustard

2 tablespoons dry white wine

Freshly ground pepper to taste

2 cups fresh bread crumbs

8 tablespoons peanut, vegetable, or corn oil

PHILADELPHIA SCRAPPLE

4	pounds pigs' knuckles
½	pound not-too-lean pork chop with bone
12	cups water
½	pound beef or calf's liver
	Salt to taste
½	teaspoon freshly ground pepper
2	small, dried, hot red peppers
1	tablespoon leaf sage
⅛	teaspoon grated nutmeg or mace
2½	cups yellow cornmeal

Scrapple is, to my mind, one of the greatest regional American specialties. The name derives from the word "scrap" and relates to scraps or odd parts of the pig from which it is made. Scrapple is of Pennsylvania Dutch origin; it was first made by the early German settlers in that state.

1. Combine the pigs' knuckles, pork chop, water, liver, salt, pepper, dried red peppers, sage, and nutmeg in a kettle. Bring to the boil and simmer, partly covered, for about 2 hours, or until the knuckle meat is fork-tender.

2. Remove the pigs' knuckles and pork and liver from the kettle. Set aside.

3. Strain the cooking liquid and discard the spices. There should be about 11 cups.

4. Remove the bones from the pigs' knuckles and pork chop. Keep all the meat, fat, skin, and so on. Put the pieces of knuckle, pork chop, liver, and so on into the container of a food processor. Take care that no trace of bone is added. Or grind the mixture in a food grinder. As it is processed or ground, scrape it into a large kettle. Add 8 cups of the reserved cooking liquid and stir to blend. Bring to the boil.

5. Spoon the cornmeal into a bowl. Add the remaining 3 cups of cooking liquid. Blend well with a wire whisk. Add this to the boiling ground mixture, stirring to prevent lumping. Add salt to taste.

6. Place the kettle on a metal pad and let it simmer over low heat for about 30 minutes. Stir often from the bottom. Cornmeal has a tendency to lump and/or stick as it cooks if it is not stirred often.

7. Pour the mixture evenly into two loaf pans (measuring 9 x 5 x 2¾ inches). Let stand until cool. Refrigerate until set. To cook, cut the loaves into ½-inch-thick slices. Dredge lightly in flour and sauté in bacon fat or butter.

Yield: 2 loaf pans.

SMITHFIELD, VIRGINIA, OR COUNTRY HAM

1. Place the ham in a large kettle or roasting pan and add cold water to cover. Soak for about 24 hours, changing the water often.

2. Preheat the oven to 300 degrees.

3. Drain the ham and trim or scrape off all mold on the "face" side (this is opposite the skin side).

4. It is not essential, but you will facilitate carving the ham after cooking if you run a boning or other knife around the contours of the hipbone on the underside of the ham. Run the knife down deep around the bone, but do not remove the bone at this time.

5. Place the ham in a roaster with 10 cups of water and cover closely with a lid or heavy-duty aluminum foil. Place in the oven and bake for 20 to 23 minutes to the pound. Remove the ham from the oven, leaving the heat on.

6. Using the fingers, pull against the hipbone that was carved around earlier. Run the carving knife around the bone and pull with the fingers to remove it.

7. Increase the oven heat to 425 degrees.

8. Slice away the skin from the ham, leaving a thick layer of fat. Using a sharp knife, score the ham at 1-inch intervals, making a diamond-shaped pattern. Stud the fat with cloves. Sprinkle the surface with the brown sugar and bake for 15 minutes.

Yield: 12 to 20 servings.

1 cured Smithfield, Virginia, or country ham (14 to 16 pounds)
40 to 60 whole cloves
½ cup brown sugar

RED-EYE GRAVY

Red-eye gravy, to those unaccustomed to the nobler things in life, requires first a good, well-cured country ham. Smithfield and genuine Virginia hams are ideal for this.

Take a slice of uncooked ham with most or much of the fat left on. Fry the ham in its own fat until nicely browned on both sides. When it is cooked, transfer the ham to a warm platter and add boiling black coffee to the skillet, scraping to dissolve the brown particles that cling to the bottom and sides.

That is red-eye gravy, which you pour over the ham and serve.

The name derives from the fact that a circle or oval of liquid fat with a slightly reddish cast will form on the surface of the gravy when it is slightly reduced. This is the "eye" of the name.

BAKED FRESH HAM

1 fresh ham with bone in (about 14 pounds), or 1 boneless fresh ham (about 9 pounds)

Salt and freshly ground pepper to taste

1 tablespoon dried rosemary

2 garlic cloves, finely minced

2 tablespoons corn, peanut, or vegetable oil

2 onions, peeled and left whole

2 cups fresh or canned chicken stock

1. Preheat the oven to 400 degrees.

2. Using a sharp knife held parallel to the bone, score the fat from one side to the other. Continue scoring at 1-inch intervals from the bottom to the top of the fat layer. Sprinkle the ham on all sides with the salt and pepper.

3. Chop the rosemary as fine as possible and blend with the garlic. If you have a spice mill, grind the two together. In any event, rub the ham all over with the mixture.

4. Brush the ham on all sides with oil. Arrange the ham fat side up in a large roasting pan. Place in the oven and bake for 1 hour, or 45 minutes for a boneless ham. Reduce the oven heat to 350 degrees and place the onions in the pan. Bake for 1½ hours longer, basting often with the pan drippings. As the ham bakes, rotate the pan in the oven so that it bakes evenly.

5. After 2½ hours total baking time (2¼ hours for boneless ham), pour off the fat from the pan and return the ham to the oven. Continue baking, basting and rotating the pan occasionally, for about 30 minutes.

6. Pour off all the fat from the pan. If the ham has a bone in, you will facilitate carving if you pull out the very thin bone from the short end of the ham. If the ham is done, it should come out easily. Add the chicken stock to the pan and return the ham to the oven. Continue baking for about 15 minutes. If you use a meat thermometer, the temperature at the thickest part of the ham should register 165 degrees. Transfer the ham to a warm platter.

7. Line a saucepan with a sieve and pour the pan juices into it. Skim off the fat. Bring the pan juices to the boil and serve with the ham.

Yield: 10 to 18 servings.

ROAST SUCKLING PIG

Two of the best roast suckling pigs we've ever eaten were in Puerto Rico: once, when the animal was hand-turned out of doors for several hours on a wooden spit over hot coals; the second was a decade later in the home of the governor of Puerto Rico, Carlos Romero-Barcelo, and his American-born wife, Kate. Their chef, Jesús Villalba, cooked the pig in the oven with a minimum of effort, and the results were admirable—a crisp, crusty skin with a tantalizing flavor and moist, tender, well-done meat. This is his version, stuffed with rice and fresh pigeon peas.

1. Wash the pig well and dry inside and out.

2. Blend the oil, salt, garlic, oregano, and pepper. Prick the pig all over and massage the pig inside and out with the garlic mixture. Put in a pan, cover with cheesecloth, and let stand for several hours.

3. Preheat the oven to 350 degrees. Place the pig in a roasting pan feet side down and bake for about 1 hour and 10 minutes. Baste often. If at any point any part of the pig starts to burn (ears, feet, etc.), cover that part with foil.

4. Reduce the oven heat to 250 degrees and bake for about 1 hour and 10 minutes longer, basting often. Increase the oven heat to 400 degrees and bake for 20 to 30 minutes, basting. Remove the pig from the oven. Remove the cheesecloth.

5. Fill the stomach cavity of the pig with the rice mixture. Keep the stuffing intact with a sheet of aluminum foil. There may be an excess of rice. This may be heated later and served on the side.

6. Before serving, preheat the oven once more to 350 degrees. Place the stuffed pig back in the oven on a roasting pan and bake for 20 minutes longer.

Yield: 12 or more servings.

One 13- to 15-pound suckling pig

½ cup peanut, vegetable, or corn oil

¼ cup salt

2 garlic cloves, peeled and mashed to a fine purée

1 tablespoon crushed dried oregano

Freshly ground pepper to taste

Rice with pigeon peas (see following recipe)

RICE WITH PIGEON PEAS

2 cups fresh green pigeon peas, or one 16-ounce can, available in Spanish markets

Salt to taste

3 tablespoons olive oil

1 cup finely chopped onion

1 teaspoon finely minced garlic

1 cup chopped sweet green pepper

¼ cup diced raw, not-too-lean, cured ham, preferably unsmoked

1 tablespoon chopped fresh coriander

1 cup cubed tomatoes

2 cups fresh or canned tomato sauce, put through a sieve if fresh

1 cup drained pimiento-stuffed green olives

2 tablespoons drained capers

4 cups rice

⅓ cup canned coconut cream

4 cups fresh or canned beef broth

1. If the peas are fresh, put them in a kettle with water to cover and salt to taste. Bring to the boil and simmer until tender, 45 minutes to 1 hour. If they are canned, drain them.

2. Heat the oil in a skillet and add the onion, garlic, green pepper, ham, and coriander leaves. Cook, stirring, until the onion is wilted. Add the tomatoes, pigeon peas, tomato sauce, olives, and capers. Stir and add the rice. Stir to blend well and add the coconut cream and beef broth.

3. Cover closely with aluminum foil and bring to the boil. Simmer for 20 minutes. Discard foil. The rice is now ready to be used as a stuffing for roast suckling pig.

Yield: About 8 cups, or enough to use as a stuffing for a small roast suckling pig.

RABBIT IN RED WINE SAUCE

1. Preheat the oven to 350 degrees.

2. Sprinkle the rabbit pieces with the salt and pepper. Set aside.

3. Drop the salt pork into cold water to cover. Bring to the boil and simmer for about 1 minute. Drain. Cook the pieces in one or two heavy skillets until the slices are rendered of their fat and crisp. Remove the pieces with a slotted spoon and set aside.

4. Add the rabbit pieces to the fat and brown on all sides. If two skillets are used, combine the pieces in one skillet after browning.

5. Add the garlic, onions, mushrooms, and carrot and cook, stirring, for about 5 minutes. Tie the bay leaf, thyme sprigs, and parsley in a bundle and add it. If blood is not available for later use, sprinkle the flour over all and stir to coat the pieces of rabbit. Add the wine and water and bring to the boil on top of the stove. Cover and place in the oven. Bake for about 45 minutes if the rabbit is small, about 1 hour and 15 minutes if large.

6. If rabbit blood is to be used, add a small amount of the hot sauce to the blood. Gradually stir this mixture into the sauce and simmer gently, stirring, for about 1 minute. Remove the herb bundle and sprinkle the rabbit with the browned pieces of salt pork.

Yield: 4 to 8 servings.

One 2½- to 4-pound rabbit, cut into serving pieces

Salt and freshly ground pepper to taste

¼ pound thinly sliced salt pork, cut into ¼-inch strips

2 teaspoons finely chopped garlic

16 very small white onions, peeled, or 1 cup finely chopped onion

⅓ pound small button mushrooms, left whole, or larger mushrooms, quartered and sliced

1 carrot, trimmed, scraped, and cut into rounds

1 bay leaf

2 fresh thyme sprigs, or ½ teaspoon dried

3 parsley sprigs

¼ cup flour (to be used only if rabbit blood, indicated below, is not available)

3 cups dry red Burgundy

1 cup water

¾ to 1 cup rabbit blood (blended with the juice of ½ lemon to prevent coagulation)

RABBIT WITH MUSTARD SAUCE

One 3- to 3½-pound
young rabbit, cleaned

4 tablespoons butter

Salt and freshly ground
pepper to taste

¾ pound carrots,
trimmed, scraped, and
cut into 2-inch lengths

¾ pound small white
onions, peeled,
about 10

3 tablespoons Dijon
mustard

1 cup plus 2 tablespoons
dry white wine

½ pound mushrooms, left
whole if small,
otherwise sliced or
quartered

1 cup fresh or canned
chicken broth

1 bay leaf

1 garlic clove, peeled and
left whole

1. Preheat the oven to 425 degrees.

2. Cut the rabbit into five large pieces: the forelegs with thighs attached, the hind legs with thighs attached, and the meaty breast portion. Set the liver aside.

3. Melt the butter in a baking dish large enough to hold the rabbit pieces in one layer. Add the rabbit pieces. Sprinkle with the salt and pepper and turn the pieces in the butter. Place the rabbit skinned side down.

4. Meanwhile, put the carrots and onions in a saucepan and add cold water to cover and salt to taste. Bring to the boil and simmer for about 5 minutes. Drain and set aside.

5. Put the rabbit in the oven. Do not cover. Bake for 30 minutes and turn the rabbit pieces skinned side up.

6. Blend the mustard and 2 tablespoons wine in a small mixing bowl. Brush the rabbit all over with half the mustard mixture. Add the liver. Return to the oven and let bake for about 5 minutes. Turn the rabbit pieces.

7. Scatter the mushrooms, the blanched carrots, and onions around the rabbit pieces. Brush the rabbit pieces, including the liver, with the remaining mustard. Pour the remaining 1 cup wine and the broth around the rabbit pieces. Add the bay leaf and garlic.

8. Bake for 30 minutes longer, basting occasionally, and reduce the oven heat to 375 degrees. Continue roasting and basting for about 15 minutes, or until tender.

Yield: 6 servings.

FILLET OF VENISON

1. Cut the fillet crosswise in half and put the pieces in a bowl. Add the salt, pepper, celery, onion, leeks, carrots, rosemary, thyme, parsley, bay leaf, marjoram, and wine. Cover closely and refrigerate or place in a very cold place for two to three days (if pressed for time, overnight will do).

2. Remove the venison pieces. Strain the marinating liquid, reserving separately both the marinating solids and the liquid.

3. Heat 1 tablespoon butter in a saucepan and add the reserved solids (vegetables and herbs). Cook for about 5 minutes, stirring often. Add the reserved liquid and let boil over high heat for about 10 minutes, or until the liquid is reduced to about ¾ cup.

4. Blend the arrowroot and 2 teaspoons Cognac and stir this into the sauce. Put the sauce through a fine sieve into a small saucepan, pressing to extract as much liquid as possible from the solids. Discard the solids. Set the sauce aside.

5. Heat the remaining butter in a skillet and add the two well-drained pieces of venison fillet. Cook to brown one side over high heat for about 2 minutes. Turn and brown quickly on the other side. Reduce the heat to moderate and continue cooking, turning the pieces as necessary so that they cook evenly, for 8 to 10 minutes. Take care that the pieces do not overcook or they will become dry. The meat should remain slightly rare. Transfer the pieces of meat to a serving dish.

6. Pour all the fat from the skillet and add the 2 tablespoons of Cognac. Add the strained sauce and the cream. Bring to the boil, stirring. If desired, strain the sauce through a fine sieve.

7. The venison fillet may be covered with a thin and somewhat tough or fatty layer. Cut this away and discard it. Carve the flesh on the bias into thin slices and serve with the sauce.

Yield: 6 servings.

---

1 fillet or boneless loin of venison

Salt and freshly ground pepper to taste

¾ cup coarsely chopped celery

⅔ cup coarsely chopped onion

¾ cup coarsely chopped leeks

½ cup cubed carrots

2 fresh rosemary sprigs, or 1 teaspoon dried

3 fresh thyme sprigs, or ½ teaspoon dried

2 fresh parsley sprigs

1 bay leaf

½ teaspoon dried marjoram

2 cups dry red wine, preferably a fine Burgundy

3 tablespoons butter

¾ teaspoon arrowroot or cornstarch

2 teaspoons plus 2 tablespoons Cognac

¼ cup heavy cream

RAGOUT OF VENISON

2 quarts, approximately, marinade for game (see following recipe)

5 pounds shoulder of venison, cut into 2- or 3-inch cubes

2 to 4 tablespoons peanut, vegetable, or corn oil

¼ cup flour

Salt and freshly ground pepper to taste

4 tablespoons currant jelly

10 small white onions

1 teaspoon butter

1 teaspoon sugar

2 tablespoons vegetable oil

½ pound mushrooms, thinly sliced

1. Prepare the marinade and add the venison pieces. Stir and cover with foil. Refrigerate for 4 or 5 days, no longer.

2. Preheat the oven to 400 degrees.

3. Remove the meat from the marinade and set it aside. Drain the vegetables, reserving the solids and the liquid. There should be about 4 cups liquid.

4. Heat 2 tablespoons of oil in one or two medium-size skillets. Brown one third of the meat at a time. As the meat is browned, transfer it to a kettle. Use more oil as necessary to cook the meat. The total time for browning the meat should be about 10 minutes.

5. Add a little more oil to a skillet and cook the reserved solids over high heat for about 5 minutes. Add this to the meat.

6. Sprinkle the flour over all and stir to coat the pieces more or less evenly. Cook for about 3 minutes and add the reserved liquid. Add the salt and pepper. Bring to the boil and cover. Place the kettle in the oven and bake for 2 hours.

7. Remove from the oven, tilt the kettle, and skim off the excess fat from the surface. Add the jelly and stir until dissolved. Simmer for 5 minutes on top of the stove.

8. Meanwhile, peel the onions and combine them in a saucepan with water to barely cover, salt to taste, the butter and sugar. Cook until the liquid evaporates and the onions start to take on a brown glaze.

9. Heat the oil in a skillet and add the mushrooms. Sprinkle with salt and pepper to taste and cook, stirring as necessary, for about 10 minutes.

10. Add the onions to the skillet and cook for about 5 minutes. Sprinkle this mixture over the venison and cook for 10 minutes.

Yield: 12 or more servings.

MARINADE FOR GAME

4¼ cups red wine vinegar

½ teaspoon dried marjoram

4 juniper berries, crushed

1 bay leaf

1 teaspoon dried rosemary

2 whole cloves

¼ teaspoon dried thyme

10 peppercorns

1 cup coarsely chopped celery

1 cup thinly sliced carrots

1 cup quartered small onions

2 parsley sprigs

Salt to taste

1. Combine in a saucepan ¼ cup of the red wine vinegar, the marjoram, juniper berries, bay leaf, rosemary, cloves, thyme, and peppercorns. Bring to the boil and simmer for about 5 minutes.

2. Empty the mixture into a stainless steel or enamel bowl and add the remaining ingredients. Use as a marinade for game.

Yield: 2 quarts, approximately, or enough marinade for 5 pounds of venison.

FISH AND SHELLFISH

It has always struck us odd that so many Americans seem intimidated by the cooking of fish, for, to us at least, it is one of the easiest of all forms of cookery. In the baked fish recipe outlined here, for example, the fillets are simply brushed with mustard, sprinkled with bread crumbs, and dotted with butter before cooking. In the sautéed fish recipe, a simple breading technique is used and the fillets, once cooked, may be served as is or, even better—but more complicated—with a mustard hollandaise. Easiest of all is to steam or poach the fillets, then serve with that delicious butter sauce called beurre blanc.

BAKED FISH FILLETS

1. Preheat the oven to 400 degrees.

2. Cut each fillet into three pieces.

3. Butter a baking dish large enough to hold the pieces in one layer with the 2 tablespoons of butter. Sprinkle with the salt, pepper, and shallots.

4. Arrange the fish pieces over the shallots and sprinkle with half of the wine. Blend the remaining wine with the mustard and brush the tops of the fish with the mixture. Sprinkle each piece of fish with 1½ teaspoons of the bread crumbs and dot each piece with ½ teaspoon of butter. Bake in the oven for 5 minutes.

5. Turn the broiler to high and run the baking dish under it. Broil until the fish flakes easily when tested with a fork. Do not overcook. Sprinkle with chopped parsley. Serve each portion with a lemon wedge.

Yield: 4 servings.

4 striped bass, fluke, flounder, or sole fillets, 1½ to 2 pounds

2 tablespoons plus 6 teaspoons butter

Salt and freshly ground pepper to taste

2 tablespoons finely chopped shallots or scallions

½ cup dry white wine

2 teaspoons Dijon mustard

6 tablespoons fresh bread crumbs

¼ cup finely chopped parsley

Lemon wedges

BREADED FISH FILLETS

2 pounds fish fillets, such as striped bass, sole, or flounder

¾ cup flour

Salt and freshly ground pepper to taste

1 egg, lightly beaten

3 tablespoons plus 1 teaspoon peanut, vegetable, or corn oil

2 tablespoons water

¾ cup fresh bread crumbs

1 tablespoon butter

Lemon wedges

Mustard hollandaise (see recipe page 771), optional

1. Cut the fish into serving pieces.
2. Combine the flour, salt, and pepper.
3. Beat the egg with 1 teaspoon of the oil, the water, and salt and pepper to taste.
4. Coat the fish pieces all over in the seasoned flour. Dip them well into the egg, then coat them all over with the crumbs.
5. In a heavy skillet, heat the remaining 3 tablespoons of oil and the butter and cook the fish pieces until golden brown on one side. Turn and cook on the other side, basting frequently with the oil and butter in the skillet. It is impossible to give an exact cooking time, because it depends on the thickness of the fish. Cooking time may range from 5 minutes for flounder to 10 minutes for bass. Serve with lemon wedges or mustard hollandaise. Accompany the fish with steamed potatoes.

Yield: 4 to 6 servings.

STEAMED FISH FILLETS WITH BEURRE BLANC

4 boneless fish fillets, such as striped bass, red snapper, and so on, about ½ pound each

Salt and freshly ground pepper to taste

1 tablespoon finely chopped herbs, such as fresh basil or tarragon

Beurre blanc (see recipe page 773)

1. Place the fish fillets skin side down in the top of a steamer. Sprinkle with salt and pepper. Sprinkle with chopped basil or tarragon.
2. Pour water in the bottom of the steamer and bring to a high boil.
3. Place the steamer top securely over the boiling water and cover closely. Let steam for 3 to 5 minutes. Steaming time will depend on the thickness of the fillets.
4. Serve with hot beurre blanc.

Yield: 4 servings.

BAKED SALTWATER FISH WITH TARRAGON

1. Preheat the oven to 425 degrees.

2. Wipe the fish and pat it dry inside and out.

3. Melt 2 tablespoons of the butter in a large skillet and add the onion, leeks, and garlic. Cook briefly, stirring, until the onion is wilted. Add the tomatoes, salt, and pepper. Cook for about 5 minutes.

4. Add half of the tarragon, all of the wine, and the bay leaf. Simmer, stirring occasionally, for about 5 minutes.

5. Rub a baking dish large enough to hold the fish with the remaining 2 tablespoons of butter. Sprinkle with salt and pepper.

6. Put the fish in the baking dish. Pour and scrape the tomato sauce around the fish. Sprinkle the fish with salt and pepper. Sprinkle the remaining tarragon over the fish.

7. Cover the dish closely with foil and place in the oven. Bake for 25 to 30 minutes, basting occasionally.

8. Pour and scrape the tomato sauce into a skillet or casserole. Cook down to about half.

9. Transfer the fish to a warm serving dish. Pour the tomato sauce over the fish and sprinkle with the chopped basil or parsley.

Yield: 4 to 6 servings.

One 3½-pound (cleaned weight, gills removed) fish, such as weakfish, striped bass, or red snapper

4 tablespoons butter

1 cup finely chopped onion

1 cup finely chopped leeks

1 teaspoon finely minced garlic

4 cups peeled, cored, and cubed tomatoes

Salt and freshly ground pepper to taste

1 tablespoon finely chopped fresh tarragon, or 1½ teaspoons dried

1 cup dry white wine

1 bay leaf

Chopped fresh basil or parsley

BAKED WHOLE FISH À LA GRECQUE

One 4- to 5-pound whole fish, such as striped bass, sea bass, or weakfish (sea trout)

Salt and freshly ground pepper to taste

¼ cup olive oil

4 lemon slices

1 fresh thyme sprig, or ½ teaspoon dried

1 medium-size onion, peeled and thinly sliced, about 2 cups

1 garlic clove, finely minced

1 teaspoon dried oregano

⅔ cup dry white wine

12 littleneck clams, the smaller the better, optional

1. Preheat the oven to 400 degrees.

2. Sprinkle the fish inside and out with the salt and pepper. Place in a roasting pan and pour the olive oil over it. Arrange the lemon slices on top and cover with the sprig of thyme.

3. Scatter the onion rings around the fish and add the garlic and oregano.

4. Place the roasting pan on top of the stove to heat the bottom briefly without cooking the fish. Place the fish in the oven and bake for 10 minutes.

5. Pour the wine around the fish. Add the clams and bake for 20 minutes longer, basting.

Yield: 6 servings.

PANACHÉ DE POISSON (MIXED STEAMED FISH FILLETS WITH VEGETABLES)

The word *panaché* means "mixed or assorted." When this dish is prepared at the Troisgros restaurant in Roanne, an assortment of fish is used and three or more kinds of fish are served with each portion. If you can find a mixture of fish for the recipe, well and good; otherwise, simply use one or two kinds of fish.

1. Cut the fish into 8 or more individual portions, enough to serve 2 or more portions per person. The pieces should be of more or less equal size. Arrange the pieces skin side down in a steamer (steamers such as used in Chinese or other Asian cookery are good for this). Arrange the fish pieces in one layer. You will probably need two tiers to hold the fish.

2. Sprinkle the fish with the salt and pepper. Put water into the bottom of the steamer and set the tier or tiers in place. Set aside until ready to cook.

3. Drop the peas into boiling salted water and cook for about 30 seconds, no longer. Drain and put immediately into cold water to chill quickly. Drain. Set aside.

4. Pick over the snow peas and pull off any strings from the top and bottom. Drop the snow peas into boiling salted water and cook for about 30 seconds. Drain and put immediately into cold water to chill quickly. Drain. Set aside.

5. Cut the carrots into 1½-inch lengths. Cut the pieces into ¼-inch slices. Stack the slices and cut each slice into ¼-inch strips (julienne). Discard the center strips or core of each carrot. There should be about 1 cup when ready. Drop the strips into boiling salted water and cook for 30 seconds, no longer. Drain and put them immediately into cold water to chill quickly. Drain.

6. Core and peel the tomatoes. Cut them into slices and then into ½-inch cubes. There should be about 1½ cups.

7. When ready to serve, bring enough water to cover the vegetables to the boil. Add salt to taste.

8. Set the steamer over moderate heat and bring water in the bottom of the steamer to the boil. Remember that the fish when steamed cooks very quickly, 30 seconds to 1 minute. If the fish steams longer, it will be dry.

9. Prepare the butter sauce and set aside.

10. When the fish is properly cooked, drop all the vegetables, including the tomatoes, into the boiling water. This is just to heat

2½ pounds nonoily, white-fleshed fish fillets, boneless but with skin left on

Salt and freshly ground pepper to taste

1 cup shelled fresh new peas, or 1 package frozen green peas

⅓ pound fresh snow peas

2 large carrots, about ½ pound

2 large ripe, unblemished tomatoes, about 1 pound

Beurre nantais (see recipe page 774)

them through. Do not cook or the tomatoes will disintegrate. Drain quickly and well.

11. Arrange the fish on individual serving dishes and spoon equal amounts of vegetables over the pieces. Spoon hot butter sauce over each serving.

Yield: 4 to 6 servings.

FLOUNDER FILLETS WITH MUSTARD

8 small, skinless, boneless flounder fillets, about 1 pound

Salt and freshly ground pepper to taste

1 tablespoon peanut, vegetable, or corn oil

2 tablespoons mayonnaise, preferably homemade

1 tablespoon Dijon mustard

2 teaspoons finely chopped parsley

4 lemon or lime wedges

1. Preheat the broiler to high.

2. Place the fillet halves on a flat surface. Sprinkle with salt and pepper and brush with the oil. Arrange the fillets on a baking sheet. Blend the mayonnaise, mustard, and parsley. Brush it evenly over the fillets.

3. Place the fillets under the broiler, 3 or 4 inches from the source of heat. Broil for about 1 minute, or until golden brown on top and the fish is just cooked through. Serve with lemon wedges.

Yield: 4 servings.

FISH CREOLE

1. Preheat the oven to 450 degrees.
2. Cut the fish into 6 individual serving pieces and set aside.
3. Melt 2 tablespoons of the butter in a saucepan and add the onion. Cook, stirring, until wilted and add the garlic and sweet peppers. Sprinkle with salt and pepper to taste. Toss well and add the tomatoes, capers, Tabasco, and parsley. Cover and cook for 15 minutes. Uncover and cook for 5 minutes longer.
4. Rub a baking dish with the remaining butter and sprinkle with salt and pepper. Add the fish pieces and spoon the sauce over. Bake for 15 minutes.

Yield: 6 servings.

1¾ pounds skinless, boneless fish fillets such as sea trout, sea bass, cod, red snapper, or hake

3 tablespoons butter

1 cup thinly sliced onion

1 teaspoon chopped garlic

3 cups chopped green and red sweet peppers

Salt and freshly ground pepper to taste

2 cups chopped fresh tomatoes, or one 17-ounce can imported peeled tomatoes, preferably with tomato paste and basil

2 tablespoons capers

Tabasco sauce to taste

¼ cup finely chopped parsley

FISH STEAKS WITH OIL AND LEMON SAUCE

1. Preheat the broiler or prepare the charcoal for grilling.
2. Have the fish ready and set it aside.
3. Blend the lemon juice, salt, and dried oregano. Gradually add the oil while stirring with a fork. Add a generous amount of pepper. This sauce is known as a salmoriglio sauce.
4. When the broiler or charcoal grill is quite hot, place the fish under the broiler or on the grill. The fish should be quite close to the source of heat. It must cook quickly. Cook for about 1 minute on one side. Turn carefully but quickly and cook for 1 minute or slightly longer on the other side. Do not overcook or the fish steaks will become dry.
5. Transfer the fish to a warm platter and ladle the salmoriglio sauce over it.

Yield: 4 servings.

2 pounds swordfish, salmon, or tilefish, cut crosswise into ½-inch-thick steaks

Juice of half a lemon (at least 2 tablespoons)

Salt to taste

1 teaspoon dried oregano

¼ cup olive oil

Freshly ground pepper to taste

Stir-Fried Fish with Tree Ears

3 tablespoons dried tree ear mushrooms

1 pound skinless, boneless gray sole fillets

4 tablespoons dry sherry

½ cup plus 1½ tablespoons cornstarch

1½ cups fresh or canned chicken broth

Salt to taste

1 tablespoon sugar

1 cup peanut, vegetable, or corn oil

1. Put the tree ears in a mixing bowl and add boiling water to cover. Let stand for at least 30 minutes.

2. Cut each fillet in half lengthwise. Cut each fillet half on the diagonal into 2-inch pieces.

3. Put the fish in a bowl and add 1 tablespoon of the sherry.

4. Put ½ cup of the cornstarch on a plate. Dredge each piece of fish on both sides in the cornstarch. Set aside.

5. Blend a little of the chicken broth with the remaining cornstarch, salt, and sugar. Blend with the remaining broth and set aside.

6. Drain the tree ears and put them in a saucepan. Add cold water to cover. Bring to the boil and simmer for 1 minute. Drain. Squeeze to extract excess moisture. Set aside.

7. Heat the oil in a wok and, when it is very hot, add two or three pieces of fish at a time. Cook over very high heat for about 15 seconds and remove. The fish pieces should not brown. Do not overcook.

8. Pour off all but 1 teaspoon of the oil from the wok. Add the broth mixture and the remaining 3 tablespoons of sherry. Cook, stirring, until thickened.

9. Add the tree ears and fish and cook, stirring gently, for about 1 minute. Transfer to a hot serving dish.

Yield: 8 servings with other Chinese dishes.

SAUTÉED FRESH ROE

1. The size of the roe may vary greatly from 2 to 6 or more inches in length. Prick the roe in several places with a needle or pin.

2. Sprinkle with the salt, pepper, and flour. Shake to remove any excess flour.

3. Melt the butter in a skillet large enough to hold the roe in one layer. When the butter is quite hot, add the roe. Reduce the heat. Cook until nicely golden on one side. Cooking times will vary depending on the size of the roe, from 3 to 8 minutes to a side. Turn the roe and cook over gentle heat until golden and cooked through.

4. Remove the roe to a serving dish. Add the garlic to the skillet and cook briefly without browning. Add the lemon juice, stir, and pour the pan sauce over the roe. Serve sprinkled with chopped parsley and lemon wedges.

Yield: 4 or more servings.

1 pound fresh roe from flounder, herring, weakfish, or other fish

Salt and freshly ground pepper to taste

Flour for dredging

2 tablespoons butter

1 teaspoon finely minced garlic

Juice of ½ lemon

Finely chopped parsley for garnish

Lemon wedges for garnish

BLUEFISH ANDALOUSE

2 tablespoons olive or corn oil

1 pound boneless bluefish fillets

1 cup thinly sliced onion

1 teaspoon finely minced garlic

1½ cups thinly sliced green pepper

½ teaspoon saffron stems, or ¼ teaspoon powdered

1 bay leaf

1 fresh thyme sprig, or ½ teaspoon dried

2 cups chopped ripe tomatoes

1 teaspoon red wine vinegar

1 tablespoon finely chopped parsley

Some of the most sought-after dishes in the world are those that can be made in advance and served hours or even a day later. Two classic examples follow, both made with bluefish. One is seasoned with tomatoes and a touch of saffron; the other with white wine and spices. Both are buffet dishes that actually improve after several hours of refrigeration, preferably overnight.

1. Preheat the oven to 400 degrees.

2. Spread 1 tablespoon of the oil on the bottom of a baking dish large enough to hold the fillets in one layer. Arrange the fillets skin side down in the dish. If the fillets are large, it may be necessary to cut them into two or three pieces.

3. Heat 1 tablespoon of the oil in a saucepan and add the onion, garlic, green pepper, saffron, bay leaf, and thyme. Cook, stirring often, for about 5 minutes.

4. Add the tomatoes, vinegar, and parsley and cook, stirring occasionally, for about 10 minutes.

5. Ladle the sauce over the fish.

6. Bring to the boil on top of the stove. Place in the oven and bake for 15 minutes.

7. Remove from the oven and let stand in the marinade until cool. Chill if desired. Serve cold.

Yield: 4 servings.

BLUEFISH IN WHITE WINE

1. Preheat the oven to 400 degrees.

2. If the fillets are small, arrange them skin side down in one layer in a shallow baking dish. If the fillets are large, it may be necessary to cut them into two or three pieces before putting them in the dish.

3. Cut a few lengthwise ridges down the side of the lemon using a lemon peeler or knife. This is only for a decorative effect. Trim off the ends of the lemon. Cut the lemon into 8 or 10 thin slices and remove the seeds. Arrange the slices over the fish.

4. Combine the water, wine, vinegar, sugar, onion, bay leaf, cloves, hot red pepper, peppercorns, and thyme in a saucepan. Bring to the boil and simmer for 10 minutes.

5. Pour the sauce over the fish and place the dish on the stove. Bring just to the boil. Place in the oven and bake for 15 minutes.

6. Remove the fish and let stand in the marinade until cool. Chill if desired. Serve cold.

Yield: 4 servings.

1 pound boneless bluefish fillets

1 lemon

½ cup water

¼ cup dry white wine

2 tablespoons white vinegar

1 teaspoon sugar

1 small onion, cut in half and thinly sliced, about 1 cup

1 bay leaf

3 whole cloves

⅛ teaspoon crushed hot red pepper flakes

12 peppercorns

1 fresh thyme sprig, or ½ teaspoon dried

BLUEFISH COOKED IN FOIL

A friend of mine, Arthur Gloka, a captain with a major airline, taught me this recipe. You envelop the fish in aluminum foil, bake it in the oven (you could cook it over charcoal), and when you unwrap the fish the skin comes off attached to the foil. The only seasoning necessary is a little garlic, sliced wafer-thin.

1. Preheat the oven to 500 degrees.

2. Wrap the fillet, or two fillets, in one layer of heavy-duty aluminum foil. The fish must be tightly enclosed and sealed in the foil. Wrap the package neatly and seal the ends, tucking them under.

3. Place the fish on the bottom rack of the oven and bake for 10 minutes.

4. If you open the foil and invert the fish onto a plate, the skin will remain stuck to the foil. Heat the butter and garlic and pour over the fish.

Yield: 2 servings.

1 large, boneless bluefish fillet with skin on, or 2 boneless bluefish fillets weighing 1 pound

4 tablespoons butter

1 small peeled garlic clove, sliced wafer-thin

Sybil Arant's Catfish Baked with Cheese

6 to 8 catfish fillets, about 2 pounds

½ cup freshly grated Parmesan cheese

¼ cup flour

Salt and freshly ground pepper to taste

1 teaspoon paprika

1 egg, lightly beaten

1 tablespoon milk

4 tablespoons butter, melted

¼ cup sliced almonds

Like most Southerners, I adore catfish. I'm not certain that my mother ever prepared catfish at home, however. She was too aristocratic for that. Red snapper, yes; but catfish was too common, something to be enjoyed outdoors on Sunday outings. Eating deep-fried catfish was a ritual, and the menu was always the same: the cornmeal-coated catfish with its golden brown crusty exterior and moist white inner flesh; deep-fried hush puppies; deep-fried potatoes; and coleslaw. And tomato ketchup. Deep-fried catfish without ketchup is like a hot dog without mustard. Now that catfish are being raised in freshwater ponds, they are available frozen all over the country and can be used in any recipe calling for a white nonoily fish. Even after freezing and defrosting, catfish remain snow white and as firm as when taken from the water.

1. Preheat the oven to 350 degrees.
2. Wipe the catfish dry.
3. Blend together the cheese, flour, salt, pepper, and paprika.
4. Combine the egg and milk in a flat dish.
5. Dip the fillets in the egg mixture and then coat with the cheese mixture. Arrange the fillets in one layer in a baking dish and pour the butter over all. Sprinkle with the almonds. Place in the oven and bake for 20 minutes.

Yield: 6 to 8 servings.

CATFISH FILLETS IN WHITE WINE SAUCE

1. Preheat the oven to 400 degrees.

2. Pat the catfish pieces dry. Rub a baking dish (a dish measuring about 2 x 13 x 8 inches is ideal) with 1 tablespoon of the butter. Arrange the fillets in the buttered dish in one layer.

3. Add the wine. Scatter the mushrooms over all and sprinkle with salt and pepper to taste. Place in the oven and bake for 10 minutes.

4. Meanwhile, melt the remaining butter in a saucepan and add the flour, stirring with a wire whisk. Add the milk, stirring with the whisk. When blended and smooth, remove from the heat.

5. Pour the liquid from the baked fish into the sauce, stirring. Bring to the boil and cook, stirring often, for about 5 minutes. Stir in the lemon juice. Pour the sauce over the fish and bake for 10 minutes longer. Sprinkle with Parmesan cheese and parsley. Serve hot.

Yield: 6 servings.

- 6 catfish fillets, about 2 pounds
- 5 tablespoons butter
- ½ cup dry white wine
- ½ pound mushrooms, thinly sliced, about 2 cups
- Salt and freshly ground pepper to taste
- 2 tablespoons flour
- ½ cup milk
- Juice of ½ lemon
- 2 tablespoons freshly grated Parmesan cheese
- 2 tablespoons finely chopped parsley

DEEP-FRIED CATFISH

1. Heat the oil for deep frying.

2. Cut each fillet in half crosswise.

3. Combine the cornmeal, salt, and pepper.

4. Dredge the fillets in the cornmeal. Pat to make the cornmeal adhere. Drop the fillets in the oil and cook for 5 to 10 minutes, or until crisp and brown. Serve with lemon halves, ketchup, and hush puppies.

Yield: 2 to 4 servings.

- Fresh corn oil to cover
- 3 catfish fillets, about 1 pound
- ½ cup white cornmeal
- Salt and freshly ground pepper to taste
- Lemon halves
- Tomato ketchup
- Hush puppies (see recipe page 744)

POACHED COD STEAKS WITH MUSTARD AND PARSLEY SAUCE

4 cod steaks, about ¾ pound each and about 1 inch thick

½ cup milk

3 cups water

Salt and freshly ground pepper to taste

8 parsley sprigs tied with string

1 bay leaf

8 peppercorns, crushed

2 tablespoons finely chopped shallots

2 tablespoons red wine vinegar

1 tablespoon cold water

4 tablespoons butter

1 tablespoon Dijon mustard

4 tablespoons finely chopped parsley

1. Arrange the fish steaks in one layer in a casserole in which they fit comfortably. Add the milk and water. The liquid should cover the steaks, but barely. Add the salt, pepper, parsley, bay leaf, and peppercorns. Bring to the boil. Let simmer for 5 minutes and turn off the heat. Let stand for 3 minutes or longer until ready to serve.

2. Combine the shallots and vinegar in a very heavy, small saucepan and cook until most of the vinegar evaporates. Let cool briefly and add the water. Start adding the butter gradually, beating vigorously and rapidly with a wire whisk. Take care that the sauce does not boil at any point because it will curdle, but it must be very hot, just below the boiling point. If it starts to get too hot, remove the saucepan from the heat. When it is creamy and smooth and lightly thickened, add the mustard and parsley.

3. Carefully drain the steaks and serve with the sauce spooned over.

Yield: 4 servings.

COD FLORENTINE

1. Preheat the oven to 375 degrees.

2. Prepare the mornay sauce and set aside.

3. If bulk spinach is used, pick it over well. Discard any tough stems. Rinse the leaves thoroughly to rid them of all sand. Drop the spinach into boiling water to cover. Return to the boil and simmer for about 2 minutes. Drain and run the spinach under cold running water. Squeeze the spinach between the hands to extract excess moisture. Chop the spinach coarsely. Set aside.

4. Butter a baking dish with 2 tablespoons of butter. Sprinkle with the shallots, salt, and pepper.

5. Cut the cod into 6 pieces of approximately the same weight. Arrange the pieces neatly over the baking dish. Sprinkle with salt, pepper, and the wine. Cover with foil. Bring the wine to the boil on top of the stove, then put the dish in the oven. Bake for 12 to 15 minutes, or just until the fish flakes easily when tested with a fork.

6. Meanwhile, heat the remaining 1½ tablespoons of butter in a skillet and add the onion. When it wilts, add the chopped spinach, salt, and pepper. Cook for about 1 minute, no longer.

7. Spoon the spinach into an oval baking dish and smooth it over the bottom. Carefully transfer the baked cod pieces to the spinach, arranging them neatly over it. Cover and keep warm.

8. Pour the wine liquid from the baked fish into a saucepan and reduce it quickly over high heat to about ¼ cup. Add this to the mornay sauce and stir. Bring to the boil.

9. Spoon the hot sauce over the fish, smoothing it to coat the fish evenly. Sprinkle with the Parmesan cheese and bake, uncovered, until bubbling throughout and the fish is nicely browned on top.

Yield: 6 servings.

2½ cups mornay sauce (see recipe page 779)

2 pounds bulk or two 10-ounce packages fresh spinach

3½ tablespoons butter

1 tablespoon finely chopped shallots

Salt and freshly ground pepper to taste

1¾ to 2 pounds skinless, boneless cod or striped bass fillets

½ cup dry white wine

3 tablespoons chopped onion

3 tablespoons freshly grated Parmesan cheese

BROILED COD FILLETS

2 cod fillets or codfish
   steaks
2 tablespoons butter
   Salt and freshly ground
   pepper to taste
½ cup fresh bread crumbs
½ teaspoon paprika

1. Preheat the oven to 450 degrees.
2. Grease the bottom of a baking dish with 1 tablespoon of the butter.
3. Arrange the fillets skin side down on the dish and sprinkle with the salt and pepper.
4. Scatter the bread crumbs on a piece of wax paper. Hold a small sieve over the crumbs. Put the paprika through the sieve and blend paprika and crumbs. Sprinkle the fish fillets with the crumbs and melt and dribble the remaining butter over all. Broil about 6 inches from the heat until golden brown. Then bake for 5 to 10 minutes.

Yield: 2 servings.

COD STEAKS WITH PERNOD

2¾ pounds cod steaks,
   each about 1 inch
   thick, skinned and
   boned
4 tablespoons butter
2 tablespoons finely
   diced shallots
2 tablespoons finely
   chopped onion
1 garlic clove, finely
   minced
½ cup dry white wine
   Juice of ½ lemon
1 tablespoon finely
   chopped parsley
1 cup peeled fresh or
   canned tomatoes
   Salt and freshly ground
   pepper to taste
½ cup heavy cream
1 tablespoon Pernod,
   Ricard, or other anise-
   flavored liqueur
   Freshly chopped
   parsley for garnish

1. Cut the cod into 6 or 8 serving pieces. Set aside.
2. Melt 2 tablespoons of the butter in a skillet large enough to hold the cod in one layer. Add the shallots, onion, and garlic. Cook until wilted. Add the wine and cook until most of it evaporates. Add the lemon juice, parsley, and the tomatoes. Add the salt and pepper to taste. Cook for 10 minutes.
3. Add the cod in one layer. Sprinkle with salt and pepper and cover. Bring to the boil and simmer for about 5 minutes. Add the cream and shake the skillet gently to blend. Handle the cod with care as it tends to flake and break. Cook for about 3 minutes.
4. Carefully pour the sauce from the skillet into a saucepan. Boil it down for about 5 minutes and add the Pernod. Swirl in the remaining butter and pour this over the fish. Serve in hot soup plates. Serve sprinkled with chopped parsley.

Yield: 6 servings.

CODFISH FRITTERS

1. Put the cod in a bowl and add cold water to cover. Let stand for several hours or overnight, changing the water if the cod is very salty. Drain well. Flake the cod with the fingers, discarding any bones. Chop the flesh fine. There should be about ½ cup.

2. Put the flour in a bowl and add the pepper (the taste of pepper should be a bit pronounced). Add the salt and oregano. Gradually add the cold water, stirring with a whisk to prevent lumping. This batter should not be runny, nor too thick. Add the chopped cod, chilies, and coriander. Stir and refrigerate for several hours.

3. Heat about ⅛ inch of the oil in a skillet. Add the batter, about 1 tablespoon to a fritter. Cook until golden brown on one side. Turn and cook until golden brown on the other side. Drain on absorbent towels.

Yield: About 24 fritters.

¼ pound dried salt cod

2 cups flour

½ teaspoon freshly ground pepper

Salt to taste

1 teaspoon crushed, dried oregano

1½ cups cold water, approximately

1 tablespoon chopped hot, or mildly hot, green or red fresh chilies

1 tablespoon chopped fresh coriander

Peanut, vegetable, or corn oil for shallow frying

GROUPER WITH LEAF SPINACH

20 thin, skinless,
    boneless, crosswise
    slices of fresh grouper
    (about 2 pounds)

Salt and freshly ground
pepper to taste

2 pounds fresh spinach,
    picked over to remove
    any tough stems or
    blemished leaves, or
    2 packages (10 ounces
    each) fresh spinach

2 cups water

2 tablespoons butter

⅛ teaspoon freshly grated
    nutmeg

⅓ cup flour

4 tablespoons corn,
    peanut, or vegetable oil

4 tablespoons olive oil

Juice of ½ lemon

1. Preheat the oven to 500 degrees.

2. Each grouper slice should be about ¼ inch thick. Sprinkle the slices with the salt and pepper and set aside.

3. Rinse the spinach leaves thoroughly to rid them of all sand. Drain. Put the water in a kettle and bring to the boil. Add salt to taste and the spinach. Stir down to wilt.

4. Bring to the boil, stirring occasionally, and cook for about 5 minutes. Empty the spinach into a colander and drain. Press with the back of a wooden spoon to extract most of the liquid. Squeeze between the hands to extract additional moisture.

5. Put the spinach on a flat surface and coarsely chop. Heat the butter in a skillet and add the spinach. Add the salt, pepper, and nutmeg. Cook, tossing and stirring, just to heat through. Keep warm and set aside briefly.

6. Dredge the fish slices on both sides with the flour and pat to make the flour adhere. Shake off the excess.

7. Use a nonstick skillet and add half of the corn and olive oils. When they are quite hot and starting to smoke, add half the fish slices. Cook over high heat for 1 minute and 15 seconds on one side, and turn the pieces. Cook for about 10 seconds, no longer, on the second side.

8. Pour off any fat from the skillet and wipe out the skillet. Add the remaining oils to the skillet and cook the remaining batch of fish as before.

9. Scoop out the spinach onto the center of a preheated ovenproof plate. Smooth it over. Arrange the fish pieces symmetrically over the spinach. Place the fish in the oven and bake for 10 seconds, no longer. Sprinkle with the lemon juice and serve.

Yield: 4 servings.

BARBECUED MACKEREL

1. Prepare a charcoal grill and have it ready. The coals must be white-hot but not overly plentiful, or the food will cook too fast. Arrange the grill 6 to 8 inches over the coals.

2. Sprinkle the fish with the salt and pepper and brush lightly with the oil.

3. Arrange the fish on the grill and cook until lightly browned on one side. Turn and baste the top side with sauce. Cook, turning the fish and basting as necessary, until the fish flakes easily with a fork, 20 to 25 minutes.

4. Give the fish a final brushing with the sauce and remove to a serving dish.

Yield: 2 to 4 servings.

2 fresh, cleaned mackerel (about 1 pound each)

Salt and freshly ground pepper to taste

2 tablespoons peanut, vegetable, or corn oil

Country barbecue sauce (see recipe page 794)

MACKEREL WITH WHITE WINE AND TOMATOES

1. Preheat the oven to 400 degrees.

2. In a saucepan, heat 1 tablespoon of the oil and add the onion. Cook, stirring, until wilted. Add the carrot rounds, garlic, salt, pepper, vinegar, white wine, cloves, bay leaf, and tomatoes. Cook for 20 minutes and let cool.

3. Select a baking dish large enough to hold the mackerel in one layer. Rub the bottom of the dish with the remaining 1 tablespoon of the oil and sprinkle with salt and pepper. Arrange the mackerel in the dish. Arrange the lemon slices over the fish and sprinkle with the lemon juice. Sprinkle with salt and pepper to taste.

4. Spoon the tomato and wine sauce over the fish and cover with a piece of buttered wax paper cut to fit the baking dish. Bake for 15 to 20 minutes, just until the fish flakes easily when tested with a fork. Baking time will depend on the size of the fish.

Yield: 10 or more servings.

Note: Mackerel fillets may be used in this recipe, but time will have to be adjusted accordingly.

2 tablespoons olive oil

1 cup thinly sliced onion

¼ cup thin carrot rounds

2 garlic cloves, finely minced

Salt and freshly ground pepper to taste

2 tablespoons white vinegar

2 cups dry white wine

3 whole cloves

1 bay leaf

1 cup fresh or canned peeled tomatoes

5 pounds cleaned whole mackerel (see note)

10 thin lemon slices

3 tablespoons lemon juice

BLACKENED REDFISH

3   teaspoons salt

½   teaspoon cayenne

½   teaspoon freshly
    ground white pepper

¼   teaspoon freshly
    ground black pepper

¼   teaspoon dried thyme

¼   teaspoon dried basil

¼   teaspoon dried oregano

2   teaspoons paprika

8   skinless, boneless
    fillets of fish,
    preferably redfish,
    pompano, or tilefish,
    about ¼ pound each
    (see note)

8   tablespoons butter,
    melted

Paul Prudhomme is that rarity in the world of food—a celebrated, internationally known chef who just happens to have been born in the United States. When Mr. Prudhomme visited my kitchen, he demonstrated numerous Louisiana specialties, including jambalaya and chicken gumbo, dirty rice, red beans with rice, and his own invention, this specialty of specialties, blackened redfish. Because there were no redfish or red snapper in our local market, he chose tilefish, and it worked admirably as a substitute.

1. Combine the salt, cayenne, white pepper, black pepper, thyme, basil, oregano, and paprika in a small bowl.

2. Dip the fish pieces on both sides in butter. Sprinkle on both sides with the seasoned mixture.

3. Heat a black iron skillet over high heat for about 5 minutes or longer (the skillet cannot get too hot) until it is beyond the smoking stage and starts to lighten in color on the bottom.

4. Add two or more fish pieces and pour about a teaspoon of butter on top of each piece. The butter may flame up. Cook over high heat for about 1½ minutes. Turn the fish and pour another teaspoon of butter over each piece. Cook for about 1½ minutes. Serve immediately. Continue until all the fillets are cooked.

Yield: 4 servings.

Note: Redfish and pompano are ideal for this dish. If tilefish is used, you may have to split the fillets in half. Place the fillet on a flat surface, hold the knife parallel to the surface and split in half through the center from one end to the other. The weight of the fish may vary from 1 to 1½ pounds, depending on your skillet, but they must not be more than about 1½ inches thick.

BEAN SAUCE HOT FISH

1. Prepare the rice two days before as indicated in the recipe.

2. Rinse the fish and pat dry.

3. Heat the oil in a wok or casserole large enough to hold the fish. When it is almost smoking, add the fish and cook for about 1 minute. Drain and set aside. Pour off and reserve the oil.

4. Heat ½ cup of reserved oil in a wok or skillet and add the pork, stirring to break up lumps. When the meat changes color, add the ginger, garlic, and red pepper, stirring. Add the chili paste and bean paste. Cook for about 1 minute and add the cup of fermented rice and salt. Cook, stirring, over high heat and add ½ cup of the water. Cook over high heat, stirring, for about 10 minutes.

5. Meanwhile, heat 2 tablespoons of oil in a pan large enough to hold the fish and add the fish. Add the remaining 1 cup of water and cover. Steam for 8 to 10 minutes. Drain. Transfer the fish to a serving dish.

6. Add the scallions to the pork sauce and pour the sizzling hot sauce over the fish. Serve.

Yield: 8 servings with other Chinese dishes.

1 cup fermented rice (see following recipe)

One 1¾- to 2-pound red snapper

Peanut, vegetable, or corn oil for deep frying

½ pound ground pork

½ cup finely chopped ginger

2½ tablespoons finely chopped garlic

¼ pound fresh hot red peppers, seeded and chopped, about ¾ cup

1½ tablespoons chili paste with garlic, available in Asian markets

½ cup bean paste, available in Asian markets

Salt to taste

1½ cups water

1 cup chopped scallions

FERMENTED RICE

¾ **pound glutinous rice**

½ **wine ball, or wine cube (available in Asian markets)**

1½ **teaspoons flour**

1. Soak the rice overnight in cold water to cover, then drain.

2. Line a steamer top or a colander with cheesecloth and add the drained rice. Cover and steam for 1 hour.

3. Crush the wine ball or cube on a flat surface, using a mallet or rolling pin. When it is crushed fine like a powder, blend well with the flour. Set aside.

4. Rinse the rice delicately in lukewarm water, working gently with the hands to separate the grains. The rice should be at about body temperature when it is ready. If it is too warm at this time, it will ferment too quickly. If it is cold, it will not ferment.

5. When the rice is right, drain it well. Sprinkle it with the wine ball–and-flour mixture and work gently to mix thoroughly. Spoon the rice into a thin bowl and smooth the top with the fingers.

6. Using the fingers, make a hole or well in the center, about 1 inch in diameter. Pat the top of the rice with wet fingers to smooth it, but do not disturb the hole. You will see later when you uncover the rice that the hole accumulates liquid as the rice stands.

7. Cover the bowl well and then carefully wrap it in blankets. Set the blanket-covered bowl in a warm (but not too warm) place and let it stand for 24 hours. If properly made and all the elements are right, liquid will have accumulated in the hole.

8. Spoon the rice and liquid into mason jars and seal loosely. Let it stand until room temperature, then refrigerate. The fermented rice keeps for weeks in the refrigerator, but you should loosen the tops occasionally to make sure too much gas is not accumulating inside the jars.

Yield: 1½ pints.

Grilled Salmon and Tuna with Anchovy Butter

1. Preheat a charcoal grill to very hot.
2. Cut the tuna across the grain into six equal portions, each about ¾ inch thick.
3. Cut the salmon into six individual portions.
4. Combine the tuna and salmon in a mixing bowl and add the oil. Stir to coat the fish pieces with the oil.
5. Put the fish pieces on the grill and cook for about 1 minute on one side. Turn and cook the fish on the other side for 1 to 2 minutes longer.
6. Scatter the onions (broken into rings) over a hot serving dish. Arrange the fish pieces over the onions. Smear the anchovy butter on top. Garnish, if desired, with whole anchovy fillets and serve.

Yield: 6 servings.

1 pound fresh tuna fillet
1 pound fresh salmon fillet
2 tablespoons olive oil
Grilled onion slices (see following recipe)
¾ cup anchovy butter (see following recipe), at room temperature
12 whole anchovy fillets, optional

GRILLED ONION SLICES

1. Preheat a charcoal grill to very hot. Trim off the ends of the onions. Peel the onions and cut into ¼-inch-thick slices. Put the slices in a bowl and add the olive oil. Set aside until ready to cook.
2. Put the onion slices on the grill and cook for about 45 seconds. Turn them with a spatula or tongs. They will probably divide into rings. Cook until tender, 2 or 3 minutes, turning often.

Yield: 6 servings.

3 to 4 medium-size red onions
¼ cup olive oil

ANCHOVY BUTTER

1. Pound the anchovy fillets in a mortar or chop as fine as possible.
2. Put the anchovies in a small bowl and add the butter, lemon juice, and pepper. Blend well.

Yield: ¾ cup.

6 to 8 anchovy fillets packed in oil and drained
6 tablespoons butter, at room temperature
Juice of ½ lemon
Freshly ground pepper to taste

SAUMON CHAMBORD
(SALMON IN RED WINE SAUCE)

2 pounds salmon with skin and bone (this may be a whole salmon or a portion, such as the tail or a center cut)

Salt and freshly ground pepper to taste

4 tablespoons butter

½ cup thinly sliced onion

¼ cup finely chopped shallots

½ cup thinly sliced mushrooms

2 fresh parsley sprigs

1½ cups dry red wine, preferably a Burgundy

¼ teaspoon dried thyme

1 bay leaf

2 teaspoons flour

4 whole mushrooms

Juice of ½ lemon

Almost all the fish flourishing in American waters are associated with the seasons: cod in winter, trout in the spring, and so on. If ever a fish smacked gloriously of summer, it is the elegantly pink, seductively flavored salmon. It is one of the very few fish that seem to team well with a red wine sauce.

1. Preheat the oven to 350 degrees.

2. Sprinkle the salmon with the salt and pepper.

3. Use 1 tablespoon of the butter to grease a flameproof baking dish large enough to hold the salmon comfortably.

4. Place the salmon in the dish and scatter around it the onion, shallots, sliced mushrooms, parsley, wine, thyme, and bay leaf.

5. Cover the dish closely with foil. Place the dish on top of the stove and bring the cooking liquid to the boil. Place the dish in the oven and bake for 30 minutes. Remove the foil.

6. Transfer the fish to a warm platter. Pour and scrape the cooking liquid and vegetables into a saucepan and bring to the boil. Cook the liquid down to about ¾ cup. Pour the liquid and vegetables into a strainer. Press the solids to extract as much liquid as possible. Discard the solids. Pour the liquid into a saucepan.

7. Carefully pull off and discard the skin of the fish. Scrape away and discard the dark flesh that coats the pink flesh of the salmon. When turning the fish, turn it carefully so that the flesh does not break.

8. Transfer the fish to a serving dish.

9. Bring the cooking liquid to the boil.

10. Blend 2 tablespoons of the butter and the flour in a small mixing bowl.

11. Meanwhile, put the whole mushrooms in a small saucepan and add water to cover and the lemon juice. Bring to the boil. Simmer for 1 minute. Drain.

12. Add the butter-flour mixture to the cooking liquid, stirring constantly. Cook until smooth and thickened, about 1 minute. Remove from the heat and swirl in the remaining 1 tablespoon of butter.

13. Arrange the whole mushrooms in the center of the salmon. Spoon the sauce over and serve.

Yield: 4 to 6 servings.

POACHED SALMON

1. Combine all the ingredients for the court bouillon in a fish cooker or a kettle large enough to hold the fish. Bring to the boil and simmer, covered, for about 20 minutes. Let cool.

2. Wrap the whole salmon or salmon piece in cheesecloth or a clean towel and tie neatly with string. Lower it into the fish cooker and cover. Bring to the boil and simmer gently for exactly 20 minutes. The cooking time will be the same for a whole salmon or a large center section. Let stand briefly and serve hot, or let cool completely until ready to use if it is to be served at room temperature.

3. Remove the salmon and untie it. Remove the cheesecloth or towel. Place the salmon carefully on a flat surface and pull and scrape away the skin. Scrape away the thin dark brown flesh that coats the main pink flesh.

4. Decorate and garnish the salmon as desired. As a suggestion, drop large tarragon sprigs in boiling water and drain immediately. Chill instantly in ice water. Pat dry. Garnish the surface of the salmon with halved cherry tomatoes and tarragon leaves. Arrange around the salmon small Boston lettuce cups filled with quartered hard-cooked eggs wedged neatly between quartered small tomatoes. Serve with lemon wedges and mayonnaise sauces such as cucumber mayonnaise, mustard mayonnaise, anchovy mayonnaise, or sauce verte, and cucumber salad with dill.

Yield: 12 to 24 servings, depending on the size of the salmon and whether served as an appetizer, buffet dish, or main course.

THE COURT BOUILLON:

24 cups water

1 bottle dry white wine

1½ cups coarsely chopped carrots

1½ cups coarsely chopped celery

3 cups chopped onions

4 garlic cloves, unpeeled but cut in half

1 hot red pepper

10 dill sprigs

6 fresh parsley sprigs

Salt to taste

1 bay leaf

1½ cups coarsely chopped leeks

THE SALMON:

1 whole, cleaned salmon, up to 7½ pounds, or use 1 large section of salmon such as the tail section or center cut, about 3½ pounds

THE GARNISHES:

Tarragon sprigs

Cherry tomatoes, halved

Boston lettuce

Hard-cooked eggs, quartered

Small tomatoes, quartered

Lemon wedges

COULIBIAC OF SALMON

Brioche dough (see
recipe page 395)

Salmon and
mushrooms with
velouté (see recipe
page 396)

Fourteen 7-inch crêpes
(see recipe page 397)

Rice and egg filling
(see recipe page 397)

INGREDIENTS USED IN
ASSEMBLY:

2 egg yolks

2 tablespoons cold water

2 tablespoons butter, at
   room temperature

¾ pound plus
   4 tablespoons butter,
   melted and hot

It is not easy to explain precisely what a coulibiac of salmon is. The easiest way out would be to define it as a pâté of salmon. Such a definition is woefully inapt. It is no mere trifle, no ordinary pâté, something to be dabbled with while awaiting a second course or third or fourth. A coulibiac is a celestial creation, manna for the culinary gods and a main course unto itself.

A coulibiac admittedly demands patience, time, talent, and enthusiasm, and if you are possessed of these, what a magnificent offering to those invited to your table. Actually, any cook who is skilled enough to prepare a brioche dough, a standard French crêpe, and a cream sauce is equal to the task.

1. Have all the ingredients for the coulibiac ready.

2. Remove the salmon-and-mushroom mixture from the refrigerator. Using a knife, cut it in half lengthwise down the center.

3. Remove the brioche dough from the bowl and with floured fingers shape it into a thick, flat pillow shape. Place the brioche dough on a lightly floured board and roll it into a rectangle measuring about 21 by 18 inches. The rectangle, of course, will have slightly rounded corners. Arrange 8 crêpes, edges overlapping in a neat pattern, over the center of the rectangle, leaving a border of brioche dough.

4. Sprinkle the crêpes down the center with a rectangle of about one third of the rice mixture. Pick up half the chilled salmon and carefully arrange it mushroom side down over the rice mixture. Sprinkle with another third of the rice mixture. Top this, sandwich fashion, with another layer of the chilled salmon filling, mushroom side up. Sprinkle with the remaining rice. Cover with 6 overlapping crêpes.

5. Bring up one side of the brioche. Brush it liberally with a mixture of 2 beaten yolks and 2 tablespoons of cold water. Bring up the opposite side of the brioche dough to enclose the filling, over-lapping the two sides of dough. Brush all over with the egg yolk. Trim off the ends of the dough to make them neat. Brush with the yolk and bring up the ends, pinching as necessary to enclose the filling.

6. Butter a baking dish with 2 tablespoons of butter. Carefully turn the coulibiac upside down onto the baking dish. This will keep the seams intact. Brush the coulibiac all over with the yolk. Using a small, round, decorative cookie cutter, cut a hole in the center of the coulibiac. This will allow steam to escape. Brush around the hole with the yolk. Cut out another slightly larger ring of dough to

surround and outline the hole neatly. Roll out a scrap of dough and cut off strips of dough to decorate the coulibiac. Always brush with the beaten yolk before and after applying the pastry cutouts.

7. Roll out a 6-foot length of aluminum foil. Fold it over into thirds to make one long band about 4½ inches in height. Brush the band with 4 tablespoons of the melted butter. Arrange the band neatly and snugly around the loaf, buttered side against the brioche. The purpose of the band is to prevent the sides of the loaf from collapsing before the dough has a chance to firm up while baking. Fasten the top of the band with a jumbo paper clip. Run a cord around the center of the foil band to secure it in place. Run the cord around three times and tie the ends. Make certain the bottom of the loaf is securely enclosed with foil. Set the pan in a warm, draft-free place for about 30 minutes.

8. Meanwhile, preheat the oven to 400 degrees.

9. Place the loaf in the oven and bake for 15 minutes. Reduce the oven heat to 375 degrees and bake for 10 minutes longer. Cover with a sheet of aluminum foil to prevent excess browning. Continue baking for 20 minutes (for a total baking time at this point of 45 minutes). Remove the foil and continue baking for 15 minutes more.

10. Remove the coulibiac from the oven. Pour ½ cup of the melted butter through the steam hole into the filling. Serve cut into 1-inch slices with the remaining hot melted butter on the side.

Yield: 16 or more servings.

BRIOCHE DOUGH

¾ cup milk
¼ teaspoon sugar
3 packages granular yeast
4 to 4½ cups flour
Salt to taste
1 cup egg yolks (about 12)
8 tablespoons butter, at room temperature

1. Pour the milk into a saucepan and heat it gradually to lukewarm. Remove from the heat. If the milk has become too hot, let it cool to lukewarm.

2. Sprinkle the milk with the sugar and yeast and stir to dissolve. Cover with a towel. Let stand for about 5 minutes and place the mixture in a warm place (the natural warmth of a turned-off oven is good for this) for about 5 minutes. It should ferment during the period and increase in volume.

3. Place 4 cups of flour with the salt in the bowl of an electric mixer fitted with a dough hook, or use a mixing bowl and wooden spoon. Make a well in the center and pour in the yeast mixture, the cup of yolks, and butter. With the dough hook or wooden spoon, gradually work in the flour until well blended. Then beat vigorously until the dough is quite smooth and can be shaped into a ball.

4. Turn the dough out onto a lightly floured board and knead until it is smooth and satiny, about 10 minutes. As you work the dough,

continue to add flour to the kneading surface as necessary to prevent sticking, but take care not to add an excess or the finished product will be tough.

5. Lightly butter a clean mixing bowl and add the ball of dough. Cover with a clean towel and let stand in a warm place for about 1 hour, or until double in bulk. Punch the dough down. Turn it out once more onto a lightly floured board. Knead it for about 1 minute and return it to the clean bowl. Cover closely with plastic wrap and refrigerate overnight.

6. The next morning, punch the dough down again and continue to refrigerate, covered, until ready to use.

SALMON AND MUSHROOMS WITH VELOUTÉ

THE SALMON AND MUSHROOMS:

2 skinless, boneless salmon fillets, each weighing about 1½ pounds

2 tablespoons butter

2 tablespoons finely chopped onion

2 tablespoons finely chopped shallots

Salt and freshly ground pepper to taste

¾ pound fresh mushrooms, thinly sliced

¼ cup finely chopped fresh dill

2 cups dry white wine

THE VELOUTÉ:

2 tablespoons butter

3 tablespoons flour

⅛ teaspoon cayenne

3 tablespoons lemon juice

5 egg yolks

1. Preheat the oven to 400 degrees.

2. Using a sharp carving knife, cut each fillet on the bias into slices about ⅓ inch thick. Each fillet should produce about 12 slices.

3. Select a heatproof rectangular baking dish. It should be just large enough to hold two rows of slightly overlapping slices (a dish measuring 13½ × 8½ × 2 inches is suitable). Rub the bottom of the dish with the 2 tablespoons of butter and sprinkle with the onion, shallots, salt, and pepper. Arrange two parallel rows of salmon slices, the slices slightly overlapping, over the onion and shallots. Sprinkle with salt to taste. Sprinkle somewhat liberally with pepper. Scatter the mushrooms over the salmon. Sprinkle the mushrooms with fresh dill and pour the wine over all. Cover with aluminum foil and bring to the boil on top of the stove. Place the dish in the oven and bake for 15 minutes.

4. Remove the dish, uncover, and pour the accumulated liquid into a saucepan. Carefully spoon off most of the mushrooms and transfer them to another dish. Bring the cooking liquid to the boil over high heat. Tilt the dish containing the salmon. More liquid will accumulate as it stands. Spoon or pour this liquid into the saucepan containing the cooking liquid.

5. For the velouté, melt the 2 tablespoons of butter in a saucepan and stir in the flour, using a wire whisk. When blended, add the cooking liquid, stirring rapidly with the whisk. Cook for about 5 minutes, stirring often. Add the mushrooms and continue cooking for about 20 minutes, adding any liquid that accumulates around the salmon. Add the cayenne and lemon juice. Beat the yolks with a whisk and scrape them into the mushrooms, stirring vigorously. Cook for about 30 seconds, stirring, and remove from the heat. Add salt and a generous amount of pepper to taste.

6. Spoon and scrape this sauce—it should be quite thick—over the salmon. Blanket the salmon all over with an even layer of the sauce, but try to avoid having it spill over the sides of the salmon. Smooth the sauce over. Let cool. Grease a neat rectangle of wax paper with butter. Arrange this, buttered side down, on the sauce-covered salmon and refrigerate until thoroughly cold.

CRÊPES

1½ cups flour
3 large eggs
Salt and freshly ground pepper to taste
1¾ cups milk
2 tablespoons butter, melted
1 tablespoon finely chopped fresh parsley
1 tablespoon finely chopped fresh dill

1. Place the flour in a mixing bowl and make a well in the center. Add the eggs, salt, and pepper and, stirring, gradually add the milk.

2. Put the mixture through a sieve, running the whisk around inside the sieve to remove lumps. Add the melted butter, the parsley, and dill. Use to make crêpes.

Yield: About fourteen 7-inch crêpes.

Note: Leftover crêpes may be frozen. Interlayer them with rounds of wax paper, wrap in foil, and freeze.

RICE AND EGG FILLING

3 hard-cooked eggs
1¾ cups firmly cooked rice
¼ cup finely chopped parsley
1 tablespoon finely chopped fresh dill
Salt and freshly ground pepper to taste
1½ cups chopped, cooked vesiga (see following instructions), optional

Chop the eggs and put them in a mixing bowl. Add the remaining ingredients and blend well.

VESIGA FOR COULIBIAC

½ pound vesiga

Salt to taste

One of the classic—but optional—ingredients for a coulibiac of salmon is called vesiga. It is a ropelike, gelatinous substance, actually the spinal marrow of sturgeon. The vesiga, after cleaning, must be simmered for several hours until tender. It is then chopped and looks like chopped aspic. It has a very bland flavor and its principal contribution to the dish is its slightly tender but chewy texture.

Vesiga is by no means a staple item, but it is often available from fish stores in metropolitan areas.

1. Wash the vesiga in cold water. Split it as necessary for thorough cleaning. Drain the vesiga and place it in a saucepan. Add water to cover and salt to taste. Bring to the boil.

2. Simmer for 4 hours, replacing the liquid as it evaporates. Drain the vesiga and chop it. It will be translucent and look like chopped aspic.

WEAKFISH WITH CAPERS AND RED WINE VINEGAR

1½ pounds weakfish (sea trout) or other fish, filleted but with skin left on

2 tablespoons milk

Salt and freshly ground pepper to taste

¼ cup flour

¼ cup peanut, vegetable, or corn oil

4 tablespoons butter

¼ cup drained capers

1 teaspoon red wine vinegar

1 tablespoon finely chopped parsley

1. Cut the fish fillet into four serving pieces of equal size.

2. Put the milk in a flat dish and add the fish. Sprinkle with the salt and pepper. Turn the fish pieces on all sides in the milk.

3. Lift the pieces from the milk and dip into the flour seasoned with salt and pepper.

4. Heat the oil in a skillet large enough to hold the fish in one layer without crowding. Cook for 3 to 6 minutes, or until golden brown on one side. Cooking time will depend on the thickness of the fish. Turn the pieces and cook for 2 to 3 minutes. Baste occasionally as the pieces cook.

5. Remove the fish to a warm serving platter. Wipe out the skillet.

6. Add the butter to the skillet and heat, swirling the butter around. When it starts to brown, add the capers and cook for about 2 minutes, shaking the skillet occasionally.

7. Add the vinegar and cook for about 10 seconds. Spoon the mixture over the fish. Sprinkle with parsley and serve.

Yield: 4 servings.

SEA BASS WITH FRESH FENNEL

1. Heat the butter in a baking dish large enough to hold the fish. Stir in the olive oil and garlic. Let cool briefly and add the fish, turning it in the mixture. Sprinkle with salt and pepper.

2. Cut off enough of the fennel leaves to stuff the fish lightly. Add this to the cavities.

3. Cut off the tops of the fennel bulbs and trim the base. Pull off and discard the tough outer leaves. Cut the bulbs into quarters and arrange these around the fish.

4. When ready to cook, preheat the oven to 375 degrees. Place the fish in the oven and bake for 30 minutes, basting both the fish and fennel frequently. Cook until the fish flakes easily when tested with a fork.

Yield: 6 to 8 servings.

6 tablespoons butter

3 tablespoons olive oil

6 garlic cloves, finely minced

Two 1½- to 2-pound sea bass or other small whole fish, cleaned and with head intact but with gills removed

2 fennel bulbs with leaves

Salt and freshly ground pepper to taste

GRILLED MARINATED SHAD WITH HERBS

1 boneless fillet of shad

Salt and freshly ground pepper to taste

2 tablespoons olive oil

2 tablespoons lemon juice

½ teaspoon finely crumbled bay leaf

½ teaspoon dried thyme

¼ teaspoon paprika

Lemon wedges for garnish

The availability of shad in this country usually begins early in February in the rivers around Florida. The fish travels up the Altamaha and Ogeechee rivers in Georgia, through the waters of the Carolinas, then the Chesapeake and the Delaware and, eventually, it is found in some unpolluted sections of the Hudson (shad will neither swim nor spawn in polluted waters for lack of oxygen). The season ends in Connecticut near the end of May. So we always take advantage of the short season for this glorious fish and its roe.

1. Put the fillet on a platter and sprinkle it with the salt and pepper. Add the oil and turn the fish to coat it.

2. Add the lemon juice, bay leaf, and thyme and spread around. Cover and let stand for 1 hour.

3. Preheat the broiler to high.

4. Remove the shad from the platter and arrange it skin side down in a baking dish. Pour the marinade into a small saucepan and keep it warm. Sprinkle the fish with paprika and brush the top to coat it evenly. Place under the broiler about 4 inches from the source of heat and broil for about 5 minutes. Cut the fish in half lengthwise.

5. Transfer the fish to two hot serving dishes. Spoon a little of the marinade over each serving. Serve with lemon wedges.

Yield: 2 servings.

SHAD STUFFED WITH SHAD ROE NANTAISE

1. Preheat the oven to 400 degrees.

2. Cut the shad roe in half, slicing through the membrane. Remove and discard the membrane. Put the roe on a flat surface and add the shallots, coarsely chopped hard-cooked egg, and ¼ cup chopped parsley. Chop together to blend well.

3. Put the crumbs in a mixing bowl and add the milk. Stir to blend. Add the roe mixture, salt, and pepper.

4. Open up the fillets skin side down. Sprinkle with salt and pepper. You will note that there are two flaps to each fillet. Open these up and spread one fillet with the roe filling, smoothing it over. Bring up the sides of the fillet. Cover with the other fillet, letting the flaps of the fillet fall down and overlap the stuffed fillet.

5. Tie the "package" neatly with string in four or five places to keep the fillets and filling intact.

6. Butter a baking dish large enough to hold the stuffed fish. Use about 2 tablespoons of the butter. Sprinkle with salt and pepper.

7. Arrange the fish fillets in the dish. Dot with the remaining butter. Place in the oven and bake for 15 minutes. Spoon 1 tablespoon of dry white wine over the fish and continue baking, basting often with the pan juices, for about 15 minutes.

8. Pour the remaining wine over all and continue baking and basting for 15 minutes longer. It is imperative that you baste often as the fish cooks.

9. Remove the fish from the oven and remove the strings. Using the fingers, pull off and discard the skin of the fish from the top. The skin comes off easily. Baste the fish. Garnish with the lemon slices and sprinkle with the chopped parsley. It is now ready to be carved crosswise and served.

Yield: 6 to 8 servings.

1 pair shad roe

1½ tablespoons finely chopped shallots

1 hard-cooked egg, coarsely chopped

¼ cup finely chopped parsley

1 cup fresh bread crumbs

½ cup milk

Salt and freshly ground pepper to taste

2 shad fillets, about 1½ pounds

4 tablespoons butter

½ cup dry white wine

8 thin lemon slices for garnish

Chopped parsley for garnish

HERBED MARYLAND SHAD (OVEN-STEAMED SO YOU CAN EVEN EAT THE BONES)

One 4-pound shad, dressed

Salt and freshly ground pepper to taste

4 to 5 cups water

1 cup white wine

2 celery ribs, coarsely chopped

1 small onion, chopped

2 bay leaves

Beurre nantais (see recipe page 774), optional

Shad is, of course, one of the boniest fish to be found in river or ocean. For years, we have been asked about a technique for cooking shad in which the whole fish is baked until the bones are "dissolved" as a result of the prolonged cooking. When we came across such a recipe in a throwaway brochure from the Seafood Marketing Authority in Annapolis, Maryland, we tested the recipe in our own kitchen and, much to our surprise, it works admirably. In fact, it drew raves— "melted" bones and all. We added a delicious herb butter sauce.

1. Preheat the oven to 300 degrees.

2. Wash the shad and dry it with paper towels. Sprinkle the fish inside and out with the salt and pepper.

3. Put the fish on the rack of a baking pan. Add 4 cups of water and the wine to a level just under the fish. Add the remaining ingredients, except the sauce. If necessary, add the fifth cup of water to prevent burning.

4. Cover tightly and steam for 5 hours. Baste often. Serve sliced crosswise through the bones. Serve, if desired, with herb butter sauce.

Yield: 6 servings.

Note: The secret of softening the bones is to make sure the pan cover fits tight and to cook the fish for the full amount of time. If these directions are followed exactly, even the large backbone will be soft enough to be eaten, and most of the small splinter bones will disappear.

SHAD WITH MUSHROOMS AND TOMATOES

1. Split the fillet in half crosswise. Sprinkle the pieces with the salt and pepper and place in a small flat basin of milk. Remove the fish pieces from the milk without draining. Put the pieces in the flour to coat on both sides.

2. Heat the corn or other oil in a frying pan and add the fish pieces, skin side up. Cook 1½ to 2 minutes over high heat, or until golden brown on one side. Carefully turn the pieces and continue cooking on the second side over moderately low heat for 3 to 4 minutes. Transfer the pieces to two warm serving plates.

3. Slice the mushrooms thin. There should be about 2 cups.

4. Heat the olive oil in a skillet and add the mushrooms and salt and pepper to taste. Cook, stirring, for about 2 minutes. Add the garlic and butter and swirl and stir around until the butter melts.

5. Meanwhile, heat the tomatoes in a small saucepan and cook down for about 5 minutes.

6. Spoon half of the tomatoes onto each fish piece. Pour the mushrooms over and sprinkle with the parsley.

Yield: 2 servings.

1 boneless fillet of shad
Salt and freshly ground pepper to taste
¼ cup milk
½ cup flour
¼ cup corn, peanut, or vegetable oil
¼ pound mushrooms
3 tablespoons olive oil
1 teaspoon finely minced garlic
1 tablespoon butter
½ cup imported canned tomatoes, crushed
2 tablespoons finely chopped parsley

SHAD ROE POACHED IN BUTTER

1. Trim off excess membranes. Do not split the pair of roe in half although it may separate as it cooks. Puncture the roe in several places with a pin. Sprinkle with the salt and pepper.

2. Melt the butter in a small skillet or casserole with a tight-fitting lid. Add the roe, cover, and let cook over gentle heat for about 3 minutes. Using a spatula, carefully turn the roe. Cover and let simmer for 8 or 10 minutes on the second side.

3. If the roe has not split, divide it carefully. Transfer the pieces to 2 hot serving plates. Spoon a little butter over each. Sprinkle with parsley and serve with lemon wedges.

Yield: 2 servings.

1 pair of shad roe
Salt and freshly ground pepper to taste
4 tablespoons butter
1 tablespoon finely chopped parsley
Lemon wedges

RAIE AU BEURRE NOIR (SKATE WITH BLACK BUTTER)

2 poached skate wings
  (see following
  instructions)
½ cup white vinegar
1 teaspoon crushed black
  peppercorns
2 bay leaves
2 fresh thyme sprigs, or
  ½ teaspoon dried
  Salt and freshly ground
  pepper to taste
¼ pound butter, clarified
4 tablespoons drained
  capers
1 tablespoon red wine
  vinegar
2 tablespoons finely
  chopped parsley

There are scores, if not hundreds, of fish swimming around in American waters that are all but unknown on the American table, often because fishermen toss them back into the sea. But some are startlingly good and can be purchased in season in fish markets. One of the greatest and tastiest fish known to man is skate, known in France as raie. *Raie au beurre noir,* or skate with black butter sauce, is a supreme invention.

1. After draining and trimming the skate as indicated in the preparation instructions, transfer the wings to a wide utensil that will hold them in one layer.

2. Add water to cover, the white vinegar, peppercorns, bay leaves, and thyme. Bring just to a gentle, rolling boil and turn off the heat.

3. Drain the fish and transfer it to a hot platter. Sprinkle with the salt and pepper.

4. Melt the butter in a large skillet and cook, shaking the skillet and swirling the butter around over high heat. When the butter becomes quite brown, watch it carefully. Continue cooking until the butter starts to become a very dark brown ("black"). Add the capers and wine vinegar. Shake the skillet to blend and pour this over the skate. Sprinkle with parsley and serve with hot boiled potatoes.

Yield: 4 servings.

HOW TO PREPARE SKATE FOR COOKING

Leave the skate wings whole; cut off and discard the connecting tail portion. Put the wings in a large, wide utensil and add water to cover. Bring the fish to the boil and simmer for 2 minutes. Drain quickly and run under cold water until cold.

Remove the wings to a flat surface lined with absorbent paper towels. Using a knife, gently and carefully scrape away the skin from one side. Discard it. Turn the wings and scrape away the skin from the second side. Also scrape away any red streaks across the center of one side.

Using a heavy knife, chop and trim off the tips of the outside bones that rim the wings. Return the wings to the utensil and refrigerate until ready to use.

STRIPED BASS WITH ONIONS, TOMATOES, AND PEPPERS

1. Place the fish on a dish and prick the skin all over with a fork. Sprinkle all over with the juice of the limes. Stuff the cavity of the fish with the lime halves. Let stand for 3 hours. Remove the lime halves.

2. Preheat the oven to 375 degrees.

3. Sprinkle the fish all over with the salt and pepper and place it on a large baking dish. It may be necessary to cut off the head to make the fish fit the pan.

4. Heat the oil in a saucepan and add the onions and garlic. Cook until wilted. Add the tomatoes, capers, olives, jalapeño peppers, oregano, bay leaf, salt, and pepper. Simmer for about 10 minutes.

5. Pour the sauce over the fish and place in the oven. Bake, uncovered, for about 30 minutes. Turn the fish carefully and continue baking for 30 to 40 minutes longer, or until the flesh flakes easily when tested with a fork. Serve garnished with lime wedges and coriander sprigs, if desired.

Yield: 8 or more servings.

One 4-pound fish, such as striped bass, red snapper, or weakfish (sea trout) with head left on but gills removed

2 limes

Salt and freshly ground pepper to taste

3 tablespoons olive oil

2 cups thinly sliced onion

3 tablespoons finely chopped garlic

4 cups diced, peeled tomatoes

3 tablespoons drained capers

20 to 24 stuffed green olives

2 or more jalapeño peppers, drained, seeded, and coarsely chopped

1 teaspoon chopped fresh oregano, or ½ teaspoon dried

1 bay leaf

Lime wedges for garnish

Fresh coriander sprigs for garnish, optional

STRIPED BASS IN PHYLLO PASTRY

5 cups loosely packed
spinach leaves

2 tablespoons finely
chopped chervil,
parsley, or fresh sage
leaves

1 tablespoon olive oil

¼ cup finely chopped
shallots

¾ cup shucked, drained
oysters, about 12

Salt and freshly ground
pepper to taste

¾ cup clarified butter
(see note)

12 leaves phyllo pastry

6 teaspoons fine fresh
bread crumbs,
approximately

6 center-cut fillets of
striped bass with skin
on, about ½ pound
each

1. Preheat the oven to 450 degrees.

2. Pick over the spinach leaves to remove any tough stems. Rinse and drain well. Combine with the chervil.

3. Heat the oil in a large heavy skillet and add the shallots. Cook briefly, stirring. Add the spinach and cook, stirring, until the spinach is wilted. Spoon out onto a chopping block.

4. Add the oysters, salt, and pepper to the spinach. Finely chop using a heavy knife.

5. Brush a baking dish with the butter.

6. Arrange the phyllo pastry in one stack on a clean cloth. Brush with the butter. Sprinkle with the crumbs. Turn the pastry sheet over and brush with the butter. Sprinkle with the crumbs. As you work, keep the pastry sheets covered with a lightly dampened cloth to prevent them from drying out.

7. Arrange the fish fillets one at a time on a flat surface, skin side down. Slice them crosswise and slightly on the bias. Make four parallel gashes almost but not to the skin.

8. Arrange one fish fillet, skin side down, on the center of two sheets of the pastry. Spoon 1 tablespoon or so of the oyster and spinach mixture inside each gash. Sprinkle with salt and pepper. Lift up the pastry and fold it over and over to enclose the fillet. Cut off excess pastry, leaving about 2 inches of phyllo to fold under. Fold the edges under, envelope fashion. Repeat with the other fillets. Brush the top of the "packages" with butter and arrange them on the buttered baking dish.

9. Place in the oven and bake for 20 minutes, or until well puffed and browned.

Yield: 6 servings.

Note: To clarify butter, place the butter in a heatproof glass measuring cup and let it melt slowly in a 200-degree oven. Do not stir the butter. Pour off the clear, golden liquid on top, leaving the white milky substance at the bottom. The clear liquid is clarified butter.

STRIPED BASS FILLET WITH OYSTERS

It is obvious that in our profession we are occupied with the sheer pleasure of dining well. Once in a while, one is faced with a moment of daring, a new experience, a quickened emotion not unlike diving into a cold swimming pool before the sun has prepared you for it.

When we dined at the Restaurant Girardet in the small town of Crissier in Switzerland, we had such an experience. Freddy Girardet is one of the great creative forces in the world of chefs today, and our meal was unforgettable, not a dish to be faulted. We dined on an elaborate succession of his creations, one of which was loup de mer aux huîtres, or loup de mer with oysters. When Pierre Franey recreated the Girardet dishes in our kitchen, he substituted striped bass for the loup de mer, which is not available in American waters. It remains just as glorious.

1. Cut the fillet into six portions of approximately equal weight, slicing slightly on a diagonal. Place the pieces on a flat surface and pound lightly with a flat mallet.

2. Coat a baking dish with the butter and sprinkle with the salt and pepper. Arrange the fish pieces over the bottom. Sprinkle with salt and pepper. Refrigerate until ready to cook.

3. Prepare the vegetables and drop them into boiling salted water. Simmer for about 5 minutes and drain.

4. Preheat the oven to 450 degrees.

5. In a heated saucepan, heat the wine and fish stock and liquid from the oysters if there is any. Bring to the boil.

6. Pour 1½ cups of the wine mixture over the fish and place in the oven. Bake for 3 to 5 minutes. Do not overcook. Pour off and add the cooking liquid to the original wine mixture. Keep the fish covered with foil.

7. Add the oysters to the liquid and cook briefly, about 1 minute. Scoop out the oysters and arrange equal amounts of them over the portions of fish.

8. Meanwhile, reduce the cooking liquid to about 1 cup. Add the cream and boil over high heat for about 5 minutes. Add the drained vegetables and chopped chives. Spoon the sauce over the oysters and fish and serve piping hot.

Yield: 6 servings.

One 1½-pound skinless, boneless fillet of striped bass

1 tablespoon butter

Salt and freshly ground pepper to taste

½ cup carrot cut into very fine julienne strips (approximately the size of toothpicks)

¼ cup very fine julienne strips of leeks

½ cup very fine julienne strips of celery root (or use stalk celery)

1 cup dry white wine

1 cup fish stock (see recipe page 801)

24 shucked oysters with their liquid

1 cup heavy cream

1 tablespoon finely chopped chives

POACHED STRIPED BASS

One 3-pound (cleaned weight) striped bass, with head and tail left on but with gills removed

14 cups water

1 cup dry white wine

2 cups coarsely chopped onions

1½ cups coarsely chopped celery

1 cup coarsely chopped carrots

4 fresh parsley sprigs

2 bay leaves

3 small garlic cloves, left whole

Salt to taste

8 peppercorns

1 small dried, hot, red pepper

Tomato wedges, hard-cooked egg wedges, parsley, lemon wedges, dill sprigs, and so on for garnish

1. Wrap the fish in cheesecloth or a clean dish towel. Tie it with string in three or four places.

2. Set the rack of the fish poacher in place. Add the water, wine, onions, celery, carrot, parsley, bay leaves, garlic, salt, peppercorns, and red pepper to the fish poacher. Cover and bring to the boil. Let simmer for 20 minutes. Remove from the heat and let the liquid cool.

3. Put the fish in the poacher and cover. Bring gently to the boil. At the boil, cook for 8 minutes. Remove from the heat. Uncover and let stand (see note) until the fish and cooking liquid become luke-warm.

4. Lift up the rack and let the fish drain. Cut off and discard the string. Unwrap the cheesecloth or towel enclosing the fish. Using a paring knife, neatly and carefully pull and scrape away the line of bones along the back side of the fish. Use the knife and fingers to pull and scrape away the skin from the topside of the fish. Scrape and pull away the small bones at the belly (underside) of the fish. The fatty, brownish-gray flesh on top of the fish should be scraped away also. It has an oily taste.

5. Lift up the cheesecloth or towel on which the fish rests. Transfer the fish, skinned side down, onto a serving platter. Remove and discard the cheesecloth. Repeat the skin removal from the other side of the fish. Scrape away the brownish-gray flesh and so on. Remove the skin from the cheek of the fish. Clean the rim of the platter.

6. Decorate the fish with one or more garnishes such as lemon wedges, tomato wedges, and so on. Serve with a sauce based on mayonnaise, such as anchovy mayonnaise, cucumber mayonnaise, or sauce rémoulade.

Yield: 6 or more servings.

Note: The fish could be served hot after standing in the cooking liquid for about 10 minutes after the heat is turned off. Serve with hollandaise sauce or simply melted butter, lemon, and herbs.

Striped Bass with Spices

1. Cut off the heads of the fish and neatly trim the end of each tail.

2. Select a flameproof oval baking dish large enough to accommodate both fish. Do not add the fish. Select six pieces of bamboo (cut-off chopsticks may be used). Arrange them crosswise, evenly spaced, over the bottom of the baking dish to support the fish and prevent them from lying directly on the bottom of the dish.

3. Add the oil, water, ginger, turmeric, cumin, paprika, cayenne, and salt. Bring to the boil on top of the stove.

4. Arrange the fish in the dish. Baste the fish for about 3 minutes with the simmering sauce.

5. Cover closely with foil and continue cooking for 20 minutes. Uncover and add the butter and lemon juice. Continue cooking for 10 minutes and sprinkle the parsley on top of each fish. Arrange the lemon and tomato slices on the fish and baste with the sauce. Serve.

Yield: 6 servings.

---

2 striped bass, about 1½ pounds each, cleaned weight

½ cup peanut oil

2 cups water

2 teaspoons ground ginger

2 teaspoons ground turmeric

2 teaspoons ground cumin

1 teaspoon paprika

¼ teaspoon cayenne

Salt to taste

2 tablespoons butter

6 tablespoons lemon juice

1 cup finely chopped parsley

6 thin, seeded lemon slices

6 round slices of cherry tomatoes

BROILED SWORDFISH WITH MUSTARD

1 swordfish steak, about
1¼ pounds and 1 inch
thick

Salt and freshly ground
pepper to taste

2 tablespoons butter

2 teaspoons Dijon
mustard

1 teaspoon mustard
seeds

Lemon wedges

Melted butter, optional

1. Preheat the broiler to high.

2. Sprinkle the swordfish with the salt and pepper.

3. Heat the butter in a baking dish large enough to hold the sword-fish. Brush the steak on both sides with the mustard and sprinkle with the mustard seeds.

4. Place the steak 4 or 5 inches from the source of heat. Broil for 3 or 4 minutes.

5. Turn the fish and broil on the second side for 4 or 5 minutes. Do not overcook. Serve with lemon wedges and, if desired, melted butter poured over.

Yield: 2 servings.

PAN-FRIED TROUT

Perhaps we find portents in curious places, but why is it that trout figures more often in English poetry than any other fish? Lord Byron spoke of "trout not stale." And trout, according to Shakespeare, "must be caught with tickling." Tennyson spoke of "here and there a lusty trout." We prefer to think it has more to do with the elegant taste of the fish than with iambic pentameter and such.

We would by all means nominate trout as one of the supreme beings of lakes, creeks, and rivers. It has a sweet delicacy of flavor, an uncommon texture that makes it, in our minds, the rival of carp, tuna, cod, and weakfish (which sometimes goes by the fancy name of sea trout, yet is unrelated to the true trout) and other fine foods with fins that swim in ocean waters.

4 trout, 8 to 10 ounces each, cleaned but with head and tail on

Salt and freshly ground pepper to taste

Flour for dredging

⅓ cup peanut, vegetable, or corn oil

3 partly cooked, peeled potatoes, cut into ¼-inch slices, about 3 cups

1 small onion, peeled and sliced

Lemon wedges

1. Sprinkle the trout on all sides with salt and pepper. Dredge lightly in flour.

2. Meanwhile, heat the oil in a large iron skillet over a hot charcoal fire. Or heat it on the stove.

3. When the oil is hot and almost smoking, add the fish and cook until crisp and golden brown on one side. Turn and cook until crisp and golden on the other side. Continue cooking until the fish is cooked through. Cooking time will depend on the size of the fish.

4. As the fish cook, push them to one side and add the potatoes and onion. Cook, turning the potatoes and onion slices until browned and golden on both sides. Remove the fish and serve with lemon wedges. Serve with the potatoes and onions.

Yield: 4 servings.

TROUT MEUNIÈRE WITH PECANS

Four 10-ounce trout
(see note)

¼ cup milk

Salt and freshly ground
pepper to taste

½ cup flour

¼ cup peanut, vegetable,
or corn oil

5 tablespoons butter

½ cup pecan halves

Juice of 1 lemon

2 tablespoons finely
chopped parsley

1. Using a pair of kitchen shears, cut off the fins from the back and sides of the trout. Leave the head and tail intact.

2. Place the trout in a large pan and add the milk, salt, and pepper. Turn the trout in the mixture.

3. Remove the trout without patting dry and dredge on all sides in flour seasoned with salt and pepper.

4. Heat the oil and 1 tablespoon of the butter in a large heavy skillet and add the trout, lining them up neatly in the pan. Cook for about 8 minutes, or until golden and cooked on one side. Turn and cook for 8 minutes longer. Baste often. The basting is important to keep the trout juicy.

5. Remove the trout to a warm platter. Sprinkle with salt and pepper.

6. Pour off the fat from the pan and wipe out the skillet. Add the remaining 4 tablespoons of butter and, when melted, add the pecans. Cook, shaking the pan and stirring, until the butter becomes the color of hazelnuts. Do not burn. Add the lemon juice and pour the sauce over the fish. Serve sprinkled with chopped parsley.

Yield: 4 servings.

Note: The 10-ounce weight specified here is arbitrary. Larger or smaller trout may be cooked in the same manner, but adjust the cooking time accordingly.

Truites au Bleu (Trout cooked in court bouillon)

This simple yet elegant preparation gets its name from the fact that the vinegar gives a blue color to the trout.

Four 10-ounce trout
4 quarts water
1 cup white vinegar
1 bay leaf
Salt to taste
10 peppercorns
Lemon wedges
Melted butter

1. Using a pair of kitchen shears, cut off the fins from the back and sides of the trout. Leave the head and tail intact.

2. Using a long needle such as a trussing needle, run a string through the eyes of the trout, then through the tail. Tie the head and tail together. The reason for this is simply appearance. When trout are freshly caught, they are killed and dressed and dropped into boiling water immediately. These trout will curve naturally through muscle and nerve reaction.

3. Combine the water and vinegar in a fairly wide casserole. There should be enough liquid to cover the trout when they are added. Add the bay leaf, salt, and peppercorns. Bring to the boil and simmer for 10 minutes.

4. Drop the trout into the simmering water. Simmer for 5 minutes. Drain the trout and serve with lemon wedges and hot melted butter.

Yield: 4 servings.

FISH AND CHIPS

4   large Idaho potatoes,
    about 2 pounds

6   cups peanut, vegetable,
    or corn oil

½   cup flour

    Salt and freshly ground
    pepper to taste

8   small, skinless,
    boneless flounder or
    other fish fillets, about
    2 pounds

    Batter for fish (see
    following recipe)

    Oil for deep frying

    Malt vinegar

1. Trim the potatoes with a swivel-bladed vegetable scraper. Drop them into cold water to prevent discoloration. Cut the potatoes into ½-inch-thick slices. Cut the slices into ½-inch strips. Drop into cold water and drain.

2. Heat about 6 cups of oil in a deep fryer. A wok is also good for this. Drop a few strips of the potato into the hot oil and cook for 1½ to 2 minutes. Drain on absorbent towels. Continue until all the strips have been precooked and drained.

3. Blend the flour, salt, and pepper. Dredge the fillets in the flour. Dip the fish fillets, one at a time, in the batter and drop them into the oil (preheated to 350 degrees). You may cook three or four fillets at one time. Cook until puffed and browned. Turn the pieces as they cook. Total cooking time for each fillet is 1½ to 2 minutes. Please note that after a few pieces of fish are cooked, you should let the oil come back to its original heat. As the fish pieces are added, the oil heat is diminished. Continue until all the fish is cooked and drained.

4. Before cooking the potatoes a second time, bring the oil temperature to about 400 degrees (slightly higher than for the fish). Add the potatoes, one batch at a time. Cook for 1½ to 2 minutes, or until crisp. Drain. Continue cooking and draining until all the potatoes are used. Serve the batter-fried fish with the potatoes.

5. Serve with malt vinegar and salt on the side so that guests may flavor the fish according to their own tastes.

Yield: 4 servings.

BATTER FOR FISH

1   cup cold water

½   teaspoon yellow food
    coloring

2   tablespoons corn oil

1   teaspoon salt

1   cup flour

1   teaspoon baking
    powder

1. Combine the cold water, food coloring, oil, and salt in a mixing bowl. Gradually add the flour, stirring rapidly with a wire whisk.

2. Just before using, stir in the baking powder, making certain it is evenly blended in the batter.

Yield: Enough batter for 8 fish fillets.

FINNAN HADDIE

Since we first encountered finnan haddie on a breakfast menu at the Connaught Hotel in London, it has been our long-held notion that this smoked-fish delicacy is one of the consummate breakfast foods. Give us a platter of choice finnan haddie, freshly cooked in its bath of water and milk, add melted butter, a slice or two of hot toast, and a pot of steaming Darjeeling tea and you may tell the butler to dispense with the caviar, truffles, and nightingales' tongues.

The proper way to poach finnan haddie is to place it (defrosted if frozen) in a skillet with water to barely cover. Add about ½ cup milk and, if desired, 1 bay leaf, 2 cloves, and 2 slices of onion. Bring to the boil but do not boil. Let the haddock simmer gently for about 2 minutes, or until the fish is piping hot. Do not cook long or it will toughen and become fibrous. Drain the fish, spoon it onto hot plates, and pour hot melted butter over it. Serve immediately with lemon halves on the side and a pepper mill for those who wish it. After a first course of freshly squeezed orange juice, serve the fish with buttered, boiled potatoes, buttered toast, marmalade, and tea or champagne. Breakfast coffee is not a suitable drink with smoked fish.

FRENCH-FRIED SQUID

2 pounds squid, cleaned
   (see following
   instructions)
½ cup milk
2 cups flour
   Salt and freshly ground
   pepper to taste
6 cups oil
   Juice of ½ lemon

Squid is a delicacy that I would place in the highest category of good things to eat from the sea. They are often referred to as voracious predators because they enthusiastically consume large and small fish as well as other squid. I feel equally voracious when faced with a platter of deep-fried squid rings or squid in wine sauce.

1. Cut the squid bodies into ½-inch rounds and the tentacles into bite-size pieces. There should be about 3 cups.

2. Put the squid in a bowl. Pour the milk over the squid.

3. Put the flour in a flat dish and add the salt and pepper. Blend well. Drain the squid lightly and add to the flour. Dredge thoroughly, shaking off excess flour.

4. Pour oil—about 1 inch deep—into a heavy skillet. Heat the oil until it is quite hot but not smoking (375 degrees). Add the squid pieces, a few at a time, to the skillet without crowding. Cook until crisp and lightly golden, about 2 minutes for each batch. Remove squid pieces and drain on paper towels. Continue cooking in batches until all the pieces are cooked. Serve sprinkled with lemon juice.

Yield: 4 to 6 servings.

HOW TO CLEAN SQUID

1. Twist and pull off the head of the squid. As you do this you will also pull out much of the interior of the body. This may include an ink sac, which is used in many European recipes but not for the recipes given here. Discard the pulled-out material.

2. Pull out and discard the semihard, translucent, sword-shaped pen.

3. Using a knife, cut off the tentacles from the head of the squid (just in front of the eyes).

4. Using the fingers, pop out the round, hard beak in the center of the tentacles. Discard the beak.

5. The tentacles are wholly edible. If they are long, you may want to cut them in half or into smaller lengths.

6. Rub off the brown skin of the squid, holding the squid under cold running water. Use coarse salt while rubbing and pulling with the fingers.

7. Rinse the squid inside and out to remove any remaining material from inside the body. Drain the squid thoroughly and set aside.

CALAMARI ALLA NANNI (SQUID IN WINE SAUCE)

1. Heat the oil in a large kettle and add the garlic, scallions, and bay leaves. Add the anchovies along with the oil in which they are packed. Simmer for about 5 minutes and add the remaining ingredients except the liqueur. Cover and let simmer for 1 hour.

2. Stir in the Pernod, if used, and serve hot with rice.

Yield: 12 or more servings.

⅔ cup olive oil

6 garlic cloves, finely chopped

⅓ cup finely chopped scallions

4 bay leaves

One 2-ounce can flat anchovies

6½ pounds fresh squid, thoroughly cleaned and cut into 1-inch rounds

½ cup chopped fresh parsley

½ cup chopped fresh basil

¾ cup dry white wine

½ teaspoon dried oregano

1 pound peeled, cored, crushed fresh tomatoes, about 1½ cups, or use canned imported tomatoes

Salt and freshly ground pepper to taste

1 tablespoon Pernod or other anise-flavored liqueur, optional

BROILED EEL WITH MUSTARD BUTTER

THE EEL:

One 1¼- to 1½-pound
skinned eel (cleaned
weight)

3 tablespoons butter

THE MUSTARD BUTTER:

4 tablespoons butter, at
room temperature

Juice of ½ lemon

2 teaspoons Dijon
mustard

3 tablespoons finely
chopped parsley

¼ teaspoon Worcester-
shire sauce

Tabasco sauce to taste

Salt and freshly ground
pepper to taste

1. Preheat the broiler to its highest heat.

2. Using a sharp knife, score the eel flesh top and bottom. To do this, make shallow ⅛-inch parallel incisions at ½-inch intervals. Cut the eel into 6-inch lengths.

3. In a baking dish, gently melt the 3 tablespoons of butter and add the eel pieces. Sprinkle with salt and pepper and turn the eel pieces in the butter until coated all over.

4. Place the dish of eel 4 to 6 inches from the source of heat and broil for 1½ to 2 minutes. Turn the pieces and cook for 2 to 3 minutes longer. Pour off all the fat that has accumulated in the pan.

5. To make the mustard butter, combine all the ingredients for the butter and beat rapidly with a whisk or wooden spoon until well blended. Spoon equal amounts over the fish sections and serve immediately.

Yield: 6 servings.

FRIED EEL

1 or 2 skinned and
cleaned eel, about 1¼
pounds total weight

Milk to cover

Salt and freshly ground
pepper to taste

¼ teaspoon Tabasco
sauce

½ cup flour

Oil for deep frying

1 large bunch parsley

Lemon wedges

Tartar sauce (see
recipe page 769)

1. Cut the eel into 3-inch lengths. Place in a mixing bowl and add milk to cover, salt, pepper, and Tabasco sauce.

2. Drain well. Dredge the eel pieces in flour seasoned with salt and pepper.

3. Heat the oil in a deep fryer or a skillet and, when it is hot and almost smoking, add the eel pieces. Cook, stirring occasionally and turning the pieces, until golden brown and cooked through. Drain on paper towels.

4. Trim off and discard the parsley stems. If the parsley is totally clean, do not wash it. If it is rinsed, it must be patted thoroughly dry. Add the parsley and deep fry until crisp. It will darken as it cooks. Drain well and serve with the eel pieces. Serve with lemon wedges and tartar sauce.

Yield: 6 or more servings.

FROGS' LEGS CREOLE

1. Prepare one pair of frogs' legs at a time. Slip one leg in between the two muscles of the lower part of the other leg to keep the frogs' legs flat.

2. Soak the legs briefly, about 5 minutes, in the milk.

3. Drain the legs but do not dry, then dredge each pair in flour seasoned with salt and pepper.

4. Meanwhile, pour the tomatoes into a saucepan and simmer until thickened, 20 to 30 minutes. Season to taste with salt and pepper.

5. In a large skillet, heat the oil and 2 tablespoons of the butter. Cook the legs until golden on one side, then turn and cook the other side until golden.

6. Lightly butter a heatproof serving dish and arrange the frogs' legs on it in a symmetrical fashion. Spoon the tomato sauce neatly over the centers of the frogs' legs.

7. Discard the fat from the skillet and wipe out the skillet with paper towels. Melt the remaining butter in the skillet and add the garlic. When the butter is hot and foaming, pour it over the frogs' legs. Sprinkle with parsley and serve.

Yield: 4 to 6 servings.

12 large pairs frogs' legs, or 24 small pairs

1 cup milk

1 cup flour, approximately

Salt and freshly ground pepper to taste

1 can (28 ounces) peeled tomatoes, drained

½ cup vegetable or salad oil

6 tablespoons butter

1 tablespoon finely chopped garlic

¼ cup finely chopped parsley

WASH-BOILER CLAMBAKE

24 pounds wet seaweed, or enough to fill an 18-gallon wash boiler

Two 3½- to 4-pound chickens, quartered

Peanut, vegetable, or corn oil

2 teaspoons paprika

Salt and freshly ground pepper to taste

24 or more cherrystone or littleneck clams

17 red-skinned "new" potatoes, about 2½ pounds

3 or 4 quahog or chowder clams (for flavor only)

Eight 1¼ pound lobsters

16 ears of corn, unshucked

½ pound butter, melted

4 lemons, cut into wedges

Tabasco sauce

Worcestershire sauce

Blessed are those who live by the sea, for theirs is the kingdom of shellfish and seaweed, the two principal ingredients of an old-fashioned clambake. Clambakes where we live in East Hampton come in two sizes: the large, traditional, back-breaking affair with pits to dig and rocks to fire and sand to sweep; and the more recently evolved wash-boiler clambake for smaller gatherings. The latter, of course, may lack the color of the original, but we can state emphatically that the results are more or less equal. And there is one vast and important difference. The marvelous old-fashioned clambake demands 600 pounds of seaweed. With the wash-boiler type, you can settle for a child's portion—twenty-four pounds.

1. Gather the seaweed and have it ready.

2. Make a large wood fire in a grill, improvised if need be, on which the wash boiler will sit.

3. Make a charcoal fire for grilling the chicken pieces.

4. Place the chicken in a large dish and add enough oil to coat the pieces. Sprinkle with paprika, salt, and pepper and rub well. Grill the chicken pieces quickly first on one side, then the other until they are golden brown but not cooked. Tie 2 pieces of chicken in each of 4 cheesecloth bags.

5. Make individul cheesecloth packages of clams, 3 or more per serving.

6. Put about a sixth of the seaweed in the bottom of the wash boiler. Add the chicken in cheesecloth. Cover with the same amount of seaweed and add all but one of the potatoes. Add more seaweed and the packaged clams. Add the quahogs. Add more seaweed and the lobsters. Add more seaweed and the corn. Add a final layer of seaweed and place the reserved potato directly in the center. Cover closely with a lid. Weight the lid down with heavy stones. Cook over a good fire for 1¼ to 1½ hours, or until the potato on top is tender without being mushy.

7. Serve all the foods simultaneously with melted butter, lemon wedges, and the sauces. Cold beer, but of course. Plus ice cream or watermelon.

Yield: 8 servings.

CLAM FRITTERS

1. To prepare the clams, chop them on a flat surface or put them through a food grinder, using the medium blade. Put the clams in a mixing bowl.

2. Add the egg, lemon juice, parsley, baking soda, and flour and stir.

3. Blend the clam juice and milk and add this gradually to the clam mixture, stirring constantly. Add only enough of the clam juice and milk to make a batter that is not too runny. Add the butter, cayenne, and pepper.

4. Heat an eighth of an inch of oil in a skillet and drop the batter, about 2 tablespoons, into the oil. Continue adding batches of batter without letting the sides touch. Turn the fritters as they brown and continue cooking until cooked through. Continue cooking until all the batter is used. Serve hot with shrimp sauce.

Yield: 4 servings.

1 cup chopped clams

1 egg, lightly beaten

1 teaspoon lemon juice

1 tablespoon finely chopped parsley

1 teaspoon baking soda

1 cup flour

¼ cup clam juice

¼ cup milk

4 teaspoons butter, melted

Pinch of cayenne

Freshly ground pepper to taste

Oil for shallow frying

Shrimp sauce (see recipe page 783)

DEEP-FRIED SOFT-SHELL CRABS

1. Sprinkle the crabs on all sides with salt and pepper.

2. Break the egg into a flat dish and add the water, salt, and pepper. Beat to blend well.

3. In a separate flat dish, blend the flour, salt, and pepper to taste.

4. Place the bread crumbs in a third flat dish.

5. Dip the crabs first in egg, then in flour, and finally in crumbs, turning and patting so that the crumbs adhere.

6. Heat the fat for deep frying and add the crabs. Cook, turning as necessary, until crisp and golden brown. Drain on absorbent towels. Serve hot with lemon wedges and tartar sauce.

Yield: 4 servings.

4 soft-shell crabs

1 egg

3 tablespoons water

Salt and freshly ground pepper to taste

½ cup flour

1½ cups fresh bread crumbs

Fat for deep frying

Lemon wedges

Tartar sauce (see recipe page 769)

SOFT-SHELL CRABS MEUNIÈRE

4   soft-shell crabs

¼   cup milk

Salt and freshly ground
pepper to taste

½   cup flour

½   cup peanut, vegetable,
or corn oil

Juice of ½ lemon

4   thin slices from a
peeled lemon, seeds
removed

2   tablespoons chopped
parsley

1. Put the crabs in a shallow dish in one layer and add the milk, salt,
   and pepper. Turn the crabs in the milk.

2. Season the flour with salt and pepper.

3. Heat the oil in a heavy skillet large enough to hold the crabs in one
   layer.

4. Dip the crabs immediately from the milk into the flour, turning to
   coat well.

5. Heat the oil until quite hot and add the crabs, belly side up. Cook
   for 4 to 5 minutes (more or less depending on the size of the
   crabs) and turn. Cook until golden on both sides and cooked
   through. Transfer the crabs to a warm serving platter and sprinkle
   with lemon juice. Garnish neatly with lemon slices and sprinkle with
   parsley.

Yield: 4 servings.

POACHED CRABS

4   large hard-shell blue
crabs, about 1¼
pounds each

1   quart water

½   teaspoon ground
allspice

4   whole cloves

1   tablespoon whole black
peppercorns

4   hot dried red peppers

1   teaspoon celery seeds

Salt to taste

1. Set the crabs aside until ready to cook.

2. Put the water, allspice, cloves, peppercorns, peppers, celery seeds,
   and salt in a kettle and bring to the boil.

3. Put in the crabs and cover closely. Cook for 10 minutes. Drain and
   set the crabs aside until cool enough to handle.

Yield: 4 boiled crabs that, when picked over, will yield 1 pound of
meat plus more edible, nonmeaty portions such as the coral, liver, and
roe.

DEVILED CRAB

Deviled dishes, meaning those with special spices and generally containing dry mustard, were commonplace in my childhood. Although deviled foods are a part of a national pattern in American kitchens (you will also find foods "à la diable" or devil's style in French cookery), I have always considered deviled—or well-spiced—dishes, such as the following recipe for crabmeat, to be particularly Southern. The dish is seasoned with those two most basic Southern staples, Tabasco and Worcestershire sauces, seasonings my mother could not have cooked without. It can be made with any kind of crab—blue crab, Dungeness, Alaskan king, or whatever.

1. Pick over the crabmeat to remove any trace of shell or cartilage. Place the crabmeat in a mixing bowl.

2. Chop the eggs and add them to the crab. Add the parsley.

3. Heat 2 tablespoons of the butter in a skillet and add the onion, celery, and green pepper. Cook, stirring, until the onion is translucent. Add to the crabmeat mixture along with the chopped pimiento.

4. Fold in 1½ cups of the bread crumbs and moisten with the clam juice and sherry. Add the scallions, Tabasco, Worcestershire, salt, and pepper.

5. Beat the egg lightly and add it to the crab mixture. Fold all the ingredients together until well blended.

6. Pile equal parts of the mixture into 8 or 10 crab shells, scallop shells, or ceramic ramekins. Smooth over the tops and brush each with mustard. Sprinkle with the remaining bread crumbs. Dot with the remaining butter.

7. When ready to cook, preheat the oven to 400 degrees.

8. Place the shells on a baking sheet and bake for 20 to 30 minutes, until piping hot throughout and golden brown on top. Serve with lemon wedges.

Yield: 4 to 6 servings.

1 pound lump crabmeat

2 hard-cooked eggs

¼ cup chopped parsley

2 tablespoons plus 2 teaspoons butter

½ cup finely chopped onion

¾ cup finely chopped celery

⅓ cup finely chopped sweet green pepper

3 tablespoons chopped pimiento

2 cups bread crumbs

¼ cup fresh or bottled clam juice

2 tablespoons dry sherry

1½ teaspoons chopped scallions or chives

¼ teaspoon Tabasco sauce, or to taste

¼ teaspoon Worcestershire sauce, or to taste

Salt and freshly ground pepper to taste

1 egg

¼ cup hot mustard (see recipe page 782)

Lemon wedges

CARIBBEAN-STYLE STUFFED CRABS

4 tablespoons butter, approximately

4 scallions, chopped

1 teaspoon chopped garlic

1 hot green chili, finely chopped, seeds optional, or use dried red pepper flakes to taste

1 tablespoon curry powder

¾ to 1 pound crabmeat, finely shredded (this does not have to be lump or fancy crab; snow crab, flaked crabmeat, or even canned crab may be used)

2 tablespoons finely chopped fresh coriander, optional

2 tablespoons finely chopped fresh parsley

Salt and freshly ground pepper to taste

6 to 8 tablespoons crab liquid, or bottled clam juice

2 cups fresh bread crumbs

Lime wedges for garnish

1. Preheat the oven to 400 degrees.

2. Melt the butter in a wide, shallow saucepan or skillet. When melted, add the scallions, garlic, and chili. Add the curry powder and blend. Add the crabmeat. Add the coriander, if desired, and parsley. Add the salt and pepper. Add enough crab liquid to moisten properly. If you want a richer—and better—dish, add 2 to 4 more tablespoons of butter. Add the bread crumbs and blend well.

3. Remove from the heat and use the mixture to fill 4 to 8 clam shells.

4. Bake for 10 to 15 minutes, until piping hot and nicely brown. Serve with lime wedges.

Yield: 4 to 8 servings.

BROILED MARYLAND CRAB CAKES

1. Preheat the broiler to moderate.
2. Handle the crabmeat as little as possible to avoid breaking up the large, firm lumps. Remove any pieces of shell or cartilage, however.
3. Blend the mayonnaise, egg white, and cracker crumbs in a mixing bowl. Add the crab and fold gently to blend without breaking up the lumps of meat. Using slightly moistened fingers, divide the mixture into 8 equal portions. Shape each portion into a patty. Coat the patties all over with bread crumbs, pressing to make the crumbs adhere. Refrigerate until ready to use.
4. Heat 1 tablespoon of butter in a skillet large enough to hold the crab cakes. Turn them in the butter to coat top and bottom. Place under the broiler and broil about 4 inches from the flame, turning once, until nicely browned and cooked through, about 5 minutes. Serve 2 crab cakes with equal portions of melted butter.

Yield: 4 servings.

1 pound crabmeat, preferably lump or backfin

1 cup freshly made mayonnaise

1 egg white

3 to 4 tablespoons very fine cracker crumbs

½ cup fine fresh bread crumbs or cracker crumbs

1 tablespoon butter

4 tablespoons butter, melted and still hot

CRAB FRITTERS

1. Put the flour in a mixing bowl and add salt and pepper to taste, olive oil, nutmeg, and Tabasco to taste. Add the yolks of the eggs and gradually add the milk, stirring constantly with a whisk. Add the scallions and fold in the crabmeat. Beat the egg whites until stiff and fold them in.
2. Heat the ½ cup of oil in a heavy skillet and add spoonfuls of the crab mixture. The quantity of each spoonful is optional. The fritters may be very small, only a tablespoon or so, or rather large, 4 tablespoons. Cook until brown on one side, turn and cook until brown on the other. Drain on paper towels. Serve with tomato sauce.

Yield: 20 to 40 fritters.

1½ cups flour

Salt and freshly ground pepper to taste

2 tablespoons olive oil

¼ teaspoon grated nutmeg

Tabasco sauce

2 eggs, separated

1 cup milk

1 cup finely chopped scallions

1 pound crabmeat, lump or backfin, picked over well

½ cup peanut, vegetable, or corn oil

Fresh tomato sauce (see recipe page 784)

FLOWERS AROUND THE SNOW (STIR-FRIED CRAB)

8 large egg whites, about 1¼ cups

1½ tablespoons cornstarch

1¼ cups milk

2 teaspoons salt

2 teaspoons sugar

¾ pound fresh, picked-over crabmeat (see note)

½ cup chives cut into ½-inch lengths, preferably Chinese chives (available in Asian markets), which are flatter and more flavorful than Western chives

½ cup peanut, vegetable, or corn oil, plus oil for deep frying

One 2-ounce package bean threads (cellophane noodles)

1 tablespoon dried rose petals, optional

1. Put the egg whites in a mixing bowl. Beat lightly with a fork or chopsticks.

2. Separately blend the cornstarch with ½ cup of the milk, a little at a time. When blended, add this to the eggs. Add the remaining milk. Add the salt and sugar and beat well. Add the crab and half of the chives and blend well. Set aside.

3. When ready to serve, heat the oil for deep frying. Break the bean threads into three portions. Set one portion aside for another use. Add the other portions, one at a time, to the hot oil. Cook for about 2 seconds on one side and turn. Cook for about 2 seconds and turn. Quickly lift from the oil and place on a round serving platter. Repeat with the second portion.

4. Heat the ½ cup of oil in a wok and, when hot, add the egg white mixture. Cook, using a flat stirring spoon and stir gently and slowly, pushing the mixture from the outside toward the center. Use a lifting and folding motion. Cook, stirring and lifting gently from the bottom, for 3 or 4 minutes.

5. Transfer to the center of the fried bean threads. Garnish with the rose petals, if desired, and the remaining chives.

Yield: 8 servings with other Chinese dishes.

Note: It is preferable to use part crab roe from female crabs, but this is generally found only in crabs that you steam and pick out yourself.

CRAB GUMBO

1. Drop the corn into boiling water to cover and return the water to the boil. Remove from the heat and let stand for 5 minutes. Drain. Cut the kernels from the cob and set aside.

2. Heat the bacon fat in a skillet. Cut the okra, fresh or frozen, into ½-inch lengths. Add to the skillet and cook, stirring often, for 10 to 15 minutes, or until it is quite dry.

3. Meanwhile, heat the butter and add the onion, garlic, celery, and green pepper. Cook, stirring, until the onion is wilted.

4. Add the tomatoes, salt, pepper, Worcestershire sauce, broth, and water. Add the Tabasco and bring to the boil. Simmer for 40 minutes.

5. Stir in the crab and corn and heat thoroughly.

6. When ready to serve, add the sherry and parsley. Heat thoroughly and serve with hot cooked rice.

Yield: 6 or more servings.

4 to 6 ears of corn

2 tablespoons bacon fat or vegetable oil

¾ pound fresh young okra, or use one 10-ounce package frozen

2 tablespoons butter

¾ cup finely chopped onion

1 teaspoon finely chopped garlic

¾ cup finely chopped celery

½ cup finely chopped green pepper

4 tomatoes, cored and chopped, about 4 cups

Salt and freshly ground pepper to taste

1 teaspoon or more Worcestershire sauce

2 cups fish broth, or use 2 cups bottled clam juice

1 cup water

Tabasco sauce to taste

½ pound or more crabmeat, preferably lump or backfin

5 tablespoons dry sherry

¼ cup finely chopped parsley

CRAWFISH ÉTOUFFÉE

⅓ cup corn, peanut, or vegetable oil

⅓ cup flour

¼ cup finely chopped sweet green pepper

¼ cup finely chopped celery

½ cup finely chopped onion

1 teaspoon finely minced garlic

1½ cups fish stock (see recipe page 801)

2 tablespoons butter

½ cup finely chopped scallions

3 pounds crawfish tails (see following instructions)

¼ cup crawfish fat

Salt and freshly ground pepper to taste

1 tablespoon finely chopped fresh basil

⅛ teaspoon cayenne

2 tablespoons fresh lemon juice

1. Heat the oil in a heavy kettle and add the flour. Cook, stirring almost constantly, for about 20 minutes, or until the flour becomes reddish brown. Take care that the flour does not burn or it will develop a bitter taste.

2. Add the green pepper, celery, and onion. Cook, stirring, about 5 minutes. Add the garlic and stir. Add the stock, stirring with a wire whisk until thickened.

3. Heat the butter in a wide saucepan and add the scallions and crawfish tails. Cook, stirring, about 1 minute. Add the thickened sauce, crawfish fat, salt, and pepper and stir. Cook, stirring often, for about 8 minutes. Add the basil, cayenne, and lemon juice. Serve with rice.

Yield: 4 servings.

TO REMOVE CRAWFISH TAIL AND FAT

Turn the crawfish upside down. Break or twist the tails from the main body. Inside the shell there will be a creamy white mass that you should scoop out with the tip of a knife or a small spoon. This is crawfish fat. Break open the tail portions and pull away the tail meat.

BROILED LOBSTERS WITH TARRAGON

1. Preheat the broiler.

2. Place each lobster, shell side up, on a flat, heavy surface. Plunge a sharp heavy kitchen knife into the midsection of the lobster where the tail and body meet. This will kill the lobster instantly. Cut the lobster in half lengthwise, cutting first through the tail, then through the body. Discard the tough sac near the eyes.

3. Remove the soft liver and coral from the body of the lobsters and put them in a small mixing bowl. Set aside.

4. Arrange the lobster halves cut side up on a baking dish.

5. To the coral and liver add the bread crumbs, butter, tarragon, cream, salt, and pepper to taste. Blend well.

6. Spoon equal portions of the filling into the cavity of each lobster half.

7. Sprinkle each lobster half with salt and pepper. Brush the tops of each lobster half, filling included, with the oil.

8. Place the lobsters under the broiler, about 6 inches from the source of heat. It may be necessary to use two racks to do this. In that case, place one baking dish under the broiler about 6 inches from the source of heat. Place the other on a second rack below. Bake and broil, alternating the placement of the dishes on the racks, for about 5 minutes.

9. Turn the oven temperature to 400 degrees and continue baking for 10 minutes longer. Garnish with parsley sprigs. Serve with melted butter and lemon wedges.

Yield: 4 to 8 servings.

4 lobsters, about 1¾ pounds each

½ cup fine fresh bread crumbs

4 tablespoons butter, at room temperature

2 tablespoons finely chopped fresh tarragon, or 1 tablespoon dried

¼ cup heavy cream

Salt and freshly ground pepper to taste

⅓ cup peanut, vegetable, or corn oil

Parsley sprigs for garnish

¼ pound butter, melted

Lemon wedges

Lobster and Vegetables in Court Bouillon

1 small onion

2 heart of celery stalks

1 small carrot

1 cup thinly sliced green part of leeks

½ cup coarsely chopped onion

½ cup coarsely chopped celery

½ cup coarsely chopped carrot

2 cups water

1 cup dry white wine

½ teaspoon dried thyme

1 bay leaf

6 fresh parsley sprigs

6 whole black peppercorns, crushed

Salt to taste

Two 1½-pound live lobsters

2 tablespoons butter

1. Peel the onion and cut it lengthwise in half. Cut each half crosswise into very thin slices. There should be about ½ cup. Set aside.

2. Trim the celery and cut it crosswise into ⅛-inch slices. Set aside.

3. Trim and peel the carrot. Use a lemon peeler to make lengthwise ridges around the carrot. Cut the carrot into thin rounds. Set aside.

4. Combine in a large kettle half of the leeks, the coarsely chopped onion, coarsely chopped celery, coarsely chopped carrot, water, wine, thyme, bay leaf, 2 parsley sprigs, peppercorns, and salt. Cover and bring to the boil. Simmer for 15 minutes.

5. Add the lobsters and cover closely. Cook for exactly 7 minutes.

6. Remove the lobsters. Strain the cooking liquid. Discard the solids.

7. Put the thinly sliced onion, celery slices, and carrot rounds in a saucepan. Add the remaining leeks. Add the strained cooking liquid. Bring to the boil and cook over high heat for about 5 minutes.

8. Split the lobsters in half. Remove and discard the tough sac near the eyes. Crack the claws. Arrange a lobster half and 1 claw in a soup bowl.

9. Pluck off enough small bits of parsley leaves from each of the remaining sprigs to make ½ cup.

10. To the vegetables and liquid add the butter bit by bit, swirling it into the sauce. Cook for about 1 minute. Add the parsley bits.

11. Pour the sauce over the lobster and serve hot.

Yield: 4 servings.

Baked Lobsters with Vegetables

1. In the saucepan, bring to the boil enough water to amply cover the potatoes. Add salt to taste and a bit more than seems logical. Add the potatoes and simmer until cooked but still a bit firm to the bite, 10 to 15 minutes. Drain well.

2. In a saucepan, bring to the boil enough water to cover the green beans amply. Add salt as indicated above. Add the beans and cook until tender but still a bit firm to the bite, about 10 minutes. Drain and rinse under cold water until well chilled. Drain well.

3. Bring enough water to the boil to cover the peas thoroughly. Add salt as indicated above. Add the peas and simmer for 4 minutes or longer, until tender but still firm. Drain and rinse under cold running water. Drain well.

4. Combine the carrots and turnips and add cold water to cover. Add salt to taste and bring to the boil. Cook as above, about 10 minutes. Drain and rinse until cold. Drain well.

5. Plunge a knife into the center of each lobster where the tail and body meet. This will kill the lobster instantly. Cut the lobsters in half at midsection between the carcass and tail. Cut the tail section into 3 pieces. Cut the carcasses in half lengthwise. Remove and reserve the soft coral and liver portion of the lobster. Discard the sac. Crack the claws.

6. Heat 4 tablespoons of the butter and the oil in a large, heavy casserole or Dutch oven and add all the lobster pieces. Cook for 3 to 4 minutes. Add the shallots and onions and stir. Add the blanched vegetables—potatoes, green beans, peas, carrots, and turnips. Add salt and pepper to taste. Cook for about 5 minutes, stirring to blend the flavors.

7. Add the wine and broth and cover. Cook for about 10 minutes. Remove from the heat. Using a lid to hold the solids in place, drain off the liquid into a large, heavy saucepan. Bring the liquid to the boil and let simmer for about 15 minutes.

8. Meanwhile, add the remaining 2 tablespoons of butter to the coral and liver and blend well with the fingers. Add the flour and blend well. Add to the sauce, stirring vigorously. Bring to the boil and cook, stirring constantly, for about 5 minutes.

9. Pour this mixture over the lobster mixture and bring to the boil. Cook, stirring, for about 5 minutes. Serve.

Yield: 10 servings.

1½ cups small potatoes, peeled and quartered or cut into chunks
Salt

¾ pound green beans, trimmed at the ends and cut into 1-inch lengths

1 cup shelled peas, the fresher the better

1½ cups carrots cut into bâtonnets

1 cup fresh turnips cut into bâtonnets

3 or 4 live lobsters, about 1½ pounds each

6 tablespoons butter

¼ cup olive oil

⅓ cup finely chopped shallots

8 to 10 very small white onions, peeled and cut into quarters or eighths
Freshly ground pepper

¾ cup dry white wine

1¼ cups chicken broth, preferably freshly made

3 tablespoons flour

BAKED LOBSTER WITH HERB BUTTER

One 1- to 1½-pound lobster
1 teaspoon olive oil
Salt and white pepper
¼ pound butter, melted
1 tablespoon finely chopped shallots
1 tablespoon finely chopped parsley
1 teaspoon finely chopped fresh tarragon

1. Preheat the oven to 450 degrees.
2. Turn the lobster on its back and split it lengthwise. Remove and discard the small sac inside the lobster near the eyes.
3. Arrange the lobster halves, split side up, in a baking dish and brush with the oil. Sprinkle with the salt and pepper.
4. Bake for 15 minutes and remove.
5. Combine the butter with the remaining ingredients. Using a fork, lift up the tail sections from the shell. Spoon the butter into the shell and replace the tails in the shells. Serve immediately.

Yield: 2 servings.

MOULES MARINIÈRE (MUSSELS IN WHITE WINE)

2½ pounds (about 2 quarts) cleaned mussels
2 tablespoons butter
2 tablespoons finely chopped onion
1 tablespoon finely chopped shallots
1 small garlic clove, finely minced
2 tablespoons finely chopped parsley
Freshly ground pepper to taste
¾ cup dry white wine

One of the most fascinating discussions we ever engaged in took place while mussel gathering one gray day on Duxbury Bay in Massachusetts with C. Graham Hurlburt. Mr. Hurlburt, in addition to being director of administrative services at Harvard, was an expert on the edible blue mussel and experiments in cultivation. The thing that really intrigued us was the gentleman's comparison of mussels and T-bone steaks. The protein content of both is virtually the same, he informed us. Steak, however, has four times more calories than mussels and eighteen times more fat. How, we've been pondering ever since, can anything so positively nutritious be so positively delectable.

1. Run the mussels under cold running water, rubbing the shells together to remove any foreign matter that may still cling to them. Drain well.
2. Heat the butter in a kettle and add the onion, shallots, and garlic. Cook until wilted and add the mussels. Add half the parsley, pepper to taste, and wine. Cover closely and cook for about 5 minutes, or until the mussels are opened. Discard any mussels that don't open. Serve in soup bowls sprinkled with the remaining parsley.

Yield: 2 to 4 servings.

STEAMED MUSSELS WITH TOMATOES AND BASIL

1. Scrub the mussels thoroughly under cold running water. Drain.

2. Heat the oil in a small kettle and add the onion and garlic. Cook until the onion is wilted and add the tomatoes and wine. Cook over high heat to reduce slightly and add the mussels. Cover closely and steam until the mussels have opened, about 5 minutes. Discard any mussels that don't open. Sprinkle with parsley and basil.

3. Arrange one or two crusts in the bottom of each of 4 soup bowls. Spoon the mussels into the bowls and serve piping hot.

Yield: 4 servings.

3 quarts (3½ pounds) fresh mussels

5 tablespoons olive oil

¼ cup finely chopped onion

2 garlic cloves, finely minced

1 cup fresh, peeled, chopped tomatoes

1 cup dry white wine

2 tablespoons finely chopped parsley

1 tablespoon finely chopped fresh basil

4 to 8 provençale crusts (see following instructions)

PROVENÇALE CRUSTS

Preheat the oven to 400 degrees. Brush 4 to 8 thin rounds of French bread with olive oil on both sides. Place on a baking sheet and bake until crisp, turning once.

MUSSELS WITH SAFFRON CREAM

3 pounds (about 2½ quarts) cleaned mussels

2 tablespoons butter

3 tablespoons finely chopped leeks

2 tablespoons finely chopped onion

1 garlic clove, finely minced

1 tablespoon finely chopped shallots

1 teaspoon loose saffron stems

2 tablespoons white wine vinegar

Salt and freshly ground pepper to taste

¼ cup finely chopped parsley

½ cup heavy cream

1. Scrub the mussels thoroughly. Drain and set aside.

2. Melt the butter in a kettle and add the leeks, onion, garlic, and shallots. Cook for about 1 minute and add the saffron. Cook about 2 minutes, stirring, and add the vinegar and mussels. Add the salt and pepper and cover closely. Cook for about 1 minute.

3. Add the parsley and cream and cover. Cook for about 5 minutes, or until the mussels open. Discard any mussels that don't open. Serve in hot soup bowls.

Yield: 4 servings.

MUSSELS VINAIGRETTE

1. Put the mussels in a large, heavy metal casserole and scatter half the onions over all. Sprinkle with the pepper. Do not add salt or liquid.

2. Put the casserole on the stove and cover. Cook over high heat for 6 to 10 minutes, or until the moment the steam starts to escape from the casserole. Shake the casserole so that the mussels are redistributed. Remove from the heat as soon as the mussels are open. Discard any mussels that don't open. Take care not to overcook or the mussels will fall out of the shells. Pour off the cooking liquid immediately. Let stand, uncovered, until ready to serve.

3. When ready to serve, put the mussels in a large salad bowl and scatter the remaining onions over all.

4. Spoon the sauce over the mussels and toss with finely chopped parsley.

Yield: 6 or more servings.

6 quarts (6 pounds) mussels, well scrubbed

2 cups coarsely chopped red onions

½ teaspoon freshly ground pepper

Sauce vinaigrette (see following recipe)

½ cup finely chopped parsley

Spoon the mustard into a mixing bowl and add the vinegar. Start beating with a wire whisk and gradually beat in the oils. Add salt and pepper to taste.

Yield: About 1¼ cups.

LA PETITE FERME'S SAUCE VINAIGRETTE

2 tablespoons Dijon mustard

6 tablespoons red wine vinegar

6 tablespoons peanut oil

6 tablespoons olive oil

Salt and freshly ground pepper to taste

OYSTERS FRIED IN CORNMEAL

24 large, shucked oysters with their liquor

½ cup cornmeal, preferably yellow although white may be used

½ teaspoon freshly ground pepper

⅛ teaspoon cayenne

⅛ teaspoon paprika

Salt to taste

Corn, peanut, or vegetable oil for deep frying

Whenever considering oysters, my thoughts turn to one of the finest books that I have encountered about a single food—*The Glorious Oyster,* printed in England and edited by Hector Bolitho.

One learns from the book, for example, that the oyster is the most tranquil of animals and can be rather eccentric. It tells of an oyster that learned to whistle, another that became a mousetrap, and it explains that in certain lands oysters grow on trees. It is their talent for laziness that makes them, as one expert put it, the most tender and delicate of seafoods.

Oysters, apparently, know no national boundaries, provided the land is surrounded by saltwater. And their culinary uses, of course, know no bounds. We enjoy them Southern style, coated with cornmeal and deep-fried.

1.   Drain the oysters briefly.

2.   Combine the cornmeal, pepper, cayenne, paprika, and salt. Blend well.

3.   Heat the oil to 375 degrees.

4.   Dredge the oysters in the cornmeal mixture. Drop them, a few at a time, into the hot oil and cook, stirring often, until they are golden brown all over, less than 2 minutes depending on size. Do not overcook. Remove and drain.

5.   Let the oil return to the proper temperature before adding successive batches. Serve, if desired, with tartar sauce, mayonnaise, or, Southern style, with tomato ketchup flavored with Worcestershire sauce, a dash of Tabasco, and lemon juice.

Yield: 2 servings.

STIR-FRIED OYSTERS AND SHRIMP

For years we had heard of Danny Kaye's prowess as a chef, particularly in the province of Chinese cooking, but tended to regard it with some skepticism. One more touch of Hollywood, we mused. His talents, however, wildly exceeded his billing. With only one helper in what was undoubtedly the finest Chinese kitchen of any private home anywhere, he regaled us with a banquet of surpassing excellence. This stir-fried oyster and shrimp dish and the batter-fried scallops are just two of our favorites from Danny's repertory.

1. Place the oysters in a bowl and add the flour and water to cover. Stir the oysters in the liquid. Drain well and run under several changes of cold water. Drain well. The flour will both cleanse and plump the oysters. They must be rinsed well before draining.

2. Drop the oysters into barely simmering water. Turn off the heat. Let stand for 1 minute and drain. Set aside. Repeat with the shrimp.

3. Heat the oil in a wok or skillet over high heat. Add the ginger and scallions and cook, stirring, for about 5 seconds. Add the oysters and shrimp and stir rapidly. Cook for about 15 seconds. Add the soy sauce, sesame oil, salt, and pepper to taste, stirring constantly.

4. Blend the cornstarch with the water and stir it into the dish. Cook for 15 seconds, stirring quickly, and serve.

Yield: 8 servings with other Chinese dishes.

1 cup raw oysters

¼ cup flour

½ pound shrimp, shelled and deveined

2 tablespoons peanut, vegetable, or corn oil

One 2-inch piece fresh ginger, peeled and cut into fine shreds

5 scallions, trimmed and cut into 2-inch lengths

1 teaspoon light soy sauce

¼ teaspoon sesame oil

Salt and freshly ground pepper to taste

1½ tablespoons cornstarch

1½ tablespoons water

BATTER-FRIED SCALLOPS

2 cups whole bay
   scallops or quartered
   sea scallops
½ cup flour
½ cup cornstarch
1 egg white
1 tablespoon peanut,
   vegetable, or corn oil
1 tablespoon white
   vinegar
1 teaspoon baking soda
½ cup or more water
   Flour for dredging
   Peanut, vegetable, or
   corn oil for deep frying
2½ cups sweet and sour
   sauce (see following
   recipe)

Scallops are, conceivably, my favorite bivalve, with an incredible versatility where preparation is concerned. At lunch I once asked a very young neighbor as he speared his fork into a large platter of broiled scallops what it was that he admired so much about the bay scallops. With scarely a pause he answered, "No bones." Now that is putting it simplistically.

1. Rinse and drain the scallops well.
2. In a mixing bowl, combine the flour, cornstarch, egg white, 1 tablespoon of oil, vinegar, and baking soda. Mix well.
3. Gradually add the water, stirring constantly with a wire whisk. Add enough water to make a thick, pancakelike batter.
4. Dredge the scallops in flour.
5. Heat the oil almost to smoking and, if desired, test one scallop by dipping it in the batter and frying to determine if the batter is too thick. If so, stir in a little more water.
6. Add the scallops to the batter and quickly drop them one at a time into the hot oil. Deep fry, stirring and turning with a strainer, making sure that the scallops do not stick together. Remove and drain well. Pour onto a serving dish. Pour the heated sweet and sour sauce over and serve.

Yield: 8 servings.

SWEET AND SOUR SAUCE

1 cup sugar
¾ cup white vinegar
½ cup plus 3 tablespoons
   water
¾ cup pineapple juice
1½ tablespoons cornstarch
½ teaspoon red food
   coloring

1. Combine the sugar, vinegar, ½ cup water, and pineapple juice in a saucepan. Bring to the boil and simmer, stirring, until the sugar dissolves.
2. Blend the cornstarch with the remaining water and stir into the sauce. Stir in the food coloring.

Yield: About 2½ cups.

BROILED SCALLOPS

1. Preheat the broiler to high.
2. Select a large, flat baking dish with a low rim. Put the butter in it and place under the broiler until the butter melts and is bubbling hot without browning.
3. Add the scallops and stir to coat with the butter. Add the crumbs, salt, and pepper and stir until scallops are coated with crumbs.
4. Place the scallops about 3 inches from the source of heat and broil. Do not close the broiler door as the scallops cook. Broil for 5 minutes without stirring or turning. Serve hot with lemon wedges.

Yield: 4 servings.

3   tablespoons butter
1   pound sea or bay scallops
2   tablespoons fine fresh bread crumbs
    Salt and freshly ground pepper to taste
    Lemon wedges

Deep-Fried Scallops

1 pound sea or bay
   scallops
1 egg
1 teaspoon peanut,
   vegetable, or corn oil
   Salt to taste
1 tablespoon water
   Flour for dredging
1 cup fine fresh bread
   crumbs
   Oil for deep frying
   Lemon wedges

1. If the scallops are freshly opened, rinse and drain them.

2. Combine the egg, 1 teaspoon of oil, salt, and water in a dish, such as a pie plate.

3. Dredge the scallops lightly on all sides in flour. Turn them in the egg mixture until coated. Dredge them on all sides in the bread crumbs. Arrange them on a rack so that they do not touch. The scallops may be prepared to this point about an hour in advance or they may be cooked immediately.

4. Heat the oil for deep frying and add the scallops. Cook them quickly, stirring with a slotted spoon, until golden brown. Drain on absorbent towels. Serve with cucumber mayonnaise, tartar sauce, or a cocktail sauce. Serve garnished with lemon wedges.

Yield: 4 to 6 servings.

Scallops with Shallot Butter and Pine Nuts

1. Preheat the oven to 450 degrees.
2. Rinse the scallops and pat them dry.
3. Work the butter with the fingers until it is soft. Add the shallots, salt, pine nuts, parsley, bread crumbs, and lemon juice.
4. Add equal amounts of scallops to each of 8 scallop shells or ramekins. Top the scallops with equal portions of the butter. Place on a baking dish and bake for 10 minutes, or until piping hot and bubbling.

Yield: 8 servings.

1 pound fresh bay scallops

¼ pound butter

3 tablespoons finely chopped shallots

Salt to taste

2 tablespoons pine nuts

1 tablespoon chopped parsley

⅓ cup fine fresh bread crumbs

1 tablespoon lemon juice

COQUILLES ST. JACQUES (SCALLOPS WITH MUSHROOMS IN CREAM SAUCE)

4 tablespoons butter

1 tablespoon finely chopped shallots

2 cups thinly sliced mushrooms

Salt and freshly ground pepper to taste

½ cup dry white wine

1 pound sea or bay scallops

2 tablespoons flour

½ cup milk

1 cup plus 2 tablespoons heavy cream

Pinch of cayenne

1. Melt 1 tablespoon of the butter in a saucepan and add the shallots. Cook briefly, stirring, and add the mushrooms. Cook until wilted and add the salt, pepper, and wine.

2. Add the scallops and bring to the boil. Cook until all the scallops are heated through, stirring gently as necessary. Take care not to let the scallops overcook or they will toughen.

3. Using a slotted spoon, remove and set aside the scallops and mushrooms. Reserve the liquid. There should be about ¾ cup of liquid.

4. Melt 2 tablespoons of the butter in a saucepan and add the flour, stirring rapidly with a wire whisk. When blended add the reserved liquid, stirring until thickened and smooth. Add the milk and 1 cup of the cream. Cook for about 5 minutes. Add salt and pepper to taste and a pinch of cayenne.

5. Whip the remaining 2 tablespoons of heavy cream. Fold it into the sauce.

6. Use 6 individual scallop shells or ramekins. Spoon equal portions of the scallops and mushrooms into each shell. Spoon the sauce over the scallop mixture.

7. Preheat the broiler to high. Place the filled shells under the broiler about 6 inches from the source of heat and bake until a nice brown glaze forms on top. As the scallops broil, turn occasionally for even browning, about 5 minutes. Serve immediately.

Yield: 6 servings.

SCALLOPS IN A TOMATO AND GARLIC SAUCE

1. Drop the tomatoes into boiling water to cover and let stand for exactly 12 seconds. Drain and peel.

2. Cut away and discard the cores of the tomatoes. Cut each tomato in half and squeeze gently to extract most of the seeds and the soft pulp containing them.

3. Cut each tomato into ½-inch cubes. There should be about 2½ cups.

4. Heat the oil in a skillet and add the garlic. Cook briefly, stirring, about 30 seconds. Add the tomatoes and lemon juice and cook over high heat for about 6 minutes, or until the sauce is quite thick. Remember that the scallops when added will give up a considerable amount of liquid.

5. Meanwhile, combine the scallops, paprika, salt, and pepper.

6. Add the scallops to the tomato sauce. Add the ½ cup chopped parsley and the pepper flakes. Cook for about 1½ minutes. Do not overcook.

7. Pour the mixture into a serving dish. Cover with overlapping lemon slices. Sprinkle with chopped parsley for garnish.

Yield: 4 servings.

2 or 3 large ripe tomatoes, totaling about 1 pound

4 tablespoons olive oil

1 tablespoon finely minced garlic

2 tablespoons lemon juice

2 cups (1 pint) fresh bay scallops

½ teaspoon paprika

Salt and freshly ground pepper to taste

½ cup finely chopped parsley

¼ teaspoon hot red pepper flakes

4 thin seeded lemon slices

Chopped parsley for garnish

SCALLOPS AND SHRIMP ON SKEWERS

20 sea or bay scallops, about ¾ pound

20 shrimp, about ¾ pound

Salt and freshly ground pepper to taste

2 tablespoons peanut, vegetable, or corn oil

Tabasco sauce to taste

1 teaspoon dried rosemary

2 tablespoons lemon juice

1 garlic clove, finely minced

1 lemon slice

½ cup fine fresh bread crumbs

Melted butter for basting

Lemon wedges

1. Place the scallops and shrimp in a mixing bowl and add the salt, pepper, oil, and Tabasco sauce. Chop the rosemary and add it. Add the lemon juice, garlic, and lemon slice. Blend well and refrigerate for at least half an hour.

2. Arrange the scallops and shrimp alternately on 4 skewers. If using wood skewers, soak in water first to prevent burning. Dredge in bread crumbs.

3. To grill, brush a hot, fired grill with oil and add the skewers. Brush occasionally with melted butter. Turn after 2 minutes and continue to turn frequently while grilling, a total of about 10 minutes.

4. To broil, place the skewers on a baking dish and broil 6 inches more or less from the source of heat. Broil for about 5 minutes and turn. Brush frequently with melted butter. Broil for about 10 minutes. Serve with lemon wedges.

Yield: 4 servings.

SHRIMP AMÉRICAINE

This sauce américaine is an enormously simplified version of the real thing, which involves cooking lobsters in the shell, crushing and pressing the shells in a sieve and so on. But it is equally delectable. This sauce can be made ahead and refrigerated or frozen.

1. Peel and devein the shrimp. Rinse well and drain thoroughly.

2. Bring the sauce to the boil, but do not let it cook.

3. Melt the butter in a large kettle or casserole. Add the shallots and cook briefly, stirring.

4. Add the shrimp and sprinkle with the salt, pepper, and cayenne. Cook the shrimp, stirring gently, for about 5 minutes, or until they lose their raw look. Sprinkle with 1 cup of Cognac and ignite it (if it does not flame, do not worry). Stir and add half of the tarragon. Stir.

5. Add the sauce and stir to blend. Bring to the boil. Do not cook more than a minute. It is important, however, that the dish be piping hot throughout.

6. The liquid from the shrimp will probably thin the sauce. Thicken the sauce by blending the additional 3 tablespoons of Cognac with the arrowroot. Stir in gently. Stir in the remaining tarragon and serve.

Yield: 30 servings.

15 pounds raw shrimp in the shell

14 cups sauce américaine (see following recipe)

½ pound butter

¾ cup finely chopped shallots

Salt and freshly ground pepper to taste

¼ teaspoon cayenne, optional

1 cup Cognac

½ cup finely chopped fresh tarragon, or ¼ cup dried

3 tablespoons Cognac, optional

2 tablespoons arrowroot or cornstarch, optional

SAUCE AMÉRICAINE

4 tablespoons butter

1½ cups finely chopped onions

½ cup finely chopped shallots

2 teaspoons finely minced garlic

1 cup finely chopped celery

1 cup finely diced carrots

¼ cup flour

2 cups dry white wine

2 cups fish stock (see recipe page 801), or bottled clam juice

10 cups fresh or canned imported Italian tomatoes, crushed

¼ cup tomato paste

1 teaspoon dried thyme

1 bay leaf

⅓ cup packed fresh tarragon leaves

Salt and freshly ground pepper to taste

¼ teaspoon cayenne

1. Melt the butter in a kettle or large casserole. Add the onions, shallots, garlic, celery, and carrots. Cook, stirring, for about 5 minutes. Sprinkle with flour and stir to coat the vegetables evenly.

2. Add all of the remaining ingredients, stir, and bring to the boil. Cook, stirring, for about 20 minutes.

3. Put the sauce through a food mill, pressing to extract as much of the liquid from the solids as possible.

Yield: 14 cups.

BATTER-FRIED SHRIMP

Many years ago, when we attended a hotel school in Switzerland, we first discovered the miracle known as a beer batter. Although a can of flat beer may be the bane of those who dote on a frosty and lively brew, it is a liquid of considerable merit to a knowledgeable cook. It yields a crisp, puffy, gossamer coating to such good things as shrimp, brains, and assorted vegetables.

1. Peel and devein the shrimp but leave the last tail segment intact. Refrigerate until ready to use.
2. Prepare the beer batter well in advance.
3. Combine the shrimp with the cornstarch, sherry, parsley, and salt to taste.
4. When ready to cook, heat the oil. Add a few shrimp at a time to the batter and, using a two-pronged fork, drop them, one at a time, into the hot oil. Cook, turning as necessary, to brown evenly. Drain on paper towels. Sprinkle with salt.
5. Serve immediately with lemon wedges and any desired sauce such as hot mustard, marmalade and mustard sauce, or soy and ginger dip.

Yield: 4 to 6 servings.

1½ pounds shrimp

Beer batter (see following recipe)

1½ tablespoons cornstarch

1 tablespoon dry sherry

2 tablespoons finely chopped fresh parsley

Salt to taste

Peanut, vegetable, or corn oil for deep frying

Lemon wedges

1. Place the flour in a bowl and stir in the beer, salt, and oil. Stir to blend roughly. There should be a few small lumps. Cover the bowl with plastic wrap and let stand in a warm place for about 3 hours.
2. Stir in the egg yolk.
3. When ready to cook, beat the white until stiff and fold it in.

BEER BATTER

¾ cup flour

½ cup beer, at room temperature

Salt to taste

1 teaspoon peanut, vegetable, or corn oil

1 egg, separated

SHRIMP STEAMED IN BEER WITH DILL

1 pound shrimp, about 30

1 bay leaf

6 fresh dill sprigs

1 garlic clove

8 whole peppercorns, crushed

1 teaspoon ground allspice

1 dried hot red pepper pod

½ to 1 cup beer

   Salt to taste

2 small celery ribs with leaves

Do not peel the shrimp. Put them in a saucepan or deep small skillet and add the remaining ingredients. Cover and bring to the boil. Bring to a rolling boil and remove from the heat. Serve the shrimp with melted butter.

Yield: 2 to 4 servings.

SHRIMP CREOLE

It is conceivable that the first Creole dish I ever sampled (how many decades ago!) and the one I have eaten most often because of my affection for it is shrimp Creole. The following is one of the most basic and best recipes for the dish. It is made with what Paul Prudhomme has referred to as the "holy trinity" of Creole foods: chopped celery, green pepper, and onion. It is a recipe that served me well, long before I became professionally involved in the food field, when I set up a bachelor kitchen in Chicago after my years in military service.

1. Shell and devein the shrimp. Rinse and pat dry. Set aside.

2. Melt the butter in a saucepan and add the onion. Cook, stirring, until the onion is wilted and add the celery, green pepper, and garlic. Cook briefly, stirring. The vegetables must remain crisp.

3. Add the tomatoes, thyme, bay leaf, Tabasco, lemon rind, salt, and pepper. Simmer for 10 minutes uncovered.

4. Add the shrimp and cover. Cook for 3 to 5 minutes, no longer. Add the chopped parsley, lemon juice, and, if desired, more Tabasco sauce to taste. Serve with rice.

Yield: 2 to 4 servings.

1   pound fresh shrimp

3   tablespoons butter

¾   cup coarsely chopped onion

3   small celery ribs, coarsely chopped

1   sweet green pepper, cored, seeded, and coarsely chopped

3   garlic cloves, finely minced

2   cups canned tomatoes, preferably Italian peeled tomatoes

2   sprigs fresh thyme, or ½ teaspoon dried

1   bay leaf

Tabasco sauce to taste

½   teaspoon grated lemon rind

Salt and freshly ground pepper to taste

2   tablespoons finely chopped parsley

Juice of ½ lemon

CURRIED SHRIMP

6 pounds raw shrimp, peeled and deveined

2 tablespoons butter

Salt and freshly ground pepper to taste

1 tablespoon curry powder

3 cups curry sauce (see following recipe)

Chutney

1. Prepare the shrimp and set aside.

2. Melt the butter in a 4- to 5-quart kettle and add the shrimp. Add the salt and pepper. Sprinkle with curry powder and cook briefly, stirring, just until the shrimp lose their raw look.

3. Add the curry sauce and cook, stirring constantly from the bottom to prevent sticking, 3 to 5 minutes, until piping hot throughout. If desired, the sauce may be thinned a little with chicken broth or heavy cream. It should not be necessary, however. Serve with rice and chutney.

Yield: 24 servings.

CURRY SAUCE

4 tablespoons butter

2 cups finely chopped onion

1 cup finely chopped celery

2 tablespoons finely minced garlic

2 bay leaves

4 to 6 tablespoons curry powder

1 tablespoon ground turmeric

½ cup flour

5 cups rich chicken broth (see recipe page 800)

3 tablespoons tomato paste

Salt and freshly ground pepper to taste

2 bananas, peeled and mashed, about 1¼ cups

2 apples, peeled, cored, and finely diced, about 2 cups

1. Select a large heavy kettle, preferably one with a 9-quart capacity. Melt the butter in the kettle and add the onion, celery, and garlic. Cook, stirring, until wilted. Add the bay leaves, curry powder, turmeric, and flour and stir with a wire whisk.

2. Add the broth and tomato paste, stirring rapidly with the whisk. Add salt and pepper. Let simmer for about 5 minutes.

3. Add the bananas and apples and stir. Cook for about 20 minutes, stirring often from the bottom.

4. Put the sauce through a food mill, pressing to extract as much liquid as possible from the solids. Or, less preferably, purée the sauce using a food processor or a blender.

Yield: About 8 cups.

GARIDES MI FETA
(SHRIMP BAKED WITH FETA CHEESE)

1. Preheat the oven to 350 degrees.

2. Put the tomatoes in a saucepan and cook until reduced to about 2 cups. Stir often to prevent burning and sticking.

3. Shell and devein the shrimp and set aside.

4. Heat the olive oil in another saucepan or deep skillet and add the garlic, stirring. Add the tomatoes, using a rubber spatula to scrape them out.

5. Add the fish broth, oregano, pepper flakes, capers, and salt and pepper to taste.

6. Heat the butter in a heavy saucepan or skillet and add the shrimp. Cook briefly, less than 1 minute, stirring and turning the shrimp until they turn pink.

7. Spoon equal portions of half the sauce in four individual baking dishes and arrange 6 shrimp plus equal amounts of the butter in which they cooked in each dish. Spoon remaining sauce over the shrimp.

8. Crumble the cheese and scatter it over all. Place the dishes in the oven and bake for 10 to 15 minutes, or until bubbling hot.

9. Remove the dishes from the oven and sprinkle each dish with 1 tablespoon ouzo, if desired, and ignite it. Serve immediately.

Yield: 4 servings

3 cups imported canned Italian plum tomatoes

1 pound shrimp, about 24

¼ cup olive oil

1 teaspoon finely chopped garlic

¼ cup fresh fish broth or bottled clam juice

1 teaspoon crushed dried oregano

1 teaspoon dried red pepper flakes

2 tablespoons drained capers

Salt and freshly ground pepper to taste

3 tablespoons butter

¼ pound feta cheese

¼ cup ouzo, a Greek anise-flavored liqueur, optional

SHRIMP PILAF

2	pounds shrimp
6	strips of bacon
½	cup finely chopped onion
¼	cup finely chopped sweet green pepper
1¾	cups canned tomatoes, partly drained and crushed
1	cup long-grain rice
3	tablespoons butter
	Salt and freshly ground pepper to taste
6	drops Tabasco sauce
⅛	teaspoon ground mace

1. Peel and devein the shrimp.

2. Bring 6 cups water to the boil in a saucepan. Add the shrimp. Cover and cook for about 2 minutes, no longer. Turn off the heat.

3. Drain the shrimp, but reserve 1½ cups of the cooking liquid. Use this liquid to cook the rice for the pilaf.

4. Cook the bacon in a skillet until crisp. Drain. When the bacon is cool, crumble it and set aside.

5. Pour off all but 1 tablespoon of the bacon fat from the skillet. Add the chopped onion and green pepper to the skillet and cook until wilted.

6. Add the tomatoes and cook, stirring occasionally, about 5 minutes.

7. Add the rice and reserved 1½ cups cooking liquid. Stir to blend. Cover and simmer for 17 minutes.

8. Add the butter and stir until the butter is melted and blended. Add the salt, pepper, Tabasco, and mace. Stir. Add the shrimp and bacon. Stir from the bottom to blend. Reheat gently.

Yield: 8 or more servings.

HUNAN SHRIMP

1. Peel the shrimp and split them in half. Rinse well to remove the dark vein. Pat dry.

2. Place the shrimp in a mixing bowl and add 1½ tablespoons of the sherry, the egg whites, and 1½ tablespoons of the oil. Stir in a circular motion until the whites become bubbly and add half the salt and 1½ tablespoons of the cornstarch. Stir to blend.

3. Prepare the scallions and ginger and set aside.

4. Combine the remaining 3 tablespoons sherry, remaining 1 tablespoon cornstarch blended with the water, soy sauce, vinegar, sugar, remaining salt, sesame oil, and chicken broth.

5. Heat the remaining 4 cups of oil in a wok or skillet and add the shrimp, one at a time. Cook for about 1 minute and scoop out, leaving the oil in the wok continuously heating. Return the shrimp to the oil and cook for about 30 seconds. Drain wok completely.

6. Return about 1 tablespoon of the oil to the wok and add the scallions and ginger, stirring constantly. Cook for about 5 seconds and add the shrimp and the vinegar mixture. Toss and stir until piping hot and the shrimp are coated evenly. Serve garnished with coriander leaves if desired.

Yield: 4 to 8 servings.

10 giant shrimp, about 1¼ pounds, available in Chinese fish markets

4½ tablespoons dry sherry

2 egg whites

4 cups plus 1½ tablespoons peanut, vegetable, or corn oil

½ teaspoon salt

2½ tablespoons cornstarch

2 scallions, white part only, trimmed and shredded

5 very thin slices fresh ginger, shredded

2 tablespoons water

2 tablespoons soy sauce

2½ tablespoons white vinegar

2 tablespoons sugar

½ teaspoon sesame oil

⅓ cup chicken broth

½ cup loosely packed fresh coriander

SHRIMP IN COCONUT MILK

1 pound small shrimp, peeled and deveined

1 tablespoon peanut, vegetable, or corn oil

1 garlic clove, very thinly sliced

1 small onion, halved and thinly sliced, about ½ cup

1 mild or hot fresh green chili, cut on the diagonal into thin slices, about ⅓ cup

2 salam leaves, available in Asian food shops

1 thin slice laos root, available in Asian food shops

Salt to taste

1 teaspoon sugar

1 tablespoon tamarind liquid (see note)

½ cup coconut cream (see instructions page 800)

1 tomato, cut into wedges, about ¾ cup

1. Prepare the shrimp and set aside.

2. Heat the oil and add the garlic, onion, and chili. Cook, stirring, for about 30 seconds. Add the shrimp and stir until they redden.

3. Add the salam leaves and laos root and stir. Add the salt, sugar, and tamarind liquid. Cook, stirring, for about 1 minute.

4. Add the coconut cream and bring to the boil. Add the tomato wedges and simmer for about 5 minutes. Do not overcook.

Yield: 6 or more servings with other Indonesian dishes.

Note: To make tamarind liquid, blend 2 tablespoons tamarind seeds (available in Asian food shops) with ¼ cup water. Let stand for 30 minutes. Using the fingers, work the mixture until the soft solids loosen from the seeds. Put through a strainer, pushing as much of the soft solids through as possible.

TEMPURA

2 egg yolks

2 cups ice water

2 cups plus about 3 tablespoons flour, sifted

Oil for deep-frying

Foods to be deep-fried (see following suggestions)

Salt to taste

Lemon wedges for garnish

Tempura dip (see following recipe)

It has been observed that all the world's cuisines can be categorized according to their most characteristic cooking medium: Chinese cooking is based on oil, French on butter, and Japanese on water. It has long been a source of puzzlement that, where the Japanese kitchen is concerned, there is one outstanding exception, and that is tempura. On a trip to Osaka, we found out why. Shizuo Tsuji, the distinguished head of the largest hotel school in Japan, told us that tempura was brought into Japan by Portuguese priests who came to Japan in the sixteenth century. Tempura's original form was probably what the French call beignets and the English call fritters.

1. Place the yolks in a mixing bowl and beat well, preferably with chopsticks.

2. Add the ice water, stirring constantly. When well blended, add 2 cups of flour all at once, stirring. Do not overblend. The batter, when ready, should be fairly lumpy.

3. Heat oil to the depth of about 2 inches in a utensil suitable for deep frying. When it is very hot but not smoking, add any combination of the ingredients listed below and prepared as indicated. Cook batter-coated foods until golden but not browned.

4. Lift from the fat and drain on absorbent paper towels. As the foods are added and cooked, it is important to skim the surface of the oil to remove any loose bits of batter and particles of food that rise to the top. If the batter seems too thin at any point, sprinkle the surface with a tablespoon of flour and stir briefly, leaving it lumpy.

5. Continue cooking until all the foods are deep fried. Sprinkle the tempura lightly with salt and garnish with lemon wedges. Serve with the tempura dip.

Yield: Any number of servings, depending on the quantity of foods cooked.

FOODS TO BE DEEP-FRIED

The single essential ingredient of any tempura is shrimp. All the other batter-fried foods are side dishes. Here are some of the ingredients that may be dipped in batter and deep-fried for the tempura:

Shrimp: Peel the shrimp but leave the last tail segment intact. Make slight gashes in the shrimp at ½-inch intervals on the underside. When ready to cook, dip lightly in flour, then in batter, and deep-fry. Drain and serve hot.

Squid: Clean the squid thoroughly or buy them cleaned. All the inner digestive tract should be eliminated as well as all bone or cartilage. The outer mottled skin, as well as the very fine, transparent under skin, should be pulled away and discarded. Rinse the flesh and pat it dry. Cut the squid into strips measuring about 4 inches by 1 inch. Score on the underside. When ready to cook, coat lightly in flour and dip in batter. Deep-fry, drain, and serve hot.

Fresh mushrooms: In Japan there are numerous varieties of wild mushrooms included in an elaborate tempura. They include matsutake or pine tree mushrooms; enikodake, delicate, long-stemmed, white-fleshed mushrooms with a tiny cap, generally fried in bundles; and shiitake, the large black mushroom caps common in Japanese and Chinese cookery, which, if not available fresh, may be soaked from the dried state, squeezed, and patted dry. They may then be floured, dipped in batter, and deep-fried. Drain and serve hot.

Fish: Almost any white-fleshed, nonoily fish may be cut into bite-size pieces and used. Conger eel, which is quite fatty, is, on the other hand, a frequent addition to a tempura. Sometimes the skinless, boneless eel is used, sometimes whole small fillets. Very small fish are frequently used whole, while some small fish are sometimes butterflied, boned, and used.

All these are dipped in flour, then in batter, and deep-fried, drained, and served hot.

Onions: Cut onions into ½-inch-thick slices and skewer with toothpicks to keep the rings intact. Dip in flour, then batter, and fry. Drain and serve hot.

There are also special foods—deep-fried without batter—that may be added to an elaborate tempura:

Shrimp: Peel the shrimp, leaving the last tail segment intact. Dip the peeled portion in flour, then in egg white, then liberally in a choice of crushed almonds, fine cracker crumbs, white sesame

seeds, or finely chopped bean thread (cellophane noodles). Deep-fry, drain, and serve hot.

Small fish fillets with green noodles: Break enough Japanese green noodles (green soba) into fine pieces to make ½ cup. Dip fillets in flour, then egg white, then coat with noodles. Deep-fry. This gives a porcupine effect. Serve hot.

Small fish fillets with egg noodles: Break enough Japanese egg noodles (udon) into fine pieces to make ½ cup. Dip fillets in flour, then in egg white, then coat with noodles. Deep-fry. This gives a porcupine effect. Serve hot.

Miniature eggplant: The eggplant must be very small (no more than 3 inches in length). Leave the eggplant whole and with stems on. Slice them from bottom to center, about half way up, at ¼-inch intervals. Deep-fry until cooked through.

Miniature hard-shell crab (very small soft-shell crabs could be substituted): If the miniature crabs are available, break off and discard the tiny "apron" on the front of each. Drop the crab into very hot fat. Cook for 30 seconds or less and drain. Serve as is.

Scallops: Use bay scallops or cut ocean scallops into bite-size pieces. Skewer or not, as desired. Dip in flour, then in egg white, then liberally in a choice of crushed almonds, fine cracker crumbs, white sesame seeds, or finely chopped bean thread (cellophane noodles). Deep-fry, drain, and serve hot.

Shrimp "toast" sandwiches: Blend enough raw shrimp to make ½ cup of purée. Stir in half an egg yolk and salt to taste. Cut trimmed white bread slices in half or into quarters. Spread one piece with the shrimp mixture, cover with another slice, sandwich fashion, and cook in very hot oil until brown on one side. Turn and brown on the other. Drain, cut into small squares, and serve hot.

Japanese cooks also prepare deep-fried gingko nut meats stuffed with the same shrimp mixture as for toast. The gingko nuts are sliced down the center without cutting through. The opening is sprinkled lightly with flour and filled with a small portion of the shrimp mixture. The gingko nut meats are skewered and deep-fried.

TEMPURA DIP

2½ cups dashi (see recipe
   page 802)

½ cup dark soy sauce

½ cup mirin (sweet sake),
   available in wine and
   spirit shops near Asian
   communities

1 cup well-packed
   katsuobushi, shaved
   bonito flakes, available
   in most Japanese
   grocery stores

   Grated Japanese white
   radish, available in
   Asian markets

Combine the dashi, dark soy sauce, and mirin and bring to the
boil. Add the katsuobushi and stir. Remove from the heat immediately. Let stand for about 30 seconds, skimming the surface as necessary. Strain. Serve with grated radish on the side so that guests
may add their own.

Yield: About 3½ cups.

STEWS AND CASSEROLES

Many decades of observing the cooking and dining patterns of Americans has led me to the conclusion that cooks have one need that, if met, would put them in a state of absolute nirvana in the kitchen. Particularly those cooks with a desire to entertain guests and relax over cocktails with them. The need is for a dish, subtly seasoned and tempting, that can be made hours or even days in advance, or, for that matter, frozen and defrosted on schedule. The answer, of course, is stews, braised dishes, and casseroles. Many in this chapter will also feed a crowd, a boon during holiday seasons.

Beef Braised with Red Wine

1. Preheat the oven to 400 degrees.

2. Sprinkle the beef on all sides with salt and pepper to taste. Heat 1 tablespoon oil in a deep, heavy casserole or Dutch oven. Brown the meat on all sides for 15 or 20 minutes, turning often. When ready, the beef should have a nice mahogany color without being burned.

3. Scatter the cubed onion, carrot, celery, and garlic around the meat. Stir and add the wine, beef broth, bay leaf, thyme, parsley, and cloves. Cover closely and place in the oven. Bake for 1½ hours.

4. Reduce the oven heat to 350 degrees. Continue baking for ½ hour.

5. Meanwhile, combine the onions, turnips, carrots, and celery to be used for the garnish in a kettle of cold water to cover and salt to taste. Bring to the boil. Simmer for about 2 minutes and drain.

6. Heat the butter in a large kettle and cook the sautéed vegetables and mushrooms, swirling the skillet and stirring the vegetables, for about 5 minutes, or until they start to take on a golden color.

7. Remove the meat from the oven and cool the meat briefly. Pour off the cooking liquid and strain through a sieve, pressing the vegetables with the back of a wooden spoon to extract as much of the juices as possible.

8. Remove the string from the meat and return the meat to the casserole. Add the vegetables and the strained sauce. Cover and return to the oven. Bake for 30 minutes longer.

Yield: 6 servings.

THE BRAISED BEEF:

    One 3½- to 4-pound boneless chuck roast, tied with string
    Salt and freshly ground pepper to taste

1 tablespoon peanut, vegetable, or corn oil

1 large onion, cut into ½-inch cubes

1 carrot, trimmed, scraped, and cut into ½-inch cubes

2 celery ribs, trimmed, cut in half, and cut into ½-inch cubes

1 garlic clove, finely minced

2 cups dry red wine

1 cup beef broth

1 bay leaf

3 fresh thyme sprigs, or ½ teaspoon dried

4 fresh parsley sprigs

2 whole cloves

THE VEGETABLE GARNISH:

10 or 12 small white onions, about ½ pound, peeled

2 or 3 white turnips, about ½ pound, peeled, and quartered

3 carrots, about ½ pound, trimmed, scraped, halved, and cut into 2-inch lengths

2 celery ribs, trimmed, quartered lengthwise, and cut into 2-inch lengths

1 tablespoon butter

¼ pound fresh mushrooms, halved, quartered, or left whole, depending on size

BEEF AND MUSHROOMS IN RED WINE

4 pounds lean, boneless chuck steak

⅓ cup plus 2 tablespoons peanut, vegetable, or corn oil

Salt and freshly ground pepper to taste

⅛ teaspoon ground cloves

2 cups coarsely chopped onions

2 bay leaves

¼ teaspoon dried thyme

3 tablespoons flour

3 cups dry red wine

1 cup water

½ pound carrots, preferably baby carrots

¾ pound fresh mushrooms

2 tablespoons Cognac

¼ teaspoon freshly grated nutmeg

There was a time when the one great French dish known to almost all Americans was something called beef bourguignonne. Over the years its popularity has faded. Nonetheless it is one of the great basic recipes in Western cuisine. Here is our version made with mushrooms and the slightest hint of nutmeg.

1. Trim the beef of all fat. Cut it into 2-inch cubes.

2. Heat the ⅓ cup of oil in a kettle and add the cubed beef. Sprinkle with the salt and pepper.

3. Cook over relatively high heat, stirring the beef so that the cubes brown evenly. As the meat cooks, it will give up a good deal of liquid. Cook over high heat until most of the liquid has evaporated.

4. Add the cloves, onions, bay leaves, and thyme and stir. Cook for about 5 minutes.

5. Sprinkle with the flour and stir so that the pieces are evenly coated.

6. Add the wine and water. Bring to the boil. Cover closely and simmer for about 1½ hours. Uncover the kettle and let the meat continue to simmer for about 10 minutes. Meanwhile, prepare the carrots and mushrooms.

7. If the carrots are very small, trim and scrape them. If large, cut them into quarters lengthwise and cut each length in half. Put the carrots in a saucepan and add water to cover. Bring to the boil and simmer for 5 minutes. Drain and add them to the stew.

8. Rinse the mushrooms under cold water. Drain well. If the mushrooms are quite small, leave them whole. Otherwise, cut them into quarters or halves.

9. Heat 2 tablespoons of oil in a large skillet and, when it is quite hot, add the mushrooms. Cook, shaking the skillet and stirring, over high heat. When the mushrooms start to brown, drain them in a sieve and add them to the stew.

10. Simmer the stew for about 5 minutes. Add the Cognac, nutmeg, and a generous grinding of pepper. Serve with noodles or rice.

Yield: 8 servings.

CARBONNADE FLAMANDE
(BEEF AND ONIONS COOKED IN BEER)

1. Preheat the oven to 325 degrees.

2. Place the meat on a flat surface. Cut it into slices about ¾ inch thick. Cut the slices into strips about 2 inches wide. Cut the strips into 2-inch lengths. Set aside.

3. Cut the bacon into small pieces. Cook the pieces in a large skillet until lightly browned and crisp. Using a perforated spoon, transfer the pieces to a large heavy casserole, leaving the fat in the skillet.

4. Peel and quarter the onions. Cut each quarter into thin slices. There should be about 7 cups. Set aside.

5. Add the butter to the fat in the skillet. Add one quarter of the cubed meat and cook over high heat, turning the pieces so that they cook evenly. As the meat browns, transfer the pieces to the casserole. Add more meat and continue cooking until all the meat is browned and added to the casserole.

6. Add the onions to the skillet and cook, stirring occasionally, until lightly browned. Add the onions to the meat.

7. Add the garlic, salt, pepper, thyme, bay leaves, sugar, beer, and broth.

8. Spread the bread on both sides with the mustard. Place the slices on top of the stew. Cover closely. Bring to the boil. Place in the oven and bake for 1½ to 2 hours. Cooking time will depend on the tenderness of the meat.

9. Stir the vinegar into the sauce and place on top of the stove. Simmer for about 2 minutes. Pour the stew into a sieve and strain the sauce into a saucepan. Skim off the fat and bring back to the boil. Arrange the meat on a warm serving platter and spoon the sauce over the meat.

Yield: 6 servings.

---

3 pounds boneless chuck in one piece

¼ pound lean bacon

3 large onions, about 1½ pounds

3 tablespoons butter

3 garlic cloves, finely chopped

Salt and freshly ground pepper to taste

2 fresh thyme sprigs, or ½ teaspoon dried

2 bay leaves

1 tablespoon brown sugar

2 cups light beer

1 cup fresh or canned beef broth

3 slices French bread, crusts removed

3 tablespoons Dijon mustard

2 tablespoons red wine vinegar

MASMAN BEEF CURRY

4 large potatoes, about 1 pound, peeled and dropped into cold water

1 medium-size onion, about ½ pound

2¾ cups coconut cream, preferably fresh (see instructions page 800)

2 pounds beef stew meat, cut into 1½-inch cubes

2 tablespoons curry powder

3 tablespoons fish sauce, available in Asian markets

¼ cup sugar

¾ cup shelled peanuts

1½ cups fresh or canned, unsweetened coconut milk

1½ cups water

When Amnuay Nethongkome came into our kitchen to cook his native Thai dishes, he was the saucier at Le Cirque, one of Manhattan's chicest dining establishments. Prior to that he had been at Maxwell's Plum under Jean Vergnes and at Luchow's—a long way from Bangkok. Mr. Nethongkome and his Thai-born wife regaled us with dishes made with lemongrass, dried lime leaves, and that thin essence of anchovy called fish sauce, which they use in quantity. The Nethongkomes subsequently opened a Thai restaurant in Miami.

1. Cut the potatoes into ½-inch-thick rounds and set aside in cold water.

2. Quarter the onion lengthwise. Cut the onion into lengthwise shreds. There should be about 1½ cups.

3. Heat the coconut cream in a large skillet and add the beef cubes. Bring to the boil and cook uncovered, stirring occasionally, for about 20 minutes, or until the liquid is thickened and saucelike. Remove the pieces of meat and set aside. Add the curry powder and stir rapidly with a whisk.

4. Add the fish sauce and stir well. Add the sugar. Stir.

5. Return the meat to the sauce. Cook for 10 minutes.

6. Add the onions, drained potato rounds, and peanuts. Add the canned coconut milk and water. Cover and bring to the boil. Cook for 45 minutes to 1 hour, until the meat is tender.

7. Spoon out the beef onto a warmed serving platter. Allow the sauce to rest for a minute, then skim off the surface fat and pour the sauce over the meat before serving.

Yield: 10 servings.

CALIFORNIA CASSEROLE

1. Preheat the oven to 350 degrees.
2. Cook the meat in oil until it loses its red color. Add the garlic, salt, pepper, onion, green pepper, and chili powder. Cook for 5 minutes, or until onion is wilted.
3. Add Worcestershire, Tabasco, tomatoes, kidney beans, and rice and turn into a buttered 2-quart casserole. Bake, uncovered, for 45 minutes.
4. Sprinkle with olives and cheese and bake for 15 minutes longer, or until the cheese has melted.

Yield: 8 servings.

1 pound ground round steak

1 tablespoon peanut oil

1 garlic clove, finely minced

Salt and freshly ground pepper to taste

1 large onion, finely chopped

1 green pepper, cored, seeded, and chopped

1 tablespoon chili powder

1 tablespoon Worcestershire sauce

Tabasco sauce to taste

One 16-ounce can Italian plum tomatoes

One 16-ounce can kidney beans

¾ cup rice

¼ cup chopped stuffed green olives

¾ cup shredded Cheddar cheese

PICADILLO (A MEAT STEW WITH OLIVES AND CAPERS)

1 cup dried currants

4 tablespoons peanut, vegetable, or corn oil

3 cups finely chopped onions

2 to 4 tablespoons finely chopped garlic

3 cups chopped green peppers

One 10-ounce jar stuffed green olives

Three 3½-ounce jars capers, drained

½ cup white vinegar

Salt to taste

1 tablespoon freshly ground pepper

¾ teaspoon cinnamon

1 teaspoon ground cloves

2 bay leaves

Tabasco sauce

6 pounds ground round or chuck

12 cups peeled, chopped tomatoes

Freshly cooked rice

There are some dishes in this world that are all but impossible to describe because their contents change from home to home and country to country. I would place picadillo (*picadinho* in Brazil) in this category, for I have never found two versions closely allied. The only ingredients that seem common to all picadillos are ground meat, tomatoes, and onions. Some versions include eggs and red wine, some raisins and vinegar, and so on. In Texas, picadillo is frequently served as a dip with tortilla chips, although it is good served in a bowl like chili.

1. Place the currants in a bowl and add warm water to cover. Let stand until they plump, about half an hour.

2. Meanwhile, heat half of the oil in a very large kettle and add the onions, garlic, and green peppers. Cook, stirring, until wilted. Add the green olives, capers, vinegar, salt to taste, pepper, cinnamon, cloves, bay leaves, and Tabasco sauce to taste. Cook, stirring, for about 10 minutes.

3. In a large casserole or Dutch oven, heat the remaining oil and add the meat. Cook, stirring with the side of a wooden spoon to break up all lumps. Cook only until the meat loses its red color.

4. Add the green olive mixture and stir to blend.

5. Drain the currants and add them.

6. Add the tomatoes and cook, stirring often, for about 1 hour. Skim off the fat as it rises to the surface. Serve hot with rice.

Yield: 18 or more servings.

MACARONI AND BEEF CASSEROLE

1. Preheat the oven to 450 degrees.

2. Drop the macaroni into boiling salted water and simmer until the macaroni is barely tender. Do not overcook because the dish will bake later in the oven. Drain in a colander and place under cold running water.

3. In a skillet, heat 1½ tablespoons of the butter and add the onion and green pepper. Cook, stirring, until the onion is wilted. Add the meat and cook, stirring, until it loses its red color. If there is an accumulation of liquid fat in the skillet, drain well in a large sieve. Return the meat mixture to the skillet. Add the basil, oregano, and tomatoes. Cook for 3 minutes.

4. In a saucepan, heat the remaining 2 tablespoons of butter and stir in the flour, using a wire whisk. Add the milk, stirring rapidly with the whisk. Cook, stirring, for about 5 minutes. Remove the sauce from the heat and stir in the Cheddar cheese. Stir until it melts. Add the salt and pepper, nutmeg, and cayenne.

5. Spoon the macaroni into a baking dish. Ours measured 7 × 10 × 2½ inches. Spoon the meat mixture over the macaroni and pour the cheese sauce over all. Sprinkle with Parmesan cheese and bake for 30 minutes, or until hot and bubbling throughout. Run under the broiler briefly to glaze.

Yield: 4 to 6 servings.

1½ cups elbow macaroni

3½ tablespoons butter

¾ cup chopped onion

¼ cup finely chopped green pepper

1 pound chopped ground chuck or round

1 teaspoon dried basil

1 teaspoon dried oregano

½ cup drained tomatoes

3 tablespoons flour

2 cups milk

2 cups (about 10 ounces) cubed Cheddar cheese

Salt and freshly ground pepper to taste

¼ teaspoon grated nutmeg

Cayenne to taste

Grated Parmesan cheese

MOUSSAKA À LA GRECQUE
(AN EGGPLANT AND MEAT CASSEROLE)

6 tablespoons olive oil

3 cups finely chopped onions

3 cups rich, concentrated but not too salty beef broth

3 pounds lean ground chuck

Salt and freshly ground pepper to taste

2 cups tomato sauce, approximately (see following recipe)

3 large eggplants, about 4 pounds total weight

3 cups water

¾ cup dry red wine

2 quarts béchamel sauce, approximately (see following recipe)

¼ cup fine fresh bread crumbs

4 cups freshly grated cheese, preferably a combination of Parmesan and pecorino (use twice as much Parmesan as pecorino), or use all Parmesan

2 eggs, lightly beaten

Milk

1. Preheat the oven to 400 degrees.

2. Heat 4 tablespoons of the oil in a large kettle and add the onions. Cook, stirring, until wilted and add ½ cup beef broth. Cook, uncovered, until most of the liquid has evaporated. Add the ground meat and stir briefly. Add the remaining broth and cook, breaking up any lumps with the side of a wooden spoon. Add very little salt. Remember that the meat will become saltier as the broth cooks down. Add pepper to taste. Cover closely and let simmer for about 1½ hours.

3. As the meat cooks, prepare the tomato sauce and set aside.

4. Meanwhile, trim off the ends of the eggplant but do not peel it. Cut the eggplant lengthwise into slices about ⅛ inch thick. Save the outside, unpeeled slices of the eggplant along with the inside slices. Select a baking pan, preferably an enameled pan measuring about 17 × 11½ × 2 inches. Arrange the unpeeled outside slices of eggplant against the inside of the pan, resting them upright, slices slightly overlapping. Arrange more slices of eggplant, standing them upright and edges slightly overlapping. Arrange them in neat rows, one against the other, until all the slices are used. They probably won't fill the pan. Add 3 cups of water and cover closely with foil. Bake for 35 minutes and remove. Uncover and pour off most of the liquid from the pan. Let the eggplant slices stand until cool.

5. When the meat has cooked the specified time, select a small wire strainer and a small ladle. Dip the strainer into the meat, pressing down to allow the liquid to accumulate in the center of the strainer. Use the ladle to scoop out most of the liquid. Specifically, scoop out and discard all but about 1 cup of liquid.

6. Add the tomato sauce and red wine to the meat sauce and continue cooking for about 1 hour, or until the meat sauce is quite thick. Remove from the heat and let cool slightly while proceeding to the béchamel sauce.

7. Rub the pan in which the eggplant slices were baked with 2 tablespoons of oil. Sprinkle with bread crumbs and shake to coat the bottom and sides of the pan. Shake out the excess.

8. Discard the sliced, outside ends of the eggplant. Arrange about half the remaining slices of eggplant over the crumb-coated pan, edges slightly overlapping. Sprinkle with ¾ cup of cheese.

9. Beat the eggs with ¼ cup of the grated cheese and stir it into the meat sauce. Bring to the boil, stirring.

10. Spoon the meat sauce over the layer of eggplant, smoothing the top with a rubber spatula. Sprinkle the meat with another ¾ cup of cheese. Arrange a second layer of eggplant over, edges slightly overlapping. There may be too many slices. Use for another purpose. Sprinkle the second layer of eggplant with ¾ cup of grated cheese. Spoon the béchamel sauce over the top and smooth it over with a spatula. Sprinkle with ¾ cup of cheese.

11. When ready to cook the moussaka, preheat the oven to 350 degrees. Place the pan in the oven and bake for 40 to 45 minutes, or until the topping is barely set in the center. Remove the moussaka from the oven and let cool for 30 minutes or longer.

12. Although the moussaka could be served directly from the oven, it is infinitely preferable to refrigerate it overnight before serving. This will allow the moussaka layers to become firm prior to cutting into serving pieces.

13. After refrigeration, remove the moussaka and cut it into 12 to 20 pieces of more or less equal size. When ready to serve, preheat the oven to 500 degrees. Pour a thin layer of milk into the bottom of 1 or more baking pans. Disposable aluminum foil baking pans are good for this. Arrange 2 or more squares of moussaka in each pan and bake until piping hot throughout, about 15 minutes. The pieces should be almost but not quite touching. Transfer the squares to individual dishes, sprinkle with more cheese, and serve immediately.

Yield: 12 to 20 pieces.

Combine all the ingredients for the tomato sauce in a saucepan and cook, uncovered, for about 30 minutes.

Yield: About 2 cups.

TOMATO SAUCE

2 cups tomato purée

Salt and freshly ground pepper to taste

1 tablespoon grated nutmeg

½ teaspoon ground cinnamon

2 tablespoons sugar

BÉCHAMEL SAUCE

½ pound butter

¾ cup flour

½ cup cornstarch

7 cups hot milk

3 eggs, lightly beaten

¼ teaspoon nutmeg

1. Heat the butter in a 3-quart saucepan. When melted, add the flour, stirring with a wire whisk. Add the cornstarch and stir to blend.

2. Add about one third of the milk, stirring rapidly with the whisk. Quickly add another one third, stirring rapidly and constantly, covering all the bottom and sides of the saucepan. Add the last of the milk, stirring rapidly and constantly.

3. When thickened and smooth, remove from the heat. Beat the eggs and nutmeg and add to the saucepan, stirring with the whisk. Cook briefly, stirring constantly.

Yield: About 2 quarts.

OXTAIL RAGOUT WITH MUSHROOMS

6 pounds oxtail, cut into pieces

Salt and freshly ground pepper to taste

2 cups coarsely chopped onions

2 cups coarsely chopped celery with leaves

2 garlic cloves, finely minced

1 teaspoon dried thyme

1 bay leaf

6 tablespoons flour

1 bottle (3 cups) dry red Burgundy

2 cups water

3 cups fresh or canned beef broth

1 cup whole tomatoes, peeled and crushed

4 whole cloves

6 fresh parsley sprigs

10 or 12 whole carrots, about 1¼ pounds

1 pound mushrooms

2 tablespoons butter

1. Preheat the oven to 375 degrees.

2. The oxtail pieces should be well trimmed, leaving only a light layer of fat all around each piece. Sprinkle with salt and pepper. Use one or two large heavy skillets and add the oxtail pieces, fat side down. It is not necessary to add additional fat. Brown the pieces well on all sides, turning the pieces often, for 40 to 45 minutes.

3. Transfer the pieces to a large deep casserole or Dutch oven and continue cooking, without adding liquid or fat, for about 10 minutes longer, stirring and turning the pieces in the casserole. Pour off any fat that accumulates.

4. Add the onion, celery, garlic, thyme, and bay leaf and stir to distribute the ingredients. Sprinkle the flour evenly over the surface and stir to coat the ingredients. Add the wine, water, beef broth, tomatoes, salt, pepper, cloves, and parsley.

5. Cover and bring to the boil on top of the stove. Place the casserole in the oven and bake for 2 hours.

6. Meanwhile, trim and scrape the carrots. Quarter the carrots lengthwise and cut the pieces into 1½-inch lengths. There should be about 4 cups. Drop the carrots into boiling salted water to cover and cook for about 5 minutes. Drain and set aside.

7. If the mushrooms are large, quarter or slice them. Heat the butter in a skillet and add the mushrooms with salt and pepper to taste. Cook, stirring, for about 5 minutes. Set aside.

8. When the oxtail is tender, remove the pieces to a large bowl. Add the carrots and mushrooms. Put the sauce in which the oxtails cooked through a fine sieve, pushing the solids through as much as possible. Return the sauce to the casserole, add the oxtails and vegetables, and cook briefly until piping hot.

Yield: 8 to 12 servings.

MEAT WITH BEANS AND PARSLEY, PERSIAN STYLE

American cooks, by and large, have never been great experimenters with herbs and spices. Rosemary is not, as it is for the Italians, a basic part of our culinary heritage. And neither is tarragon, which could be called a herbal basic of the French kitchen. Cumin and coriander are foundations of Middle Eastern cooking, and ginger is an integral part of a good deal of Chinese food preparation.

But there is one herb that seems to be indigenous to the cooks of this nation, whether they are *cordons bleus* or neophytes. That herb is parsley, perhaps the most innocent of all herbs where flavor is concerned, but also by far the most versatile. That is not to say parsley is without flavor, but it does not have the positive assertiveness of, say, coriander or mint.

That is one reason why we are fascinated with recipes and dishes in which parsley becomes a dominant factor. One of them is a Persian creation, known as gormeh sabzee, that we discovered many years ago in Iran. It is a cubed meat dish made with lamb, beef, or veal that calls for no less than 12 cups (the amount varies from kitchen to kitchen, but it is always an abundant quantity) of the herb.

1. Put the beans in a large saucepan or kettle and add 4 cups of the water, the salt, and pepper. Stick the onion with the cloves and add it to the beans. Bring to the boil and let simmer, partly covered, for about 1 hour and 15 minutes, or until tender.

2. In a large casserole or Dutch oven, melt 4 tablespoons of the butter and add the parsley and scallions. Cook, stirring often, for about 5 minutes.

3. Melt the remaining 2 tablespoons of butter in a large skillet and add the meat. Add salt and pepper to taste. Cook, turning the cubes of meat often, until lightly browned. Add the parsley and scallion mixture and the remaining 3 cups of water. Add the lemon juice and the quartered lemon. Bring to the boil. Cover and simmer for 45 minutes to 1 hour, or until the meat is almost totally tender.

4. Add the beans and stir to blend. Continue cooking until the meat is tender, about 10 minutes longer.

Yield: 8 or more servings.

1 pound light red kidney beans

7 cups water

Salt and freshly ground pepper to taste

1 medium-size onion, peeled

2 whole cloves

6 tablespoons butter

12 cups finely chopped parsley

5 cups finely chopped scallions, green part and all

3 pounds veal, beef, or lamb, cut into 1-inch cubes

⅓ cup lemon juice

1 lemon, cut into quarters

INDIA HOUSE LAMB CURRY

6 pounds lean, boneless shoulder of lamb, cut into 1½-inch cubes

½ cup peanut, vegetable, or corn oil, approximately

¾ pound carrots, scraped, quartered, and thinly sliced, about 2 cups

5 celery ribs without leaves, coarsely chopped, about 2 cups

½ pound onions, coarsely chopped, about 2 cups

2 large, tart apples, about ½ pound, peeled, cored, and cut into ½-inch cubes, about 4 cups

½ cup canned sweetened, shredded, dried coconut

1 tablespoon finely chopped garlic

4 bay leaves

1 teaspoon dried thyme

8 tablespoons curry powder, more or less to taste

½ cup flour

7 tablespoons tomato paste

8 cups fresh or canned chicken broth

1 cup chutney

1 cup heavy cream

1. Preheat the oven to 400 degrees.

2. Use two skillets for this, one to brown the meat in batches, the other to receive the meat after the cubes are browned.

3. Pour about ¼ cup of the oil into the first skillet to brown the meat. Add about one quarter of the cubed meat and cook to brown on all sides. When browned, transfer the pieces to the second skillet. Continue cooking in the second skillet. Add a second batch of meat, cook to brown, and so on until all the pieces are browned. Add more oil as necessary to the first skillet.

4. When all the pieces are browned, add any remaining oil, or 2 tablespoons, to the first skillet. Add the carrots, celery, and onions and cook, stirring occasionally.

5. As the vegetables cook in the first skillet, add the cubed apples and coconut to the meat. Add the cooked vegetables, garlic, bay leaves, thyme, curry powder, flour, and tomato paste to the meat. Stir to blend well. Add the chicken broth and stir to blend. Add the chutney. Bring to the boil. Cover and place in the oven.

6. Bake for 1 hour. Transfer the pieces of lamb to a casserole.

7. Put the sauce, a little at a time, into the container of a food processor or blender and blend to a fine purée. As the sauce is processed and smooth, add it to the lamb pieces. Bring to the boil and add the cream. Bring to the boil again and serve hot.

Yield: 12 to 16 servings.

LAMB CURRY WITH YOGURT

1. Heat the oil and butter in a heavy casserole. Add the lamb, onions, garlic, and ginger. Cook, stirring, until the meat loses its raw look and the onions are wilted.

2. Add the curry powder, cinnamon, cumin, turmeric, ground coriander, cardamom, bay leaves, ½ cup of the yogurt, salt, and pepper to taste. Bring to the boil.

3. Cover and cook, stirring often, for about 1 hour and 10 minutes, or until the lamb is fork-tender. Add the remaining yogurt and chopped fresh coriander. Heat briefly and serve with hot rice.

Yield: 6 to 8 servings.

1 tablespoon peanut, vegetable, or corn oil

2 tablespoons butter

4 pounds cubed lamb, preferably from the leg

2 cups finely chopped onions

1 tablespoon finely chopped garlic

2 tablespoons finely chopped fresh ginger

1 tablespoon curry powder

¼ teaspoon ground cinnamon

1 teaspoon ground cumin

½ teaspoon ground turmeric

1 teaspoon ground coriander

½ teaspoon ground cardamom

2 bay leaves

1 cup plain yogurt

Salt and freshly ground pepper to taste

2 tablespoons finely chopped fresh coriander

IRISH STEW

1 rack of lamb, with chine bone removed, about 1¼ pounds boned weight (see note)

2 or 3 large onions, about 1¼ pounds

5 medium potatoes, about 2 pounds

5½ cups cold water

Salt and freshly ground pepper to taste

One of the most amusing days of my life was spent in my kitchen with Sean Kinsella, the chef-owner of the distinguished Mirabeau restaurant on the banks of Dublin Bay in Dublin. He prepared an incredible and delicately flavored Irish stew, and pointed out that the simpler the stew the better it is. His contained no carrots, no turnips, or other extraneous vegetables so common to the usual preparation in this country. The stew was thickened at the end with mashed potatoes. It turns out to be a delight—just the simple and excellent flavor of lamb with onions.

1. Please note that this is as much a thin soup as it is a stew. It will be thickened only with mashed potatoes. It should be served in soup bowls with a knife, fork, and soup spoon.

2. Cut away almost all the fat from the top of the ribs and pull away the thin layer of meat and fat on top of each rack. This layer is connected by a thin membrane. Cut away the thin layer of meat and fat from the tops of the ribs, leaving the meaty loin intact. Discard the meat trimmings.

3. Cut between the ribs, separating the ribs into chops. Set aside.

4. Cut each onion into six segments of more or less equal size. Set aside.

5. Peel the potatoes and drop them into cold water to prevent discoloration. Cut three of the potatoes crosswise in half. Cut the remaining two potatoes into quarters. Leave the potatoes in cold water until ready to use.

6. Run the lamb under cold water until the water runs clear. Drain well. Arrange the chops neatly over the bottom of a casserole and add the 5½ cups of cold water. Add the salt and pepper and bring to the boil.

7. At the moment the liquid comes to the boil, strain the cooking liquid and set it aside.

8. Run the chops under cold water to chill well. Drain.

9. Return the chops to a clean casserole or kettle. Cover with the onion wedges.

10. Drain the potato halves and quarters. Arrange the halved potatoes around the sides of the casserole over the chops.

11. Skim off all the scum and fat from the reserved liquid. Add the liquid to the chops in the casserole.

12. Cover the contents of the casserole with several layers of wax paper and bring to the boil. The paper must touch the top of the stew. Cook for about 30 minutes.

13. Meanwhile, put the quartered potatoes in a saucepan with cold water to cover and bring to the boil. Cook for about 20 minutes over high heat until potatoes are almost falling apart and most of the liquid evaporates.

14. Add the potato liquid to the stew. Put the potatoes through a ricer or food mill. Add the mashed potatoes, stirring them gently into the stew. Cover the top of the stew once more with wax paper and continue cooking over very gentle heat for 10 minutes.

Yield: 6 servings.

Note: Ask the butcher to cut away the chine bone. This is the backbone attached to the meaty part of the racks, away from the rib tips.

Navarin d'Agneau (A Ragout of Lamb)

2¼ pounds lean shoulder
of lamb, cut into 2-inch
cubes and including a
few rib bones

Salt and freshly ground
pepper to taste

2 carrots

2 celery ribs

1 or 2 white turnips

2 potatoes

2 cups water

½ cup chopped onion

1 garlic clove, finely
minced

½ cup dry white wine

2 tablespoons tomato
paste

1 bay leaf

2 fresh thyme sprigs, or
½ teaspoon dried

½ cup frozen peas

1. Sprinkle the meat with the salt and pepper and set aside.

2. Trim the carrots, celery, turnips, and potatoes, peeling as necessary. Quarter the carrots and cut them into 1½-inch lengths. Cut
the celery into pieces of the same size. Cut the turnips into
½-inch slices. Cut the slices into pieces the same size as the
carrots.

3. Cut the potatoes into ½-inch slices. Cut the slices into "sticks"
the size of french-fried potatoes. Drop into cold water.

4. Heat a skillet large enough to hold the meat in one layer. Do not
add fat. The meat has enough fat. Add the cubes of meat and
cook to brown well on all sides, turning as necessary as the pieces
give up fat. The browning will take from 10 to 15 minutes.

5. Transfer the pieces of meat to a heavy casserole and heat briefly,
stirring.

6. Pour off the fat from the kettle in which the meat was browned.
Add 1 cup of the water and stir to dissolve the brown particles
that may cling to the bottom and sides of the kettle. Set aside.

7. Add the onion and garlic to the meat and stir. Add the wine and
cook briefly. Add the skillet liquid. Add the remaining cup of
water, tomato paste, bay leaf, and thyme. Bring to the boil and
cook for 1 hour.

8. Meanwhile, cover the carrots, celery, and turnips with cold water
and bring to the boil. Drain and set aside.

9. Drain the potatoes. Put them in a saucepan, cover with cold
water, and bring to the boil. Drain.

10. When the stew has cooked for 1 hour, add the carrots, celery, and
turnips. Cook for 20 minutes. Add the potatoes and cook for
5 minutes longer. Add the peas and continue to cook for 5 minutes, or until the potatoes are tender.

Yield: 6 to 8 servings.

Lamb Stew, Moroccan Style

1. Heat a large heavy skillet or wide casserole until very hot. Do not add fat. Add the lamb and cook over high heat, stirring the pieces to prevent sticking. Cook for about 10 minutes, stirring often, until meat is nicely browned.

2. Transfer the meat to another dish. Add the onion to the skillet. Cook for about 5 minutes, stirring. Add the zucchini, eggplant, hot pepper, salt, and pepper. Cook, stirring, for about 2 minutes.

3. Return the meat to the skillet and stir. Add the cumin, coriander, tomatoes, water, salt, and pepper to taste. Cover closely and cook over low heat for about 1 hour.

4. Uncover and cook for about 5 minutes longer to reduce the sauce a bit.

Yield: 6 or more servings.

4 pounds lamb, cut into 2-inch cubes

Salt and freshly ground pepper to taste

1 large onion, peeled and cut into 1-inch cubes, about 2 cups

2 zucchini, trimmed and cut into 1-inch cubes, about 3 cups

1 eggplant, trimmed, peeled, and cut into 1½-inch cubes, about 4 cups

1 small hot dried red pepper

1 teaspoon ground cumin

1 teaspoon crushed coriander seeds

2 cups canned tomatoes with tomato paste

3 cups water

LAMB STEW WITH BEANS

1 pound small white
dried beans, preferably
California small white
beans or Minnesota
pea beans

2¼ pounds lean shoulder
of lamb, cut into 2-inch
cubes and including a
few rib bones

Salt and freshly ground
pepper to taste

¾ cup chopped onion

2 garlic cloves, finely
minced

One 14-ounce can
tomatoes with tomato
paste

10 cups water

2 fresh thyme sprigs, or
½ teaspoon dried
thyme

1½ bay leaves

1 small onion stuck with
2 cloves

1 large carrot, trimmed
and scraped

1. Soak the beans overnight in cold water to cover to a depth of 2 inches.

2. Sprinkle the lamb with the salt and pepper. Heat a skillet large enough to hold the meat in one layer. Do not add fat. The meat has enough fat. Add the cubes of meat and cook to brown well on all sides, turning as necessary as the pieces give up fat. The browning will take from 10 to 15 minutes.

3. Transfer the pieces of meat to a heavy casserole and sprinkle with onion and garlic. Cook briefly. Add the tomatoes, 2 cups of the water, thyme, 1 bay leaf, salt, and pepper. Cover and cook for about 1½ hours.

4. Pick over the beans to remove any foreign material. Put the beans in a saucepan and add the remaining 8 cups water, half a bay leaf, onion stuck with cloves, and whole carrot. Bring to the boil and simmer 1 to 1½ hours, skimming the surface as necessary. Test for doneness.

5. When the lamb is tender and cooked, drain the beans and remove the bay leaf and thyme sprigs. Remove carrot and cut it into ½-inch dice. Add the beans and carrot to the lamb stew. Cover and cook for 10 minutes.

Yield: 8 servings.

SHEPHERD'S PIE

1. Prepare the lamb and set it aside.

2. Heat 1 tablespoon of the butter in a casserole and add the onions, garlic, and thyme. Cook briefly until the onions wilt. Add the meat and bay leaf. Cook, stirring to break up lumps in the meat. Add salt and pepper to taste and sprinkle with the flour. Add the tomatoes and water, stirring. Cover and cook for 30 minutes. Add the parsley.

3. Meanwhile, peel the potatoes. Cut them into quarters and put them in a saucepan. Cover with cold water and add salt to taste. Bring to the boil and simmer until tender, about 20 minutes.

4. Drain the potatoes and put them through a food mill. Bring the milk to the boil. Add the milk to the potatoes and beat in the remaining butter.

5. Spoon the lamb stew into a baking dish (a dish measuring about 8½ × 13½ × 2 inches is a suitable size). Top with the mashed potatoes and smooth them over. Sprinkle with cheese.

6. When ready to cook, preheat the oven to 400 degrees.

7. Bake for 20 minutes. Run under the broiler to glaze. Serve hot.

Yield: 6 to 8 servings.

2½ pounds raw or cooked ground lamb
 3 tablespoons butter
 2 cups chopped onions
 2 teaspoons finely chopped garlic
 ½ teaspoon thyme
 1 bay leaf
   Salt and freshly ground pepper
 2 tablespoons flour
 1 cup crushed tomatoes
 ½ cup water
 ¼ cup finely chopped parsley
 2 pounds potatoes
 2 cups milk
 ½ cup grated Gruyère or Swiss cheese

Couscous

2¾ pounds meaty but bony parts of lamb, such as neck or shoulder, but preferably the shank, cut into 2-inch pieces with bone

10 medium-size onions, about 2½ pounds

1½ tablespoons salt

4 quarts plus 1 cup cold water

4 teaspoons finely ground pepper

2 teaspoons ground dried ginger

¼ teaspoon ground saffron

3 pounds medium-grain couscous

3 teaspoons olive oil, approximately

One 3-pound whole, fresh pumpkin, or use acorn squash

2 pounds carrots

1 pound seedless raisins

1 can (2 cups) chickpeas

½ cup sugar

¼ pound butter, at room temperature

People of taste who dote on Moroccan cooking tend to find it among the most sensual foods on earth. It is without question one of the world's great cuisines. A steaming platter of perfectly prepared couscous, to our palate, is about as close as one need come to feasting on heavenly manna.

The name involves two things. Couscous is a fine, blond-colored cereal that resembles grain. It is also the finished dish in which these grains are cooked and served with a sweet and savory meat sauce. This version, with lamb and pumpkin, is from Paula Wolfert, who lived for ten years in North Africa and has written extensively on Moroccan cuisine.

1. Put the lamb in a kettle, preferably into the bottom of a couscousière (couscous cooker).

2. Peel the onions and cut them in half lengthwise. Place each half cut side down and cut them into slices about ½ inch thick. There should be 7 or 8 cups. Add the onions to the kettle. Add the salt, 4 quarts of water, pepper, ginger, and saffron and bring to the boil. Cook for 45 minutes.

3. Meanwhile, put the couscous in a large bowl and add cold water to cover, stirring constantly with the hands to prevent the grains from sticking and to thoroughly moisten all the grains. Immediately pour the couscous into the top steamer of the couscousière, or into a colander that will fit closely inside a kettle, and let drain. Some of the grains may fall through. Empty the grains into a very large, open bowl. Let dry for about 10 minutes.

4. The grains will cake together. Using the fingers, break up the grains, working well to break up all lumps so that all the grains are totally separate.

5. Remove the cover from the stew. Add the steamer to the top of the couscousière. When the steam starts to rise in the holes of the steamer, add about one fourth of the couscous grains. When the steam is again apparent, add the remaining couscous. Cook for 15 minutes.

6. Remove the steamer from the stew and transfer the couscous once more to the large bowl.

7. Blend 1 cup of cold water and salt to taste. Spoon this over the couscous and, using a large metal spoon, toss the grains and spread them out so that the grains will cool quickly. Let stand for half an hour.

8. Grease the hands with oil and toss the grains, breaking up any lumps. Do this three times, oiling the hands each time before working the grains.

9. Return the couscous to the steamer and replace it over the stew. Let steam for 30 minutes. Remove the couscous again and, using the back of the spoon, spread out once more in the large bowl. Let dry once more.

10. Cut the pumpkin into eighths. Peel it. Scrape away and discard the seeds. Cut the pumpkin flesh into 3-inch pieces. There should be about 8 cups.

11. Trim and scrape the carrots. Depending on size, cut the carrots into 2-inch lengths, or split in half and cut into pieces about 2 inches long. There should be about 6 cups.

12. At this point the stew may be taken off the stove and set aside for several hours until ready for a final cooking. Cover the couscous with damp paper towels.

13. When ready for the final cooking, add the pumpkin, carrots, raisins, chickpeas, and sugar to the stew. Add more salt and pepper to taste. Bring to the boil and cook for 10 minutes. Put the steamer on the kettle. Add the couscous. Steam for 20 minutes.

14. Distribute the butter over the top of the couscous and let it melt down.

15. Pour and spoon the couscous out into a large (very large) round or oval platter. Make a well in the center and spoon about one third of the stew into the center. Spoon some of the outside couscous onto the stew. Add more couscous. More stew. Spoon up more couscous. More stew and so on.

16. Serve with any leftover stew on the side (there will be quite a bit).

Yield: 12 or more servings.

COUSCOUS WITH CHICKEN

½ cup dried chickpeas

2 tablespoons butter

One 2½-pound chicken, cut into serving pieces

½ teaspoon ground cumin

1 tablespoon finely grated fresh ginger

½ teaspoon ground turmeric

¼ teaspoon saffron stems, optional

2 teaspoons finely chopped garlic

Salt and freshly ground pepper

1 leek, trimmed, rinsed, and cut into small cubes, about ¾ cup

1 cup tomatoes cut into quarters

6 very small white onions, quartered

4 cups chicken broth

2 celery ribs, trimmed and cut into 1½-inch lengths, optional

3 small carrots, peeled, trimmed, and cut into 1-inch lengths

1 red or green sweet pepper, cored, seeded, and cut into 2-inch cubes

3 very small turnips, cut into quarters

2 small zucchini, trimmed and cut into 1-inch cubes

Couscous (see following recipe)

Hot pepper sauce (see following recipe)

This is one of the best and simplest recipes for couscous, made with chicken instead of the more traditional lamb.

1. Soak the chickpeas for at least 6 hours in water to cover. Drain and cook in water to cover about 2 inches above the peas for about 15 minutes, or until tender.

2. Heat the butter over low heat in a casserole and add the chicken. Turn the pieces in the butter and sprinkle with the cumin, ginger, turmeric, saffron, if used, garlic, salt, and a generous grinding of pepper. Cook, stirring, until the chicken starts to lose its raw color.

3. Add the leek, tomatoes, onions, and chicken broth and bring to the boil. Simmer for 20 minutes.

4. Add the celery, if used, carrots, and sweet pepper and continue cooking for about 5 minutes. Add the turnips and cook for 5 minutes. Add the zucchini and drained chickpeas and cook for 5 minutes.

5. Press a sieve into the broth and scoop out 3 cups of broth for the couscous.

6. To serve, spoon a generous amount of couscous into individual soup bowls. Serve the chicken and vegetables on top. Ladle a generous amount of broth over each serving. Take a spoonful of the hot broth and add as much hot sauce as you desire. Stir to dissolve. Spoon this over each serving.

Yield: 6 servings.

1. Put the couscous in a saucepan. Pour the hot broth over it. Cook over low heat, stirring, for about 2 minutes. Cover and remove from the heat.

2. Let stand for 10 minutes, or until ready to serve. Before serving, fluff the couscous with a fork.

Yield: 6 servings.

Note: Quick-cooking couscous is available in packages in supermarkets. For this recipe, do not use bulk, long-cooking couscous.

COUSCOUS (THE CEREAL)

1½ cups couscous cereal (see note)

3 cups strained liquid from the couscous with chicken (see preceding recipe)

1. Combine the pepper flakes and water in a small saucepan. Bring just to the boil, stirring.

2. Remove from the heat and add the oil and coriander.

Yield: About 6 tablespoons.

Note: The traditional hot pepper sauce served with couscous is called harissa. It is available in stores that specialize in imported foods and many supermarkets.

HOT PEPPER SAUCE

2 tablespoons crushed hot red pepper flakes

3 tablespoons water

1 tablespoon olive oil

½ teaspoon ground coriander

CHICKEN AND SAUSAGE GUMBO

1 chicken (2½ pounds),
   cut into serving pieces
   Salt to taste
1 teaspoon finely ground
   black pepper
1¼ teaspoons finely
   ground white pepper
1 teaspoon dry mustard
1½ teaspoons cayenne
1½ teaspoons paprika
2 teaspoons finely
   minced garlic
1 teaspoon filé powder,
   optional
1½ cups flour
2½ cups corn, peanut, or
   vegetable oil
¾ cup finely chopped
   onion
¾ cup finely chopped
   celery
¾ cup finely chopped
   sweet green peppers
9 cups fresh or canned
   chicken stock
1¾ cups chopped or thinly
   sliced smoked sausage
   such as kielbasa (see
   note)
1 bay leaf
2 cups cooked rice

1. Put the chicken pieces in a bowl. Blend the salt, black and white peppers, mustard, cayenne, paprika, 1 teaspoon of the garlic, and filé powder. Rub 4 teaspoons of the mixture over the chicken. Reserve 2 teaspoons of the spice mixture and discard the rest.

2. Put the flour and the reserved spice mixture in a bowl. Blend well.

3. Heat a 10-inch black iron skillet and pour in the oil. Dredge the chicken pieces in the flour mixture to coat well, shaking off the excess. Reserve the leftover flour.

4. When the oil is hot and almost smoking, add the chicken pieces skin side down. Cook for about 2 minutes on one side, until golden brown. Turn and cook for about 3 minutes on the second side, until nicely browned. Drain thoroughly on paper towels.

5. Pour off all but 1 cup of fat from the skillet. Heat this oil over high heat until it is almost smoking and add the reserved seasoned flour. Stir rapidly and constantly with a wire whisk until the mixture starts to look like dark chocolate. Do not burn. This is a roux.

6. Add the chopped onion, celery, and green peppers to the roux and stir to blend well. Remove from the heat without allowing it to burn.

7. Meanwhile, bring the stock to a boil in a large saucepan.

8. Add about ½ cup of the roux mixture to the stock, stirring rapidly with the whisk. Continue adding the roux mixture to the stock, ½ cup at a time, always stirring rapidly and constantly.

9. Add the smoked sausage and stir. Cook over high heat, stirring often from the bottom, about 15 minutes.

10. Add the chicken pieces, bay leaf, and the remaining teaspoon garlic. Continue cooking for about 40 minutes.

11. Remove the chicken pieces. Cut the meat from the bones and discard the bones. Cut the chicken meat into cubes and add it to the gumbo. Serve with rice spooned into the gumbo.

Yield: 6 or more servings.

Note: The smoked pork sausage traditionally used to prepare this dish is smoked andouillete, which is common in Louisiana.

TURKEY GUMBO

1. Discard the turkey skin. Scrape the herbs and all the stuffing from the turkey carcass carefully, especially if sage was used. Break up the carcass. Put it in a tall straight-sided 4-quart soup pot and add the water to cover. If that amount doesn't cover, the pot is too wide. Bring to the boil and skim off the foam. When the broth is clear, add the carrot, whole onion, and celery. Cover and simmer for 1 hour.

2. Remove the carcass. Pick off meat and dice it. Discard the vegetables. Strain and skim stock and return the turkey meat to it.

3. Heat 2 tablespoons of the butter with the bacon or ham. In the combined fat slowly sauté the garlic, chopped onion, green pepper, and okra until golden brown and okra is no longer stringy, about 25 minutes. Add to the stock along with tomatoes, thyme, bay leaf, and cayenne.

4. Simmer gently for 30 minutes, adjusting seasoning as you do so.

5. Heat the remaining 4 tablespoons of butter in a small heavy-bottomed saucepan. When bubbling, add the flour and stir until smooth. Cook very, very slowly, stirring almost constantly, for about 10 minutes, or until the roux is a dark coffee color. The flour will seem to take a long time before it begins to color, but once it does it burns quickly, so give it your undivided attention. When the roux is a good dark espresso color (but not burned), cool slightly, then stir it into the simmering gumbo. Cook for 30 minutes more.

6. Adjust the seasoning and serve in a bowl with a mound of white rice heaped in the center of each serving.

Yield: 8 or more servings.

1 turkey carcass with meat
2 to 2½ quarts water
1 large carrot
1 large onion
2 celery ribs with leaves
6 tablespoons butter
2 tablespoons minced raw bacon or lean ham
1 garlic clove, minced
1 large onion, chopped
1 sweet green pepper, seeded and chopped
1 pound okra, sliced
3 cups chopped canned tomatoes
1 teaspoon dried thyme
1 large bay leaf
Pinch of cayenne
3 tablespoons flour
Salt to taste
Steamed white rice

PORK AND GREEN CHILI STEW

3 pounds lean pork, cut into 2-inch cubes

Salt and freshly ground pepper to taste

2 tablespoons lard or vegetable oil

2 cups finely chopped onions

1 tablespoon finely chopped garlic

1 tablespoon crumbled dried oregano

Two 15¼-ounce cans tomatillos, available in Spanish markets

One 4-ounce can chopped green chilies, available in Spanish markets

2 tablespoons finely chopped fresh coriander, plus whole coriander leaves for garnish

2 cups fresh or canned chicken broth

Sour cream

1. Sprinkle the pork with salt and pepper.

2. Heat the lard in a large heavy skillet in which the cubed pork will fit in one layer. When the fat is very hot, add the pork and cook, stirring the pieces often, over very high heat. Cook until browned on all sides.

3. Add the onion and garlic and cook, stirring, until the onion is wilted. Sprinkle with oregano and stir.

4. Drain the tomatillos. Blend with the chilies in a food processor or blender. Add this to the stew. Add the chopped coriander leaves.

5. Add salt and pepper to taste. Add the broth and bring to the boil. Cover and cook for 1¼ hours, or until the pork is fork-tender.

6. Garnish with sprigs of fresh coriander. Serve with sour cream on the side.

Yield: 8 or more servings.

PORK AND POTATO STEW

1. Cook the sausages in a heavy casserole or Dutch oven. When they start to give up their fat, add the neck bones and pork chops. Cook, stirring and turning, to brown well.

2. Add the tomatoes, water, carrots, salt, and pepper to taste and cook for 45 minutes. Add the remaining ingredients and cook for another 45 minutes, or until all the meats are tender.

Yield: 4 to 6 servings.

Note: Pork chops, boneless pork, or spareribs, all cut into 2- or 3-inch cubes, may be substituted for the neck bones.

4 links sweet or hot Italian sausage

2 pounds pork neck bones (see note), cut into 3- or 4-inch pieces

2 shoulder pork chops, each cut into thirds

One 17-ounce can whole tomatoes, preferably Italian peeled tomatoes

1 cup water

4 carrots, thinly sliced

Salt and freshly ground pepper

5 potatoes, about 1½ pounds, peeled and cut into 1½-inch cubes

2 onions, about ½ pound, thinly sliced

½ teaspoon dried basil

½ teaspoon dried oregano

Jambalaya

¼ pound salt pork, cut into small cubes

¾ pound hot link sausages, such as chorizos or hot Italian sausages

4 cups finely chopped onions

3 cups finely chopped celery

3 tablespoons finely minced garlic

4 cups chopped sweet green peppers

1 cup chopped sweet red peppers

3 pounds porkette (smoked boneless pork butt) or a cooked ham in 1 thick slice

3 bay leaves

3 fresh thyme sprigs, or 1 teaspoon dried

1 can (35 ounces) imported Italian tomatoes

1 cup finely chopped parsley

Salt and freshly ground pepper to taste

Tabasco sauce to taste

1 quart shucked oysters with their liquor

4 cups fish stock (see recipe page 801) or bottled clam juice

4 cups water

5 cups rice

5 pounds raw shrimp, shelled and deveined

1½ pounds fresh bay scallops

There is some dispute as to the exact origin of the name *jambalaya*, the excellent blend of rice and other ingredients including—depending on your recipe—sausage, shrimp, crawfish, and ham, among other things. In the most definitive book on Creole and Cajun cooking. *Chef Paul Prudhomme's Louisiana Kitchen*, the author quotes the *Acadian Dictionary*, written by Rita and Gabrielle Claudet and published in Houma, Louisiana, in 1981. Jambalaya, the dictionary declares, "comes from the French 'jambon' meaning ham, the African 'ya' meaning rice, and the Acadian [language] where everything is 'à la.' " If you really want to be authentic, the ham used in a basic jambalaya is a Cajun specialty called tasso. It is a highly seasoned ham and rarely found outside Louisiana.

1. Using a large kettle or Dutch oven, cook the salt pork cubes, stirring often, until rendered of fat.

2. Cut the sausages into ½-inch-thick slices and add them to the kettle. Cook for about 8 minutes, stirring occasionally, and add the onions. Cook, stirring often, until wilted, and add the celery, garlic, green peppers, and red peppers.

3. Cut the porkette or ham into 1-inch cubes and add it to the kettle. Add the bay leaves, thyme, tomatoes, parsley, salt, pepper, and Tabasco sauce. Continue cooking. Drain the oysters and add the liquor, ½ to 1 cup, to the pot.

4. Add 2 cups of the fish stock and 2 cups of the water. Cook, stirring once or twice from the bottom, about 10 minutes.

5. Add the rice and stir gently. Cover and cook for about 15 minutes. If necessary, add a little more stock and water to prevent sticking and to keep the jambalaya from becoming too dry.

6. Add the remaining stock and water, the shrimp, scallops, and oysters. Cook, stirring often from the bottom, 15 to 20 minutes. If necessary, add more liquid to prevent scorching and drying out.

7. Serve with a bottle of Tabasco sauce on the side.

Yield: 24 or more servings.

CHOUCROUTE GARNIE

1. Drain the sauerkraut and press to extract most of the liquid. If you wish a milder dish, run cold water over it and drain again, pressing. Set aside.

2. Heat the lard in a large heavy skillet.

3. Sprinkle the spareribs with the salt and pepper. Add them to the lard and brown on all sides. Scatter the onion and garlic between the ribs and cook briefly, stirring.

4. Put the sauerkraut over and around the ribs. Pour the broth and wine over all. Place the pork butt in the center of the sauerkraut.

5. Add the cloves, juniper berries or gin, caraway seeds, bay leaf, salt, and pepper. Bring to the boil and cover. Cook for about 30 minutes and add the potatoes. Cover again and cook for 15 minutes longer.

6. Add the kielbasa and cover again. Cook for 15 minutes longer, or until the sausage is piping hot throughout.

Yield: 6 to 8 servings.

4 pounds sauerkraut

2 tablespoons lard, bacon fat, or vegetable oil

2 pounds country-style spareribs

Salt and freshly ground pepper to taste

1 cup finely chopped onion

1 garlic clove, finely minced

2 cups fresh or canned chicken broth

1 cup dry white wine

2 pounds smoked pork butt

2 whole cloves

8 juniper berries, or ½ cup dry gin

½ teaspoon caraway seeds

1 bay leaf

12 small white potatoes, scrubbed and peeled

1¼ pounds kielbasa (Polish sausage)

CASSOULET

2 pounds dried pea beans marked "no soaking necessary"

3 quarts water

1 onion stuck with 4 cloves

1 bay leaf

1 carrot, trimmed and scraped

Salt and freshly ground pepper to taste

¾ pound slab of lean salt pork with rind

1 garlic sausage (cotechine)

3 tablespoons goose fat or peanut oil

1 tablespoon finely chopped garlic

2 cups chopped onions

One 35-ounce can tomatoes

Lamb stew (see following recipe)

½ preserved goose in its fat (see recipe page 245)

Roast pork (see following recipe)

3 tablespoons bread crumbs made from toasted bread

4 tablespoons butter, melted

It is one of the great mysteries of gastronomy why the greatest wine and food regions on earth happened to be allotted to France. It is as though nature, untold centuries ago, played some gigantic dice game that bestowed on Burgundy and Bordeaux the most fertile soil for wine. Strasbourg got geese and the Périgord truffles. Normandy was awarded apples and cream. Provence got the olive groves, garlic fields, and the fruits of the Mediterranean for the express purpose of contriving a dish called bouillabaisse.

In the southwest area of France there is a small arc defined by three towns that fell heir to a peculiar endowment. These towns in the region called Languedoc are Toulouse, Castelnaudary, and Carcassonne. Together they are responsible and celebrated for the cassoulet, one of the three greatest winter dishes known to man (the other two are onion soup and sauerkraut).

Over the years, cassoulet has sparked more controversy and produced more heat than a pyromaniacal maître d'hôtel flaming his crêpes. The contretemps in this casserole includes the kinds of beans to be used. To prepare a true cassoulet, must the beans come from Pamiers or Sazères, as some connoisseurs aver? Are the white haricots of Soissons acceptable?

The three main meats for a cassoulet (pork, lamb or mutton, and goose) vary from Castelnaudary to Toulouse to Carcassonne. Could you combine all three? Can you add partridge? Must or may you add preserved goose, duck, pork, and so on?

These are arguments that will, happily, never be concluded, and there will always be a body of fortunate jurists sitting at table and sampling them all with knife, fork, or spoon in hand and that blissful grin that can derive only from dining well.

1. Pick over the beans and wash them well. Place the beans in a kettle with the water, onion, bay leaf, carrot, salt, pepper, and salt pork. Prick the garlic sausage in several places with a 2-pronged fork and add it. Bring to the boil and simmer for 30 minutes.

2. Remove the garlic sausage and set aside. Continue cooking the beans for 30 minutes and remove the salt pork.

3. Slice off and reserve the salt pork rind. Cut the rind into ¼-inch dice and set aside. Return the salt pork meat to the kettle.

4. Heat the goose fat in a saucepan and add the diced pork rind. Add the garlic and chopped onion. Cook for about 10 minutes without browning. Add the tomatoes and let simmer, stirring often, for about ½ hour.

5. When the beans are tender, drain them but reserve the beans,

salt pork, and cooking liquid. Discard the whole onion and bay leaf. Put the beans in a kettle and add the tomatoes and the lamb stew, including broth meat and sauce. Stir to blend and add salt and pepper to taste. Cover and simmer for about 10 minutes.

6. Cut the salt pork into neat, ¼-inch-thick slices and set aside.

7. Skin the garlic sausage and cut into neat, ¼-inch-thick slices and set aside.

8. Heat the goose, including the gizzard and wing if they are present. Remove the pieces and cut or pull the meat from the bones. Slice the meat as neatly as possible.

9. Cut the pork from the bones and slice it neatly. Save the pan juices from the roasting pan. Pour off the fat.

10. Spoon about a third of the beans into a large casserole and arrange the pork slices over all. Add the pan juices.

11. Add a cup of the bean liquid to the remaining beans. Spoon half the remaining beans over the pork. Arrange the sliced preserved goose over all. Add all the remaining beans. Arrange the sliced salt pork and garlic sausage over the top. Scatter the bread crumbs over the top and dribble the butter over.

12. When ready to cook, preheat the oven to 400 degrees and bake for 30 minutes. If the casserole seems too dry, add a little more bean liquid as the cassoulet cooks. When ready to serve, the cassoulet should be piping hot and bubbling throughout.

Yield: 12 or more servings.

LAMB STEW

3 pounds shoulder of
  lamb with bone, cut
  into 2-inch cubes
2 tablespoons oil or
  goose fat
  Salt and freshly ground
  pepper to taste
1 cup finely chopped
  onion
2 garlic cloves, finely
  minced
1 cup dry white wine
2 cups water
3 tablespoons tomato
  paste
1 fresh thyme sprig, or
  1 teaspoon dried
4 parsley sprigs
½ bay leaf

1. Use a heavy skillet and brown the lamb on all sides in the oil.
   Sprinkle with the salt and pepper and add the onion and garlic.
   Stir to blend. Carefully pour off all fat.
2. Return the skillet to the heat and add the remaining ingredients.
3. Cover closely and cook for 1 hour and 15 minutes, or until the
   lamb is fork-tender.

Yield: 6 to 8 servings, or enough for one large cassoulet.

ROAST PORK

One 3-pound center-
  cut pork loin
Salt and freshly ground
  pepper to taste

1. Preheat the oven to 425 degrees.
2. Sprinkle the pork all over with the salt and pepper. Place the pork,
   fat side down, in a baking dish and bake for about 20 minutes.
   Turn the pork and continue cooking for about 20 minutes. If it
   starts to brown too quickly, cover loosely with a sheet of aluminum foil. Continue baking for about 20 minutes, or until thoroughly cooked and tender.

Yield: 4 servings, or enough for one large cassoulet.

BLANQUETTE DE VEAU

Blanquettes and fricassees are stews that are enriched with cream and egg yolks. The word *blanquette* derives from *blanchir*, which in French means to cook without browning. With a fricassee, from *fricasser*, which means to cut up and fry, on the other hand, the meat is cooked until it starts to brown.

One of the most unusual blanquettes we've ever sampled came to us from Aline Landais, a young Frenchwoman living in America. It is made with veal and cauliflower, a distinctive combination that we have tried on several occasions and each time the result has been uncommonly appealing.

1. Preheat the oven to 350 degrees.

2. Place the meat in a kettle and add cold water to cover. Bring to the boil. When the water boils vigorously, drain the meat and run it under cold running water until thoroughly chilled.

3. Return the meat to the kettle and add 5 cups of chicken broth. Add the onion stuck with cloves, whole garlic cloves, bay leaf, salt, and half the nutmeg. Tie the peppercorns and thyme in a cheesecloth bag and add it. Bring to the boil on top of the stove.

4. Cover and place in the oven. Bake for 1 hour.

5. Meanwhile, cut away and discard the core from the cauliflower. Break the cauliflower into florets, each piece about 1¼ inches in diameter. Set aside.

6. Prepare the small onions and celery in separate batches. Prepare the mushrooms and sprinkle with lemon juice to prevent discoloration.

7. Put the cauliflower in a saucepan and add enough of the chicken broth to barely cover. Simmer briefly until tender but still firm to the bite. Drain but reserve the liquid. Similarly, cook the onions and celery in separate batches but always saving and using the same liquid.

8. Put the mushrooms in a saucepan and cover with the same liquid. Bring just to the boil and drain.

9. After the veal has cooked for 1 hour, add the carrot rounds and celery. Bake for 30 minutes longer, or until the meat is tender.

10. Pour the cooking liquid from the kettle into a saucepan. There should be 4 cups. Cook over high heat and reduce the liquid to 3 cups. Add the heavy cream. Combine this with the meat, cauliflower, onions, celery, and mushrooms. Bring to the boil.

5 pounds boneless shoulder of veal, cut into 1½- or 2-inch cubes

7 cups fresh or canned chicken broth, approximately

1 medium onion stuck with 4 cloves

2 whole garlic cloves, unpeeled

1 bay leaf

Salt to taste

½ teaspoon freshly grated nutmeg

1 teaspoon peppercorns

½ teaspoon dried thyme

1 medium-size head of cauliflower

16 to 24 small white onions, the smaller the better, peeled

1 cup celery sticks measuring about ½ inch thick and 1½ inches long

½ pound fresh mushrooms, left whole if small, or cut into halves or quarters if large

Juice of ½ lemon

1 cup thin carrot rounds

1 cup heavy cream

½ cup sour cream

4 egg yolks, lightly beaten

1 tablespoon lemon juice

1 tablespoon lime juice

⅛ teaspoon cayenne

11. Blend the sour cream with the beaten egg yolks. Add the remaining nutmeg, lemon and lime juices, and cayenne. Stir this into the liquid around the meat, stirring over gentle heat just until the sauce comes to the boil. Do not boil for more than a few seconds or the sauce will curdle. Remove the cheesecloth bag.

Yield: 8 to 12 servings.

FRICASSEE OF VEAL

1. Cut the breast of veal into 2-inch cubes, chopping through the bone. Or have this done by the butcher. The bone is important.

2. Place the cubed breast of veal and the stewing veal in a large mixing bowl and place under the cold water tap. Let the water run in a trickle for 1 hour. This will whiten the meat. Drain.

3. Heat the butter in a heavy casserole and add the meat. Cook for 5 minutes and sprinkle with salt and pepper to taste. Add the chopped onion, half the nutmeg, and the garlic. Tie the thyme, bay leaf, parsley, and cloves in a cheesecloth bag and add it. Add the chicken broth, wine, and cayenne and cover closely. Bring to the boil and cook 45 minutes.

4. Add the carrots, whole onions, and mushrooms and cook for 45 minutes longer.

5. Drain off about 4 cups of the cooking liquid and bring it to the boil. Cook over high heat until reduced almost by half.

6. Blend the cream with the egg yolks, salt, pepper, and the remaining nutmeg.

7. Add the reduced hot mixture to the egg-and-cream mixture, stirring rapidly. Return this to the veal, stirring, but do not boil or it will curdle. Bring just to the boil, however. Remove the cheesecloth bag.

Yield: 10 to 12 servings.

One 4-pound breast of veal

4 pounds stewing veal, cut into 2-inch cubes

4 tablespoons butter

Salt and freshly ground pepper to taste

1 onion, finely chopped

¼ teaspoon grated nutmeg, or more to taste

1 garlic clove, finely minced

6 fresh thyme sprigs, or 1 teaspoon dried

1 bay leaf

6 parsley sprigs

2 cloves

2 cups fresh or canned chicken broth

1 cup dry white wine

⅛ teaspoon cayenne

3 carrots, scraped, quartered, and cut into 2-inch lengths

36 small white onions, the smaller the better, peeled and left whole

¾ pound fresh mushrooms, quartered if large or left whole if small

1 cup heavy cream

6 egg yolks

CURRIED VEAL

4½ to 5 pounds boneless
veal (neck or shoulder
meat of veal is good for
this), cut into 2-inch
cubes

Salt and freshly ground
pepper to taste

2 tablespoons butter

1½ cups chopped onions

2 garlic cloves, finely
minced

½ cup finely chopped
celery

¼ cup curry powder

1 banana, peeled and cut
into small dice, about 1
cup

1 apple, peeled and cored
and cut into small dice,
about 1 cup

1½ cups fresh or canned
chicken broth

½ cup canned tomatoes
with tomato paste

1. Sprinkle the meat with salt and pepper.
2. Heat the butter in a large heavy casserole and add the onions and
   garlic. Add the meat and stir well. Cook briefly until the meat
   loses its pink color. Sprinkle with celery and stir. Add the curry,
   stirring to blend. Add the banana, apple, chicken broth, and tomatoes. Mix well. Cover. Cook the veal, stirring occasionally, until
   the meat is fork-tender, about 1½ hours. Skim off any excess fat
   from the sauce and serve.

Yield: 6 to 8 servings.

VEAL STEW WITH EGGPLANT

1. Sprinkle the veal with the salt and pepper.

2. Heat the oil in a large heavy skillet. It should be large enough to hold the meat in one layer. Brown the meat on all sides, turning the pieces as necessary. This will take 15 or 20 minutes.

3. Add the onions and garlic. Cook briefly, stirring, and sprinkle with the flour. Stir so that meat is coated evenly.

4. Add the eggplant, zucchini, and green peppers. Stir and add the tomatoes, wine, and chicken broth. Add salt and pepper to taste. Stir in the tomato paste, thyme, and water. Bring to the boil. Cover and cook for 1 hour and 15 minutes.

Yield: 8 or more servings.

3 pounds lean veal, cut into 2-inch cubes

Salt and freshly ground pepper to taste

½ cup peanut, vegetable, or corn oil

2 cups diced onions

1 tablespoon finely chopped garlic

¼ cup flour

4 cups diced eggplant

2 cups sliced zucchini

3 cups diced green peppers

3 cups diced tomatoes

1 cup dry white wine

2 cups fresh or canned chicken broth

3 tablespoons tomato paste

1 fresh thyme sprig, or 1 teaspoon dried

1 cup water

Hungarian Goulash

2 tablespoons corn oil

4 cups sliced onions, about 1 pound

4 pounds boneless veal or pork, cut into 2-inch cubes

1 to 3 tablespoons paprika (see note)

2 tablespoons finely chopped garlic

Salt and freshly ground pepper to taste

2 tablespoons flour

2½ cups fresh or canned chicken broth

1½ cups cored, seeded green peppers cut into 1-inch strips

1 cup sour cream, at room temperature, optional

1. Preheat the oven to 350 degrees.

2. Heat the oil in a Dutch oven or deep, heavy saucepan and add the onions. Cook, stirring, until wilted. Add the veal and stir. Cook, stirring often, until the veal loses its red color.

3. Sprinkle with the paprika and stir. Cook for 5 minutes and sprinkle with the garlic, salt, and pepper. Stir briefly and sprinkle with the flour. Stir to coat the pieces of meat and add the chicken broth. Bring to the boil. Cover with a round of wax paper and put the lid on. Place in the oven and bake from 1½ to 2 hours. Cooking time will depend on the quality of the veal. Best-quality veal cooks more rapidly than that of a lesser quality. Pork cooks quickly.

4. Meanwhile, drop the green pepper strips into boiling water and blanch for about 15 seconds. Drain immediately and set aside.

5. Thirty minutes before the stew is fully cooked, sprinkle with the pepper strips. Continue cooking until veal is tender.

6. If desired, add the sour cream. Preferably, it should be beaten with a whisk before adding and stirred in gradually. Serve the stew, if desired, with spaetzli (see recipe below).

Yield: 8 or more servings.

Note: The best Hungarian paprika is available in bulk. It comes in three strengths: sweet, medium, and hot. It should be added to taste.

SPAETZLI

2 cups sifted flour

3 eggs

⅔ cup milk

Salt to taste

⅛ teaspoon grated nutmeg

2 tablespoons butter

1. Place the flour in a mixing bowl. Beat the eggs and add them to the flour, stirring with a wire whisk or a beater. Gradually add the milk, beating or stirring constantly. Add salt and nutmeg.

2. Bring a large quantity of water to a boil in a kettle and add salt. Pour the spaetzli mixture into a colander and hold the colander over the boiling water. Press the mixture through the holes of the colander with a rubber spatula or large spoon. The spaetzli are done when they float on the top. Drain the noodles and spoon them onto a clean towel or paper towels to dry briefly.

3. Heat the butter in a skillet and, when it is hot, add the spaetzli, tossing and stirring for 3 to 5 minutes. Serve hot.

Yield: 4 to 6 servings.

HOMINY AND CHICKEN CASSEROLE FOR A CROWD

1. Heat the oil in a saucepan with a capacity of approximately 6 quarts and add the onions and garlic. Cook, stirring, until wilted. Add the beef, breaking up lumps with the side of a heavy metal spoon. Cook, stirring, until the meat loses its raw look.

2. Add the tomatoes, tomato paste, chicken broth, peppers, oregano, salt, and pepper. Cook, stirring often, for 30 or 40 minutes, or until thickened. Add the sauce suprême and stir.

3. Meanwhile, preheat the oven to 350 degrees.

4. Butter two 8-quart casseroles and add a layer of hominy, a layer of chicken, a layer of sauce, and a layer of cheese in each. Continue making layers, ending with a layer of cheese.

5. Place the casseroles in the oven and bake for 45 minutes, or until piping hot and bubbling throughout.

Yield: 20 to 24 servings.

2 tablespoons olive oil

3 cups finely chopped onions

3 tablespoons finely minced garlic

1½ pounds ground beef

3½ cups imported canned tomatoes

½ cup tomato paste

2 cups chicken broth from poached chicken thighs (see following recipe)

½ cup, more or less, finely chopped seeded fresh or canned jalapeño peppers

2 teaspoons dried oregano

Salt and freshly ground pepper to taste

5 cups sauce suprême (see recipe page 779)

4 teaspoons butter

Six 29-ounce cans hominy, drained, about 18 cups

6 cups shredded chicken made from poached chicken thighs (see following recipe)

6 cups grated sharp Cheddar cheese, about 1½ pounds

POACHED CHICKEN THIGHS

20 chicken thighs, about 6 pounds

2 cups water

2 bay leaves

1 teaspoon dried thyme

2 medium-size onions, each stuck with 2 cloves

1¼ cups coarsely chopped celery

6 fresh parsley sprigs

Salt to taste

14 whole black peppercorns

1. Combine the thighs, water, bay leaves, thyme, onions, celery, parsley, salt, and peppercorns in a 3- or 4-quart kettle. Bring to the boil, partly covered, and simmer for 20 minutes.

2. Remove from the heat and let stand until ready to use. Remove the thighs, strain the broth, and skim off the fat.

Yield: 20 cooked thighs, plus 2 cups broth.

CHICKEN AND RICE, CARIBBEAN STYLE

1. Put the chicken in a dish and massage with salt, pepper, and lime juice.

2. Heat 2 tablespoons of the butter in a large heavy skillet and add the chicken, skin side down. As it starts to brown, add the tomato paste and sugar and continue cooking over high heat until lightly browned, about 10 minutes. Turn the pieces as they cook.

3. Add the onion, celery, and garlic and cook for about 1 minute. Add the Worcestershire sauce. Stir and cook for about 5 minutes. Add the tomatoes. Cook for about 15 minutes. Add half the broth and stir. At boil, set aside.

4. Meanwhile, combine the rice and remaining chicken broth in a separate saucepan and bring to the boil. Cover and cook for about 15 minutes, or until the liquid is absorbed.

5. As the chicken and rice cook, heat the remaining 2 tablespoons of butter in a small skillet and add the chopped cabbage. Cook and stir over low heat for about 10 minutes, until the cabbage is tender. Take care that it does not burn.

6. Before serving, add the rice and cabbage to the chicken. Stir to blend. Bring to the boil and serve.

Yield: 4 to 6 servings.

One 3-pound chicken, cut into serving pieces

Salt and freshly ground pepper to taste

3 tablespoons lime juice

4 tablespoons butter

1 tablespoon tomato paste

1 teaspoon sugar

¾ cup finely chopped onion

½ cup finely chopped celery

1 teaspoon finely minced garlic

2 teaspoons Worcestershire sauce

1 cup chopped fresh or canned tomatoes

3 cups fresh or canned chicken broth

1 cup rice

1 pound cabbage, cored and chopped or finely shredded, about 4 cups

BRUNSWICK STEW

One 9- to 10-pound
capon, or use 2 or 3
chickens with 10
pounds total weight,
cut into serving pieces

Salt and freshly ground
pepper to taste

4   tablespoons butter

3   cups thinly sliced
    onions

2   cups diced sweet green
    peppers, seeded

2   cups diced celery

1   tablespoon finely
    minced garlic

2   dried, hot, red pepper
    pods

3   bay leaves

1   cup coarsely chopped
    fresh parsley

8   cups water

4   cups peeled, chopped
    tomatoes

Two 10-ounce
packages frozen cut
okra

10 or more ears fresh corn
    on the cob, or use
    three 10-ounce
    packages frozen whole
    kernel corn

4   cups shelled baby lima
    beans, or use three
    10-ounce packages
    frozen baby lima beans

¼   cup Worcestershire
    sauce

The name of the following dish is derived from the place of its origin, Brunswick County, Virginia. The dish was originally made with squirrel, but chicken makes a practical and palatable substitute. The dish was created in the early 1800s, and one source states specifically in the year 1828 at a political rally. Some authorities state that only onions were used in the original recipe and that corn and lima beans (which to my taste are essential to the goodness of the dish) were added with the passage of time.

1. Sprinkle the chicken pieces with the salt and pepper. Heat the butter in two large skillets and brown the chicken pieces on all sides. Or use one skillet and do this in several steps.

2. Remove the chicken and add the onions, peppers, celery, and garlic. Cook until the vegetables give up their liquid. Cook until the liquid evaporates and the vegetables start to brown.

3. Return the chicken to the skillet or skillets and add the hot pepper pods, bay leaves, parsley, water, tomatoes, and okra. Cover and cook for 15 minutes.

4. Meanwhile, drop the corn into boiling water and cover. When the water returns to the boil, remove it from the heat. Let stand, covered, for 5 minutes. Drain and let cool.

5. Add the lima beans to the stew and continue cooking for 15 minutes. Uncover and continue cooking for 10 minutes, or until beans are tender.

6. Cut and scrape the kernels off the cob. There should be about 6 cups. Add this to the stew. Add salt and pepper to taste. Stir in the Worcestershire sauce and serve piping hot.

Yield: 18 or more servings.

MY MOTHER'S CHICKEN SPAGHETTI

Curiously, the first Thanksgiving dinner I recall in sum was a non-turkey dinner when I was a child in Mississippi and my mother had a boardinghouse.

At the time of my birth, my father had been a fairly prosperous plantation owner. Shortly before I reached my teens, he lost everything, as the family saying went. Although my mother fancied herself every bit the Southern belle, which she was, in those days Southern belles could open boardinghouses and still maintain status and face. Hers was probably the most elegant table in the entire Mississippi Delta. It was set with her family silver (it had been buried under the smokehouse the day the Yankees came). Each place at the large oval table, which could accommodate twelve to fourteen, was set with a silver goblet in which ice water and sometimes iced tea were served. My father, meanwhile, resorted to raising animals for milk and food.

There were two holidays each year when my mother stipulated that meals would not be served to boarders, all of whom went to visit relatives or friends anyway: Christmas and Thanksgiving.

The nonturkey Thanksgiving came about because the three children in the family announced that they were bored with the daily diet of poultry. Chicken was the least expensive food item in the South and it was served at my mother's table almost invariably once and sometimes twice a day. A vote was taken. Almost in unison we asked for mother's baked spaghetti, a dish made with chicken, ground beef, mushrooms, cheese, tomatoes, and a cream sauce. Thus we had spaghetti fresh from the oven for Thanksgiving dinner, reheated for supper.

One of the stipulations in the recipe, which I believe was strictly my mother's own creation, is that all the ingredients be combined at least 4 hours before baking.

1. Place the chicken with neck, gizzard, heart, and liver in a kettle and add chicken broth to cover and the salt. Bring to the boil and simmer until the chicken is tender without being dry, 35 to 45 minutes. Let cool.

2. Remove the chicken and take the meat from the bones. Shred the meat, cover, and set aside. Return the skin and bones to the kettle and cook the stock down for 30 minutes or longer. There should be 4 to 6 cups of broth. Strain and reserve the broth. Discard the skin and bones.

3. Meanwhile, put the tomatoes in a saucepan and cook down to half the original volume, stirring.

4. Melt 3 tablespoons of the butter in a saucepan and add the flour, stirring to blend with a wire whisk. When blended and smooth,

One 3½-pound chicken with giblets

Fresh or canned chicken broth to cover

Salt to taste

3 cups imported Italian peeled tomatoes

7 tablespoons butter

3 tablespoons flour

½ cup heavy cream

⅛ teaspoon grated nutmeg

Freshly ground pepper to taste

½ pound fresh mushrooms

2 cups finely chopped onions

1½ cups finely chopped celery

1½ cups chopped green pepper

1 tablespoon or more finely minced garlic

¼ pound ground beef

¼ pound ground pork

1 bay leaf

½ teaspoon hot red pepper flakes, optional

1 pound spaghetti or spaghettini

½ pound Cheddar cheese, grated, 2 to 2½ cups

Freshly grated Parmesan cheese

add 1 cup of the reserved hot broth and the cream, stirring rapidly with the whisk. When thickened and smooth add the nutmeg, salt, and pepper to taste. Continue cooking, stirring occasionally, for about 10 minutes. Set aside.

5. If the mushrooms are very small, leave them whole. Otherwise, cut them in half or quarter them. Heat 1 tablespoon of the butter in a small skillet and add the mushrooms. Cook, shaking the skillet occasionally and stirring the mushrooms, until they are golden brown. Set aside.

6. Heat the remaining 3 tablespoons of butter in a deep skillet and add the onion. Cook, stirring, until wilted. Add the celery and green pepper and cook, stirring, for about 5 minutes. Do not overcook. The vegetables should remain crisp-tender.

7. Add the garlic, beef, and pork and cook, stirring and chopping down with the edge of a large metal spoon to break up the meat. Cook just until the meat loses its red color. Add the bay leaf and red pepper flakes, if desired. Add the tomatoes and the white sauce made with the chicken broth. Add the mushrooms.

8. Cook the spaghetti or spaghettini in boiling salted water until it is just tender. Do not overcook. Remember that it will cook again when blended with the chicken and meat sauce. Drain the spaghetti and run under cold running water.

9. Spoon enough of the meat sauce over the bottom of a 5- or 6-quart casserole to cover it lightly. Add about one third of the spaghetti. Add about a third of the shredded chicken, a layer of meat sauce, a layer of grated Cheddar cheese, and another layer of spaghetti. Continue making layers, ending with a layer of spaghetti topped with a thin layer of meat sauce and grated Cheddar cheese.

10. Pour in up to 2 cups of the reserved chicken broth or enough to almost but not quite cover the top layer of spaghetti. Cover and let the spaghetti stand for 4 hours or longer. If the liquid is absorbed as the dish stands, add a little more chicken broth. Remember that when this dish is baked and served, the sauce will be just a bit soupy rather than thick and clinging.

11. When ready to bake, preheat the oven to 350 degrees.

12. Place the spaghetti casserole on top of the stove and bring it just to the boil. Cover and place it in the oven. Bake for 15 minutes and uncover. Bake for 15 minutes longer, or until the casserole is hot and bubbling throughout and starting to brown on top. Serve immediately with grated Parmesan cheese on the side.

Yield: 12 or more servings.

CHICKEN AND RICE CASSEROLE, INDIAN STYLE

1. The chicken should be cut into flat pieces, each about 3 inches square.

2. Heat ½ cup of the oil in a casserole and cook the chicken pieces sprinkled with the salt and paprika until they lose their raw look. Set aside.

3. Heat the remaining cup of oil in a heavy casserole and cook the onions, stirring, until golden brown, about 20 minutes.

4. Wash the rice well and cover with cold water. Let stand for half an hour.

5. Cover the raisins with cold water and let stand.

6. Place the casserole with onions on low heat. Add the cumin seeds, bay leaves, whole cloves, garlic slivers, and drained raisins. Cook, stirring, for 3 minutes. Add the yogurt and salt to taste.

7. Drain the rice and add it to the casserole along with the chicken pieces and any liquid that may have accumulated. Add the crushed cardamom seeds and chicken stock. Sprinkle with kewra, if desired. Cover and cook for 15 minutes.

8. Meanwhile, preheat the oven to 250 degrees.

9. Do not uncover and do not stir, but pick up the casserole firmly with both hands and toss to redistribute the chicken and the rice. Or, if the casserole is too heavy and seems unwieldy, uncover it and gently stir the rice with a rubber spatula to redistribute it.

10. Place the casserole in the oven and bake for 30 minutes.

11. It is preferable to scoop the rice mixture from the casserole to a rice dish with a saucer so that the rice grains do not become sticky.

Yield: 8 to 12 servings.

Note: Kewra is a white spirit that smells vaguely and pleasantly like nasturtiums. It is available in bottles in Indian stores.

2 pounds skinned, boneless chicken breasts

1½ cups peanut, vegetable, or corn oil

Salt to taste

¼ teaspoon paprika

4 cups thinly sliced onions

3 cups short-grain rice, preferably purchased in Indian markets

¾ cup raisins

1 tablespoon crushed cumin seeds

6 bay leaves

6 whole cloves

½ teaspoon slivered garlic

¼ cup thick yogurt (see following instructions)

1 teaspoon crushed cardamom seeds

4¼ cups chicken stock (see following recipe)

½ teaspoon kewra (see note), optional

THICK YOGURT

Line a bowl with cheesecloth. Empty the contents of 1 pint of plain commercial yogurt into the cheesecloth. Bring up the edges of the cheesecloth and tie with a long string. Suspend the cheesecloth bag with the string over the bowl. Let stand for about 2 hours.

INDIAN-STYLE CHICKEN STOCK

The bones of a 3-pound chicken

Water to cover

Salt to taste

2 cinnamon sticks, each about 1½ inches

4 crushed brown cardamom pods

Combine all the ingredients in a saucepan. Bring to the boil and cook, uncovered, for about 45 minutes. Strain.

Yield: About 5 cups.

PAELLA

1. Heat the oil in a paella pan or a wide, shallow, heatproof casserole. When it is very hot, add the garlic and cook, stirring, until it is golden brown. Remove the garlic with a slotted spoon and discard it.

2. Add the onion and cook, stirring, for about 3 minutes. Depending on the source of heat, it will be necessary to shift the pan around so that the foods cook evenly.

3. Add the tomatoes and cook, stirring, for about 5 minutes. Add the sausages and cook for about 1 minute, stirring. Add the shrimp and cook until they turn bright red. Add the capers and tomato paste. Stir briefly and add the clams and scallops. Add the oysters and cook, stirring, for about 2 minutes. Add 5 cups of the chicken broth, the bay leaves, and oregano.

4. Gradually sprinkle the rice into the pan so that it is evenly distributed. After the rice is added, the paella must be stirred constantly until the dish is finished. But do not stir the rice in a circular fashion. Instead, using a wooden spoon, dip it into the paella and stir gently back and forth in a small area. Move the spoon to another part of the pan and stir gently back and forth. Continue, taking care that all areas of the paella are stirred. Add the Tabasco.

5. After the rice has been cooking for 8 or 10 minutes, add 2 more cups of hot chicken broth and continue stirring in the above-mentioned fashion. Cook for about 5 minutes and distribute the chicken over the rice, pushing it into the stew.

6. Continue cooking and stirring and, if the dish seems to become dry, add more hot broth gradually. The dish should not be soupy. The paella is ready when the rice is tender. Remove the bay leaves. Garnish the paella and serve.

Yield: 12 to 18 servings.

¼ cup olive oil

4 garlic cloves, thinly sliced

¾ cup coarsely chopped onion

1½ cups unpeeled tomatoes, cored and cut into cubes

3 chorizos or Spanish sausages, cut into ¼-inch slices

2 cups raw, shelled, and deveined shrimp

¼ cup capers

⅓ cup tomato paste

12 cherrystone clams

1½ cups bay scallops

1 cup drained oysters

7 to 8 cups fresh hot chicken broth (see following recipe)

2 bay leaves

1 teaspoon dried oregano

2½ cups long-grain rice

Tabasco to taste

6 cups cubed, shredded chicken (see following recipe)

Garnish (see following directions)

CHICKEN AND BROTH FOR PAELLA

One 3-pound chicken

9 cups unsalted chicken broth made from the bony parts of chicken, or use water

½ teaspoon freshly ground pepper

Salt to taste

½ teaspoon chopped Spanish saffron

2 large onions, cut into quarters

2 celery ribs with leaves

1. Place the chicken in a kettle and add the remaining ingredients. Bring to the boil and simmer until the chicken is tender.

2. Strain and reserve the broth and the chicken.

3. Remove the meat from the chicken and discard the bones. Cut the meat into bite-size pieces and set aside.

Yield: About 8 cups of broth and 1 chicken.

HOW TO GARNISH PAELLA

The traditional garnishes for a paella include pimientos, generally cut into lozenges or strips; cooked green peas; Spanish olives stuffed with pimientos, and hard-cooked eggs, cut into wedges. The egg yolks may be put through a sieve and sprinkled over all. A piece of seafood such as a clam in the shell is centered in the pan. It is surrounded with wedges of egg white like the spokes of a wheel, with lozenges of pimiento in between. A cup of cooked peas generally serves as a border around the paella. The olives, approximately a cup, are scattered at random.

Paul Prudhomme's Seafood Gumbo

1. Put the oil and flour in a heavy kettle. Cook, stirring with a wire whisk or flat wooden spoon, until the flour goes through several changes of color: beige, light brown, dark brown, light red, and a slightly darker red. You must keep stirring constantly. The cooking will take 5 minutes or slightly longer. This is a roux. Set aside.

2. Melt the butter in a saucepan and add the onion, green peppers, celery, and garlic. Cook, stirring, until the vegetables are wilted. Add the sausage and stir.

3. Add the oregano, thyme, bay leaves, cayenne, white and black peppers, salt, tomatoes, and seafood stock. Bring to the boil and simmer for 15 minutes.

4. Add the tomato and sausage mixture to the roux. Bring to the boil, stirring, and cook for 1 hour.

5. If the blue crabs are used, pull off and discard the apron at the base on the underside of each crab. Cut the crabs in half and pull off and discard the spongy "dead man's fingers." Cut each crab half in two and add to the kettle. Simmer for 1 minute.

6. Add the shrimp and crabmeat. Stir. Cover and set aside for 15 minutes. Serve with rice.

Yield: 8 or more servings.

Note: To be genuinely authentic, the sausage should be a smoked andouillete, which is common in Louisiana.

- ¾ cup peanut, vegetable, or corn oil
- 1 cup flour
- 2 tablespoons butter
- 3½ cups finely chopped onions
- 3 cups finely chopped green peppers
- 2 cups finely chopped celery
- 1 tablespoon finely minced garlic
- 1½ pounds Polish sausage (kielbasa), cut into ½-inch cubes (see note)
- ¼ teaspoon dried oregano
- ½ teaspoon dried thyme
- 2 bay leaves
- ½ teaspoon cayenne
- ¼ teaspoon freshly ground white pepper
- ½ teaspoon freshly ground black pepper
- Salt to taste
- 2 cups chopped fresh or canned imported tomatoes
- 2 quarts seafood stock (see following recipe)
- 4 live blue crabs, optional
- 2 pounds shrimp, shelled and deveined (use the shells for seafood stock)
- 1 pound lump crabmeat

SEAFOOD STOCK

4 pounds fish bones,
preferably with head
on but gills removed

3 quarts water

1½ cups coarsely chopped
onions

1½ cups coarsely chopped
celery

2 cups coarsely chopped
cored tomatoes

Shells from 2 pounds
of shrimp

1. Combine all the ingredients in a kettle. Bring to the boil. Cook the stock down until about 2 quarts of liquid are left.

2. Cook for 5 to 7 hours longer, but always keep the liquid replenished so that it remains at approximately 2 quarts. Strain and discard the solids.

Yield: 2 quarts.

CHINESE CABBAGE CASSEROLE

It is as basic as chopsticks to say that the greatest obstacle in the preparation of a Chinese dinner is the ability to organize dishes in a manner that permits the home cook to join guests at table while maintaining a cool presence. Our friend and colleague, Virginia Lee, suggested this vegetable casserole as one of the dishes for such a dinner because it simmers for almost an hour, leaving the cook free to attend the wok for other dishes to be stir-fried just before serving.

14	dried mushrooms
	One 2½- to 3-pound Chinese cabbage
1	cup peanut, vegetable, or corn oil
	Salt to taste
1	teaspoon sugar
3	fat pads fresh bean curd
1	large piece of chicken fat, or 3 tablespoons melted chicken fat or corn oil

1. Place the mushrooms in a bowl and add boiling water to cover. Let stand half an hour or longer. Drain and cut off and discard the tough stems. Set the whole mushrooms aside.

2. Pull off and discard a few of the large outer leaves of the cabbage. Pull off the remaining leaves and stack them two at a time on a flat surface. Neatly trim the leaves into rectangles, trimming away the tops, bottoms, and sides of the leaves. Cut the leaves into long strips about 1 inch wide.

3. Heat half the oil in a large wok or skillet and add the cabbage strips. Cook over high heat, stirring and turning the cabbage, for about 5 minutes. Add the salt and sugar and cook briefly, stirring, for about 1 minute longer. The cabbage should remain crisp-tender. Transfer the pieces of cabbage to a casserole, arranging them neatly. Add the cabbage juices.

4. Cut each bean curd pad into 4 slices.

5. Wipe out the wok and add the remaining oil. Heat the oil until it is quite hot and add the bean curd slices. Cook for about 5 minutes over high heat until golden brown on one side (it will look like pale French toast or a slightly overcooked omelet). Turn the slices and drain.

6. Arrange the bean curd slices, edges slightly overlapping, around the rim of the cabbage. Arrange the mushrooms in a layer and piled in the center of the bean curd. If a piece of chicken fat is available, place it over the mushrooms to prevent them from drying out. Or brush with melted chicken fat or oil. Cover closely and let simmer for about 50 minutes.

Yield: 12 servings with other Chinese dishes.

PASTA

There is probably not one person in a thousand in this country who knows that the countless sauces destined for pasta cannot, in the classic sense, be used arbitrarily with all pasta regardless of shape, size, color, and texture. Put otherwise, you cannot serve, indiscriminately, all sauces with any kind of pasta.

The rules for which sauce goes with which shape pasta cannot be reduced to a simple, absolute formula. But generalizations are very much in order, particularly when they come from Marcella Hazan, an expert on Italian cuisine who has frequently visited our kitchen and shared her knowledge and enthusiasm.

Generally speaking, she says, sauces that contain pieces of things—things like chopped meat, peas, ham, and so on—go well with a pasta that has a hole (like macaroni), or a shape that catches pieces, spiral shapes for example, and shells.

Very thin sauces are destined for pasta like spaghetti or vermicelli. But there is one exception. If the sauce has a base of olive oil and contains clams, scallops, chopped fish, or seafood, pasta strands such as spaghetti would be quite suitable. Think of linguine with clam sauce.

Homemade pastas go best with sauces that must be absorbed, which is to say sauces that cling—like the cream and cheese sauce tossed with fettuccine and known as Alfredo. You would never—or shouldn't—serve packaged spaghetti with that sauce.

Like most Italian cooks, Mrs. Hazan is firm in her belief that homemade pasta rolled by hand is superior to that prepared by machine. As a concession, she agreed to prepare pasta in my kitchen using a machine.

HOMEMADE PASTA

1. Empty the flour onto a wooden or Formica surface. Make a well in the center and neatly build up a "wall" to surround the eggs. Start beating the eggs with a fork, gradually incorporating the flour.

2. Do not let the eggs overflow; keep the wall built around by pushing with the fingers toward the center. Continue stirring and incorporating flour until all of the flour is added.

3. When the eggs have lost their fluidity (will not overflow the walls), start pushing the flour into the egg mixture, kneading gently, and continue working the flour all over the surface to incorporate all the flour.

4. Remove the pasta. Wash and dry the board and start kneading again by hand. It will get more elastic. Turn the ball of dough as it is kneaded until it has the texture of satiny, nonsticky modeling clay. Wrap in plastic. Let it rest 8 minutes. When you open it, the pasta will seem sticky again. Do not add more flour.

5. Remove the pasta from the plastic wrapping and shape it into a ball. Cut it into 5 pieces of more or less equal size. Set the pasta machine opening to wide (No. 6). Flatten each of the 5 pieces of pasta dough. Run the pieces through the machine, one at a time, without changing the setting. Arrange them on a clean cloth as they are put through. Reduce the setting to the next smaller opening and put the pieces through. When the pasta has gone through the No. 4 opening, stop rolling.

6. Cut each strip of pasta crosswise at the center point. This will make ten pieces. Reduce the opening by half and put the ten strips of pasta through the opening. Let them dry on the cloth, turning from time to time. Let dry for 30 minutes, more or less (see note). Put the sheets of pasta through any desired cutter to produce the shape and/or width you desire. The sheets of pasta when rolled out fine may also be cut by hand for widths the cutters cannot accommodate.

Yield: 1 pound of pasta, or 4 to 6 servings.

Note: One way to test whether the pasta is dry enough is to put one small sheet of pasta through the fine cutter of the machine. If the strands stick together and have to be pulled apart with the fingers, the pasta should be allowed to dry longer.

1¾ cups semolina (durum wheat flour)

3 large eggs (¾ cup)

Pasta with Scallops

1½ pints scallops

⅓ cup plus 4 tablespoons olive oil

2 teaspoons finely chopped garlic

2½ tablespoons finely chopped flat-leaf parsley

Salt to taste

¼ teaspoon finely chopped hot red pepper flakes

2 pounds homemade tonnarelli (see recipe below and double it), or use spaghetti or vermicelli, cooked until al dente and drained

¼ cup toasted bread crumbs

1. Cut each scallop into quarters. Set aside.

2. Heat ⅓ cup of the oil in a wide saucepan and add the garlic. Cook briefly, stirring, without browning. Add the scallop pieces and parsley and 3 tablespoons of the oil, stirring. Add the salt and hot red pepper flakes. Cook for about 1 minute and set aside.

3. Toss the pasta with the scallops and add the remaining tablespoon of oil. Serve sprinkled with toasted bread crumbs.

Yield: 8 servings.

HOMEMADE TONNARELLI (A FINE CUT PASTA)

Prepare the recipe for homemade pasta. When the sheets of pasta have been dried briefly as indicated, put them through the fine cutter of the machine. If the pasta is not to be used immediately, take a few strands of pasta and wrap them around the fingers, bird's nest fashion. Let stand until thoroughly dry like store-bought pasta. They will later be easier to handle.

To cook, drop the pasta into boiling salted water. Cook until just tender, less than a minute after the water returns to the boil. Drain.

Yield: 1 pound of tonnarelli.

PENNE WITH HAM AND ASPARAGUS

1. Using a swivel-bladed vegetable scraper, scrape the sides of the asparagus, starting about 2 inches from the top. Cut off the ends of the spears about 1 inch from the bottom.

2. Split the ham slice in half. Cut the halves into ½-inch-thick strips.

3. Bring enough water to the boil to cover the asparagus spears when they are added. Add the asparagus and cook for about 2 minutes and drain. When cool enough to handle, cut the asparagus into 1-inch lengths.

4. Heat half the butter in a small skillet and add the ham. Cook, stirring and shaking the skillet, until the ham is piping hot.

5. Heat the remaining butter in a skillet and add the asparagus. Cook briefly, stirring, until all of the liquid evaporates, no longer. Add the cream and bring to the boil. Cook for about 5 minutes, until the sauce is thickened. Add the ham.

6. Cook the pasta until al dente. Serve tossed with the pasta sauce and grated Parmesan cheese.

Yield: 8 servings.

1½ pounds fresh asparagus
One 6-ounce boiled ham slice, about ¼ inch thick
2 tablespoons butter
1 cup heavy cream
1½ pounds penne
Grated Parmesan cheese

FETTUCCINE WITH PROSCIUTTO AND PEAS

1. Drop the peas into boiling water. If fresh, they should cook in 1 or 2 minutes. If frozen, they should cook in 10 seconds, or just until the peas are no longer sticking together. Drain and run briefly under cold water. Drain again and return to a saucepan. Add the cream and prosciutto and set aside.

2. Cook the pasta until al dente. Drain quickly.

3. Put the butter in a hot serving dish for tossing the pasta. Add the hot pasta.

4. Heat the cream briefly. Add the peas and prosciutto in the cream to the pasta. Add the cheese, nutmeg, salt, and pepper. Toss well and serve hot.

Yield: 4 servings.

1¼ cups freshly shelled peas, or one 10-ounce package frozen peas
½ cup heavy cream
¼ cup finely shredded prosciutto
1 pound fettuccine
4 tablespoons butter, cut into small pieces
¾ cup freshly grated Parmesan cheese
⅛ teaspoon grated nutmeg
Salt and freshly ground pepper to taste

SPAGHETTI PRIMAVERA

1   bunch broccoli

2   small zucchini

4   asparagus spears, each
    about 5 inches long

1½ cups green beans,
    trimmed and cut into
    1-inch lengths

    Salt to taste

½   cup fresh or frozen
    green peas

¾   cup fresh or frozen
    snow peas

1   tablespoon peanut,
    vegetable, or corn oil

2   cups thinly sliced
    mushrooms

    Freshly ground pepper
    to taste

1   teaspoon chopped hot,
    fresh, red or green
    chilies, or about
    ½ teaspoon dried red
    pepper flakes

¼   cup finely chopped
    parsley

6   tablespoons olive oil

1   teaspoon finely
    chopped garlic

3   cups cubed ripe
    tomatoes

6   fresh basil leaves,
    chopped, about ¼ cup

1   pound spaghetti or
    spaghettini

4   tablespoons butter

2   tablespoons fresh or
    canned chicken broth

½   cup heavy cream,
    approximately

⅔   cup grated Parmesan
    cheese

⅓   cup pine nuts

This inspired blend of pasta and crisp-tender vegetables, such as zucchini, mushrooms, broccoli, and green beans, is a creation of Italian origin that flourished in one of New York's most popular luxury French restaurants, Le Cirque. Although the dish is called spaghetti primavera—spaghetti with a springtime air—it can be served all year and can be reproduced easily in the home.

1. Trim the broccoli and break it into bite-size florets. Set aside.

2. Trim off and discard the ends of the zucchini but do not peel. Cut the zucchini into quarters. Cut each quarter into 1-inch or slightly longer lengths. There should be about 1½ cups, no more. Set aside.

3. Cut each asparagus spear into thirds. Set aside.

4. Cook each of the green vegetables separately in boiling salted water to cover. The essential thing is to cook each vegetable so that it remains crisp-tender. Cook the broccoli, zucchini, green beans, and asparagus for about 5 minutes. Drain well, run under cold water to chill, and drain thoroughly. Combine them in a mixing bowl.

5. Cook the peas and snow peas for about 1 minute if fresh, or 30 seconds if frozen. Drain, chill, and drain again. Combine all the vegetables in the mixing bowl.

6. Heat the peanut oil in a skillet and add the mushrooms. Add salt and pepper to taste, shaking the skillet and stirring. Cook for about 2 minutes. Add the mushrooms to the vegetables. Add the chopped chilies and parsley.

7. Heat 3 tablespoons of the olive oil in a saucepan and add half the garlic, the tomatoes, salt, and pepper to taste. Cook for about 4 minutes, stirring gently so as not to break up the tomatoes more than is essential. Add the basil, stir, and set aside.

8. Heat the remaining 3 tablespoons of olive oil in a large skillet and add the remaining garlic and the vegetable mixture. Cook, stirring gently, just to heat through.

9. Drop the spaghetti into boiling salted water. Cook until al dente. The spaghetti when ready must retain just a slight resilience in the center. Drain well.

10. Melt the butter in a utensil large enough to hold the drained spaghetti and vegetables. Add the chicken broth, ½ cup cream, and cheese, stirring constantly. Cook gently on and off the heat until smooth. Add the spaghetti and toss quickly to blend. Add

half the vegetables and pour in the liquid from the tomatoes, tossing and stirring over very low heat.

11. Add the remaining vegetables and, if the sauce seems too dry, add about ¼ cup more cream. The sauce should not be soupy. Add the pine nuts and give the mixture one final tossing.

12. Serve equal portions of the spaghetti mixture in four to eight hot soup or spaghetti bowls. Spoon equal amounts of the tomatoes over each serving. Serve immediately. Four portions will serve as a main course; six to eight as an appetizer.

Yield: 4 to 8 servings.

COLD SPAGHETTI PRIMAVERA

4 asparagus spears

1 or 2 zucchini, about ½ pound

½ cup fresh green peas

1 cup broccoli cut into small florets

Salt to taste

½ pound spaghetti

¼ pound sliced mushrooms, about 1½ cups

2 cups cubed tomatoes

3 tablespoons chopped fresh basil

¼ cup chopped fresh parsley

1½ cups freshly made mayonnaise

2 teaspoons finely minced garlic

2 tablespoons white vinegar

Freshly ground pepper to taste

½ cup toasted pine nuts

1. Trim and scrape the asparagus. Cut each spear on the bias into 1-inch lengths.

2. Trim off the ends of the zucchini. Slice it lengthwise into quarters. Cut each quarter crosswise into ½-inch-thick pieces. There should be about 2 cups.

3. Use separate saucepans to cook the asparagus, zucchini, peas, and broccoli. Add enough water to each saucepan to cover the vegetables when added. Add salt to taste.

4. Add the vegetables to the saucepans and bring to the boil. Cook each vegetable until crisp-tender. Cook the peas and asparagus for 1 minute or longer, depending on age. Cook the broccoli and zucchini for 5 minutes or less. As the vegetables are cooked, drain them. Set aside.

5. Break the spaghetti strands in half. Cook the spaghetti in boiling salted water until tender, about 7 minutes. Drain and run briefly under cold running water. Drain thoroughly.

6. Put the spaghetti in a mixing bowl and add the cooked vegetables, mushrooms, tomatoes, fresh basil, and parsley. Blend the mayonnaise, garlic, and vinegar in a small bowl. Add this to the spaghetti and vegetable mixture. Add salt and pepper to taste. Toss to blend.

7. Sprinkle with pine nuts and serve at room temperature.

Yield: 8 servings.

FETTUCELLE WITH TUNA AND ANCHOVIES

Alfredo Viazzi came to professional cooking relatively late in life, but became one of the most successful chefs and restaurant owners in New York. He demonstrated his Merlin-like ways with pasta many times in our kitchen, and we include here three of his specialties.

1. Heat the oil and 2 tablespoons of the butter in a casserole. Add the garlic and cook briefly without browning. Add the anchovies and stir. Add the tomatoes and pepper to taste and cook for about 10 minutes.

2. Add the capers, olives, and tuna. Stir to blend. Add the remaining butter and cook for about 10 minutes. Add parsley and salt to taste.

3. Cook the fettucelle until al dente and drain. Serve with the sauce.

Yield: 4 servings.

3 tablespoons olive oil
4 tablespoons butter
1 tablespoon chopped garlic
8 fillets of anchovy, minced
1 cup drained, crushed, Italian plum tomatoes
Freshly ground pepper
⅓ cup drained capers
¾ cup pitted, imported red olives, such as Greek calamati, Spanish Alfonso, or Italian gaeta
1½ cups canned, undrained tuna
1 tablespoon finely chopped parsley
Salt to taste
1 pound fettucelle

Green Tagliarini with Four Cheeses

4 tablespoons butter

¼ teaspoon freshly ground white pepper

¼ pound fontina cheese, cubed

¼ pound Gorgonzola cheese, cubed

¼ pound Bel Paese cheese, cubed

¾ cup grated Parmesan cheese

1 cup heavy cream

1 pound green tagliarini

Salt to taste

1. Melt the butter in a deep saucepan and add the pepper. Add the fontina, Gorgonzola, and Bel Paese cheeses. Stir until the cheeses melt. Stir in the Parmesan cheese and heavy cream.

2. Drop the tagliarini into salted boiling water and cook, stirring frequently, until tender, about 7 minutes. Drain the tagliarini and toss in the cheese mixture.

Yield: 4 to 6 servings.

Spaghetti Carbonara

¼ pound pancetta or lean bacon

2 medium-size onions, finely chopped

3 tablespoons olive oil

Salt and freshly ground pepper to taste

5 tablespoons chopped flat-leaf parsley

½ cup chopped prosciutto

½ pound diced fontina or fontinella cheese

1 pound spaghetti

4 eggs, beaten

Grated Parmesan cheese

1. Cut the pancetta or bacon into 1-inch pieces. Cook in a small skillet until crisp. Drain on paper towels and set aside.

2. Sauté onions in the olive oil. When wilted, add the salt, pepper, parsley, prosciutto, pancetta, and fontina. (If fontinella is used, add to sauce the last few minutes.) Cover and simmer over low heat, stirring often, for 5 to 10 minutes.

3. Cook the spaghetti in boiling salted water until al dente. Drain, place in a serving bowl, add eggs and toss well. Add sauce and toss again. Serve immediately with grated Parmesan cheese.

Yield: 6 servings.

Green Tagliarini with Chicken Livers and Prosciutto

1. Heat the butter in a skillet or casserole and add the onion and carrots. When bubbling, sprinkle with the salt and pepper to taste. Cook gently and without browning for about 8 minutes.

2. Add the parsley and nutmeg. Add the veal and cook, stirring to break up any lumps. When the meat loses its red color, add the chicken livers and cook, stirring, for about 1 minute. Add salt to taste and the sherry. Cook for about 1 minute, stirring, and add the chicken broth. Simmer for about 3 minutes. Add the tomatoes and cook for about 5 minutes.

3. Heat the oil in another skillet and cook the prosciutto for about 3 minutes, stirring. Add to the sauce and continue to cook for about 20 minutes. Serve hot with the cooked pasta.

Yield: 4 to 6 servings.

4 tablespoons butter

½ cup finely chopped onion

¼ cup finely diced carrots

Salt and freshly ground pepper to taste

2 tablespoons chopped parsley

⅛ teaspoon grated nutmeg

½ pound ground meat, preferably veal, although pork or beef might be used

¼ pound chicken livers, cut into ½-inch cubes

1 tablespoon dry sherry

⅓ cup fresh or canned chicken broth

1 cup drained, crushed, peeled, imported Italian plum tomatoes

1 tablespoon olive oil

¼ pound prosciutto, shredded, about 1 cup loosely packed

1 pound tagliarini, cooked until al dente

Penne Modo Mio
(Pasta with Cauliflower and Ham)

2   tablespoons butter

2   tablespoons olive oil

2   cups thinly sliced
    onions

1   teaspoon finely
    chopped garlic

1½ cups cubed boiled ham

2   tablespoons chopped
    fresh basil

2   tablespoons chopped
    fresh parsley

1   cup dry white wine

    Salt and freshly ground
    pepper to taste

½   pound penne

2   cups peeled, raw
    potatoes, cut into
    ½-inch cubes

4   cups cauliflower
    (1 small), broken or
    cut into florets

½   cup grated Parmesan
    cheese

The "mio" in this recipe title is one of our most prized acquaintances, Ed Giobbi. Ed's kitchen is one of those places we always visit with bounding enthusiasm and keen appetite because, although he is a painter and sculptor by profession, he is a splended and inventive cook who goes about his hobby with the cool dexterity of a croupier shuffling cards. He also believes that pasta can be one of the most gratifying and healthy ways to eat economically. This and the following four recipes are ample and delicious proof of his thesis.

1. Have all the ingredients cut, chopped, measured, and ready to cook before starting this dish. Have a kettle of water at the boil for the pasta.

2. Heat the butter and oil in a skillet and add the onions. Cook, stirring, until golden. Add the garlic, ham, basil, parsley, wine, salt, and pepper and continue cooking.

3. Simultaneously, as soon as the onions start to cook, add the penne or rigatoni and potatoes to the boiling water. Add salt and pepper to taste. Let return to the boil, stirring often so that the pasta does not stick. Let cook for about 4 minutes.

4. Add the cauliflower and continue cooking for 4 to 5 minutes, or until the pasta is just cooked. Do not overcook. When done, drain immediately and add the pasta mixture to the ham mixture. Toss with half the grated Parmesan cheese. Serve with the remaining cheese on the side.

Yield: 8 servings.

PASTA WITH ASPARAGUS

1. Have all the ingredients for this recipe prepared and ready to cook before starting to cook. Bring about 3 quarts of water to the boil and have it ready for the pasta.

2. Cut the asparagus into lengths about 2 inches long. If the stalks are thick, cut them in half or quarter them. Leave the tips intact. Heat the butter in a skillet and add the asparagus pieces, salt, and pepper. Cook for 4 to 5 minutes, or until crisp-tender and lightly browned. Remove from the heat.

3. Heat the oil in a deep skillet and add the garlic. Cook until lightly browned and remove and discard the garlic. Add the tomatoes, parsley, basil, and salt and pepper to taste. Cook, stirring, for about 10 minutes.

4. Meanwhile, add the pasta and salt to the water and, when it returns to the boil, cook for about 7 minutes, or until tender. Do not overcook.

5. Just before the pasta is done, turn off the heat under the tomatoes and add the beaten eggs, stirring vigorously so that they blend into the sauce without curdling. Do not boil the sauce after the eggs are added.

6. Add the asparagus to the tomato sauce and stir to blend.

7. Drain the pasta immediately. Add the tomato sauce and asparagus and toss with half the cheese. Serve piping hot with the remaining cheese on the side.

Yield: 8 or more servings.

1½ pounds fresh asparagus

3 tablespoons butter

Salt and freshly ground pepper to taste

2½ tablespoons olive oil

2 whole garlic cloves

2 cups canned Italian plum tomatoes put through a sieve

1 tablespoon finely chopped fresh parsley

1 tablespoon finely chopped fresh basil

¾ pound penne, rigatoni, or other tubular pasta

2 eggs plus 1 egg yolk, beaten well with a fork

½ cup grated Parmesan cheese

PASTA WITH BROCCOLI

½ pound fresh broccoli (see note)

½ pound spaghettini or linguine

5 tablespoons olive oil

2 to 3 garlic cloves, finely chopped

½ teaspoon hot red pepper flakes, approximately

2 cups water, approximately

Salt to taste

Grated Parmesan cheese

This recipe is incredibly easy to make, but there are a couple of pitfalls that must be guarded against. When the pasta and vegetables are cooked, the pasta must be stirred often to keep the strands from sticking to themselves and to the bottom of the pan. It is best to stir gently but often with a plastic spatula to prevent this.

1. Trim off and reserve the bud clusters at the top of the broccoli stems. Leave part of the stem attached to the base of each cluster. If the clusters are very large, cut them in half. Reserve the stems as well.

2. Unless the broccoli is very young and tender, pare or peel off the outer skin of the stems. If the stems are large, slice them in half lengthwise. In any event, cut the stem sections into 2-inch lengths. Combine and set aside the prepared broccoli pieces.

3. Break the pasta into 2- or 3-inch lengths. Set aside.

4. Heat the oil in a heavy, not too large skillet or casserole, 9 or 10 inches in diameter. Add the garlic and cook briefly. Add the hot pepper flakes, pasta, and broccoli. Add 1 cup of water and, when it boils, stir the ingredients to make certain the pasta does not stick to itself or the bottom of the pan.

5. Cover the pan and continue cooking but stirring often and adding water as it is absorbed, about ¼ cup at a time. Add salt to taste. When this dish is ready, the pasta will be cooked, the broccoli crisp-tender, and most of the liquid will be absorbed. The "sauce" that clings to the pasta will be minimal. The total cooking time is 10 to 12 minutes. Do not overcook or the pasta will become mushy.

6. Serve immediately in hot soup plates with Parmesan cheese on the side.

Yield: 4 appetizer servings or 2 main dishes.

Note: Broccoli di rape, a tender, delicious and somewhat bitter Italian green, may be substituted for the broccoli.

COLD PASTA AND BROCCOLI WITH PESTO

1. Prepare the pesto and have it ready.

2. Cut the broccoli into small florets. Trim the stalks and stems of the broccoli and cut both into bite-size lengths. Steam the broccoli pieces over boiling water or cook in boiling salted water until crisp-tender. Do not overcook. Set aside.

3. Cook the rigatoni in boiling salted water until al dente. The pasta must be tender and in no sense mushy. Drain but reserve a little of the boiling pasta water to dilute the pesto.

4. Heat the oil in a saucepan and add the garlic and blanched broccoli. Sprinkle with pepper flakes. Cook, stirring gently, just to heat through. Remove from the heat.

5. Meanwhile, core the tomato and cut the tomato into bite-size wedges.

6. Put the rigatoni in a bowl. Add 1 or 2 tablespoons of the hot pasta water to the pesto and stir until slightly thinned. Do not make it soupy. Pour this over the rigatoni. Add salt to taste. Add the broccoli and tomato and toss to blend. Serve at room temperature.

Yield: 8 to 10 servings.

4 to 6 tablespoons pesto genovese (see following recipe)

1 bunch of broccoli
  Salt

1 pound rigatoni or any tubular pasta, preferably imported

3 tablespoons olive oil

1 garlic clove, finely chopped

½ teaspoon or more hot red pepper flakes, optional

1 firm ripe tomato

PESTO GENOVESE (BASIL AND NUT SAUCE FOR PASTA)

2 cups fresh basil

½ cup olive oil

2 tablespoons pine nuts (pignoli)

2 garlic cloves, peeled

Salt to taste

½ cup grated Parmesan cheese

2 tablespoons grated Romano pecorino cheese (or increase the quantity of Parmesan by this amount)

3 tablespoons butter, at room temperature

1. Remove all tough stems from the basil. To measure, pack the leaves gently but somewhat firmly in a measuring cup without crushing the leaves.

2. Empty the basil into the container of a food processor or blender. Add the olive oil, pine nuts, garlic, and salt and blend on high speed. Using a rubber spatula, scrape the sides down occasionally so that it blends evenly. Pour the mixture into a bowl and beat in the grated cheeses by hand. Beat in the softened butter.

3. Let stand until the pesto is at room temperature. When the pasta is cooked, and before draining, quickly add and stir 1 or 2 tablespoons of the hot pasta water into the pesto. Toss with the hot drained pasta and serve.

Yield: Enough sauce for 1 pound pasta.

HOW TO FREEZE PESTO

Prepare the pesto and spoon it into a plastic container or freezer jar, filling the container almost to the brim. Seal and freeze. When ready to serve, defrost overnight in the refrigerator.

Broccoli, Tuna, and Rigatoni Salad

1. Drop the rigatoni into a kettle of boiling salted water. When the water returns to the boil, cook for about 10 minutes, or until just tender. Drain and run briefly under cold running water. Drain well.

2. Put the rigatoni in a mixing bowl.

3. Drop the broccoli into a saucepan of boiling salted water and cook until tender, about 5 minutes. Do not overcook. Drain well.

4. Add the broccoli, the remaining ingredients, and salt to taste to the rigatoni. Toss well. Serve at room temperature.

Yield: 8 or more servings.

½ pound rigatoni or ziti

Salt to taste

2 cups broccoli florets

2 cups cubed tomatoes

One 8-ounce can tuna fish packed in olive oil, preferably imported

Freshly ground pepper to taste

3 to 4 tablespoons red wine vinegar

½ cup olive oil

¼ teaspoon hot red pepper flakes

½ cup finely chopped parsley

½ cup thinly sliced red onion

SPAGHETTI WITH EGGPLANT

5 tablespoons olive oil

2 garlic cloves, finely minced

4 cups peeled tomatoes, preferably imported if canned

4 tablespoons tomato paste

¾ cup water

1 teaspoon sugar

Salt and freshly ground pepper to taste

½ cup chopped parsley

1 tablespoon finely chopped fresh basil

1½ pounds eggplant

½ pound or more spaghetti

¾ cup grated Parmesan cheese

1. Heat 1 tablespoon of the oil in a saucepan and add the garlic. Cook, stirring, without browning and add the tomatoes, tomato paste, water, sugar, salt, pepper, parsley, and basil. Stir to blend. Partly cover and cook, stirring frequently, for about 45 minutes.

2. Meanwhile, cut off the ends of the eggplant. Peel the eggplant and cut it into ½-inch cubes.

3. Heat the remaining oil in a large skillet and, when it is very hot, add the eggplant and salt to taste. Cook the eggplant, tossing, until it is nicely browned and tender. Add the eggplant to the tomato sauce and cover. Cook for 30 to 40 minutes, or until the eggplant blends with the sauce.

4. Cook the spaghetti until al dente and drain. Serve hot with the sauce. Serve grated Parmesan cheese on the side. This sauce is excellent when reheated.

Yield: 6 to 8 servings.

PASTA WITH FIELD MUSHROOMS

1. If necessary, rinse the mushrooms and pat them dry. Cut them into bite-size pieces.

2. Heat the oil in a large skillet and add the mushrooms, stirring. Cook about 5 minutes and add half the butter and the shallots. Cook over high heat for about 5 minutes.

3. Add the chicken broth and bring to the boil. Add the fontina cheese and cook over high heat for 5 or 6 minutes. Add the remaining butter and toss. Add the Parmesan and toss. Add the ¼ cup finely chopped basil and the thyme and toss.

4. Serve with cooked pasta garnished with the coarsely chopped basil.

Yield: 6 main-course servings or 12 first-course servings.

1¼ pounds mushrooms, preferably shiitaki

¾ cup olive oil

½ pound butter

¾ cup thinly sliced, lightly chopped shallots

2¼ cups freshly made chicken broth

½ pound imported fontina cheese at room temperature, cut into ¼-inch cubes, about 1¼ cups

¼ pound freshly grated Parmesan cheese

¼ cup finely chopped fresh basil

1 teaspoon dried thyme

1½ pounds pasta (penne, fettuccine, ditalini, pappardelle), cooked until al dente

½ cup coarsely chopped fresh basil

PASTA WITH FUNGHI TRIFOLATI (MUSHROOMS WITH GARLIC, OIL, AND PARSLEY)

½ ounce dried Italian mushrooms

⅔ cup olive oil

2 teaspoons finely chopped garlic

3 tablespoons finely chopped parsley

1 pound fresh mushrooms, finely chopped, about 6 cups

Salt and freshly ground pepper to taste

1 pound fettuccine, cooked until al dente

1. Put the dried mushrooms in a mixing bowl and add warm water to cover. Let stand for half an hour or longer until the mushrooms are soft. Remove the soaked mushrooms but save all their liquid. Squeeze to extract as much liquid as possible but save this liquid, too. Line a sieve with one layer of a kitchen towel. Strain the liquid. Chop the soaked mushrooms on a flat surface. They should be chopped fairly fine. Combine the strained mushroom liquid and the chopped mushrooms in a skillet. Bring to the boil and cook until all the liquid has evaporated.

2. Heat the olive oil in a deep skillet or casserole and add the garlic. Cook, stirring, without browning. Add the parsley. Add the fresh mushrooms and cook for about 1 minute, stirring. Add the dried mushrooms. Add the salt and pepper. Cook until the mushrooms give up their liquid. Continue cooking until the liquid (not the oil) evaporates.

3. Toss with the cooked fettuccine.

Yield: 4 to 6 servings.

Note: This pasta sauce is also excellent served as a vegetable.

SPAGHETTI WITH TOMATO SAUCE AND PEPPERS

1. Remove the cores from the tomatoes. Cut the tomatoes into 1-inch cubes. There should be about 4 cups.

2. Heat the oil in a saucepan and add the onion, garlic, green pepper, and hot red pepper. Cook, stirring often, for about 5 minutes.

3. Add the tomatoes, bay leaf, thyme, and salt and pepper. Bring to the boil and simmer for 20 minutes.

4. Spoon and scrape the mixture into the container of a food processor or blender. Blend to a fine purée. Add the basil and reheat. Swirl in the butter. Serve over spaghetti. This sauce freezes well.

Yield: 4 servings.

3 fresh ripe tomatoes, about 1¾ pounds, or 4 cups canned tomatoes

2 tablespoons olive or corn oil

¾ cup finely chopped onion

1 tablespoon finely chopped garlic

¾ cup finely chopped green pepper

¼ teaspoon crushed hot red pepper flakes

1 bay leaf

¼ teaspoon dried thyme

Freshly ground black pepper to taste

1 tablespoon chopped fresh basil

1 tablespoon butter

1 pound spaghetti, cooked until al dente

PASTA WITH TOMATOES, BASIL, AND HOT PEPPERS

4 pounds ripe tomatoes, peeled

½ cup olive oil

1 cup thinly sliced, lightly chopped shallots

10 fresh basil stems tied in a bundle

Salt to taste

2 or more dried hot red peppers, crushed

4 tablespoons butter

2 pounds pasta (ditalini, penne, spaghetti, fettuccine), cooked until al dente

3 cups freshly grated Parmesan cheese

30 fresh basil leaves

1. Cut the tomatoes into small wedges. There should be about 12 cups.

2. Heat the oil in a large skillet and add the shallots. Cook, stirring, until golden brown. Add the basil stems and tomatoes. Add salt to taste and hot red peppers.

3. Cook, stirring, for about 7 minutes and add the butter. Cook for 2 minutes and remove from the heat.

4. Put the pasta in a large hot bowl. Remove the bundle of basil stems and add three quarters of the sauce. Add 2 cups of the cheese and toss. Garnish with basil leaves and serve with the remaining sauce and Parmesan cheese on the side.

Yield: 6 main-course servings or 12 first-course servings.

PENNE ARRABBIATA (PENNE WITH TOMATO AND HOT CHILI SAUCE)

1. Place the mushrooms in a mixing bowl and add warm water to cover. Let stand, stirring occasionally, until softened.

2. Meanwhile, put the tomatoes and basil in a saucepan and bring to the boil. Add the hot, dried red pepper, salt, and pepper. (If using hot red pepper flakes, add them later.) Some cooks recommend puréeing the tomatoes in a food mill or food processor before or after cooking down. Others prefer mashing them down with a spoon as they cook for a bulkier texture.

3. Cook, stirring occasionally from the bottom to prevent sticking, for about 45 minutes, or until reduced to about 3½ cups. If the sauce becomes too thick as it cooks down, add some of the mushroom liquid or water.

4. Heat the oil in a small, deep skillet and add the pancetta. Cook, stirring, until brown but not crisp.

5. Add the garlic and stir. Cook briefly. Meanwhile, squeeze the soaked mushrooms to extract most of the liquid and add them, stirring. Cook, stirring, for about 3 minutes. Add the cooked-down tomatoes, salt, and pepper to taste. If desired, add hot crushed red pepper flakes. For a richer sauce, stir in 1 or 2 more tablespoons of olive oil.

6. Cook and drain the penne. Serve with the sauce and grated Parmesan cheese.

Yield: 4 to 6 servings.

1 pound, about 1½ cups, dried Italian mushrooms

4½ cups fresh or canned tomatoes

6 to 8 fresh basil leaves

1 hot, dried red pepper or ½ teaspoon hot red pepper flakes

Salt and freshly ground pepper to taste

¼ cup olive oil

¼ pound pancetta, cut into ½-inch cubes

1 or 2 teaspoons finely minced garlic

1 pound penne or other tubular pasta

Grated Parmesan cheese

Ragu Abruzzese (A Meat and Tomato Sauce for Pasta)

1 cup vegetable oil

2½ pounds veal and beef bones, preferably a few marrow bones included

Salt and freshly ground pepper to taste

2¼ pounds flank steak, cut into ½-inch-thick rectangles, measuring about 2 by 4 inches

¼ pound butter

¾ cup finely chopped heart of celery

1½ cups chopped onions

½ cup chopped shallots

3 garlic cloves, chopped

3 bay leaves

2 cups dry red wine

4 quarts tomatoes, put through a sieve or food mill to eliminate seeds

1 cup tomato paste

1½ cups water

1 fresh rosemary sprig, or 1 tablespoon dried, tied in a cheesecloth bag

¾ cup Italian mushrooms

The chefs of Italy are equally as chauvinistic about distinguishing the places of their birth as gastronomic spawning places as are the French. Just as French chefs claim that the gastronomic center of France (if not the universe) is Lyons, many Italian chefs claim that the mountainous Abruzzi region of Italy has produced the preponderance of great Italian chefs.

Luigi Nanni, a fine Italian chef, is from Abruzzi and maintains that poor regions tend to produce fine cooks who must exercise the greatest skill with such bounty as they have. Signor Nanni led us though a blissful meal in our home that proved his great skill. One of the dishes was an exceptional pasta bathed in his Abruzzese tomato sauce.

1. Heat the oil in a heavy kettle and add the bones. Sprinkle with the salt and pepper and cook, stirring occasionally, until nicely browned, 10 or 15 minutes.

2. Add the meat and cook, stirring occasionally, for about 30 minutes, or until browned. Pour off fat from kettle.

3. Add the butter, celery, onions, shallots, garlic, and bay leaves. Cook for about 20 minutes, stirring occasionally. Add the wine and simmer for 10 minutes. Add the tomatoes, tomato paste, and water. Cook for about 30 minutes and add the rosemary. Cook for about 1 hour longer.

4. Remove the bones. The meat clinging to the bones is excellent for nibbling on.

5. Remove and discard the bay leaves and cheesecloth bag.

6. Cover the mushrooms with water and bring to the boil. Simmer about 1 minute. Drain and add to the tomato sauce. Cook briefly. This sauce is now ready to be served with almost any form of pasta. The meat may be served with the sauce or separately after the pasta course. This sauce will keep for several days in the refrigerator and much longer if reheated occasionally. It freezes well.

Yield: About 4 quarts of sauce.

PASTA WITH GINGER AND GARLIC

One of the oddest, tastiest, and most intriguing recipes for pasta we've found in a long time was sent to us by Joe Famularo, an executive with McGraw-Hill publishers and a cookbook author. Joe, a fine cook, dispatched the recipe to us pursuant to one more suggestion that noodles may have first been created in China. "I don't know the origin of this dish," he wrote, "but my father cooked it religiously and swore it was an old ancestral recipe from Potenza in Italy. I often accused him of inventing it, however, for he was born on Mott Street—a street that quietly divided Little Italy from Chinatown."

1. Heat water in a kettle to cook the pasta.

2. Meanwhile, heat the oil in a saucepan and add the carrot. Cook for about 3 minutes, stirring occasionally. Add the garlic, ginger, scallion, oregano, salt, pepper flakes, and vermouth. Cook for about 5 minutes. Add the 1 cup of water. Bring to the boil and simmer until the pasta is cooked (do not cook the sauce more than 15 minutes total cooking time).

3. Cook and drain the pasta and return it to the kettle. Add the butter. Add three quarters of the ginger sauce. Toss.

4. Serve the pasta in hot bowls, with about 1 tablespoon of remaining sauce spooned on top. Serve Parmesan cheese separately.

Yield: 4 to 6 servings.

1 pound vermicelli, spaghettini, or spaghetti

½ cup olive oil

½ cup finely diced carrot

1 tablespoon finely chopped garlic

2 tablespoons finely chopped fresh ginger

2 tablespoons chopped scallion

1 teaspoon dried oregano
   Salt to taste

¼ to ½ teaspoon hot red pepper flakes

½ cup dry vermouth

1 cup water

4 tablespoons butter
   Grated Parmesan cheese

KIDNEYS AND MUSHROOMS WITH BUCATINI

1½ pounds veal or lamb
    kidneys
    Salt and freshly ground
    pepper to taste
¼ cup peanut, vegetable,
    or corn oil
2 tablespoons butter
½ pound mushrooms,
    quartered or thinly
    sliced
¼ cup finely chopped
    shallots
½ cup Marsala wine
1½ cups heavy cream
2 tablespoons Dijon
    mustard
1 pound bucatini,
    perciatelli, or
    spaghetti, cooked until
    al dente
    Freshly grated
    Parmesan cheese

1. Split the kidneys lengthwise through the center. Cut away and discard the center core. Cut the kidneys into ½-inch cubes. Sprinkle with salt and pepper and set aside.

2. Heat the oil in a heavy skillet and, when it is quite hot and almost smoking, add the kidneys. Cook, stirring, for about 1½ minutes. Drain thoroughly in a colander, discarding the oil.

3. Add the butter to the skillet and, when it is hot, add the mushrooms. Add salt to taste. Cook, stirring, for about 2 minutes.

4. Add the shallots and wine. Cook until the wine has reduced by half and add the cream. Bring to a rolling boil and add the mustard. Turn off the heat and add the kidneys and blend.

5. Serve with cooked bucatini and grated Parmesan cheese on the side.

Yield: 6 to 8 servings.

Spaghetti with Smoked Salmon in Cream

1. Stack the salmon slices. Cut the slices into 1-inch cubes. Set aside.
2. Cook the peas briefly in boiling salted water. When just tender, drain. Set aside.
3. Melt the butter in a skillet and, when it is hot, add the salmon cubes. Cook quickly, stirring. Add the cream and cook over high heat for about 1 minute.
4. Add the peas, pepper, nutmeg, and basil.
5. Heat the sauce briefly and serve with the spaghetti.

Yield: 4 servings.

¼ pound smoked salmon, cut into thin slices
½ cup green peas, preferably fresh
Salt
1 tablespoon butter
¾ cup heavy cream
Freshly ground pepper to taste
⅛ teaspoon grated nutmeg
2 tablespoons loosely packed, shredded, fresh basil leaves
1 pound spaghetti or spaghettini, cooked until al dente

Cold Spaghetti with Garlic and Anchovies

1. Heat ⅓ cup of the olive oil in a small skillet. Add the garlic and cook, stirring, without browning.
2. Add the mushrooms and cook until the mushrooms wilt. Add the chopped anchovy fillets. Stir and remove from the heat.
3. Add the lemon juice, black pepper, olives, and pepper flakes and stir. Set aside.
4. Cook the spaghetti until al dente. Drain and toss with the remaining 1 tablespoon of olive oil. Add the anchovy sauce and toss. Let stand until lukewarm.

Yield: About 6 servings.

⅓ cup plus 1 tablespoon olive oil
2 teaspoons finely chopped garlic
1 cup thinly sliced mushrooms
⅓ cup chopped anchovy fillets
Juice of 1 lemon
Freshly ground pepper to taste
½ cup imported black olives, pitted
¼ teaspoon crushed hot red pepper flakes
1 pound spaghetti

SHRIMP AND PEAS WITH PASTA SALAD

48 cooked, peeled, and deveined shrimp

1 pound tubular pasta, such as penne

2½ cups spicy mayonnaise (see recipe page 766)

2 cups cooked fresh or frozen peas (see note)

½ cup finely chopped herbs, such as basil, dill, and parsley, either separate or blended

¾ cup finely chopped scallions

2 to 4 tablespoons tarragon wine vinegar, according to taste

¼ cup drained capers

Salt and freshly ground pepper to taste

Finely chopped parsley for garnish

1. Cut the shrimp in half crosswise.

2. Cook the pasta until al dente. Drain and let cool.

3. Combine the shrimp and pasta in a mixing bowl and add the remaining ingredients except the chopped parsley. Blend well. Serve sprinkled with chopped parsley.

Yield: 10 to 12 servings..

Note: If frozen peas are used, empty them frozen into a sieve and pour boiling hot water over them. Let drain. Further cooking is not necessary.

SPAGHETTI WITH MUSSELS, SICILIAN STYLE

1. Put the mussels in a kettle and add the wine, thyme, bay leaf, parsley, and pepper. Cover tightly and cook until the mussels open, tossing occasionally as they cook, about 5 minutes. Discard any mussels that don't open. Remove from the heat. Strain the mussel liquid and set aside.

2. Heat the oil in a saucepan and add the garlic. Cook briefly and add the capers and olives. Remove from the heat. Stir in the chopped parsley and ¼ cup of the reserved mussel liquid. Add pepper to taste and a little salt. Add the hot red pepper flakes.

3. Remove the mussels from the shells. If desired, remove and discard the small rubberlike bands around the mussels.

4. Add the mussels to the sauce. Heat briefly and serve with the spaghetti.

Yield: 4 servings.

Note: A dark, heavy olive oil is recommended for this dish.

2 quarts mussels, well scrubbed

¼ cup dry white wine

2 fresh thyme sprigs, or ½ teaspoon dried

1 bay leaf

2 fresh parsley sprigs

Freshly ground pepper to taste

¼ cup olive oil (see note)

1 teaspoon finely chopped garlic

2 tablespoons drained capers

¼ cup pitted black olives, preferably imported

¼ cup finely chopped parsley

Salt to taste

½ teaspoon hot red pepper flakes

1 pound spaghetti or spaghettini, preferably imported, cooked until al dente

LINGUINE AND CLAM SAUCE

18 cherrystone clams
 4 cups water
    Salt to taste
 1 pound linguine
½ cup heavy cream
 4 tablespoons butter
 1 tablespoon finely
    chopped garlic
 4 tablespoons finely
    chopped parsley
 3 tablespoons finely
    chopped basil
 1 teaspoon chopped
    fresh thyme leaves, or
    ½ teaspoon dried
    Freshly ground pepper
    to taste
½ cup grated Parmesan
    cheese

1. Open and drain the clams and reserve both clams and juice. Chop the clams. There should be about 1 cup of clams and 1½ cups of juice.

2. Pour the juice into a kettle and add the water and salt. Bring the liquid to the boil and add the linguine. The clam sauce requires less time than the linguine.

3. As the linguine cooks, heat the cream in a saucepan just to the boil.

4. Meanwhile, heat the butter in another saucepan and add the clams, garlic, parsley, basil, thyme, and pepper. Do not add salt at this time. Add the cream.

5. When the linguine is done, drain it in a colander. Pour it onto a large hot platter and add the sauce immediately, tossing. Add the cheese and salt to taste, tossing with a fork and spoon. Serve very, very hot with a pepper mill on the side.

Yield: 4 to 6 servings.

Spaghetti alla Puttanesca with Clams

One of the most amusing names in the Italian cooking repertory is spaghetti alla puttanesca, or spaghetti whore's style. My friend Ed Giobbi, the artist and cookbook author, avers the name originated with the ladies of the night in Naples. It is said that the scent of the ingredients—tomatoes, garlic, anchovies, and olives—would tempt passersby.

1. Heat the oil in a deep heavy skillet and add the garlic. Cook without browning for about 30 seconds. Add the tomatoes, half the parsley, basil, oregano, red pepper flakes, capers, and olives. Cook over moderately high heat for about 25 minutes. Stir frequently.

2. Meanwhile, drain the anchovies and chop them coarsely. Rinse the clams under cold running water until clean.

3. When the sauce is ready, add the anchovies and remaining parsley. Cook, stirring, for about 1 minute.

4. Add the clams and cover the skillet closely. Cook for about 5 minutes, or until all the clams are opened.

5. Serve piping hot with freshly cooked spaghetti.

Yield: 6 servings.

¼ cup olive oil

1 tablespoon finely minced garlic

4 cups peeled, chopped tomatoes, preferably fresh, or imported Italian plum tomatoes

⅓ cup finely chopped parsley

2 tablespoons finely chopped fresh basil

1 teaspoon dried oregano

½ teaspoon red pepper flakes, or more to taste

2 tablespoons drained capers

18 pitted imported black olives

Two 2-ounce cans flat anchovies

24 littleneck clams, the smaller the better

1 pound spaghetti, cooked until al dente

Scungilli (Conch) with Diavolo Sauce and Linguine

Two 35-ounce cans imported Italian peeled tomatoes

¼ **cup olive oil**

4 **tablespoons finely chopped garlic**

½ **cup dry white wine**

1½ **teaspoons dried oregano**

Salt to taste

1 **teaspoon freshly ground pepper**

3 **tablespoons butter**

3 **cups cooked, cleaned, sliced conch (see note and following recipe)**

¼ **to 1 teaspoon hot red pepper flakes, according to strength desired**

1½ **pounds linguine, cooked until al dente**

A great personal favorite among oddments from the sea is conch, which Italians call scungilli. Living in the Hamptons, I have had access to scungilli already prepared—in a tomato sauce with linguine, or in a zesty, piquant salad. The chef of these good things is Eduardo Giurici, who came into my kitchen to demonstrate the simple (if time-consuming) method for cooking scungilli.

1. Empty the tomatoes into a large bowl and crush well with the hands.

2. Heat the oil in a wide, not too deep casserole and add 3 tablespoons of the garlic. Cook, stirring, until the garlic is lightly browned. Do not burn. Add half the wine and cook until the wine has almost evaporated. Add the tomatoes.

3. Bring to the boil. Add 1 teaspoon of the oregano, salt to taste, and the pepper. Cook over high heat, stirring often with a wooden spoon so that the tomatoes do not stick. Cook for 20 minutes. This sauce should not be dark, but thick and reddish. When ready, there should be about 7 cups.

4. Melt the butter in a saucepan or small casserole and add the remaining tablespoon of garlic. Cook, stirring, until the garlic is lightly browned. Do not allow it to burn.

5. Add the conch and remaining wine. Cook down briefly and add the remaining oregano, salt, pepper, and hot red pepper flakes. Continue cooking until the wine is reduced by half. Add the tomato sauce and heat through. Put the drained linguine in a large serving bowl and toss with the sauce.

Yield: 6 servings.

Note: Canned scungilli, or conch, is available at many stores that specialize in Italian foods. It is an excellent product and can be substituted for the fresh. It is, however, fairly expensive. Drain well before using.

1. The conch may be sandy so wash them before cooking. Put them in a basin with warm water and rub them carefully to remove surface sand. Drain.

2. Put the conch in one or two large kettles. Add hot water from the tap to barely cover. Do not add salt. Bring to the boil and cook for 1 hour. Drain well.

3. Remove the conch from the shell, using a two-pronged fork. Holding the body in one hand, remove and discard the soft, flabby portions that hang and cling to the body at the bottom and inside. Split open the body sac with the fingers and pull out the inside organ. Discard it. Hold the conch under cold running water and scrub off as much of the black coating as possible. Feel all over for traces of sand.

4. Return the conch meat to a clean kettle and add water to cover about 5 inches above the surface of the conch. Do not add salt. Put on the stove and bring to the boil. Cook for 4 hours, or until tender. If the conch are quite large, it may be necessary to cook them for up to 5 hours.

5. At this point you may freeze the conch meat. Cover closely and freeze the entire batch, or divide into portions, wrap tightly, and freeze.

6. When ready to serve, place the conch pieces, one at a time, on a flat surface and cut into ¼-inch-thick slices.

Yield: About 6 cups.

COOKED CONCH

16 large conch, each about ¾ pound (total weight is 10 to 11 pounds)

Pasta with Sausages and Pork

2 hot Italian sausage links

4 sweet Italian sausage links

1 ready-to-cook braciole, about ¾ pound

1 pound spareribs, cut into 3- or 4-inch squares, or 1 pound boneless pork, left whole

One 35-ounce can tomatoes, preferably Italian peeled tomatoes

One 6-ounce can tomato paste

¾ cup water

½ cup finely chopped onion

2 garlic cloves, finely minced

Salt and freshly ground pepper to taste

½ teaspoon hot red pepper flakes, more or less to taste

2 teaspoons dried oregano

1 pound pasta such as ziti, fusilli, shells, or rigatoni

½ cup grated cheese, preferably Romano

1. Brown the sausages in a large heavy skillet. When they start to give up their fat, add the braciole and spareribs. Cook until all the meats are well browned on all sides.

2. Meanwhile, strain the tomatoes and add them to a kettle large enough to hold the meats. Add the tomato paste. Rinse out the can with the water and add the water.

3. Transfer the meats to the kettle and pour off all but 2 tablespoons of fat from the skillet. Add the onion and cook until transparent. Add the garlic and brown lightly. Add this to the kettle. Add the salt, pepper, pepper flakes, and oregano. Partly cover. Cook, stirring often from the bottom to prevent sticking and burning, for a total of 2½ hours, skimming the surface as necessary to remove fat and scum.

4. Cook the pasta until al dente. Drain the pasta and return it to the pot. Add a little sauce and ½ cup cheese. Toss lightly to coat.

5. Place the meat on a platter. Spoon a cup or so of sauce on the bottom of a hot, deep serving dish. Add the pasta and spoon a little more sauce on top. Serve the remaining sauce on the side. Serve, if desired, with additional grated cheese.

Yield: 6 to 10 servings.

BAKED RIGATONI

1. Heat 2 tablespoons of the butter in a heavy skillet and add the onions. Cook, stirring, until wilted. If the mushrooms are tiny, leave them whole. Otherwise, quarter them or slice them, depending on size. Add the mushrooms to the onions and cook, stirring frequently, until the mushrooms give up their liquid. Cook further until the liquid evaporates.

2. In a separate skillet, cook the pork or sausage meat (take the skins off) until rendered of its fat. Use a wooden spoon to break up any lumps. Add the meat to the mushroom mixture and stir it in. Sprinkle with garlic, fennel (omit the fennel if sausages are used), basil, sage, oregano, and red pepper. Cook for about 3 minutes, stirring. Add the tomatoes, salt, pepper, water, and chicken broth. Simmer for 1 hour, stirring frequently.

3. Add the chopped parsley and simmer for 15 minutes longer. Stir in the olive oil and set aside to cool.

4. Drop the rigatoni or ziti into a large quantity of boiling salted water and cook, stirring rapidly to make certain that the pieces of pasta float free and do not stick to the bottom. Cook for about 8 minutes. Do not cook longer because the pasta will be baked later. Immediately drain the pasta in a colander and run cold water over it. Drain well.

5. Preheat the oven to 400 degrees.

6. Spoon a thin layer of sauce into a 13½ × 8¾ × 1¾-inch baking dish. Add a single layer of rigatoni. Scatter half the mozzarella over it and sprinkle with 1 tablespoon of the Parmesan. Continue making layers of sauce, pasta, mozzarella, and Parmesan, ending with a layer of sauce and Parmesan. Use only about ½ cup of Parmesan for the dish. The remainder will be served with the finished dish.

7. Dot the casserole with the remaining butter and bake, uncovered, for 30 minutes, or until bubbling hot throughout. Run the dish briefly under the broiler to give it a nice brown glaze. Serve the dish cut into squares with Parmesan cheese on the side.

Yield: 8 to 12 servings.

---

5 tablespoons butter

2 cups chopped onions

1 pound mushrooms

1 pound ground pork or Italian sausages

1 teaspoon finely minced garlic

¾ teaspoon fennel seeds

1 tablespoon finely chopped fresh basil

¾ teaspoon crushed sage

¾ teaspoon dried oregano

1 dried red pepper, chopped, optional

6 cups peeled Italian plum tomatoes

Salt and freshly ground pepper to taste

1 cup water

1 cup fresh or canned chicken broth

¼ cup finely chopped parsley

2 tablespoons olive oil

1 pound rigatoni or ziti

½ pound mozzarella cheese, cut into ½-inch cubes

2 cups grated Parmesan cheese

LASAGNE WITH SEAFOOD IN A CREAM TOMATO SAUCE

1 tablespoon butter

1 tablespoon finely chopped shallots

¾ pound raw shrimp, peeled

1 pint scallops

Salt and freshly ground pepper to taste

½ cup dry white wine

2 cups thinly sliced mushrooms

2 cups béchamel sauce (see recipe page 778)

1 cup crushed canned tomatoes

½ cup heavy cream

¼ teaspoon crushed hot red pepper flakes

3 tablespoons finely chopped parsley

9 lasagne strips

4 small skinless, boneless flounder fillets, about 1 pound total weight

1 cup grated Gruyère or Swiss cheese

Lasagne is a first-rate solution to the dilemma of what to serve a party of 10 or more that is festive enough to be special yet can be made and served in one dish—thus minimizing the cleanup process. The problem, however, is that in America most people's lasagne is apt to taste very much like that of their neighbors: a standard compendium of lasagne noodles, meat sauce, and mozzarella and ricotta cheeses.

The fact is that with a little imagination the flavors and textures of baked lasagne can achieve a far greater latitude than most home cooks believe—from a blend of seafood in a light tomato and cream sauce to a fine, lusty blend of chicken with sausage and beef. And these lasagne dishes may be prepared in advance.

1. Melt the butter in a large skillet and add the shallots. Cook for about 30 seconds and add the shrimp and scallops. (If the scallops are bay scallops and small, leave them whole. Otherwise, cut them into small, bite-size pieces.) Sprinkle with the salt and pepper.

2. When the shrimp start to turn pink, add the wine. Cook, stirring briefly, just until the wine comes to the boil.

3. The moment the wine boils, turn off the heat. Using a slotted spoon, transfer the seafood to a mixing bowl.

4. Bring the cooking liquid to the simmer and add the mushrooms. Cook for about 5 minutes and add the béchamel sauce, stirring.

5. Add the tomatoes and simmer for about 5 minutes. Add the cream, pepper flakes, and salt and pepper. Add the parsley. Add any liquid that may have accumulated around the shrimp and scallops to the sauce.

6. Preheat the oven to 375 degrees.

7. Cook the lasagne according to taste.

8. Butter the bottom and sides of a lasagne pan (a pan measuring 9½ × 13½ × 2 inches is suitable).

9. Spoon a layer of the sauce over the bottom. Add half the shrimp and scallops.

10. Spoon some of the sauce over the shrimp and scallops.

11. Cover with 3 strips of lasagne.

12. Add a layer of flounder. Add salt and pepper and a thin layer of sauce.

13. Cover with 3 strips of lasagne.

14. Scatter the remaining shrimp and scallops over and spoon a light layer of sauce over this, leaving enough sauce for a final layer.

15. Cover with 3 strips of lasagne. Spoon a final layer of sauce over this.

16. Place in the oven and bake for 30 minutes.

Yield: About 10 servings.

Chicken, Sausage, and Beef Lasagne

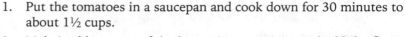

2   cups tomatoes
5   tablespoons butter
4   tablespoons flour
2   cups chicken broth
1   cup heavy cream
    Salt and freshly ground
    pepper to taste
⅛   teaspoon grated
    nutmeg
½   pound hot or sweet
    Italian sausages
1   cup finely chopped
    green pepper
1   cup finely chopped
    celery
1   cup finely chopped
    onion
1   to 2 tablespoons finely
    chopped garlic
½   pound ground sirloin
2   cups thinly sliced
    mushrooms
    Tabasco sauce to taste
1   teaspoon Worcester-
    shire sauce
1   cup frozen or very
    fresh green peas
9   lasagne strips
2   cups shredded,
    skinless, boneless
    cooked chicken
2   cups grated Cheddar
    cheese
¼   cup freshly grated
    Parmesan cheese

1. Put the tomatoes in a saucepan and cook down for 30 minutes to about 1½ cups.

2. Melt 3 tablespoons of the butter in a saucepan and add the flour, stirring with a wire whisk. When blended, add the broth, stirring rapidly with the whisk. Cook for about 10 minutes, stirring occasionally. Add the cream, salt, pepper, and nutmeg.

3. Remove and discard the skin of the sausages. Add the flesh to a skillet and cook, stirring with the side of heavy metal kitchen spoon to break up any lumps. Cook until the meat loses its raw color. Drain off and discard the fat. Set the meat aside.

4. Melt the remaining 2 tablespoons of butter in a skillet and add the green pepper, celery, onion, and garlic. Cook, stirring briefly, until crisp-tender.

5. Add the beef and cook, cutting down with the sides of a heavy metal kitchen spoon to break up any lumps. Add the sausage meat and mushrooms and cook briefly. Add salt and pepper to taste.

6. Add the tomatoes to the cream sauce. Pour this combined sauce over the meat mixture and stir to blend. Add the Tabasco and Worcestershire sauce and salt and pepper to taste. Add the peas and bring to the boil.

7. Preheat the oven to 375 degrees.

8. Cook the lasagne according to taste. Drain.

9. Butter a lasagne baking dish (a dish measuring about 9½ × 13½ × 2 inches is suitable).

10. Arrange 3 lasagne strips over the dish. Add a layer of chicken and spoon some of the meat sauce over. Add about a third of the grated Cheddar cheese.

11. Cover with 3 lasagne strips.

12. Add a layer of chicken and another layer of meat sauce and grated cheese.

13. Add a third layer of lasagne. Add the remaining chicken and spoon the remaining meat sauce over all. Sprinkle with the remaining grated Cheddar cheese.

14. Bake for 30 minutes. Serve with grated Parmesan cheese on the side.

Yield: 10 or more servings.

LASAGNE WITH RICOTTA AND SAUSAGES

1. Preheat the oven to 375 degrees.

2. Remove and discard the skins from the sausages. Heat the oil in a skillet and add the sausage meat. Cook, stirring to break up the meat. When the sausage has given up its fat, drain off all but about 1 tablespoon of oil from the skillet. Add the garlic and pork to the sausage, stirring to break up the pork. Cook, stirring, until the pork turns white. Add the wine and bring to the boil over high heat. Cook, stirring, until the wine evaporates. Add the tomato sauce, salt and pepper.

3. Bring a large quantity of salted water to the boil and add the lasagne strips, one at a time. Cook until almost tender. Add a quart of cold water to the pot. Drain and spread the strips on a damp cloth.

4. Lightly grease a lasagne pan measuring approximately 13 × 8 × 2 inches. Add a layer of lasagne.

5. Beat the ricotta with the hot water to make it spreadable. Spread about a third of the ricotta over the lasagne. Spread a layer of the meat sauce over this and sprinkle with about ¼ cup of the cheese. Continue making layers, ending with a layer of lasagne sprinkled with a final quarter of the cheese. Pour the melted butter over all and bake for 15 to 20 minutes, or until the lasagne is piping hot and bubbling throughout.

Yield: 4 to 6 servings.

1 pound sweet or hot Italian sausages

1 tablespoon olive oil

1 garlic clove, finely minced

½ pound ground lean pork

½ cup dry white wine

3 cups tomato sauce (see following recipe)

Salt and freshly ground pepper to taste

12 lasagne strips

2 cups ricotta cheese

¼ cup hot water

1 cup grated Parmesan cheese

4 tablespoons butter, melted

TOMATO SAUCE

2 tablespoons olive oil

4 tablespoons butter

1½ cups chopped onions

1 tablespoon chopped garlic

¼ pound fresh mushrooms, finely chopped

¾ cup finely chopped carrots

2 tablespoons finely chopped fresh parsley

1 tablespoon finely chopped fresh basil

6 sprigs fresh thyme, or 1 teaspoon dried

1 teaspoon sugar

1 whole clove

½ cup dry white wine

4 cups chopped fresh or canned tomatoes

Salt and freshly ground pepper to taste

1. Heat the oil and 2 tablespoons of the butter in a heavy casserole and add the onions, garlic, mushrooms, carrot, parsley, basil, thyme, sugar, and clove. Cook, stirring, until the mixture is almost dry but still moist, about 10 minutes.

2. Add the wine and cook, stirring, over high heat until wine evaporates. Add the tomatoes, salt, and pepper and bring to the boil. Partly cover and simmer for 1 hour.

3. Put the mixture through a food mill, pushing through as much of the vegetable solids as possible. Stir in the remaining butter and bring to the boil.

Yield: About 3 cups.

SPINACH RAVIOLI

1. Place the flour in a mixing bowl and make a well in the center. Beat the eggs lightly and add them to the well. Sprinkle with salt to taste. Add the water. Work well with the fingers until the dough can be handled easily. Wrap in wax paper and refrigerate.

2. Drop the spinach into boiling water to cover and cook for about 1 minute. Drain immediately. When cool enough to handle, squeeze the spinach until most of the moisture is pressed out. There should be about ¾ cup of spinach. Put in a mixing bowl.

3. Add the egg, parsley, ricotta, nutmeg, and the ¾ cup Parmesan cheese. Add the garlic, salt, and pepper to taste and blend well with the fingers.

4. Divide the dough into four pieces. Roll out the dough by hand, if you are expert in pasta-making, or use a pasta machine and roll out the dough according to the manufacturer's instructions.

5. There are numerous techniques for filling pasta for ravioli. The simplest is to use a ravioli-maker that can be purchased in stores where first-class cooking equipment is sold. The commonest has 12 metal indentations. The surface should be lightly floured. As the dough is rolled out, a rectangle of dough is laid over the surface and a small amount of filling, about 1½ teaspoons, is spooned into the dough-covered indentations. Another rectangle of dough is laid over, stretching the dough gently, if necessary, to cover the entire pan, and a small rolling pin is run over this to seal the filling while simultaneously cutting out patterns of ravioli, which may be separated. Or the dough can be rolled out, small mounds of filling added at intervals. This can be covered with another sheet of dough and a ravioli cutter used to outline the dumplings.

6. As the ravioli are made, arrange them in one layer on a dry floured kitchen towel.

7. When ready to serve, drop the ravioli into rapidly boiling salted water. Cook until ravioli rise to the top, stirring gently on occasion. Partly cover and continue to cook for 10 to 15 minutes. Cooking time will depend on thickness of dough. Drain well.

8. As the ravioli cook, heat the butter in a saucepan. Pour off about 2 tablespoons into another saucepan and add the sage. Cook for about 30 seconds. Add the remaining butter and pour hot over the ravioli. Serve Parmesan cheese on the side.

Yield: 8 dozen ravioli, or 6 to 8 servings.

THE DOUGH:

4 cups flour

5 large eggs, or 1¼ cups, plus 2 egg yolks

Salt

½ to 2 tablespoons cold water

THE FILLING:

¾ pound bulk spinach, or 1 10-ounce package fresh spinach

1 large egg, beaten

2 tablespoons finely chopped parsley

1 cup ricotta cheese

¼ teaspoon grated nutmeg

¾ cup grated Parmesan cheese

¼ teaspoon finely minced garlic

Salt and freshly ground pepper to taste

THE SERVICE:

4 tablespoons butter

5 leaves fresh or dried sage, snipped in half

Grated Parmesan cheese

GNOCCHI DI PATATE

3 large potatoes,
preferably Idaho
potatoes, about
1¾ pounds

Salt to taste

2 egg yolks

1¾ to 2 cups flour

4 tablespoons butter,
melted

Grated Parmesan
cheese

2 cups tomato and onion
sauce (see recipe
following)

Freshly ground pepper

1. Place the potatoes in a kettle and add cold water to cover. Add the salt and bring to the boil. Simmer until the potatoes are tender but not mushy. Drain and let cool.

2. Peel the potatoes. Put them through a ricer or food mill. Or put them through a meat grinder using the medium blade. Add egg yolks and blend well.

3. Scoop the flour onto a flat surface. Start kneading the potatoes, adding the flour gradually. Add only enough flour to make a firm, soft, and delicate dough. If too much flour is added they become tough when cooked. Knead thoroughly, then shape the dough, rolling with the palms to make a thick sausage shape about 12 inches long. Using a knife or pastry scraper, cut the roll into 11 equal slices. Roll each slice into a long cigar shape. Cut each cigar into 18 or 19 pieces. These pieces will resemble miniature pillows. Flour the pieces and set aside until ready to cook.

4. Drop the pieces of dough, half of them at a time, into a large quantity of boiling salted water and let cook until they rise to the surface. Drain quickly and chill under cold running water. Drain well.

5. When ready to serve, drop the pieces once more into a large quantity of boiling salted water. When they float the second time, drain them and return them to the pot. Add the melted butter and cheese. Add the sauce and sprinkle with pepper. Serve with additional sauce on the side.

Yield: 6 or more servings.

TOMATO AND ONION SAUCE

8 cups canned tomatoes,
preferably imported
from Italy

¼ pound lard

3 cups thinly sliced
onions

⅓ pound prosciutto, cut
into very thin strips,
about 1½ cups

Salt and freshly ground
pepper to taste

¼ cup freshly snipped
basil

1. Using the hands, crush the tomatoes.

2. Heat the lard and add the onions. Cook, stirring often, until the onions are golden brown, about 20 minutes.

3. Add the prosciutto and cook for 5 minutes. Add the tomatoes and cook for about 2 hours, stirring often to prevent sticking. Add the salt, pepper, and basil.

Yield: About 6 cups of sauce.

BARBARA TROPP'S TANGY NOODLES

1. Toss and separate the fresh uncooked noodles by hand to release any tangles. Do not break them.

2. Bring a generous quantity of water to the boil. Add the noodles, stirring with chopsticks or wooden spoons to separate. Cook, stirring occasionally, for 3 or 4 minutes. Do not overcook or they will become soggy and sticky. Drain immediately in a colander. Run under cold water until chilled. Shake off excess water.

3. Put the noodles in a clean bowl or dry pot.

4. Combine the sesame oil, soy sauce, vinegar, sugar, salt, and hot oil in a mixing bowl. Blend well.

5. Pour the sauce over the noodles and mix well, preferably with the hands. Add the scallions and toss again.

6. Cover and set aside for several hours at room temperature. Or store overnight in the refrigerator. Serve in individual bowls with more chopped scallions, if desired. The noodles can be refrigerated several days, but they are best on the second day. Serve at room temperature.

Yield: 6 to 8 servings.

1 pound fresh long, thin Chinese egg noodles, available in Asian supermarkets and grocery stores

3½ tablespoons Chinese or Japanese sesame oil

3½ tablespoons dark soy sauce

1½ tablespoons vinegar, preferably Chinese black vinegar, or use red wine vinegar

2 tablespoons sugar

2 teaspoons kosher salt

½ to 1 tablespoon hot chili oil

5 or 6 tablespoons thinly cut scallion rings, green parts and all

SALMON AND NOODLE CASSEROLE

2 cups freshly cooked or canned skinless, boneless salmon

¼ pound (about 3 cups) broad noodles

Salt to taste

2 tablespoons butter plus butter for greasing the pan

½ cup finely chopped onion

½ cup diced sweet red or green pepper

2 tablespoons flour

2 cups milk

¼ teaspoon grated nutmeg

Freshly ground pepper to taste

¼ pound grated Cheddar cheese, about ½ cup

2 tablespoons finely chopped parsley

2 tablespoons freshly grated Parmesan cheese

1. Preheat the oven to 400 degrees.

2. Pick over the salmon to remove all traces of skin and bones. Set aside.

3. Bring enough water to the boil to cover the noodles when they are added. Add the salt. Add the noodles and bring to the boil again. Let simmer for about 5 minutes until almost but not quite tender. Drain and run briefly under cold water. Drain. There should be about 3 cups.

4. Meanwhile, melt the butter in a saucepan and add the onion and diced pepper. Cook briefly, stirring, until the onion is wilted. Add the flour, stirring with a wire whisk until the mixture is blended and smooth. Add the milk, stirring rapidly with the whisk, then add the nutmeg and salt and pepper to taste.

5. Remove from the heat and add the Cheddar cheese. Stir until melted. Add the salmon, noodles, and parsley. Stir gently to blend.

6. Lightly grease a 1½-quart baking dish and pour in the creamed mixture. Sprinkle with the Parmesan cheese. Place the dish in the oven and bake for 15 minutes. If desired, run the dish briefly under the broiler to brown the top.

Yield: 4 to 6 servings.

NOODLES WITH HOT MEAT SAUCE FOR A CROWD

1. Heat a wok and add half the oil. Add half the pork and cook quickly over high heat, stirring and chopping down to break up any lumps. Cook only until the pork loses its raw look.

2. Add ⅔ cup of the brown bean sauce and half the chili paste with garlic. Cook, stirring rapidly, for 1 to 2 minutes. Add half the sugar and half the sherry and cook for 1 minute longer over high heat.

3. Turn the mixture into a 4-quart casserole.

4. Rinse and wipe out the wok, and repeat the procedure using the remaining half of the corn oil, pork, brown bean sauce, chili paste with garlic, sugar, and sherry. Add the second batch to the first. Let stand to room temperature. Refrigerate for up to 3 days (or the mixture may be frozen in small batches up to a month or longer).

5. When ready to serve, bring to room temperature. Reheat the sauce gently. Twenty minutes before serving, bring a large kettle of water to the boil. Add the noodles and cook for 4 minutes.

6. Drain the noodles and cut them into shreds of manageable length. Pour the noodles into a heated, heatproof serving dish.

7. Add the scallions to the simmering sauce and stir. Pour the sauce over the hot noodles and toss to blend. Serve with the three garnishes, letting guests help themselves.

Yield: 25 to 30 servings.

Note: These ingredients are available in Asian groceries and supermarkets.

1 cup corn, peanut, or vegetable oil

4 pounds ground pork, preferably not too lean and not too finely ground

1⅓ cups brown bean sauce (see note)

2 tablespoons bottled chili paste with garlic (see note)

4 tablespoons sugar

4 tablespoons dry sherry

2 pounds fresh Chinese egg noodles (see note)

1 cup minced scallions, green parts and all

GARNISHES:

4 cups picked-over bean sprouts

3 cups peeled, seeded, and shredded cucumbers

¾ cup hot chili oil (see note)

Vegetables

RATATOUILLE

1. Heat 4 tablespoons of the oil in a large heavy skillet or casserole and, when it is quite hot, add the eggplant. Cook, stirring, for about 3 minutes. Remove with a wooden spoon and put it in a colander. Add the zucchini to the skillet and cook, stirring, for about 3 minutes. Add it to the eggplant.

2. Add the remaining oil to the skillet and add the onions. Cook, stirring, until wilted and add the green peppers. Cook, stirring, for about 3 minutes. Add the garlic, thyme, and bay leaf. Add the eggplant, zucchini, salt, and pepper. Cook, stirring, for about 5 minutes. Add the tomatoes and stir. Cover closely and cook for 20 minutes.

3. Uncover and cook for about 10 minutes to reduce the liquid that will have accumulated. Serve hot or cold.

Yield: 6 to 8 servings.

5 tablespoons olive oil

1 eggplant, about ¾ pound, cut into 1-inch cubes

1 or 2 zucchini, about ¾ pound, cut into 1-inch cubes

2 or 3 onions, about ¾ pound, coarsely chopped

2 or 3 green peppers, about ½ pound, cut into 1-inch cubes

1 tablespoon chopped garlic

2 fresh thyme sprigs, or ½ teaspoon dried

1 bay leaf

Salt and freshly ground pepper to taste

3 or 4 tomatoes, about 1½ pounds, cut into cubes

BAKED VEGETABLES, CATALAN STYLE

8 large leeks, about
   2½ pounds
3 eggplants, about
   2 pounds
3 or 4 large onions,
   about 2 pounds
5 large sweet green or
   red peppers, about
   1¾ pounds
   Salt and freshly ground
   pepper to taste
8 tablespoons olive oil

1. Preheat the oven to 500 degrees.

2. Cut off the threadlike root ends of the leeks. Trim off portions of the upper green stems of each leek, leaving about 12 inches, including white bottom portions plus part of green. Leave leeks whole but rinse away as much sand and soil as possible from between inner leaves. Pat dry. Line a baking dish with aluminum foil and arrange the leeks in one layer.

3. Line a second large baking dish with foil. Arrange whole eggplants, onions, and peppers in one layer.

4. Place both baking dishes in the oven and bake for 1 hour, turning the vegetables at 15 minute intervals so they bake evenly.

5. At the end of the hour, check the vegetables. If the green peppers are tender and slightly browned, remove them. Or continue cooking until they are tender and can be peeled.

6. If at the end of the hour the leeks are slightly charred and are tender, remove them. Wrap in foil and let stand for ½ hour or so until they can be handled.

7. Let the onions continue to bake up to 1½ hours, or until the inner flesh is tender to the touch.

8. Peel the peppers, cutting or pulling away and discarding the core and seeds. Cut the flesh of each pepper lengthwise into strips, each about ½ inch wide. Arrange the strips in a small serving dish.

9. Peel the eggplants. Discard peel and seeds. Cut the flesh into strips about the same size as the peppers. Arrange the strips in a second serving dish.

10. Remove and discard the browned outer skin of each onion. Cut the onions into strips about the same size as the eggplants and peppers. Stack the strips in a third serving dish.

11. Remove the leeks from the foil. Trim off and discard the tough browned outer leaves. Split the tender inner portions of each in half lengthwise. Cut crosswise in half. Arrange the strips in a fourth serving dish.

12. Sprinkle the vegetables lightly with salt. Sprinkle with pepper to taste. Spoon equal amounts of the oil over each vegetable. Serve as a side dish with grilled meats or fish. Leftover vegetables are excellent.

Yield: 4 to 8 servings.

SAUTÉED CARROTS, TURNIPS, AND SNOW PEAS

1. Scrape and trim the carrots. Cut the carrots crosswise into 1½-inch lengths. Cut the pieces into ¼-inch slices. Cut slices into batons about ¼ inch wide. There should be about 1½ cups.

2. Trim and scrape the turnips. Cut the turnips in half. Cut each half crosswise into ¼-inch-thick slices. Stack the slices; cut them into batons about the same size as the carrots. There should be about 2 cups.

3. Trim off and discard the tips of the snow peas. There should be about 1 cup of peas.

4. Melt the butter in a heavy skillet. Add the carrots and turnips. Cook the vegetables, stirring, for about 1 minute. Add the snow peas and cook, stirring, for about 5 minutes until crisp-tender.

5. Add the salt and pepper and the vinegar. Cook briefly and stir well.

Yield: 4 servings.

2 large carrots, about ½ pound

2 large white turnips, about ½ pound

½ pound fresh snow peas

2 tablespoons butter

Salt and freshly ground pepper to taste

1 tablespoon red wine vinegar

VEGETABLE CROQUETTES

1　small eggplant, about ¾ pound, peeled

1　small zucchini, about ½ pound, ends trimmed

1　sweet red or green pepper, cored and seeded

2　tablespoons peanut, vegetable, or corn oil

1　cup finely chopped onion

1　teaspoon finely minced garlic

1　cup peeled and seeded ripe tomatoes cut into ¼-inch cubes

1　bay leaf

½　teaspoon dried thyme

1　cup cooked rice

3　tablespoons butter

5　tablespoons plus ¼ cup flour

1　cup chicken broth

½　cup milk

4　egg yolks

　　Salt and freshly ground pepper to taste

½　cup finely chopped fresh parsley

1　teaspoon grated fresh ginger

1　egg

3　tablespoons water

1　cup fine fresh bread crumbs

　　Oil for deep frying

Croquettes, crisp and crunchy on the outside, moist within, are usually composed of leftover meats, poultry, or fish. But one of our favorites is made with chopped fresh vegetables and cooked rice. The croquettes are an ideal accompaniment to meat, poultry, and fish dishes and do not require a sauce.

1. Cut the eggplant into ¼-inch cubes. There should be about 3 cups.

2. Cut the zucchini into ½-inch cubes. There should be about 2 cups.

3. Cut the pepper into ½-inch pieces.

4. Heat the 2 tablespoons of oil in a large heavy skillet and add the onion, garlic, and sweet pepper pieces. Cook, stirring, until wilted.

5. Add the eggplant, zucchini, tomato, bay leaf, and thyme and cook, stirring, about 5 minutes, or until the liquid from the tomato has evaporated. Do not brown the vegetables. Add the rice.

6. Melt the butter in a saucepan and add the 5 tablespoons of flour, stirring with a wire whisk. Add the broth and milk, stirring vigorously with the whisk. When blended and smooth, cook for about 5 minutes, stirring. Add the egg yolks and cook, stirring, for about 30 seconds. Add the salt and pepper.

7. Stir the sauce into the vegetable mixture. (Remove the bay leaf.) Add the parsley and fresh ginger. Let stand until thoroughly cooled.

8. Divide the mixture into 20 equal portions. Shape each portion into a ball. Roll the balls in the remaining ¼ cup of flour. Mold them into the desired form: spheres, cylinders, pyramids, or flat cakes.

9. Beat the egg with the water. Roll the croquettes in the egg mixture and then in the bread crumbs. Press to help the crumbs adhere. Shake off any excess.

10. Heat the oil for deep frying. Add the croquettes a few at a time and cook for about 4 minutes, or until golden brown.

Yield: 4 to 6 servings.

VEGETABLE KOORMA

1. Cook each batch of vegetables in boiling salted water until just tender. Drain each batch as it is cooked and combine in a mixing bowl. Set aside.

2. Put the cashews into the container of a food processor or blender and blend to a purée. Add the yogurt, coconut, and water and blend to a paste.

3. Heat the oil in a large saucepan and, when it is quite hot but not smoking, add the cloves, small pieces of cinnamon, and cardamom seeds. Add the onion and cook until wilted. Add the tomatoes and stir. Cook for about 5 minutes. Add the turmeric, ground coriander, cumin, and salt.

4. Add the cooked vegetables and the yogurt and cashew mixture. Stir in half the fresh coriander. Cover and heat gently until piping hot throughout, about 5 minutes. Serve sprinkled with more fresh coriander.

Yield: 8 servings.

Note: Available in Indian shops.

1 cup cauliflower florets

1 cup fresh or frozen green peas

1 cup string beans cut into ½-inch lengths

1 cup diced carrots

1 cup peeled and diced potatoes

¾ cup unroasted peeled cashew nuts (see note)

¾ cup yogurt

1 cup unsweetened finely shredded coconut (see note)

¼ cup water

6 tablespoons sesame oil

6 whole cloves

5 small broken pieces cinnamon stick

3 small cardamom seeds

1½ cups coarsely chopped onion

2 cups cubed unpeeled tomatoes

¼ teaspoon ground turmeric

½ teaspoon ground coriander

½ teaspoon ground cumin

2 teaspoons salt

4 tablespoons chopped fresh coriander

ARTICHOKES VINAIGRETTE

Cut off the stems of the artichokes, using a sharp knife, to produce a neat, flat base. As the artichokes are cut, rub any cut surfaces with lemon to prevent discoloration. Slice off the top "cone" of the artichoke, about 1 inch from the tip.

Using a pair of kitchen scissors, cut off the sharp tips of the leaves, about ½ inch down.

Place in a kettle and add cold water to cover and salt to taste. For each 2 quarts of water, add the juice of 1 lemon. Cover and bring to the boil. Cook for 45 minutes.

Drain the artichokes. Using a melon ball scoop, hollow out the fuzzy choke in the center. Arrange them bottom side up on a rack to drain. Let cool. Chill. They are now ready to be served with cold sauces such as vinaigrette or mayonnaise.

STUFFED ARTICHOKES

There is definitely a hierarchy among greens—who could contemplate okra or cabbage in sophisticated realms—and if I should rank them, artichokes would certainly be at the top of the list. Although I like them whole, either hot or cold, one of my favorite ways to serve them is pared of their leaves. The neatly turned heart at the bottom of the artichoke makes a fancy and flavorful cup for any number of stuffings.

1. Prepare the artichokes for stuffing and preheat the oven to 350 degrees.

2. Heat 1 tablespoon of the oil in a skillet and add 1 cup of the onions. Cook, stirring, until wilted. Add the pork and 1 clove of minced garlic. Cook, stirring, until the meat changes color. Add the parsley, bay leaf, salt, pepper, thyme, bread crumbs, and red pepper flakes. Blend well. Stuff the artichokes throughout, that is to say, in the hollowed-out cavity and between the leaves, pushing the stuffing down toward the bottom.

3. Cook the bacon in a casserole large enough to hold the artichokes in one layer. When rendered of fat, add the remaining ½ cup of onion and remaining 1 clove of minced garlic. Add the artichokes, bottom side down. Dribble the remaining oil over the artichokes and pour the chicken broth around them. Sprinkle with salt and pepper. Bring to the boil and cover closely. Place in the oven and bake for 1 hour.

Yield: 4 servings.

4 large artichokes prepared for stuffing (see instructions)
3 tablespoons olive oil
1½ cups finely chopped onions
½ pound ground pork
2 garlic cloves, finely minced
3 tablespoons finely chopped parsley
1 small bay leaf
Salt and freshly ground pepper to taste
½ teaspoon dried thyme
1½ cups fresh bread crumbs
Hot red pepper flakes to taste
2 slices bacon, cut into small pieces
1½ cups fresh or canned chicken broth

HOW TO PREPARE WHOLE ARTICHOKES FOR STUFFING

Cut off the stems of the artichokes, using a sharp knife, to produce a neat, flat base. As the artichokes are cut, rub any cut surface with lemon to prevent discoloration. Slice off the top "cone" of the artichoke about 1 inch from the tip.

Using a pair of kitchen scissors, cut off the sharp tips of the leaves, about ½ inch down.

Use a melon ball scoop and hollow out the fuzzy choke in the center, taking care to remove all of it. Turn the artichokes upside down and press down to open up the center and facilitate stuffing. Turn right side up and stuff as desired.

ARTICHOKE BOTTOMS WITH TOMATOES AND MUSHROOMS

8 large artichoke bottoms prepared for stuffing (see following instructions)

2 tablespoons olive oil

½ pound mushrooms, sliced thin, about 3 cups

Salt and freshly ground pepper to taste

1 tablespoon finely chopped garlic

2 cups chopped imported canned tomatoes with liquid

⅛ teaspoon hot red pepper flakes

2 tablespoons finely chopped parsley

½ cup freshly grated Parmesan cheese

1. Prepare the artichoke bottoms and set aside.
2. Preheat the oven to 425 degrees.
3. Heat the oil in a skillet and add the mushrooms. Cook, stirring, until they give up their liquid. Cook until the liquid has evaporated and they start to brown. Add the salt, pepper, and garlic and cook briefly.
4. Add the tomatoes and cook down, stirring often, for about 8 minutes. Add the pepper flakes and parsley.
5. Spoon equal portions of the mixture into the artichoke shells. Arrange in a baking dish. Sprinkle with equal amounts of cheese. Bake for 5 minutes.

Yield: 8 servings.

HOW TO PREPARE ARTICHOKE BOTTOMS

Cut off the stems of the artichokes, using a sharp knife to produce a neat, flat base. Rub any cut surfaces with lemon to prevent discoloration. Trim all around until the base is smooth and white.

Place the artichoke on its side on a flat surface. Slice off the top, leaving a base about 1½ inches deep. Using a paring knife, trim around the sides and bottom to remove the green exterior that remains. Don't remove the fuzzy choke yet; it comes out easily when the artichokes are cooked.

They are now ready to be cooked in a blanc légume, or vegetable whitener, a blend of water and flour. Use enough to barely cover the artichoke bottoms. For each 6 cups of water use ¼ cup of flour.

Place a sieve over the saucepan in which the artichokes will be cooked. Add the flour. Pour cold water over the flour, rubbing to dissolve it. Add salt to taste. Add the artichoke bottoms and bring to the boil. Cover the pot closely and cook for about 25 minutes.

If the artichokes are not to be used immediately, let them rest in the cooking liquid. Before using, drain the artichoke bottoms and pull or scrape out the chokes.

ARTICHOKE BOTTOMS WITH OYSTERS AND SPINACH

1. Prepare the artichoke bottoms and arrange them stemmed side down in a baking dish.

2. Preheat the oven to 450 degrees.

3. Melt the butter in a saucepan and add the scallions. Cook briefly, stirring. Add the spinach and cook, stirring, until wilted. Add the salt and pepper.

4. Divide the spinach mixture in half. Use half to stuff the artichoke shells, an equal portion in each.

5. Return the remaining spinach mixture to the stove and add the cream. Bring to the boil and cook for 2 minutes. Add the oysters and cook briefly, just until edges curl, 30 or 40 seconds. Do not overcook. Arrange 1 oyster on top of each spinach-filled artichoke bottom. Spoon the spinach in cream over all.

6. Sprinkle each portion with cheese. Bake for 8 minutes.

Yield: 8 servings.

8 large artichoke bottoms prepared for stuffing (see preceding instructions)

2 tablespoons butter

1 cup finely chopped scallions

2 pounds bulk spinach, or two 10-ounce packages fresh spinach, cleaned and stems removed

Salt and freshly ground pepper to taste

½ cup heavy cream

8 oysters

¼ cup freshly grated Gruyère or Parmesan cheese

ASPARAGUS MILANESE

1. Preheat the broiler. Using a swivel-bladed vegetable peeler, scrape the asparagus, starting about 2 inches from the top of tips. Line up the tips of the asparagus spears uniformly on a flat surface. Cut off the ends 3 or 4 inches from the bottom. Discard the ends.

2. Place the asparagus in a skillet large enough to hold them and add cold water to cover. Add salt to taste. Bring to the boil and simmer from 1 to 5 minutes. Cooking time will depend on the size of the asparagus and how crisp you wish them to remain. Preferably they should be crisp-tender, not limp. Drain immediately.

3. Arrange the asparagus uniformly in a heatproof dish. Sprinkle with butter and cheese. Sprinkle with pepper to taste and glaze them until golden brown under the broiler.

Yield: 6 to 8 servings.

24 to 32 asparagus spears

Salt to taste

2 to 4 tablespoons butter, melted

½ to ¾ cup grated Parmesan cheese

Freshly ground pepper to taste

ASPARAGUS WITH HORSERADISH SAUCE

1 tablespoon fresh
   horseradish

2 tablespoons water

4 tablespoons butter, cut
   into 4 pieces

16 to 18 hot, freshly
   cooked asparagus
   spears

Combine the horseradish and water in a saucepan and stir. Do not boil but heat almost to the boiling point. Add the butter, piece by piece, and swirl it around until the sauce is well blended and smooth. Serve the hot sauce over the asparagus.

Yield: 4 to 6 servings.

ASPARAGUS WITH CHOPPED EGGS AND BUTTERED CRUMBS

3 pounds asparagus
   spears, about 30

   Salt to taste

1 hard-cooked egg,
   sieved or finely
   chopped

   Freshly ground pepper
   to taste

4 tablespoons butter

½ cup fine fresh bread
   crumbs

   Finely chopped parsley
   for garnish

1. Using a swivel-bladed vegetable peeler, scrape the asparagus spears starting about 2 inches from the top. Line up the asparagus spears and cut off about 1 inch of the tough bottom portions. Discard the ends. In a skillet bring enough water to the boil to cover the asparagus when added. Add the asparagus and salt and bring to the boil. Simmer until crisp-tender, 3 to 6 minutes, depending on the size of the asparagus. Drain.

2. While hot, arrange the asparagus on a serving dish. Sprinkle neatly with the chopped or sieved egg, salt, and pepper. Heat the butter in a heavy skillet and add the bread crumbs. Cook over high heat, swirling the crumbs in the butter until the crumbs and butter are hazelnut brown. Pour the mixture over the asparagus and serve sprinkled with chopped parsley.

Yield: 6 servings.

CHINESE NEW YEAR BEAN SPROUTS

If you eat large bean sprouts at the beginning of the Chinese New Year, "no matter how rough the road, your path will be smoothed." That's what Virginia Lee told us, and we wouldn't question her.

1. Rinse the bean sprouts and drain well.

2. Pour boiling water over the mushrooms and let stand for about 20 minutes. Drain and squeeze dry. Trim off the stems.

3. Cut the bamboo shoots into 12 pyramid shapes, each about 1½ inches tall. Rinse and drain.

4. Heat 3 tablespoons of the oil in a wok or skillet and add the bean sprouts. Cook for about 30 seconds and add the mushrooms. Cook for 20 seconds and add the bamboo shoots. Add the chicken broth, salt, sherry, sugar, and dark soy sauce. Cook over high heat, stirring, for about 6 minutes. Turn off the heat.

5. Arrange the pieces of bamboo shoot in an oval on a small oval serving dish. Arrange the bean sprouts in the center. Leave the mushrooms in the wok.

6. Add the remaining 1 teaspoon of oil to the wok and cook the mushrooms for about 45 seconds. Arrange the mushrooms over the bean sprouts and serve.

Yield: 8 servings with other Chinese dishes.

3 cups large bean sprouts
10 dried black mushrooms
1 or 2 pieces bamboo shoot
3 tablespoons plus 1 teaspoon peanut, vegetable, or corn oil
½ cup chicken broth
1½ teaspoons salt
1 tablespoon dry sherry
1 teaspoon sugar
½ teaspoon dark soy sauce

GREEN BEANS WITH MUSTARD SAUCE

1. Cut or snap off the ends of the beans, but leave the beans whole. Let stand in cold water until ready to use. Drain the beans and, preferably, steam them in a vegetable steamer for about 5 minutes. Or cook them briefly in a large quantity of boiling water about the same length of time. The important thing is not to overcook them. They must remain crisp-tender.

2. As the beans cook, spoon the mustard into a small bowl and add the salt, pepper, and lemon juice. Stir to blend and whisk in the oil. Drain the beans. Add the mustard sauce to the beans and toss to coat well. Serve piping hot in a hot serving dish.

Yield: 12 servings.

2 pounds green beans
1 tablespoon Dijon mustard
Salt and freshly ground pepper to taste
Juice of one lemon
⅓ cup olive oil

GREEN BEANS, PEASANT STYLE

1½ pounds green beans
⅛ pound salt pork
1 gallon water
½ cup salt
3 tablespoons butter
2 tablespoons finely
     chopped shallots
1 teaspoon finely
     chopped garlic
¼ cup chopped parsley

1. Cut or snap off the ends of the beans. Cut or snap the beans into 2-inch lengths. There should be about 5 cups. Add the beans to a basin of cold water and let stand until ready to use. Thinly slice the salt pork and cut the slices into small strips about the size of paper matches. Set aside.

2. Bring the water to the boil and add the salt. That volume of salt will help keep the beans green. Drain the beans and add them. When the water returns to the boil, cook the beans over high heat for about 5 minutes. Take care not to overcook. The beans must remain crisp. Drain them and put them into a basin of cold running water. Let chill in the water. Drain well.

3. Heat the butter in a large saucepan and add the salt pork. Cook until quite crisp. Add the shallots and beans and stir. Cook for about 2 minutes to heat the beans thoroughly. Add the garlic and parsley, toss and serve.

Yield: 8 to 12 servings.

Bean Curd with Ginger

1. Cut the bean curd into ½-inch cubes.
2. Soak the tree ears in warm water until they soften. Drain and coarsely chop.
3. Heat the oil in a wok or skillet and, when it is very hot, add the ginger, garlic, and scallions.
4. Add the bean curd, stirring quickly. Add the tree ears, chopped chilies, and peas, if desired, and stir. Add the soy sauce, sugar, and vinegar and toss. Spoon the mixture onto a serving dish and sprinkle the sesame oil over all.

Yield: 4 servings.

---

3 pads fresh bean curd

8 tree ear mushrooms, available in Chinese markets

2 tablespoons peanut, vegetable, or corn oil

1 tablespoon finely chopped fresh ginger

1½ tablespoons finely chopped garlic

¾ cup chopped scallions

1 teaspoon chopped fresh hot chilies, or ½ teaspoon crushed hot red pepper flakes

½ cup cooked peas, optional

1 tablespoon soy sauce

1 teaspoon sugar

1 tablespoon red wine vinegar

1 teaspoon sesame oil

BEETS IN SOUR CREAM
AND MUSTARD SAUCE

1¼ to 1½ pounds fresh
   beets
   Salt to taste
2 small red onions
1 tablespoon Dijon
   mustard
2 teaspoons white
   vinegar
½ cup sour cream
   Freshly ground pepper
   to taste

1. Cut off the leaves of the beets, but leave an inch or so of the beet top intact. Do not cut off the root ends. Wash the beets well and place in a kettle. Add cold water to cover and salt to taste. Bring to the boil and simmer until the beets are tender. This may take anywhere from 20 minutes to 1 hour depending on the size and age of the beets.

2. Drain the beets and let cool. When cool, trim off and discard the ends of the beets. Peel the beets and cut them into ¼-inch-thick or slightly smaller slices. Place the slices in a mixing bowl. Peel and slice the onions and add them to the bowl. Combine the remaining ingredients and blend well. Pour this mixture over the beets and toss well.

Yield: 6 to 10 servings.

POLISH-STYLE BEETS

7 or 8 fresh beets, about
   2 pounds
3 tablespoons butter
2 teaspoons lemon juice
   Salt to taste
¼ cup sour cream
   Freshly ground pepper
   to taste
¼ teaspoon sugar,
   optional

1. Trim off the ends of the beets. Peel the beets with a knife or swivel-bladed vegetable peeler. If the beets are very large, cut them into quarters. Cut small beets in half. If they are very small, leave them whole. Put the beets in a large saucepan and add water to cover. Bring to the boil and simmer for 30 to 45 minutes, or until tender. Drain.

2. Mash or blend the beets. Do not make them into a fine purée. The texture should be a little coarse. Add the butter, lemon juice, and salt. Stir in the sour cream and pepper. If the beets are not sweet enough, add the sugar. Serve warm.

Yield: 6 to 10 servings.

ITALIAN STYLE BROCCOLI

1. Cut the broccoli into bite-size florets. The pieces should not be too small or they will disintegrate. You may cut the broccoli stalks into 1½-inch lengths. Trim the sides and split the pieces in half lengthwise.

2. Heat the oil in a skillet and add the garlic and hot red pepper. Cook briefly without browning the garlic.

3. Add the broccoli and water and cover closely. Cook over low heat for about 10 minutes, or until the broccoli is tender. Stir the pieces occasionally so that they cook evenly. If necessary, add a couple of more tablespoons of water. When ready, the broccoli should be green and tender and all the water evaporated.

4. Serve, if desired, with lemon or vinegar.

Yield: 4 servings.

1 bunch broccoli, about 1½ pounds
2 tablespoons olive oil
1 to 2 teaspoons finely minced garlic
¼ teaspoon crushed hot red pepper flakes
⅓ cup water

BROCCOLI DI RAPE

1. If the broccoli di rape is bright green, young, and tender, it may be simply trimmed at the base and cooked. If it is a bit large and starting to lose its bright green color, it will be necessary to scrape the outside of the stems. The stems, if small, may be left whole. Or they may be cut into smaller pieces.

2. Rinse the broccoli di rape and drain without patting dry. It will steam in the water that clings to the leaves without adding more liquid. Put the broccoli di rape in a heavy kettle with a tight-fitting lid and add the remaining ingredients. Cover closely and simmer over low heat for about 5 minutes. Serve immediately and, if desired, with lemon wedges.

Yield: 4 servings.

1¼ pounds broccoli di rape (also sold as plain rabe or rapi)
Salt and freshly ground pepper to taste
½ teaspoon hot red pepper flakes
¼ cup olive oil
1 garlic clove, finely chopped

THREE-MILE HARBOR STUFFED SWEET AND SOUR CABBAGE

1 large or 2 small cabbages, about 3 pounds total

1 pound ground chuck

1 teaspoon peanut or vegetable oil

2 cups finely chopped onions

1 garlic clove, finely minced

1 cup fine fresh bread crumbs

1 egg, lightly beaten

¼ cup finely chopped parsley

1 cup drained imported canned tomatoes

Salt and freshly ground pepper to taste

One 28-ounce can tomatoes with tomato paste

½ cup white vinegar

¼ cup sugar

1 teaspoon paprika

1. Cut the core from the cabbage and drop the cabbage into a kettle of cold water to cover. Bring to the boil and cook for 5 minutes. Drain well.

2. Put the meat in a mixing bowl and set aside.

3. Heat the oil in a small skillet and add the onions and garlic. Cook, stirring, until wilted. Remove from the heat and let cool slightly.

4. Add half the onion mixture to the beef. Add the bread crumbs, egg, and parsley. Add the 1 cup of imported tomatoes, the salt, and pepper. Blend thoroughly with the hands.

5. Separate the leaves of the cabbage. Place one large leaf on a flat surface and cover the center with a small leaf. Add about 3 tablespoons of the meat mixture to the center and fold the cabbage leaves over, tucking in the ends. There should be about 18 cabbage rolls in all.

6. Do not drain the tomatoes with tomato paste but crush them.

7. Add half the crushed tomatoes to the bottom of a baking dish large enough to hold the stuffed cabbage rolls close together, in one layer.

8. Cover the tomato layer with the stuffed cabbage.

9. Blend the remaining crushed tomatoes with the remaining onion mixture, vinegar, and sugar. Spoon this over the stuffed cabbage. Sprinkle with paprika.

10. Preheat the oven to 350 degrees.

11. Cover the dish closely and bring to the boil on top of the stove. Bake for 1 hour and 15 minutes. Uncover and bake for about 20 minutes longer.

Yield: 6 to 8 servings.

STUFFED CABBAGE AVGOLEMONO

Lemon is the vanilla of Greek cooking. We have certain Greek friends who would sooner do without salt than the juice of a freshly squeezed lemon. This fondness is nowhere more apparent in the Greek kitchen than in those celebrated dishes that bear the name avgolemono (avgo, meaning egg, plus lemon). One of the best uses to which it can be put is as a sauce for a delectable stuffed cabbage.

2	heads cabbage, about 2 pounds each
	Salt to taste
1½	cups milk
¼	cup raw rice
1	pound ground lamb
⅓	cup finely chopped onion
3	tablespoons chopped fresh dill, or 1 teaspoon dried
½	teaspoon ground cinnamon
	Freshly ground pepper to taste
6	tablespoons olive oil
1	teaspoon dried oregano
2	garlic cloves, chopped
½	cup coarsely chopped onion
2½	cups fresh or canned chicken broth
3	egg yolks
⅓	cup lemon juice

1. Pull off the tough outer leaves from the head of cabbage. Use a knife to cut away the tough white center core. Drop the cabbage into boiling salted water to cover and let cook for about 5 minutes, or until the leaves separate easily. Invert the cabbage in a colander and let stand until cool and thoroughly drained.

2. Combine 1 cup of the milk and the rice in a small saucepan and bring to the boil. Stir and cover. Cook over low heat until all the liquid is absorbed and the rice is very soft. Stir as necessary. Uncover and let cool.

3. Combine the lamb with the rice, finely chopped onion, dill, cinnamon, salt and pepper to taste, 2 tablespoons of the olive oil, remaining ½ cup of milk, and oregano.

4. Separate the leaves of cabbage and pat dry. Use a sharp knife to make a V cut at the tough center end of each large leaf. Leave the tender smaller leaves intact. Rinse out a large square of cheesecloth in cold water, then squeeze dry and place on a flat surface. In the center place a large cabbage leaf, curly edge up. Arrange a smaller cabbage leaf in the center of the large leaf. Spoon 1 or 2 tablespoons of the filling into the center of the small leaf.

5. Bring the 4 corners of cheesecloth together and twist the ends together over a bowl. This will shape the leaves into a compact round. Remove the cabbage ball from the cheesecloth. It will not be necessary to use any string. Continue making the balls until all the cabbage leaves and filling are used. Shred any remaining cabbage leaves.

6. Heat the remaining 4 tablespoons of oil in a heavy casserole or Dutch oven large enough to hold the stuffed cabbage rolls in one layer. Add the garlic, coarsely chopped onion, salt to taste, and shredded cabbage. Arrange the stuffed cabbage seam side down and sprinkle with salt and pepper to taste. Add the chicken broth and bring to the boil. Cover and cook until the cabbage is tender, 1 to 1½ hours.

7. Pour off and save the cooking liquid. Keep the cabbage warm. Skim fat from cooking liquid. Pour reserved cooking liquid into a

saucepan and reduce it to about 1½ cups. Beat the yolks and lemon juice together. Add them, off heat, to the sauce, stirring rapidly. Return sauce to the burner and bring it just to the boil, stirring, but do not boil or it will curdle. Serve the sauce over the cabbage.

Yield: 16 to 18 cabbage rolls.

Braised Sweet and Sour Cabbage

1 small cabbage, about 2 pounds

2 tablespoons butter

¼ cup finely chopped shallots or onion

3 tablespoons brown sugar

2 tablespoons red wine vinegar

Salt and freshly ground pepper to taste

½ teaspoon aniseed

1. Cut the cabbage into wedges. Cut away and discard the core. Place the wedges on a flat surface and slice, cutting them crosswise into shreds. There should be about 10 cups.

2. Heat the butter in a casserole and add the shallots. Cook briefly and add the cabbage. Cover and cook for about 5 minutes.

3. Add the brown sugar, vinegar, salt, pepper, and aniseed. Cover closely and cook, stirring occasionally, for about 1¼ hours.

Yield: 8 servings.

CHINESE EGGS WITH CABBAGE

One of the first Chinese dishes that anyone learns to appreciate in America is that old standby, egg fu yung. Here is an exotic variation made with cabbage and flavored with both mustard and curry powder.

1. Heat 1 tablespoon of the oil in a wok and, when it is hot and almost smoking, add the cabbage. Cook, stirring, over high heat until cabbage is wilted and browned, about 4 minutes.

2. Reduce the heat and continue cooking and stirring until the cabbage seems a bit dry, about 4 more minutes. Transfer the cabbage to one side of a platter.

3. Heat 1 more tablespoon of oil in the wok and add the onions. Cook until the onions wilt and are golden brown, about 4 minutes. Transfer the onions to the other side of the platter.

4. Heat another tablespoon of oil and add the eggs, stirring until scrambled and firm. Transfer the eggs to the platter. Wipe out the wok.

5. Heat the fourth tablespoon of oil in the wok and add the mustard and curry powder. When the powders are bubbling, add the cabbage, onions, and eggs. Add the rice. Cook, stirring to blend the ingredients, for about 1 minute. The ingredients must be piping hot when ready. Transfer the mixture to a platter.

Yield: 6 servings.

4 tablespoons peanut, vegetable, or corn oil

5 cups shredded cabbage, about ¾ pound

2 cups thinly sliced onions

2 eggs

1½ teaspoons dried mustard

1½ teaspoons curry powder

2 cups cooked rice

BENGALESE CABBAGE WITH MUSTARD SEEDS AND COCONUT

1 coconut

6 tablespoons mustard oil (see note)

1 teaspoon whole black mustard seeds (see note)

2 bay leaves

1 medium-size cabbage (3 to 3½ pounds), cored and finely shredded

¾ teaspoon salt

1 hot green pepper, cut into fine, long strips resembling cabbage strips

1. When buying a coconut, shake it and make sure it has liquid inside. This liquid is not needed in the recipe, but it insures a moist interior. Crack the coconut open with a hammer and pry away the meat by sliding a pointed knife between it and the hard shell. Cut off the brown skin of the meat and discard it. Wash the white meat and finely grate it. You need about ⅓ cup.

2. Heat the oil in a wide casserole over a medium-high flame. When the oil is hot, add the mustard seeds and bay leaves. As soon as the bay leaves darken and the mustard seeds begin to pop (this takes just a few seconds), add the shredded cabbage. Turn the heat to medium. Stir and cook for about 5 minutes, or until the cabbage wilts. Add the salt and hot pepper strips. Stir and cook for 3 to 5 minutes more. Turn off the heat. Sprinkle with grated coconut, mix well, and serve.

Yield: 4 to 6 servings.

Note: Mustard oil and black mustard seeds are available at Indian food shops.

How to Make Sauerkraut

25 pounds white cabbage
½ pound pure granulated salt (noniodized)

1. Remove and discard the outer leaves and any other bruised or otherwise blemished leaves of the cabbage. Cut the cabbage into halves, then into quarters. Cut away the white tough center cores. Using a shredder or sharp slicer, cut the cabbage into fine shreds about the thickness of a penny.

2. In a kettle combine 5 pounds of the shreds with 3 tablespoons of the salt. Blend well and let stand for 15 minutes or so, until the cabbage wilts and gives up part of its liquid. Transfer this to a large sterilized crock. Add alternate layers of cabbage and salt, pressing down gently but firmly after each layer is added until the juice comes to the surface. Continue until the crock is filled to within 3 or 4 inches of the top.

3. Cover the cabbage with a clean white cloth such as a double layer of cheesecloth, tucking in the sides against the inside of the container. Add a free-floating lid that will fit inside the crock and rest on the cabbage. Failing this (perhaps even preferably), add a clean, heavy plastic bag containing water to rest on top of the cabbage. Whatever method is used the lid or covering should extend over the cabbage to prevent exposure to the air. Air will cause the growth of film yeast or molds. The lid will also act as a weight and should offer enough weight to keep the fermenting cabbage covered with brine. Store the crock at room temperature. The ideal temperature is from 68 to 72 degrees.

4. When fermentation occurs, gas bubbles will be visible in the crock. Total time of fermentation is 5 to 6 weeks.

Yield: Enough for about 9 quarts.

HOW TO PRESERVE FRESH SAUERKRAUT

When the sauerkraut has fermented sufficiently, empty it into a large kettle and bring it just to the simmer. Do not boil. The correct simmering temperature is from 185 to 210 degrees. Remove the sauerkraut from the heat and pack it into hot sterilized jars. Cover with hot juice to about ½ inch from the top of the rim. Close and seal the jars with a lid and screw top. Put in a water bath and boil pint jars for 15 minutes, quart jars for 20 minutes. The sauerkraut is now ready to be stored. It will keep on the shelf for months.

SAUERKRAUT WITH CARAWAY

2 pounds sauerkraut

2 tablespoons lard or vegetable oil

1 cup finely chopped onion

1 garlic clove, finely minced

1 tablespoon sugar

2 teaspoons crushed caraway seeds

2 cups fresh or canned chicken broth

Salt and freshly ground pepper to taste

1 small raw potato

1. Put the sauerkraut in a colander and squeeze or press to remove most of the liquid.

2. Melt the lard in a heavy casserole and add the onion and garlic. Cook, stirring, until the onion is translucent. Add the sauerkraut, sugar, caraway seeds, chicken broth, salt, and pepper. Cover and cook for 45 minutes.

3. Peel and grate the potato. There should be about ⅓ cup. Stir this into the sauerkraut. Cover and cook for 15 minutes longer.

Yield: 6 servings.

RED CABBAGE ALSATIAN STYLE

2 pounds red cabbage

3 tablespoons peanut, vegetable, or corn oil

2 whole cloves, crushed

1 tablespoon red wine vinegar

2 tablespoons brown sugar

Salt and freshly ground pepper to taste

3 tablespoons butter

1. Pull off and discard any tough or wilted outer leaves from the cabbage. Trim away and discard the core from the cabbage. Shred the cabbage. There should be about 10 cups.

2. Heat the oil in a heavy skillet and add the cabbage. Cook, stirring, to wilt. Add the cloves, vinegar, sugar, salt, and pepper. Cook for 10 to 15 minutes, stirring often. Stir in the butter and serve.

Yield: 10 or more servings.

BRAISED RED CABBAGE WITH CHESTNUTS

1. Preheat the oven to 450 degrees.

2. Pull off and discard any blemished outer leaves from the cabbage. Quarter the cabbage and shred it.

3. Using a sharp paring knife, make an incision around the perimeter of each chestnut, starting and ending on either side of the "top-knot" or stem end. Place the chestnuts in one layer in a baking dish just large enough to hold them. Place them in the oven and bake for about 10 minutes, or until they open. Let the chestnuts cool just until they can be handled. Peel them while they are hot.

4. Heat the salt pork in a heavy saucepan large enough to hold the cabbage. When the salt pork is rendered of its fat, add the onion and cook briefly.

5. Meanwhile, peel and core the apples and cut them into quarters. Thinly slice the apple quarters. There should be about 4 cups. Add the apples to the saucepan. Add the wine and bring it to the boil. Add the cabbage, salt, and pepper to taste. Add the brown sugar and chestnuts and cover. Simmer for 10 minutes, stirring occasionally. Make sure that the mixture does not stick and burn.

6. Place the saucepan in the oven and bake for 30 minutes. Reduce the oven heat to 375 degrees and bake for 1 to 1¼ hours, or until the cabbage is thoroughly tender. Stir occasionally as it cooks. Stir in the butter and vinegar and blend well. Serve piping hot.

Yield: 8 to 12 servings.

One 3-pound red cabbage
12 chestnuts
¼ pound salt pork, cut into small cubes
¼ cup finely chopped onion
3 cooking apples, about 1 pound
1 cup dry white wine
Salt and freshly ground pepper to taste
2 tablespoons dark brown sugar
2 tablespoons butter
1 tablespoon red wine vinegar

CARROTS VICHY

1½ pounds carrots,
   trimmed and scraped
   Salt and freshly ground
   pepper to taste
1 teaspoon sugar
¼ cup water
4 tablespoons butter
   Chopped parsley

One of the most amusing stories I know about the names of food concerns Vichy. It is, of course, the famous spa that, during the Nazi occupation of France in the Second World War, acquired so bad a reputation that some hotels in this country changed the name Vichyssoise on their menus to De Gaulloise.

In any event, the most famous dish that bears the name is carrots Vichy. They are, I am told, a frequent part of the Vichy diet and there they are made with the famed local mineral water. Actually the dish consists of thin carrot rounds cooked until glazed with sugar, a little water, and butter.

Equip a food processor with the slicing blade and slice the carrots. There should be about 4 cups. You may, of course, slice them very thin by hand. Put them in a skillet and add salt and pepper, sugar, water (Vichy water if you want to be authentic), and butter. Cover with a round of buttered wax paper and cook over moderately high heat, shaking the skillet occasionally. Cook for about 10 minutes, or until carrots are tender, the liquid has disappeared, and they are lightly glazed. Take care they do not burn. Serve sprinkled with chopped parsley.

Yield: 6 servings.

CAULIFLOWER POLONAISE

1 medium-size head of
   cauliflower
   Water to cover
½ cup milk
   Salt to taste
4 tablespoons butter
½ cup fine fresh bread
   crumbs
1 hard-cooked egg, finely
   chopped
1 tablespoon chopped
   parsley

1. Trim the cauliflower and put it in a kettle with cold water to cover about 1 inch above the top of the cauliflower. Add the milk and salt and bring to the boil. Simmer, uncovered, for 15 minutes, or to the desired degree of doneness. By all means do not overcook the cauliflower. It must be tender and not mushy. Drain the cauliflower and put it on a hot serving dish.

2. Melt the butter in a small skillet and, when it is quite hot, add the bread crumbs. Cook, shaking the skillet, until they start to brown. Add the egg. Cook, tossing everything, for about 10 seconds and add the parsley. Cook, tossing and stirring, for about 1 minute. When ready, the mixture should be thick and foamy. Do not let it burn. Pour the sauce over the cauliflower and serve.

Yield: 6 to 8 servings.

BATTER-FRIED CAULIFLOWER

1. Break the cauliflower into florets.

2. Drop the cauliflower into boiling water with salt to taste. When the water returns to the boil, cook for about 2 minutes. Drain and run under cold water. Drain well and set aside.

3. Add the cauliflower to the fritter batter, turning to coat well.

4. Heat the oil for deep frying and, when it is quite hot, add the batter-coated cauliflower pieces one at a time. Do not crowd the pieces in the oil. Cook, turning the pieces occasionally, for about 2 minutes, or until crisp outside and golden brown.

5. Remove with a slotted spoon and drain on paper towels.

6. Add the remaining cauliflower pieces and cook until done. Sprinkle with salt to taste. Serve hot with tomato sauce.

Yield: 4 to 8 servings.

1 cauliflower, about 1¼ pounds

Salt to taste

Fritter batter (see following recipe)

Oil for deep frying

Fresh tomato sauce (see recipe page 784)

FRITTER BATTER

Sift the flour into a mixing bowl. Add the oil and salt. Add the eggs and stir with a wire whisk. Add the water gradually, beating with the whisk.

Yield: About 2 cups.

1½ cups flour

3 tablespoons peanut, vegetable, or corn oil

1 teaspoon salt

2 large eggs

½ cup water

CHAYOTES STUFFED WITH SHRIMP

3 chayotes, ¾ to 1 pound each

Salt to taste

¾ pound raw shrimp in the shell

4 tablespoons butter

1 cup finely chopped onion

1 teaspoon finely minced garlic

2 tablespoons flour

1 cup milk

2 teaspoons finely chopped fresh ginger, optional

¼ cup finely chopped scallions

1 egg yolk

Freshly ground pepper to taste

½ cup fine fresh bread crumbs

¼ cup finely chopped parsley

½ cup grated Cheddar cheese

Chayotes enjoy considerable popularity on the tables of Louisiana in general and New Orleans specifically, where they are known as mirlitons. They resemble a pale green quince and have a pleasant crunchy texture like that of a not-too-ripe melon. Its flavor makes it a natural for almost any assertive flavors you wish to employ.

1. Split the chayotes lengthwise in half. Put in a kettle of cold water and add the salt. Bring to the boil and simmer for about 10 minutes. Do not overcook or the vegetables will become mushy. Drain and run briefly under cold water. Drain again.

2. Using a spoon or melon ball cutter, scoop out the flesh and seeds of each half, leaving a shell of about ⅛ inch thick or slightly thicker. Set the shells aside. Chop flesh and seeds fine. There should be about 1 cup. Set aside.

3. Peel and devein the shrimp and coarsely chop. There should be about 1¼ cups. Set aside.

4. When ready to cook, preheat the oven to 425 degrees.

5. Melt half the butter in a saucepan and add the onion and garlic. Cook, stirring, until wilted. Sprinkle with the flour and stir to distribute evenly. Add the milk, stirring rapidly with a wire whisk.

6. When the sauce is thickened and smooth, add the chopped pulp. Bring to the boil, stirring, and add the ginger and scallions.

7. Remove from the heat and stir in the egg yolk. Let stand to room temperature. Stir in the shrimp, salt, pepper, ¼ cup of the bread crumbs, and the parsley.

8. Use the mixture to stuff the chayote halves. Pile up and smooth over.

9. Blend the remaining ¼ cup of bread crumbs and cheese. Sprinkle the tops with the mixture, patting to help it adhere. Dot with the remaining 2 tablespoons of butter.

10. Arrange the stuffed halves in a lightly buttered baking dish and bake for 20 minutes.

Yield: 6 servings.

Chayotes Stuffed with Cheese

1. Split the chayotes lengthwise in half. Put them in a kettle of cold water with the salt. Bring to the boil and let simmer for about 10 minutes. Do not overcook or the vegetable will become mushy. Drain and run briefly under cold water. Drain again.

2. Using a spoon or melon ball cutter, scoop out the flesh and seeds of each half, leaving a shell about ⅛ inch thick or slightly thicker. Set the shells aside. Chop flesh and seeds fine. There should be about 1 cup.

3. When ready to cook, preheat the oven to 425 degrees.

4. In a mixing bowl, combine the chopped pulp with 1 cup of the bread crumbs, 2 cups of the cheese, the egg, garlic, scallions, pepper flakes, salt, and pepper to taste.

5. Use this mixture to fill the chayote halves. Pile the filling up and smooth it over.

6. Combine the remaining ½ cup of cheese with the remaining ½ cup of bread crumbs. Sprinkle the tops with the mixture, patting to help it adhere. Dot the tops of each half with butter.

7. Arrange the stuffed halves in a lightly buttered baking dish and bake for 20 minutes.

Yield: 6 servings.

3 chayotes, ¾ to 1 pound each

Salt to taste

1½ cups fine fresh bread crumbs

2½ cups finely grated Muenster cheese

1 egg, lightly beaten

2 teaspoons finely minced garlic

¼ cup finely chopped scallions

¼ teaspoon hot red pepper flakes

Freshly ground pepper to taste

2 tablespoons butter

BUTTERED WHOLE CHESTNUTS

2 pounds chestnuts
3 tablespoons butter
Salt to taste
¾ cup fresh or canned chicken broth
1 tablespoon sugar

1. Preheat the oven to 400 degrees.

2. Using a sharp paring knife, make an incision around the perimeter of each chestnut, starting and ending on either side of the "top-knot" or stem end. Place the chestnuts in one layer in a baking dish just large enough to hold them. Place them in the oven and bake for about 10 minutes. Let the chestnuts cool just until they can be handled. Peel them while they are hot.

3. Place the chestnuts in a saucepan and add the butter, salt, broth, and sugar. Cover and cook over low heat, stirring frequently, for 10 to 15 minutes. Place them in the oven and bake, stirring occasionally, for 25 to 30 minutes, or until thoroughly tender.

Yield: 6 to 8 servings.

PURÉE OF CHESTNUTS

2 pounds chestnuts
Salt to taste
2 cups fresh or canned chicken broth
1 celery rib, quartered
1 small fennel bulb, halved (optional)
2 tablespoons butter
1 cup hot milk
½ cup hot heavy cream

1. Using a sharp paring knife, make an incision around the perimeter of each chestnut, starting and ending on either side of the "top-knot" or stem end. Put the chestnuts in a skillet with water to cover and the salt. Bring to the boil and simmer for 15 to 20 minutes, or until the shells can be easily removed with the fingers. Drain. When cool enough to handle, peel the chestnuts. Remove both the outer shell and the inner peel.

2. Return the chestnuts to the saucepan and add the chicken broth, celery, and fennel, if desired. Simmer, covered, for 20 to 30 minutes, or until the chestnuts are done. Drain.

3. Put the chestnuts through a food mill or ricer and, while they are still hot, beat in the butter, hot milk, and hot cream. Serve hot.

Yield: 8 to 12 servings.

Put enough water in a kettle to cover the shucked corn. Do not add salt. Bring the water to the boil and add the corn and cover. When the water returns to the boil, remove the kettle from the heat. Let the corn stand in the water for at least 5 minutes and serve.

The corn may stand in the water for as long as 20 minutes without damage to its flavor and quality.

CORN AND PIMIENTOS VINAIGRETTE

Cut and scrape the kernels of corn from the cob. There should be about 2 cups. Put in a mixing bowl. Add the pimientos, onion, garlic, and parsley. Blend the remaining ingredients with a wire whisk. Pour over the corn mixture and toss to blend.

Yield: 4 to 6 servings.

4 ears of cooked corn

½ cup pimientos cut into ¼-inch cubes

½ cup finely chopped onion

½ teaspoon minced garlic

¼ cup finely chopped parsley

1 teaspoon Dijon mustard

1 tablespoon red wine vinegar

Juice of ½ lemon

5 tablespoons olive oil

Salt and freshly ground pepper to taste

CORN PUDDING

8 to 10 ears of uncooked corn
½ cup heavy cream
2 egg yolks
2 whole eggs
½ cup grated Cheddar cheese
⅛ teaspoon grated nutmeg
   Salt and freshly ground pepper to taste
1 to 2 tablespoons diced green chilies, optional
1 tablespoon butter

Although there is nothing more delectable than fresh corn on the cob slathered with sweet butter, we have, since childhood, had a special fondness for grated corn dishes and corn pudding.

1. Preheat the oven to 375 degrees.

2. Grate and scrape the corn off the cob. There should be about 2½ cups. Put the corn pulp in a mixing bowl and add the cream, yolks, whole eggs, cheese, nutmeg, salt, pepper, and green chilies. Beat well.

3. Butter a baking dish with the butter (we used a 9-inch ceramic pie plate) and pour in the corn batter. Bake for 25 minutes. Serve hot.

Yield: 6 servings.

CORN FRITTERS

4 ears of cooked corn, or 2 cups frozen whole corn kernels, defrosted
2 eggs, separated
6 tablespoons flour
   Salt and freshly ground pepper to taste
⅓ cup milk
4 tablespoons peanut, vegetable, or corn oil
2 tablespoons butter

1. If fresh corn is available, cut off the kernels with a sharp knife. There should be 2 cups.

2. Put the corn kernels in a mixing bowl and add the egg yolks. Add the flour, salt, and pepper and blend with a spoon. Stir in the milk.

3. Beat the whites until stiff and fold them in.

4. Heat the oil and butter in a skillet, and when it is hot spoon about 4 mounds of batter into the fat. Add only enough at a time to fill the skillet. Cook for 3 to 4 minutes, or until golden on one side. Turn with a spatula and cook until golden on the other side, 3 to 4 minutes. Transfer to paper towels, but serve quickly while they are still hot.

Yield: About 16 fritters.

SUCCOTASH WITH HOMINY

1. Preheat the oven to 475 degrees.

2. Open up the tops of each corn cob to expose the cornsilks. Chop off and discard the top of each ear to remove most of the corn silks. Drop the corn into cold water to cover and let stand for 5 minutes. Drain.

3. Reshape the husks and wrap two at a time in aluminum foil. Arrange them on a baking sheet and place in the oven. Bake for 15 minutes.

4. Shuck the corn cobs, discarding any remaining cornsilks. Cut away the kernels and set aside.

5. Heat the butter in a casserole and add the scallions and peppers. Cook briefly, stirring, and add the hominy. If fresh lima beans and peas are used, add them and cook until tender. If frozen peas are used, run them under the hot water tap until defrosted. Drain and add them to the casserole along with the corn. Cook, stirring, for about 1 minute and stir in the chives.

Yield: 6 servings.

6 unshucked ears of corn on the cob

8 tablespoons butter

½ cup finely chopped scallions

½ cup finely chopped sweet yellow pepper

½ cup finely chopped sweet red pepper

2 cups drained canned hominy

½ cup fresh or frozen baby lima beans

½ cup fresh or frozen field peas or lady peas, or use any tender, small white peas

¼ cup finely minced chives

PARSLEYED CUCUMBER OVALS

Trim off the ends of the cucumbers. Cut the cucumbers into 2-inch lengths. Quarter each section lengthwise. Using a paring knife, carefully trim the pieces, cutting away the green skin and the seeds and leaving only the firm flesh. The pieces are now ready to cook, although if you want to "turn" them, as French chefs do, neatly round the ends of each piece with a knife. Place the pieces in a saucepan and add boiling water to cover and the salt. Cook for 1 minute and drain. Return the cucumbers to the saucepan and add the butter, salt, and pepper to taste. Toss until butter melts. Sprinkle with parsley. Serve not.

Yield: 4 servings.

2 large, firm, fresh cucumbers

Salt to taste

1 tablespoon butter

Freshly ground pepper to taste

2 tablespoons finely chopped parsley

Eggplant Stuffed with Prosciutto and Cheese

THE EGGPLANT:

1½ pounds eggplant
    Flour for dredging
3 large eggs
2 tablespoons finely
   chopped parsley
   Oil for deep frying

THE FILLING:

½ pound mozzarella
   cheese
½ cup finely shredded
   prosciutto
1 egg
2 cups ricotta cheese
¼ cup grated Parmesan
   cheese
1 tablespoon finely
   chopped parsley
   Salt and freshly ground
   pepper to taste
2 to 3 cups marinara
   sauce (see recipe
   page 787)

1. Preheat the oven to 500 degrees.

2. Trim off the ends of the eggplant and cut the eggplant lengthwise into 12 center-cut slices. Discard the trimmings. Dredge the slices in flour to coat on all sides. Shake off excess. Beat the eggs with parsley and dip the slices in egg to coat well. Fry the slices, a few at a time, in hot oil, for about 3 minutes for each batch. Drain well.

3. Cut the mozzarella into ¼-inch slices. Cut the slices into ¼-inch strips. Cut the strips into ¼-inch cubes. Combine the mozzarella with the remaining ingredients for the filling except the marinara sauce.

4. Place the fried eggplant slices on a flat surface. Add equal amounts of filling toward the base of each slice. Roll to enclose the filling. Spoon about ½-inch of marinara sauce over a baking dish large enough to hold the stuffed slices. Arrange them over the sauce. Cover with more sauce and place in the oven. Bake for about 10 minutes.

Yield: 8 to 12 servings.

EGGPLANT AU GRATIN

1. Preheat the oven to 425 degrees.
2. Peel the eggplant and cut the flesh into 1-inch cubes, more or less. Drop the cubes into boiling salted water and cook for about 5 minutes. Drain well.
3. Meanwhile, slice the mushrooms. There should be about 3 cups. Heat 1 tablespoon of the butter in a skillet and add the mushroom slices. Sprinkle with salt and about 1 teaspoon lemon juice. Cook, stirring and tossing, until wilted and the juices come out. Continue cooking until the liquid evaporates. Set aside.
4. Melt 1½ tablespoons of butter in a saucepan and add the flour, stirring with a wire whisk. Add the half-and-half, stirring rapidly with the whisk. When blended and smooth, add salt and pepper to taste, the remaining lemon juice, nutmeg, and Tabasco. Stir in the mushrooms and eggplant. Stir in the egg. Spoon the mixture into a baking dish (we used an 8 × 1-inch pie plate). Sprinkle with a mixture of crumbs and cheese and dot with the remaining tablespoon of butter. Bake for 30 to 40 minutes and then brown under the broiler.

Yield: 4 to 6 servings.

1 eggplant, about 1 pound
Salt to taste
½ pound fresh mushrooms
3½ tablespoons butter
Juice of ½ lemon
1½ tablespoons flour
¾ cup half-and-half
Freshly ground pepper to taste
¼ teaspoon grated nutmeg
Tabasco sauce to taste
1 egg, lightly beaten
2 tablespoons bread crumbs
2 tablespoons grated Parmesan cheese

STRANGE FLAVOR EGGPLANT

1½ pounds eggplant, preferably the Chinese long variety

1 tablespoon finely minced garlic

1 tablespoon finely chopped fresh ginger

1 large scallion, trimmed and cut into 1-inch lengths

¼ to ½ teaspoon hot red pepper flakes

2½ tablespoons soy sauce

2½ to 3 tablespoons loosely packed light brown sugar

1 teaspoon rice vinegar

2 tablespoons hot water

2 tablespoons corn or peanut oil

1 teaspoon Chinese or Japanese sesame oil

1 tablespoon chopped scallion, or fresh coriander sprigs for garnish

Barbara Tropp, whose expertise in Chinese cooking came about by way of studying Chinese poetry and art in Taiwan, explained to us that this dish comes from the word *guai*, which in Chinese poetry can mean "odd or weird." In cooking, however, "strange" flavor refers to an ineffable and delicious blend of flavors—spicy, subtle, sweet, tart, and tangy all at the same time.

1. Preheat the oven to 475 degrees.

2. Rinse the eggplants and pat dry. Prick them all over with a fork.

3. Arrange the eggplants on a baking dish or cookie sheet. Put the dish in the center of the oven and bake until the eggplants are wilted and collapse when pressed. Turn once as they bake. This will take 20 to 40 minutes or longer. Let stand until cool enough to handle.

4. Pull off and discard the skin of each eggplant. Cut the flesh into pieces and put in the container of a food processor or blender. Blend until smooth. Scrape the eggplant into a bowl.

5. Add the garlic, ginger, and 1-inch lengths of scallion to the container of a food processor or blender. Blend thoroughly. Scrape into a bowl and add the pepper flakes.

6. Combine the soy sauce, sugar, vinegar, and water, stirring to dissolve the sugar.

7. Heat a wok and add the corn oil. Add the garlic mixture and cook, stirring, for about 20 seconds. Do not burn.

8. Add the sugar mixture and stir. When the liquid boils, add the eggplant. Stir to blend. Bring to the simmer.

9. Add the sesame oil and stir. Scrape the mixture into a serving dish. Garnish with chopped scallion or sprigs of fresh coriander. Serve hot, cold, or lukewarm.

Yield: 4 servings.

SPICED EGGPLANT

1. Place the eggplants on a hot charcoal grill or wrap them in heavy-duty aluminum foil and bake in a very hot (500-degree) oven for about 20 minutes. If the eggplants are grilled, turn them often over the hot coals. Cook until the eggplants are capsized and thoroughly tender throughout. Remove and let stand until cool enough to handle.

2. Melt the butter in a saucepan. When the eggplant are cool, pull away the skin, scraping off and saving the tender inside pulp. Scoop the tender pulp into the saucepan with the butter. Discard the skins. Add the onions to the eggplant and cook for 10 minutes, stirring often and taking care that the mixture does not stick to the bottom and burn.

3. Add the salt and tomatoes. Add the ginger, peppers, and paprika and cook, stirring often while scraping the bottom to prevent scorching. Cook for about 15 minutes and remove from the heat. Add the chopped coriander. Serve hot, lukewarm, or at room temperature.

Yield: 4 to 8 servings.

2 eggplants, about 1 pound each

4 tablespoons butter

2 cups finely chopped onions

Salt to taste

1 cup ripe tomatoes, cored and cut into thin wedges

½ cup fresh ginger, cut into small cubes or thin sticks the size of matchsticks

¾ cup sliced hot green peppers, or use hot red pepper flakes to taste

1 teaspoon sweet paprika

3 tablespoons chopped fresh coriander, optional

BRAISED ENDIVES

8 firm, perfect,
  unblemished endives,
  about 1½ pounds

1 tablespoon butter

  Juice of ½ lemon

½ cup water

1 teaspoon sugar

  Salt and freshly ground
  pepper to taste

Among the handful of vegetables and salad greens that most appeal to our palates is one of the most difficult to cultivate, Belgian endive. Endive is cultivated by hand, as it has been for the past 125 years, on the Flemish flatlands that surround Brussels. The vegetable defies harvesting by machine. The seeds are sown by hand and, when they produce roots at the end of six weeks, the roots must be dug up and replanted in a blend of sand and soil that offers both heat and humidity, plus total darkness. It is this combination of factors that produces a premature, straight, smooth, and fragile-crisp endive.

As if this were not labor enough, the endive is then harvested, replanted, and covered with deep-layered mounds of loamy earth. Weeks later, the ready-to-market endive is again brought to the surface by hand, washed, spun-dried, and packaged to be sold at home or shipped overseas.

An average harvest is estimated at about 80,000 tons a year; of this, more than 550 tons are exported to the United States for the delectation of those who cherish the finer things of the table. Although endive is best known and enjoyed in this country as a salad ingredient, it is a remarkably versatile vegetable.

1. Trim off the darkened ends of each endive. Put the endives in one layer in a heavy skillet.

2. Add the butter, lemon juice, water, sugar, salt, and pepper and cover closely. Bring to the boil and simmer for 25 minutes.

Yield: 4 servings.

BAKED ENDIVES WITH PARMESAN CHEESE

8 cooked, well-drained
  endives (see preceding
  recipe for braised
  endives)

2 tablespoons butter

¼ cup freshly grated
  Parmesan cheese

1. Preheat the oven to 425 degrees.

2. Drain the endives well on paper towels.

3. Using 1 tablespoon of the butter, lightly butter the bottom and sides of a baking dish large enough to hold the endives close together in one layer. Add the endives. Sprinkle with the cheese and dot with the remaining butter.

4. Bake for 15 minutes. Run briefly under the broiler until browned and nicely glazed.

Yield: 4 servings.

FENNEL AU GRATIN

Fennel is a crisp, aromatic vegetable that is more closely identified with the Italian table than any other. It is established that it was known in England, however, long before the Norman Conquest and that for centuries it has been traditional throughout Europe for use with both fresh and salted fish. Although it is delicious eaten out of hand as a cold appetizer, it is an enormously versatile vegetable when cooked.

1. Preheat the oven to 400 degrees.

2. Cut off the tops of the fennel bulbs and trim the base. Pull off and discard any tough outer leaves. Cut the remaining fennel into quarters if they are large, or in half if they are small. Drop the fennel into enough boiling water to cover and, when the water returns to the boil, simmer for 15 to 20 minutes, or until almost tender.

3. Drain the fennel and arrange the pieces symmetrically, cut side down, on a baking dish. Dot with the butter. Add salt, pepper, and chicken broth. Sprinkle with cheese and bake for 30 minutes.

Yield: 6 to 8 servings.

3 to 6 fennel bulbs
4 tablespoons butter
  Salt and freshly ground pepper to taste
1 cup fresh or canned chicken broth
½ cup grated Parmesan cheese

FRIED FENNEL

3 fennel bulbs
Salt to taste
2 eggs, beaten
1½ cups fine, dry,
   unflavored bread
   crumbs
Oil for frying

1. Cut off the tops of the fennel bulbs and trim the base. Pull off and discard any tough outer leaves. Cut the remaining fennel into slices slightly less than ½ inch thick. Rinse well and drain.

2. Bring 3 quarts of water to the boil and add the salt. Add the fennel slices. Cook until tender yet firm, 6 to 10 minutes. Drain and cool.

3. Dip the slices first in egg, then in bread crumbs. Heat about ½ inch of oil in a heavy skillet and, when the oil is quite hot, add the slices. Do not crowd them but cook as many as possible at one time. Cook until golden brown on one side, turn and cook until golden on the other. Drain on paper towels. Sprinkle with salt and serve hot.

Yield: 4 servings.

MIXED SOUTHERN GREENS

The standard item of soul food that appeared almost daily at my mother's table were one form of greens or another, always cooked with pieces of pork, sometimes salted, sometimes smoked. The greens were of a common garden variety, such as mustard greens, collard greens, and turnip greens. These would be put on to boil with a great quantity of water and salt and allowed to cook for hours. Once cooked, the liquid is much treasured by Southern palates. It is called "pot likker," and you sip it like soup with corn bread. If you want to be fancy, you can always make cornmeal dumplings to float on top of the cooking liquid.

1. Pick over the greens to remove any tough stems and veins. Wash and drain thoroughly. Use only the tender leaves, cutting or breaking them into 2-inch pieces.

2. Put the bacon in a very large heavy kettle or casserole and cook, stirring, until rendered of fat and browned. Add the onion, celery, and sweet green pepper. Cook, stirring, for about 5 minutes.

3. Add the greens, stirring. Cover closely and cook, stirring, until greens are wilted. Add the ham hocks, salt, pepper, vinegar, and dried hot pepper. Cover and cook for about 15 minutes.

4. Add the water, cover, and let simmer for about 1½ hours.

Yield: 8 to 12 servings.

7 pounds mixed greens (they may include collards, kale, and turnip greens)

¾ pound slab of lean bacon, cut into ¼-inch cubes

1 cup finely chopped onion

½ cup finely chopped celery

¾ cup chopped sweet green pepper

2 ham hocks (about ¾ pound each)

Salt and freshly ground pepper to taste

2 tablespoons red wine vinegar

1 or 2 dried hot red peppers, broken into pieces

2 cups water

JERUSALEM ARTICHOKES (SUN CHOKES) WITH TOMATOES

1 pound Jerusalem artichokes, about 8

3 tablespoons olive oil

1 tablespoon finely minced garlic

1 cup drained, imported canned tomatoes

2 tablespoons finely chopped parsley

Salt and freshly ground pepper to taste

One of the most abundant, curiously neglected and oddly named foods in America is the Jerusalem artichoke. It is not an artichoke at all, as we know the more sophisticated globe artichoke. The Jerusalem version is actually related to the sunflower, called *girasole* in Italian. And, at least according to folk etymology, girasole, through some slip of nomenclature, turned into Jerusalem. In today's French kitchens it is known as a *topinambour,* again for an unusual reason: At approximately the same time that it was introduced into that country, there was an exhibition featuring a tribe from Brazil known as *topinambours.* The vegetable was thus christened and the name stuck. Whatever it is called (most recently sun choke), it is delicious and, when in season, readily available from California.

1. Using a small regular or swivel-bladed paring knife, peel the artichokes. Cut them into ¼-inch-thick slices. There should be about 3 cups.

2. Heat the oil in a saucepan and add the artichoke slices. Cook, stirring and tossing in the oil, for about 2 minutes. Add the garlic and cook, stirring and tossing, for about 30 seconds. Add the tomatoes, parsley, salt, and pepper. Stir and cover. Cook for 8 to 10 minutes and serve.

Yield: 4 servings.

If we had to produce a list of our favorite vegetables for cold weather, it would certainly include the leek, that delectable green and white root of such a hearty nature that it can be left in the ground all winter if the temperature does not drop beyond 10 below. Although it is a member of the onion family, it has a subtle, irresistible flavor and certainly leaves no aftertaste.

HOW TO PREPARE LEEKS FOR COOKING WHOLE

Trim off the root ends of the leeks at the very base. Cut off the tops of the leeks crosswise at the center. Remove any bruised outside leaves. Split lengthwise, inserting a knife about 1 inch from the base. Give it a ¼-inch turn and make another lengthwise cut. This allows the leaves to be opened up. Drop the leeks into a basin of cold water and let stand until ready to use.

Shake the leeks to make certain they are cleared of inner dirt or sand. Tie with string into bunches. Bring enough salted water to the boil to cover the leeks. Add the leeks and cook for 10 minutes. Drain in a colander and let cool. Do not refrigerate.

LEEKS AU GRATIN

1. Preheat the oven to 450 degrees.

2. Drain the leeks well and let them cool.

3. Melt 2 tablespoons of the butter and add the flour, stirring with a wire whisk. When blended, add the milk, stirring rapidly with the whisk. Add the salt, pepper, nutmeg, and cayenne and blend. Remove from the heat and add the yolks, stirring briskly.

4. Arrange the leeks close together in a row and cut them crosswise into 4 pieces of equal length. Heat the remaining 1 tablespoon of butter in a skillet and add the pieces of leeks. Sprinkle with salt and pepper. Cook briefly, tossing to heat evenly. Arrange the leeks in a baking dish (a dish that measures 6½ × 10 × 1½ inches is suitable). Spoon the sauce over and sprinkle with cheese. Bake for 10 minutes, or until piping hot and bubbling throughout. They should be nicely glazed on top.

Yield: 4 to 6 servings.

6 cooked leeks

3 tablespoons butter

1 tablespoon plus 2 teaspoons flour

1½ cups milk

Salt and freshly ground pepper to taste

⅛ teaspoon grated nutmeg

A pinch of cayenne

2 egg yolks

¼ cup grated Gruyère, Swiss, or Parmesan cheese

LEEKS WITH POTATOES

1. Trim off the ends of the leeks. Slice them down the center and rinse well between the leaves. Finely chop the leeks. There should be about 4 cups.

2. Peel the potatoes and drop them into cold water. Drain and cut them in half lengthwise. Place one half cut side down and cut it lengthwise at ½-inch intervals to resemble French fries. Thinly slice the strips into crosswise pieces. There should be about 4 cups. Drop these into cold water to prevent discoloration. Drain.

3. Heat the butter and add the leeks and garlic. Cook, stirring often, for about 5 minutes, or until the liquid evaporates. Sprinkle with the salt and pepper. Add the broth and potatoes. Cook, stirring occasionally, for about 1 hour. Add the nutmeg, cayenne, and cream and serve hot or cold.

Yield: 6 servings.

3 large leeks

4 large potatoes, about 1¾ pounds

2 tablespoons butter

1 teaspoon finely minced garlic

Salt and freshly ground pepper to taste

6 cups fresh or canned chicken broth

⅛ teaspoon freshly grated nutmeg

Pinch of cayenne

½ cup heavy cream

SAUTÉED MUSHROOMS

12 or more mushrooms,
   about ½ pound
3 tablespoons butter
   Salt and freshly ground
   pepper to taste
2 teaspoons Worcester-
   shire sauce
   Juice of ½ lemon

1. Trim the stems off the mushroom caps. Reserve both stems and caps. Rinse the caps and stems in cold water and drain immediately. Pat dry.

2. Heat the butter in a skillet large enough to hold the mushroom pieces in one layer. Add the mushroom pieces and cook, stirring and shaking the skillet, turning the pieces so that they cook evenly. Sprinkle with the salt and pepper. Cook until nicely browned all over. They will give up liquid. Cook until this liquid evaporates. Sprinkle with the Worcestershire sauce, stirring and shaking the skillet. Sprinkle with the lemon juice. Toss quickly and serve hot.

Yield: 2 to 4 servings.

MUSHROOMS WITH SHALLOTS AND PARSLEY

1 pound fresh
   mushrooms
¼ cup peanut, vegetable,
   or corn oil
   Salt and freshly ground
   pepper to taste
2 tablespoons butter
1½ tablespoons finely
   chopped shallots
1 tablespoon chopped
   parsley
¼ cup fine fresh bread
   crumbs

1. Rinse and drain the mushrooms. Cut them into quarters. Heat the oil in a heavy skillet and, when it is hot and almost smoking, add the mushrooms. Add salt and pepper. Cook over high heat, shaking the skillet and stirring, until the mushrooms are nicely browned all over. Drain in a sieve.

2. Heat the butter in a clean, heavy skillet and add the mushrooms, shallots, parsley, and bread crumbs. Cook, tossing and stirring, for about 1 minute. When ready, the crumbs should be dry and crisp. This is an excellent accompaniment for grilled lamb, poultry, or steak, and also goes well with grilled tomatoes.

Yield: 4 servings.

MUSHROOMS IN MARSALA WINE

1. Soak the dried mushrooms in the lukewarm water for 30 minutes. Line a small sieve with cheesecloth and add the mushrooms. Strain and reserve the soaking liquid. Squeeze the mushrooms in the sieve to extract their juices.

2. Heat the oil in a casserole and add the soaked, drained mushrooms, garlic, and rosemary. Cook, stirring, for about 1 minute. Add the reserved soaking liquid and cook down over high heat until most of the liquid evaporates.

3. Add the fresh mushrooms and cook, stirring often, until the mushrooms are wilted. Add the Marsala and cook, stirring occasionally but gently, until the wine is almost but not quite evaporated. Serve hot or at room temperature.

Yield: 4 servings.

1 ounce dried mushrooms, preferably imported Italian boletus mushrooms

1 cup lukewarm water

¼ cup olive oil

½ teaspoon finely minced garlic

½ teaspoon dried rosemary

1 pound mushrooms, thinly sliced, about 6 cups

½ cup Marsala wine

MUSHROOMS STUFFED WITH SPINACH AND ANCHOVIES

1. Preheat the oven to 400 degrees.

2. Remove stems and reserve the caps from the mushrooms. Chop the stems. There should be about 1 cup.

3. Pick over the spinach to remove any tough stems. Rinse the leaves well and drop them into boiling water to cover. Simmer for about 1 minute and drain in a colander. Chill under cold running water and drain. Press the spinach between the hands to remove most of the moisture. Chop the spinach. There should be about 1 cup.

4. Empty the oil from the anchovy can into a saucepan and add the chopped mushroom stems. Cook, stirring, for about 5 minutes and add the spinach and garlic. Chop the anchovies and add them. Stir to blend thoroughly. Stir in the cream and bring just to the boil. Remove from the heat and let cool.

5. Meanwhile, place the mushrooms hollow side down in a buttered baking dish. Brush with half the melted butter and place in the oven for 10 minutes. Remove and let cool.

6. Stuff the cavity of each mushroom with the mixture, heaping it up and smoothing it over. Arrange the mushrooms in the baking dish and sprinkle with Parmesan cheese and the remaining melted butter. Place in the oven and bake for 20 minutes.

Yield: 6 servings.

12 large mushrooms

1 pound bulk spinach

One 2-ounce can anchovies

½ teaspoon chopped garlic

½ cup heavy cream

3 tablespoons butter, melted

¼ cup grated Parmesan cheese

BRAISED CHINESE MUSHROOMS FOR A CROWD

48 large to 60 medium-size unbroken dried Chinese mushrooms

¾ pound shrimp, peeled, deveined, and finely chopped

¾ pound ground pork, preferably not too lean and not too finely ground

6 water chestnuts, preferably fresh, finely minced, about ½ cup

¼ cup finely chopped scallions, green parts and all

2 teaspoons finely minced fresh ginger

3 tablespoons light soy sauce

3 tablespoons dry sherry

3 tablespoons cornstarch

¾ teaspoon plus ¼ teaspoon sugar

1 teaspoon sesame oil

Salt and freshly ground pepper to taste

6 tablespoons corn, peanut, or vegetable oil

1½ cups fresh or canned chicken broth

1½ tablespoons oyster sauce

1. Put the mushrooms in a large bowl and add hot water to cover. Let stand for 1 hour or longer.

2. Rinse and dry the mushrooms. Cut off and discard the stems.

3. In a mixing bowl, combine the shrimp, pork, water chestnuts, scallions, ginger, soy sauce, sherry, cornstarch, ¾ teaspoon of the sugar, the sesame oil, salt, and pepper. Blend well.

4. Fill each mushroom cap with an equal portion of the mixture, mounding and smoothing over the tops.

5. Heat 3 tablespoons of the oil in each of two large skillets. Add the mushrooms stuffing side down and brown lightly. Turn the mushrooms carefully in both skillets and carefully pour off the oil from both skillets.

6. Blend the broth, oyster sauce, and the remaining ¼ teaspoon of sugar. Pour an equal portion of this into each skillet. Bring the liquid to the simmer and cover closely. Cook over low heat for about 15 minutes, basting once during cooking. If the liquid starts to evaporate, add a few drops of water and continue cooking.

7. Give the mushrooms one final basting. Transfer them to a dish in one layer. Pour the remaining liquid over all. Let cool uncovered. Cover and refrigerate.

8. When ready to serve, preheat the oven to 300 degrees. Heat the mushrooms in their cooking liquid for 15 minutes. These mushrooms are good even at room temperature.

Yield: 20 to 25 servings.

OKRA WITH TOMATO SAUCE

One of the best okra dishes I have ever sampled came about during a visit to Chapel Hill, North Carolina, where it was difficult to find a soul-food restaurant. I discovered Dip's Country Kitchen, and enjoyed this simply made but delectable dish of okra with tomato sauce.

2 pounds fresh baby okra, or 2 packages (10 ounces each) frozen whole okra

4 cups canned tomatoes

2 tablespoons butter

Salt and freshly ground pepper to taste

1. Wash the okra well in cold water, whether fresh or frozen. If frozen is used, continue rinsing until the okra is defrosted. Drain well.

2. Put the okra in a saucepan and add about ½ cup cold water. Bring to the boil and cover. Let cook about 7 minutes.

3. Meanwhile, blend the tomatoes thoroughly in the container of a food processor or blender.

4. Drain the okra and add the tomatoes, butter, salt, and pepper. Bring to the boil, partly cover, and cook until the okra is tender, about 10 minutes.

Yield: 4 to 6 servings.

KAY AHUJA'S INDIAN OKRA AND ONIONS

1. Rinse the okra in cold water and drain well. If the stem ends are tough, cut them off and discard. Cut the okra into ½-inch lengths. There should be about 4 cups.

2. Heat the oil in a skillet and add the onions. Cook over medium heat, stirring, until wilted. Continue cooking until somewhat caramelized but not burned.

3. Add the salt, pepper, cayenne, turmeric, coriander, and cumin.

4. Add the okra and cover closely. Cook over low heat until tender, for 5 to 10 minutes.

Yield: 4 servings.

1 pound fresh baby okra

¼ cup peanut, vegetable, or corn oil

2½ cups thinly sliced onions

Salt and freshly ground pepper to taste

¼ teaspoon cayenne

¼ teaspoon ground turmeric

½ teaspoon ground coriander

¾ teaspoon ground cumin

ONIONS STUFFED WITH HAM

8 onions, about ½ pound each

Salt and freshly ground pepper to taste

8 slices bacon, cut into ½-inch cubes

¼ cup finely chopped onion

2 teaspoons finely chopped garlic

¼ pound finely chopped ham

6 tablespoons fine fresh bread crumbs

1 tablespoon heavy cream

1 egg, lightly beaten

¼ teaspoon grated nutmeg

¼ cup finely chopped parsley

2 tablespoons grated Parmesan cheese

2 tablespoons peanut, vegetable, or corn oil

¼ cup fresh or canned chicken broth

1. Preheat the oven to 400 degrees.

2. Peel the onions. Cut off a thin slice from the bottom and top of each onion. Using a melon ball cutter, hollow out the center of each onion, leaving a shell about ½ inch thick all around and on the bottom. Drop the onions into boiling water and simmer for about 10 minutes. Drain. Sprinkle the inside of each onion with salt and pepper to taste.

3. Meanwhile, cook the bacon in a skillet until rendered of fat. Add the chopped onion and garlic and cook until wilted. Remove from the heat and add the ham, 4 tablespoons of the crumbs, cream, egg, nutmeg, parsley, salt, and pepper. Return to the heat, stirring, for about 1 minute, or until heated through. Do not cook. Let the filling cool slightly.

4. Stuff the cavities of the onions with the filling, piling it up over the top. Sprinkle with a blend of the remaining bread crumbs and cheese and sprinkle with the oil. Arrange the onions on a buttered baking dish and pour the broth around them. Place in the oven and bake for 45 minutes, basting occasionally. If necessary, cover loosely with foil to prevent overbrowning.

Yield: 4 servings.

Puréed Parsnips and Carrots

1. Cut the parsnips in half lengthwise. Cut each half crosswise into ½-inch-thick pieces. There should be about 3 cups.

2. Cut the carrots crosswise into rounds about ¼ inch thick. Combine the carrots and parsnips in a saucepan. Add water to cover, salt, and pepper. Bring to the boil and cook for about 5 minutes, or until tender. Do not overcook.

3. Drain thoroughly. Put the vegetables into the container of a food processor and process or, preferably, into a conical food mill and pass the vegetables through into a saucepan.

4. Reheat while stirring the butter, milk, salt to taste, and nutmeg into the mixture. When piping hot, remove from the heat and serve.

Yield: 6 or more servings.

4 medium-size parsnips, about 1 pound, trimmed and scraped

4 to 5 carrots, about ½ pound, trimmed and scraped

Salt and freshly ground pepper to taste

2 tablespoons butter

½ cup milk

⅛ teaspoon grated nutmeg

Garden Peas with Mint

Put the peas in a heavy saucepan and add 2 tablespoons of the butter, the salt, pepper, and water. Cover closely and cook for about 5 minutes, or until the peas are just tender. Sprinkle with the mint and swirl in the remaining butter.

Yield: 6 servings.

2½ to 3 cups freshly shelled peas

4 tablespoons butter

Salt and freshly ground pepper to taste

2 tablespoons water

2 teaspoons chopped fresh mint

Snow Peas and Abalone Mushrooms

½ pound snow peas

¼ cup thinly sliced bamboo shoots

One 10-ounce can abalone mushrooms (see note)

One 10-ounce can golden mushrooms (see note)

¾ cup fresh or canned chicken broth

1 tablespoon cornstarch

¼ cup oyster sauce

1 teaspoon sugar

1 tablespoon dark soy sauce

7 tablespoons peanut, vegetable, or corn oil

1. Trim the snow peas and rinse well. Drain. Combine with the bamboo shoots. Set aside.
2. Rinse and drain the two kinds of mushrooms. Set aside.
3. Blend the chicken broth with the cornstarch. Set aside.
4. Blend the oyster sauce, sugar, and soy sauce. Set aside.
5. Heat 6 tablespoons of the oil in a wok or skillet and, when very hot, add the bamboo shoots and snow peas. Cook over very high heat for about 30 seconds. Using a slotted spoon, scoop out the vegetables. Add the mushrooms to the wok and cook, stirring, over very high heat for about 45 seconds. Scoop the mushrooms out with the spoon. Add the remaining tablespoon of oil to the wok and add the oyster sauce mixture. Add the chicken broth and cornstarch mixture. When it boils up, add the snow peas and mushroom mixtures. Stir to blend and serve.

Yield: 4 to 6 servings.

Note: Both the mushrooms are available in cans in Chinese markets.

Sautéed Sweet Peppers

3 sweet red peppers

3 sweet green peppers

2 tablespoons peanut, vegetable, or corn oil

1. Using a sharp knife, cut the peppers down the sides to produce large slices. Discard the core and seeds and inner veins. Stack a few slices at a time and cut them into very fine, julienne strips. There should be about 4 cups.
2. Heat the oil in a very heavy skillet and add the peppers. Do not add salt or other seasonings. Cook over very high heat, tossing and stirring until peppers are crisp and piping hot, a minute or longer.

Yield: 6 servings.

PICADILLO-STUFFED SWEET PEPPERS

If anyone were to study our enthusiasms, they would find a well-defined fondness for stuffed vegetables. There is every reason to presume that the first version came about through some fortuitous deployment of a leftover food, such as a roast. Chances are that the result was so eminently delectable that the stuffing became an end in itself, as with this Tex-Mex-inspired filling for sweet peppers.

1. Split the peppers in half lengthwise and remove the cores. Bring a large quantity of water to the boil and add the peppers. Cook for about 30 seconds and drain well.

2. Heat 1 tablespoon of the olive oil in a saucepan and add the whole almonds. Cook, shaking the skillet and stirring, until the almonds are golden brown. Remove with a slotted spoon and set aside.

3. To the oil remaining in the saucepan, add the onions and garlic. Cook until wilted. Add the meat and cook, stirring and chopping down with the side of a metal spoon to break up the lumps. Add the chili powder, chopped jalapeños, tomato sauce, salt and pepper, cinnamon, cloves, and raisins. Cook for about 3 minutes and add the reserved whole almonds.

4. Rub the bottom of a large baking dish with the remaining tablespoon of olive oil. Arrange peppers over it, split side up. Sprinkle inside lightly with salt and pepper. Fill the cavities with the picadillo. Sprinkle the fillings with the ground almonds.

5. When ready to cook, preheat the oven to 375 degrees. Bake for about 15 minutes.

Yield: 4 to 6 servings.

- 6 large red or green sweet peppers
- 2 tablespoons olive oil
- ⅓ cup whole blanched almonds
- 1½ cups finely chopped onions
- 1 tablespoon finely chopped garlic
- 1 pound lean ground beef
- 1 tablespoon chili powder, optional
- 1 tablespoon chopped jalapeño pepper with seeds
- 1 cup fresh tomato sauce (see recipe page 784), or use 1 cup drained canned tomatoes
- Salt and freshly ground pepper to taste
- ¼ teaspoon ground cinnamon
- ⅛ teaspoon ground cloves
- ¼ to ½ cup seedless raisins
- 3 tablespoons ground blanched almonds

TARRAGON- AND PORK-STUFFED PEPPERS

4 large green peppers

Salt and freshly ground pepper to taste

1 pound leftover roast pork

¼ pound fresh mushrooms, rinsed and drained

6 tablespoons butter

1½ cups finely chopped onions

2 garlic cloves, finely minced

2 fresh thyme sprigs, finely chopped, or ½ teaspoon dried

½ bay leaf, finely chopped

2 tablespoons finely chopped parsley

1 tablespoon finely chopped fresh tarragon, or 1 teaspoon dried, crushed

1 cup cooked rice

2 eggs

¼ cup pine nuts, optional

¼ cup fresh bread crumbs

¼ cup grated Parmesan cheese

2 cups peeled tomatoes, preferably Italian plum tomatoes if canned ones are used

½ cup fresh or canned chicken broth

1. Split the peppers in half lengthwise and remove the cores. Sprinkle the insides with the salt and pepper.

2. Put the pork through a meat grinder fitted with a coarse blade, or chop it fine. There should be about 4 cups. Put the meat in a mixing bowl.

3. Put the mushrooms through the grinder. Melt 1 tablespoon of the butter in a skillet or saucepan and add the mushrooms, 1 cup of the onion, and half the garlic. Cook, stirring, until the mushrooms give up their liquid. Cook until most of the liquid evaporates. Add the thyme, bay leaf, parsley, and tarragon.

4. Add the mushroom mixture to the pork. Add the rice, eggs, salt, pepper, and the pine nuts. Blend well. Stuff the pepper halves with the mixture and sprinkle with the bread crumbs and cheese.

5. With 3 tablespoons of the butter, grease a flameproof baking dish large enough to hold the peppers. Add the remaining ½ cup of onion and garlic and sprinkle with salt and pepper. Arrange the peppers in the dish. Blend the tomatoes in a blender and pour them around the peppers. Add the chicken broth. Sprinkle salt and pepper over all. Melt the remaining 2 tablespoons of butter and dribble it over the peppers.

6. Preheat oven to 350 degrees. Bring the dish to the boil on top of the stove, then place it in the oven. Bake for 45 minutes. Serve the peppers with the natural tomato sauce in the pan.

Yield: 8 servings.

Steamed Rutabaga

1. Pare the rutabaga and cut into 1-inch cubes. There should be about 5 cups.
2. Place the rutabaga in a saucepan and add the butter and water. Cover as tightly as possible. Bring the liquid to the boil and cook over low heat until all the liquid has evaporated and the rutabaga is tender. Check occasionally to make certain the rutabaga does not burn toward the end. Pour the lemon juice over the rutabaga.
3. Turn the rutabaga out into a serving dish and sprinkle with parsley.

Yield: 6 to 8 servings.

1½ pounds rutabaga
4 tablespoons butter
3 cups water
3 tablespoons lemon juice
Chopped parsley for garnish

Rutabaga and Sweet Potato Casserole

1. Preheat the oven to 350 degrees.
2. Peel the rutabaga and sweet potatoes. Cut both in half, then into 2-inch chunks.
3. Place the rutabaga in a saucepan and the potatoes in another saucepan. Cover both with cold water and add salt. Bring to the boil and cook until tender. The potatoes will require less cooking than the rutabaga. Drain well.
4. While hot, put the vegetables through a food mill into a mixing bowl. Stir in the salt and pepper to taste, 2 tablespoons of the butter, nutmeg, and cream.
5. Spoon the mixture into a baking dish, dot with the remaining butter, and bake 20 minutes. At the last minute, run the dish under the broiler to glaze.

Yield: 4 to 6 servings.

2 pounds rutabaga
¾ pound sweet potatoes
Salt and freshly ground pepper to taste
3 tablespoons butter, at room temperature
¼ teaspoon grated nutmeg
⅓ cup heavy cream

Spinach Purée

3 pounds fresh spinach,
   or three 10-ounce
   packages
4 cups water
   Salt to taste
2 tablespoons butter
   Freshly ground pepper
   to taste
½ cup heavy cream
⅛ teaspoon grated
   nutmeg

1. Pick over the spinach. Tear off and discard any tough steams. Discard any blemished leaves. Rinse the spinach well and drain.
2. Bring the water to the boil and add the salt. Add the spinach and cook, stirring often, for about 5 minutes. Drain well and let cool. Squeeze the spinach between the hands to remove the excess moisture. Divide it into 4 balls. Blend in a food processor or blender. There should be about 3 cups.
3. Heat the butter and add the spinach, salt, pepper, and cream. Add the nutmeg and serve piping hot.

Yield: 8 or more servings.

Acorn or Butternut Squash with Minted Green Peas

2 acorn or butternut
   squash, about 1½
   pounds each
2 tablespoons butter,
   melted
¼ cup brown sugar
1 teaspoon
   confectioners' sugar
1 teaspoon ground
   ginger
1 10-ounce package
   frozen small green
   peas
1 tablespoon butter
2 teaspoons chopped
   fresh mint
   Salt and freshly ground
   pepper to taste

1. Preheat the oven to 375 degrees.
2. Split the squash, lengthwise or crosswise, in half. Scrape out and discard the seeds. Cut off a thin slice from the bottom of each half so that it will rest firmly upright in a pan.
3. Brush the rims and cavity of each squash with the melted butter.
4. Blend the sugars and ginger and sprinkle each half, rim and cavity, with equal portions of the mixture. Arrange the halves on a baking sheet and bake for 1 hour.
5. Meanwhile, put the peas in a sieve and run hot water over them for 15 seconds, or until defrosted. Put the peas in a small skillet. Add the butter, mint, salt, and pepper. Cook briefly until heated throughout. Do not overcook. Fill the squash halves with the peas and serve immediately.

Yield: 4 servings.

SPAGHETTI SQUASH

Who would have believed that horticulturists would one day create a new vegetable, the inside of which when cooked would turn out to be "spaghetti." Not only that, a vegetable innately tasty and well textured. I like it freshly cooked even unsauced. It is best, however, with a little butter and salt and pepper or a meat and tomato sauce. As a matter of fact, spaghetti squash is delicious served with almost any sauce that is suitable for pasta, including pesto.

1 medium-size spaghetti squash, about 2½ pounds
2 tablespoons butter
Salt and freshly ground pepper to taste

1. Pierce the squash all over with the tines of a fork.
2. Put the squash in a kettle and add cold water to cover. Bring to the boil and cook for 30 minutes.
3. Place the squash in the sink and slice it in half crosswise. Let it drain.
4. Using a heavy metal spoon, scrape the spaghetti-like strands into a bowl and serve tossed with butter, salt, and pepper. Or the squash can be served with a tomato sauce.

Yield: 6 servings.

BROILED TOMATOES

1. Preheat the broiler to high.
2. Cut the core from each tomato. Cut each tomato crosswise in half. Arrange the halves, cut side up, on a rack and sprinkle with salt and pepper. Stud each tomato half with equal portions of the garlic slivers. Sprinkle with oil.
3. Place the tomatoes under the broiler and broil for about 5 minutes, or until the garlic slivers start to burn. Discard the garlic slivers and sprinkle with chopped basil.

Yield: 4 servings.

2 ripe tomatoes (about ¾ pound)
Salt and freshly ground pepper to taste
2 garlic cloves, cut into thin slivers
1 tablespoon olive oil
1 tablespoon finely chopped fresh basil

CURRY-STUFFED TOMATOES

⅓ cup dark raisins

8 ripe but firm tomatoes, about 4 pounds

2 tablespoons butter

¼ cup finely chopped celery

¾ cup finely chopped onion

1 teaspoon minced garlic

2 tablespoons curry powder

2 bay leaves

1 pound finely ground lean lamb

Salt and freshly ground pepper to taste

¼ cup fine bread crumbs

1. Put the raisins in a bowl and add warm water to cover. Set aside for 30 minutes.

2. Slice about half an inch off the tops of the tomatoes. Set the tops aside.

3. Using a melon ball cutter or a spoon, scoop out the inside of each tomato, leaving a shell about ⅓ inch thick. Chop and reserve the scooped-out pulp.

4. Melt 1 tablespoon of the butter in a wide saucepan and add the celery, ½ cup of the onion, and the garlic and cook, stirring, until the onion is wilted. Add the curry powder and bay leaves. Add the lamb and cook, stirring and breaking up the lumps in the meat with the side of a heavy metal spoon.

5. Add the chopped tomato pulp, salt, and pepper. Cook, stirring often, for about 30 minutes.

6. Drain the raisins and add them. Cook for 5 minutes longer.

7. Preheat the oven to 400 degrees.

8. Butter a baking dish large enough to hold the tomatoes in one layer with the remaining butter. Sprinkle with the remaining ¼ cup chopped onion. Chop the reserved tops of the tomatoes, cutting away and discarding the cores. Sprinkle the chopped tomatoes over the onions.

9. Sprinkle the inside of the tomatoes with salt and pepper to taste. Stuff the tomatoes with the curried lamb.

10. Arrange the stuffed tomatoes over the chopped tomatoes and onion. Sprinkle the tops of the stuffed tomatoes with bread crumbs.

11. Place the tomatoes in the oven and bake for 30 minutes.

Yield: 4 to 8 servings.

TOMATOES STUFFED WITH RICE AND SAUSAGE

1. Preheat the oven to 375 degrees.

2. Remove the stems from the tomatoes. Split the tomatoes in half for stuffing. Gently squeeze each tomato half, letting the seeds, juice, and pulp fall into a small bowl. Reserve. Sprinkle each tomato half with the salt and pepper and set aside.

3. Remove the sausage meat from the casings. Heat the oil in a skillet and add the onion and garlic. Cook briefly and add the sausage meat, breaking up any lumps with the side of a heavy kitchen spoon. Cook until the meat changes color. Add the reserved tomato seeds, juice, and pulp. Cook until the liquid evaporates. Let cool briefly. Add the rice, parsley, basil, pine nuts, and half the cheese. Add the egg, salt, and pepper to taste and blend well. Let cool.

4. Lightly oil a baking dish. Arrange the tomato halves cut side up. Spoon the filling into and over the tops of the tomato halves, piling it up and rounding it with the fingers. Sprinkle with the remaining cheese. Bake for 30 minutes. Serve hot or cold.

Yield: 6 to 12 servings.

6 small, ripe but firm tomatoes, about 1½ pounds

Salt and freshly ground pepper to taste

½ pound sweet or hot Italian sausages, about 4

1 tablespoon olive oil

½ cup finely chopped onion

1 garlic clove, finely minced

1½ cups cooked rice

2 tablespoons finely chopped parsley

1 tablespoon finely chopped basil

3 tablespoons pine nuts

¼ cup grated Parmesan cheese

1 egg, lightly beaten

PIPERADE (A TOMATO AND PEPPER DISH)

5 green peppers, about 1½ pounds

5 large ripe tomatoes, about 2½ pounds

2 or 3 onions, about ¾ pound

¾ cup plus 1 tablespoon peanut, vegetable, or corn oil

1 garlic clove, finely minced

Salt and freshly ground pepper to taste

⅛ pound thinly sliced prosciutto or other ham, cut into shreds or cubes

1 tablespoon finely minced garlic

2 bay leaves

3 eggs

1. Core and seed the peppers. Cut them into thin strips. There should be about 5 cups. Set aside.

2. Core and peel the tomatoes. Cut them into eighths. There should be about 5 cups. Set aside.

3. Peel the onions and cut them in half. Then cut the onions into very thin slices. There should be about 3 cups. Set aside.

4. Heat ¼ cup of the oil in each of 3 skillets. Add the peppers to one skillet, the tomatoes to another, and the onions and minced garlic clove to the third. Cook the peppers, onions, and garlic until they are browned without burning. Cook the tomatoes until they are somewhat reduced and saucelike. Add the peppers and onions to the tomatoes. Add the salt and pepper.

5. Heat the remaining tablespoon of oil in a skillet and add the ham. Cook for about 30 seconds and add to the tomatoes. Add the garlic and the bay leaves. Cook for about 15 minutes.

6. Turn the heat to very low and add the eggs one at a time, stirring constantly. The trick is to incorporate the eggs into the tomato sauce, stirring as to prevent curdling. The heat must be gentle. After the eggs are added, do not cook further but serve immediately.

Yield: 8 to 12 servings.

FRIED GREEN TOMATOES

1½ pounds green tomatoes

Tabasco sauce to taste

6 tablespoons flour

6 tablespoons cornmeal

Coarse salt and freshly ground pepper to taste

½ teaspoon cayenne

¾ cup peanut or vegetable oil, approximately

Green tomatoes have always seemed to me to be one of the most curious of foods to be cooked. I have always wondered if they were first plucked and cooked because some gardener simply could not wait for the summer harvest when they were sweet, red, and luscious.

1. Cut the tomatoes in slices about ¼ inch thick. Sprinkle the slices with Tabasco.

2. Combine the flour and cornmeal with salt, black pepper, and cayenne. Put in a plastic bag. Add the tomato slices, a few at a time, and toss to coat with the flour mixture. Shake off the excess.

3. Heat about ¼ inch of oil in a skillet and fry the tomatoes, adding them a few at a time, without overcrowding, until golden brown on each side. Drain on paper towels.

4. Serve immediately. If kept, the tomatoes will turn soggy.

Yield: 4 servings.

SAUTÉED TURNIPS

1. Peel the turnips and cut them into quarters. Cut each quarter crosswise into very thin slices. There should be about 4 cups.

2. Heat the oil and butter in a heavy skillet and add the turnips. Add the salt and pepper. Cook, tossing the skillet and stirring the pieces of turnip so that they cook evenly.

3. When the pieces start to take on color, add the caraway seeds and stir. Cover closely and cook for about 5 minutes.

4. Uncover, sprinkle with garlic, and cook briefly until all liquid evaporates.

Yield: 4 servings.

4 or 5 medium-size white turnips, about 1½ pounds
1 tablespoon olive oil
1 tablespoon butter
Salt and freshly ground pepper to taste
1 teaspoon caraway seeds
1 teaspoon finely chopped garlic

FRIED ZUCCHINI

1. Trim off the ends of the zucchini. Cut the zucchini into 3-inch lengths. Cut each length into ¼-inch-slices. Cut the slices into ¼-inch strips. Drop the strips into cold water and let stand briefly.

2. Drain the zucchini well. Place in a bowl, sprinkle with enough flour to coat the pieces, and toss well with the hands. Put the eggs in a large bowl. Add the floured zucchini and mix well with the hands until the pieces are coated.

3. Heat the oil until it is hot and almost smoking. Add a portion of the zucchini, half of it or less at a time, and cook, stirring to separate the pieces, for 6 or 7 minutes, or until crisp. Drain on a clean towel. Serve hot sprinkled with salt.

Yield: 6 or more servings.

3 zucchini, about ½ pound each
Flour for dredging
3 eggs, beaten
Oil for deep frying
Salt to taste

Zucchini and Tomato Casserole

3 medium-size red peppers, about ½ pound, optional

6 medium-size zucchini, about 1¾ pounds

4 large ripe tomatoes, about 2½ pounds

1 large onion, about ½ pound

⅓ cup plus ¼ cup olive oil

½ cup water

1 tablespoon finely minced garlic

Salt and freshly ground pepper to taste

1 teaspoon dried thyme, or 4 fresh thyme sprigs broken into small pieces

1. If the peppers are to be used, preheat the broiler. Place the peppers under the broiler and roast until they are burnt on one side. Turn and roast on the other side. Continue turning until roasted all over, top and bottom. Put in a plastic bag to cool. Peel. Discard the stems and seeds. Cut the peppers into thin strips. There should be about ¾ cup.

2. Trim off the ends of the zucchini. Using a swivel-bladed vegetable cutter, trim off the sides of each zucchini, leaving intervals of green to make a pattern. Cut the zucchini on the bias into ¼-inch slices. There should be about 7 cups.

3. Remove the cores from the tomatoes. Cut each tomato into slices about ⅓ inch thick.

4. Peel the onion and cut it in half crosswise. Cut each half into very thin slices. There should be about 2 cups. Put the onion in a heavy saucepan.

5. Add ⅓ cup of the oil and the water to the onion. Bring to the boil and cook over relatively high heat for 10 or 12 minutes. When ready, the onion will be nicely glazed and lightly browned. Do not burn.

6. Preheat the oven to 350 degrees.

7. Spoon the onion over the bottom of an oval or rectangular baking dish (a dish that measures about 13½ × 8 × 2 inches is ideal). Sprinkle the garlic and pepper strips over the onion.

8. Arrange a layer of tomatoes, letting them lean at an angle against the sides of the baking dish. Arrange a layer of zucchini against the tomatoes. Continue making layers until all the tomatoes and zucchini are used. Sprinkle with the salt and pepper and the thyme. Dribble the remaining ¼ cup of oil over all.

9. Place in the oven and bake for 30 minutes. Increase the oven temperature to 475 degrees and continue baking for about 45 minutes. At this point the top of the vegetables will be quite dark. Press the vegetables down with a flat pancake turner. Return to the oven and continue baking for 15 minutes. Serve hot or cold.

Yield: 4 to 6 servings.

ZUCCHINI PROVENÇALE

1. Peel the onions and cut them in half. Thinly slice each half. There should be about 2½ cups.

2. Trim off the ends and peel the zucchini. If they are small, cut them in half lengthwise. Cut each quarter or half into 1-inch pieces. There should be about 6 cups.

3. Place the oregano in a small skillet and toast over moderate heat, shaking the skillet and stirring to prevent burning. Cook just until lightly toasted. Do not burn or the oregano will be bitter. Crush or grind the oregano and set it aside.

4. Heat the oil in a heavy saucepan and add the onions. Cover closely and cook without browning, stirring occasionally, for about 20 minutes. Add the zucchini and the garlic. Cover and cook very gently, stirring often to prevent scorching, for about 45 minutes. By that time the vegetables will be very tender. Stir vigorously with a spoon to make a purée.

5. Beat the eggs and add them. Cook for about 2 minutes over moderate heat, stirring, and turn off the heat. Add salt, pepper, and nutmeg. Stir in the toasted oregano and serve piping hot.

Yield: 6 to 8 servings.

½ pound onions

2 pounds zucchini

1 teaspoon loosely packed dried oregano

2 tablespoons olive oil

½ teaspoon finely minced garlic

3 eggs

Salt and freshly ground pepper to taste

Grated nutmeg to taste

MUSHROOM-AND-CHEESE-STUFFED ZUCCHINI

14 small zucchini, each about 6 inches in length

¾ cup olive oil

1½ cups chopped onion

1½ cups finely diced fresh mushrooms

3 garlic cloves, finely minced

1 cup cream cheese

3 eggs

2 cups grated Parmesan cheese

2 cups finely chopped parsley

Salt and freshly ground pepper to taste

4 hot chilies, chopped, optional

1. Preheat the oven to 350 degrees.

2. Cut the zucchini in half lengthwise. Using a melon ball scoop or a spoon, scoop out the flesh of each zucchini half, leaving a shell about ¼ inch thick. Set the zucchini halves aside. Chop the pulp and set aside.

3. Heat the oil and add the onion. Cook, stirring often, until the onion is wilted. Add the mushrooms and garlic. Cover and cook until the mushrooms give up their juices. Add the chopped zucchini pulp. Cook over high heat, uncovered, stirring until the liquid evaporates. Add the cream cheese, eggs, 1½ cups of the Parmesan cheese, the parsley, salt, pepper, and hot chilies. Cook, stirring often, for about 10 minutes. Let cool.

4. Stuff the zucchini shells with equal parts of the mixture. Sprinkle with the remaining ½ cup Parmesan. Arrange in a baking dish and bake for 10 minutes, or until piping hot. Run under the broiler to brown briefly.

Yield: 14 to 28 servings.

ZUCCHINI AND TOMATOES, GUJARATI STYLE

1. Prepare the zucchini and tomatoes and set aside.
2. Heat the oil in a kettle and, when it starts to smoke, add the cumin seeds. Stir briefly and add the hing, coriander, cumin, turmeric, paprika, garam masala, and salt. Add the zucchini and tomatoes and stir gently to blend without breaking the slices. Add the water and cover. Cook over gentle heat for 10 minutes. Serve sprinkled with chopped fresh coriander.

Yield: 8 servings.

8 cups thinly sliced zucchini, about 1¼ pounds

1 cup cored and cubed tomatoes

3 tablespoons sesame oil

2 teaspoons whole cumin seeds

¼ teaspoon hing, available in Indian food shops

1½ teaspoons ground coriander

1½ teaspoons ground cumin

¼ teaspoon turmeric

1 tablespoon paprika

1 teaspoon garam masala (see recipe page 793)

1 teaspoon salt

2 tablespoons water

4 teaspoons chopped fresh coriander

Rice, Potatoes, and Beans

A PERFECT BATCH OF RICE

Producing a perfect dish of Western-style rice requires a certain attention to detail—the proportion of rice to liquid and the cooking time should be exact. But these two requirements are easy to learn because they are constant, no matter what the other ingredients. The liquid should measure one and one-half times the quantity of rice, and it should be cooked on top of the stove or baked in the oven for exactly seventeen minutes. Ignore those package directions that sometimes call for twice as much liquid as rice. It defeats the purpose of properly cooked rice.

3 tablespoons butter
½ cup finely chopped onion
2 cups rice
Salt to taste
Cayenne or Tabasco sauce to taste
3 cups fresh or canned chicken broth
Parsley sprigs
1 bay leaf
1 fresh thyme sprig, or ½ teaspoon dried

1. Preheat the oven to 400 degrees.

2. Heat 2 tablespoons of the butter in a saucepan and add the onion. Stir and cook until the onion wilts.

3. Add the rice and stir until the grains are coated.

4. Add the salt. Add a pinch of cayenne or Tabasco sauce and the broth.

5. Add a bouquet garni consisting of a small bundle of the parsley sprigs, bay leaf, and thyme.

6. Let the broth come to the boil. At the boil, cover closely and place in the oven. Set a kitchen timer for exactly 17 minutes and bake the rice for precisely that long.

7. Remove and discard the bouquet garni. Add the remaining 1 tablespoon of butter and toss to blend.

Yield: 8 servings.

Note: The rice can also be cooked for the same amount of time on top of the stove, provided the saucepan has a tight cover.

This recipe is easily divided simply by reducing all ingredients by half. The basic formula is 1 cup of rice for each 1½ cups liquid.

RICE VARIATIONS

Saffron rice: Crumble 1 teaspoon of loosely packed stem saffron. Add it to the saucepan and stir just before adding the raw rice.

Cumin rice: Use 1 finely minced garlic clove and 1 teaspoon of ground cumin. Add it to the saucepan and stir just before adding the raw rice.

RICE FOR A CROWD

12 tablespoons butter
1 cup finely chopped onion
8 cups long-grain rice
12 cups fresh or canned chicken broth
6 fresh parsley sprigs
2 bay leaves
4 fresh thyme sprigs, or 1 teaspoon dried
  Salt
  Tabasco sauce

1. Melt 8 tablespoons of the butter in a large kettle with a tight-fitting lid.
2. Add the onion and cook until wilted. Add the rice and stir. Add the broth. Tie the parsley, bay leaves, and thyme into a bundle and add the bundle to the rice. Add salt and Tabasco sauce to taste.
3. Bring the broth to the boil. Cover tightly and cook over low heat for exactly 17 minutes. Uncover and remove the bundle of spices. Dot with the remaining 4 tablespoons of butter and fluff the rice with a fork until the butter is incorporated.

Yield: 30 servings.

RISOTTO

4 tablespoons butter
3 tablespoons finely chopped onion
1 garlic clove, finely minced
2 cups arborio rice
1 teaspoon chopped saffron stems
  Salt and freshly ground pepper to taste
5 cups fresh or canned chicken broth
½ cup dry white wine
¾ cup grated Parmesan cheese

1. Heat 2 tablespoons of the butter in a fairly large casserole. Add the onion and garlic and cook until the onion is wilted. Add the rice, saffron, salt, and pepper and stir to coat the grains.
2. Meanwhile, heat the broth and keep it at the simmer.
3. Add the wine to the rice and cook, stirring occasionally, until all the wine has evaporated.
4. Add 1 cup of the hot broth to the rice mixture and cook, stirring occasionally and gently, until all that liquid has been absorbed. Add ½ cup more of the broth and cook, stirring occasionally, until it is absorbed.
5. Continue cooking the rice in this fashion, adding ½ cup of broth each 3½ to 4 minutes, just until each ladle is absorbed. Remember that the rice must cook gently.
6. When all the broth has been added and absorbed, fold in the remaining butter and the cheese. When the rice is done, it should be tender but retain a small bite. The total cooking time should be from 25 to 28 minutes.

Yield: 8 servings.

RICE WITH ZUCCHINI

1. Preheat the oven to 400 degrees.
2. Trim off and discard the ends of the zucchini. Do not peel the vegetable. Cut the zucchini into 1½-inch cubes. Set aside.
3. In a large heavy casserole, heat the oil and add the onions, thyme, bay leaf, salt, and pepper. Cover tightly. Cook until the onions are tender but not brown.
4. Add the zucchini, rice, and chicken broth. Bring to the boil on top of the stove. Cover and bake in the oven for 17 minutes—no longer. Remove the bay leaf and serve.

Yield: 6 to 8 servings.

1½ pounds zucchini
¼ cup olive oil
3 cups coarsely chopped onions
3 fresh thyme sprigs, or ½ teaspoon dried
1 bay leaf
Salt and freshly ground pepper to taste
1 cup rice
1 cup fresh or canned chicken broth

RICE VALENCIANA

1. Heat the butter in a saucepan and add the sweet pepper. Cook, stirring, for about 5 minutes. The cubes must remain crisp-tender. Add the diced ham and cook to heat through, for about 1 minute. Add the peas and remove from the heat.
2. Pour and scrape the rice into a hot bowl. Add the ham mixture and toss to blend evenly.
3. If desired, spoon and scrape the mixture into a 5-cup mold, packing it down firmly with the back of a wooden spoon. When filled, pack down one final time with a spoon or spatula.
4. Invert a round plate over the mold. Turn the mold and plate over. Tap the mold with a piece of metal or wood. Do not unmold until ready to serve. Lift up the mold and serve immediately or the rice will fall apart as it stands.

Yield: 8 servings.

1 tablespoon butter
1⅓ cups cubed sweet red or green pepper
⅔ cup diced ham
1 cup cooked fresh or frozen peas
2 cups cooked rice

MUSHROOM RICE WITH TURMERIC

¾ pound mushrooms

4 tablespoons butter

½ cup finely chopped onion

1 garlic clove, finely minced

½ teaspoon ground turmeric

1 cup rice

1 bay leaf

1¼ cups fresh or canned chicken broth

Salt and freshly ground pepper to taste

1. Preheat the oven to 400 degrees.

2. Remove the stems from the mushrooms. Cut the mushroom caps into ½-inch cubes. There should be about 2 cups.

3. Heat 2 tablespoons of the butter in a saucepan with a tight-fitting lid and add the onion and garlic. Cook for about 2 minutes and add the mushrooms. Cook for about 5 minutes, stirring. Sprinkle with the turmeric and add the rice and bay leaf. Stir until the rice is coated and add the chicken broth, salt, and pepper. Cover closely and bring to the boil on top of the stove.

4. Bake for exactly 17 minutes. Remove the cover and discard the bay leaf. Using a two-pronged fork, stir in the remaining butter while fluffing the rice.

Yield: 4 to 6 servings.

SPANISH RICE

¼ pound lean bacon

1 cup finely chopped onion

1 cup finely chopped celery

1 cup finely chopped sweet green peppers

3½ cups long-grain rice

4 cups canned tomatoes with their liquid

Salt and freshly ground pepper to taste

1½ teaspoons sugar

¼ teaspoon Tabasco sauce

1. Preheat the oven to 325 degrees.

2. Cut the bacon into small cubes. Put the cubes in a skillet and cook, stirring, until the pieces are crisp and browned. Remove the pieces using a slotted spoon. Set the bacon aside and leave the fat in the skillet.

3. To the fat remaining in the skillet, add the onion, celery, and green peppers. Cook, stirring, until the onion is wilted. Add the rice and stir.

4. Put the tomatoes with their liquid in the container of a food processor and blend thoroughly. Add this to the rice and stir. Add the salt, pepper, sugar, and Tabasco.

5. Bring to the boil, stirring, and cook for about 5 minutes.

6. Pour and scrape the rice mixture into a casserole and cover. Bake, stirring occasionally, for about 1 hour, or until the rice is tender and the liquid is absorbed.

Yield: 12 to 16 servings.

DIRTY RICE

One of the most humorous names ever applied to a dish, Southern or otherwise, is "dirty rice," a well-known Louisiana dish of Cajun inspiration. It is called that because of the darkened color of the rice, once the dish is made. The color comes from the other ingredients, which include the chopped-up livers and gizzards of a chicken. I find this dish absolutely delectable.

1. Put the livers and gizzards in separate piles on a flat surface and chop until fine, or use a food processor but do not blend to a purée. The gizzards and livers must retain their character.

2. Heat the oil in a skillet until it is almost smoking. Add the eggplants and cook, stirring, for about 5 minutes.

3. Add the pork and stir with a heavy metal spoon, chopping down with the sides of the spoon to break up lumps. Add the gizzards. Cover closely and cook for about 10 minutes.

4. With the spoon, mash down on the eggplant pieces. Add the green peppers, celery, and onion. Cover and continue cooking over high heat for about 10 minutes. Stir from the bottom to scrape up the brown particles. Add the cayenne, salt, white pepper, and black pepper. Cook, stirring always from the bottom to incorporate the dark brown matter that sticks to the bottom of the skillet, about 10 minutes.

5. Add the broth and stir to clean the bottom. Cover and cook for about 20 minutes. Uncover and stir in the livers. Cook for about 5 minutes. Add the rice and cover. Cook for 15 to 20 minutes, or until the rice is tender. Stir in the scallions and serve.

Yield: 10 to 12 servings.

1 pound chicken livers

1 pound chicken gizzards

10 tablespoons peanut, vegetable, or corn oil

6 cups peeled and cubed eggplants

1 pound ground pork

1½ cups finely chopped sweet green peppers

1 cup finely chopped celery

1 cup finely chopped onion

1 teaspoon cayenne

Salt to taste

1 teaspoon white pepper

1½ teaspoons freshly ground black pepper

6½ cups fresh or canned chicken broth

1 cup long-grain rice

1 cup chopped scallions

RICE WITH DILL, PERSIAN STYLE

2 cups long-grain rice
¼ cup salt
One 10-ounce package frozen baby lima beans
12 tablespoons butter
2 tablespoons water
1 or 2 Idaho potatoes
1¾ cups chopped fresh dill (1 large bunch, tough stalks discarded)

1. Several hours before cooking the rice, wash it and rinse several times. Place it in a mixing bowl and add cold water to a depth of about 1 inch above the top of the rice. Add the salt and let stand about 1½ hours before cooking.

2. Drain the water into a large, heavy kettle. Add about 3 more quarts of water and bring to a vigorous boil. Add the drained rice and lima beans. Bring back to the boil and cook for 5 to 7 minutes, testing the grains frequently for state of doneness. The grains are ready when they are tender on the outside but have a tiny hard core in the center. Drain immediately or the rice will overcook.

3. Meanwhile, melt the butter with the 2 tablespoons of water in a saucepan. Set aside.

4. Similarly, as the rice cooks, peel the potato or potatoes and cut into ¼-inch slices. There should be enough slices to cover the bottom of the same heavy kettle when the slices are placed snugly together without overlapping and in one layer.

5. Pour enough melted butter into the kettle to barely cover the bottom and arrange the potatoes over it. Spoon about a fourth of the rice over the potatoes and add about a fourth of the dill. Carefully stir the rice with a spoon to blend in the dill.

6. Do not disturb the potatoes at any point until the dish is fully cooked. Continue adding rice and dill layers, stirring to blend after each addition. Shape the rice-dill mixture into a cone-shaped mound. Pour the remaining butter evenly over the rice. Place the kettle on the heat and cook over medium heat for 5 minutes, or until steam comes through the center. Cover with a heavy bath towel folded so that it fits the top of the pot. Cover this with the lid and place a weight over the lid so that no steam can escape as the rice cooks. Reduce the heat and cook for 45 minutes to 1 hour.

7. When ready to serve, spoon the rice onto a large platter and garnish with the potato slices, bottom side up. The bottoms should be golden brown and crisp. Test the potatoes before removing. If the potatoes haven't browned, uncover and cook over medium heat for a few minutes until browned.

Yield: 8 servings.

Note: This rice can be cooked ahead and reheated by pouring a little boiling water over the rice and steaming for 15 minutes longer.

RED BEANS WITH RICE

1. Rinse the beans and drain well. Put them in a kettle with 6 cups of the water and cover. Bring to the boil and cook for about 30 minutes, or until the beans are almost mealy.

2. Meanwhile, put the pork cubes in a skillet and cook until the pork is rendered of much of its fat. Cover closely and cook over high heat, stirring occasionally, until it is browned and crisp. Add the ham, onions, green peppers, celery, bay leaves, 1½ teaspoons of the garlic, the thyme, basil, cayenne, white pepper, salt, and paprika. Cook, stirring often, for about 30 minutes.

3. Add the pork and vegetables to the beans. Add 4 cups of the water to the skillet in which the pork and vegetables cooked and stir to dissolve the brown particles that cling to the bottom and sides of the skillet. Bring to the boil and add to the beans. Cook for about 20 minutes and add 4 more cups of water. Cover and continue cooking for about 30 minutes and add 2 more cups of water. Cover and continue cooking for about 1½ hours. It is imperative that you stir the bean mixture from the bottom often or it will stick.

4. Meanwhile, combine the rice and remaining 4 cups of water in a saucepan or kettle and bring to the boil. Add the salt. Cover and cook for 10 minutes. Turn off the heat and let the rice stand for about 15 minutes.

5. Chop the parsley and remaining teaspoon of chopped garlic together and stir it into the beans.

6. Spoon rice into individual serving plates and add beans as desired.

Yield: 12 servings.

---

1 pound dried red kidney beans

20 or more cups water

1 pound lean salt pork, cut into 1½-inch cubes

¾ pound smoked ham, cut into ½-inch cubes

2½ cups finely chopped onions

2½ cups finely chopped green peppers

1½ cups finely chopped celery

2 bay leaves

2½ teaspoons finely minced garlic

½ teaspoon dried thyme

¼ teaspoon dried basil

¼ teaspoon cayenne

¼ teaspoon freshly ground white pepper

Salt to taste

1 teaspoon paprika

2 cups rice

¼ cup chopped parsley

STEAMED WILD RICE

1 cup wild rice
2 cups boiling water
  Salt and freshly ground
  pepper to taste
3 tablespoons butter

1. Place the rice, water, salt, pepper, and 1 tablespoon of the butter in the top of a double boiler.
2. Cover and steam the rice for 1 hour. Fluff the rice with a fork, stirring in the remaining butter.

Yield: 6 to 8 servings.

WILD RICE WITH SHALLOTS

1 cup wild rice
5 cups cold water
  Salt to taste
4 tablespoons butter
2 tablespoons finely
  chopped shallots
½ cup finely diced celery
  Freshly ground pepper
  to taste

1. Run cold water over the rice and drain until the water runs clear.
2. Put the rice in a saucepan and add the water and salt.
3. Bring to the boil and simmer for 1 hour. At this point the rice grains should be puffed open. If not, remove from the heat and let the rice stand in the hot cooking water until puffed.
4. When ready, drain the water off and cover tightly.
5. Melt half the butter in a small skillet and add the shallots and celery. Cook, stirring often, for about 5 minutes. The celery should retain some of its crispy texture.
6. Add the celery, shallots, and salt and pepper to taste to the rice and stir.
7. Just before serving, add the remaining butter and reheat, stirring from the bottom.

Yield: 6 servings.

POLENTA

2 cups coarse cornmeal,
   preferably imported
   from Italy (see note)
8½ cups water
   Salt to taste
1 tablespoon olive oil

There are three foods of consummate goodness that may be served as either a main course or a side dish in the Italian kitchen. These are pasta, rice in the form of risotto, and polenta. Of the three, polenta, which is a form of cornmeal mush, is relatively little known and appreciated in this country. A pity, too, for polenta has scores of delectable uses. It can be served piping hot the moment it is taken from the stove, or it can be chilled, cut into various shapes, sprinkled with butter and cheese, and baked for a sumptuous side dish. It is also delectable when topped with Gorgonzola cheese and baked. Although cornmeal that is produced commercially in this country can be used to prepare polenta, it is far better to use cornmeal (sold as raw polenta) imported from Italy.

1. Measure the cornmeal and set aside.
2. Put the water in a heavy casserole and bring to a full rolling boil over high heat. Add the salt.
3. Start stirring vigorously with a wire whisk. Gradually add the cornmeal in a thin, steady stream. One must stir rapidly as the meal is added to prevent lumping. Stir constantly for at least 5 minutes, covering the inside of the casserole, bottom and sides, to blend well and prevent lumping.
4. At the end of 5 minutes, turn the heat to moderately low and continue cooking, stirring quite often with a heavy wooden spoon all around the bottom and sides.
5. At the end of 15 or 20 minutes, a light crust will start to form on the bottom of the casserole. Add the olive oil and continue stirring with the spoon. For this quantity of cornmeal, the total cooking time should be about 20 minutes.
6. To unmold quickly, invert the casserole on top of a clean, flat surface. Traditionally, Italian cooks use a string to cut the polenta into serving portions. Hold a string taut at both ends and slip it carefully under the bed of polenta, holding the string close against the flat surface. Slide the string under the polenta to a distance of from 1 to 2 inches. Bring it up quickly to make a long slice. Repeat, pushing the string farther away from you and bringing it up to make a second long slice. Repeat. Now, turn the string and repeat slicing in the other direction.
7. Serve hot with any of various savory stews. Or chill the polenta and bake it later with cheese on top.

Yield: 6 to 10 servings.

Note: Imported cornmeal (referred to as raw polenta) is widely available in specialty shops that offer imported foods and in grocery stores that specialize in Italian foods.

Polenta with Gorgonzola Cheese

2 to 3 cups cooked polenta

¼ pound Gorgonzola cheese

4 tablespoons butter

10 or 12 sage leaves, preferably fresh

Freshly grated Parmesan cheese

1. Preheat the oven to 450 degrees.
2. Cut off enough freshly made polenta to cover the bottom of an oval baking dish measuring 10 × 7 × 1½ inches. Press it down to make a solid layer. Cover with half of the Gorgonzola cheese, crumbled. Add the remaining polenta and press down.
3. Melt the butter and add the sage leaves. Let simmer over very low heat for about 1 minute without browning.
4. Cut the remaining cheese into 4 or 5 small triangles and press them into the top of the top layer of polenta. Pour the butter over the top and arrange the sage leaves around the polenta. Press the leaves down in the butter or they will burn. Sprinkle with Parmesan cheese.
5. Place in the oven and bake for about 5 minutes. Run under the broiler for about 2 minutes, or until bubbling and piping hot.

Yield: 4 servings.

Egi Maccioni's Gorgonzola-Mascarpone Cheese with Polenta

4 cups water

Salt to taste

1 cup fine or coarse ground cornmeal, preferably imported

4 tablespoons butter

Six ¼-inch-thick slices Gorgonzola-Mascarpone cheese

1. Bring the water to the boil with the salt. Add the cornmeal while stirring vigorously with a wire whisk.
2. Continue cooking, stirring often and rapidly with the whisk, taking care to stir well over the bottom and sides so that the mixture cooks evenly and does not lump. Stir in the butter.
3. Very hot plates are essential for the success of this dish. Heat six plates and place one slice of the cheese on each. Spoon an equal portion of the cornmeal mixture over each serving and serve immediately.

Yield: 6 servings.

HOMINY AND CHEESE CASSEROLE

One of the staples of my childhood was whole hominy in one form or another. There is a good deal of confusion in the minds of those who were not raised on it as to the difference between whole hominy and hominy grits. Whole hominy is made from the whole dried kernels of corn with the hull and germ removed. The kernels may be white or yellow. If dried kernels are used, they must be soaked or well simmered before using. Originally, the dried kernels were soaked in wood-ash lye and then well washed. That is why it is sometimes referred to as lye hominy. Canned hominy is excellent, and a lot more expedient to use than dried hominy. If you enjoy the flavor of tortillas, you will like the flavor of hominy, for they are both corn products and the flavors are very much akin.

Hominy grits are the whole grains of dried corn that have been ground and milled. Breakfast in the South without grits borders on the unthinkable, preferably served as a side dish with an egg or eggs over light, fried country ham, and red-eye gravy.

1 can whole white or yellow hominy

1 cup grated Cheddar cheese

1 can (4 ounces) chopped green chilies

½ cup sour cream

Salt and freshly ground pepper to taste

¼ cup heavy cream

1. Preheat the oven to 350 degrees.

2. Drain the hominy. There should be about 3 cups. Set aside ¼ cup cheese for the topping.

3. Put a layer of hominy on the bottom of a 4-cup casserole. Start forming layers of chilies, sour cream, the remaining ¾ cup cheese, the salt, and pepper. Pour on the heavy cream.

4. Sprinkle the reserved ¼ cup cheese on top and bake for 25 minutes.

Yield: 4 servings.

Fried Grits

2 cups water

2 cups plus 2 tablespoons milk

Salt to taste

1 cup regular or quick-cooking grits

3 eggs

1 cup fine fresh bread crumbs

2 tablespoons butter, or more

As a child of the South (and one who has not infrequently been described as having cornmeal mush in his mouth), I feel notably secure in stating that grits, that celebrated Southern cereal, constitutes a plural noun. I staunchly defend this opinion, but I do feel moved to give the opposition a moment of self-defense.

A fellow Mississippian, who shall go nameless, has written to me as follows:

"I wonder whether you have quietly fallen victim of a Yankee malaise, one that causes even editors of dictionaries, alas, to refer to grits as a plural noun. Never mind what these Yankee dictionaries say, come back home where grits is *it*, not them. Do Yankees refer to those oatmeal? Does one eat one grit or many? Isn't it supposed, at least by tradition, to be a singularly singular noun? Please say it's so.

"I remember, growing up on the Mississippi Gulf Coast, laughing with smirking pleasure over Yankees' references to grits as 'them' and 'those.' I do not recall whether any of them referred to the finer-ground cousin of grits, cornmeal, as 'them' or 'those' cornmeal, but maybe I was not listening.

"Until I hear better, I am going to assume that you remain well, and the dictionary usage for grits was insinuated (or were insinuated) into your otherwise impeccable article by some scurrilous (Yankee) copy editor.

"P.S.: Now, repeat after me: 'I like grits. It is good. I eat it (not them) whenever possible.'"

1. In a saucepan, combine the water and 2 cups of the milk with salt and gradually add the grits, stirring often. Cook until done, according to package directions. Regular grits require 25 to 30 minutes of slow cooking; quick-cooking grits will take 3 to 5 minutes.

2. Remove from the heat. Lightly beat 2 of the eggs, then beat them into the grits. Pour the mixture into an 8-inch-square pan. Chill until firm.

3. Cut the mixture into 1½-inch squares.

4. Beat the remaining egg and milk and dip each square into it. Coat with the bread crumbs.

5. Heat the butter in a skillet and cook the grits squares until golden brown on both sides, turning once.

Yield: 8 servings.

BAKED GRITS

1. Preheat the oven to 350 degrees.
2. Cook the grits according to package directions. Regular grits require 25 to 30 minutes of slow cooking; quick-cooking grits will take 3 to 5 minutes.
3. Stir in the cheese, butter, eggs, and milk and pour into a buttered 3-cup baking dish. Bake for 40 minutes or longer, or until set.

Yield: 6 to 8 servings.

1 cup regular or quick-cooking grits

½ pound sharp Cheddar cheese, grated

¼ pound butter

3 eggs, well beaten

⅓ cup plus 1 tablespoon milk

GRITS CASSEROLE

1. Preheat the oven to 350 degrees.
2. Bring the milk just to the boil in a heatproof casserole and add the ¼ pound of butter. Stir in the grits and continue to cook until it is the consistency of cereal.
3. Remove from the stove and add the salt and pepper. Beat with an electric beater and add the remaining 4 tablespoons butter.
4. Stir in the Gruyère until melted. Sprinkle Parmesan on top. Place in the oven and bake for 1 hour, until crusty on top.

Yield: 8 servings.

1 quart milk

¼ pound plus 4 tablespoons butter

1 cup regular grits

1 teaspoon salt

½ teaspoon freshly ground pepper

1 cup chopped Gruyère cheese

½ cup grated Parmesan cheese

Puréed Potatoes

2 pounds potatoes
Salt to taste
1 cup milk
4 tablespoons butter, at
  room temperature
¼ teaspoon grated
  nutmeg

1. Peel the potatoes and quarter them or cut them into 2-inch cubes. Place the potatoes in a saucepan and add cold water to cover and salt and simmer for 20 minutes, or until tender.

2. Drain the potatoes and put them through a food mill or ricer. Return them to the saucepan.

3. Meanwhile, bring the milk to the boil.

4. While the milk is being heated, use a wooden spoon and add the butter to the potatoes while beating. Add the salt and nutmeg and beat in the hot milk.

Yield: About 6 servings.

Potatoes Mont d'Or

6 potatoes, about
  2 pounds
Salt to taste
1 cup milk
6 tablespoons butter
Freshly ground pepper
  to taste
⅛ teaspoon grated
  nutmeg
2 eggs, separated
3 tablespoons grated
  Parmesan cheese

1. Preheat the oven to 350 degrees.

2. Peel the potatoes and cut them into thirds. Drop them into a saucepan with cold water to cover and salt to taste. Bring to the boil and simmer for about 20 minutes, until tender.

3. Drain the potatoes well, leaving them in the saucepan. Place the potatoes in the oven to dry for about 5 minutes.

4. Meanwhile, bring the milk just to the boil.

5. Press the potatoes through a food mill into a saucepan and beat in the butter, salt, pepper, and nutmeg.

6. Add the egg yolks and beat them in. Beat in the hot milk.

7. Beat the whites until stiff and fold them into the potatoes. Spoon the mixture into a baking dish (we used an oval dish that measured 8 × 14 × 2 inches) and smooth the top. Or, if you want to be fancy, spoon half the mixture into a baking dish and pipe the remainder through a pastry tube. Sprinkle with cheese and bake for 20 minutes. Brown under the broiler until glazed. Serve piping hot.

Yield: 8 or more servings.

STRAW POTATOES

1. Peel the potatoes and drop them into cold water to cover.
2. Cut the potatoes into about ⅛-inch-thick slices with a knife or potato slicer. Stack the slices, a few at a time, and cut the potatoes into shreds about ⅛ inch thick. Drop the shreds into cold water as they are prepared.
3. Drain the potatoes well into a colander.
4. Heat the oil to about 360 degrees in a cooker for deep-frying. Add the potatoes, a few handfuls at a time, and cook them, stirring frequently, until they are crisp and golden brown. Drain on absorbent towels and sprinkle with the salt.

Yield: 8 servings.

4 large potatoes (about 1½ pounds)
Oil for deep frying
Salt to taste

SAUTÉED POTATOES

1. Rinse the potatoes and put them in a kettle. Add cold water to cover and the salt. Simmer for 30 to 45 minutes, or until tender. Drain immediately.
2. Peel the potatoes. Cut each in half and cut each half into slices about ⅓ inch thick.
3. In a large heavy skillet, heat the oil and butter. Add the potatoes, salt, and pepper. Cook, tossing and stirring with care, until the potatoes are golden brown, 15 to 20 minutes. Sprinkle with garlic, toss, and spoon onto a hot dish. Serve sprinkled with chopped parsley.

Yield: 8 or more servings.

3 pounds fairly large potatoes
Salt to taste
¼ cup peanut, vegetable, or corn oil
3 tablespoons butter
Freshly ground pepper to taste
1 teaspoon finely minced garlic
1 tablespoon chopped parsley

POTATO CAKES

5 potatoes, about
1¾ pounds
Salt to taste
2 eggs, lightly beaten
2 tablespoons flour
⅛ teaspoon grated
nutmeg
½ cup Gruyère or Swiss
cheese, cut into the
finest possible dice
4 tablespoons oil

1. Peel the potatoes and grate them, using the fine blade of the grater. Spoon the potatoes into cheesecloth and squeeze to extract most of the moisture. There should be about 1¾ cups of pulp remaining.

2. Empty the potato pulp into a bowl and add the salt, the eggs, flour, nutmeg, and cheese and blend well.

3. Heat the oil in a skillet and drop the potato mixture into the skillet, using about 3 tablespoons at a time. Cook until golden on one side; turn and cook on the other side.

Yield: 6 to 8 servings.

BAKED SLICED POTATOES
WITH GRUYÈRE CHEESE

2½ pounds potatoes
Butter
2 garlic cloves, peeled
2 cups milk
1 cup heavy cream
Salt and freshly ground
pepper to taste
Grated nutmeg to taste
1 cup grated Gruyère or
Swiss cheese

1. Preheat the oven to 375 degrees.

2. Peel the potatoes and cut them into very thin slices. As they are sliced, drop them into cold water. Drain. There should be 6 or 7 cups.

3. Rub a baking dish (an oval one measuring about 14 × 8 × 2 inches is convenient) with butter and a peeled clove of garlic. Crush both cloves of garlic lightly and put them in a saucepan.

4. Add the milk, cream, salt, pepper, and nutmeg to the garlic cloves and bring to the boil. Strain this mixture over the potatoes. Discard the garlic. Sprinkle the top with the grated cheese. Place in the oven over a baking sheet to catch any drippings. Bake for about 1 hour, or until the potatoes are tender and the cheese is golden.

Yield: 8 or more servings.

BAKED POTATOES WITH SHRIMP

There are few vegetables that have more virtues than potatoes. They are delectable served hot or cold, but the flavor of a potato depends to a great extent on the flavors and textures of the foods with which it is combined. Put it in league with a garlic-tinged sauce; a chopping of parsley, chives, or scallions; or a purée of leeks or other vegetables, and there is a flavor explosion of the most refined and delectable sort.

We thought of this recently in creating a series of luncheon or supper dishes with baked potatoes as a base. From childhood we have found stuffed baked potatoes with a topping of cheese irresistible. Why not, we wondered, blend them with an assortment of savory ingredients such as shrimp, ground pork with rosemary, or oysters and those Creole vegetables, onions, green pepper, and celery? The results were all to the good.

1. Preheat the oven to 400 degrees.

2. Arrange the potatoes on a baking sheet and place them in the oven. Bake for about 1 hour, or until done.

3. Meanwhile, shell and devein the shrimp. Cut the shrimp into small cubes.

4. Melt 1 tablespoon of the butter in a saucepan and add the shrimp and mushrooms. Cook, stirring, for about 1 minute. Add the sherry and stir. Remove from the heat.

5. When the potatoes are done, slice off the top of each, about half an inch from the top. Carefully scoop out the center of each potato to make a boat for stuffing. Put the scraped out potato pulp into a saucepan or bowl and mash well and uniformly. Add this to the shrimp mixture. Add the cream and 1 tablespoon of the butter and cook briefly, stirring. Add salt and pepper and a few drops of Tabasco. Blend.

6. Fill the potato boats with the mixture, piling it up and smoothing it over.

7. Arrange the potatoes, stuffed side up, in a baking dish. Sprinkle with cheese. Melt the remaining tablespoon of butter and pour it over the potatoes. Bake for 15 minutes.

Yield: 4 servings.

4 large Idaho baking potatoes, about ½ pound each

½ pound raw shrimp in the shell

3 tablespoons butter

1 cup coarsely diced mushrooms

2 tablespoons dry sherry

¼ cup heavy cream

Salt and freshly ground pepper to taste

A few drops of Tabasco sauce

1 tablespoon freshly grated Parmesan cheese

BAKED POTATOES WITH OYSTERS

4 large Idaho baking
potatoes, about
½ pound each

4 tablespoons butter

¼ cup finely chopped
onion

¼ cup finely chopped
green pepper

¼ cup finely chopped
celery

¼ cup heavy cream

Salt and freshly ground
pepper to taste

⅛ teaspoon grated
nutmeg

¼ cup finely chopped
scallions

½ pint shucked oysters

1 tablespoon fine fresh
bread crumbs

1. Preheat the oven to 400 degrees.

2. Arrange the potatoes on a baking sheet and place in the oven. Bake for about 1 hour, or until done.

3. Meanwhile, melt 1 tablespoon of the butter in a saucepan and add the onion, green pepper, and celery. Cook, stirring, until the vegetables are wilted but still crisp.

4. When the potatoes are done, slice off the top of each, about half an inch from the top. Carefully scoop out the center of each potato to make a boat for the stuffing. Put the scraped out potato pulp into the saucepan and mash well and uniformly with the green pepper mixture. Add the cream, 2 tablespoons of the butter, the salt, pepper, nutmeg, and scallions. Blend well.

5. Cut each oyster in half if they are large and add them to the potato mixture. Cook, stirring, over moderate heat for about 2 minutes.

6. Fill the potato boats with the mixture, piling it up and smoothing it over.

7. Sprinkle the top of each potato with bread crumbs. Arrange the potatoes, stuffed side up, in a baking dish. Melt the remaining tablespoon of butter and pour it over the crumbs. Bake for 15 minutes.

Yield: 4 servings.

BAKED POTATOES STUFFED WITH PORK

1. Preheat the oven to 400 degrees.

2. Arrange the potatoes on a baking sheet and place in the oven. Bake for about 1 hour, or until done.

3. Meanwhile, melt 1 tablespoon of the butter in a saucepan and add the onion and celery. Cook, stirring, until the vegetables are wilted. Add the pork, sage, salt, and pepper and cook, stirring down with the side of a heavy metal spoon to break up any lumps, until the meat loses its raw look.

4. When the potatoes are done, slice off the top of each, about half an inch from the top. Carefully scoop out the center of each potato to make a boat for the stuffing. Put the scraped out potato pulp into the saucepan and mash well and uniformly with the meat mixture. Add the milk, 3 tablespoons of the butter, salt and pepper to taste, and the parsley and blend thoroughly.

5. Fill the potato boats with the mixture, piling it up and smoothing it over.

6. Arrange the potatoes stuffed side up in a baking dish. Melt the remaining tablespoon of butter and brush the tops of each potato with it. Hold a sieve over the top of each potato and sprinkle the paprika through the sieve onto the tops of the potatoes.

7. Return the potatoes to the oven and bake for 15 minutes.

Yield: 4 servings.

4 large Idaho baking potatoes, about ½ pound each

5 tablespoons butter

¼ cup finely chopped onion

¼ cup finely chopped celery

⅓ pound very lean ground pork

2 teaspoons crumbled leaf sage, or ½ teaspoon ground

Salt and freshly ground pepper to taste

⅓ cup milk

3 tablespoons finely chopped parsley

½ teaspoon paprika

SPICED POTATOES

7   cups peeled, cooked
    potatoes, cut into
    1-inch cubes

¼   cup sesame oil

2   teaspoons black
    mustard seeds

2   teaspoons urad dal
    (small white lentils)

⅛   teaspoon hing,
    available where
    imported spices are
    sold

1   teaspoon chopped
    fresh ginger

¼   cup coarsely chopped,
    mildly hot, fresh chilies

5   to 6 curry leaves,
    available in Indian food
    shops

¼   teaspoon ground
    turmeric

2   teaspoons salt

2   teaspoons lemon juice

2   tablespoons chopped
    fresh coriander

1. Prepare the potatoes and set them aside.

2. Heat the oil in a kettle and add the mustard seeds. When they crackle, add the lentils and cook for about 30 seconds.

3. Add the hing, ginger, chilies, curry leaves, turmeric, and salt. Cook, stirring, for about 30 seconds. Add the potatoes and stir gently until they are coated. Turn carefully so as not to break up the potato pieces.

4. Sprinkle with lemon juice and half the coriander. Toss gently to blend. Serve sprinkled with more fresh coriander.

Yield: 8 servings.

CANDIED SWEET POTATOES

1. Put the unpeeled potatoes in a saucepan and add cold water to cover. Bring to the boil and cook until barely soft, about 15 minutes. Drain.

2. Cool the potatoes and peel them. Slice them and arrange the slices, slightly overlapping, in a buttered baking dish.

3. Preheat the oven to 350 degrees.

4. In a saucepan, combine ⅔ cup of the brown sugar, water, and butter. Bring to the boil and let simmer for 5 minutes, stirring occasionally. Add the vanilla.

5. Pour the syrup evenly over the potatoes and sprinkle with the remaining brown sugar. Place in the oven and bake for 30 minutes, basting several times with the syrup.

Yield: 4 to 6 servings.

4 medium-size sweet potatoes (about 1½ pounds)

⅔ cup plus 1 tablespoon firmly packed brown sugar

¼ cup water

3 tablespoons butter

1 teaspoon pure vanilla extract

ORANGE AND SWEET POTATO CASSEROLE

6 sweet potatoes (about 2 pounds)
4 tablespoons butter
6 tablespoons firmly packed brown sugar
3 tablespoons dark rum
Salt to taste
¾ cup sectioned mandarin oranges, regular oranges, or tangerines, seeds and membranes removed and discarded
2 tablespoons coarsely chopped pecans

1. Put the potatoes in a kettle with water to cover and bring to the boil. Cook until tender, 30 minutes or longer. Cooking time will depend on the size of the potatoes. Drain.

2. Preheat the oven to 375 degrees.

3. Peel the potatoes and cut them into cubes. Put them through a food mill or potato ricer into a mixing bowl. Add 2 tablespoons of the butter, 4 tablespoons of the brown sugar, the rum, and salt. Beat thoroughly.

4. Add half the oranges to the mixture and fold them in. Turn this mixture into a buttered 2-quart casserole. Smooth over the top. Arrange the remaining orange pieces neatly over the top.

5. Combine the remaining butter, brown sugar, and pecans and sprinkle this over the top.

6. Place in the oven and bake for 30 minutes.

Yield: 6 servings.

SWEET POTATO PURÉE WITH WALNUTS AND GINGER

6 to 8 sweet potatoes (about 3 pounds)
½ cup ginger preserves
3 tablespoons dark rum
2 tablespoons butter
1 cup chopped walnuts, preferably black walnuts
¾ cup milk

1. Preheat the oven to 350 degrees.

2. Put the potatoes in a baking dish and bake for 1 to 2 hours, depending on the size of each potato. Press with the fingers and remove each potato as it becomes soft.

3. When all the potatoes are cooked, let them rest until cool enough to handle. Split each potato in half and scoop out the flesh.

4. Put the flesh through a fine sieve or potato ricer. There should be about 3 cups. Put this in a saucepan.

5. Combine the preserves and rum in a small saucepan. Bring to the boil, stirring. Add this to the potatoes. Add the butter, walnuts, and milk and heat to the boiling point, stirring.

Yield: 6 to 8 servings.

FALAFEL

1. Put the peas in a bowl and add water to cover to a depth of about 2 inches above the peas. Soak overnight.
2. Put half the peas in the container of a food processor and add portions of garlic, onion, cumin, ground coriander, fresh chopped coriander, and parsley. Add the salt, pepper, cayenne, and baking powder.
3. Blend one portion at a time to a fine purée. Empty the mixture into a mixing bowl and proceed with another batch. Continue until all the ingredients are used. The mixture will be manageable but moist.
4. Shape the mixture into balls about the size of a walnut. Flatten the pieces to make biscuit shapes.
5. Heat the oil for deep frying. Add the falafel and cook, turning once, until nicely browned and cooked throughout.

Yield: About 36 pieces.

½ pound dried chickpeas
1 large garlic clove
1 large onion, about ⅓ pound, peeled and thinly sliced
½ teaspoon ground cumin
½ teaspoon ground coriander
1 tablespoons chopped fresh coriander
6 fresh parsley sprigs
Salt and freshly ground pepper to taste
⅛ teaspoon cayenne
¼ teaspoon baking powder
Oil for deep frying

FAU (PURÉE OF BEANS, RUSSIAN STYLE)

1. Put the beans through a food mill or use a food processor to blend.
2. Pour the purée into a bowl.
3. Cut the onions in half and slice each half as thin as possible. There should be about 4 cups loosely packed.
4. Heat the oil in a skillet and add the onions. Cook, stirring, until the onions are nicely browned. Spread the onions evenly over the puréed beans. Sprinkle lightly or heavily with cayenne and serve at room temperature.

Yield: 4 to 6 servings.

2 20-ounce cans cannellini beans, undrained
4 yellow onions, about 1 pound, peeled
⅓ cup peanut, vegetable, or corn oil
Cayenne to taste

FLAGEOLETS

1 pound dried flageolets
7 cups water
Salt to taste
1 bay leaf
1 carrot, scraped
1 garlic clove, peeled but left whole
1 onion, peeled and stuck with 2 cloves
1 garlic clove, finely minced
2 tablespoons finely chopped parsley
3 tablespoons butter

1. Put the flageolets in a mixing bowl and add cold water to cover to a depth of about 1 inch above the top of the beans. Let soak for several hours or overnight.

2. Drain the beans and put them in a saucepan. Add the 7 cups of water. Add the salt, bay leaf, carrot, whole clove of garlic, and the onion. Bring to the boil and cook until tender. This may take from 1 to 1½ hours, depending on the age of the beans and soaking time.

3. Remove and discard the bay leaf, carrot, whole clove of garlic, and onion. Add the minced garlic, parsley, and butter. Bring to the boil, uncovered, and cook for 5 minutes.

Yield: 8 or more servings.

LENTIL PURÉE

1 pound lentils
¾ pound potatoes, peeled and cut into eighths
1 small onion, stuck with 2 cloves
1 garlic clove, peeled
1 bay leaf
6 cups water
Salt and freshly ground pepper to taste
1 cup half-and-half
2 tablespoons butter

1. Combine the lentils, potatoes, onion, garlic, bay leaf, water, salt, and pepper in a saucepan. Bring to the boil and simmer for 30 minutes, or until the lentils are tender. Drain.

2. Pour the lentil mixture into a food mill and pass it through into a saucepan. Discard any solids left in the food mill.

3. Add ¾ cup of the half-and-half, the butter, and salt to taste. Beat well to blend. Smooth the surface and pour the remaining ¼ cup of half-and-half on top to prevent a skin from forming. When ready to serve, heat thoroughly and stir to blend.

Yield: 8 to 10 servings.

LENTILS WITH SMOKED HAM

1. Heat 1 tablespoon of the butter in a small kettle or deep saucepan and add the ham and coarsely chopped onion. Cook briefly until the onion wilts.

2. Add the lentils, water, broth, bay leaf, thyme, salt, and pepper and simmer for 30 to 40 minutes. Discard the bay leaf and ham.

3. Meanwhile, heat the remaining butter in a saucepan and add the leek and finely chopped onion. Add the garlic and cook, stirring, for about 5 minutes. Add the tomatoes and cover. Simmer for about 15 minutes.

4. Combine the lentils with the tomato sauce. Cover and cook for about 15 minutes. Serve sprinkled with chopped parsley and sliced cotechini, or garlic sausage, if desired.

Yield: 6 to 8 servings.

3 tablespoons butter

¼ pound smoked ham slice, fat left on, cut into quarters

¼ cup coarsely chopped onion

½ pound dried lentils

2 cups water

4 cups fresh or canned chicken broth

½ bay leaf

1 fresh thyme sprig or ¼ teaspoon dried

Salt and freshly ground pepper to taste

1 finely diced leek

½ cup finely chopped onion

1 garlic clove, finely minced

1 cup tomatoes, fresh or canned

Chopped parsley for garnish

Sliced cotechini, or garlic sausage, for garnish, optional

LIMBO DAL (LEMON LENTILS)

1¼ cups peanut, vegetable, or corn oil

2 onions, halved and thinly sliced, about 1½ cups

4 2-inch pieces of cinnamon stick

2 pounds red lentils, available in specialty food stores

1 tablespoon chopped fresh ginger

5 cups fresh or canned chicken broth

5 cups water

Salt to taste

1 teaspoon cayenne

Juice of 1 lemon

The squeezed, seeded shell of 1 lemon including skin and pulp

½ cup chopped onion

1 garlic clove, finely minced

1 hot green chili, chopped, with seeds

4 bay leaves

½ cup chopped fresh coriander

Dal, the traditional lentil dish of India, is described by Ismail Merchant as a "rich man's, poor man's dish and every household has its own version. It is a must with any meal, and if you don't offer it, something is wrong." Mr. Merchant, a Bombay-born movie producer and one of the best Indian cooks in Manhattan, offered us his version of dal, made special with lemon.

1. Heat ¾ cup of the oil in a large saucepan and add the sliced onions. Cook to wilt and add the cinnamon pieces and lentils. Add the ginger and cook, stirring often, for about 10 minutes. Add the broth and water, salt to taste, and cayenne. Bring to the boil and simmer for about 10 minutes.

2. Add the lemon juice and lemon shell and cook for about 50 minutes longer, stirring often.

3. Heat the remaining ½ cup of oil and add the onion, garlic, chili, and bay leaves. Cook, stirring, until the onions are browned. Add this mixture including the oil to the lentils. Sprinkle with chopped coriander and serve hot.

Yield: 12 or more servings.

PINTO BEANS

1 pound dried pinto beans

1 large onion, chopped

½ pound chunk salt pork

Salt to taste

Soak the beans in water to cover for about 1 hour, then drain them. Cover again with water about 2 inches above the beans, add the onion and salt pork, and simmer until the beans are tender, about 2 hours. Add salt to taste.

Yield: 8 servings.

FRIJOLES RANCHEROS

1. Set the beans and bean liquid aside.
2. Heat the oil in a saucepan and add the onion and garlic. Cook until the onion wilts. Add the green pepper and chopped chilies and cook, stirring, for about 1 minute. Add the beans and bean liquid. Add the tomatoes, cinnamon, clove, salt, and pepper. Cover and simmer for 20 minutes.

Yield: 4 to 6 servings.

1 cup drained, cooked pinto beans (see preceding recipe)

¼ cup liquid in which beans cooked

¼ cup olive oil

1 cup finely chopped onion

2 teaspoons finely minced garlic

¾ cup cored, seeded, diced, sweet green pepper

2 tablespoons chopped hot, fresh chilies, preferably jalapeños

2 cups cored, unpeeled, diced tomatoes

One 1-inch piece stick cinnamon, or ½ teaspoon ground

1 whole clove

Salt and freshly ground pepper to taste

ROMAN BEANS WITH OIL

1. Put the beans in a bowl and add water to cover to a depth of about 2 inches above the top layer of beans. Soak overnight.
2. Heat the oil and add the garlic. Cook briefly. Drain the beans and add them. Add the water, sage, salt, and pepper. Cook, uncovered, for about 1 hour. Serve as a vegetable with a generous amount of olive oil sprinkled over each serving. Serve the beans with their pot juice spooned over.

Yield: 6 to 8 servings.

1 pound dried Roman, or cranberry, beans

¼ cup olive oil plus more olive oil for garnish

1 tablespoon finely minced garlic

6 cups cold water

2 to 4 sage leaves, the number will depend on size and potency of leaves

Salt and freshly ground pepper to taste

FRIJOLES DE OLLA
(BLACK BEANS IN A POT)

1　pound dried black
　　beans

⅛　pound lean salt pork,
　　cut into 1-inch cubes

½　onion, coarsely
　　chopped

10　cups water

　　Salt to taste

1.　Wash the beans and drain them. Put them in a kettle with the pork, onion, and water. Do not add salt. Bring to the boil and simmer for 1 hour.

2.　Add salt and continue cooking for about 2 hours longer.

Yield: About 8 servings.

Note: These beans are best if they are allowed to simmer awhile the second day.

Salads

We don't often write about nutrition because we believe that any well-planned meal, by definition, will be well balanced in the nutritional sense. Salads are part and parcel of good nutrition and, with rare exceptions, should have a place in almost every major meal year in and year out. Someone is bound to ask what the exceptions are and one answer is: following a platter of sauerkraut.

BASIC SALAD DRESSING

Combine all the ingredients in a small jar. Close and shake until thoroughly blended. Serve over salad greens.

Yield: About ⅓ cup.

2 tablespoons red wine vinegar or lemon juice

6 to 8 tablespoons peanut, vegetable, or olive oil

Salt and freshly ground pepper to taste

MUSTARD VINAIGRETTE

1. Put the mustard in a bowl and add the vinegar, salt, and pepper.
2. Start blending with a wire whisk, gradually adding the oil. Stir vigorously as the oil is added. Stir in the garlic.

Yield: About 1 cup.

2 teaspoons Dijon mustard

1 tablespoon wine vinegar

Salt and freshly ground pepper to taste

¾ cup olive oil

1 teaspoon finely minced garlic

SALAD DRESSING WITH FRESH HERBS

1 tablespoon Dijon
mustard

2 teaspoons red wine
vinegar

Salt and freshly ground
pepper to taste

½ cup olive oil, or a
combination of olive
oil and peanut,
vegetable, or corn oils

1 teaspoon chopped
fresh tarragon

1 teaspoon chopped
fresh chives

1 teaspoon chopped
fresh chervil, optional

½ teaspoon finely minced
garlic, optional

1. Put the mustard and vinegar in a mixing bowl.
2. Add the salt and pepper. Start stirring with a wire whisk.
3. When thoroughly blended, stir vigorously with the whisk and gradually add the oil.
4. Stir in the herbs and the finely minced garlic, if using.

Yield: About ⅔ cup.

VERMOUTH VINAIGRETTE

1½ tablespoons Dijon
mustard

1 tablespoon red wine or
malt vinegar

¼ cup dry white
vermouth

½ cup olive oil

2 tablespoons finely
chopped shallots

Salt and freshly ground
pepper to taste

1. Put the mustard and vinegar in a mixing bowl and add the vermouth while beating with a wire whisk.
2. Add the oil gradually, beating vigorously with the whisk. Add the shallots, salt, and pepper.

Yield: About 1 cup.

CREAMY SALAD DRESSING

1. Beat the egg yolk and put 1 teaspoon of it in a mixing bowl. Add the mustard, Tabasco, garlic, salt, pepper, and vinegar.

2. Using a wire whisk, beat vigorously to blend the ingredients. Still beating, gradually add the oil. Continue beating until thickened and well blended.

3. Add the lemon juice and beat in the heavy cream. Taste the dressing and add more salt, pepper, mustard, or lemon juice to taste.

Yield: ¾ cup.

1 egg yolk

2 or 3 teaspoons Dijon mustard

Dash of Tabasco sauce

½ teaspoon finely chopped garlic

Salt and freshly ground pepper to taste

1 teaspoon vinegar

½ cup olive oil

1 or 2 teaspoons fresh lemon juice

1 teaspoon heavy cream

RUSSIAN DRESSING

I rather doubt that you will find a recipe for Russian dressing in any Russian cookbook, and it seems quite definitely of American origin. To the best of my knowledge you won't find it in the French repertory of cooking under sauce Russe or otherwise. It is my belief that the original recipe for the dressing contained caviar, in addition to mayonnaise, chili sauce, horseradish, and grated onion, and that that is the source of the name.

Combine all the ingredients in a mixing bowl. Blend well.

Yield: About ¾ cup.

½ cup mayonnaise

1 tablespoon chili sauce or ketchup

1 teaspoon finely chopped onion

½ teaspoon prepared horseradish

¼ teaspoon Worchestershire sauce

1 tablespoon finely chopped parsley

1 tablespoon black or red caviar, optional

THOUSAND ISLAND DRESSING

1   cup mayonnaise

¼   cup chili sauce or
    ketchup, or equal parts
    of each

1   hard-cooked egg,
    chopped

1   tablespoon finely
    chopped onion

2   tablespoons finely
    chopped pimiento-
    stuffed green olives

½   cup finely chopped
    heart of celery

2   tablespoons finely
    chopped sweet pickles

    Lemon juice to taste

    Salt and freshly ground
    pepper to taste

2   teaspoons finely
    chopped parsley

Legend has it that Thousand Island dressing was created many years ago by the executive chef of the Drake Hotel in Chicago. He concocted the mayonnaise dressing with many chopped foods such as olives, pickles, and egg, and when his wife saw it she remarked that it looked like the Thousand Islands, near Ontario, New York, that they had recently visited.

Combine all the ingredients in a mixing bowl and blend well. Serve on lettuce, on hard-cooked egg halves, seafood, and so on.

Yield: About 1½ cups.

ASPARAGUS WITH THAI DRESSING

1. Cut off and discard any tough ends of the asparagus spears. Cut the spears on the bias into 1-inch lengths. Put the asparagus pieces into the top of a vegetable steamer. Steam them, closely covered, for 4 minutes or less, or until crisp-tender.

2. Put the garlic in a mortar and grind to a paste with a pestle. Add the fish sauce, lime juice, oil, hot pepper flakes, and pepper and blend well.

3. In a mixing bowl, combine the mint, coriander, and onion rings. Add the asparagus. Spoon the sauce over all. Toss well.

4. Arrange a ring of lettuce leaves around the border of a round plate or serving dish. Spoon the asparagus salad in the center.

Yield: 4 to 6 servings.

Note: Fish sauce, called nuoc mam or nam pla, is available in bottles in Asian groceries and supermarkets.

1½ pounds asparagus spears

½ garlic clove

1 tablespoon fish sauce (see note)

1 tablespoon lime juice

3 tablespoons peanut, vegetable, or corn oil

¼ teaspoon hot red pepper flakes

½ teaspoon freshly ground pepper

½ cup loosely packed fresh mint leaves

½ cup loosely packed, coarsely chopped fresh coriander

½ cup loosely packed onion rings

Lettuce leaves for garnish

Avocado Mousse with Chilies

4 ripe, firm, unblemished avocados, about 3 pounds combined weight

8 tablespoons lime juice

¼ cup water

2 tablespoons (envelopes) unflavored granular gelatin

1½ cups freshly made mayonnaise

One 4-ounce can chopped green chilies, drained, about ⅓ cup

One 8-ounce package cream cheese

1 to 4 canned jalapeño peppers, drained and chopped

¼ cup finely chopped fresh coriander

Salt and freshly ground pepper to taste

1 teaspoon peanut, vegetable, or corn oil

1. Peel the avocados. Cut them in half and discard the pits. Quickly cut the halves into 1-inch cubes and add 1 tablespoon of the lime juice. Toss to prevent discoloration. There should be about 6 cups.

2. Blend the water with the gelatin in a saucepan. Heat gently, stirring, until the gelatin dissolves.

3. Put the mayonnaise in a mixing bowl and add the gelatin mixture and chopped chilies. Blend well.

4. Combine the cubed avocado, the remaining lime juice, and cream cheese in the container of a food processor. Blend thoroughly. Add the chopped peppers, coriander, salt, and pepper to taste. Blend well.

5. Brush the inside of a 6-cup ring mold with the oil.

6. Spoon the avocado mixture into the prepared mold. Cover the mousse with a ring of wax paper. Refrigerate overnight.

7. To unmold, surround the mold with hot towels to loosen the mousse. Unmold onto a round serving dish. Serve with mayonnaise, if desired.

Yield: 8 or more servings.

STRING BEAN AND PEPPER SALAD WITH CUMIN VINAIGRETTE

1. Trim or break off the ends of the beans. Remove the strings if any.

2. Bring enough water to the boil to cover the beans when they are added. Add the beans. When the water returns to the boil, cook until the beans are tender, about 10 minutes. Drain well. Put them in a mixing bowl.

3. Put the pepper under the broiler and turn frequently until the skin is charred on all sides. Remove and put in a paper bag until cool enough to handle. Pull off the skin, cut the pepper in half, and remove the seeds. Put each half of the roasted pepper on a flat surface. Cut it into very thin strips about ¼ inch wide. There should be about ½ cup. Add them to the beans. Add the chopped onion.

4. Put the mustard, vinegar, salt, and pepper in a small mixing bowl. Start stirring with a wire whisk while gradually adding the oil. Add the cumin.

5. Stir and add the sauce to the bean mixture. Sprinkle with parsley and toss. Serve at room temperature.

Yield: 4 to 6 servings.

1 pound string beans
1 sweet red or green pepper
½ cup finely chopped onion
1 teaspoon Dijon mustard
1 tablespoon red wine vinegar
Salt and freshly ground pepper to taste
⅓ cup olive oil
¼ teaspoon ground cumin
¼ cup finely chopped parsley

Green Beans Vinaigrette

1 pound fresh green beans

Salt to taste

1 tablespoon finely chopped shallots

1 tablespoon Dijon mustard

Freshly ground pepper

1 tablespoon red wine vinegar

6 tablespoons peanut, vegetable, or corn oil

¼ cup finely chopped fresh dill, optional

1. Trim off the ends of the green beans. Cut the beans into 2-inch lengths. Drop them into boiling salted water and simmer for 2 to 5 minutes. The important thing is not to overcook them. They must remain crisp-tender. Drain well.

2. Meanwhile, combine all the remaining ingredients except the dill in a small saucepan and heat over very low heat, stirring with a whisk, until the sauce is lukewarm. Do not cook and do not heat too far in advance.

3. Arrange the warm beans on 4 salad plates and spoon equal amounts of sauce over. Sprinkle with dill, if desired. Serve warm.

Yield: 4 servings.

Three-Bean Salad

One 16-ounce can cut wax beans

One 16-ounce can cut green beans

One 16-ounce can kidney beans

¼ cup sugar

½ cup cider vinegar

Salt and freshly ground pepper to taste

¼ cup peanut, vegetable, or corn oil

¼ cup finely chopped onion

2 tablespoons finely chopped parsley

Empty the beans and drain well. Place the beans in a mixing bowl. Add the sugar and vinegar and toss until the sugar is dissolved. Add all the remaining ingredients. Toss well and chill until ready to serve.

Yield: About 6 cups.

PICKLED BEETS AND ONIONS

1. Place the beets in a saucepan and add cold water to cover. Add the salt and bring to the boil. Partly cover and simmer until the beets are tender throughout. The cooking time will vary from 15 to 45 minutes or longer, depending on the size and age of the beets. Let cool in the cooking liquid.

2. Remove the beets and slip off the skins under cold running water. Slice the beets. There should be about 2 cups. Place them in a mixing bowl.

3. Add about 1 teaspoon of salt, pepper to taste, sugar, and vinegar and stir until the sugar is dissolved. Taste the marinade and add more salt, sugar, or vinegar to taste.

4. Peel and slice the red onion. Add it to the mixing bowl and stir until the beets and onion are well intermingled.

Yield: 3 to 4 cups.

1 pound raw beets, trimmed

Salt and freshly ground pepper to taste

2 teaspoons sugar

2½ tablespoons wine vinegar

1 red onion, about ½ pound

BEET AND TUNA SALAD

10 medium-size beets, about 2 pounds

18 small, red-skinned potatoes, about 2 pounds

Salt to taste

1½ cups finely chopped onion

Two 7-ounce cans solid white tuna packed in oil, drained and flaked

One 2-ounce can flat anchovies, drained and chopped

2 tablespoons Dijon mustard

¼ cup red wine vinegar

9 tablespoons corn, peanut, or vegetable oil

Freshly ground pepper to taste

⅓ cup finely chopped parsley

2 tablespoons finely chopped fresh dill

1. Put the beets in one kettle and the potatoes in a second. Add cold water to cover and salt to taste to each kettle. Bring to the boil. Cook the potatoes for about 25 minutes and the beets for 25 to 45 minutes, or until each vegetable is tender. Drain and let cool.

2. Peel both the beets and potatoes.

3. Slice the beets and potatoes into a large mixing bowl. There should be about 5 cups of potatoes and 4 cups of beets. Add the onion, tuna, and anchovies.

4. Put the mustard in a mixing bowl and add the vinegar, stirring with a wire whisk. Gradually add the oil, stirring vigorously with the whisk. Season to taste with the pepper.

5. Pour the sauce over the salad. Add the parsley and dill and toss to blend.

Yield: 8 to 12 servings.

CREAMY COLESLAW

1. Remove the core from the cabbage. Cut the cabbage into 2-inch cubes. Put the cubed cabbage, one batch at a time, in the container of a food processor. Process until finely chopped. As the cabbage is chopped, put it into a mixing bowl. There should be about 8 cups.

2. Cut the carrots into ½-inch rounds. Put the rounds into the container of the food processor. Process until finely chopped.

3. Put the egg yolk, mustard, vinegar, salt, and pepper into a mixing bowl. Start beating with a wire whisk while adding the oil gradually until the mixture thickens like a mayonnaise.

4. Add the poppy seeds, celery seeds, sugar, Tabasco sauce, and onion. Stir. Add the cabbage and carrot and blend thoroughly. Chill.

Yield: 12 servings.

1 head cabbage, 2 pounds

2 small carrots, trimmed and scraped

1 egg yolk

1 teaspoon Dijon mustard

2 tablespoons white vinegar

Salt and freshly ground pepper to taste

1 cup peanut, vegetable, or corn oil

1 teaspoon poppy seeds or caraway seeds

½ teaspoon celery seeds, optional

1 teaspoon sugar

⅛ teaspoon Tabasco sauce

2 tablespoons finely minced onion

CARROT SALAD

1 pound fresh carrots,
about 12

1 large garlic clove,
peeled but left whole

Salt

¼ cup lemon juice

⅛ teaspoon ground
cinnamon

½ teaspoon ground cumin

½ teaspoon paprika

⅛ teaspoon cayenne

¼ cup olive oil

Chopped parsley for
garnish

1. Trim and scrape the carrots and put them in a kettle.
2. Add water to cover, and the garlic and salt to taste. Bring to the boil and cook for 10 minutes. Drain. Cut the carrots into ½-inch cubes. There should be about 2½ cups.
3. Combine the lemon juice, salt to taste, cinnamon, cumin, paprika, and cayenne in a mixing bowl and blend. Add the carrot cubes and half the oil. Stir to blend and set aside.
4. Spoon into a serving dish and sprinkle the remaining oil over the top. Sprinkle with chopped parsley and serve.

Yield: About 6 servings.

MOROCCAN CARROT SALAD

1 pound carrots,
trimmed and scraped

¼ cup olive oil

3 tablespoons lemon
juice

1 garlic clove, finely
minced

½ teaspoon cumin

¼ teaspoon dried mint
leaves

Salt and freshly ground
pepper to taste

½ teaspoon
confectioners' sugar, or
more to taste

¼ teaspoon cayenne

1. Use the julienne cutter of a food processor to cut the carrots into fine shreds. Or cut the carrots on a flat surface into ⅛-inch-thick slices. Stack the slices and cut them into very fine strips. There should be about 6 cups.
2. Blend the remaining ingredients and pour the sauce over the carrots. Toss to blend.

Yield: 10 or more servings.

CELERY AND MUSHROOMS WITH CORIANDER

1. Trim off the ends of the celery stalks. Scrape the stalks as necessary. Cut each stalk crosswise into 1½-inch lengths. There should be about 2½ cups. Set aside.

2. Rinse and drain the mushrooms. Set aside.

3. Peel the onions and cut them into quarters. There should be about ¾ cup.

4. Cut the pepper into matchlike strips about 1 inch long.

5. Pour the olive oil into a saucepan and add the lemon juice, vinegar, coriander seeds, cloves, salt, peppercorns, bay leaf, and thyme. Add the celery, mushrooms, onions, and pepper. Cover closely and cook, shaking the pan occasionally, about 10 minutes.

6. Pour the mixture into a mixing bowl and let cool. Chill. Serve cold or at room temperature.

Yield: 4 or more servings.

8 celery stalks, approximately
½ pound small mushrooms
4 very small white onions
½ sweet red or green pepper
2 tablespoons olive oil
¼ cup lemon juice
¼ cup white wine vinegar
2 teaspoons coriander seeds
2 whole cloves
  Salt to taste
½ teaspoon whole black peppercorns
1 bay leaf
¼ teaspoon dried thyme

CORN SALAD WITH HAM AND CHEESE

1   slice cooked ham, about ½ inch thick

1   slice Gruyère cheese, about ¼ inch thick

4 to 6   hearts of celery stalks

24   small pimiento-stuffed green olives

2   cups peeled, seeded, and diced ripe tomatoes

1   cup cooked corn cut from the cob

¾   cup finely chopped parsley

1   cup coarsely chopped onion

¾   cup mustard vinaigrette (see recipe page 659)

Next to the New World itself, corn is, to my mind, the greatest discovery brought about by Christopher Columbus. It not only offers sustenance in the form of breads, puddings, tortillas, and the like, but it is, when properly cooked, quite simply one of the most irresistible foods known. It also gives dimension to a summery ham-and-cheese salad, the inspiration for which came, oddly enough, from a small food shop on an island in the French West Indies.

1. Cut the ham into strips ½ inch wide. Cut the strips into ½-inch cubes. There should be about 2 cups.

2. Cut the cheese into ¼-inch strips. Cut the strips into ¼-inch cubes. There should be about 1 cup.

3. Finely dice the celery. There should be about 1½ cups.

4. Cut the olives in half crosswise.

5. In a large salad bowl, combine all the ingredients and toss well with the vinaigrette.

Yield: 6 or more servings.

CUCUMBER SALAD

2   fresh, firm cucumbers, about ¾ pound

¼   cup sugar

    Salt to taste

5   tablespoons white vinegar

5   tablespoons water

1   tablespoon very thinly sliced shallots

1   tablespoon finely shredded seeded hot fresh red pepper

¼   cup chopped fresh coriander

1. Peel the cucumbers. Quarter the cucumbers lengthwise and cut into thin slices. There should be about 2 cups.

2. Combine the sugar, salt, vinegar, water, and shallots in a saucepan. Bring to the boil and stir until the sugar dissolves. Remove from the heat and reserve.

3. Combine the cucumbers and shredded hot red peppers in a bowl. Pour the sugar syrup over all and stir. Sprinkle with coriander. Cover and refrigerate for 2 to 3 hours.

Yield: 4 to 6 servings.

Cucumber Salad with Dill

1. If the cucumbers are new and unwaxed, there is no need to peel them. Otherwise, peel them. Cut into thin slices and put in a mixing bowl. There should be 6 cups. Add 6 tablespoons of the vinegar, ½ cup of the sugar, 3 teaspoons of the salt, and the dill. Cover and refrigerate for 1 hour or longer.

2. Drain. Add the remaining 1 tablespoon of vinegar, 1 teaspoon of salt, and 1 teaspoon of sugar. Blend well.

Yield: 12 or more servings.

2 to 4 large cucumbers
7 tablespoons white wine vinegar
½ cup plus 1 teaspoon sugar
4 teaspoons salt
2 tablespoons chopped fresh dill

Cucumber and Yogurt Salad

1. Line a bowl with cheesecloth and empty the yogurt into it. Bring the edges of the cheesecloth together and tie to make a bag. Suspend the bag over the bowl and let drain for 1 hour or longer. The yogurt will become thick like sour cream.

2. Empty the yogurt into a clean bowl and add the remaining ingredients. Blend thoroughly. Chill well.

Yield: 4 to 6 servings.

3 cups plain yogurt
1 cup peeled, seeded, diced cucumber
Salt to taste
2 garlic cloves, finely minced
1 tablespoon chopped fresh dill
¼ cup olive oil
2 teaspoons wine vinegar

SPICY CUCUMBER SALAD

2 large cucumbers
1½ teaspoons salt
3 tablespoons soy sauce
½ teaspoon crushed red pepper, or ¼ teaspoon cayenne
1 teaspoon sesame oil
1 tablespoon vinegar

1. Wash the cucumbers and pat dry. Pound the cucumbers lightly all over with a cleaver.

2. Trim off the ends. Peel the cucumbers and cut them lengthwise into quarters. Cut or scrape away and discard the seeds.

3. Cut each cucumber strip into 1½-inch lengths. Trim the corners of each piece to make them neater. Put the pieces in a bowl and add 1 teaspoon of the salt. Let stand for 10 minutes.

4. Drain the cucumbers well and add the remaining ingredients. Chill and serve.

Yield: 4 servings.

BELGIAN ENDIVE AND FENNEL VINAIGRETTE

6 heads Belgian endive
1 fennel bulb
2 tablespoons fresh lemon juice
1 tablespoon Dijon mustard
6 tablespoons olive oil
Salt and freshly ground pepper to taste

1. Trim off the bottoms of the endive. Cut the endive into 1-inch lengths or cut it lengthwise into thin shreds. Drop the pieces into cold water. This will keep them from turning dark. Drain and spin dry or pat dry. Put in a plastic bag and chill.

2. Trim the fennel and slice it thin. Cut the slices into fine pieces. Rinse, drain, and spin or pat dry. Chill.

3. Combine the fennel and endive in a chilled mixing bowl. Blend the remaining ingredients and pour it over all. Add more lemon juice or oil to taste. Toss and serve on chilled salad plates.

Yield: 4 to 6 servings.

FENNEL AND AVOCADO VINAIGRETTE

1. Cut off the tops of the fennel bulbs and trim the base. Pull off and discard any very large, tough outer leaves. Cut the remaining fennel lengthwise into about twelve ½-inch slices. Arrange the slices in one layer in a serving dish.

2. Blend the garlic, oregano, vinegar, oil, salt, and pepper. Beat rapidly with a whisk or fork. Add the tomato cubes. Set aside.

3. Arrange 1 anchovy fillet on each of the fennel slices.

4. When ready to serve, peel the avocado and slice in half. Discard the pit. Cut the avocado lengthwise into ½-inch-thick slices and arrange these around the fennel. Add the olives. Beat the sauce lightly and pour it over all.

Yield: 4 to 6 servings.

2 fennel bulbs

1 tablespoon finely chopped garlic

1 teaspoon dried oregano

7 teaspoons red wine vinegar

6 tablespoons olive oil

Salt and freshly ground pepper to taste

1 cup cubed, peeled, seeded fresh tomatoes, optional

12 flat fillets of anchovies

1 ripe, unblemished avocado

24 black olives

JERUSALEM ARTICHOKES AND SHRIMP VINAIGRETTE

1 pound Jerusalem artichokes, or sun chokes, about 8

Salt to taste

1 tablespoon Dijon mustard

2 tablespoons red wine vinegar

½ cup olive oil

Freshly ground pepper to taste

1½ pounds shrimp, cooked, shelled, and deveined

½ cup finely chopped red onion

1 teaspoon finely minced garlic

¼ cup teaspoon hot red pepper flakes

¼ cup finely chopped parsley

1. Using a small regular or swivel-bladed paring knife, peel the artichokes. If the artichokes are very large, cut them in half. Ideally, the artichokes or pieces of artichokes should be of uniform size or the size of the smallest whole artichoke.

2. Put the artichokes in a saucepan. Add cold water to cover and salt to taste. Bring to the boil and simmer for 10 to 15 minutes, or until tender but still a little crisp. Drain well.

3. While the artichokes are still warm, cut them into ¼-inch-thick slices. Put them in a bowl.

4. Put the mustard and vinegar in a small bowl. Start beating with a wire whisk while gradually adding the oil. Beat in salt and pepper to taste.

5. Add the shrimp, onion, garlic, pepper flakes, and parsley to the artichokes. Pour the sauce over all and stir to blend. Serve warm.

Yield: 4 to 6 servings.

LEEKS VINAIGRETTE WITH ANCHOVY AND PIMIENTO

Arrange the leeks on a serving dish. Pour the vinegar and oil in a small mixing bowl and beat briskly with a wire whisk. Add the anchovies, garlic, salt, and pepper and beat well to blend. Fold in the pimiento and parsley and spoon the sauce over the leeks.

Yield: 4 servings.

- 8 cooked leeks
- 2 teaspoons red wine vinegar
- 4 tablespoons olive oil
- 3 anchovies, chopped
- 1 garlic clove, finely minced

  Salt and freshly ground pepper to taste
- 2 tablespoons diced pimiento
- 2 tablespoons finely chopped parsley

MUSHROOM AND AVOCADO SALAD

1. Blend the oil, vinegar, mustard, salt, pepper, parsley, and garlic thoroughly with a wire whisk.
2. Pour the sauce over the mushrooms and toss until well blended.
3. Peel the avocado and cut it in half. Remove and discard the pit. Cut the avocado into 1-inch cubes. Add the cubes to the mushroom mixture and toss gently to blend. Serve at room temperature.

Yield: 4 to 6 servings.

- ¼ cup olive oil
- 2 tablespoons red wine or tarragon vinegar
- 2 teaspoons Dijon mustard

  Salt and freshly ground pepper to taste
- 2 tablespoons finely chopped parsley
- ½ teaspoon finely minced garlic
- ½ pound mushrooms, thinly sliced, about 2½ cups
- 1 firm but ripe unblemished avocado

Mushroom and Pepper Salad

1 large sweet red pepper,
  about ½ pound

1 large sweet green
  pepper, about ½ pound

¾ cup celery cut
  crosswise into ¼-inch
  pieces

2 large unblemished
  endives

¼ pound mushrooms,
  thinly sliced, about 2
  cups

¼ cup chopped scallions

2 tablespoons lemon
  juice

1 tablespoon red wine
  vinegar

3 tablespoons olive oil

¼ teaspoon sugar

1. Cut away the core of each pepper.

2. Bring enough water to the boil in a saucepan to cover the peppers when added. Add the peppers and cook for 2 minutes, no longer. Remove the peppers but leave the water in the saucepan.

3. Using a paring knife, pull off the skin of the red pepper. The green pepper will not skin properly.

4. Cut the peppers lengthwise into quarters. Remove any veins and seeds. Cut the quartered peppers into ¼-inch crosswise strips.

5. Add the celery to the boiling water and simmer for about 30 seconds. Drain.

6. Trim off the base of the endives. Cut the endives, crosswise into ¼-inch pieces.

7. Combine the peppers, mushrooms, celery, endives, and scallions in a salad bowl.

8. Put the lemon juice and vinegar in a small mixing bowl and gradually beat in the oil and sugar. Beat well with a wire whisk. Pour the sauce over the mushroom mixture. Toss and serve.

Yield: 4 servings.

MARINATED MUSHROOMS

1. Crush the coriander seeds and put them in a saucepan large enough to hold the mushrooms. Add the oregano. Tie the marjoram, fennel, sage, thyme, bay leaf, and garlic in a small square of cheesecloth. Add the cheesecloth bag to the saucepan and add the water, lemon juice, olive oil, vinegar, salt, and pepper. Bring to the boil and cook over high heat for 5 minutes.

2. Meanwhile, rinse the mushrooms in cold water and drain them well. If the mushrooms are very small, leave them whole. Otherwise, cut them in half or quarter them, depending on size.

3. Add the mushrooms to the saucepan and return to the boil. Cover and cook over high heat for 7 to 8 minutes, shaking the saucepan to redistribute the mushrooms so that they cook evenly. Uncover and cook for about 5 minutes longer over high heat.

4. Spoon the mushrooms, cooking liquid, and cheesecloth bag into a mixing bowl and cover. Let cool. Chill overnight. Remove and discard the cheesecloth bag. Serve the mushrooms cold or at room temperature. Garnish, if desired, with lemon wedges or parsley.

Yield: 6 to 8 servings.

1 teaspoon coriander seeds

½ teaspoon dried oregano

½ teaspoon dried marjoram

½ teaspoon dried fennel seeds

1 teaspoon dried sage leaves, crushed

½ teaspoon dried thyme

1 bay leaf, broken

1 large garlic clove, crushed but unpeeled

¼ cup water

2 tablespoons lemon juice

3 tablespoons olive oil

1 tablespoon distilled white vinegar

Salt and freshly ground pepper to taste

1 pound mushrooms, the smaller the better

Lemon wedges or parsley for garnish

HEARTS OF PALM SALAD

Two 14-ounce cans hearts of palm

½ pound fresh mushrooms

20 cherry tomatoes, cut in half

1 small red onion, peeled and cut into thin slices

1 small garlic clove, finely minced

¼ cup lime juice

½ cup olive oil or more to taste

¼ cup finely chopped parsley

Salt and freshly ground pepper to taste

1. Drain the hearts of palm. Cut the pieces into ¾-inch rounds and put them in a salad bowl.

2. Slice the mushrooms thin and add them. Add the tomatoes, onion rings, garlic, lime juice, olive oil, parsley, salt, and pepper. Toss and, if desired, add more oil.

Yield: 6 to 8 servings.

SWEET PEPPERS, MOROCCAN STYLE

3 or 4 large sweet green or red peppers, preferably a combination of both, about 1 pound

½ teaspoon ground cumin

1 tablespoon lemon juice

2 tablespoons olive oil

¼ teaspoon finely chopped garlic

⅛ teaspoon cayenne

¼ teaspoon paprika

2 tablespoons chopped parsley

Salt and freshly ground pepper to taste

1. Preheat the broiler or use a charcoal grill. Put the peppers under the broiler or on the grill and cook, turning often, until the skin is shriveled and partly blackened. Remove. Put the peppers in a paper bag and let stand until cool enough to handle. Peel off the skins.

2. Split the peppers in half. Remove and discard the stems and seeds. Place the halves on a flat surface. Cut into strips or cut them into fairly large, bite-size pieces. There should be about 1½ cups.

3. Put the pieces in a mixing bowl and add all the remaining ingredients. Toss to blend. Serve at room temperature.

Yield: About 4 servings.

POTATO SALAD WITH BACON AND ONION

1. Put the potatoes in a kettle and add cold water to cover and the salt. Bring to the boil and cook until tender, 15 to 20 minutes. Remove from the heat and drain.

2. As soon as the potatoes are cool enough to handle, peel them. Cut them into ¼-inch-thick slices and put them in a mixing bowl.

3. Meanwhile, cook the bacon until crisp. Drain on absorbent paper towels. Chop coarsely. Set aside.

4. Add the onion, parsley, salt, and pepper to the potatoes. Add the vinegar and oil and half the bacon and toss.

5. Spoon into a salad bowl and garnish with the remaining bacon bits and small heart of romaine lettuce leaves or other greens.

Yield: 6 to 8 servings.

2 pounds new red-skinned potatoes

Salt to taste

6 slices lean bacon

4 tablespoons finely chopped onion

3 tablespoons finely chopped parsley

Freshly ground pepper

1 tablespoon wine or herb vinegar

5 tablespoons peanut, vegetable, or corn oil

Lettuce leaves for garnish

POTATO SALAD WITH WALNUTS AND ANCHOVY MAYONNAISE

1. Put the potatoes in a kettle and add water to cover and the salt. Bring to the boil and simmer for 20 minutes, or until tender. Drain.

2. When the potatoes are still hot but cool enough to handle, peel them. Cut them into ¼-inch-thick slices. There should be about 6 cups. Put the slices in a bowl.

3. Add the walnuts, mayonnaise, and chopped dill. Toss and serve while still warm.

Yield: 8 or more servings.

2 pounds Idaho, Long Island, or Maine potatoes

Salt to taste

1 cup broken walnut meats

¾ cup anchovy mayonnaise (see recipe page 768)

¼ cup chopped dill or parsley

POTATO SALAD WITH FINES HERBES

2 pounds new red-
   skinned potatoes

Salt to taste

¼ cup finely chopped
   shallots

1 garlic clove, finely
   minced

2 tablespoons chopped
   fresh chives

3 tablespoons finely
   chopped parsley

1 tablespoon chopped
   fresh tarragon, or
   1 teaspoon dried

¼ cup dry white wine

1 teaspoon red wine or
   herb vinegar

3 tablespoons walnut oil,
   or use peanut,
   vegetable, or corn oil

Freshly ground pepper
   to taste

Lettuce leaves for
   garnish

There is nothing in the world wrong with the traditional potato salad that Grandma used to make. Tossed with some homemade mayonnaise, a bit of celery and onion, it makes a grand addition, as it has for many generations, to picnics and church socials, to backyard barbecues and covered-dish suppers. But there are potato salads and potato salads. Infinitely more sophisticated than Grandma's version are the "warm" potato salads, made sometimes with a splash of dry white wine, sometimes with oil and vinegar, sometimes with bacon, and often with an unexpected piquant herb such as tarragon. They add a bit of class to an informal meal, indoors or out.

1. Put the potatoes in a kettle and add cold water to cover and the salt. Bring to the boil and cook until tender, 15 to 20 minutes. Remove from the heat and drain.

2. As soon as the potatoes are cool enough to handle, peel them. Cut them into ¼-inch-thick slices and put them in a mixing bowl.

3. Add the shallots, garlic, chives, parsley, tarragon, wine, vinegar, oil, salt, and pepper. Toss well. Garnish with heart of romaine lettuce leaves or other greens. Serve, if desired, with garlic sausages (see following recipe).

Yield: 6 to 8 servings.

GARLIC SAUSAGES

2 uncooked garlic
   sausages (cotechini),
   about 1 pound each

2 bay leaves

½ teaspoon dried thyme

1. Put the sausages in a kettle and add cold water to cover.

2. Add the bay leaves and thyme and bring to the boil. Let simmer for 30 minutes. Serve sliced, hot or cold.

Yield: 6 to 8 servings.

SWEET POTATO SALAD

1. Cook the sweet potatoes until soft; drain. When cool enough to handle, peel, quarter lengthwise, then cut into cubes. Place in a mixing bowl and sprinkle with lime juice. Chill.

2. Peel, core, and dice the apples. Add to the potatoes together with the celery and nuts. Add enough mayonnaise to coat well. Chill before serving.

Yield: 4 to 6 servings.

1½ pounds sweet potatoes (about 3 large)

Juice of 4 limes

2 large apples

1 cup thinly sliced and then chopped celery

6 ounces coarsely chopped cashews or pecans

1 cup freshly made mayonnaise, approximately

SLICED TOMATOES WITH HERBED VINAIGRETTE SAUCE

1. Cut away and discard the core from the tomatoes. Slice the tomatoes and arrange them in a serving dish. Sprinkle with the salt and pepper.

2. Blend the remaining ingredients, adding salt and pepper to taste. Pour over the tomatoes and serve.

Yield: 4 servings.

2 red, ripe, unblemished tomatoes

Salt and freshly ground pepper to taste

1 tablespoon red wine vinegar

3 tablespoons olive oil

1 tablespoon finely chopped chives

1 tablespoon finely chopped parsley

TOMATOES AND ONIONS WITH GORGONZOLA SALAD DRESSING

2 or 3 large ripe
  tomatoes, about
  1½ pounds
1 large Bermuda onion,
  about 1 pound
1 tablespoon vinegar
3 tablespoons olive oil
  Salt and freshly ground
  pepper to taste
¼ pound Gorgonzola
  cheese, at room
  temperature

1. Core the tomatoes and thickly slice them. Peel the onion and cut it into thick slices. Arrange alternate and slightly overlapping slices of tomatoes and onion on a serving dish.

2. Combine the vinegar, oil, salt, and pepper in a bowl and blend well. Add the cheese and cut it into the dressing, which should be slightly lumpy. Pour the salad dressing over all and serve.

Yield: 4 servings.

FRESH MOZZARELLA WITH TOMATOES AND ANCHOVIES

¾ to 1 pound fresh
  mozzarella
12 slices ripe tomatoes
36 flat anchovy fillets
4 to 6 tablespoons olive
  oil
  Freshly ground pepper
  to taste
  Fresh basil sprigs

Cut the mozzarella into 12 more or less equal slices and arrange them on a serving dish. Place 1 slice of tomato atop each. Garnish each serving with 3 flat anchovy fillets. Sprinkle each serving with olive oil. Add a few turns of the peppermill and serve at room temperature, garnished with basil.

Yield: 6 to 12 servings.

Moroccan Tomato Salad

1. Cut the pepper into strips about ½ inch wide. Cut the strips crosswise into thin slices. There should be about ⅓ cup.

2. Put the pepper in a bowl and add the remaining ingredients. Blend. Chill.

Yield: 4 to 6 servings.

1 small green pepper, cored, seeded, and deveined

1½ cups cored, peeled, and seeded tomatoes, cut into ½-inch cubes

1 tablespoon finely chopped parsley

1 tablespoon finely chopped onion

¼ teaspoon finely minced garlic

½ teaspoon finely minced fresh coriander

Salt to taste

¼ teaspoon cayenne

½ teaspoon ground cumin

1 tablespoon white vinegar

2 tablespoons peanut oil

CHEZ PANISSE'S BAKED GOAT CHEESE WITH LETTUCE SALAD

8 rounds of very soft, mild goat cheese, about half an inch thick

1 cup olive oil, preferably virgin oil

   Salt and freshly ground pepper to taste

8 fresh thyme sprigs, or any desired herbs such as oregano, rosemary, sage, or finely minced garlic

1 cup fresh bread crumbs

8 cups loosely packed assorted salad and herb greens such as arugula, mesclun, or mâche

1 tablespoon red wine vinegar

1. Arrange the goat cheese rounds on a shallow dish.

2. Pour ¾ cup of the olive oil over all. Sprinkle with the salt and pepper. Turn the rounds in the oil. Arrange or sprinkle the fresh herbs over all.

3. Dip the rounds all over in the bread crumbs, patting to make the crumbs adhere. Arrange the rounds on a baking dish. Refrigerate for 15 minutes or longer.

4. When ready to cook, preheat the oven to 450 degrees.

5. Strain the herbs from the oil and reserve the oil.

6. Place the baking dish in the oven and bake for 10 to 12 minutes.

7. Meanwhile, put the salad and herb greens in a salad bowl. Blend the vinegar, the reserved oil, and the remaining ¼ cup oil, salt, and pepper. Pour the dressing over the greens and toss well.

8. Transfer the greens to a flat serving dish. Arrange the cheese rounds around and serve immediately.

Yield: 4 to 8 servings.

GREEK SALAD

1. Rub a large salad bowl with salt and garlic. Discard the garlic.
2. In the salad bowl, combine the lettuce, celery, radishes, scallions, cucumber, green pepper, olives, and cheese.
3. Beat the olive oil with the lemon juice and pour over the salad. Toss and season with the salt and pepper. Sprinkle the salad with the oregano and parsley.
4. Arrange the anchovy fillets radiating from the center with the tomato wedges. Garnish with parsley sprigs.

Yield: 12 or more servings.

Salt to taste
1 garlic clove
2 heads Boston lettuce, shredded
1 romaine lettuce, shredded
3 celery hearts, diced
6 radishes, sliced
1 bunch scallions, sliced
1 cucumber, thinly sliced
1 sweet green pepper, cut into thin rings
12 oil-cured black olives
½ pound feta cheese, diced
½ cup olive oil
Juice of 2 lemons
Salt and freshly ground pepper to taste
½ teaspoon dried oregano
1 tablespoon minced parsley
8 anchovy fillets
3 tomatoes, cut into wedges
Parsley sprigs for garnish

Spicy Orange Salad, Moroccan Style

3 large, seedless oranges
1/8 teaspoon cayenne
1 teaspoon paprika
1/2 teaspoon minced garlic
3 tablespoons olive oil
1 tablespoon vinegar
   Salt and freshly ground pepper to taste
1/3 cup freshly chopped parsley
12 pitted black olives, preferably imported Greek or Italian olives

1. Peel the oranges, paring away all the exterior white pulp. Cut the oranges into eighths. Cut each segment into 1-inch pieces. Set aside.
2. Place the cayenne, paprika, garlic, olive oil, vinegar, salt, and pepper to taste in a salad bowl and blend well with a wire whisk. Add the oranges, parsley, and olives. Toss gently to blend and serve cold or at room temperature.

Yield: 4 servings.

Herbed Cottage Cheese Salad

3 cups curd-style cottage cheese
1/2 cup mayonnaise
3/4 cup finely chopped scallions
2 tablespoons finely chopped onion
1/4 cup chopped chives
1/4 cup finely chopped parsley
1 cup finely diced cucumber
1 tablespoon chopped fresh basil
1/2 cup coarsely chopped radish
   Lemon juice to taste
   Salt and freshly ground pepper to taste

Place the cottage cheese in a mixing bowl. Add the mayonnaise and blend. Add the remaining ingredients and blend well.

Yield: About 4 cups.

BLACK BEAN SALAD

1. Bring 3 quarts of water to the boil. Add the beans and return to the boil. Remove from the heat and let stand for 1 hour.

2. Return the beans to the boil and simmer for 1½ to 2 hours, until beans are soft but not mushy.

3. Meanwhile, cook the salt pork in a heavy skillet until the fat is rendered and the pork is crisp. Remove the pork with a slotted spoon and set aside. To the fat in the skillet add the onions and cook for 5 minutes, stirring. Add the green peppers, garlic, and oregano and continue cooking, stirring, until the onion is golden. Add this to the beans. Add the red wine and bring to the boil. Simmer for ½ hour. Let cool.

4. Combine the ingredients for the vinaigrette sauce and stir it into the beans. Add more salt and pepper to taste, if desired, and chill.

Yield: 8 to 12 servings.

THE BEANS:

2 pounds dried black beans, preferably turtle beans

½ pound salt pork, cut into small cubes

2 cups finely chopped onions

1 cup chopped sweet green pepper

1 tablespoon finely chopped garlic

½ teaspoon dried oregano

1 cup dry red wine

THE VINAIGRETTE SAUCE:

2 tablespoons red wine vinegar

6 tablespoons olive oil

1 garlic clove, finely minced

1 teaspoon Dijon mustard

Salt and freshly ground pepper to taste

WHITE BEANS VINAIGRETTE

1 cup dried white beans
   such as white kidney
   beans or pea beans

4 cups water

1 cup finely chopped
   onion

1 teaspoon finely minced
   garlic

2 tablespoons finely
   chopped parsley

2 tablespoons finely
   chopped basil

   Salt and freshly ground
   pepper to taste

3 tablespoons red wine
   vinegar

½ cup olive oil

1. Unless the package specifies no soaking, put the beans in a bowl
   and add water to cover to about 2 inches above the top of the
   beans. Soak overnight.

2. Drain the beans. Put them in a kettle and add 4 cups of water.
   Bring to the boil and simmer for 50 minutes to 1 hour, or until the
   beans are tender. Drain well.

3. Put the beans in a mixing bowl and add the remaining ingredients.
   Blend gently but well. Serve warm.

Yield: 8 servings.

LENTIL SALAD

1. Combine the lentils, onion, carrot, whole garlic clove, thyme, bay leaf, parsley sprigs, water, salt, and pepper. Bring to the boil and simmer for 30 minutes, or until tender. Drain.

2. Remove the carrot and cut it into cubes. Set aside.

3. Remove and discard the bay leaf, parsley, thyme sprigs, the onion stuck with clove, and the whole garlic clove.

4. Spoon the lentils into a mixing bowl and add the cubed carrot, the chopped onion, chopped parsley, chopped garlic, wine vinegar, and oil. Add salt and pepper to taste. Toss to blend well. Serve garnished with the tomato wedges.

Yield: 8 or more servings.

½   pound dried lentils

1   small onion stuck with 1 clove

1   carrot, trimmed and scraped

1   garlic clove, peeled and left whole

2   fresh thyme sprigs, or ½ teaspoon dried

1   bay leaf

3   fresh parsley sprigs

3   cups water

Salt and freshly ground pepper to taste

½   cup finely chopped onion

4   tablespoons finely chopped parsley

1   garlic clove, finely minced

1   tablespoon wine vinegar

4   tablespoons olive oil

Tomato wedges for garnish

LENTIL AND SCALLION SALAD

2 small smoked pork hocks, or ½ pound smoked pork

6 cups water, approximately

1 pound lentils

Salt to taste

¼ cup chopped scallions

4 to 6 tablespoons olive oil

2 to 3 tablespoons wine vinegar

Freshly ground pepper to taste

¼ to 1 teaspoon dry mustard

1. Put the pork hocks in a large saucepan and add the water. Bring to the boil and cover. Simmer for 1½ hours.

2. Remove the pork from the saucepan and skim off any fat. Add the lentils and salt. Bring to the boil and simmer, covered, for about 25 minutes, or until tender. It may be necessary to add more water to the saucepan. The lentils, as they cook, should be almost but not quite covered with the boiling liquid. When the lentils are tender, drain them. They must not be cooked to a mushy stage.

3. Let the lentils cool.

4. Cut the meat off the pork hocks and add it to the lentils. Add the remaining ingredients with salt to taste. Blend well and let stand for several hours to develop the flavor.

Yield: 6 or more servings.

TABBOULEH

¾ cup fine bulgur

1 cup diced, seeded tomatoes

1 cup finely chopped parsley

½ cup chopped scallions

1 tablespoon chopped fresh mint

½ cup fresh lemon juice

½ cup olive oil

Salt and freshly ground pepper to taste

Romaine lettuce leaves for garnish

1. Put the bulgur in a sieve and let cold water run over it. Transfer the bulgur to a mixing bowl and add cold water to cover to a depth of about 1 inch above the top of the wheat. Let soak for about 15 minutes.

2. Line a sieve with cheesecloth and drain the cracked wheat. Bring up the edges of the cheesecloth and squeeze to extract most of the moisture.

3. Put the bulgur in a mixing bowl and add all the remaining ingredients except the lettuce leaves. Toss to blend thoroughly.

4. Arrange the lettuce leaves around a salad bowl. Spoon in the salad and serve.

Yield: 8 or more servings.

WARM FISH SALAD WITH CAPERS

1. Make neat, symmetrical, generous arrangements of endive leaves, watercress, and lettuce leaves on four large dinner plates. Arrange equal portions of shredded lettuce in the center of each arrangement.

2. Cut each fish fillet lengthwise down the center. Cut each fillet half crosswise in two.

3. Put the milk in a small dish and add the fish pieces, salt, and pepper. Stir to coat each piece of fish evenly.

4. Put the flour in a flat dish and dredge the pieces of fish in the flour, turning to coat evenly.

5. Heat the corn oil over high heat and add a few pieces of fish at a time. Do not crowd them in the skillet. Cook for about 45 seconds on one side until golden brown. Turn quickly and cook until golden on the second side, about 30 seconds.

6. Arrange 4 fish pieces close together on each of the salad arrangements.

7. Heat the olive oil in a skillet and, when it is quite hot, add the capers. Cook over high heat for 30 seconds, no longer. Add the vinegar, swirl it around, and pour an equal portion of the caper mixture over each serving of fish.

Yield: 4 servings.

- 1 head Belgian endive
- 1 bunch watercress
- 8 heart of lettuce leaves
- 1 cup finely shredded heart of lettuce
- 4 small skinless, boneless fillets of fish, such as flounder, sea bass, or sole, about ¾ pound
- 2 tablespoons milk
  Salt and freshly ground pepper to taste
- ½ cup flour
- ¼ cup corn, peanut, or vegetable oil
- ⅓ cup olive oil
- ⅓ cup drained capers
- ¼ cup raspberry or red wine vinegar

CRAB AND YOGURT MAYONNAISE SALAD

1. Handle the crabmeat as little as possible to avoid breaking up the large, firm lumps. Remove any pieces of shell or cartilage, however. Put the crabmeat in a bowl and add ½ cup of the yogurt and watercress mayonnaise. Stir gently to blend.

2. Arrange the lettuce leaves in a circular pattern on a serving dish, stem sides toward the center. Pile the crab salad in the center.

3. Garnish around the sides of the crabmeat with slices of radish and cucumber, arranging them symmetrically.

4. Put the egg through a sieve. Sprinkle it over the crabmeat. Serve with the remaining yogurt and watercress mayonnaise on the side.

Yield: 4 servings.

- 1 pound lump crabmeat
- 2 cups yogurt and watercress mayonnaise (see recipe page 768)
- 8 to 10 Boston lettuce leaves
- 3 radishes, cut into thin slices for garnish
- 12 cucumber slices
- 1 hard-cooked egg

LOBSTER AND ASPARAGUS SALAD

2 to 4 live 1-pound lobsters, preferably female

Salt to taste

16 asparagus spears, ends trimmed

2 tablespoons imported mustard with green peppercorns

1 tablespoon raspberry or other berry vinegar

¼ cup virgin olive oil

2 tablespoons walnut oil

Freshly ground pepper to taste

3 cups mesclun or shredded Boston lettuce leaves

8 raw mushrooms, sliced

4 fresh coriander sprigs

1. Bring enough water to the boil to cover the lobsters when they are added. Add the salt. Add the lobsters. When the water returns to a full rolling boil, remove the kettle from the heat. Let stand for 15 minutes.

2. Drain the lobsters. Cut off the tails and claws. Crack the tails and claws and remove the meat. Cut the tail meat in half lengthwise. Leave the claw meat whole. Discard the shells.

3. Bring enough water to the boil in a skillet to cover the asparagus spears when they are added. Add salt to taste. Add the asparagus spears and simmer for about 2 minutes, or until crisp-tender. Drain. Run under cold water and drain again.

4. Put the mustard in a small bowl and add the vinegar, stirring with a wire whisk. Gradually add the oil, and salt and pepper to taste, beating vigorously with the wire whisk.

5. Arrange a bed of lettuce in the center of four dinner plates. Arrange the lobster pieces on the lettuce. Garnish with asparagus spears and overlapping slices of raw mushrooms. Spoon the sauce over all.

6. Garnish with sprigs of fresh coriander and serve at room temperature.

Yield: 4 servings.

CHIFFONADE OF LOBSTER CHEZ DENIS

1. If live lobsters are used, drop them into vigorously boiling salted water and cover. Cook for 10 minutes and remove from the heat. Let stand for about 15 minutes. Drain and let cool.

2. When the lobsters are cool enough to handle, crack them and remove the meat from the claws and tail. Reserve and set aside any red coral. There should be about 2 cups of meat and coral. Refrigerate until ready to use.

3. Place the yolk in a mixing bowl and add the vinegar, mustard, tomato paste, salt, pepper, and cayenne. Gradually add the oil, beating vigorously with a wire whisk. Beat in the lemon juice, tarragon, and Cognac.

4. Add the lobster, foie gras, if desired, and tomatoes to the mayonnaise and fold them in with a rubber spatula. This may be done in advance and refrigerated for an hour or so.

5. When ready to serve, stack the romaine lettuce leaves and cut them into the finest possible shreds, using a heavy sharp knife. There should be about 2 cups loosely packed shreds. Add this to the salad and fold it in. Serve immediately before the shreds wilt.

Yield: 6 to 8 servings.

Two 1½-pound live lobsters, or 2 cups cubed cooked lobster meat

1 egg yolk

1 tablespoon white wine vinegar

1 tablespoon Dijon mustard

1 tablespoon tomato paste

Salt and freshly ground pepper to taste

⅛ teaspoon cayenne or Tabasco sauce to taste

1 cup olive oil

Juice of ½ lemon

1 teaspoon chopped fresh tarragon

2 teaspoons Cognac

½ cup cubed foie gras, optional

¾ cup cubed, seeded tomatoes

6 to 12 leaves fresh, crisp unblemished romaine lettuce leaves, rinsed and patted dry

LOBSTER SALAD À L'AJA

3 cups cubed lobster
meat

2 cups peeled, seeded,
and cubed tomatoes

2 cups cubed firm but
ripe avocado

Juice of 1 lime

2 cups freshly made
mayonnaise

Salt and freshly ground
pepper to taste

1 hard-cooked egg, finely
chopped

Finely chopped red
coral from the lobsters,
if available

Dill or parsley sprigs
for garnish

1. Combine the lobster meat, tomatoes, avocado, lime juice, mayonnaise, salt, and pepper. Toss well.

2. Arrange the salad on a platter and sprinkle with the chopped egg and chopped coral. Garnish with dill or parsley sprigs.

Yield: 8 to 12 servings.

OCTOPUS SALAD

There are many people who find an octopus preparation a bit bizarre. We can assure them that this one is not. It is delectable. And octopus, fresh or frozen, is widely available in communities with a large Greek population. Squid is also a delectable foundation for a salad as is conch, or scungilli, one of my personal favorites.

1. Cut away and discard the "beak" and "mouth" of the octopus. Remove and discard the viscera and the ink sac.

2. Bring enough water to the boil to cover the octopus when it is added.

3. Drop the octopus into the water and cook for 5 seconds. Remove the octopus but leave the water boiling. Drop the octopus into a basin of cold water and let stand for 1 minute.

4. Return the octopus to the boiling water for 5 seconds. Remove it a second time, leaving the water boiling. Chill briefly in cold water.

5. Add the white wine vinegar to the boiling water. Add the octopus a third time, cover closely, and cook for 1 hour. Drain and let cool.

6. It is not essential to clean away the skin and suckers (suction cups) of the octopus, for they are edible. It is better, however, for appearance's sake. If you want to remove the skin and tentacles, it is easier if you cut off the tentacles before cleaning.

7. Cut the tentacles and meaty center portion of the octopus into bite-size pieces and place in a bowl. There should be about 4 cups.

8. Add the remaining ingredients and blend well. Cover and refrigerate for several hours before serving.

Yield: 6 to 8 servings.

One 3-pound octopus

2 tablespoons white wine vinegar

1 teaspoon finely minced garlic

½ cup coarsely chopped onion, preferably red

¼ cup lemon juice

3 tablespoons red wine vinegar

6 tablespoons olive oil

Salt to taste

A generous grinding of black pepper

¼ cup finely chopped parsley

SQUID SALAD

2 pounds squid, cleaned
¼ cup dry white wine
  Salt and freshly ground
  pepper to taste
2 garlic cloves, peeled
  and left whole
1 hot red pepper, or
  ¼ teaspoon hot red
  pepper flakes
1 bay leaf
4 fresh parsley sprigs
2 teaspoons finely
  minced garlic
3 tablespoons finely
  chopped parsley
2 tablespoons lemon
  juice
1 tablespoon red wine
  vinegar
¼ cup olive oil
½ cup finely chopped red
  onion

1. Cut the bodies of the squid into rings about ½ inch wide. Cut the tentacles into bite-size pieces. There should be about 3½ cups.

2. Put the squid in a saucepan or small kettle and add the wine, water to cover, salt, pepper, garlic cloves, red pepper, bay leaf, and parsley sprigs. Bring to the boil. Cover and cook for about 1 minute, or just until squid pieces firm up. Drain and chill.

3. Put the squid in a mixing bowl and add the remaining ingredients. Toss and serve chilled.

Yield: 4 or more servings.

Note: Freshly cooked shelled shrimp are also excellent in a salad with squid. Simply substitute a portion of shrimp for any given quantity of the squid.

SCUNGILLI (CONCH) SALAD

3 cups cooked, cleaned,
  sliced conch (see
  method for cooking
  page 547)
1 tablespoon finely
  chopped garlic
4 to 6 tablespoons lemon
  juice
3 tablespoons olive oil
½ teaspoon hot red
  pepper flakes
½ teaspoon crushed dried
  oregano
¼ cup finely chopped
  parsley
  Salt to taste

1. Put the sliced conch in a bowl and add the garlic. Toss. Add the lemon juice and toss. Add the remaining ingredients. Toss well.

2. Taste and add more lemon juice, oil, salt, and so on if desired.

Yield: 4 to 6 servings.

Note: This salad may be covered closely and will keep for 3 or 4 days in the refrigerator.

SALMON SALAD WITH VEGETABLES

1. Drop the peas into cold water with salt to taste. Bring to the boil and simmer for 1 to 2 minutes, or until barely tender. Do not overcook. Drain and set aside.

2. Bring enough water to the boil to cover the carrots, celery, and turnips when added. Add salt to taste. Add the carrots and simmer for about 3 minutes.

3. Add the celery and turnips and simmer for 1 or 2 minutes longer. Drain. Run under cold water to chill. Drain well on a clean towel.

4. Put the peas, turnips, celery, and carrots in a large mixing bowl.

5. Add the mayonnaise, Tabasco sauce, onion, Worchestershire sauce, and dill. Add salt and pepper to taste and toss.

5. Put the vegetables in mayonnaise in a serving dish. Surround it with the tomato wedges and pile the salmon on top.

Yield: 6 servings

1 cup fresh peas
  Salt to taste
1 cup scraped and cubed carrots
½ cup diced celery
1 cup peeled and cubed turnips
1 cup freshly made mayonnaise
¼ teaspoon Tabasco sauce
½ cup thinly sliced onion
½ teaspoon Worchestershire sauce
¼ cup finely chopped fresh dill
  Freshly ground pepper to taste
1 large ripe tomato, cored, seeded, and cut into eighths
4 cups poached salmon cut or broken into large bite-size pieces

SCALLOPS WITH MAYONNAISE SAUCE

¼ cup water

¼ cup dry white wine

1 bay leaf

1 fresh thyme sprig, or
¼ teaspoon dried

2 fresh parsley sprigs

Salt and freshly ground
pepper to taste

2 cups (1 pint) fresh bay
scallops

1 egg yolk

2 teaspoons Dijon
mustard

⅛ teaspoon Tabasco
sauce

¼ teaspoon Worcester-
shire sauce

1 tablespoon finely
chopped shallots

1 cup peanut, vegetable,
or corn oil

2 cups mesclun or
Boston lettuce cut into
fine shreds
(chiffonade)

2 hard-cooked eggs, each
cut in half, for garnish

4 tomato wedges for
garnish

1 tablespoon finely
chopped parsley for
garnish

1. In a saucepan combine the water, wine, bay leaf, thyme, parsley sprigs, salt, and pepper. Bring to the boil and add the scallops. When the cooking liquid returns to the boil, let simmer, stirring occasionally so that the scallops cook evenly. Cook for about 1 minute and drain, taking care to reserve 2 tablespoons of the cooking liquid. Set the scallops aside until cool.

2. Combine the egg yolk, mustard, Tabasco sauce, Worcestershire sauce, and shallots in a mixing bowl. Add salt and pepper to taste.

3. Start beating with a wire whisk while gradually adding the oil. Continue beating until all the oil is added. Beat in the 2 table-spoons of reserved cooking liquid.

4. Arrange the lettuce over the bottom of a serving dish. Spoon the scallops in the center. Spoon the mayonnaise over all. Garnish with the egg halves and tomato wedges. Serve sprinkled with chopped parsley.

Yield: 4 to 6 servings.

SHRIMP WITH TARRAGON AND ANCHOVY MAYONNAISE

1. Place the shrimp in a saucepan and add cold water to cover. Add the allspice, hot red pepper, and salt to taste. Bring to the boil and simmer for 1 minute. Remove the shrimp from the heat and let cool. Drain, shell, and devein the shrimp.
2. Combine the mayonnaise with the lemon juice, chopped anchovies, and tarragon. Cut the shrimp in half and add them. Chill and serve cold.

Yield: 6 or more servings.

1½ pounds raw shrimp, about 36

12 whole allspice

1 dried hot red pepper
Salt to taste

1 cup freshly made mayonnaise

2 teaspoons fresh lemon juice, or more to taste

6 anchovies, finely chopped

1 tablespoon chopped fresh tarragon

CHESA GRISCHUNA SHRIMP

At a glorious picnic on the grass at Tanglewood (actually on an 8 × 10-foot Persian rug set on the lawn with overstuffed pillows to sit on), we were served this unusual chilled shrimp by Marianne Lipsky and her husband, Karl. They explained that the recipe had come from one of their favorite restaurants, the Chesa Grischuna, in Klosters, Switzerland.

1. Arrange the lettuce in a crystal bowl and put the shrimp on top and set aside.
2. Put the mayonnaise in a bowl and add the horseradish and ketchup.
3. Core and peel the apple. Cut it into very thin slices. Stack the slices and cut into very thin strips. Cut the strips into the finest possible dice to make 1 cup. Add this to the mayonnaise.
4. Whip the cream until stiff and fold it in. Add salt, pepper, Worcestershire sauce, Tabasco, and sherry. Blend well.
5. Spoon the sauce over the shrimp and serve cold.

Yield: 15 to 20 servings.

4 cups shredded iceberg lettuce

3 pounds cooked shrimp, shelled, deveined, and chilled

1½ cups mayonnaise, preferably freshly made

½ cup freshly grated horseradish

¾ cup ketchup

1 tart green apple, preferably a Granny Smith

½ cup heavy cream
Salt and freshly ground pepper, preferably Tellicherry, to taste

1 teaspoon Worcestershire sauce

½ teaspoon Tabasco sauce

3 tablespoons dry sherry

SHRIMP RÉMOULADE

THE SHRIMP:

2 pounds fresh shrimp in the shell

16 allspice

1 large garlic clove, peeled and crushed

12 peppercorns, crushed

Salt to taste

THE RÉMOULADE SAUCE:

2 tablespoons Creole mustard, available in shops specializing in fine foods

1 tablespoon tarragon wine vinegar

Salt and freshly ground pepper to taste

1 cup olive oil

1 tablespoon paprika

½ cup finely chopped celery

1 cup chopped scallions

1 teaspoon chopped garlic

½ cup chopped parsley

2 tablespoons horseradish, preferably fresh

2 tablespoons anchovy paste

⅛ teaspoon cayenne

2 tablespoons lemon juice

Tabasco sauce to taste

THE GARNISH:

Shredded romaine lettuce

Lemon wedges

1. Put the shrimp in a saucepan and add water to cover. Add the allspice, garlic, peppercorns, and salt. Bring gradually to the boil. Simmer for about 1 minute and remove from the heat. Let stand until cool. Peel and devein the shrimp. There should be about 4 cups.

2. For the sauce, put the mustard and vinegar in a mixing bowl and add the salt and pepper. Beat with a wire whisk and gradually add the oil, stirring constantly. Stir in the remaining ingredients for the sauce.

3. Put about ½ cup of shredded romaine on each of 8 salad plates. Arrange an equal number of shrimp on the lettuce. Spoon the sauce over to completely cover the shrimp. Serve with lemon wedges.

Yield: 8 servings.

SHRIMP WITH ORANGES
AND ROSEMARY VINAIGRETTE

1. Put the celery in a saucepan and add cold water to cover and salt to taste. Bring to the boil and simmer for about 30 seconds. Drain and set aside to let cool.

2. Arrange alternating, overlapping slices of oranges and shrimp on a bed of watercress. Sprinkle with the chopped celery.

3. Blend the vinegar with the oil, paprika, salt, pepper, garlic, and rosemary. Pour the sauce over the salad and serve at room temperature.

Yield: 4 servings.

1 cup chopped celery

Salt to taste

3 oranges, peeled and sliced

1½ pounds cooked shrimp

1 bunch watercress, rinsed and drained well

2 tablespoons red wine vinegar

6 tablespoons olive oil

½ teaspoon paprika

Salt and freshly ground pepper to taste

½ teaspoon chopped garlic

1 teaspoon chopped fresh rosemary leaves, or ½ teaspoon dried

SHRIMP AND FRUIT WITH CURRIED YOGURT MAYONNAISE

3½ cups cooked, shelled, deveined shrimp

¾ cup orange sections cut into bite-size pieces

2 cups peeled, seeded papaya or mango cut into bite-size cubes

½ cup white seedless grapes

½ cup banana cut into ½-inch cubes

1⅔ cups curried yogurt mayonnaise (see recipe page 767)

Juice of ½ lemon

6 cantaloupe halves, seeded

6 mint sprigs for garnish

1. Cut the shrimp into bite-size cubes. There should be about 2½ cups. Put the cubes in a bowl.

2. Add the orange sections, papaya, grapes, banana, ½ cup of the mayonnaise, and the lemon juice. Toss to blend.

3. Pile equal portions of the fruit salad into the cantaloupe halves. Spoon a little additional mayonnaise on top of each serving. Garnish each with a mint sprig. Serve the remaining mayonnaise on the side.

Yield: 6 servings.

COLD SHRIMP SALAD WITH FETA CHEESE

1. Arrange the onion rings in the bottom of a salad bowl. Arrange the shrimp over the onions. Sprinkle with feta cheese and cover with watercress.

2. Drop the cherry tomatoes into boiling water to cover and let stand for exactly 12 seconds. Drain quickly and run under cold water. Drain well. Use a small paring knife and pull away the skin of each tomato. Garnish the salad bowl with the tomatoes.

3. Combine the remaining ingredients in a bottle and shake well. Pour the dressing over the salad and toss well.

Yield: 4 servings.

12 thin slices red onion

24 cooked shrimp, shelled and deveined

½ cup crumbled feta cheese

1 bunch watercress, trimmed, rinsed, and shaken dry

24 cherry tomatoes, or 16 wedges of standard-size ripe tomatoes

3 tablespoons finely chopped fresh dill, optional

3 tablespoons fresh lemon juice

3 tablespoons olive oil

Salt and freshly ground pepper to taste

1 garlic clove, finely minced

Tabasco to taste

Seafood and Orzo Salad

1 live 2½-pound lobster

½ pound large shrimp

Salt to taste

½ cup orzo

2 cups freshly made mayonnaise

2 teaspoons dry mustard

1 teaspoon finely chopped fresh dill

1 teaspoon chopped fresh chives

Juice of 1 lemon

2 tablespoons finely chopped parsley

Freshly ground pepper to taste

4 large ripe tomatoes

One of the best tasting and most interesting types of pasta is called orzo, which is most closely identified with Greek cooking. The word for the pasta in Greek is *kritharaki*, and both it and orzo mean "barley," which refers to the shape of the grain, although orzo, like most pasta, is made from wheat flour. Orzo also has more or less the same shape and size as pine nuts or long grains of rice.

Leon Lianides, former proprietor of the well-known Coach House Restaurant in Manhattan and our favorite authority on Greek cooking, used the pasta in a seafood salad of his own invention.

1. Bring enough water to the boil to cover the lobster and shrimp when added. Add the salt. Add the lobster and shrimp and cook for 10 minutes.

2. Remove the lobster and shrimp and run under cold water to chill.

3. Strain the cooking liquid and return it to the boil. Add the orzo and cook for 10 minutes, or until tender. Drain. Chill.

4. Remove the meat from the lobster, and shell and devein the shrimp. Cut the lobster meat and shrimp into small, bite-size pieces.

5. Combine the mayonnaise, mustard, dill, chives, lemon juice, and half the parsley in a bowl. Add salt and pepper to taste. Blend well.

6. Fold in the lobster, shrimp, and orzo. Cover and refrigerate until ready to serve.

7. Remove the cores from the tomatoes. Cut the tomatoes partly into quarters, but do not cut them all the way to the bottom. Open up each tomato and fill with the orzo mixture. Serve sprinkled with the remaining finely chopped parsley.

Yield: 4 servings.

ANYTHING MAYONNAISE SALAD

1. If a cooked solid such as chicken, veal, lamb, pork, or beef is used, cut it into small, bite-size cubes. If shrimp are used, leave them whole. If crabmeat is used, leave it in lumps or shred it. There should be about 3 cups.

2. Bring about 3 cups of water to the boil. Add the carrots and cook for about 5 minutes. Add the zucchini and cook both vegetables a minute longer. Add the celery and cook for 1 more minute. Do not overcook. The vegetables must remain a bit firm. Drain well. Let cool.

3. Put the vegetables and meat in a mixing bowl and add the shallots, garlic, salt, pepper, and parsley. Add the mayonnaise and blend.

4. Arrange a border of lettuce leaves around a serving dish. Spoon the salad into the center of the dish. Garnish with tomato and egg wedges.

Yield: 6 servings.

3 cups cubed or shredded cooked foods such as meat, poultry, fish or seafood

1 cup cubed carrot

1 cup cubed zucchini or other squash

¾ cup cubed celery

1½ tablespoons finely chopped shallots

1 garlic clove, finely minced

Salt and freshly ground pepper to taste

1 tablespoon finely chopped parsley

1½ cups freshly made mayonnaise

Lettuce leaves for garnish

Tomato wedges for garnish

Hard-cooked egg wedges for garnish

CHICKEN SALAD WITH GRAPES

2 firm, ripe, but not too sweet apples

2 cups white seedless grapes

2 teaspoons curry powder

2 tablespoons chicken broth

1 egg yolk

2 teaspoons Dijon mustard

2 tablespoons lemon juice

Salt and freshly ground pepper to taste

1½ cups peanut, vegetable, or corn oil

Tabasco sauce to taste

¼ teaspoon Worcestershire sauce

4 cups cooked, skinless, boneless chicken breast cut into neat, bite-size pieces

¾ cup walnuts

1 cup finely diced heart of celery

Boston lettuce leaves

1 basil or parsley sprig for garnish

1. Core and peel the apples. Cut them into quarters. Cut each quarter crosswise into thin slices. There should be about 2 cups.

2. If the grapes are large, cut each in half lengthwise. Set aside.

3. Combine the curry powder and broth in a small saucepan. Bring to the boil, stirring. Set aside. Let cool.

4. Put the egg yolk in a mixing bowl and add the mustard, lemon juice, salt, and pepper. Start beating with a wire whisk while gradually adding the oil. Add the Tabasco sauce to taste and Worcestershire sauce. Beat in the curry mixture.

5. Combine the chicken, apples, grapes, walnuts, and celery in a mixing bowl. Add the curried mayonnaise and fold it in.

6. Arrange the lettuce leaves on a serving dish and pile the salad in the center. Garnish with a sprig of fresh basil or parsley.

Yield: 8 to 10 servings.

LESLIE NEWMAN'S LOTOS
SALAD FOR A CROWD

1. Bring enough water to the boil to cover the chicken breasts when added. Cut the breasts in half and add them to the water. When the water returns to the boil, cover and simmer for 6 minutes. Remove from the heat and let stand for 15 minutes.

2. Remove the chicken pieces and plunge them into a basin of water with ice cubes. Let stand for 15 minutes. Remove the chicken and pat dry.

3. You may use the bean sprouts as they are purchased. It is more refined, however, if you pull off the curlicues and seed portions of each. There should be 4 cups plucked sprouts. Put the sprouts in a mixing bowl.

4. Cut the cucumbers lengthwise into strips. Cut the strips into spaghetti like shreds. There should be about 4 cups. Add them to the mixing bowl, along with the pepper strips and shredded pork.

5. Remove and discard the skin and bones of the chicken breasts. Shred the meat. There should be about 3 cups. Add this to the bowl.

6. Drop the noodles into a large quantity of boiling water. Cook for 4 minutes. Drain well and rinse under cold water until chilled. Drain once more. Cut into shreds of manageable length and put the noodles into a second bowl. Add the corn oil and sesame oil. Chill.

7. Combine the noodles and the pork, chicken, and vegetable mixture. Add the sesame sauce and toss. Add the coriander and blend. Serve immediately.

Yield: 20 to 25 servings.

Note: The chicken may be poached and chilled, then stored tightly wrapped in the refrigerator overnight. You may also prepare the remaining ingredients and store them tightly covered in the refrigerator. Blend the foods when ready to serve.

2 unskinned, unboned whole chicken breasts, about 1¾ pounds

1¼ pounds fresh bean sprouts

2 cucumbers, peeled

2 sweet red or green peppers, cored, seeded, and cut into thin strips, about 2 cups

2 cups shredded roast pork (purchased or homemade)

2 pounds fresh Chinese egg noodles

1 tablespoon corn, peanut, or vegetable oil

1½ teaspoons sesame oil

3⅓ cups rich sesame sauce (see following recipe)

½ cup chopped fresh coriander

RICH SESAME SAUCE

¼ cup sesame paste (tahini)

½ cup crunchy peanut butter

½ cup freshly brewed tea or water

2 tablespoons chili oil

2 tablespoons sugar

¾ cup light soy sauce

½ cup sesame oil

2 tablespoons finely minced garlic

¼ cup red wine vinegar

2 tablespoons Chinese black rice vinegar, available in Asian groceries and supermarkets

6 tablespoons corn, peanut, or vegetable oil

1½ tablespoons ground roasted Sichuan peppercorns (see note)

Freshly ground pepper to taste

1 cup finely chopped scallions, green parts and all

1. Combine the sesame paste and peanut butter in a mixing bowl. Start beating with a wire whisk while gradually adding the tea. Stir until smooth.

2. Add all the remaining ingredients except the chopped scallions. Cover and refrigerate. This sauce may be made as far in advance as 24 hours. Stir in the scallions just before serving. This can also be used as a cold sauce on cold noodles or poached chicken.

Yield: About 3⅓ cups, sufficient for 20 to 25 servings.

Note: Place the peppercorns in a heavy skillet and cook over moderately low heat for about 3 minutes, or until dark brown and aromatic. Grind to a powder using a coffee or spice grinder, or blender.

MANY FLAVOR DUCK SALAD

1. Cut the ducks into quarters and pull the bones from the meat. Cut away and discard the skin and any fat. The ducks may be prepared to this point a day or longer in advance. If they are not to be used immediately, wrap the pieces in foil or plastic wrap and refrigerate or freeze. Cut the meat when it is at room temperature or defrosted into 1-inch-wide shreds.

2. Meanwhile, preheat the oven to 325 degrees. Put the pine nuts in an ovenproof skillet and toss them in ½ teaspoon of the corn oil. Place in the oven and bake for 10 to 15 minutes, or until golden brown. Cool.

3. Put the nuts in a large mixing bowl and add the duck, peppers, and cabbage.

4. Put the remaining ¾ cup of corn oil in a saucepan and add the chopped scallions, ginger, ground Sichuan pepper, pepper, and chili peppers.

5. Combine the dark soy sauce, hoisin sauce, honey, garlic, and chili paste with garlic in a small bowl.

6. Bring the corn oil mixture to the simmer and cook for 1 minute, no longer. Add the soy sauce mixture and stir. Remove from the heat. Pour this simmering liquid over the salad. Toss, blending well, and serve immediately.

Yield: 25 servings.

Three 5- to 6-pound ducks red-cooked (see recipe page 239)

½ cup pine nuts

½ teaspoon plus ¾ cup corn, peanut, or vegetable oil

3 sweet red or green peppers, cored, seeded, and cut into 1-inch pieces

12 cups shredded Shandong (white-ribbed Chinese cabbage)

1½ cups minced scallions, green parts and all

1½ tablespoons minced fresh ginger

1 tablespoon ground roasted Sichuan peppercorns (see note with preceding recipe)

Freshly ground pepper to taste

3 fresh hot chili peppers, seeded and finely chopped

9 tablespoons dark soy sauce

4½ tablespoons hoisin sauce

3 tablespoons honey

2 tablespoons finely minced garlic

2 teaspoons bottled chili paste with garlic

Salade de Poulet Troisgros (Green Salad with Sautéed Sliced Chicken)

One 4-pound chicken, or 2 pounds skinless, boneless chicken breasts

⅓ cup salad sauce, approximately (see following recipe)

16 cups mixed, loosely packed salad greens (use any tender greens in season such as oak leaf lettuce, red leaf lettuce, or mesclun)

2 teaspoon coarsely chopped fresh tarragon

2 teaspoons coarsely chopped fresh basil

1 teaspoon finely chopped fresh chervil or parsley

Salt and freshly ground pepper to taste

5 teaspoons peanut, vegetable, or corn oil

¼ cup chopped scallions

4 teaspoons red wine vinegar

1 small black truffle, cut into fine strips, optional

2 teaspoons truffle liquid, optional

When Jean Troisgros comes to your home and prepares a salad as the first course, it belies the notion that salad served before the main course is an enormously unsophisticated and childish concept, as we once wrote. Here was this titan of the kitchen, one of the most celebrated chefs of Europe, giving the gastronomic lie to such a thought. But this was no mundane tossing together of a few lettuce leaves. It was an inspired orchestration of greens and herbs and quickly sautéed thin medallions of chicken.

1. Cut the whole chicken into serving pieces, separating the legs and thighs. Remove the skin and bone from the breast meat. Remove the skin and bone from the thigh meat. Cut the liver, if used, into ½-inch cubes. Use the wings, carcass, and legs for another purpose, such as soup.

2. Set the pieces of chicken (or the skinless, boneless chicken breasts) on a flat surface and pound lightly. Cut the pieces on the bias into very thin slices. As the slices are cut, arrange them in one layer on a sheet of wax paper. Cover with another sheet of wax paper and pound lightly with a flat mallet. Do not break the meat. Set aside.

3. Prepare the salad sauce in a salad bowl.

4. Add the salad greens to the bowl and sprinkle with tarragon, basil, and chervil.

5. When ready to serve, sprinkle the cubed liver and the chicken slices with salt and pepper.

6. Heat 2 teaspoons of the oil in a small skillet and, when it is very hot and almost smoking, add the liver pieces. Cook quickly, tossing and stirring until lightly browned all over, for about 30 seconds. Add the scallions and 2 teaspoons of the vinegar. Stir quickly over high heat and pour this over the salad greens. Add the truffles and truffle juice, if desired. Toss well. Spoon the greens onto 4 or 6 salad plates. Set aside.

7. Heat the remaining oil in a large skillet and add the chicken slices. Cook for about 30 seconds on one side and turn the pieces. Cook for about 30 seconds on the other side. Arrange equal amounts of chicken neatly over each serving of salad.

8. Add the remaining vinegar to the skillet. Stir. At the boil, pour this over the salad and serve.

Yield: 4 to 6 servings.

Combine the garlic, salt, pepper, mustard, and vinegar in a salad bowl large enough to contain 16 cups of salad greens when tossed. Using a wire whisk, gradually add the oil, stirring.

Yield: About ⅓ cup.

SALAD SAUCE

½ teaspoon finely minced garlic

Salt and freshly ground pepper to taste

1 tablespoon Dijon mustard

5 teaspoons red wine vinegar

5 tablespoons oil, preferably walnut oil

Daniel Fuchs's Duck and String Bean Salad

One 4- to 5-pound roast duck (see recipe page 234)
1 pound string beans
2 unblemished sweet red peppers
2 ripe tomatoes
14 lychee nuts
1 mango, peeled and seeded
½ cup macadamia nuts
3 tablespoons lemon juice
½ to ¾ cup walnut oil (or use Chinese or Japanese sesame oil)
Salt and freshly ground pepper to taste
2 tablespoons chopped fresh coriander

When the word *salad* is bandied about, the image that springs to mind is a simple concoction of one or more varieties of greens tossed together in a bowl. The fact is that some of the most interesting salads in the modern vein are fairly substantial, salads that can easily serve as a main course any season of the year. These salads also are great for party giving because they stand nobly as a buffet item.

One of the most interesting that we have sampled in many a day is an exotic creation, the concept of Daniel Fuchs when he was the chef of Maxwell's Plum restaurant in Manhattan. This salad is made with mango, macadamia nuts, sweet peppers, lychee nuts, and roast duck.

1. Cut the meat from the duck, discarding the skin and bones. Cut the meat into neat, bite-size portions. There should be about 2 cups. Set aside.

2. Trim off the ends of the beans. Cut the beans into 2-inch lengths and drop them into a saucepan of boiling water. When the water returns to the boil, let simmer for 4 minutes. Drain and run the beans briefly under cold running water. Drain thoroughly.

3. Core and seed the peppers. Cut the peppers into thin lengthwise shreds. Drop the shreds into boiling water. When the water returns to the boil, drain. Run briefly under cold water. Drain thoroughly. Set aside.

4. Remove the cores from the tomatoes. Cut the tomatoes in half and remove the seeds. Cut the tomato halves into thin strips. Set aside.

5. Cut the lychee nuts into quarters. Cut the mango flesh into thin strips. There should be about 2 cups.

6. Combine the duck meat, beans, peppers, tomatoes, nuts, mango, and the remaining ingredients in a mixing bowl and blend well. Serve at room temperature.

Yield: 8 or more servings.

Duck Liver Salad with Hot Vinaigrette Sauce

1. Cut the duck livers in half.
2. Melt the butter in a heavy skillet and, when it is very hot, add the livers. Sprinkle with the salt and pepper.
3. Cook over high heat, stirring and turning the livers gently in the sizzling butter, for about 3 minutes. Remove the livers to a hot dish.
4. To the skillet add the oil and shallots. Cook briefly, stirring. Add the vinegar and let it boil up.
5. Arrange a small bed of chicory leaves over each of 4 serving plates. Arrange the livers on top. Spoon the pan sauce over all.

Yield: 4 servings.

4 to 8 duck livers, about 1 pound

4 tablespoons butter

Salt and freshly ground pepper to taste

3 tablespoons hazelnut oil

3 tablespoons finely chopped shallots

3 tablespoons red wine vinegar

Hearts of chicory leaves

BREADS

FRENCH BREAD DOUGH

This French bread dough is easily made and produces some of the best bread we've encountered from home ovens. The recipe was evolved from one given to us by Jane Phalen, a friend and neighbor. She, in turn, got the recipe from the chef-owner of a one-star restaurant, the Château Philip in St. Nicolas de la Balerme. We used it for long loaves and also for pain de mie, the French sandwich bread that is made in black tin pans with sliding lids.

7	cups flour, approximately
½	cup milk
2	cups lukewarm water
1½	tablespoons salt
4	tablespoons butter
2	envelopes granular yeast

1. Place 7 cups of flour in a mixing bowl or, preferably, in the bowl of an electric mixer outfitted with a dough hook.

2. Combine the milk and 1¾ cups of water in a saucepan. Add the salt and butter and heat, stirring, just until the butter melts. Do not boil. Let cool.

3. Combine the yeast with the remaining ¼ cup of lukewarm water and stir to dissolve. Add the yeast to the flour, stirring constantly with the dough hook or with a wooden spoon.

4. Add the liquid, stirring constantly with the dough hook or beating vigorously with the spoon. Knead with the dough hook for about 5 minutes. Or turn the dough out onto a lightly floured board and knead for about 10 minutes, adding flour as necessary, but always using as little flour as possible.

5. Shape the dough into a ball and put it in a large, clean mixing bowl. Stretch plastic wrap over the bowl and place in a warm place until double in bulk, 2 to 3 hours.

6. Shape and bake the dough according to any method outlined below.

FRENCH BREAD BAKED IN OVAL MOLDS

1. Prepare the dough as outlined. When double in bulk, turn it out onto a lightly floured board and knead briefly. Divide in half or in thirds and shape it into 2 or 3 long ropes, approximately the same length as the bread molds.

2. Grease the molds lightly and arrange one length of dough in each. Cover loosely with a clean dry kitchen towel and let rise in a warm place until double in bulk, about 1 hour. Remove the towel and give the dough 3 parallel and diagonal slashes across the top with a razor or very sharp knife.

3. Preheat the oven to 450 degrees. Bake for 45 minutes for the double-loaf mold or for 40 minutes for the triple-loaf mold, turning the molds as necessary so that the loaves brown evenly. Remove from the oven and place the loaves on a rack to cool.

Yield: 2 or 3 loaves.

Note: This bread is improved by introducing steam into the oven. You may use a pan on the bottom of the oven and pour boiling water into it the moment the mold is placed in the oven.

FRENCH SANDWICH LOAVES

1. Prepare the dough as outlined. When double in bulk, turn it out onto a lightly floured board and knead briefly. Divide it in half and shape into 2 oval loaves. Place each of these into buttered sandwich bread pans (see note), measuring about 10½ × 3¾ × 3½-inches, and seal with the lids.

2. Let rise until the pan is filled with dough, about 1 hour. Do not open the pans, but slide the lid gently just a fraction of an inch and you can tell if dough is sticking to the top.

3. Preheat the oven to 450 degrees. Bake for 45 minutes. Remove cover, unmold onto a rack, and let cool.

Yield: 2 loaves.

Note: French sandwich bread pans are available in good kitchen supply stores.

FRENCH BREAD ROLLS

1. Prepare the dough as outlined. When double in bulk, turn it out onto a lightly floured board and knead briefly. Sprinkle two baking sheets liberally with cornmeal. Cut or pull off pieces of dough, about ½ cup or slightly more in volume. Shape these into smooth rounds and arrange them on the baking sheets. Cover loosely with a clean, dry towel. Let rise until double in bulk.

2. Preheat the oven to 450 degrees. Remove the towel. Using a razor or very sharp knife, cut a cross in the top of each roll. Place in the oven and bake until browned and cooked through, 35 to 40 minutes. Remove from the oven and remove the rolls. Place on a rack to cool.

Yield: 16 to 20 bread rolls.

Note: These rolls are improved by introducing steam into the oven. You may use a pan on the bottom of the oven and pour boiling water into it the moment the baking sheets are placed in the oven.

FRENCH BREAD (CLYDE BROOK'S VERSION)

1. Combine the water and yeast in a warm mixing bowl and stir to dissolve. Add the salt, sugar, and 4 cups of the flour and stir and beat with the hands until well blended. Add more flour, about ½ cup at a time, mixing and stirring with the hands. The dough will be sticky.

2. Continue adding flour until the dough leaves the sides of the bowl almost clean. The dough at the proper point will be lumpy and sticky. Use only as much flour as necessary to achieve this.

3. Turn out the dough onto a well-floured board. Knead for about 10 minutes. Quickly fold the dough toward you. Quickly push it away with the heels of the hands and give the dough a quarter turn. As you knead, spoon a little more flour onto the board so the dough does not stick. Continue kneading, pushing the dough away and giving it a quarter turn and flouring the board lightly until the dough is smooth and pliable. Shape into a ball.

4. Place the ball of dough in a greased warm bowl and turn it in the bowl to cover lightly with the grease. Cover the bowl with a clean towel and set the bowl in a warm place. The temperature should be 85 to 90 degrees. Let stand until double in bulk. The rising time will take from 1 to 1½ hours (or longer if the temperature is too low).

5. If bread molds are to be used, grease enough molds for 2 or 3 loaves with oil or lard. Or grease a baking sheet with oil or lard and sprinkle lightly with cornmeal.

6. Punch down the dough when it is double in bulk and turn it onto an unfloured surface. Slice the dough into 2 or 3 equal parts.

7. Using the hands, shape one portion of dough at a time on a flat surface. Roll the dough into a long ropelike shape. Roll the dough back and forth under the palms until it is more or less uniform in diameter from one end to the other. Each "rope" should be about 1 inch shorter than the molds or the baking sheet.

8. Place the dough in the molds or on baking sheet. Place uncovered in a warm place (85 to 90 degrees) and let stand until double in bulk.

9. Preheat the oven to 450 degrees.

10. Holding a razor blade on the bias, slash each loaf 3 or 4 times lightly on the top. The slashes should be about ⅛ inch or slightly deeper. If desired, the dough may be brushed lightly with water, milk, or lightly beaten egg or egg whites. This is to give color.

11. Place the loaves in the oven and bake for 15 minutes. Reduce the

2½ cups water (105 to 115 degrees for granular yeast; 80 to 85 degrees for fresh yeast cake)

1 package granular yeast (or crumble 1 fresh yeast cake)

1 tablespoon salt

1 tablespoon sugar, optional

7 or more cups flour

oven heat to 350 degrees and continue baking for 30 minutes or longer. If the loaves should expand and join each other at the sides, pull them apart and reverse their positions in the molds.

12.   Remove the loaves from the oven and remove them from the molds or baking sheet. Place them on racks so that air can circulate freely.

Yield: 2 or 3 loaves.

SOURDOUGH FRENCH BREAD (SUE GROSS'S VERSION)

1. Combine in a warm bowl the sourdough starter, 1 cup of the warm water, and 2 cups of the flour. Stir to blend and cover with plastic wrap. Let stand overnight in a warm but not hot place.

2. Dissolve the yeast in the remaining cup of warm water. Add the yeast to the starter mixture. Add the salt and 4 cups of flour and stir to blend well.

3. Turn out the mixture onto a lightly floured board and knead patiently, adding more flour to the kneading surface as necessary. Knead for 10 to 15 minutes, or until the dough is smooth and elastic. Shape the dough into a ball.

4. Rub a mixing bowl lightly with oil or lard and add the ball of dough. Flop it around in the bowl until it is coated with grease.

5. Cover with a cloth and let stand in a warm place. The temperature should be 85 or 90 degrees. Let stand until double in bulk. The rising time will take from 1 to 1½ hours (or longer if the temperature is too low).

6. If bread molds are to be used, grease enough molds for 3 loaves with oil or lard. Or grease a baking sheet with oil or lard and sprinkle lightly with cornmeal.

7. Punch down the dough when it is double in bulk and turn it onto an unfloured surface. Slice the dough into 3 equal parts.

8. Using the hands, shape one portion of dough at a time on a flat surface. Roll the dough into a long ropelike shape. Roll the dough back and forth under the palms until it is more or less uniform in diameter from one end to the other. Each "rope" should be about 1 inch shorter than the molds or the baking sheet.

9. Place the dough in the molds or on baking sheet. Place the molds uncovered in a warm place (85 to 90 degrees) and let stand until double in bulk.

10. Preheat the oven to 450 degrees.

11. Holding a razor blade on the bias, slash each loaf 3 to 4 times lightly on the top. The slashes should be about ⅛ inch or slightly deeper. If desired, the dough may be brushed lightly with water, milk, or lightly beaten egg or egg whies. This is to give color.

12. Place the loaves in the oven and bake for 15 minutes. Reduce the oven heat to 350 degrees and continue baking for 30 minutes or longer. If the loaves should expand and join each other at the sides, pull them apart and reverse their positions in the molds.

1 cup sourdough starter (see following recipe)

2 cups warm water (the temperature should be about 80 degrees)

6 cups flour, plus flour for kneading

1 package granular yeast

1 tablespoon salt

Oil or lard

13. Remove the loaves from the oven and remove them from the molds or baking sheet. Place them on racks so that air can circulate freely.

Yield: 3 loaves.

SOURDOUGH STARTER

1 package granular yeast

2 cups warm water (the temperature should be between 110 and 115 degrees)

2 cups flour

1. Empty the yeast into a warm mixing bowl and stir in the water. Stir until the yeast is dissolved.

2. Add the flour and stir well until it is blended. Cover with plastic wrap and let stand at room temperature for about 48 hours. When ready, the starter will be bubbly with a somewhat yellowish liquid on top.

3. When part of the starter is removed to make bread, the remainder must be fed with more flour and water. Add 1 cup of flour and 1 cup of water to replace the 1 cup of starter removed. Stir and cover with more plastic wrap. Let stand in a warm place for 1 hour or more or until bubbling action is renewed. The starter may be used and replenished for years and it improves with age. Store starter in the refrigerator in a mixing bowl covered with plastic wrap or in a jar with a loose-fitting lid.

Yield: About 3 cups of starter.

FOOD PROCESSOR FRENCH BREAD

1. In a mixing bowl, blend the yeast with 4 tablespoons of lukewarm water. Stir to dissolve the yeast.

2. In a saucepan, combine 1 cup of the water with the butter. Heat slowly until the butter melts (a thermometer is not essential, but the best temperature for this is 95 to 110 degrees).

3. To the container of a food processor add 3½ cups unsifted flour and 1 teaspoon of salt. Blend the flour and salt by activating the motor on and off three times. Add the dissolved yeast mixture and the water-and-butter mixture. Process until the dough becomes a ball and clears the sides of the container, 5 to 10 seconds.

4. Lightly flour a clean surface and turn out the dough onto it. With floured fingers, knead the dough quickly and gently. This is primarily for shaping the dough. Do not add an excess of flour at any time. Shape the dough into a ball.

5. Put the ball of dough in a lightly buttered mixing bowl. Cover with a clean cloth and place the bowl in a warm place. Let stand until double in bulk, about 1 hour.

6. Turn out the dough onto a lightly floured surface and knead gently. Shape into a ball and return the dough to the bowl. Cover and let stand for about 1 hour, or until double in bulk.

7. After the dough has risen in the bowl the second time, turn it out onto a lightly floured surface. Flatten with the fingers into a rough rectangle. Fold one third of the dough toward the center of the rectangle. Roll like a jelly roll and transfer the loaf to a baking sheet with the seam on the bottom and the ends folded under. The dimensions of the loaf at this time are approximately 13½ inches long, 3½ inches wide, and 2 inches high. Cover with a clean cloth and return to a warm place. Let stand until double in bulk, 30 minutes or longer.

8. As the dough rises, preheat the oven to 450 degrees.

9. Using a razor blade, make three parallel, diagonal gashes on top of the bread. Immediately place the pan in the oven. Put 4 ice cubes on the floor of the oven. Bake for 5 minutes and add 4 more ice cubes as before. Turn the pan on which the bread bakes so that the loaf bakes evenly.

10. Bake for 10 minutes (a total at this point of 15 minutes baking time) and reduce the oven heat to 400 degrees. Bake for 20 minutes longer. Transfer the bread to a rack and let cool.

Yield: 1 large loaf.

1½ envelopes granular yeast

1 cup plus 4 tablespoons lukewarm water

2 tablespoons butter

3½ cups flour, plus flour for rolling out the dough

1 teaspoon salt

CALIFORNIA SOURDOUGH
WHOLE WHEAT BREAD

1 recipe for whole wheat sourdough sponge (see following recipe)

¼ cup all-natural dark molasses

1 tablespoon salt

3 tablespoons solid white shortening

2½ to 3 cups flour

Probably the best bread maker in America today is Bernard Clayton, Jr., a writer who has spent years traveling in France and the United States gathering the formulas and techniques of bread making. We visited him in his home in Bloomington, Indiana, where he indulges his passion for breads of all kinds, and where he shared his recipes and techniques with us. One of the great faults in bread making, Mr. Clayton maintains, is impatience. "Thirty minutes resting time for bread is a crime against nature. Two hours is much better and you have only to smell the dough to know the difference." We offer three of Mr. Clayton's excellent recipes here, and another, for kugelhopf, on page 754.

1. In a large bowl, combine the sponge, molasses, and salt. Beat well with a wooden spoon. Add the shortening and beat vigorously, about 50 strokes.

2. Add 2½ to 2¾ cups of the flour, kneading well inside the bowl. Turn the dough out onto a lightly floured board and continue kneading. If the dough feels moist, continue adding flour while kneading brusquely. Beat it and slam it down on the flat surface. Knead for about 6 minutes.

3. Let warm water run in a large bowl. When warm, drain and wipe dry. Lightly grease the bowl with shortening.

4. Shape the dough into a ball and put it in the bowl. Cover tightly with plastic wrap. Let stand in a warm place for about 1½ hours, or until more than double in bulk.

5. Lightly grease the insides of two loaf pans (pans that measure 8½ × 4½ × 2½ inches are suitable).

6. Turn out the dough onto a lightly floured board and knead briefly.

7. Divide the dough in half. Shape each half into a ball, then into an oval shape. Fold the dough in half over itself lengthwise and pinch the ends to seal. Place the dough seam side down in the pans and cover with wax paper. Let the dough rise for 30 minutes, or until it has risen about 2 inches above the rims of the pans.

8. Preheat the oven to 375 degrees.

9. Using a sharp blade, make a gash lengthwise down the center of each loaf. Make smaller, leaflike gashes on either side of the lengthwise gash. Place in the oven and bake for about 40 minutes. As the loaves bake, turn the pans around at least once for even cooking.

Yield: 2 loaves.

WHOLE WHEAT SOURDOUGH SPONGE

1. This sponge must be made at least three days before using.
2. Combine all the ingredients in a large bowl. Stir well. Cover the bowl tightly with plastic wrap and let stand in a warm place.
3. Stir the mixture down once a day as it stands, always replacing the plastic wrap.

Yield: Enough sponge to produce 2 loaves of bread.

- 2 cups warm water
- 2 packages granular yeast
- ⅓ cup instant nonfat dry milk
- 3 cups whole wheat flour

OLD MILWAUKEE RYE BREAD

1 recipe for sponge for rye bread (see following recipe)

1 envelope granular yeast

1 cup warm water

¼ cup all-natural dark molasses

2 tablespoons caraway seeds

2 eggs

1 tablespoon salt

1 cup medium rye flour

3 tablespoons solid white shortening

5 to 5½ cups all-purpose flour

1 tablespoon milk

1. Stir down the sponge. Dissolve the yeast in the water. Add the yeast to the sponge, stirring. Add the molasses and 1 tablespoon of the caraway seeds. Stir to blend.

2. Add one lightly beaten egg and salt and blend once more. Add the rye flour and blend. Add the shortening and beat to blend. Add 2 cups of the all-purpose flour and blend with a wooden spoon. Gradually add 2 more cups, kneading constantly. Add more flour, about 2 tablespoons at a time, until the dough has a proper pliable and workable consistency.

3. Turn out the dough onto a lightly floured board and knead for about 6 minutes or longer. Knead brusquely, not gently. Beat and slam the dough down on the board. Knead and beat the dough for about 10 minutes. When ready, the dough should weigh about 3½ pounds.

4. Let warm water flow into a large bowl until the bowl is heated. Drain and dry thoroughly. Grease the dough with shortening. Shape the dough into a ball and add it to the bowl. Cover tightly with plastic wrap. Set aside to let rise for 1 hour or longer, or until double in bulk.

5. There are several methods of shaping the bread before baking. If long bread tins or molds are to be used, grease them. Otherwise, use a nonstick baking sheet, ungreased.

6. Divide the dough into 4 portions of equal weight. Roll each piece into a long sausage shape on a flat surface, rolling with the palms of the hand. The shapes should be about 15 inches long. Cover loosely with wax paper and set aside to rise, about 1 hour, or until double in bulk.

7. Preheat the oven to 375 degrees.

8. Using a sharp blade, make several diagonal gashes on top of each loaf. Brush the tops with 1 egg beaten with milk. Sprinkle with the remaining 1 tablespoon caraway seeds.

9. Place in the oven and bake for about 40 minutes, or until crisp crusted and cooked through.

Yield: 4 loaves.

SPONGE FOR RYE BREAD

1 package granular yeast
1½ cups warm water
2 cups medium rye flour
1 tablespoon caraway seeds

1. Combine the yeast and water in a large bowl. Stir to dissolve. Add the flour and caraway seeds and stir to blend. Cover lightly with plastic wrap.
2. Although this sponge is usable after 6 hours, it is best left to stand at room temperature from 1 to 3 days. Three days will give a more sour taste, which many people prefer.

Yield: Enough sponge for 2 to 4 loaves of rye bread.

COTTAGE CHEESE OR CLABBER BREAD

7½ to 8 cups flour
1 envelope granular
   yeast
1 tablespoon salt
10 large eggs
2 cups cottage cheese
¼ pound sweet butter,
   cut into small pieces
1 egg, lightly beaten
1 tablespoon milk

1. Combine 2 cups of the flour, the yeast, and salt in a bowl and stir to blend. Make a well in the center. Add the 10 eggs and beat vigorously with a wooden spoon until well blended. Add the cottage cheese and beat to blend well.

2. Gradually beat in the pieces of butter and 2 more cups of flour. Beat to blend. Add 2 more cups of flour. Beat to blend.

3. Start adding more flour, about 2 tablespoons at a time, beating and kneading constantly. When a total of 7½ cups of flour have been added, turn out the dough onto a lightly floured surface and knead, adding as much flour to the surface as necessary to make a pliable, easily workable dough. Knead for about 10 minutes or longer, always dusting the board and dough with flour as necessary. Beat and slam the dough down as you work. This dough, when ready, should weigh about 5 pounds.

4. Let warm water flow into a large bowl until the bowl is heated. Drain and dry thoroughly. Grease the bowl with shortening.

5. Shape the dough into a ball and add it to the bowl. Cover tightly with plastic wrap and let stand for 1½ to 3 hours, or until double in bulk. Do not rush the rising. It may not quite achieve a double bulk. Lightly grease three 9-inch cake pans with sides 1 inch high.

6. Turn out the dough onto a lightly floured surface and knead briefly. Divide the dough into three portions of equal weight. Make a ball of each piece and work the dough, folding it from the outer rim to the center. Press down the folded-in edges. Pat into a circle. Center them, folded-in side down, into the greased pans. Pat the dough to make it smooth to the edges of each pan. Cover loosely with wax paper and let stand for about 2 hours, until double in bulk.

7. Preheat the oven to 375 degrees.

8. Brush the tops of the bread with egg beaten with milk. Place in the oven and bake for 45 minutes. Pay particular attention to the bread as it bakes the last 10 minutes. Take care it does not burn.

Yield: 3 loaves.

Tjasa Sprague's Whole Wheat Bread

1. Place the yeast in a large mixing bowl and add the water. Stir to dissolve. Add the honey and salt. Add the milk and stir to blend well.

2. Add the whole wheat flour and beat with a wire whisk (or use an electric mixer) for 5 minutes.

3. Add the all-purpose flour and beat with a wooden spoon 50 times. If necessary, add more flour, but the dough should remain a little sticky. Scrape the dough out onto a floured surface and turn to coat lightly with flour. Shape the dough into a ball.

4. Grease a large mixing bowl and add the ball of dough. Cover with a clean towel and let stand at room temperature overnight.

5. Turn out the dough onto a floured board and knead briefly. Shape it into a ball. Grease a deep skillet (preferably an 8-inch skillet with a 14-cup capacity) or use a casserole of the same size. Add the ball of dough.

6. Let the dough rise until double in bulk, an hour or longer.

7. Preheat the oven to 425 degrees. When the dough has risen, place it in the oven and bake for 1 hour, or until nicely browned.

Yield: 1 large loaf.

One ¾-ounce cube
of fresh yeast, or
1 envelope granular
yeast

1 cup lukewarm water
2 tablespoons honey
2 tablespoons salt
3 cups milk
4 cups whole wheat flour
4 cups all-purpose flour,
approximately

**Butter for greasing the
bowl and pan**

ITALIAN RYE BREAD

2 packages granular
   yeast
1¾ cups lukewarm water
1 teaspoon sugar
2 tablespoons plus
   1 teaspoon olive oil
1 cup rye flour
4 cups all-purpose flour
   Salt
1 teaspoon fennel seeds
1 tablespoon cornmeal
1 egg
2 teaspoons water

1. Combine in the container of a food processor the yeast, ¼ cup of the lukewarm water, sugar, and 2 tablespoons of the olive oil. Process for about 5 seconds.

2. Add the rye flour, all-purpose flour, salt to taste, fennel seeds, and the remaining 1½ cups of lukewarm water. Blend thoroughly.

3. Lightly flour a flat surface and turn the dough out onto it. Knead briefly and shape into a smooth ball. Lightly flour the inside of a bowl and add the ball of dough. Cover with a clean cloth and place in a warm but not too hot place. Let rise until double in bulk, about 1½ hours.

4. Turn out the dough onto a lightly floured surface and knead briefly. Shape it into a ball and return it to the bowl. Cover and let rise a second time, about 1 hour.

5. Divide the dough in half. Roll out each half into a rectangle measuring about 15 inches long and 12 inches wide. Roll each half of dough like a long jelly roll, pressing lightly to seal the bottom seam. Tuck in and press the ends to make them smooth.

6. Lightly oil a baking sheet with a little of the remaining 1 teaspoon of oil and sprinkle with the cornmeal. Arrange the loaves on this. Brush the dough with the remaining oil. Cover with a clean cloth and let stand for about 30 minutes, or until double in bulk.

7. Preheat the oven to 425 degrees.

8. Beat the egg with the 2 teaspoons of water and brush the surface of the dough all over with a little of the mixture. Using a very sharp knife or razor, slash the top of the bread. Place in the oven and bake for 25 to 30 minutes.

Yield: 2 loaves.

BEER RYE BREAD

1. Heat the beer in a saucepan until it just bubbles. Add the lard, brown sugar, molasses, salt, orange rind, and caraway seeds. Cool to lukewarm.
2. In a large mixing bowl, dissolve the yeast in the warm water. Add the lukewarm beer mixture. Beat in the rye flour and enough all-purpose flour to make a soft dough.
3. Turn out the dough on a heavily floured board and knead it until it is smooth and elastic. Place the dough in a greased bowl, turning it until it is greased all over. Cover and let rise in a warm place until double in bulk.
4. Punch down the dough and knead again. Divide the dough in half and shape into 2 round or long oval shapes on a greased baking sheet. Slash the top of the loaves with a sharp knife. Let rise until double in bulk.
5. Preheat the oven to 350 degrees.
6. Place the loaves in the oven and bake for 40 to 45 minutes, or until done.

Yield: 2 loaves.

3 cups beer
⅓ cup lard or bacon fat
½ cup firmly packed light brown sugar
½ cup light molasses
1½ tablespoons salt
2 tablespoons grated orange rind
2 tablespoons caraway seeds
2 packages granular yeast
½ cup warm water
5 cups unsifted rye flour
5 to 6 cups unsifted all-purpose flour

SOUTHERN CORN BREAD

There are more recipes for corn bread than there are magnolia trees in the South. This is a family standard.

1. Preheat the oven to 350 degrees.
2. Sift the flour, cornmeal, baking soda, and salt into a mixing bowl. Beat the eggs until foamy and stir them into the dry mixture. Stir in the buttermilk and 1 cup of the whole milk.
3. Heat the butter in a 9 × 2-inch black skillet, and when it is very hot but not brown, pour in the batter. Carefully pour the remaining 1 cup of whole milk on top of the batter without stirring. Place the dish in the oven and bake for 50 minutes, or until set and baked through. Slice into wedges.

Yield: 8 servings.

Note: If this is to be used as a stuffing, it is best if it is made a day or so ahead.

⅓ cup sifted flour
1½ cups sifted cornmeal
1 teaspoon baking soda
½ teaspoon salt
2 eggs
1 cup buttermilk
2 cups whole milk
1½ tablespoons butter

JALAPEÑO CORN BREAD

1 can (8½ ounces) cream-style corn

1 cup yellow cornmeal

3 eggs

1 teaspoon salt

½ teaspoon baking soda

¾ cup milk

⅓ cup corn oil

1 cup grated sharp Cheddar cheese

¼ cup chopped jalapeño peppers

2 tablespoons butter

I have no earthly idea how or when I came by this recipe for a corn bread made with jalapeño peppers, Cheddar cheese, and cream-style corn. It is, however, to my mind one of the great adventures in taste. It is excellent when used as a replacement for regular corn bread in a poultry stuffing.

1. Preheat the oven to 400 degrees.

2. In a mixing bowl, combine the corn, cornmeal, eggs, salt, baking soda, milk, oil, ½ cup of the cheese, and the jalapeño peppers. Blend well.

3. Meanwhile, put the butter in a 1½-quart casserole (preferably a glazed Mexican earthenware casserole) or a 9-inch skillet. Place the casserole in the oven until the butter is hot but not brown. Immediately pour in the corn bread mixture. Sprinkle with the remaining ½ cup of cheese and bake for 40 minutes.

Yield: 8 servings.

CORN STICKS

½ cup yellow cornmeal

½ cup flour

2 tablespoons sugar

1½ teaspoons baking powder

Salt to taste

¾ cup plus 3 tablespoons heavy cream

2 tablepoons butter, melted

1 egg, separated

1 tablespoon butter

½ cup corn kernels freshly cut from the cob

1. Preheat the oven to 425 degrees.

2. Select a standard mold for making corn sticks. Place it in the oven until thoroughly heated.

3. Meanwhile, combine the cornmeal, flour, sugar, baking powder, and salt in a mixing bowl. Blend well.

4. Blend the cream, melted butter, and egg yolk. Add this to the cornmeal mixture, stirring to blend.

5. Melt the 1 tablespoon of butter in a small skillet and add the corn. Cook, stirring, just until heated through. Stir this into the batter.

6. Beat the egg white and fold it into the mixture.

7. Brush the corn stick mold lightly with oil. Spoon an equal portion of the filling inside each corn stick mold.

8. Bake for 15 to 20 minutes. Serve hot.

Yield: 6 to 8 corn sticks.

TORTA DE MASA

This is a fine-grained, sweet corn bread, to be served with Tex-Mex food.

1. Preheat the oven to 375 degrees.

2. Butter a loaf pan measuring 9 × 5 × 3 inches. It is not essential but it is recommended that you line the bottom of the pan with a rectangle of parchment paper, neatly cut to fit.

3. Sift together the masa harina, salt, baking powder, and sugar into the bowl of an electric mixer.

4. Start beating on low speed while slowly adding the butter. As you go along, gradually increase the speed to high.

5. Reduce the speed to low and beat in the water. Add the 6 egg yolks, beating on medium speed until well blended.

6. Beat the whites until stiff and fold them in, carefully lifting from the bottom. Pour and scrape the mixture into the prepared loaf pan. Place in the oven and bake for 45 minutes.

7. Unmold the loaf while it is still hot. Serve sliced, hot or lukewarm.

Yield: 8 to 10 servings.

Note: Masa harina is a fine-grained cornmeal available where Mexican specialties are sold. This dish may be made with regular white or yellow cornmeal, but it is imperative that you add ¾ cup of all-purpose flour. Sift together the cornmeal, flour, salt, baking powder, and sugar into the bowl of an electric mixer. Proceed with step 4.

1 cup masa harina (see note)

Salt to taste

1½ teaspoons baking powder

½ cup sugar

10 tablespoons butter, at room temperature

½ cup cold water

6 eggs, separated

HERB AND CHEESE BREAD

1½ packages granular
    yeast
¼ cup lukewarm water
4 tablespoons butter
1 cup water
3½ cups flour
    Salt to taste
1¼ cups finely chopped
    parsley
1 tablespoon finely
    chopped shallots
1 teaspoon finely
    chopped garlic
½ teaspoon crushed,
    dried oregano, optional
    Freshly ground pepper
    to taste
1 large egg, beaten but
    not frothy
2 tablespoons grated
    Parmesan cheese

1. Blend the yeast with ¼ cup of lukewarm water. Stir to dissolve. Let stand briefly in a warm place.

2. Blend 2 tablespoons of the butter and the 1 cup of water and heat briefly until the butter melts. This must not be too hot.

3. Put the flour and salt in a food processor and blend. Remove cover and add yeast and butter mixtures. Add ½ cup of the parsley. Blend until a ball forms.

4. Turn out the dough onto a lightly floured surface and knead briefly. Shape into a ball and place in a lightly buttered bowl. Cover with a clean towel and place in a warm place. Let stand until double in bulk, about 1 hour.

5. Turn the dough out once more onto a lightly floured board and knead briefly. Shape into a ball once more. Return the ball to the mixing bowl, cover, and let stand until double in bulk.

6. Heat the remaining 2 tablespoons of butter in a saucepan and add the shallots. Cook until wilted. Add the remaining parsley, garlic, oregano, if desired, salt, and pepper to taste and remove from the heat. Let cool slightly.

7. Turn out the dough once more onto a lightly floured board. Pat it flat with the fingers. Roll it out into a rectangle. Brush the top of the rectangle with a little beaten egg. Add the remaining egg to the parsley mixture.

8. Spoon the parsley and shallot mixture over the rolled out rectangle, leaving about a 2-inch border. Sprinkle with Parmesan cheese. Roll the rectangle jelly roll fashion and tuck in the ends.

9. Butter a standard loaf pan (9 × 5 × 2¾ inches) lightly. Add the dough, seam side down, and cover lightly with a clean cloth. Return to a warm, draft-free place and let stand until double in bulk, about 1 hour.

10. Preheat the oven to 425 degrees.

11. Place the pan in the oven and bake for 30 minutes. Reduce oven heat to 400 degrees and bake for 15 minutes longer.

12. Unmold onto a rack and let cool before slicing.

Yield: 1 loaf.

WHOLE WHEAT ORANGE BREAD

1. Combine the water and butter in a saucepan and heat just until the butter melts, or to a temperature of 110 degrees. If the liquid becomes hotter, let it cool to that temperature.

2. Combine 2 cups of the all-purpose flour, the yeast, salt, and brown sugar in a mixing bowl. Add the water-and-butter mixture, honey, egg, and orange rind. Blend briskly and thoroughly and work in the remaining all-purpose flour and the whole wheat flour.

3. Turn out the mixture onto a lightly floured board and knead until smooth and elastic. Shape into a ball.

4. Lightly butter a clean mixing bowl. Add the dough and turn it lightly to coat all sides. Cover the bowl with plastic wrap. Let stand in a warm place until double in bulk, about 2 hours.

5. Turn out the dough and knead it lightly. Cover and let rest for 5 to 10 minutes.

6. Shape the dough into 2 loaves. Arrange each loaf in a greased 1½-quart loaf pan (see note). Let rise again in a warm place, about 1 hour. Preheat the oven to 375 degrees. Bake for 45 minutes.

Yield: 2 loaves.

Note: If glass loaf pans are used, lower the temperature to 350 degrees.

2 cups water
4 tablespoons butter
4 cups all-purpose flour
1 package granular yeast
2 teaspoons salt
½ cup brown sugar
½ cup honey
1 egg
Grated rind of 1 orange
2 cups whole wheat flour

Nut and Seed Bread

1 cup quick-cooking oatmeal

2¾ cups cold water

1 tablespoon salt

½ cup molasses

4 tablespoons butter, melted

2 packages granular yeast

½ cup lukewarm water

⅛ teaspoon sugar

1 cup rye flour

1 cup whole wheat flour

½ cup wheat germ

⅓ cup bran flakes

1 cup plus 2 tablespoons broken walnuts or other nuts, or a combination of nuts and edible seeds such as hulled sunflower seeds, sesame seeds, pumpkin seeds

4 to 5 cups all-purpose flour

1. Combine the oatmeal and 2 cups of the cold water in a saucepan and bring to the boil. Remove from the heat.

2. Place the salt, molasses, and butter in the bowl of an electric mixer and add the oatmeal mixture. Blend and let cool to lukewarm.

3. Blend the yeast with the ½ cup of lukewarm water and sugar and stir until dissolved. Let stand in a warm place until foamy. Add this mixture plus the remaining ¾ cup cold water to the dough, beating until smooth.

4. Stir on low speed and add the rye flour, whole wheat flour, wheat germ, and bran flakes. Beat until smooth. Add the nuts and/or seeds and gradually add enough all-purpose flour to make a workable, soft dough. Turn out the dough onto a lightly floured board and knead for about 10 minutes.

5. Shape the dough into a ball and put it in a lightly greased bowl. Cover with a damp cloth and let stand until double in bulk, 45 minutes to 1 hour.

6. Punch down the dough. Divide it in two and shape each half into an oval. Put each oval in a lightly buttered standard-size loaf pan. Cover and let rise.

7. Preheat the oven to 375 degrees.

8. Place the pans in the oven and bake for 35 to 40 minutes. Turn out onto a rack to cool.

Yield: 2 loaves.

ZUCCHINI AND NUT BREAD

1. Preheat the oven to 350 degrees.
2. Beat the eggs with the sugar until pale yellow and thickened. Add the butter.
3. Sift together the flour, salt, baking powder, baking soda, and cinnamon. Fold this into the egg mixture. Stir in the vanilla, zucchini, and walnuts.
4. Spoon and scrape the mixture into a buttered loaf pan (about 9 × 5 × 2¾ inches). Bake for 1 hour, or until the bread pulls away from the sides of the pan.

Yield: 1 loaf.

3 eggs
1½ cups sugar
12 tablespoons butter, melted
3 cups flour
1½ teaspoons salt
¼ teaspoon baking powder
1 teaspoon baking soda
1 teaspoon ground cinnamon
1 tablespoon pure vanilla extract
2 cups peeled, grated zucchini
¾ cup chopped walnut meats

BANANA BREAD

⅔ cup sugar

⅓ cup peanut, vegetable, or corn oil

2 eggs, lightly beaten

1¾ cups flour

2 teaspoons baking powder

¼ teaspoon baking soda

½ teaspoon salt

⅓ teaspoon grated nutmeg

3 ripe, not too firm, unblemished bananas

⅔ cup coarsely broken walnut meats

1. Preheat the oven to 350 degrees.
2. Put the sugar and oil in the bowl of an electric mixer. Beat thoroughly to blend. Add the eggs and beat well.
3. Sift together the flour, baking powder, baking soda, salt, and nutmeg. Add this and beat well.
4. Mash the bananas to a pulp. Beat them into the batter. Fold in the walnuts.
5. Grease a standard loaf pan (9¼ × 5¼ × 2¾ inches) and pour in the batter. Bake for 1 hour.

Yield: 1 banana loaf.

Note: This bread does not slice well while warm. It is best to bake and let cool, then refrigerate before slicing. It freezes well wrapped closely in aluminum foil. It may then be heated in the foil and served.

IRISH SODA BREAD

2 tablespoons very cold butter

4 cups flour, plus a little flour for dusting the baking sheet and board

1 teaspoon salt

1 teaspoon baking soda

1½ cups buttermilk

1. Preheat the oven to 425 degrees.
2. Cut 1 tablespoon of the butter bit by bit into the 4 cups of flour. Using the fingers, quickly rub the butter into the flour. Add the salt and baking soda and empty the mixture into a flour sifter. Sift it into another bowl. Empty any ingredients remaining in the sifter into this second bowl. Stir.
3. Rub a baking sheet with the remaining butter and sprinkle with flour. Shake off any excess flour and set aside.
4. Add the buttermilk to the flour and soda mixture gradually, stirring to blend. Use the hands and knead the mixture until it holds together and can be shaped into a ball. Turn it onto a lightly floured board and knead once more quickly, handling the dough as little as possible.
5. Shape the dough into a flat disk about 8 inches in diameter. Place the disk on the prepared baking sheet. Using a sharp knife, cut a fairly deep cross in the center. Place in the oven and bake for about 45 minutes.

Yield: 1 loaf.

SALT-RISING BREAD

Salt-rising bread is one of the greatest inventions, which I think of as peculiarly Southern. It smells and tastes a little bit "cheesy" and is not to everyone's liking, but it makes excellent sandwiches and toast. Because of the timing and temperature, it takes a little practice to make a perfect loaf.

1. Place the potatoes, cornmeal, sugar, and salt in a 3-quart bowl. Add the boiling water and stir until the sugar and salt are dissolved. Cover with plastic wrap or foil. Set the bowl in a pan of warm water over the pilot light of a stove, or where it will stay at about 120 degrees, until small bubbles show in the surface, 24 hours or longer.

2. Remove the potatoes to a sieve and press out the excess moisture into a bowl or cup. Add this liquid to the potato water still in the first bowl. Discard the potatoes.

3. Add the milk, baking soda, and 4 cups of the flour to the bowl. Stir until smooth. Set the bowl again in the pan of warm water and let it stand for about 2 hours, until the dough is almost double in bulk.

4. Cut the shortening or butter into 1 cup of the remaining flour. Add this to the dough. Add enough additional flour, about 3 cups, to make a moderately stiff dough. Knead on a floured surface quickly and lightly. Do not let the dough get cold.

5. Return the dough to the bowl, grease the surface of the dough, and let it rise for about 2 hours, until double in bulk.

6. Turn out the risen dough onto a lightly floured surface and shape into 2 loaves. Place in greased loaf pans (9 × 5 × 3 inches) and grease the tops of the loaves. Let rise again for about 2 hours, until almost double in bulk or slightly above the tops of the pans. Sprinkle the tops with cornmeal, if desired.

7. About 15 minutes before the loaves have finished rising, preheat the oven to 400 degrees.

8. Bake the loaves for 15 minutes, then lower the oven temperature to 350 degrees and bake for about 35 minutes longer, or until the bread shrinks from the sides of the pans and is well browned. Cool on a rack.

Yield: 2 loaves.

2 medium-size potatoes, peeled and thinly sliced

2 tablespoons cornmeal

½ tablespoon sugar

1 teaspoon salt

2 cups boiling water

2 cups milk, scalded and cooled to lukewarm

⅛ teaspoon baking soda

8 cups sifted flour, approximately

4 tablespoons shortening or butter, at room temperature

CRACKLIN' BREAD

1½ cups cornmeal,
  preferably stone- or
  water-ground
  Salt to taste
1 teaspoon baking
  powder
1½ cups buttermilk
1 egg, lightly beaten
½ cup cracklin's (see
  following instructions)
4 tablespoons butter

When I was a child in Mississippi, my family owned an enormous cast-iron pot with four small "legs." It was used in my infancy to render pork fat, which was used for almost all the frying needs in the kitchen. When the fat was rendered, the crisp, crunchy, solid pieces were broken into pieces and eaten, to the great delight of young and old alike. These pieces were known as *cracklin's* or, to use the dictionary spelling, *cracklings*. One of the greatest uses for them was in the preparation of cracklin' bread. Cracklin's are sold today in plastic bags, but they taste awfully commercial. You can make acceptable cracklin's by rendering store-bought pork fat in your home.

1. Preheat the oven to 450 degrees.

2. Sift together the cornmeal, salt, and baking powder into a mixing bowl. Start stirring with a wire whisk while gradually adding the buttermilk. Stir in the beaten egg. When well blended, stir in the cracklin's.

3. Put the butter in a 9-inch black iron skillet and heat on top of the stove until it is quite hot but not brown. Pour half the butter into the batter and stir to blend. Pour the batter immediately into the hot skillet and place on the center rack of the oven. Bake for 30 to 35 minutes, or until the crust is golden brown.

4. Cut into wedges and serve.

Yield: 8 servings.

These crisp pieces are not the real McCoy, which are made with fresh pork fat used at hog-killing time in the South. They are, however, an acceptable substitute and work far better than the store-bought, plastic-wrapped variety. Fatback is available at supermarket meat counters.

CRACKLIN'S

½ pound fatback

1. Cut the fatback into slices and cut the slices into thin strips. Stack or align the strips and cut them into small cubes. There should be about 1 cup.
2. Put the cubes in one layer in a small skillet and barely cover with water. Bring to the boil and cook until the water evaporates. Continue cooking until the pieces are totally rendered of fat and until they are quite crisp and browned. Do not allow to burn.
3. Drain the pieces in a sieve and pour them onto paper towels to drain further.

Yield: Slightly more than 1 cup.

SPOONBREAD

This recipe was served in my home with sliced, home-cured ham or with butter to be added according to taste.

1. Preheat the oven to 350 degrees.
2. Bring 2 cups of the milk to the boil and gradually add the cornmeal in a steady stream, stirring rapidly with a wire whisk. Stir in the butter and salt. Cook over low heat, stirring almost constantly, about 10 minutes.
3. Scrape the mixture into a mixing bowl and let cool to lukewarm.
4. Beat the yolks until light and stir them into the mixture. Blend the baking powder with the remaining 1 cup of milk and stir it into the mixture.
5. Beat the egg whites until stiff and fold them into the mixture.
6. Butter a 1½-quart casserole and pour the mixture into it. Bake for 40 minutes, or until a knife inserted in the center comes out clean. Serve immediately, with butter on the side.

Yield: 6 to 8 servings.

3 cups milk
1½ cups sifted yellow cornmeal
8 tablespoons butter, melted
Salt to taste
4 eggs, separated
2 teaspoons baking powder

Hush Puppies

2 cups cornmeal, preferably water- or stone-ground

1 tablespoon flour

½ teaspoon baking soda

1 teaspoon baking powder

1 teaspoon salt

3 tablespoons finely chopped scallions

1 cup plus 3 tablespoons buttermilk

1 egg, lightly beaten

Corn, peanut, or other vegetable oil for deep-frying

There is a well-known legend about the fried corn bread known as hush puppies. Legend has it that in the days during the Civil War, Southerners would sit beside a campfire out-of-doors to prepare their meals. They would fry their cornmeal batter, and if Yankee soldiers came close, they would toss one or more of the fried cakes to their yapping dogs with the command, "Hush, puppies."

1. Sift together the cornmeal, flour, baking soda, baking powder, and salt into a mixing bowl. Add the scallions, buttermilk, and egg. Stir until thoroughly mixed.

2. Heat the oil to 375 degrees and drop the batter by spoonfuls (about 2 teaspoons) into the hot oil. Fry until golden brown. Drain and serve hot.

Yield: 6 servings.

CROISSANTS

Morning croissants and café noir are as essential to the Parisian scene as the Rive Gauche and the Champs-Élysées. Most home cooks presume the making of croissants to be beyond their scope, but it involves only two things—patience and careful chilling of the dough. The dough must be rolled, folded, and chilled several times so that the butter will not ooze out of the dough. It also helps if the surface on which the dough is rolled is cold. The ideal surface is marble, but Formica will do. Wood is not recommended.

2 tablespoons lukewarm water

2 teaspoons granular yeast

2 tablespoons sugar

1 teaspoon salt

2 tablespoons plus ¼ cup milk

1 cup plus 2 tablespoons water

14 tablespoons butter plus butter for greasing the mixing bowl and pan

4 cups flour plus flour for rolling out the dough

1 egg yolk, lightly beaten

1. Blend the lukewarm water with the yeast. Stir to dissolve and set aside briefly in a warm place.

2. Put the sugar in a small mixing bowl and add the salt. Add 2 tablespoons of the milk. Blend and set aside.

3. In a saucepan, combine the remaining ¼ cup of milk with the 1 cup of water. Add 2 tablespoons of the butter and heat gently or just until the butter is barely melted.

4. To the container of a food processor (or use the bowl of an electric mixer) add 4 cups of the flour. Add the three various liquids to the flour and blend with the processor or mix thoroughly with the mixer.

5. Lightly butter a mixing bowl and add the ball of dough. Cover and let stand in a warm place for 45 minutes to 1 hour, or until double in bulk.

6. Turn out the dough onto a lightly floured board and pat with lightly floured fingers into a rectangle. Roll it with a rolling pin until the dough rectangle measures about 7½ × 11 inches. Transfer the rectangle of dough to a lightly floured baking sheet or jelly roll pan. Cover with a clean cloth and place in the refrigerator. Chill for 30 minutes.

7. Remove the dough to a lightly floured board, preferably chilled, and roll out with a pin to another rectangle measuring about 16 × 13 inches. Dot two thirds of the rectangle of dough with the remaining 12 tablespoons of butter at room temperature (it must not be on the verge of melting). Smear the butter around but not to the margins of the dough. Do not cover the bottom third of the dough with butter.

8. Fold the unbuttered third of dough toward the center. Fold the butter-smeared top third of dough over this. Gently roll it out into a rectangle about 14 by 16 inches.

9. Fold down the top third of dough toward the center. Fold the bottom third over this. Sprinkle somewhat liberally with flour and turn the dough. Sprinkle with flour. Put the dough on the baking sheet or jelly roll pan. Cover with a cloth and chill again for 30 minutes.

10. To facilitate rolling, cut the dough crosswise in half. Refrigerate once more for 1 hour.

11. Remove half the dough and roll it out into a rectangle, about 9 × 16 inches, on a floured board. The dough should be about ¼ inch thick. Turn up the bottom third of the rectangle. Turn down the upper third of dough. Return to the baking sheet or jelly roll pan. Repeat with the other half of the dough and return to the refrigerator. Chill for 30 minutes.

12. Roll out the dough one more time to approximately the same 9 × 16-inch dimensions, using flour top and bottom but sparingly. Cut the dough down the center. Cut each half into three or four triangles. Roll up the triangles from the base toward the top. Twist into crescents. Triangles may be large or small. Half the dough will make about 7 croissants of traditional size.

13. Brush a baking sheet or jelly roll pan with butter and arrange the croissants on it. Cover with a clean towel and let rest in a warm place until double in bulk, about 30 minutes. At this point you may roll out the other half of the dough, cut it, and shape it into croissants. Or you may freeze it for future use.

14. As the dough rises, preheat the oven to 475 degrees.

15. Brush the croissants with the egg yolk beaten with 2 of the tablespoons water and place in the oven. Bake for 5 minutes and reduce the oven heat to 400 degrees. Continue baking for about 10 minutes.

Yield: About 14 croissants.

BRIOCHES

1. Combine ¾ cup of the milk and the butter in a saucepan and heat just until the butter melts, about 110 degrees. If the liquid becomes hotter, let it cool to that temperature.

2. In a mixing bowl, combine 2 cups of flour, yeast, sugar, and salt. Stir in the milk and butter mixture and 2 of the eggs.

3. Beat in 2 cups of flour and, when thoroughly blended, beat in the remaining eggs and flour. The dough will be soft and shiny. Shape into a ball.

4. Lightly butter a clean mixing bowl and add the dough. Cover with plastic wrap and let stand in a warm place until double in bulk, about 1½ hours. Punch down the dough. Cover and refrigerate overnight.

5. About 1½ hours before baking, punch the dough down once more and turn it onto a lightly floured surface. Divide the dough into approximately equal portions, each measuring about ¼ cup.

6. Nip off about one fifth of each portion and set it aside to be used as a topknot. Roll the larger portion into a ball, using the palms of the hands. Place the ball into a greased brioche tin. Use a razor blade and cut a cross on top of the ball. Roll the nipped-off portion into a teardrop shape. Arrange the teardrop, pointed side down, in the middle of the cross. Continue shaping the remaining dough in a similar manner until all the portions are used. Cover the shaped brioches and let rise until almost double in bulk.

7. Preheat the oven to 400 degrees.

8. When the brioches have risen, blend the egg yolk with the remaining 1 tablespoon of milk. Use a pastry brush and brush the top of each brioche with the mixture. Bake for 20 minutes.

Yield: 18 to 20 brioches.

¾ cup plus 1 tablespoon milk

½ pound butter

5 cups flour

2 packages granular yeast

¼ cup sugar

2 teaspoons salt

5 eggs

1 egg yolk

WATER BAGELS

THE BAGELS:

1 package granular yeast

2 cups warm water

¼ cup natural-flavored instant malted milk powder

2 tablespoons sugar

1 tablespoon salt

5¾ cups unsifted flour

THE WATER BATH:

2 quarts water

2 tablespoons natural-flavored instant malted milk powder

1 tablespoon sugar

1. Place the yeast in a warm bowl and add the water, stirring to dissolve. Add the malted milk powder and sugar and stir until dissolved. Add the salt and flour all at once. Work the dough with the fingers and hands, kneading the mass into a stiff dough. Or use a mixer equipped with a dough hook.

2. Turn out the dough onto a lightly floured board and knead until smooth. Shape the dough into a ball and place it in an ungreased bowl. Cover with plastic wrap and let rise in a warm place until double in bulk.

3. Preheat the oven to 450 degrees.

4. Bring the ingredients for the water bath to the boil.

5. Punch down the dough and divide it into 16 equal portions. Roll each portion into a ball. Pierce the center of each dough ball with the index finger. Using the fingers, shape each portion of dough into a circle like a doughnut ring.

6. If the water bath is boiling, turn off the heat. When the bagels are dropped into it, the water should be just below the boiling point.

7. Drop the bagel rounds into the just-under-boiling water and let them "cook" for about 20 seconds on a side. Immediately lift the rounds from the water, using a slotted spoon.

8. Place the bagel rounds on an ungreased baking sheet and bake for about 20 minutes, or until golden brown.

Yield: 16 bagels.

ONION-TOPPED BAGELS

½ cup dehydrated minced onion (see note), soaked in water and then squeezed dry

2 tablespoons oil

¼ teaspoon salt

½ egg white

1. There are two ways to prepare onion-topped bagels. The easiest is simply to sprinkle the bagels with dehydrated onions when they are removed from the water bath and are still wet. When using this method, the onions turn very brown, almost black when baked.

2. To produce a less dark onion topping, prepare the bagels in the basic recipe until they are ready for the oven. Combine the onion, oil, salt, and egg white and brush the mixture onto the bagels. Bake as indicated until golden brown.

Note: Chopped fresh onions do not produce a product to taste like commercially prepared bagels.

PITA BREAD

1. Dissolve the yeast in the 2 tablespoons of lukewarm water. Add the sugar and egg and stir well.
2. Sift together the flour and salt. Stir in the yeast mixture and 3 tablespoons of oil. Add the remaining ⅓ cup of lukewarm water and mix into a soft dough, adding a little more water if needed. Cover and let rise until double in bulk.
3. Punch down the dough and form into 16 flat cakes about 4 inches in diameter. Place the cakes on an oiled baking sheet and let rise until light, or almost double in bulk.
4. Preheat the oven to 375 degrees.
5. Prick the cakes with the tines of a fork, brush with water or cooking oil, and bake in the oven for 15 to 20 minutes, or until lightly browned. The pita should be puffed around the edges with a hollow in the center. Serve hot with appetizers.

Yield: 16 pita.

1 package granular yeast
2 tablespoons plus ⅓ cup lukewarm water, approximately
1 teaspoon sugar
1 egg, beaten
2 cups flour
⅛ teaspoon salt
3 tablespoons oil

BAKING POWDER BISCUITS

1. Preheat the oven to 400 degrees.
2. Combine the flour, salt, and baking powder in the container of a food processor. Add the shortening and cover. Blend while adding the water—add 5 tablespoons and, if necessary, 1 additional tablespoon. Process until a ball forms and the dough comes away from the sides of the bowl.
3. Roll out the biscuit dough to ½-inch thickness. Using a 2½-inch round biscuit cutter, cut out the biscuits. Brush lightly with heavy cream, if desired.
4. Arrange on a greased baking sheet and bake for 20 minutes, or until lightly browned on top.

Yield: 16 biscuits.

2 cups flour
Salt to taste
1 teaspoon baking powder
½ cup solid white vegetable shortening, at room temperature
5 to 6 tablespoons cold water
¼ cup heavy cream, optional

POCKETBOOK ROLLS

2 cups milk
4 tablespoons butter
4 tablespoons sugar
Salt to taste
1 tablespoon
    (2 packages) granu-
    lar yeast
¼ cup lukewarm water
5 to 6 cups sifted flour
Melted butter for
brushing rolls

Throughout my childhood, pocketbook rolls were served hot from the oven at Sunday dinner (the meal taken at midday) and on holidays and other special occasions. They are called "pocketbook" because the dough is folded over before baking and the rolls resemble small purses or pocketbooks. These rolls are not of Southern origin, although they figure largely throughout the South. They are basically Parker House rolls and were first created at the Parker House in Boston.

1. Bring the milk to the simmer. Add the butter, sugar, and salt and let stand until lukewarm.

2. Soften the yeast in the lukewarm water and add this to the milk mixture. Add enough flour to make a soft dough.

3. Turn out the dough onto a lightly floured board and let rest for 10 minutes. Knead until smooth, about 10 minutes.

4. Lightly grease the inside of a mixing bowl and add the dough, shaped into a ball. Grease the surface of the dough and cover. Let stand in a warm place until double in bulk.

5. Turn out the dough onto a lightly floured surface and knead lightly until the surface of the dough is smooth.

6. Roll the dough out to a ½-inch thickness. Lightly flour the cutting edge of a 3-inch biscuit cutter and cut out rounds. Dip the back of a table knife in flour and use this to make a crease slightly off center across each roll, taking care not to cut through the roll. Brush each roll with melted butter, and fold the larger portion over the smaller half.

7. Arrange the rolls 1 inch apart on a lightly greased baking sheet. Brush with melted butter, cover with a towel, and let stand until double in bulk, 30 to 40 minutes.

8. About 10 minutes before the rolls are ready to be baked, preheat the oven to 375 degrees.

9. Brush the rolls with a little additional melted butter and place in the oven. Bake for 15 to 20 minutes, until golden brown.

Yield: About 3 dozen rolls.

SOUTHERN BISCUITS

1. Preheat the oven to 450 degrees.

2. Combine the flour, salt, baking soda, and baking powder. Sift them together into a mixing bowl.

3. Add the lard and mix it with a pastry blender or the fingers, until it has the texture of coarse cornmeal.

4. Add the buttermilk all at once, pouring it all around and over the flour mixture.

5. Stir vigorously with a heavy wooden spoon. It will be quite soft at first, but will stiffen after a brief period. Continue beating for 1 or 2 minutes longer.

6. Scrape the dough from the sides of the bowl and shape it into a ball. Turn it out onto a lightly floured surface. Dust lightly with flour to prevent sticking. Flatten the dough gently with the hands into a thick round cake. Knead for a minute, folding the outer edge of the dough into the center of the circle, giving a light knead as you fold the sides in, overlapping each other.

7. Dust a rolling pin and the surface of the dough with flour. Roll the dough out to a ½-inch thickness. Prick the surface of the dough with the tines of a fork. Use a biscuit cutter (pressing directly down into the dough instead of wiggling it) and cut out the biscuits. Cut the biscuits as close together as possible. The scraps of dough may be gathered together and rolled out again, but the texture will not be as good.

8. Select a baking sheet, preferably one with a shiny surface. Arrange the biscuits, ½ inch apart, on the baking sheet as they are cut.

9. Place in the oven and bake for 13 minutes. Remove from the oven and let the biscuits rest for 3 or 4 minutes before serving. Serve hot.

Yield: 18 to 24 biscuits.

3 cups sifted flour
¾ teaspoon salt
½ teaspoon baking soda
4 teaspoons baking powder
⅔ cup lard
1 cup plus 2 tablespoons buttermilk

SOUTHERN BISCUIT MUFFINS

2¼ cups flour
    Salt to taste
 3 tablespoons sugar
1½ teaspoons baking
    powder
10 tablespoons butter, at
    room temperature
 1 cup buttermilk

The finest biscuits I have ever eaten were not made from a family heirloom recipe. They were not rolled out and cut with a biscuit cutter and they weren't made from a dough dropped from a spoon. They were, rather, buttermilk biscuits baked in muffin tins. This is my adaptation of that recipe.

1. Preheat the oven to 350 degrees.

2. Sift together the flour, salt, sugar, and baking powder into a mixing bowl.

3. Cut the butter into small pieces and add it. Using the fingers or a pastry cutter, work the butter into the dry ingredients until it has the texture of coarse cornmeal. Add the buttermilk and stir to blend without overmixing.

4. Spoon the mixture into a muffin tin with twelve cups, each with a ⅓-cup capacity. Place in the oven and bake for 40 to 45 minutes, until crusty and golden brown on top.

Yield: 12 biscuits.

PEARL'S SWEET POTATO BISCUITS

One of the principal cooks in my mother's boardinghouse over the years was named Pearl Hutchins. He not only cooked but acted as my personal part-time nurse. It never occurred to me in my childhood to wonder if Pearl was his given name or a nickname. One of his many fine Southern specialties was his sweet potato biscuits.

1. Preheat the oven to 450 degrees.

2. Sift together the flour, baking powder, baking soda, salt, and sugar into a mixing bowl. Add the butter and cut it in with a pastry cutter until it has the texture of coarse cornmeal. Stir in the mashed sweet potatoes.

3. Add the cream, a little at a time, stirring. Add only enough to make a soft dough.

4. Roll out the dough on a lightly floured board to ½-inch thickness. Cut the dough into rounds using a 2-inch biscuit cutter. Arrange the biscuits close together but not touching on a lightly greased baking sheet. Place in the oven and bake for about 15 minutes, or until lightly browned.

Yield: About 3 dozen.

2 cups sifted flour

2 teaspoons baking powder

½ teaspoon baking soda

Salt to taste

¼ to ½ teaspoon sugar

12 tablespoons butter

1 cup mashed, freshly cooked or canned sweet potatoes

⅓ cup heavy cream, approximately

KUGELHOPF

½ cup dark raisins

3 to 4 cups whole wheat flour, approximately

⅓ cup dark brown sugar

2 packages granular yeast

2 teaspoons salt

½ cup instant, nonfat dry milk

2 cups water

1 egg, lightly beaten

3 tablespoons vegetable oil

¼ cup roasted ground hazelnuts or almonds

1 cup all-purpose flour

Melted butter

15 whole blanched almonds and/or crushed hazelnuts or almonds

1. Put the raisins in a bowl and add warm water to cover. Let stand for about 30 minutes.

2. Combine 3 cups of the whole wheat flour, the brown sugar, yeast, salt, and dry milk in a mixing bowl. Blend well. Make a well in the center and add the water. Beat the mixture for about 50 strokes. Add the egg and beat for about 10 strokes. Beat in the oil. Add the ground hazelnuts. Drain the raisins and squeeze to extract excess liquid. Add them, beating. Add the white flour and beat the mixture with a wooden spoon. Gradually add up to 1 more cup of the whole wheat flour. Take care that you do not add an excess amount. The dough must remain pliable and easily workable when it is kneaded. Scrape out and use all the dough from the sides of the bowl.

3. Turn out the dough onto a lightly floured board. When the dough is easy to knead without adding any more flour, knead it brusquely, not gently, for at least 8 minutes. Beat and slam it against the board. Add more flour if, while kneading, the dough seems in any sense sticky.

4. Meanwhile, clean the bowl in which the dough was made. Add hot water and let stand until the dough is kneaded and ready to rest. Drain the water, wipe the bowl dry, and grease it.

5. Shape the dough into a ball and add it to the bowl. Cover with plastic wrap stretched tightly across the top.

6. Brush the inside of a 10-cup kugelhopf mold with melted butter. You may have a little too much dough for the mold. If so, butter the inside of a smaller 3-cup tin with melted butter.

7. Arrange the whole almonds in a neat circle over the bottom of the kugelhopf mold. If the smaller mold is used, sprinkle the bottom with crushed almonds.

8. Punch down the dough and knead briefly. Cut off 2½ pounds of the dough and shape it into a ball. Press down to shape it into a circle. Make a hole in the center and shape the dough by hand to resemble a very large doughnut that will fit neatly into the kugelhopf mold around the funnel. Press down. Shape the remaining dough into the smaller tin. Cover both with wax paper and set aside. Let stand for about 1 hour, or until double in bulk.

9. Preheat the oven to 375 degrees.

10. Place the molds in the oven. Bake the smaller bread for about 40 minutes, the larger for about 50 minutes.

Yield: 1 or 2 loaves.

PANETTONE (ITALIAN FEAST-DAY BREAD)

1. Put the yeast and water in a small mixing bowl. Add 1 teaspoon of the sugar and stir to dissolve the yeast. Set aside in a warm place until it foams.

2. Combine the raisins, citron, and rum in a mixing bowl. Set aside until ready to use.

3. Rinse out a large mixing bowl with hot water. Drain and dry thoroughly. Add the egg yolks and the remaining sugar. Beat with a wire whisk until pale yellow. Beat in the vanilla, lemon rind, and salt.

4. Add the yeast mixture and beat, adding the ¼ pound butter about a tablespoon at a time. Beat well.

5. Add the flour and beat briskly for 5 to 10 minutes.

6. Scrape the sides of the bowl, letting the dough rest in the center. Cover and let stand in a warm place for about 1 hour, or until double in bulk.

7. Preheat the oven to 400 degrees. Butter the inside of a 6- or 7-cup fluted mold.

8. Punch down the dough. Drain the raisins and citron and knead them briefly into the dough.

9. Turn the dough into the prepared mold. Brush the top with melted butter and place the mold in the oven. Bake for 10 minutes, then reduce the oven temperature to 325 degrees. Continue baking for about 40 minutes longer, basting often with more melted butter.

Yield: 1 loaf.

3	envelopes granular yeast
⅓	cup warm water
¼	cup sugar
½	cup dark raisins
½	cup diced citron
1	tablespoon dark rum
8	egg yolks
1	teaspoon pure vanilla extract
	Grated rind of 1 lemon
	Salt to taste
¼	pound sweet butter, at room temperature
1½	cups flour
4	tablespoons butter, melted

Pao Dolce (Portuguese Sweet Bread)

2 packages granular yeast

¼ cup lukewarm water

5 to 6 cups flour

1 teaspoon salt

5 eggs

1 cup lukewarm milk

6 tablespoons butter, melted, plus additional butter for greasing the bowl and pans

1¼ cups sugar

1 teaspoon cold water

1. Combine the yeast and lukewarm water and stir until the yeast is dissolved. Set aside.

2. Sift together the flour and salt into a large bowl and set aside.

3. Beat 4 of the eggs lightly in a small bowl.

4. Combine the milk and the melted butter in a mixing bowl. Beat in the sugar. Add the yeast mixture and the beaten eggs and stir until well blended.

5. Add about 4 cups of flour, 1 cup at a time, incorporating it with your fingers and kneading as you add it. Add enough flour to make a soft dough.

6. Turn out the dough onto a floured board and knead until smooth and elastic. Add only enough flour to make a dough that is not sticky.

7. Butter a large bowl and add the dough. Turn the dough upside down so that it is lightly covered with butter. Cover and let stand in a warm place until double in bulk.

8. Punch down the dough and knead it briefly on the floured board.

9. Divide the dough in half, on a lightly floured board, and shape each half into a flattened round shape.

10. Butter two 8-inch cake pans and add one round of dough to each.

11. Cover with a cloth and let stand until double in bulk, about 1½ hours.

12. Beat the remaining egg with the teaspoon of cold water. Brush the top of each bread lightly with a little of the mixture.

13. Fifteen minutes before the rising time is up, preheat the oven to 350 degrees.

14. Place the breads in the oven and bake for 30 to 40 minutes. Turn out onto racks to cool.

Yield: 2 loaves.

GREEK EASTER BREAD

1. In a bowl, combine ¾ cup of the lukewarm milk, the sugar, and yeast and let stand in a warm place for 10 minutes.

2. In a large bowl, combine 5½ cups flour and salt. Make a well in the center and add cooled melted butter and eggs. Add yeast mixture and blend to form a soft sticky dough. Knead, adding a little more flour as necessary, for about 5 minutes, until dough is smooth and satiny. Place in a buttered bowl and stretch a sheet of plastic wrap over the bowl. Set in a warm, draft-free place to rise until double in bulk, about 1½ hours.

3. Punch down the dough and knead for 5 minutes. Cut off 4 pieces, each piece about the size of a large egg. Place remaining dough in a round pan 10 inches in diameter and 2 inches high. Shape the small pieces of dough into twists about 5 inches long. Arrange the 4 twists from the center of the dough radiating to the edge of the dough. Put in a warm place to rise again until double in bulk, about 1 hour. Place the red egg in the center of the bread.

4. Preheat the oven to 375 degrees.

5. Brush entire surface of the bread with a wash made from the egg yolk and remaining tablespoon of milk. Bake for 30 minutes, until the bread is a deep golden brown and sounds hollow when tapped. Transfer to a rack and cool.

Yield: 12 or more servings.

Note: Color a hard-cooked egg with red Easter-egg dye according to package instructions.

¾ cup plus 1 tablespoon lukewarm milk

½ cup sugar

2 envelopes granular yeast

5½ to 6 cups flour

1 teaspoon salt

½ pound sweet butter, melted

5 eggs, lightly beaten

1 hard-cooked red egg (see note)

1 egg yolk

CHALLAH (A SWEET LEAVENED BREAD)

8½ to 9 cups flour, plus additional flour for kneading

2 packages granular yeast

2½ cups lukewarm water

½ teaspoon baking powder

½ teaspoon cinnamon

1 tablespoon salt

1 teaspoon vanilla extract

4 large eggs

¾ cup corn oil

¾ cup plus ⅛ teaspoon sugar

1 tablespoon poppy seeds or sesame seeds

1. Place 6 cups of the flour in a large mixing bowl and make a well in the center. Blend the yeast with 1 cup of the water and stir to dissolve. Add this to the well in the flour. Using a fork, start stirring around the well, gradually incorporating one fourth of the flour—no more—into the yeast mixture. When approximately that amount of flour is blended into the yeast mixture, stop stirring. There is no need to remove the fork. It will be used for further stirring. Set the bowl in a warm, not too hot place, and let stand for 45 or 50 minutes.

2. Sprinkle the baking powder, cinnamon, and salt over all. Add the vanilla, three of the eggs, the oil, and ¾ cup of sugar. Add the remaining water and blend again, first using the fork and then the hands. Add 2 cups of the flour, kneading, and if the mixture is still too sticky, add an additional cup of flour.

3. Work the mixture well with a wooden spoon to make a very stiff dough. If necessary, add more flour. Work with the hands for about 10 minutes. When the dough doesn't stick to the hands, it is ready. Shape the mixture into a rather coarse ball and cover. Let stand for about 20 minutes and turn it out onto a lightly floured board. Knead well, adding a little more flour to the board as necessary to prevent sticking. The kneading, which must be thorough and brisk, should take about 5 minutes. Flour a bowl well and add the ball, turning the dough to coat lightly with flour. Cover again and let stand for about 30 minutes.

4. Turn out the dough onto a flat surface once more and knead briefly. Using a knife, slash off about one eighth of the dough at a time. As each portion is cut off, knead quickly and shape into a ball. Flour lightly. Return each piece as it is kneaded to a bowl to rest briefly. Continue until all 8 pieces are shaped and floured.

5. Take one piece of dough at a time and place it on a flat surface, rolling briskly with the hands to make a "rope" 12 to 15 inches in length. Continue until all the balls are shaped.

6. Align the ropes vertically side by side and touching. Start working at the top of the ropes. Gather the tops of the ropes together, one at a time, pinching down to seal well. Separate the rope down the center, 4 ropes to a side. Braid the ropes as follows: Bring the extreme outer right rope over toward the center next to the inside rope on the left. Bring the extreme outer left rope over toward the center next to the inside rope on the right. Continue with this procedure until the loaf is braided and each rope has been brought to the center. As the last ropes are

brought over, it will be necessary to pull and stretch them a bit to get them to fit.

7. When the braiding is finished, gather the bottom ends of the ropes together and pinch them together just as at the top.

8. Meanwhile, generously oil the bottom and sides of a rectangular baking pan measuring about 15½ × 10½ × 2½ inches. Carefully gather up the braided loaf, using the hands and arms to help sustain the shape.

9. Cover with a towel and let stand in a warm spot for 1 hour or slightly longer, or until the loaf is well puffed and about twice the original volume.

10. Preheat the oven to 325 degrees.

11. Beat the remaining egg with the ⅛ teaspoon of sugar and, using a pastry brush, brush the loaf all over with the egg wash and sprinkle evenly with poppy or sesame seeds.

12. Place the loaf in the oven and bake for approximately 1 hour, or until well puffed, cooked through, and golden.

Yield: 1 large loaf.

STEAMED CHINESE BREAD

1 envelope granular
  yeast

2 tablespoons sugar

1 tablespoon warm but
  not melted lard

3 cups flour plus
  additional flour for
  kneading

1 cup cold water

1 teaspoon baking
  powder

1. Place the yeast, sugar, lard, ½ cup of the flour, and ½ cup of the water in a mixing bowl. Blend. Let stand for 5 minutes.

2. Add 2½ cups more of the flour and remaining ½ cup of water. Stir to blend. Knead with floured fingers (use up to ¼ cup more for kneading but as little flour as possible). Knead until the dough does not stick to the board or fingers.

3. Shape the dough into a ball and place it in a mixing bowl. Cover with a damp cloth. Let stand in a warm place for about 3 hours, or until double in bulk.

4. Remove the cloth and punch down the dough. Add the baking powder and continue kneading, using up to ¼ cup of flour but as little as possible. Knead vigorously for about 10 minutes.

5. Line a steamer at least 11 inches in diameter with a damp cloth. Shape the dough into an oval loaf about 8½ inches long. Place this on the damp cloth in the steamer, cover with the steamer lid and let rise in a warm place for about 45 minutes. Place the steamer basket over boiling water in the steamer bottom and steam for 20 minutes. When cooked, the loaf will be pure white but firm to the touch. Let cool.

6. When cool, slice the loaf lengthwise down the center. Cut crosswise into about 22 slices, each about ¾ inch thick. Let stand in the steamer basket.

7. Five minutes before serving, cover and heat over boiling water for about 5 minutes. Serve with pork and duck dishes.

Yield: 8 servings.

POORIS (PUFFED INDIAN BREAD)

1. Combine the flour and salt in a mixing bowl. Stir to blend. Add the sesame oil and work with the fingers. Gradually add the water, kneading constantly. Add only enough to make a moderately firm dough. Cover loosely and set aside for 1 hour.

2. Uncover and knead the dough for about 1 minute. Break off about ½ cup of the dough at a time. Roll it between the palms into a sausage shape. Break off pieces of this "sausage" to make small marbles of dough, each about 1 inch thick. Continue until all the dough is shaped. There should be about 38 pieces in all.

3. Heat the oil until it is almost but not quite smoking.

4. Flatten each piece of dough into a small disk about 1½ inches in diameter. Roll each piece into a thin round pancake, about 3½ inches in diameter. When rolling, use an unfloured board.

5. Drop the pieces of dough, one at a time, into the oil. Cook, tapping down on the center of each puri. They should puff in the center like a balloon. When puffed, turn each puri in the oil and cook briefly until lightly browned. Drain on absorbent towels.

Yield: About 38 pieces.

2 cups whole wheat flour
½ teaspoon salt
1 tablespoon sesame oil
⅔ cup water, approximately
Oil for deep frying

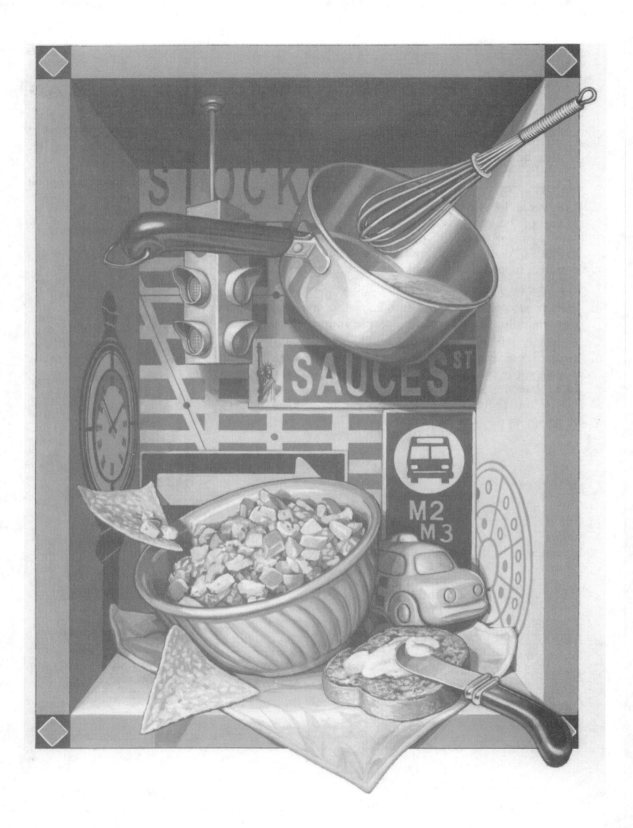

Sauces and Stocks

MAYONNAISE

1. Put the egg yolk in a mixing bowl and add the salt and pepper. Add the mustard and vinegar and beat vigorously for a second or two with a wire whisk or electric beater.
2. Add the oil gradually, beating continuously with the whisk or beater. Continue beating and adding oil until all of it is used. If the mayonnaise is not to be used immediately, beat in a tablespoon of water, which will stabilize it.

Yield: 1 cup.

1 egg yolk, at room temperature

Salt and freshly ground pepper to taste

1 teaspoon prepared mustard, preferably Dijon

1 teaspoon vinegar or lemon juice

1 cup peanut, vegetable, or corn oil

FOOD PROCESSOR MAYONNAISE

1. Place the yolks in the container of the food processor equipped with the steel or plastic blade.
2. Add the salt and mustard and activate the food processor for a split second only. If the yolks are overhomogenized, they may break down. Have the oil in the measuring cup with a pouring spout. Start the motor while simultaneously adding the oil in a thin stream. After half the oil has been added, it can be added more rapidly. Add the remaining ingredients, processing just enough to blend. Spoon into a jar and refrigerate.

Yield: About 1½ cups.

2 egg yolks

Salt to taste

2 teaspoons prepared mustard, preferably Dijon

1¼ cups peanut, vegetable, or olive oil

Freshly ground pepper to taste

2 teaspoons or more vinegar or lemon juice

HERB MAYONNAISE

1 egg yolk, at room
temperature

1 teaspoon prepared
mustard, preferably
Dijon

1 tablespoon white wine
vinegar

1 tablespoon finely
chopped parsley

1 tablespoon finely
chopped fresh tarragon

2 tablespoons finely
chopped cornichons

2 tablespoons finely
chopped drained capers

1 tablespoon finely
chopped shallots

1 cup olive oil

Salt and freshly ground
pepper to taste

1. Put the egg yolk, mustard, white wine vinegar, parsley, tarragon,
   cornichons, capers, and shallots in a mixing bowl.

2. Start beating with a wire whisk while gradually adding the oil.
   Beat until thickened. Add the salt and pepper.

Yield: 1¼ cups.

SPICY MAYONNAISE

2 egg yolks, at room
temperature

2 tablespoons red wine
vinegar

4 teaspoons prepared
imported strong
mustard

¼ teaspoon Tabasco
sauce

½ teaspoon Worcester-
shire sauce

Salt and freshly ground
pepper to taste

2 cups corn, peanut, or
vegetable oil

1. Put the yolks in a mixing bowl and add the vinegar, mustard,
   Tabasco, Worcestershire, salt, and pepper.

2. Start beating with a wire whisk and, when blended, gradually add
   the oil. Continue beating until all the oil is added and the mixture
   has thickened.

Yield: About 2¼ cups.

CURRIED YOGURT MAYONNAISE

1. Put the egg yolk, mustard, vinegar, salt, and pepper in a mixing bowl and start beating with a wire whisk. Gradually add the oil, beating vigorously with the whisk.
2. Beat in the yogurt, chutney, and curry paste. Serve with seafood, fruit salads, and so on.

Yield: About 1⅔ cups.

1 egg yolk, at room temperature

2 teaspoons prepared mustard, preferably Dijon

1 tablespoon malt vinegar

Salt and freshly ground pepper to taste

¾ cup corn, peanut, or vegetable oil

½ cup plain yogurt

¼ cup bottled chutney, chopped as fine as possible

2 tablespoons curry paste (see following recipe)

1. Heat the oil in a small saucepan and add the curry powder and flour, stirring with a wire whisk.
2. When the mixture is blended and smooth, add the broth, stirring rapidly with the whisk. When the mixture has thickened, remove it from the heat. Let cool.

Yield: About ½ cup.

Note: This paste will keep indefinitely under refrigeration.

CURRY PASTE

2 tablespoons corn, peanut, or vegetable oil

2 tablespoons curry powder

2 teaspoons flour

½ cup chicken or meat broth

Yogurt and Watercress Mayonnaise

1 egg yolk, at room
  temperature

2 teaspoons prepared
  mustard, preferably
  Dijon

2½ tablespoons malt
  vinegar

  Salt and freshly ground
  pepper to taste

¾ cup corn, peanut, or
  vegetable oil

½ cup plain yogurt

1 bunch watercress

½ cup finely chopped
  scallions

¾ cup finely diced,
  seeded cucumber

1. Put the egg yolk, mustard, 1 tablespoon of the vinegar, salt, and pepper in a mixing bowl and start beating with a wire whisk. Gradually add the oil, beating vigorously with the whisk. Beat in the yogurt and remaining vinegar.

2. Trim off and discard the tough stem ends of the watercress. Rinse and drain well. There should be about 2 cups fairly firmly packed.

3. Use a food processor or blender to purée the watercress.

4. Scrape the watercress into a length of cheesecloth or a clean kitchen towel. Squeeze to extract most of the liquid. There should be about ¾ cup of watercress solids. Add this to the mayonnaise. Add the scallions and cucumber and blend. Serve with fish or seafood, fish or seafood salads, vegetable salads, and so on.

Yield: About 2 cups.

Anchovy Mayonnaise

1 egg yolk, at room
  temperature

2 teaspoons prepared
  mustard, preferably
  Dijon

  Salt and freshly ground
  pepper to taste

1½ tablespoons white wine
  vinegar

1 cup olive oil

  A few drops of Tabasco
  sauce

¼ teaspoon Worcester-
  shire sauce

6 flat anchovy fillets,
  finely chopped

1. Put the yolk, mustard, very little salt, the pepper, and the vinegar in a small mixing bowl. Start stirring with a wire whisk.

2. Gradually add the oil, stirring constantly with the whisk. Beat until thickened and smooth. Beat in the Tabasco sauce, Worcestershire sauce, and anchovies.

Yield: About 1 cup.

TARTAR SAUCE

1. Place the yolk in a mixing bowl and add the vinegar, mustard, Tabasco, salt, and pepper. Beat vigorously for a second or two with a wire whisk or electric beater.

2. Start adding the oil gradually, beating continuously with the whisk or electric beater. Continue beating and adding oil until all of it is used. Add more salt to taste, if necessary, and the lemon juice.

3. Add the remaining ingredients and blend well.

Yield: About 1½ cups.

1 egg yolk

1 teaspoon wine vinegar

2 tablespoons prepared mustard, preferably Dijon

A few drops of Tabasco sauce

Salt and freshly ground pepper to taste

1 cup light olive oil or a combination of olive oil and peanut, vegetable, or corn oil

Lemon juice to taste

¼ cup finely chopped parsley

3 tablespoons finely chopped onion

¼ cup finely chopped cornichons or sour pickles

3 tablespoons chopped drained capers

HOLLANDAISE SAUCE

12 tablespoons butter
 3 egg yolks
 2 tablespoons cold water
    Salt to taste
 2 teaspoons lemon juice
⅛ teaspoon cayenne

1. Place a skillet on the stove and add about ½ inch of water. Bring the water to the simmer. Have ready a 1½-quart saucepan.

2. Place the butter in another saucepan and place it over very low heat (perhaps using an asbestos pad or a Flame Tamer).

3. Set the 1½-quart saucepan in the simmering water in the skillet. Place the egg yolks in the saucepan. Add the cold water, salt, and 1 teaspoon of the lemon juice. Start beating the egg yolks with a wire whisk, stirring in a back-and-forth and circular fashion, making certain that the whisk covers the bottom of the saucepan so that the yolks do not stick. It is important that the heat beneath the saucepan be moderate.

4. When the egg yolks become custardlike and thickened, start adding the melted butter.

5. Continue beating, stirring constantly and vigorously, until all the butter is added. Add the remaining lemon juice and cayenne.

Yield: About 1 cup.

BLENDER HOLLANDAISE SAUCE

¼ pound butter
 3 egg yolks
    Juice of ½ lemon
    Salt to taste
    Pinch of cayenne

1. Melt the butter and keep it hot, but do not brown.

2. Put the yolks, lemon juice, salt, and cayenne in the container of a blender. Blend on low speed, gradually adding the hot butter until the sauce is thickened and smooth.

Yield: About ¾ cup.

MUSTARD HOLLANDAISE

1. Put the mustard in a small bowl and add the salt, sugar, and water. Mix and let stand for at least 10 minutes to develop flavor.

2. Preheat the oven to 200 degrees.

3. Put the butter in a 1-quart heatproof glass measuring cup (this will facilitate pouring the butter after it is melted) and set it carefully in the oven to melt.

4. When the butter has melted, carefully skim the foam and scum off the top of the butter. Carefully pour off the clear golden liquid. Discard the milky substance on the bottom. There should be about ¾ cup of clear, liquid butter.

5. In a heavy saucepan, combine the egg yolks with the water. Place the saucepan on an asbestos pad and start whisking the yolks rapidly with the water. Whisk thoroughly until the mixture becomes thick and foamy like a custard, 5 to 10 minutes. Do not let the mixture become too hot or it will break down and curdle. Remove the saucepan from the heat and, beating vigorously, gradually add the melted butter. Add the lemon juice. Stir in the mustard according to taste.

Yield: 1¼ cups.

THE MUSTARD:

3 tablespoons dry mustard
¼ teaspoon salt
½ teaspoon sugar
2 tablespoons water

THE HOLLANDAISE:

½ pound butter
2 egg yolks
1 tablespoon water
1 tablespoon lemon juice

SAUCE BÉARNAISE

½ pound butter
2 tablespoons finely chopped shallots
2 tablespoons tarragon vinegar
1 teaspoon crushed black peppercorns
1 teaspoon dried tarragon
2 egg yolks
1 tablespoon cold water

1. Put the butter in a small heavy saucepan and let it melt slowly. Skim off the foam that rises to the top.

2. Heat the shallots, vinegar, peppercorns, and tarragon in another small heavy saucepan and cook until all the liquid evaporates. Remove from the heat and let the saucepan cool slightly.

3. Add the egg yolks and water to the shallots.

4. Return the saucepan to the stove and stir the yolk mixture vigorously over very low heat. Do not overheat or the eggs will curdle. Remove the saucepan from the heat and place it on a cold surface. Add the melted butter, ladle by ladle, stirring vigorously after each addition. Do not add the butter too rapidly and do not add the milky substance at the bottom.

Yield: About 1 cup.

SAUCE VERTE (GREEN SAUCE)

1 egg yolk
2 teaspoons prepared mustard, preferably Dijon
1 teaspoon red wine vinegar
   Salt and freshly ground pepper to taste
½ cup olive oil
2 tablespoons lemon juice
2 cups loosely packed spinach leaves
⅓ cup coarsely chopped celery
½ cup loosely packed watercress
½ cup loosely packed chopped fresh parsley

1. Put the egg yolk, mustard, vinegar, and salt and pepper into a mixing bowl. Start beating with a wire whisk. When blended and smooth, gradually add the oil, beating until smooth and thickened. Beat in the lemon juice. Set aside.

2. Drop the spinach into boiling water to cover. Cook for about 30 seconds, or until the spinach is wilted. Drain well. Squeeze to extract most of the water from the spinach. There should be about ¼ cup spinach.

3. Put the spinach, celery, watercress, and parsley into the container of a food processor. Process until smooth.

4. Line a small bowl with a square of cheesecloth. Spoon and scrape the mixture into it. Bring up the ends of the cheesecloth to make a small bag. Squeeze the juice from the spinach mixture into the bowl. Add 2 tablespoons of this to the lemon and egg sauce. Stir. Discard the remaining vegetable liquid and spinach mixture.

Yield: About ¾ cup.

SAUCE GRIBICHE

Combine all the ingredients in a mixing bowl and blend well. Serve with cold or lukewarm fish or meats.

Yield: About 2 cups.

1 cup mayonnaise
1 tablespoon finely chopped shallots
1 tablespoon finely chopped onion
1 tablespoon finely chopped chives
1 tablespoon water
2 hard-cooked eggs, pressed through a sieve
  Salt and freshly ground pepper to taste
1 tablespoon chopped parsley

BEURRE BLANC
(WHITE WINE BUTTER SAUCE)

1. Combine the shallots and wine in a saucepan and bring to a vigorous boil.
2. Let the wine cook down to about ⅓ cup. Continue cooking over moderate heat, stirring rapidly with a wire whisk. Add the butter, about 2 tablespoons at a time, stirring vigorously and constantly.
3. Add the salt and pepper and remove from the heat.

Yield: About 1¼ cups.

6 tablespoons finely chopped shallots
1½ cups dry white wine
12 tablespoons cold butter
  Salt and freshly ground pepper to taste

BEURRE ROUGE (RED WINE BUTTER SAUCE)

6 tablespoons finely chopped shallots

1½ cups red Burgundy wine

12 tablespoons butter

Salt and freshly ground pepper to taste

1. Combine the shallots and wine in a saucepan and bring to a vigorous boil.

2. Let the wine cook down to about ⅓ cup. Continue cooking over moderate heat, stirring rapidly with a wire whisk. Add the butter, about 2 tablespoons at a time, stirring vigorously and constantly. Add the salt and pepper and remove from the heat.

Yield: About 1¼ cups.

BEURRE NANTAIS (HERB BUTTER SAUCE)

2 tablespoons finely chopped shallots

1 tablespoon wine vinegar

¼ teaspoon freshly ground pepper, preferably white

1 to 2 tablespoons cold water

12 tablespoons cold butter

1 teaspoon finely chopped tarragon

1 teaspoon finely chopped fresh chervil, optional

1 teaspoon finely chopped parsley

Juice of 1 lime, or the juice of ½ lemon

Salt and freshly ground pepper to taste

1. Combine the shallots, vinegar, ¼ teaspoon pepper, and water in a 4-cup saucepan. Bring to the boil and simmer until the liquid is reduced to about half. If the mixture becomes too dry, add a little more water.

2. Cut the butter into 1-inch cubes. Add about one third of it to the sauce, stirring vigorously, and cook over low heat. Do not let this sauce boil at any point or it will curdle. Continue adding the butter, about a third at a time. Continue stirring until the butter is heated through and melted. Beat constantly until the butter sauce is piping hot.

3. Remove from the heat and stir in the tarragon, chervil, if desired, parsley and lime juice, beating. Add salt and pepper to taste and serve immediately.

Yield: About 1 cup.

SAUCE BORDELAISE (A RED WINE SAUCE)

1. Combine the shallots and wine in a saucepan and bring to the boil. Cook over high heat until all the wine has evaporated.

2. Add the meat glaze and simmer for about 2 minutes.

3. Strain the sauce through a fine-mesh sieve, pushing the solids though.

Yield: 2 cups.

3 tablespoons thinly sliced shallots

1 cup dry red wine, preferably a Bordeaux

2 cups demi-glace (see following recipe)

DEMI-GLACE (BROWN SAUCE)

4 pounds veal bones, cracked

1½ cups coarsely chopped carrot

1½ cups coarsely chopped celery

1½ cups coarsely chopped onions

2 garlic cloves, peeled

1 medium-size tomato, coarsely chopped

12 cups water

6 fresh parsley sprigs

2 bay leaves

½ teaspoon dried thyme
  Salt to taste

6 whole black peppercorns, crushed

A demi-glace is literally a half-glaze. It is often used in small quantities in the preparation of many classic French sauces, primarily in professional kitchens rather than in home cookery because it is time consuming to prepare.

A demi-glace, or brown sauce, is prepared by roasting meat bones, almost always veal bones, with vegetables and spices. These are put in a large kettle with water and cooked down for several house to a small quantity.

When strained and cooled, the sauce is quite thick. If you continue cooking that sauce down, it becomes a glace de viande. When this is cooled it is much thicker and pastelike. A little goes a long way.

You can, of course, buy acceptable demi-glaces and glaces de viande in certain specialty shops, but they are usually expensive.

1. Preheat the broiler.

2. Put the veal bones in one layer in a roasting pan. Place them under the broiler and broil until browned, about 5 minutes. Turn the pieces and continue broiling for about 5 minutes longer.

3. Scatter the carrot, celery, onions, garlic, and tomato over the bones. Broil for about 10 minutes.

4. Transfer the ingredients to a kettle and add the water, parsley sprigs, bay leaves, thyme, salt, and peppercorns. Bring to the boil and simmer over low heat for 7 hours. Skim the surface frequently during the first 2 hours.

5. Strain the liquid and discard the solids. There should be 4½ to 5 cups. At this point the stock can be frozen, if desired.

6. For the glaze, return the stock to a saucepan and continue cooking down for about 1 hour, or until it is reduced to 3 cups.

Yield: 3 cups.

SAUCE MADÈRE

1. Combine the shallots and wine in a saucepan. Bring to the boil and cook until most of the wine is reduced.

2. Add the demi-glace and cook for about 15 minutes, or until it is reduced to 2 cups. Add salt to taste.

3. Strain the sauce through a fine sieve. Swirl in the butter. If desired, add another tablespoon of Madeira to the sauce before serving.

Yield: About 2 cups.

2 tablespoons thinly sliced shallots

½ cup Madeira

3 cups demi-glace (see preceding recipe)

Salt to taste

2 tablespoons butter

BROWN CHICKEN BASE

1. Cut the chicken pieces into 2-inch lengths. Place them in a kettle and cook, stirring frequently, for about 10 minutes. It is not necessary to add fat. The chicken will cook in its natural fat. Sprinkle the chicken with salt and pepper.

2. Add the carrots, celery, onion, and garlic. Cook, stirring frequently, for 10 to 15 minutes longer, or until the chicken parts are nicely browned. Add the wine, broth, salt, and pepper, parsley, bay leaf, thyme, and tomato. Cook, uncovered, for about 1 hour, stirring frequently. Strain, using a wooden spoon to extract as much liquid from the solids as possible. Discard the solids.

Yield: About 3 cups.

Note: Leftover chicken base can be frozen.

4 pounds bony chicken parts such as wings, backs, necks

Salt and freshly ground pepper to taste

¾ cup coarsely chopped carrots

¾ cup coarsely chopped celery

1 cup coarsely chopped onion

1 garlic clove, finely minced

1 cup dry white wine

4 cups fresh or canned chicken broth

6 parsley sprigs

1 bay leaf

1 teaspoon dried thyme

½ cup chopped tomato

CRÈME FRAÎCHE
(A THICKENED FRESH CREAM)

2 cups heavy cream
2 teaspoons buttermilk

Pour the cream into a jar or mixing bowl. Add the buttermilk and stir. Cover tightly with plastic wrap and let stand in a slightly warm place for 12 hours, or until the cream is about twice as thick as ordinary heavy cream. Transfer to a jar with a tight-fitting lid and refrigerate.

Yield: 2 cups.

BÉCHAMEL SAUCE

4 tablespoons butter
4 tablespoons flour
2 cups milk
  Salt and freshly ground
  pepper to taste

1. Melt the butter in a saucepan and add the flour, stirring with a wire whisk. When blended, add the milk, stirring rapidly with the whisk. Add the salt and pepper.

2. When thickened and smooth, reduce the heat and cook, stirring occasionally, for about 5 minutes.

Yield: 2 cups.

SAUCE SUPRÊME (A BASIC CREAM SAUCE)

1. Melt the butter in a 1½- to 3-quart saucepan and add the flour, stirring with a wire whisk. When blended and smooth, add the broth, stirring rapidly with the whisk. When thickened, simmer for about 5 minutes, stirring often.

2. Add the cream, salt, and pepper. Simmer for 5 minutes longer.

Yield: About 5 cups.

6 tablespoons butter

⅓ cup flour

4 cups fresh or canned chicken broth

1⅓ cups heavy cream

Salt and freshly ground pepper to taste

MORNAY SAUCE

1. Melt the butter in a saucepan and add the flour, stirring with a wire whisk. When blended, add the milk, stirring rapidly with the whisk. When thickened and smooth, add the cream, stirring.

2. Remove from the heat and add the cheese, salt, pepper, and cayenne. Add the yolks, stirring rapidly. Heat, stirring, without boiling.

Yield: About 3½ cups.

3 tablespoons butter

4 tablespoons flour

2½ cups milk

½ cup heavy cream

¼ cup grated Gruyère or Cheddar cheese

Salt and freshly ground pepper to taste

Pinch of cayenne

2 egg yolks, lightly beaten

WATERCRESS CREAM SAUCE

6 tablespoons butter
6 tablespoons flour
3 cups fresh or canned chicken broth
1 bunch watercress
1 cup heavy cream
  Salt and freshly ground pepper to taste
¼ teaspoon grated nutmeg

1. Melt 4 tablespoons of the butter in a saucepan and add the flour, stirring with a wire whisk. When blended, add the broth, stirring rapidly with the whisk. Cook for about 20 minutes, stirring often.

2. Meanwhile, cut off and discard the tough bottom stems of the watercress. Drop the cress into a small saucepan of boiling water and simmer for about 30 seconds. Drain, squeeze to extract most of the liquid, and chop. There should be about ⅓ cup. Set aside.

3. Add the cream to the sauce. Add the salt, pepper, and nutmeg. Simmer for about 15 minutes. Strain the sauce through a very fine sieve. Return it to a saucepan and stir in the watercress. Swirl in the remaining 2 tablespoons of butter and serve piping hot.

Yield: About 3½ cups.

SAUCE DIABLE

1 tablespoon butter
2 tablespoons finely chopped shallots
¼ cup dry white wine
1 teaspoon Worcestershire sauce
½ cup chicken broth
1 tablespoon tomato paste
½ cup heavy cream
1 tablespoon extra-strong, imported prepared mustard
  Salt and freshly ground pepper to taste

1. Melt the butter in a saucepan and add the shallots. Cook briefly, stirring. Add the wine and cook down to about 2 tablespoons.

2. Add the Worchestershire sauce and chicken broth. Stir in the tomato paste and cook down by almost half. Add the cream and stir. Add the mustard, salt, and a generous grinding of pepper. Stir well to combine and serve hot.

Yield: About ¾ cup.

MUSHROOM SAUCE

1. Melt the butter in a saucepan and add the onion. When wilted, add the mushrooms and cook until they give up their liquid. Cook until the liquid evaporates and sprinkle with salt and pepper to taste.

2. Sprinkle with flour, stirring with a wire whisk. When blended, add the broth, stirring rapidly with the whisk. When blended and smooth, continue cooking, stirring occasionally, for about 15 minutes. Add the cream and simmer for about 5 minutes longer.

Yield: About 2 cups.

1 tablespoon butter

2 tablespoons finely minced onion

4 medium-size mushrooms, about ¼ pound, cut into small cubes

Salt and freshly ground pepper to taste

2 tablespoons flour

1 cup fresh or canned chicken broth

½ cup heavy cream

SAUCE RAVIGOTE

Combine the onion, capers, parsley, tarragon, chives, and vinegar in a mixing bowl. Gradually add the oil, stirring vigorously with a wire whisk. Add the salt and pepper. Serve with boiled beef or poached fish.

Yield: About 1½ cups.

3 tablespoons finely chopped onion

2 tablespoons drained capers, chopped

¼ cup finely chopped parsley

2 tablespoons finely chopped tarragon

2 tablespoons finely chopped chives

¼ cup wine vinegar

1 cup olive oil

Salt and freshly ground pepper to taste

HORSERADISH SAUCE

2 tablespoons butter
2 tablespoons flour
1 cup clear beef broth
¼ cup heavy cream
   Salt and freshly ground pepper to taste
½ cup grated fresh horseradish, or bottled horseradish to taste

1. Melt the butter in a saucepan and add the flour, stirring with a wire whisk.
2. Add the broth, stirring rapidly with a whisk. When thickened and smooth, add the cream. Add the salt, pepper, and horseradish.

Yield: About 1½ cups.

HOT MUSTARD

⅓ cup dry mustard
2 tablespoons cold water, white wine, milk, or beer
   A touch of salt

Blend the ingredients. Let stand for at least 15 minutes to develop flavor.

Yield: ¼ cup.

SAUCE PIQUANTE
(A MUSTARD AND PICKLE SAUCE)

Melt half the butter in a saucepan and add the onion and garlic. Cook until wilted and add the vinegar. Cook for about 2 minutes and add the bay leaf, brown sauce, beef broth, and pickles. Simmer for 10 minutes and stir in the mustard. Swirl in the remaining tablespoon of butter. Serve hot with tongue or pork.

Yield: About 2¼ cups.

2 tablespoons butter

⅓ cup finely chopped onion

1 garlic clove, finely mined.

1 tablespoon wine vinegar

½ bay leaf

1⅓ cups brown sauce, or canned beef gravy

½ cup fresh or canned beef broth

⅓ cup thinly sliced sour pickles, preferably imported cornichons

1 teaspoon Dijon mustard

SHRIMP SAUCE

1. Cook the shrimp in the shell for about 5 minutes in water to cover. Drain and let cool. Shell and devein the shrimp and cut them into small, bite-size pieces.

2. Melt the butter in a saucepan and add the flour, stirring with a wire whisk. Blend the clam juice and cream and add it to the saucepan, stirring rapidly with the whisk. When thickened and smooth, add the sherry, bay leaf, nutmeg, and celery seed. Add the salt and pepper. Let simmer for about 5 minutes. Serve hot.

Yield: About 1½ cups.

½ pound shrimp in the shell

2 tablespoons butter

2 tablespoons flour

¾ cup clam juice

¾ cup cream

1 tablespoon dry sherry

1 bay leaf

⅛ teaspoon grated nutmeg

½ teaspoon celery seed

Salt and freshly ground pepper to taste

FRESH TOMATO SAUCE

2 tablespoons butter

¼ cup finely chopped onion

½ teaspoon finely minced garlic

⅓ cup dry white wine

2 cups tomatoes, cored, seeded, and cut into 1-inch cubes

3 fresh basil leaves

Salt and freshly ground pepper to taste

1. Melt the butter in a saucepan and add the onion and garlic. Cook briefly, stirring. Add the wine and cook to reduce the liquid by about half. Add the tomatoes, basil, salt, and pepper. Cook for about 5 minutes.

2. Pour the mixture into the container of a blender or food processor and blend to a purée. Return the sauce to the saucepan. Reheat and serve.

Yield: About 2½ cups.

TOMATO SAUCE WITH HERBS

¼ cup olive oil

¾ cup finely chopped onion

1 or 2 garlic cloves, finely minced

6 cups crushed, imported, canned, peeled tomatoes with tomato paste

¼ cup dry white wine

½ teaspoon dried basil

¼ teaspoon dried thyme

½ teaspoon dried oregano

1 piece orange peel, white pulp removed

Salt and freshly ground pepper to taste

1 teaspoon sugar

2 tablespoons sour cream

1. Heat the oil in a large saucepan and add the onion. Cook, stirring, until the onion wilts. Add the garlic and cook briefly. Add the tomatoes, wine, basil, thyme, oregano, orange peel, salt, pepper, and sugar. Simmer over low heat for about 40 minutes, stirring occasionally to prevent sticking and burning.

2. Pour the sauce into the container of a food processor or blender and blend. Return to a saucepan and bring to the boil. Stir in the sour cream and serve.

Yield: About 4 cups.

TOMATO SAUCE WITH PEPPERS

1. Remove the cores from the tomatoes. Cut the tomatoes into 1-inch cubes. There should be about 4 cups. Set aside.

2. Heat the oil in a saucepan and add the onion, garlic, green pepper, celery, and pepper flakes. Cook, stirring often, for about 5 minutes.

3. Add the tomatoes, bay leaf, thyme, salt, and a generous grinding of pepper. Bring to the boil and simmer for 20 minutes.

4. Spoon and scrape the mixture into the container of a food processor. Blend to a fine purée. Add the basil. Reheat. If desired, swirl in the butter.

Yield: 3 cups.

3 fresh ripe tomatoes, about 1¾ pounds, or use 4 cups canned tomatoes

2 tablespoons olive oil

¾ cup finely chopped onion

1 tablespoon finely chopped garlic

¾ cup finely chopped green pepper

¾ cup finely chopped celery

¼ teaspoon hot red pepper flakes

1 bay leaf

¼ teaspoon dried thyme

Salt and freshly ground pepper to taste

1 tablespoon chopped fresh basil

1 tablespoon butter, optional

SAUCE DUGLÉRÉ
(TOMATO AND CREAM SAUCE)

1½ pounds fresh ripe
 tomatoes, or use 3
 cups imported canned
 tomatoes

 2 tablespoons butter

 2 tablespoons finely
 diced shallots

¼ cup finely diced onion

 1 tablespoon flour

 Salt and freshly ground
 pepper to taste

¼ cup dry white wine

½ cup fresh fish stock, or
 use bottled clam juice

 1 cup heavy cream

1. Core, peel, and chop the tomatoes. There should be about 3 cups.

2. Heat the butter in a saucepan and add the shallots and onion. Cook until wilted and sprinkle with flour. Add the tomatoes, salt, and pepper. Cook, uncovered, for about 15 minutes. Add the wine and fish stock and continue cooking for about 10 minutes.

3. Add the cream and bring to the boil. Serve piping hot. Serve with fish and fish mousses.

Yield: About 3½ cups.

TOMATO AND CREAM SAUCE WITH PERNOD

To the sauce Dugléré, add 1 tablespoon Pernod, Ricard, or other anise-flavored liqueur.

MARINARA SAUCE

1. Crush the tomatoes with the hands, or put them in a food processor.
2. Heat the oil in a skillet and add the garlic. Cook, stirring, until lightly browned.
3. Add the wine and cook until it has evaporated. Add the tomatoes, oregano, salt, and pepper. Cook for about 15 minutes.

Yield: About 4 cups.

4 cups imported canned tomatoes
6 tablespoons olive oil
2 teaspoons finely minced garlic
¼ cup dry white wine
1 teaspoon crushed dried oregano
Salt and freshly ground pepper to taste

MARINARA SAUCE FOR PIZZA

1. Put the tomatoes through a sieve or purée them in the container of a food processor or blender.
2. Heat the oil in a saucepan and add the garlic. Cook briefly without browning. Add the tomatoes, tomato paste, oregano, salt, and pepper. Bring to the boil and simmer for 20 minutes. Stir in the parsley.

Yield: About 2¾ cups.

2½ cups imported canned tomatoes
2 tablespoons olive oil
1 tablespoon finely minced garlic
¼ cup tomato paste
1 teaspoon dried oregano
Salt and freshly ground pepper to taste
¼ cup finely chopped parsley

SALSA

2 cups well-drained canned tomatoes, preferably imported

½ cup finely chopped red onion

2 tablespoons finely chopped fresh coriander

1 bottled pickled jalapeño pepper, drained

1 whole fresh jalapeño pepper

Salt and freshly ground pepper to taste

One of my favorite side dishes for Tex-Mex food and one that appears often on my table is this popular Mexican table sauce. There are many commercial versions, but this one is easily made and is excellent when kept tightly sealed overnight. It also makes a first-rate luncheon dish when served with canned tuna and a wedge of lemon on the side.

1. Put the tomatoes into the container of a food processor or blender. Blend until they are coarsely chopped. The tomatoes should not become too soupy. Pour the mixture into a bowl.

2. Add the chopped onion and coriander.

3. Trim off the ends of each jalapeño pepper. Do not remove the seeds. Chop the peppers and add them to the bowl. Add salt and pepper. Blend thoroughly.

Yield: About 2½ cups.

SALSA CRUDA
(RAW TOMATO AND CHILI SAUCE)

Chop the tomatoes and combine with the remaining ingredients. Stir until the ice melts. Serve with grilled meats, chicken, and chili con carne.

Yield: About 2 cups.

- 2 cups drained, canned tomatoes or fresh cubed tomatoes
- 2 tablespoons red wine vinegar
- ½ cup finely chopped onion

  Salt and freshly ground pepper to taste
- 1 or 2 fresh or canned serrano chilies, finely chopped
- 1 ice cube
- 1 tablespoon or more chopped fresh coriander

PICO DE GALLO (HOT CHILI SAUCE)

Combine all the ingredients in a mixing bowl and serve at room temperature. Serve with any Tex-Mex food, such as fajitas and chili con carne.

Yield: About 2½ cups.

- ½ cup finely chopped fresh jalapeño peppers with the seeds
- ½ cup seeded, finely diced tomatoes
- ½ cup finely chopped red onion
- 3 tablespoons finely chopped fresh coriander
- ⅓ cup finely diced avocado
- 2 tablespoons freshly squeezed lime juice

  Salt and freshly ground pepper to taste
- 1 teaspoon olive oil

Sweet and Sour Sauce

¾ cup water

½ cup sugar

¼ cup wine vinegar

1 tablespoon cornstarch

¼ cup ketchup

2 teaspoons finely minced garlic

1 tablespoon finely chopped fresh ginger, optional

¼ cup finely chopped scallions

1. Combine the water, sugar, vinegar, and cornstarch in a saucepan. Stir with a wire whisk until the cornstarch dissolves.

2. Add the ketchup, garlic, and ginger, if used. Bring to the boil, stirring. Cook until the mixture thickens. Remove from the heat and add the scallions. Serve with baked spareribs or pour the sauce over grilled foods.

Yield: About 1½ cups.

Brown Chili Sauce

2 pounds chicken necks and wings, chopped into 1-inch lengths

2 tablespoons flour

2 teaspoons ground cumin

1 tablespoon chopped garlic

3 or more tablespoons chili powder

1 tablespoon dried oregano

2 tablespoons tomato paste

1 cup fresh or canned beef broth

2 cups water

1. Put the chicken pieces in a heavy saucepan and cook, stirring often, until browned. It is not necessary to add fat, but the pieces must be stirred to prevent sticking.

2. Pour off the fat from the saucepan and sprinkle the chicken pieces with the flour, cumin, garlic, chili powder, and oregano. Stir and add the tomato paste. Stir once more and add the broth and water. Stir constantly until the sauce boils. Cook for about 40 minutes, stirring often from the bottom to prevent sticking.

3. Strain the sauce, discarding the solids, and serve hot. This sauce is good with tacos, enchiladas, hamburgers, and so on.

Yield: About 2 cups.

TARRAGON MARINADE FOR BARBECUES (FOR CHICKEN, FISH, LAMB, AND VEAL)

Put the vinegar in a small mixing bowl and add the oil, beating with a wire whisk. Add the tarragon, salt, and pepper. Blend well. Use to baste charcoal-grilled chicken, lamb, fish, and veal.

Yield: About ¾ cup.

¼ cup red wine vinegar

½ cup peanut, vegetable, or corn oil

2 teaspoons chopped fresh tarragon

Salt and freshly ground pepper to taste

LEMON MARINADE FOR BARBECUES (FOR CHICKEN, FISH, LAMB, AND VEAL)

Put the lemon juice in a small mixing bowl. Add the oil while stirring vigorously with a whisk. Add the remaining ingredients and blend well. Use to baste charcoal-grilled chicken, fish, lamb, and veal.

Yield: About 1 cup.

⅓ cup fresh lemon juice

½ cup olive oil

1 teaspoon finely minced garlic

Salt and freshly ground pepper to taste

1 teaspoon dried oregano

6 very thin, seeded lemon slices

KETCHUP SAUCE FOR BARBECUES (FOR CHICKEN, PORK, AND BEEF)

1 cup tomato ketchup

3 tablespoons lemon juice

2 tablespoons honey

1 tablespoon finely minced garlic

1 tablespoon Worcester-shire sauce

Tabasco sauce to taste

4 tablespoons butter

Salt and freshly ground pepper to taste

4 thin, seeded lemon slices

Combine all the ingredients in a saucepan and bring to the boil, stirring. Use to baste charcoal-grilled meats when they are almost done.

Yield: About 1½ cups.

SOY SAUCE MARINADE FOR BARBECUES (FOR CHICKEN, PORK, AND FISH)

½ cup soy sauce

¼ cup dry sherry

1 tablespoon finely chopped fresh ginger

2 teaspoons finely minced garlic

2 teaspoons sugar

¼ teaspoon hot red pepper flakes

Combine all the ingredients in a mixing bowl. Stir until the sugar dissolves. Use to baste charcoal-grilled chicken, pork, and fish when they are almost done.

Yield: About ¾ cup.

Texas Barbecue Sauce

1. Pour the ketchup, Worcestershire, and cider vinegar into a saucepan.
2. Cut the lemons in half. Squeeze the juice. Add the juice and rind halves to the sauce. Add the remaining ingredients and cook, stirring often, for about 30 minutes. Use as a sauce for baking or charcoal-grilling 8 pounds of spareribs or 6 pounds of chicken cut into serving pieces. Marinate the ribs or chicken parts in the sauce for 6 hours.

Yield: About 5 cups.

Note: Leftover sauce may be bottled, sealed tightly, and refrigerated. It will keep indefinitely.

1¼ cups tomato ketchup

1⅓ cups (the contents of one large bottle) Worcestershire sauce

1⅓ cups cider vinegar

2 large lemons

2 cups coarsely chopped onions

3 tablespoons unsulfured molasses

2 large garlic cloves, peeled and cut into slivers

1 bay leaf

½ teaspoon dried oregano

1 tablespoon chopped fresh basil, or half the amount dried

2 tablespoons dry mustard

½ teaspoon freshly ground pepper

4 drops of Tabasco sauce

Garam Masala

Combine all the ingredients in a small coffee grinder and blend thoroughly. The mixture may be kept for weeks if tightly sealed.

Yield: About 3 tablespoons.

1 tablespoon peeled cardamom seeds

One 2-inch stick cinnamon, crushed

1 teaspoon whole cloves

1 teaspoon whole black peppercorns

⅓ teaspoon grated nutmeg

1 teaspoon cumin seeds, optional

COUNTRY BARBECUE SAUCE

3 tablespoons peanut oil

2 cups finely chopped onions

One 16-ounce can imported plum tomatoes

1 cup ketchup or chili sauce

¼ cup white vinegar

¼ cup Worcestershire sauce

Salt to taste

1 teaspoon freshly ground pepper

1 or 2 tablespoons chili powder

½ teaspoon cayenne

1½ cups water

1 teaspoon dried oregano

1 teaspoon cumin powder

2 to 4 tablespoons honey

Heat the oil in a large deep skillet or casserole and add the onions. Cook, stirring often, until golden. Add the remaining ingredients and bring to the boil. Simmer, stirring frequently, for about 45 minutes. Let stand overnight before using. Use for basting meats when they are barbecued.

Yield: 3 to 3½ cups.

SANBAIZU SAUCE (A JAPANESE SOY AND VINEGAR SAUCE)

½ cup rice vinegar

1½ tablespoons sugar

1 teaspoon salt

1 teaspoon soy sauce

Blend the vinegar, sugar, salt, and soy sauce. Add more sugar, salt, or soy sauce according to individual taste.

Yield: About 9 tablespoons.

Nuoc Mam Sauce (Vietnamese Fish Sauce)

Combine all the ingredients and stir to blend. Place equal portions into individual bowls and serve with Vietnamese dishes. Leftover sauce may be kept refrigerated for a week or longer.

Yield: About 1½ cups.

1 cup fish sauce, available in bottles where Asian foods are sold

1 tablespoon finely chopped fresh ginger

2 garlic cloves, finely chopped

1 teaspoon hot red pepper flakes (or use a little cayenne to taste)

3 tablespoons lemon juice

2 tablespoons sugar

¼ cup water

Ketjap Manis (Indonesian Sweet Soy Sauce)

1. Put the sugar in a heavy saucepan and cook over moderate to low heat, stirring, until the sugar melts and starts to turn brown. Continue cooking, stirring constantly, until the sugar takes on a deep amber color. Take care that the sugar does not burn or it will be bitter.

2. When the sugar is properly caramelized, add the soy sauce and remaining ingredients. Bring to the boil, stirring constantly, and let simmer slowly for about 15 minutes.

3. Let cool. Pour the syrup into one or more bottles. This will keep for months if properly refrigerated.

Yield: About 3 cups.

Note: Unfamiliar ingredients can be found in shops that specialize in Asian foods.

2½ cups sugar

One 2-ounce bottle dark soy sauce

3 garlic cloves, peeled and crushed

1 piece star anise

2 salam leaves

2 slices laos

½ cup water

CARROTS AND YOGURT

1 large carrot, scraped
  and trimmed
1 cup plain yogurt
1 teaspoon sugar
¼ teaspoon ground cumin
¼ cup finely chopped
  onion
½ teaspoon finely
  chopped hot, fresh red
  or green pepper, or use
  ½ teaspoon crushed
  hot red pepper flakes

A classic Indian kitchen frequently serves a variety of yogurt sauces with curried and other foods. Three of them are offered here. Each is outstanding in its ability to stimulate and freshen the palate. One is made with carrots, the second with onion, and a third with cucumber, tomatoes, and scallions.

1. Cut the carrot into 1½-inch lengths. Cut the pieces lengthwise into very thin slices. Stack the slices and cut them into very thin strips. There should be about 1 cup.

2. Drop the strips into boiling water and cook for about 30 seconds. Drain well.

3. Combine the yogurt, carrot, and the remaining ingredients. Serve chilled.

Yield: About 1½ cups.

YOGURT AND ONION RELISH

1 cup plain yogurt
1 onion, about ¼ pound,
  peeled
  Salt to taste
½ teaspoon toasted,
  crushed cumin seeds
  (see note)

1. Spoon the yogurt into a small bowl.

2. Thinly slice the onion. Bring enough water to the boil to cover the onion slices when added. Drop in the onion slices. Stir and remove from the heat.

3. Drain immediately in a small sieve and run under cold running water until chilled. Drain once more.

4. Add the onion, salt, and cumin to the yogurt. Chill. Serve with Indian foods as a side dish.

Yield: About 2 cups.

Note: To toast the cumin seeds, put them in a small skillet and cook over moderate heat, stirring and shaking the skillet. Cook until they give off a slight aroma and are lightly browned.

Cucumber, Tomato, Scallion, and Yogurt Relish

1. Peel the cucumber. Cut the cucumber lengthwise in half and scrape out the center seeds.
2. Cut the cucumber into 1½-inch lengths. Slice the pieces lengthwise into thin slices. Stack the slices and cut them lengthwise into very thin strips. There should be about 1½ cups.
3. Combine the yogurt, cucumber, and remaining ingredients.

Yield: About 2 cups.

1 medium-size cucumber
1 cup plain yogurt
1 teaspoon sugar
¼ cup chopped scallions
¼ teaspoon cumin
Salt and freshly ground pepper to taste
½ cup peeled, seeded, cubed tomato

MANGO CHUTNEY

4 garlic cloves, crushed
10 cups cubed mangoes
2 cups chopped onions
2 pounds brown sugar
3 cups vinegar
1 cup lime juice
2 lemons, chopped, peel and all
Peel of 2 oranges
Peel of 1 grapefruit
10 pineapple slices, drained
1 tablespoon grated nutmeg
1 tablespoon cinnamon
1 tablespoon ground ginger
1 tablespoon cloves
1 tablespoon salt
1 teaspoon freshly ground pepper
1 drop of Tabasco sauce
1 cup pitted prunes or dates

Put the garlic, mangoes, onion, sugar, vinegar, and lime juice in a saucepan and simmer for 10 minutes. Add the remaining ingredients and cook until the fruit is soft, about 20 minutes. The chutney can be kept in the refrigerator for about 6 months without sterilization.

Yield: 8 pints.

FRESH GREEN CHUTNEY

Combine the coriander and chili in the container of a food processor or blender. Add the water and blend to a smooth paste. As the mixture is blended, stir down as necessary with a plastic spatula. Spoon and scrape the mixture into a mixing bowl. Add the remaining ingredients and blend well.

Yield: About 1½ cups.

1 cup loosely packed, chopped fresh coriander

1 fresh hot green chili, trimmed and sliced

3 tablespoons water

1 cup plain yogurt

Salt and freshly ground pepper to taste

½ teaspoon ground cumin (preferably made from toasted cumin seeds)

1 tablespoon lemon juice

GINGER AND GREEN CHILI SAUCE

Combine the fish sauce, lime juice, garlic, and ginger in a mixing bowl. Blend. Cut the chili on the diagonal into very thin slices. Add it to the sauce. Add the remaining ingredients and serve at room temperature with hot meats.

Yield: About 1¼ cups.

½ cup fish sauce, available in bottles where Asian foods are sold

⅓ cup freshly squeezed lime juice

1 tablespoon finely minced garlic

1 tablespoon finely minced fresh ginger

1 or 2 hot, fresh, red or green chilies, or use ½ teaspoon or more crushed red pepper flakes

1 scallion, trimmed and chopped

½ cup loosely packed chopped fresh coriander

1 tablespoon chopped fresh basil

COCONUT MILK AND COCONUT CREAM

To crack one or more coconuts, pierce the "eyes" of each coconut with an ice pick. Drain and discard the liquid. Preheat the oven to 275 degrees.

Using a hammer, crack the shell of each coconut in half. Arrange the coconut halves, cracked side up, on a baking sheet. Place in the oven and bake for 15 or 20 minutes.

Remove the coconut halves. Pry the meat from the shells. Peel away the brown skin from the meat. Cut the meat into ½-inch cubes. Two coconuts should yield about 5 cups of cubed meat.

Put the coconut meat into the container of a food processor and add 4 cups of warm water. Purée thoroughly.

Line a colander with cheesecloth. Pour in the coconut mixture. Bring up the ends of the cheesecloth and squeeze to extract as much liquid as possible. There should be about 4½ cups. The white creamlike substance that rises to the top of the liquid on standing is coconut cream. The bottom layer is coconut milk.

RICH CHICKEN BROTH

5 pounds meaty chicken bones
2 cups coarsely chopped onions
½ pound carrots, coarsely chopped, about 2 cups
1 cup coarsely chopped celery
1 garlic clove, peeled
10 fresh parsley sprigs
1 bay leaf
½ teaspoon dried thyme
10 whole black peppercorns
16 cups water

1. Put the chicken bones in a large stockpot and cover with water. Bring to the boil and drain, discarding the water. Rinse the bones thoroughly and return to the stockpot.

2. Add the remaining ingredients and bring to the boil. Reduce the heat so the broth simmers slowly. Cook for 2 hours, skimming fat and scum from the surface every 15 or 20 minutes.

3. Strain the broth through a fine sieve into a large bowl. Let cool and then cover and refrigerate.

4. Remove the fat from the top of the broth with a slotted spoon. Use the clear broth as needed. It can be frozen in convenient-size containers.

Yield: 10 cups.

BEEF BROTH

1. Place the bones in a kettle and add cold water to cover. Bring to the boil and simmer for about 2 minutes. Rinse well under cold water.

2. Return the bones to a clean kettle and add the 4 quarts of water and remaining ingredients. Simmer for 3 hours. Strain. Discard the solids. Freeze the broth in convenient-size containers.

Yield: 3 or more quarts.

5 pounds meaty neckbones of beef

32 cups (4 quarts) water

1 large carrot, trimmed and scraped

1 turnip, trimmed and peeled

1 large onion, peeled and stuck with 2 cloves

1 large celery rib, cut in half

1 garlic clove, left whole

1 bay leaf

2 fresh thyme sprigs, or ½ teaspoon dried

Salt to taste

24 peppercorns, crushed

FISH STOCK

1. Combine all the ingredients in a kettle or large saucepan.

2. Bring to the boil and simmer for 20 minutes. Strain and discard the solids. Freeze leftover stock in convenient-size containers.

Yield: About 10 cups.

3 pounds meaty fish bones, preferably with head and tail on but gills removed

8 cups water

1 cup dry white wine

2 cups coarsely chopped onions

4 fresh parsley sprigs

1 cup coarsely chopped celery

1 bay leaf

½ teaspoon dried thyme

6 whole black peppercorns

Salt to taste

½ cup chopped green part of leeks, optional

VEGETABLE BROTH

2 tablespoons olive oil

1 onion, finely chopped

3 parsnips, scraped and cut into 1-inch lengths

3 carrots, scraped and cut into 1-inch lengths

3 small white turnips, scraped and quartered

2 celery stalks, cut into 1-inch lengths

Salt and freshly ground pepper to taste

2 fresh parsley sprigs

¼ teaspoon dried thyme

1 bay leaf

Pinch of cayenne

3 cups water

1. Heat the oil in a large saucepan. Add the onion and cook, stirring occasionally, until the onion is wilted.

2. Add the parsnips, carrots, turnips, celery, salt, pepper, parsley, thyme, bay leaf, and cayenne. Stir.

3. Add the water. Cover and simmer for 1 hour. Strain and chill thoroughly.

Yield: About 3 cups.

DASHI (JAPANESE SOUP STOCK)

5 cups cold water

1 large square kombu (kelp), measuring about 7 × 7 inches (see note)

3 cups loosely packed packaged katsuobushi or dried bonito shavings (see note)

1. Place the water in a saucepan and add the kombu. Bring to the boil and immediately remove the kombu. Do not let it cook.

2. Add the katsuobushi and stir. Remove from the heat immediately. Strain through flannel.

Yield: About 5 cups.

Note: Both kombu and katsuobushi are available in Japanese markets.

DESSERTS

I am not basically a dessert man—at least, not in the passionate way of certain friends and acquaintances. I find most European pastries toothsome enough: a well-made roulade au chocolat; variations on a genoise; napoleons; éclairs; baked meringues. But these I can resist. Crêpes suzette have a certain appeal, but they do not interrupt my sleep with sweet anticipation.

No, it isn't these confections that make me salivate, that arouse the hounds of hunger at the conclusion of a meal. The dessert category that I find totally irresistible is purely and simply nursery desserts, those custards and mousses and glorious sensual puddings and sauces based on egg and cream. I am convinced that my craving for these desserts stems directly from the cradle and the years immediately following. First in a high chair, then sitting on a stack of Encyclopedia Brittanica (the telephone book in the town of my childhood was only a quarter-inch thick).

TAPIOCA PUDDING

1. Combine the milk, tapioca, and vanilla bean in a saucepan and bring to the boil, stirring constantly with a wooden spoon. Let cook for 6 to 7 minutes.

2. Combine the sugar and yolks in a mixing bowl and beat rapidly with a wire whisk until light and lemon-colored. Add a little of the hot tapioca mixture to the egg yolk mixture, stirring constantly. Return this mixture to the saucepan and, when it begins to boil, continue cooking, stirring constantly, for about 1 minute. Remove the vanilla bean. Pour the pudding into a serving dish and let cool. Chill until ready to serve.

Yield: 8 to 12 servings.

6 cups milk

½ cup quick-cooking tapioca

1 vanilla bean, or 1 teaspoon vanilla extract

½ cup sugar

3 egg yolks

BREAD-AND-BUTTER PUDDING

¾ cup mixed candied fruit or dried currants

2 tablespoons Cognac

20 slices untrimmed French bread, each slice about ⅓ inch thick

3 egg yolks

3 whole eggs

1 cup granulated sugar

3 cups milk

4 tablespoons butter, melted

Confectioners' sugar

1. Preheat the oven to 350 degrees.

2. Mix the candied fruit with the Cognac in a bowl and set aside for 30 minutes.

3. Select a heatproof baking dish. (An oval dish that measures $14 \times 18 \times 2$ inches is ideal.)

4. Slice the bread. Preferably, the diameter of the bread should not exceed 3 inches. If much larger, cut the pieces in half.

5. Combine the egg yolks, whole eggs, and sugar in a mixing bowl. Beat with a whisk until blended. Stir in the milk. Drain the Cognac from the fruit and add the Cognac to the milk mixture.

6. Scatter the fruit over the bottom of the baking dish.

7. Brush one side of each bread slice with butter. Arrange the bread slices neatly and symmetrically overlapping to cover the bottom of the dish.

8. Strain the custard over the bread slices.

9. Set the baking dish in a larger heatproof baking dish. Pour about 1 inch of water around the baking dish. Bring the water to the boil on top of the stove. Place in the oven and bake for 40 minutes to 1 hour, or until the custard is set.

10. Remove the dish to a rack and let cool. Serve sprinkled with confectioners' sugar.

Yield: 8 to 12 servings.

CHOCOLATE BREAD PUDDING

1. Preheat the oven to 375 degrees.

2. Butter the bread on both sides. Arrange the slices in one layer on a baking sheet. Bake until lightly golden on one side. Turn the slices and continue baking for about 2 minutes longer, or until totally golden on both sides.

3. Put the chocolate in a saucepan and set the saucepan in a basin of simmering water. Stir until melted.

4. Meanwhile, heat the milk almost but not quite to the boiling point. Add the chocolate, stirring.

5. Beat the whole eggs, egg yolks, and sugar until well blended. Pour in the chocolate mixture, stirring.

6. Add the milk, stirring.

7. Arrange the toast pieces slightly overlapping on the bottom of an oval dish measuring about 14 × 8 × 2 inches. Carefully ladle the chocolate mixture over all.

8. Select a baking dish large enough to hold the oval dish. Pour boiling water into the baking dish. Set the oval dish in the water and place it in the oven.

9. Bake for 30 minutes. Before serving, sprinkle the top with confectioners' sugar. Serve, if desired, with whipped cream.

Yield: 8 or more servings.

3 tablespoons butter, melted

15 slices French bread, approximately, each about ½ inch thick (there should be enough slices to cover the bottom of an oval baking dish with the slices slightly overlapping)

¼ pound (4 squares) sweet chocolate

3 cups milk

3 eggs

3 egg yolks

½ cup granulated sugar

1 tablespoon confectioners' sugar

RICE PUDDING

7 cups milk

1 vanilla bean, or
1 teaspoon pure
vanilla extract

1 cup rice

1½ cups granulated sugar

¾ cup raisins

2 large eggs

1 tablespoon butter

½ teaspoon ground
cinnamon

2 tablespoons confec-
tioners' sugar

1. Pour the milk into a saucepan and add the vanilla bean or vanilla extract. Bring to the boil and add the rice and granulated sugar. Stir often from the bottom to prevent sticking. Cook until the rice is tender, about 40 minutes.

2. Put the raisins in a small bowl and pour boiling water over them. Let stand until rice is cooked.

3. Beat the eggs. Remove the rice from the heat and add the eggs, stirring rapidly.

4. Meanwhile, preheat the oven to 400 degrees.

5. Drain the raisins and add them to the cooked rice.

6. Grease a baking dish with the butter. We used an oval dish measuring 14 × 18 × 2 inches. Pour in the rice mixture. Sprinkle with cinnamon. Place the dish in a larger flameproof dish and pour boiling water around it. Bring to the boil on top of the stove. Place the dish in the oven and bake for 30 minutes, or until custard is set. Remove from the oven and sprinkle with confectioners' sugar. Serve hot or cold.

Yield: 8 to 10 servings.

MARLBOROUGH PUDDING

1. Preheat the oven to 350 degrees.

2. Peel the apples and cut them into quarters. Carve away the core and stems. Cut the quartered apples into thin slices. Put the apples in a heavy saucepan and add the water. Cover and cook for about 5 minutes, or until the apples are tender.

3. Put the mixture into the container of a food processor or blender and blend to a purée. There should be about 1⅓ cups.

4. Pour and scrape the mixture into a saucepan and add 2 tablespoons of the butter, the eggs, sugar, heavy cream, mace, lemon rind, and lemon juice. Blend.

5. Butter a small baking dish (one measuring 10 × 7 × 1½ inches is ideal) with the remaining 1 teaspoon of butter. Pour in the apple mixture. Set the dish inside a larger heatproof dish and pour boiling water around it. Bring the water to the boil again. Place in the oven and bake for about 45 minutes, or until the custard is set in the center.

Yield: 6 servings.

3 apples, about 1¼ pounds, or use 1⅓ cups applesauce

¼ cup water

2 tablespoons plus 1 teaspoon butter

2 large eggs

½ cup sugar

½ cup heavy cream

¼ teaspoon ground mace or grated nutmeg

1 teaspoon grated lemon rind

Juice of ½ lemon

BANANAS WITH APRICOT PUDDING

3½ cups milk

Peel from half an orange

½ cup quick-cooking farina (cream of wheat)

7 tablespoons sugar

3 egg yolks

½ cup raisins

One 10-ounce jar apricot preserves

3 firm, ripe, unblemished bananas

3 tablespoons butter

3 tablespoons Grand Marnier, rum, or Cognac

¼ cup toasted, slivered, unsalted, blanched almonds

1. Pour the milk into a saucepan and start to heat.

2. Peel the orange, eliminating as much of the white pith as possible. Cut the yellow skin into very fine julienne strips. Add this to the milk and continue heating just to the boil.

3. Add the farina gradually, stirring constantly. Cook for 5 minutes, stirring occasionally. Remove from the heat.

4. Immediately blend 5 tablespoons of the sugar with the egg yolks and add this to the hot farina, stirring rapidly with a whisk. Return briefly to the heat and, stirring constantly, bring just to the boil. Do not boil. Remove from the heat.

5. Spoon equal portions of the pudding mixture into 8 small, individual dessert bowls. Smooth over the top and let cool.

6. Meanwhile, place the raisins in a small bowl or cup and add boiling water to cover. Let stand until plumped.

7. Spoon the preserves into a saucepan and heat.

8. Peel the bananas and cut them first in half, then into quarters. Cut the pieces into cubes.

9. Heat the 3 tablespoons of butter in a skillet and add the cubed bananas. Sprinkle with the remaining sugar and cook, stirring gently, for about 2 minutes. Add the Grand Marnier and spoon this over the pudding.

10. Drain the raisins and add them to the heated preserves. Spoon this over all and sprinkle with almonds.

Yield: 8 servings.

CHOCOLATE CRÈME CARAMEL

1. Preheat the oven to 350 degrees.

2. Select eight ½-cup metal or ovenproof custard molds.

3. Combine the ½ cup of sugar, the water, and lemon juice in a saucepan and bring to the boil. Let cook, bubbling, until the syrup becomes a light amber color. Take care not to let the syrup burn or it will be bitter. The moment the syrup is ready, pour equal amounts of it quickly into the 8 molds. Swirl the syrup around so that it covers the bottom of each mold. Let cool at room temperature.

4. Heat the milk with the chocolate, stirring often until the chocolate has dissolved.

5. Beat the eggs, egg yolks, and ½ cup sugar until thickened and smooth. Pour the milk mixture into the egg mixture and blend well. Strain the custard and skim off and discard surface foam.

6. Ladle the custard into the eight prepared molds. Arrange the molds in a baking dish and pour boiling water around them. Place the dish in the oven and bake until the custard is set in the center, about 30 minutes.

7. Remove the custard molds and let cool. Unmold when ready to serve.

Yield: 8 servings.

THE CARAMEL BASE:

- ½ cup sugar
- 2 tablespoons water
  Juice of ½ lemon

THE CHOCOLATE CUSTARD:

- 2 cups milk
- 4 ounces (squares) semisweet chocolate
- 4 eggs
- 4 egg yolks
- ½ cup sugar

COEUR À LA CRÈME

1 cup cottage cheese
1 cup cream cheese
½ cup sour cream
½ cup heavy cream
  Strawberry sauce (see
  following recipe)

1. The quantities listed here are for a 3-cup, heart-shaped mold. Coeur à la crème molds come in various sizes, starting with about a ½-cup volume. Quantities of ingredients for other molds will have to be adjusted accordingly.

2. In the bowl of an electric mixer, combine the cottage cheese, cream cheese, and sour cream. Beat until well blended.

3. Whip the heavy cream and fold it into the cheese mixture.

4. Line the mold completely with cheesecloth, letting the edges overlap the rim of the mold.

5. Spoon the cheese mixture into the mold, smoothing and packing it firmly into the mold. Fold the cheesecloth over the top. Cover with plastic wrap and refrigerate overnight.

6. Open up the cheesecloth and invert the mold onto the center of a platter. Carefully remove the cheesecloth.

7. Garnish with strawberry sauce and serve with additional strawberry sauce. Early recipes for this dessert call for eating the coeur à la crème with crème fraîche or heavy cream and a heavy sprinkling of sugar.

Yield: 10 or more servings.

STRAWBERRY SAUCE

Two 10-ounce packages frozen strawberries, or use 2 pints of fresh strawberries
½ cup sugar or more to taste
2 tablespoons framboise, kirsch, mirabelle, or other white liqueur made of berries

Empty the defrosted strawberries into the container of a food processor or blender. If fresh strawberries are used, remove the stems and rinse the berries well. Drain and put in the container of a food processor or blender. Add the sugar and blend to a fine purée. Add the framboise. Serve chilled in a sauceboat.

Yield: 2½ cups.

TRIFLE

1. Drop the peaches into boiling water for about 12 minutes. Drain immediately. Skin the peaches by pulling off the peel with a paring knife. Slice and pit the peaches. Add ½ cup of the sugar and refrigerate.

2. Rinse, hull, and drain the strawberries. Add ½ cup of the sugar and refrigerate.

3. Bring the milk just to the boil. Put the whole eggs and egg yolks in a mixing bowl. Beat until light and lemon-colored. Add the remaining ¼ cup of sugar. Pour half of the near-boiling milk over the eggs, beating vigorously. Return this mixture to the remaining milk and return the saucepan to the heat. Cook, stirring constantly this way and that over the bottom, using a wooden spoon. It may be best to use a heatproof pad under the saucepan. Cook the custard until it is slightly thickened, like thick cream, and coats the spoon. Strain the sauce into a mixing bowl. Add the vanilla, almond extract, and sherry. Chill.

4. Cut the poundcake into ½-inch-thick slices. Spread enough slices with apricot preserves to arrange the slices spread side up over the bottom and sides of a crystal bowl. Cut additional slices into convenient sizes as necessary to fill the empty spaces.

5. Add the peaches to the lined bowl and pour in the custard almost to the top. Spread any remaining poundcake slices with strawberry preserves and arrange spread side up on top of the cake. Arrange the strawberries on top of this. Pipe sweetened whipped cream over the top.

Yield: 8 to 12 servings.

2 large, ripe, unblemished peaches
1¼ cups sugar
1 cup red, ripe strawberries
2 cups milk
2 whole eggs
2 egg yolks
1½ teaspoons pure vanilla extract
¼ teaspoon almond extract
2 tablespoons medium-dry sherry
1 frozen poundcake, defrosted
¾ cup apricot preserves, approximately
½ cup strawberry or currant preserves, approximately
1 cup sweetened whipped cream

SHEER KHORMA (PISTACHIO AND ALMOND DESSERT)

1½ cups shelled pistachios

¾ cup almonds, shelled but with the skin on

⅛ pound Indian vermicelli

8 tablespoons butter

5 cups milk

¾ cup heavy cream

½ teaspoon saffron

5 tablespoons sugar

1. Place the pistachios and almonds in a mixing bowl and add cold water to cover. Let stand overnight. Drain and rub off the skins.

2. Place the nuts in the container of a food processor or blender and blend. Do not blend to a purée. The texture should be coarse-fine. Set aside.

3. Break the vermicelli sticks in half. Heat the butter in a large saucepan and add the vermicelli. Cook, stirring, until the vermicelli is nicely browned without burning. Add the milk and cream and bring to the boil. Add the pistachio mixture, saffron, and sugar. Cook, stirring often, for about 15 minutes.

Yield: 12 or more servings.

APPLE CHARLOTTE WITH CALVADOS

The spirit called applejack or Calvados is—to turn a phrase of Clifton Fadiman's to our own purposes—apples' leap into immortality. Although applejack or Calvados is delectable as a simple beverage and as a basis for many old-fashioned cocktails, it is also an excellent ingredient for cooking. It goes superbly with almost any roast made with apples. It is almost an essential for many tripe dishes, and it reaches what might be called its zenith in that butter-rich dessert called apple charlotte.

½ cup golden raisins

1 cup warm water

5 or 6 firm, ripe, slightly tart cooking apples, about 2 pounds

16 tablespoons butter

⅓ cup sugar

1 teaspoon grated lemon rind

4 tablespoons Calvados or applejack

7 slices white bread, trimmed of crusts

Crème anglaise (see following recipe) flavored with 1 tablespoon Calvados or applejack

1. Put the raisins in a mixing bowl and add the warm water to cover. Let soak for about 20 minutes. Drain.

2. Meanwhile, preheat the oven to 400 degrees.

3. Peel and core the apples. Cut them into quarters, then cut each quarter into ¼-inch-thick slices.

4. Heat 8 tablespoons of the butter in a large heavy skillet and, when it is melted, add the apple slices and sprinkle with sugar and lemon rind. Cook, stirring often without breaking up the slices, for about 10 minutes. Add half of the Calvados.

5. Cut 1 slice of bread into ½-inch cubes. Melt about 4 tablespoons of the butter and toss the bread cubes in it without browning. Add this and the raisins to the apples. Stir.

6. Meanwhile, rub the inside of a 4-cup charlotte mold with 1 tablespoon of the butter. Trim 1 slice of bread to fit the inside bottom of the mold. Butter it generously on top. Cut about 4 slices of bread into rectangles sufficient to line the inside bottom of the mold. Butter them generously on top. Cut about 4 slices of bread into rectangles sufficient to line the inside of the mold, each rectangle standing up close together but not overlapping. Butter the rectangles generously.

7. Spoon and scrape the apple mixture into the bread-lined mold.

8. Cut the remaining slice of bread into a round shape to fit inside the lined mold to neatly cover the apple filling. Butter this on both sides with the remaining butter. Fit the round of bread on top.

9. Place the mold in the oven and bake for 15 minutes.

10. Reduce the oven temperature to 350 degrees and bake for 15 minutes longer.

11. Remove from the oven and let stand for 15 minutes. Unmold the charlotte onto a round serving dish. Pour the remaining 2 tablespoons of Calvados over the mold. Serve with crème anglaise flavored with Calvados.

Yield: 8 servings.

CRÈME ANGLAISE (ENGLISH CUSTARD)

5 egg yolks
⅔ cup sugar
2 cups milk
⅛ teaspoon salt

1. Put the yolks in a saucepan and add the sugar. Beat with a wire whisk until thick and lemon-colored.

2. Meanwhile, bring the milk almost but not quite to the boil.

3. Gradually add the milk to the yolk mixture, beating constantly, this way and that, making certain that the spoon touches all over the bottom of the saucepan. Cook, stirring, and add the salt. Cook until the mixture has a custardlike consistency and coats the sides of the spoon. Do not let the sauce boil, or it will curdle.

4. Immediately remove the sauce from the stove, but continue stirring. Set the saucepan in a basin of cold water to reduce the temperature. Let the sauce cool to room temperature. Chill for an hour or longer.

Yield: 8 to 12 servings.

GINGERBREAD PUDDING
WITH DARK BEER SABAYON

1. Preheat the oven to 375 degrees.

2. Use 1 tablespoon of the butter to butter 8 small soufflé ramekins. Sprinkle equal amounts of sugar into each ramekin and shake to coat the sides.

3. Put the remaining 3 tablespoons of butter in a mixing bowl and add the teaspoon of sugar. Beat until well creamed.

4. Combine the gingersnaps and milk and stir briefly. Set aside.

5. Add the egg yolks to the creamed butter mixture.

6. Melt the chocolate over boiling water until completely soft.

7. Scrape the chocolate into the creamed mixture and stir to blend.

8. Squeeze the gingersnaps to extract any excess liquid. Add the gingersnaps, walnuts, and lemon rind to the yolk batter. Blend well.

9. Beat the egg whites until stiff. Add about one third of the egg whites to the gingersnap batter. Beat them in with a wire whisk. Add the remaining whites and fold them in with a spatula.

10. Fill each ramekin almost to the top with the soufflé mixture.

11. Place a double sheet of wax paper in a shallow roasting pan large enough to hold the ramekins. Arrange them in the pan. Add boiling water to cover the bottom of the ramekins by half an inch. Place the pan in the oven and bake for 25 to 35 minutes, or until well puffed. The puddings can stand in the oven with the heat turned off for an additional 10 minutes. Or they may be served immediately.

12. Unmold the puddings onto individual serving plates. Spoon the sabayon sauce over. Garnish, if desired, with strawberry slices.

Yield: 8 servings.

4 tablespoons butter

1 teaspoon granulated sugar plus sugar to coat the ramekins

1½ cups coarsely crumbled gingersnaps

¼ cup milk

4 eggs, separated

⅓ ounce sweet chocolate

½ cup broken walnuts

¼ teaspoon grated lemon rind

Dark beer sabayon sauce (see following recipe)

Strawberry slices for garnish, optional

DARK BEER SABAYON

4 egg yolks

2 tablespoons sugar

¾ teaspoon lemon juice

¼ cup dark beer

¼ cup whipped cream (measured after whipping)

1. It is best to make this in an unlined, round-bottom copper basin, but another metal bowl or saucepan will do.

2. Put the yolks, sugar, and lemon juice in the basin and beat rapidly with a wire whisk. Place the basin over gentle heat (you may set it in a water bath). Beat rapidly while adding the beer. Beat vigorously with a heavy whisk until the sauce is about four or five times its original volume.

3. Set the basin on a bed of ice cubes and continue beating until cold.

4. Fold in the whipped cream.

Yield: 8 servings.

MOUSSE AU CHOCOLAT (CHOCOLATE MOUSSE)

Once in a rare while, we discover a formula for a dish that seems the ultimate, the definitive, the ne plus ultra. Over the years we have printed recipes for a score or more desserts called mousse au chocolat. We are convinced that the finest chocolate mousse creation ever whipped up in our kitchen is the one printed here. As if you didn't know, *mousse* means "foam" in French. This mousse is the foamiest.

½ pound sweet chocolate

6 large eggs, separated

3 tablespoons water

¼ cup sweet liqueur such as chartreuse, amaretto, mandarine, or Grand Marnier

2 cups heavy cream

6 tablespoons sugar

Whipped cream for garnish

Grated chocolate for garnish

1. Cut the chocolate into ½-inch pieces and place the chocolate in a saucepan. Set the saucepan in hot, almost boiling water and cover. Let melt over low heat.

2. Put the yolks in a heavy saucepan and add the water. Place the saucepan over very low heat while beating vigorously and constantly with a wire whisk. Experienced cooks may do this over direct heat. It may be preferable, however, to use a metal disk such as a Flame Tamer to control the heat. In any event, when the yolks start to thicken, add the liqueur, beating constantly. Cook until the sauce achieves the consistency of a hollandaise or a sabayon, which it is. Remove from the heat.

3. Add the melted chocolate to the sauce and fold it in. Scrape the sauce into a mixing bowl.

4. Beat the cream until stiff, adding 2 tablespoons of the sugar toward the end of beating. Fold this into the chocolate mixture.

5. Beat the whites until soft peaks start to form. Beat in the remaining sugar and continue beating until stiff. Fold this into the mousse.

6. Spoon the mousse into a crystal bowl and chill until ready to serve. When ready to serve, garnish with whipped cream and grated chocolate.

Yield: 12 or more servings.

Bitter Chocolate Mousse

4½ ounces unsweetened chocolate

3 tablespoons extra strong coffee, preferably espresso

1 tablespoon cocoa powder

6 tablespoons heavy cream, optional

8 egg whites

4 tablespoons sugar

1. Combine the chocolate, coffee, and cocoa in a mixing bowl. Put the bowl in a skillet and add water to a depth of about 1 inch. Bring the water to the boil and heat, stirring the chocolate mixture occasionally, until the ingredients are blended and smooth.

2. Beat the mixture with a whisk. If the mixture does not become liquid, beat in the cream.

3. Beat the whites until stiff while gradually adding the sugar. Add half the whites to the chocolate mixture. Beat them in. Fold in the remaining whites.

4. Pour and scrape the mixture into an appropriate dish and chill thoroughly.

Yield: 4 servings.

LIME MOUSSE

1. Combine the ⅓ cup of sugar and water in a saucepan and bring to the boil, stirring until sugar dissolves.

2. Add the lime juice. Empty the gelatin into a small bowl and add enough water to moisten thoroughly. Stir this into the lime mixture. Bring to the boil, stirring, and remove from the heat. Let cool, but do not let the mixture set.

3. When the mixture is cool but still liquid, beat the cream until stiff with the remaining 2 teaspoons of sugar. Fold this into the lime mixture. Spoon into individual crystal glasses or molds. Chill until set. Serve with tangerine jelly.

Yield: 6 to 12 servings.

⅓ cup plus 2 teaspoons sugar
¼ cup water
1 cup freshly squeezed, strained lime juice
1 envelope unflavored gelatin
1 cup heavy cream
   Tangerine jelly (see following recipe)

1. Rub the tangerines all over with the sugar cubes, collecting as much skin oil on the cubes as possible.

2. Peel the tangerines. Cut the skin of two tangerines into very thin strips. Remove the sections. Carefully cut away and discard the membranous outer coating of each section. Remove and discard the seeds. Place the sections as they are prepared in a mixing bowl.

3. Pour the wine into a saucepan and add the sugar cubes and strips of tangerine peel. Add the gelatin and bring to the boil slowly, stirring constantly with a wooden spoon. Strain. Let cool.

4. Pour about 1½ cups of the liquid into the bottom of a crystal bowl. Chill until almost set. Arrange a circular pattern of tangerine sections in the center. Chill once more until set. Continue adding layers of the liquid and patterns of tangerine sections until all the ingredients are used. Chill until ready to serve.

Yield: 8 or more servings.

TANGERINE JELLY

4 fresh tangerines or tangelos
30 pieces cubed sugar (called hostess cubes)
2 cups dry white wine
1 envelope unflavored gelatin

LEMON SOUFFLÉ

2 large lemons
2 cups sugar
 Juice of 1 lemon
2 cups milk
½ cup flour
8 eggs, separated
1 tablespoon cornstarch

1. Peel the lemons with a swivel-bladed peeler, removing all the yellow but as little of the white of the skin as possible.

2. Place the rind on a board and cut it into the thinnest possible strips. Cut these strips into bits and chop them as small as possible. Put them into a mixing bowl and add 1 cup of the sugar. Mix well with the fingers. Cover and let stand for 24 hours.

3. Spoon the lemon rind and sugar mixture into a small saucepan. Add the lemon juice and bring to the boil. Simmer over low heat, stirring frequently, for about 10 minutes. Let cool, then chill well.

4. Generously butter a 9- or 10-cup soufflé dish and chill it in the freezer.

5. In a saucepan, combine the milk, flour, egg yolks, ½ cup of the sugar, and the cornstarch. Cook over low heat, stirring constantly, until thickened. Add the lemon mixture and bring just to the boil, stirring. Spoon this into a large mixing bowl and let it cool.

6. Preheat the oven to 400 degrees.

7. Beat the whites and, when they start to form peaks, gradually beat in the remaining ½ cup of sugar. Continue beating to make a stiff meringue.

8. Add one third of the whites to the lemon mixture and beat in with a whisk. Fold in the remaining whites with a plastic spatula. Pour the mixture into the prepared soufflé dish and place in the oven. Bake for 10 minutes and reduce the oven temperature to 375 degrees. Bake for 15 minutes longer. If you want the soufflé to be less moist in the center, bake for 10 minutes longer.

Yield: 6 to 8 servings.

BANANA SOUFFLÉ

1. Generously butter the inside of a 9- or 10-cup soufflé dish and put it in the freezer to chill.

2. In a mixing bowl, combine the 6 tablespoons of butter, the flour, and ½ cup of the sugar and work with the fingers to blend well. Shape into a ball.

3. Peel the bananas and cut into slices. Blend in a food processor or blender. There should be about 1½ cups. Pour the purée into a saucepan and add the milk, stirring to blend. Bring to the boil. Add the butter and flour ball, stirring constantly until thickened and smooth. Blend the cornstarch with the rum and stir it in.

4. Beat the yolks lightly, then beat them into the banana mixture. Cook, stirring rapidly, for about 30 seconds, then remove from the heat. Continue beating off heat for about 1 minute. Spoon the mixture into a mixing bowl, cover with a round of buttered wax paper, and let cool.

5. Meanwhile, preheat the oven to 375 degrees.

6. Beat the egg whites until they start to stand in peaks and gradually beat in the remaining ¾ cup of sugar. Continue beating the whites to the stiff meringue stage. Using a wire whisk, beat about a third of the whites into the soufflé mixture. Fold in the remaining whites with a rubber spatula.

7. Remove the soufflé dish from the freezer and sprinkle the inside with sugar. Shake the sugar around to coat the bottom and sides. Shake out the excess sugar. Spoon the banana mixture into the soufflé dish. As a safeguard you may want to place a baking dish or sheet of aluminum foil on the bottom of the oven to catch any drippings. Place the soufflé in the oven and bake for 15 minutes. Reduce the oven heat to 350 degrees and bake for 30 minutes longer.

Yield: 6 to 8 servings.

6 tablespoons butter
½ cup flour
1¼ cups sugar
½ pound ripe, sweet but firm bananas (about 4)
3 cups milk
1 tablespoon cornstarch
3 tablespoons dark rum, kirsch, or Cognac
8 eggs, separated

Frozen Strawberry Soufflé

3 cups sliced
   strawberries

1¼ cups plus
   3 tablespoons sugar

3 egg yolks

2 tablespoons framboise,
   mirabelle, kirsch, or
   other white spirit,
   optional

1½ cups heavy cream

3 or 4 whole and/or
   sliced strawberries for
   garnish

1. Blend the strawberries and ½ cup of the sugar in a skillet. Cook, stirring occasionally, until the sugar and the liquid from the berries thicken, about 10 minutes. Remove and let cool thoroughly.

2. Select a 2-quart mixing bowl that will fit snugly inside a larger saucepan. Add about 2 inches of water to the saucepan and bring to the simmer.

3. To the mixing bowl add the egg yolks and ¾ cup of the sugar and beat vigorously and thoroughly with a wire whisk or portable electric mixer, making certain to scrape around the inside bottom of the bowl with the beater.

4. Fit the mixing bowl inside the saucepan (over but not in the water), and continue beating. Beat for about 10 minutes or less, until the yolks are quite thick and pale yellow. Beat in the framboise. Add the berry mixture and fold it in. Chill thoroughly.

5. Whip 1 cup of the cream until stiff and fold in 2 tablespoons of the sugar. Fold this into the strawberry mixture.

6. Chill a 6- to 7-cup soufflé dish in the freezer.

7. Neatly tie a "collar" made of wax paper or aluminum foil around the soufflé dish. The top of the paper or foil should extend about 2 inches above the top of the dish.

8. Pour the soufflé mixture into the dish. Place in the freezer and let stand overnight.

9. Remove the wax paper. Whip the remaining ½ cup of cream. Beat in the remaining 1 tablespoon of sugar. If desired, outfit a pastry bag with a star tube and pipe the cream around the top in a fancy pattern. Decorate with whole and/or sliced strawberries.

Yield: 8 or more servings.

OEUFS À LA NEIGE (MERINGUES IN CUSTARD)

4	cups milk
1¼	cups granulated sugar
1	vanilla bean, or
1	teaspoon vanilla extract
6	eggs, separated
½	teaspoon cornstarch
	Pinch of salt
	Kirsch or rum (optional)
¼	cup water

1. Bring the milk to the boil in a skillet. Add 6 tablespoons of the sugar and the vanilla bean or vanilla extract. Stir to dissolve the sugar.

2. Beat the egg whites until stiff. While beating, gradually add 6 tablespoons of the sugar, the cornstarch, and the salt.

3. When the meringue is stiff, outfit a pastry bag with a star tube, number 4. Fill it with the meringue and pipe it out in a 2-inch circle onto a baking sheet. Pipe out the meringue to make layer upon layer on the bottom circle. This will produce a small, roundish "beehive" pattern or, if you prefer, a kind of rosette about 2 inches high. Continue making rosettes until all the meringue is used. The meringue is sufficient to produce 16 to 18 rosettes, or "eggs."

4. Using a metal spatula, transfer the rosettes, as many as the skillet will hold, into the milk.

5. Simmer for about 30 seconds on one side, then, using a slotted spoon, gently turn the eggs over. Poach the other side for 30 seconds.

6. Drain the eggs, which should be quite firm by now, on paper towels. Let cool while preparing the remainder of the recipe.

7. Strain the milk in which the eggs cooked. If a vanilla bean was used, remove it, rinse, and wipe dry, then store in sugar for another use.

8. Beat the egg yolks until light and lemon-colored. Gradually pour into the strained milk. Stir over low heat just until the custard coats the spoon.

9. The custard may be flavored with kirsch or rum. In any event, strain the custard into a wide, shallow serving dish and cover with the eggs. Chill.

10. Combine the remaining sugar with the ¼ cup of water in a saucepan. Cook until the caramel is dark amber in color, but do not let it burn.

11. Before the caramel has a chance to set, pour it in a thin thread all over the tops of the eggs.

Yield: 10 or more servings.

DACQUOISE

5 egg whites, about ¾ cup

9 tablespoons granulated sugar

1⅓ cups ground hazelnuts, almonds, or walnuts

Butter cream (see following recipe)

¼ cup confectioners' sugar, approximately

Dacquoise is, without question, one of the finest and most sought-after desserts in fine restaurants. One of the first places we ever encountered it was at the distinguished Coach House. One of the restaurants where we've most recently sampled it is the Windows on the World at the World Trade Center. A dacquoise is a layered meringue dessert made with hazel or other nuts, the layers put together with a rich butter cream. One of the finest dacquoises we've ever sampled was prepared in our kitchen by our good friend and master pastry chef, Albert Kumin.

1. Preheat the oven to 250 degrees.

2. Select one or two baking sheets of sufficient size so that three 9-inch circles can be traced on them without overlapping. Butter the baking sheet or sheets evenly. Sprinkle with flour and shake it around to coat the surface evenly. Shake off excess flour. Using a round-bottom 9-inch cake tin or false bottom and a pointed knife, outline three 9-inch circles over the flour-coated baking sheet.

3. Place the egg whites in the bowl of an electric mixer. Beat until they stand in peaks. Gradually beat in half of the granulated sugar. Continue beating until stiff. Blend 1 cup of the nuts and remaining granulated sugar. Fold this into the meringue.

4. Outfit a pastry bag with a number 4 star pastry tube. Add the meringue to the bag and squeeze out the meringue in a neat spiral to completely fill the three circles. Squeeze from the perimeter of each circle going toward the center or vice versa. Fill in any empty spots. Smooth over the meringue with a spatula. Do not discard any unused meringue, but squirt it out onto the baking sheet apart from the circles. This will be used later for garnish.

5. Place the baking sheet in the oven and bake for 45 minutes, or until firm and set. Remove from the oven and gently run a metal spatula beneath the meringues to loosen them while still warm. Let cool.

6. Select the nicest of the three meringue circles for the top layer. Use a metal spatula and smoothly spread one of the circles with butter cream. Add a second circle and spread it similarly. Add the top circle. Spread a light layer of butter cream over the top. Smoothly spread the sides of the dacquoise with butter cream.

7. Blend any leftover pieces of meringue to make fine crumbs. Blend these with the remaining ⅓ cup of ground nuts. Coat the sides of the cake with this and sprinkle any leftover mixture on top of the dacquoise. Sprinkle the top with confectioners' sugar.

8. Chill the dacquoise for an hour or longer to facilitate slicing. The dacquoise or leftover portions of it may be wrapped closely and frozen.

Yield: 12 or more servings.

BUTTER CREAM

6 egg whites, slightly more than ¾ cup
1¾ cups superfine sugar
1 pound sweet butter, at room temperature

1. Combine the egg whites in the bowl of an electric mixer. Set the bowl in a basin of boiling water and start beating with a wire whisk. Gradually add the sugar, beating rapidly with the whisk. Continue beating until the mixture is somewhat thickened. Ideally, the temperature for the mixture should be about 105 degrees. In any event, a "ribbon" should form when the whisk is lifted.

2. Transfer the bowl to the electric beater and start beating on high speed. Continue beating for about 20 minutes, or until the mixture is at room temperature. Gradually add the butter, beating constantly. This butter cream may be flavored variously (see flavored butter cream below).

Yield: 5 to 6 cups.

FLAVORED BUTTER CREAM

Mocha butter cream: Blend 1 tablespoon or more of instant or freeze-dried coffee with 1½ tablespoons Cognac or rum. Blend this into the butter cream.

Chocolate butter cream: Melt 3 ounces of sweet chocolate with 1 tablespoon of water and blend it into the butter cream.

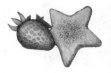

Pavlova

Butter

Flour

3 egg whites

¾ cup plus 2 tablespoons sugar

¼ teaspoon salt

1 teaspoon white vinegar

½ teaspoon pure vanilla extract

1 teaspoon cornstarch

4 kiwis or peaches, or 1 pint berries or other fruit

1 cup heavy cream

One of the most celebrated meringue desserts in the world hails, oddly enough, from Australia and New Zealand and, for some inexplicable reason, it is named for Anna Pavlova, the celebrated Russian ballerina. A Pavlova consists of a thick meringue layer served with tropical fruits (including kiwi) or berries and sweetened whipped cream.

1. Preheat the oven to 250 degrees.

2. Butter the bottom and sides of an 8- or 9-inch springform pan. Sprinkle with flour and shake to coat the bottom and sides. Shake out any excess flour.

3. Line the pan with a round of wax paper and butter the top of the paper.

4. Beat the egg whites until frothy. Continue beating while gradually adding the ¾ cup sugar and the salt. Add the vinegar and vanilla and continue beating until the meringue is stiff.

5. Sift the cornstarch over the meringue and fold it in with a rubber spatula.

6. Scrape the meringue into the prepared pan and smooth it over. Make a slight indentation extending from the center of the meringue out to about 1 inch from the sides of the pan. Build up the sides of the meringue slightly. The indentation will hold when the meringue is baked.

7. Place the pan in the oven and bake for 30 minutes. Turn off the oven heat and let the meringue rest in the oven for 1 hour longer. Remove and let stand until thoroughly cool. Unmold the meringue.

8. Peel the kiwis or peaches. Cut one of them into 10 round slices. Garnish the upper outside rim of the meringue with the slices.

9. Cut the remaining kiwis or peaches lengthwise into quarters. Cut the quarters crosswise into 1-inch pieces. Use the berries whole or sliced. Put the fruit in a bowl and add 1 tablespoon of the sugar. Stir until the sugar dissolves. Spoon this into the center of the meringue surrounded by the sliced fruit.

10. Whip the cream until frothy and add the remaining tablespoon of sugar. Continue beating until stiff. Use a pastry tube and pipe the whipped cream over the fruit. Or you may use a spatula to cover the fruit-filled meringue with the cream.

Yield: 6 to 8 servings.

PROFITEROLES (CREAM PUFFS)

There are numerous desserts in a pastrymaker's art that border on the miraculous—things that puff in the oven out of all proportion to what they were when they went in. One of the most impressive of these—and one easily within the scope of an amateur cook—is a dessert whose base is called pâte à choux in French, cream-puff paste in English. It is best known as the base for éclairs and profiteroles, or cream puffs. The pastry is piped onto a greased, floured baking sheet and baked briefly until puffed and golden brown.

1 recipe for pâte à choux (see following recipe)

1 recipe for crème patissière (see recipe page 837)

1 recipe for mocha or cocoa frosting (see following recipe)

1. Preheat the oven to 425 degrees.

2. Grease a baking sheet all over with butter and sprinkle with flour. Shake the baking sheet this way and that until the surface is coated with flour. Shake off excess.

3. Fit a pastry bag with a round tipped, number 6 pastry tube. Spoon the pâte à choux into the bag. Holding the pastry bag straight up with the tip close to the floured surface of the pan, squeeze the bag to make mounds of pastry at intervals all over the pan. There should be about 36 mounds.

4. The mounds may have pointed tips on top. To flatten these, wet a clean tea towel and squeeze it well. Open it up, fold it over in thirds. Hold it stretched directly over the mounds, quickly patting down just enough to rid the mounds of the pointed tips. Do not squash the mounds.

5. Place the pan in the oven and bake for 30 minutes, or until the cream puffs are golden brown and cooked through. Remove and let cool.

6. Outfit another pastry bag with the same number 6 pastry tube. Spoon the crème patissière into the bag. Slit a small hole in the side of each cream puff and insert the tip of the bag. Squeeze enough crème patissière into the hole to partly fill the cream puff. Decorate the top of each cream puff with frosting, using a palette knife or a pastry bag outfitted with a star tube. Chill until frosting sets.

Yield: About 36 cream puffs.

PÂTE À CHOUX (CREAM PUFF PASTE)

1 cup cold water
8 tablespoons butter
  Salt to taste
½ teaspoon sugar
1 cup flour
4 large eggs

1. Put the water in a saucepan and add the butter, salt, and sugar. Bring to the boil.

2. Add the flour all at once, stirring vigorously and thoroughly in a circular fashion with a wooden spoon until a ball is formed and the mixture cleans the sides of the saucepan.

3. Add the eggs, one at a time, beating vigorously and rapidly with the spoon until the egg is well blended with the mixture. Add another egg, beat, and so on until all 4 eggs are beaten in.

Yield: Enough cream puff paste for 36 cream puffs or 20 éclairs.

MOCHA FROSTING

2½ tablespoons butter, at room temperature
1 tablespoon powdered cocoa
1 tablespoon freeze-dried coffee or espresso
1 tablespoon boiling water
1 cup confectioners' sugar
  Pinch of salt

1. Place the butter in a small mixing bowl. Using a whisk or electric beater, start creaming the butter.

2. Add the powdered cocoa. Separately, blend the freeze-dried coffee with the boiling water.

3. Start blending the butter and cocoa and add the liquid coffee. Beat in a small pinch of salt.

4. Use as a frosting on cookies, cream puffs, and so on.

Yield: About ¾ cup.

PROFITEROLES AU CHOCOLAT

Bake the profiteroles but do not fill with pastry cream. Split them in half and scoop a small portion of ice cream onto the bottom of each cream puff. Cover with the cream puff top. Spoon the chocolate sauce over and serve immediately.

Yield: 12 or more servings

- 36 profiteroles (see preceding recipe)
- 36 small scoops of vanilla ice cream
- Chocolate sauce (see following recipe)

CHOCOLATE SAUCE

- 1 pound dark, sweet chocolate
- ⅔ cup water
- 3 tablespoons sugar
- 1 cup heavy cream
- 4 tablespoons butter

1. Break up the chocolate and put it in a saucepan. Add the water and sugar and cook, stirring as necessary, until the chocolate melts.

2. Off heat, add the cream and butter. Keep warm without boiling.

Yield: 3½ cups.

ÉCLAIRS

Follow the recipe for profiteroles (cream puffs), but rather than make mounds of pastry as indicated, pipe the pâte à choux mixture out at intervals into straight ribbons, each about 4 inches long. There should be about 20 ribbons of paste in all. Smooth over the ends of the ribbons with a spatula. Place the pan in the oven and bake for 20 minutes, or until the éclairs are golden brown and cooked through. Remove and let cool. Decorate the top of each éclair with frosting, using a palette knife or pastry bag outfitted with a star tube. Chill until frosting sets.

Yield: About 20 éclairs.

APPLE TURNOVERS

Fast puff pastry (see following recipe)

4 apples, such as McIntosh or Delicious, about 1½ pounds

2 tablespoons butter

½ cup sugar

¼ teaspoon vanilla extract

1 egg, lightly beaten

The single most complicated pastry, the one most difficult to describe with mere words, is puff pastry. It requires tedious hours of folding and chilling, and otherwise getting things together.

We have come up with what we consider a fine and far less elaborate version of puff pastry that could be referred to as *à la minute*.

The most common use for puff pastry in the French kitchen is in the preparation of mille-feuille, or thousand-leaf pastry. That is because when the pastry is rolled out and baked, it puffs into an inestimable number of flaky, thin layers, a thousand or more according to some pastry cooks.

Our hasty version of puff pastry does not shape up into that degree of puffiness, but it is rich, light, and delicate.

1. Prepare the pastry and chill as indicated in the recipe.

2. Peel the apples and quarter them. Cut away and discard the stems and cores. Cut each quarter into thin slices.

3. Melt the butter in a saucepan and add the apples and sugar. Add the vanilla, cover, and cook for about 5 minutes.

4. Roll out the chilled, folded dough on a flat, cold, floured surface. Roll it into a rectangle. Fold it like a letter.

5. Roll it out again into a thin rectangle. Using a sharp heavy knife, cut the rectangle neatly into 8 or 10 squares of approximately the same size.

6. Spoon an equal portion of the apple mixture into the center of each. Brush the edges of each square with beaten egg. Fold over one half of each square to make a triangle-shaped turnover.

7. Using the tines of a fork, press the folded-over edges to seal. As the turnovers are sealed, arrange them on a baking sheet.

8. Brush the top of each turnover with beaten egg. Make a slight slit in the top of each turnover to allow steam to escape. Refrigerate for at least 15 minutes.

9. When ready to bake, preheat the oven to 375 degrees.

10. Place the turnovers in the oven and bake for 30 to 40 minutes. Use a pancake turner or spatula and run it under the turnovers to loosen them. Serve hot or cold.

Yield: 8 to 10 turnovers.

FAST PUFF PASTRY

½ pound very cold butter
1¾ cups flour
 Salt to taste
¼ teaspoon cream of tartar
½ cup ice water

1. Cut the butter into very small cubes. Put the cubes on a plate and put the plate in the freezer. The dough may be made by hand or in the container of a food processor. It is best to chill the rolling pin before rolling out the dough.

2. If the food processor is used, put the cold butter, flour, salt to taste, and cream of tartar into the container of the processor. Work quickly. Start processing and hastily add enough water so that the dough will hold together. There will be bits of butter that are apparent in the dough.

3. If you do this by hand, combine the flour, salt, and cream of tartar on a cold, flat, smooth surface, preferably marble. Make a well in the center and add the cold butter and water. Bring the flour up to enclose and coat the butter, and start working the dough with the hands, kneading. Work rapidly to the point where the dough can be gathered together in a ball. There will be bits of butter apparent in the dough.

4. Whatever the technique used, shape the dough into a ball. Shape the ball of dough into a flat patty about 5 inches in diameter. Wrap it closely in plastic wrap and refrigerate for 15 minutes.

5. When ready to roll out the dough, sprinkle a flat cold surface with flour and lay the dough on it. Roll out the dough into a rectangle measuring roughly 18 × 12 inches. It is important that you keep the surface lightly floured as you work. Turn the pastry over once or twice as you roll it out. If the butter sticks to the surface, scrape under it with a knife, flour the surface, and continue rolling.

6. Fold one third of the rectangle toward and over the center. Brush the top and bottom of the dough with a clean, dry pastry brush to remove any excess flour. Fold down the upper third just as you would normally fold a letter before inserting it in an envelope. Brush off any excess flour top and bottom.

7. Roll the dough out into another rectangle of about the same size. Fold it a second time just as you did the first, letter-fashion. Arrange the folded dough on a lightly floured baking sheet. Cover with a clean cloth and chill for 15 to 20 minutes.

Yield: About 1 pound of pastry, or enough for 8 to 10 turnovers.

BAKED APPLES PAVILLON

5 medium to large
apples, about 2 pounds

1 cup water

½ cup sugar

2 tablespoons honey
Juice of ½ lemon

1½ cups bananas cut into
½-inch cubes, or
crushed pineapple

¼ cup chopped ginger in
syrup (sold in bottles),
or crystallized ginger,
or use an equal amount
of kumquats in syrup

2 tablespoons syrup from
the bottled ginger or
kumquats

3 cups crème patissière
(see following recipe)

2 tablespoons dark rum

3 tablespoons crumbs
made from ladyfingers
or spongecake

Years ago, when Le Pavillon was in its heyday as a restaurant of splendor and excellence, the pastry chef's baked apples occupied a place alongside the chilled oeufs à la neige, the mousses au chocolat, and the gateaux St. Honoré on the cold dessert display. These were apple halves poached in syrup, filled with fruits, and then topped with pastry cream and baked—not the sort of baked apples likely to be found in a roadside diner.

1. Peel the apples and split them in half. Using a melon ball cutter, scoop out the core of each apple. Trim away and discard the stem line leading from the core.

2. Combine the water, sugar, honey, and lemon juice in a skillet large enough to hold the apple halves in one layer. Add the apple halves and cook, turning gently once or twice so that the apples cook evenly. Poach them for 5 to 8 minutes, until just cooked. Do not overcook or they will become mushy.

3. Let the apple halves cool. Drain them upside down on a rack, but do not discard the cooking syrup.

4. Preheat the oven to 450 degrees.

5. Put the cubed bananas, chopped ginger, and ginger syrup in a saucepan. Add ½ cup of the syrup in which the apples cooked. Bring to the boil and remove from the heat. Let cool. It will thicken slightly as it stands.

6. Arrange the apple halves cored side up on a baking dish large enough to hold them in one layer.

7. Spoon equal portions of the fruit mixture into and over the center of each apple half.

8. Blend the crème patissière with the rum and ½ cup of the reserved syrup from the cooked apples.

9. Spoon the crème patissière over the filled apple halves. Sprinkle with the crumbs.

10. Place in the oven and bake for 15 to 20 minutes. Serve hot or lukewarm.

Yield: 10 servings.

1. Blend 1 cup of the milk and the cream in a saucepan and bring to the boil.

2. As the liquid is heating, put the egg yolks and sugar into a mixing bowl and beat until pale yellow. Add the cornstarch to the yolk mixture and beat well. Add the remaining ½ cup of milk and beat until blended.

3. When the milk and cream are at the boil, remove from the heat. Add the yolk mixture, beating rapidly with a wire whisk.

4. Return to the heat and bring to the boil, stirring constantly with the whisk. When thickened and at the boil, remove from the heat and let cool, stirring occasionally.

Yield: About 3 cups.

CRÈME PATISSIÈRE (PASTRY CREAM)

1½ cups milk
½ cup heavy cream
4 egg yolks
½ cup sugar
3 tablespoons cornstarch

APPLE CRISP

1½ cups brown sugar
1 cup flour
12 tablespoons butter
6 to 8 cooking apples, about 3 pounds
¼ teaspoon ground cinnamon
¼ teaspoon grated nutmeg
Grated rind of 1 lemon
Juice of ½ lemon

1. Preheat the oven to 375 degrees.
2. Combine the sugar, flour, and butter in a mixing bowl and mix well with the fingers. Set aside.
3. Peel, quarter, and core the apples. Cut the apple quarters into thin slices and place the slices in a bowl. Blend the cinnamon and nutmeg and sprinkle over the apples. Sprinkle with lemon rind. Add the lemon juice and toss with the hands to blend.
4. Arrange the slices in a not-too-shallow baking dish. Cover with the butter and sugar mixture, smoothing it over.
5. Place the dish in the oven. (If the ingredients are close to brimming over, place a pan under the dish to catch the overflow.) Bake for 1 hour.

Yield: 8 servings.

BANANAS IN GINGER SYRUP

3 or 4 bananas, about 1½ pounds
½ teaspoon ground ginger
¼ cup sugar
⅓ cup water
2 tablespoons lemon juice

1. Peel the bananas and cut them into ¼-inch-thick rounds. There should be about 3½ cups. Arrange half of the rounds close together on a flat plate. Sprinkle lightly with half of the ginger. Cover with the remaining slices and sprinkle with the remaining ginger.
2. Combine the sugar and water in a small saucepan and bring to the boil, stirring constantly until the sugar is dissolved. Add the lemon juice. Cook for 15 minutes and pour the syrup over the bananas. Let stand until cool. Chill.

Yield: 4 to 6 servings.

BING CHERRIES WITH LIQUEURS

Rinse the cherries and drain well. Place in a bowl and pour the liqueurs over them.

Yield: 8 or more servings.

2½ quarts Bing cherries with stem

⅔ cup cassis syrup, available in wine and spirits shops

⅓ cup framboise, available in wine and spirits shops

MANGO SLICES WITH CHAMPAGNE

1. Peel the mangoes. Run a knife around the perimeter of the mangoes all the way to the pit. Use a large kitchen spoon and, starting at one end, carefully push the spoon's blade around the large pit of the fruit. Repeat on the other half of the mangoes. Discard the pit.

2. Cut the mango flesh into strips. Place the strips in a bowl and sprinkle with sugar. Add the framboise and chill. Spoon the fruit and liquid into 6 serving dishes and add Champagne (or any good dry white wine) to taste.

Yield: 6 servings.

3 very ripe but firm mangoes

½ cup confectioners' sugar

¼ cup framboise

Chilled Champagne

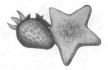

ORANGES WITH ZEST IN GRAND MARNIER SAUCE

4 unblemished, seedless oranges

½ cup water

¾ cup sugar

¼ cup orange liqueur, such as Grand Marnier or Mandarine

1. Using a swivel-bladed vegetable peeler, cut off the yellow skin of the oranges.

2. Stack the pieces of skin and, using a heavy sharp knife, cut the skin into very thin julienne strips. There should be about ¾ cup loosely packed.

3. Slice off the ends of each orange. Squeeze the juice from the end pieces and set aside.

4. Peel the oranges, removing all trace of the white pith. Set the oranges aside.

5. Combine the water, sugar, squeezed juice, and orange strips in a shallow skillet. Bring to the boil and cook for 5 minutes. Add the liqueur.

6. Arrange the oranges in a smaller saucepan and pour the syrup over them. Cover closely and cook for about 5 minutes. Turn the oranges occasionally so that they cook on all sides.

7. Remove the oranges to a platter. Cook the sauce down to about half. Strain the sauce over the oranges. Garnish the top of each orange with equal amounts of the cooked rind.

Yield: 4 servings.

BUCKWHEAT CRÊPES WITH GLAZED FRUITS

1. Preheat the oven to 350 degrees.
2. Lightly butter the bottom of a 7-inch crêpe pan. When quite hot, add 2 or 3 tablespoons of the crêpe batter. Swirl the pan around to coat the bottom of the pan evenly. Let cook until lightly browned on the bottom, about 20 seconds. Turn and cook about 15 seconds on the second side and turn out onto a platter. Continue until 12 to 16 crêpes are made.
3. Lay out 1 crêpe at a time on a flat surface. Spread each crêpe with an equal portion of glazed fruit butter. Reserve a small portion of butter for the top of the crêpes when they are all filled and arranged on the dish. Make a row of about 2 tablespoons of the orange sections down each crêpe, but reserve ½ cup of orange sections for a top garnish. Roll each crêpe as it is prepared and arrange them uniformly and close together on a heatproof baking dish. Scatter the remaining orange sections on top.
4. Dot the top of the crêpes with the reserved fruit butter. Pour the ½ cup of drained liquid from the glazed fruit over the filled crêpes.
5. Place the baking dish in the oven and bake for 10 minutes, or until the crêpes are bubbling and piping hot.

Yield: 4 to 8 servings.

- 1½ cups buckwheat crêpe batter (see following recipe)
- 12 to 16 tablespoons glazed fruit butter (see following recipe)
- 2 cups drained, seedless orange sections, preferably made from blood oranges
- ½ cup liquid from glazed fruits (see following recipe)

BUCKWHEAT CRÊPE BATTER

- 4 tablespoons butter
- 1 cup milk
- ¼ cup buckwheat flour
- ¾ cup all-purpose flour
  Salt
- ¾ teaspoon sugar
- 2 eggs
- 1 teaspoon peanut, vegetable, or corn oil
- ½ cup beer

1. Heat the butter and milk in a saucepan until the butter is melted. Stir and let cool.
2. Sift together the buckwheat flour and all-purpose flour into a mixing bowl. Add the salt, sugar, and eggs. Add the oil.
3. Stir the mixture with a wire whisk or wooden spoon. Add the milk and butter mixture gradually, stirring constantly. Stir in the beer.
4. If the mixture is lumpy, strain it through a sieve. Chill until ready to use. Leftover batter may be covered and refrigerated for later use.

Yield: About 2½ cups, or enough for 40 or more crêpes.

GLAZED FRUIT BUTTER

3 to 4 glazed fruits such as clementines or kumquats packed in syrup (see note)

8 tablespoons butter

2 teaspoons sugar

1. Remove the fruits from their packing liquid. Squeeze each fruit to remove any excess interior liquid. Put the fruits on a flat surface and chop fine. There should be ⅓ cup or slightly more. Reserve the liquid for filled crêpes.

2. Cut the butter into pieces and blend with the chopped fruits. Add the sugar and blend well.

Yield: About ¾ cup, or enough for 12 to 16 crêpes.

Note: Although almost any fruit packed in syrup is suitable for this recipe, Alice Waters of Chez Panisse prefers imported clementines packed in "eau de Provence." These are sold in specialty shops where fine imported produce is available.

SOUTHERN AMBROSIA

1. Peel the oranges. Slice them or section them with a knife. Put them in a crystal bowl.
2. Crack the coconut and remove the meat. Pare away the dark skin and finely grate the pulp. Add to the bowl and mix gently.
3. Sprinkle with confectioners' sugar and chill until ready to serve.

Yield: 6 servings.

Note: Some people add cubed bananas to the ambrosia; others add pineapple cubes, and some add a final garnish of whipped cream, but this last step is not appropriate.

4 large, heavy, sweet seedless oranges
1 fresh coconut
⅓ cup confectioners' sugar, more or less to taste

PEARS POACHED IN WHITE WINE

1. Peel and core the pears and cut each of them into eighths. Place the pears in a saucepan and add the wine and sugar.
2. Peel the lemon and cut the peel into very fine, julienne strips. Reserve the lemon for another use. Add the peel to the saucepan. Bring to the boil and simmer for 5 to 10 minutes, or until the pears are tender. Transfer the pears and lemon peel to a serving dish.
3. Bring the liquid in the saucepan to the boil and add the remaining ingredients. Bring to boil and cook for about 10 minutes. Pour the sauce over the pears. Let cool and chill.

Yield: 6 servings.

2½ pounds fresh, ripe, unblemished pears
2 cups dry white wine
½ cup sugar
1 lemon
One 2-inch length of cinnamon, or ¼ teaspoon ground
One 1-inch length vanilla, or 1 teaspoon vanilla extract
¼ cup orange marmalade
¼ cup apricot preserves

Spiced Pears

6 ripe, firm, unblemished pears, preferably Anjou, about 1½ pounds

4 cups dry red wine, preferably Burgundy

¾ cup honey

1 bay leaf

½ teaspoon whole black peppercorns

2 whole cloves

One 2-inch piece cinnamon stick

1. Remove the core from each of the pears, but leave the stem intact. Peel the pears.

2. Combine the wine, honey, bay leaf, peppercorns, cloves, and cinnamon in a saucepan. Bring to the boil.

3. Add the pears and cook, uncovered, for 45 minutes, or until the pears are tender. Remove from the heat. Let the pears cool in their cooking liquid. Cover and chill for several hours.

Yield: 6 servings.

Pears Stuffed with Gorgonzola

6 large pears, about ½ pound each

12 very thin slices of fresh ginger

1 cup dry white wine

½ cup water

3 tablespoons sugar

Juice of ½ lemon

½ pound Gorgonzola cheese, at room temperature

⅔ cup pistachio nuts

1. Peel the pears but leave the stems intact.

2. Neatly slice off the stem end of the pears about a third of the way down. Reserve both the base and top of the pears.

3. Using a melon ball scoop, scoop out the core, leaving a neat round cavity for stuffing.

4. Arrange the pear bottoms in a heavy casserole and replace the tops. Scatter the ginger around the pears and add the wine and water. Sprinkle with sugar and lemon juice. Cover with a tight-fitting lid and cook for about 10 minutes, or until tender but firm.

5. Mash the Gorgonzola with a fork until it is softened. Remove the pears from the casserole. Stuff the cavity of each pear with equal amounts of cheese. Replace the tops and set aside.

6. Cook down the liquid in the casserole until it is reduced to about ¼ cup.

7. Chop the pistachios. Dip the bottom of each pear in the syrup, then in pistachios. Return the pears, stem side up, to the casserole and spoon any remaining sauce over the pears. Add the remaining pistachios to the syrup and serve while still warm.

Yield: 6 servings.

PEARS IN CARAMEL SYRUP

1. Peel the pears, leaving the stem on. As each pear is peeled, drop it into water with lemon juice added to prevent discoloration.

2. Measure 3 cups of water into a saucepan and add 1 cup of the sugar. Bring to the boil and add the pears. Cook the pears in the liquid, turning them gently on occasion, until they are tender but firm, about 20 minutes. Carefully remove the pears and reserve the syrup. Arrange the pears neatly on a serving dish.

3. Pour 1 cup of the reserved syrup into a saucepan and add the remaining 1 cup of sugar. Bring to the boil. Cook for 5 to 10 minutes, until the syrup starts to caramelize, shaking the saucepan in a circular fashion. When quite brown but not burned, quickly remove the saucepan from the heat and add the remaining syrup. Bring to the boil again and add the coffee liqueur. Pour the sauce over the pears and chill. Serve cold with whipped cream if desired.

Yield: 8 servings.

8 firm, unblemished, ripe Comice or Anjou pears

Juice of 1 lemon

2 cups sugar

⅓ cup coffee liqueur

Whipped cream, optional

PINEAPPLE FRITTERS WITH APRICOT SAUCE

Dessert fritters offer a nice change from pies, ice creams, and other expected fare at the end of each meal. They benefit from a quickly made sauce, and we offer an excellent one made with apricot preserves.

1. Cut the pineapple rings into quarters.

2. Heat the oil to 350 degrees. Dip one piece of pineapple at a time in the batter and add it to the hot oil. Cook, turning once or twice, until the fritters are puffed and browned.

3. As the fritters are cooked, drain well on paper towels. Continue cooking until all the pineapple pieces are fried. If the batter becomes thin, it is due to the liquid given up by the fruit. You may thicken it by stirring in a little more flour.

4. Before serving, sprinkle the fritters with confectioners' sugar, using a small sieve. Serve with apricot sauce spooned over.

Yield: 8 or more servings.

8 pineapple rings

Corn, peanut, or vegetable oil for deep-fat frying

3½ cups fritter batter (see following recipe)

¼ cup confectioners' sugar

1¼ cups apricot sauce (see following recipe)

FRITTER BATTER FOR FRUIT

1¾ cups flour
1 egg
1 tablespoon sugar
Salt to taste
1 tablespoon corn, peanut, or vegetable oil
1 cup beer, at room temperature
¼ cup water
½ cup egg whites (about 4)

1. Combine the flour, egg, sugar, salt, and oil in a mixing bowl. Start blending with a wire whisk. Add the beer and water and continue beating until smooth.
2. Beat the whites until stiff and fold them in.

Yield: About 3½ cups.

APRICOT SAUCE

1 cup apricot preserves
¼ cup water
2 tablespoons kirsch, optional

1. Put the apricot preserves in a saucepan and add the water. Stir, over medium heat, until blended.
2. Put the sauce through a sieve. Return the sauce to the saucepan and reheat. Add the kirsch and serve.

Yield: About 1¼ cups.

FRESH RHUBARB WITH GRAPEFRUIT JUICE

2 pounds fresh rhubarb
¼ cup freshly squeezed or bottled fresh grapefruit juice
1½ cups sugar

1. Trim off and discard the ends of the rhubarb. By all means discard the leaves. If the rhubarb is not very young and tender, use a swivel-bladed potato scraper and scrape the outside. It is also easy to pull off the outer coating like sugar cane.
2. Cut the rhubarb stalks into 1½-inch lengths and combine the pieces in a saucepan with the grapefruit juice and sugar. Boil for 2 to 5 minutes, or just until tender. Do not overcook or it will become mush.
3. Let cool, then chill thoroughly.

Yield: 6 servings.

STRAWBERRY SHORTCAKE

1. Preheat the oven to 450 degrees.
2. Put the flour, baking powder, and granulated sugar into a sifter. Sift the mixture into a mixing bowl.
3. Add the butter and work with the fingers until well blended. Make a well in the center and add the sour cream, eggs, and vanilla. Blend well with the fingers.
4. Turn out the dough onto a lightly floured board and knead briefly.
5. Roll out the dough on a lightly floured surface into a circle about 12 inches in diameter and about ½ inch thick. Using a biscuit cutter about 3 inches in diameter, cut the dough into rounds. As the rounds are cut, arrange them on an ungreased baking sheet an inch or so apart. Gather up the remaining scraps of dough and roll out. Cut out more rounds. Continue rolling and cutting until all the dough is used. There should be 12 to 16 rounds.
6. Place in the oven and bake for 15 minutes.
7. Meanwhile, pick over the strawberries. Pick out 12 to 16 perfect, unstemmed berries and set them aside. Remove and discard the stems from the remaining berries and cut them in half. There should be about 4½ cups. Put the berries in a bowl.
8. Add the lemon juice and superfine sugar and blend well. Cover and refrigerate.
9. Split the biscuits in half. Arrange half of them on a serving dish.
10. Whip the heavy cream.
11. Using a pastry bag and star tube, pipe stars of whipped cream around the inside rim of each biscuit half. Fill the inside of the ring with the sweetened strawberry halves. Top each serving with the remaining biscuit halves. Pipe whipped cream around the inside rim of each. Fill the centers with more of the sweetened strawberries. Garnish each serving with 1 of the reserved whole strawberries.

Yield: 6 to 8 servings.

THE BISCUITS:

- 2½ cups unbleached flour
- 2 tablespoons baking powder
- 2 tablespoons granulated sugar
- 12 tablespoons butter, cut into small pieces
- 1 cup sour cream
- 2 large eggs, lightly beaten
- 1 teaspoon pure vanilla extract

THE ASSEMBLY:

- 4 pints strawberries
- 2 tablespoons fresh lemon juice
- ½ cup superfine sugar
- 2 cups heavy cream

EUGÉNIE

1 pint red, ripe
strawberries, plus
6 more for garnish

4 tablespoons kirsch or
framboise

3 cups heavy cream

5 tablespoons sugar

2 envelopes unflavored
gelatin

¼ cup cold water

1. Pick over the berries and hull them. Rinse well and drain. Pat dry.

2. Cut 1 pint of berries into eighths and place in a bowl. Add 1 table-spoon of the kirsch and set aside.

3. Lightly butter an 8-cup soufflé dish. Refrigerate.

4. Start beating the cream with a wire whisk or electric beater and, as it starts to stiffen, gradually beat in 3 tablespoons of the sugar. Continue beating the cream until stiff.

5. Soften the gelatin and water in a small saucepan and heat, stirring, until the gelatin dissolves. Scrape this into a large mixing bowl and add the remaining kirsch and 1 cup of the whipped cream, stirring rapidly with a whisk to blend well. Beat in the remaining 2 tablespoons of sugar and stir in the strawberries.

6. Add the remaining cream and fold it in with a rubber spatula. Spoon into the prepared mold. Refrigerate for several hours, or until set.

7. When ready to serve, dip the mold into a basin of hot water. Remove, dip again. Remove and dip a third time. Place a round serving dish over the mold, invert the dish and unmold the Eugénie. Garnish with the remaining strawberries, left whole or cut in half.

Yield: 10 to 12 servings.

MACEDOINE DE FRUITS (A MIXED FRUIT DESSERT)

1. Combine all the fruits in a mixing bowl and sprinkle with sugar. Blend well. Chill until ready to serve.
2. When ready to serve, add the Cognac, kirsch, and Grand Marnier. Stir to blend and serve immediately.

Yield: About 6 servings.

1½ cups seedless grapes

1½ cups peeled, seeded peaches cut into wedges

1½ cups peeled, diced apples

1½ cups seedless orange sections

1½ cups peeled pears cut into wedges

5 tablespoons confectioners' sugar

3 tablespoons Cognac

3 tablespoons kirsch

3 tablespoons Grand Marnier

PERSIAN FRUIT MÉLANGE

1 honeydew melon

1 cantaloupe

1 pint strawberries, stemmed

2 tablespoons slivered almonds

¼ cup chopped, skinless pistachios

1 cup seedless grapes

2 tablespoons rosewater

1½ cups orange juice, sweetened to taste

½ cup kirsch

Rosewater is a clear, highly aromatic flavoring that smells strongly of roses. It is much used in Middle Eastern cookery, particularly desserts, such as this Persian fruit mélange.

1. Split the honeydew melon and the cantaloupe in half and scoop out the seeds. Using a melon ball cutter, scoop out the flesh of both melons into a serving bowl.

2. Rinse the berries under cold running water and pat dry. Add them to the bowl. Add the remaining ingredients and mix gently but thoroughly.

Yield: 8 servings.

NEW YEAR'S EVE FRUIT COMPOTE

4 pounds mixed dried fruit, including, preferably, equal amounts of prunes, pears, peaches, and apples

Three 17-ounce jars Kadota figs in syrup

2 pounds (drained weight) fresh or canned dark sweet pitted cherries, about 4 cups

Sugar to taste

1 cup or more Armagnac or Cognac

4 to 6 bananas, peeled and sliced

2 cups fresh berries, such as blueberries, strawberries, or raspberries

1. If the dried fruit has pits, cut away and remove them. Cut all the fruit in half and add to a kettle or casserole. Add water to cover and bring to the boil. Simmer for 20 minutes. Let cool.

2. Pour the fruit and the cooking liquid into a mixing bowl. Cut the figs in half and add them along with their syrup to the fruit in the bowl. Add the cherries and sugar to taste. Add the Armagnac to taste.

3. Cover closely and refrigerate for at least 24 hours to ripen. When ready to serve, add the sliced bananas and berries. Add more sugar and Armagnac, if desired.

Yield: 30 servings.

HONEY BROWNIES

1. Preheat the oven to 325 degrees.
2. Melt the butter and chocolate over low heat in a heavy saucepan.
3. Beat the eggs and salt in a mixing bowl until thick and pale yellow. Add the sugar and honey gradually, beating until the mixture is light in texture.
4. Add the melted chocolate and butter and vanilla. Stir in the flour. Add the nuts. Pour the mixture into a 9-inch square pan and bake for 45 minutes, or until done. Cut into squares when cool.

Yield: About 16 brownies.

4	tablespoons butter
4	squares (ounces) unsweetened chocolate
4	eggs
½	teaspoon salt
1	cup sugar
1	cup honey
1	teaspoon vanilla extract
1	cup plus 2 tablespoons sifted flour
1	cup chopped pecans or walnuts

CHOCOLATE FUDGE COOKIES

1. Preheat the oven to 350 degrees.
2. Put the butter in a saucepan with a heavy bottom. Place the saucepan over very low heat and let stand until the butter melts. Add the grated chocolate, corn syrup, sugar, and vanilla. Stir occasionally with a wire whisk until the chocolate melts.
3. Remove from the heat and let stand for 10 minutes. Add the egg and blend well.
4. Sift together the flour, baking soda, and salt. Add it to the chocolate mixture and blend well. Scrape the mixture into a mixing bowl.
5. Line a baking sheet with a length of wax paper. Cover this with a sheet of aluminum foil.
6. Spoon 1 tablespoon of the mixture at 2-inch intervals over the foil.
7. Place in the oven and bake for 10 to 15 minutes, watching carefully that the cookies do not burn on the bottom. It may be necessary to turn the baking sheet and to shift it to a higher position in the oven to prevent burning.
8. Turn off the oven heat and open the oven door. Let the cookies rest in the oven for 5 minutes. Remove and transfer the cookies to a rack to cool.

Yield: About 2 dozen cookies.

¼	pound butter
5	ounces (5 squares) unsweetened chocolate, grated
¼	cup dark corn syrup
⅓	cup sugar
1	teaspoon vanilla extract
1	extra large egg
1	cup sifted flour
½	teaspoon baking soda
⅛	teaspoon salt, if desired

Mint Surprise Cookies

¼ pound butter

½ cup granulated sugar

¼ cup brown sugar

1 egg

1½ teaspoons water

½ teaspoon vanilla extract

1½ cups flour

½ teaspoon baking soda

½ teaspoon salt

24 thin, chocolate-covered mints, approximately

24 walnut halves, approximately

1. All of the ingredients should be at room temperature. Cream the butter and gradually add the granulated sugar, then the brown sugar. Beat in the egg, water, and vanilla.

2. Sift together the flour, baking soda, and salt. Blend into the butter mixture. Wrap in wax paper and chill for at least 2 hours.

3. Preheat the oven to 375 degrees.

4. Enclose each thin mint with about 1 tablespoon of the dough. The mints may be cut in half for a smaller cookie. Place on a cookie sheet that has been greased or lined with baking parchment. Top each cookie with a walnut half. Bake in the oven for 10 to 12 minutes, until lightly browned. Let stand a minute or so, then remove and cool on a cake rack.

Yield: About 24 cookies.

Greek Easter Cookies

½ cup sweet butter, at room temperature

½ cup confectioners' sugar

1 egg

¼ cup heavy cream

2 tablespoons orange liqueur, or brandy

3 cups flour

½ teaspoon salt

1 teaspoon baking powder

1 egg yolk

Sesame seeds

1. Preheat the oven to 350 degrees.

2. In a bowl, cream the butter and add the sugar. Beat until creamy. Add the egg, cream, and orange liqueur and beat the mixture for 5 minutes.

3. In another bowl sift together the flour, salt, and baking powder and blend into the butter mixture, ½ cup at a time, to form a soft dough.

4. Form the dough into 1½-inch balls and shape into twists. Brush the twists with egg yolk and sprinkle with sesame seeds. Place on cookie sheets and bake for 30 minutes, or until they turn a light golden color.

Yield: About 48 cookies.

POLVORONES, SEVILLE STYLE

1. Preheat the oven to 300 degrees.
2. Cream the butter until it is light-colored and fluffy, using an electric mixer or food processor.
3. Beat together the egg yolk and the 1 tablespoon of the confectioners' sugar. Add the Cognac and beat once more. Add this to the butter while beating. Scrape this mixture into a bowl.
4. Sift together the flour and cinnamon.
5. Fold the flour mixture into the egg mixture, using a rubber spatula. The dough will be a little sticky.
6. Using floured hands, shape the dough into ovals measuring about 2 inches long and ½ inch high. Arrange the ovals on an ungreased baking sheet. The dough should be enough to make about 20 cookies.
7. Place the cookies in the oven and bake for about 30 minutes. The cookies should not brown. Let cool for 2 or 3 minutes.
8. Sift 1 cup of the confectioners' sugar onto a sheet of wax paper. Reserve the remainder. Roll the warm cookies in the sugar to coat them thoroughly. Let the cookies stand until thoroughly cool. Arrange them on a dessert dish and sift the remaining confectioners' sugar over them.

Yield: About 20 cookies.

½ pound butter, at room temperature

1 egg yolk

1 tablespoon confectioners' sugar

1 tablespoon Cognac

2 cups sifted flour

½ teaspoon ground cinnamon

2 cups, approximately, confectioners' sugar for coating

TULIPES (FREE-FORM DESSERT CUPS)

6 tablespoons butter plus butter for brushing the baking sheet

¼ cup sugar

½ cup sifted flour

½ teaspoon pure vanilla extract

2 egg whites

One of the most delicate, elegant, and yet easily made of French pastries is something known in the pastry chef's kitchen as tulipes. They are fragile, brittle, wafer-thin cups into which a multitude of good things go. The fillings may consist of one or more scoops of sherbet or ice cream, either a single flavor or several; a fine layer of irresistible pastry cream topped with fresh fruits or berries, and perhaps a dusting of confectioners' sugar, and so on.

1. Preheat the oven to 425 degrees.

2. Put the 6 tablespoons of butter and sugar into a mixing bowl and beat with a wire whisk or an electric mixer until light and creamy.

3. Beat in the flour and vanilla.

4. Beat the egg whites until they stand in soft peaks. Fold the whites into the creamed mixture.

5. Select a baking sheet large enough to fit neatly in the oven. Brush the top surface with butter.

6. Using a mixing or other round bowl that is 5 inches in diameter, invert it onto the baking sheet and trace a circle in the light butter coating. Make as many separately traced circles as possible; you may be able to get only two or three to a sheet.

7. Spoon 1 or 2 tablespoons of the batter into the center of each circle. Carefully smooth the batter into one very thin layer, less than ⅛ inch thick, to cover the circle. Continue filling the circles.

8. Place the baking sheet in the oven and bake for 3 to 3½ minutes, watching carefully that the pastries do not burn. Remove the sheet from the oven and immediately lift up the circles one at a time, carefully shaping them while hot (place the brown bottom side up) in the center of a cup (a regular-shape rounded coffee cup or Chinese soup or rice bowl is suitable). When pushed into the center, the edges should be neatly fluted or ruffled. Let cool and remove from the mold. Continue until all the cups are baked and shaped.

Yield: 10 to 12 free-form dessert cups.

Tulipes aux Fraises (Dessert Pastries with Strawberries)

1. Arrange 1 dessert cup on each of 10 or 12 plates.
2. Spoon an equal portion of the pastry cream in the center of each cup. Garnish the top of the pastry cream decoratively with 3 strawberries.
3. Hold a small sieve over the top of each serving and add a little confectioners' sugar. Sprinkle the tops with sugar.

Yield: 10 to 12 servings.

Note: One may substitute almost any fresh fruit or berry in season as a garnish for the tops of these desserts. Use raspberries, peaches, seedless grapes, and so on, according to choice.

10 to 12 free-form dessert cups (see preceding recipe)

2½ cups pastry cream (see recipe page 837)

30 to 36 ripe strawberries, stems removed (see note)

Confectioners' sugar for garnish

Centimes (Meringue and Almond Cookies)

1. Preheat the oven to 350 degrees.
2. Melt the butter over gentle heat. Let it cool.
3. Put the egg whites in the bowl of an electric mixer and beat until frothy but not stiff.
4. Gradually add the confectioners' sugar to the egg whites, beating on high speed.
5. Blend the flour and almonds. Fold them into the meringue, using a rubber or plastic spatula. Fold in the melted butter and vanilla.
6. Butter 1 or 2 baking sheets. Outfit a pastry bag with a round No. 4 tube. Fill the pastry bag with the meringue mix and push small mounds onto the baking sheet, about 1 teaspoon at a time. The mounds should be about 2 inches apart. Tap the baking sheet against a flat surface so that the mounds flatten somewhat. Sprinkle the tops lightly with granulated sugar.
7. Place the baking sheets in the oven and bake for 10 minutes, or until the mounds are not sticky throughout.

Yield: About 36 cookies.

5⅓ tablespoons butter

3 egg whites

¾ cup confectioners' sugar

½ cup flour

⅓ cup blanched, grated almonds

½ teaspoon vanilla extract

¼ cup granulated sugar

TOZZETTI OR BISCOTTI (HAZELNUT COOKIES)

2 cups flour

1⅓ cups sugar

2 large eggs

1 tablespoon grated lemon rind

¼ cup anise-flavored liqueur such as Sambuca

¼ cup rum

1½ cups peeled, blanched hazelnuts, or whole or slivered almonds

2 teaspoons baking powder

Whenever one travels for mostly gatronomic reasons, some dishes will be indelibly etched in the mind. Others will demand a few bites and then be forever lost to memory. On one trip through Italy, we sampled many desserts. In retrospect, one that remains entrenched in our memories is the fine hazelnut cookies we were served in the home of Jo and Roberto Bettoja in Rome. These cookies are prepared in many places throughout the world, including Little Italy in New York. Generally, they are made of almonds. Traditionally, they are dipped into a sweet wine before eating. They are also delicious when brushed with a little anise-flavored liqueur.

1. Preheat the oven to 350 degrees.

2. Lightly oil a large baking pan and dust with flour. Shake off excess flour.

3. Combine the flour, sugar, eggs, lemon rind, liqueur, and rum in a mixing bowl and beat with a wooden spoon until thoroughly blended.

4. Beat in the hazelnuts and baking powder.

5. Using the hands, pick up half the dough and shape it into a long sausage shape. Arrange it on the prepared baking pan, off center and not too close to the edge of the pan. Arrange the other half alongside but not too close. Both masses will spread as they bake.

6. Place in the oven and bake for 1 hour. Remove the pan and let cool for about 20 minutes.

7. Carefully and gently run a spatula or pancake turner under the two pastries. Let stand until almost at room temperature. Using a serrated bread knife, cut each pastry into crosswise slices, each about 1 inch thick. Arrange these in one layer on a baking sheet and return to the oven to dry out, about 10 minutes. Let cool and store. These cookies are improved if a little anisette or other anise-flavored liqueur is poured or brushed over them in advance of serving.

Yield: About 36 cookies.

ALMOND MACAROONS

1. Preheat the oven to 325 degrees.

2. Cut the almond paste into ½-inch pieces and place in the container of a food processor fitted with a steel blade.

3. Add the sugar, two egg whites, almond extract, and salt. Blend well until smooth and no lumps remain in the almond paste.

4. The mixture should be soft but not loose. If it seems too stiff, add the remaining egg white to a mixing bowl and beat lightly. Add it, a little at a time, to the almond mixture. Blend after each addition.

5. Spoon and scrape the mixture into a bowl and beat with a wooden spoon.

6. Cut a rectangle of brown paper (from a grocery bag) to fit a cookie sheet. Drop the dough by spoonfuls onto the paper, flattening the mounds lightly with the back of a spoon. Place them about 1½ inches apart. If desired, the paste may be squeezed from a pastry bag onto the sheet. Bake for 30 minutes, or until lightly browned.

7. Cool on a rack. To remove the macaroons, dampen the bottom of the baking paper. Continue dampening slowly and lightly until the macaroons loosen easily.

Yield: 18 or more macaroons, depending on size.

Note: Almond paste is available in cans in fancy food markets and many supermarkets. Do not use almond pastry filling for macaroons.

½ pound almond paste (see note)

1 cup granulated sugar

2 or 3 egg whites

¼ teaspoon almond extract

⅛ teaspoon salt

TUILES D'AMANDE (ALMOND COOKIES)

1 cup chopped almonds
½ cup sugar
3 tablespoons flour
1 large egg
1 teaspoon vanilla
  extract

1. Preheat the oven to 375 degrees.

2. The texture of the almonds must not be too fine. The coarseness of the pieces should be like that of rice.

3. Place the almonds in a bowl and add the remaining ingredients. Blend well.

4. Grease a baking sheet with butter and sprinkle with flour. Shake off excess flour. Spoon about 1½ teaspoons of the mixture onto the prepared sheet. There should be about 32 mounds with about 2 inches of space between each. Flatten each spoonful with the tines of a dampened fork.

5. Place in the oven and bake for 8 to 10 minutes, or until golden brown. Do not let them become too dark.

6. Immediately remove them and place them top side down in a small round ring mold. The purpose of this is to give each tile a slightly curved shape. Let cool briefly and turn out onto a flat surface. Let cool and serve.

Yield: 32 cookies.

SWISS WALNUT FINGERS

1. Preheat the oven to 325 degrees.

2. Combine the ground nuts, flour, sugar, orange rind, spices, chopped citron, and egg white. Heat the honey with the Grand Marnier and add it. Blend well with the hands.

3. Shape the batter into a rectangle about 3 × 12 inches. Cut into fingers about ¾ inch thick. Place the fingers on an oiled baking sheet and bake for ½ hour.

4. For the glaze, combine the sugar, water, and Grand Marnier. Brush the mixture over the fingers and let stand until dry.

Yield: About 16 cookies.

THE COOKIES:

1 cup ground walnuts, about ¼ pound

1 cup ground almonds, about ¼ pound

½ cup flour

3 tablespoons superfine sugar

1 teaspoon grated orange rind

¼ teaspoon ground allspice

¼ teaspoon ground mace or nutmeg

¼ teaspoon ground cinnamon

½ cup chopped citron or other fruitcake mixture

1 egg white, stiffly beaten

1 tablespoon honey

1 tablespoon Grand Marnier or Cognac

THE GLAZE:

2 tablespoons confectioners' sugar

1 tablespoon water

1 tablespoon Grand Marnier or Cognac

PINE NUT COOKIES

¼ pound sweet butter

½ cup granulated sugar

1 egg yolk

1 teaspoon vanilla extract

1 cup sifted flour

½ cup toasted pine nuts

Pine nuts are, quite simply, the edible seeds of the pine tree. At times, during the "season," they may be purchased in the pine cone from which they derive. They first became commonly known in this country when America discovered pesto sauce.

The most commonly used pine nuts are small, white, and oval in shape and resemble, to a degree, the shape of puffed rice. They are smooth and slightly oily in flavor and go by many names throughout the world.

American Indians and Mexicans refer to them as piñons, pignons, pignolas, Indian nuts, and stone nuts. Italians call them pignoli. I am told that they are also referred to as pinnochio.

1. Preheat the oven to 300 degrees.

2. Cream together the butter and sugar.

3. Beat in the egg yolk, vanilla, and flour. Mix in the nuts.

4. Drop the batter, a teaspoon or so at a time, onto a buttered, floured cookie sheet. Bake for 20 to 25 minutes, or until pale golden. While still hot, remove with a spatula to a rack and let cool.

Yield: About 30 cookies.

CHOCOLATE TRUFFLES

1 pound semisweet chocolate

½ pound butter, at room temperature

6 egg yolks

6 tablespoons dark rum

¾ cup powdered cocoa

¾ cup confectioners' sugar

The only shameful thing about chocolate truffles is that they are like fresh roasted peanuts, insidiously good and, therefore, irresistible.

1. Preheat the oven to 200 degrees or lower.

2. Place the chocolate in a heatproof bowl and place the bowl in the oven. Watch carefully and remove the bowl just when the chocolate has softened.

3. Immediately beat in the butter, yolks, and rum with a wire whisk. Beat with the whisk until the mixture becomes workable. Chill the chocolate mixture briefly until it can be shaped into balls between the palms of the hands. Shape the chocolate into round balls about 1 inch in diameter and roll them in powdered cocoa and/or confectioners' sugar. Arrange the truffles on a rack and let stand in a cool place for several hours.

Yield: 80 to 90 truffles.

PECAN SUGAR COOKIES

1. Sift the flour, baking powder, and sugar together into a mixing bowl. Add the butter, eggs, lemon extract, vanilla, and pecans. Blend thoroughly with the hands.

2. Shape the dough into two rolls, each about 1½ inches thick. Wrap each roll neatly in wax paper. Chill for 30 minutes or longer.

3. Preheat the oven to 350 degrees.

4. Lightly flour a baking sheet, shaking off the excess flour.

5. Slice each roll crosswise into rounds, each about ½ inch thick, or slightly less. Arrange rounds on the baking sheet. Place in the oven and bake for 25 to 30 minutes, or until golden brown. Remove and let cool.

Yield: About 3 dozen.

2	cups flour
1½	teaspoons baking powder
½	cup sugar
¼	pound butter
2	eggs, lightly beaten
½	teaspoon lemon extract
2	teaspoons vanilla extract
¾	cup chopped pecans

CREOLE PRALINES

2 cups granulated sugar
1 cup dark brown sugar
¼ pound butter
1 cup milk
2 tablespoons dark corn syrup
4 cups pecan halves

Like a great deal of French cooking that was "borrowed" by the residents of Louisiana many years ago, pralines, Creole style, underwent a sea change in preparation from one country to the other. The classic praline of the French kitchen is made by cooking almonds, preferably whole, with sugar, until the sugar becomes liquid and then becomes caramel-colored. The mass is spooned onto a greased board and allowed to cool. When it cools it becomes brittle and can be cracked easily. The Creole version of this confection is made with pecan halves cooked with brown sugar and butter to the soft-ball stage. It is then spooned onto a flat surface. When it is cooled it is fairly soft to the bite; it is not brittle.

1. Combine all the ingredients except the pecans in a heavy 3-quart saucepan. Cook for 20 minutes, stirring constantly, after the boil is reached.

2. Add the pecans and continue cooking until the mixture reaches a temperature of 236 degrees on a candy thermometer, or forms a soft ball when dropped into cold water.

3. Arrange several sheets of wax paper over layers of newspapers.

4. Stir the praline mixture well. Drop it by tablespoons onto the sheets of wax paper. Let cool. When cool, stack the pralines in an airtight container, with wax paper between the layers.

Yield: 30 to 36 pralines.

COCONUT LAYER CAKE

1. Preheat the oven to 375 degrees.

2. Butter the inside bottom and sides of two 9-inch cake pans. Sprinkle with flour and shake to coat the insides. Shake out any excess flour.

3. Combine the 2 cups flour, baking powder, and salt in a flour sifter. Sift the ingredients into a mixing bowl and set aside.

4. Put the butter in another bowl and stir briskly with a wooden spoon until it is soft. Continue beating until it becomes glossy in appearance. Add the sugar, ¼ cup at a time, beating well after each addition. Beat until pale and most of the granulated feel of the sugar dissolves. Beat in the egg yolks.

5. Beat in the vanilla and lemon juice.

6. Add ½ cup of the sifted flour mixture and ¼ cup of the milk, stirring rapidly until blended. Continue adding flour and milk in these proportions until all is used. The last addition should be the flour.

7. Beat the whites until they stand in soft peaks and fold them into the batter, using a rubber or plastic spatula.

8. Pour and scrape equal amounts of the batter into each prepared cake pan.

9. Place the pans on the middle rack of the oven and bake for 30 minutes, or until the cakes have shrunk from the sides of the pan.

10. Remove the cakes from the oven and turn them out onto wire cake racks. Let cool for 10 minutes. Cover with a light, clean cloth and let stand until ready to frost.

11. When ready to frost, dust off any crumbs from the layers. Place one layer on a serving dish and spread over it a generous amount of frosting. Spread frosting over the top and sides. Place the second layer on top, making sure it is flush with the bottom. Frost the second layer. Pour the remaining frosting over the top and spread it over the top and around the sides. Sprinkle the grated coconut over the top and sides. A frosted coconut cake is better when served the next day.

Yield: 12 or more servings.

---

2 cups sifted flour

1 tablespoon baking powder

¼ teaspoon salt

¼ pound butter

1¼ cups superfine sugar

2 egg yolks, beaten

2 teaspoons pure vanilla extract

2 teaspoons freshly squeezed lemon juice

1 cup milk, at room temperature

3 egg whites

Boiled frosting (see following recipe)

Grated coconut, fresh (see instructions) or canned

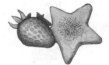

BOILED FROSTING

1 cup plus 2 tablespoons
  sugar
¼ cup cold water
3 large egg whites
1 teaspoon fresh lemon
  juice

1. Combine the sugar and cold water in a small saucepan. Let stand at room temperature for about 15 minutes.
2. Place the saucepan on the stove. Bring the mixture to the boil and cook over medium-high heat. Watch carefully as the syrup cooks. It must not discolor around the edges of the pan. Cook until the syrup spins a thread when dropped from a spoon.
3. Meanwhile, beat the egg whites until stiff and pour the hot syrup slowly into the whites, beating briskly. Continue adding and beating until the frosting holds its shape. Beat in the lemon juice. Let cool for a few minutes, but use before the icing becomes firm.

Yield: Frosting for a 2-layer cake.

GRATED FRESH COCONUT

Use one or two coconuts. It is best to use two in case one isn't sweet enough. Select large coconuts that are heavy and contain a lot of liquid.

Pierce the "eyes" of the coconut with an ice pick. Crack the shell of the coconut in several places, using a hammer or hatchet.

Pry out the flesh with a blunt knife. Pare away the dark skin. Grate the coconut using the coarse blade of a grater.

CHOCOLATE MOUSSE CAKE

One of the grandest desserts we know is a luxurious chocolate cake that is made wholly without flour. It consists of a single preparation, which is basically a chocolate mousse. Take a portion of that mousse and bake it in a springform pan. You set the remainder aside. After the baked mousse is firm, you simply frost it with the remainder.

1. Preheat the oven to 350 degrees.

2. Put the chocolate squares and butter in a saucepan. Set the saucepan in a skillet of boiling water. Keep the water at the simmer. Stir the chocolate and butter until the chocolate has melted.

3. Combine the egg yolks and sugar in the bowl of an electric mixer. Beat until the mixture is light and lemon-colored.

4. Add the chocolate sauce to the egg mixture, stirring to blend thoroughly.

5. Beat the whites until stiff but not brittle. If the whites are too stiffly beaten, they will not fold in properly.

6. Add half the egg whites to the chocolate mixture and beat. Fold in the remaining whites.

7. Butter the bottom and sides of an 8-inch springform pan. Pour three quarters of the mixture into the pan.

8. Set the remaining chocolate mixture aside. This will be used as a filling and frosting.

9. Place the pan in the oven and bake for 1 hour and 15 minutes.

10. When the cake is done, transfer it to a rack. Let stand for about 10 minutes. Remove the rim from the springform pan. Let the cake stand until thoroughly cool.

11. Spoon a portion of the reserved, uncooked chocolate mixture around the sides of the cake, smoothing it over like an icing. Build it up slightly around the top of the cake. Spoon the remainder of the mixture on top of the cake and smooth it over.

12. Hold a small sieve over the cake and spoon the cocoa into it. Sprinkle it evenly over the top of cake. Chill briefly.

13. Add the confectioners' sugar to the sieve and sprinkle it over the top of the cake.

Yield: 8 to 10 servings.

½ pound (8 squares) unsweetened chocolate

½ pound sweet butter, cut into cubes, plus butter for greasing the pan

8 egg yolks

1¼ cups sugar

5 egg whites

1 tablespoon cocoa powder

1 teaspoon confectioners' sugar

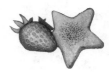

BLACK FOREST CAKE

One 10-inch chocolate spongecake (see following recipe)

½ cup plus 1 tablespoon sugar

1 cup water

2 thin orange or lemon wedges

One 8-ounce can dark sweet pitted cherries (see note)

One 16-ounce can sour cherries

⅓ cup kirsch

One 3-ounce (85-gram) bar of imported bittersweet chocolate

3 cups heavy cream

3 drops of vanilla extract

Scraped and/or grated chocolate for garnish

1. Prepare the spongecake and set aside.

2. Combine ½ cup of the sugar and the water in a saucepan. Add the orange or lemon wedges and bring to the boil. Simmer about 3 minutes and let the syrup cool. Discard wedges.

3. Drain both cans of cherries separately and set cherries aside.

4. Combine the kirsch with ⅔ cup of the syrup. Set aside.

5. Place the chocolate in a saucepan and let it melt gradually in a warm place. When it is melted, gradually add 3 tablespoons of the remaining syrup, stirring.

6. Whip the cream and beat in the remaining tablespoon of sugar and the vanilla.

7. Fold 1½ cups of the whipped cream into the chocolate mixture. Set the remaining whipped cream aside.

8. Place the cake on a flat surface and, holding a long, sharp knife parallel to the bottom of the cake, slice the cake into thirds.

9. Place the bottom slice on a serving plate and brush with some of the syrup mixture. Add about half the chocolate mixture to the slice and smooth it over. Cover with the top slice but place it bottom side up. Brush the slice with syrup and add the remaining chocolate mixture, smoothing it over.

10. Using a pastry tube, pipe 3 rings of whipped cream around the cake. Pipe one ring in the center, another in the middle and the other around the rim. Arrange sour cherries in the center and between the middle and outer rings.

11. Top with the final slice of cake. Brush it with the remaining syrup. Add whipped cream to the top, but save enough cream to make rosettes on top of the cake. Smooth the whipped cream around the top and sides of the cake. Use a No. 4 star pastry tube and pipe 12 rosettes, equally spaced, around the upper rim of the cake. Make one rosette in dead center. Garnish each rosette with one dark sweet pitted cherry. Garnish the top with scraped or grated chocolate. Refrigerate until ready to serve.

Yield: 10 servings.

Note: Fresh black Bing cherries may be poached in syrup, pitted, and used in this recipe.

1. Preheat the oven to 375 degrees.

2. Butter a round cake tin (ours measured 10 by 2 inches). Sprinkle the inside with flour and shake the flour around until the bottom and sides are well coated. Shake out any excess flour.

3. Put the eggs into the bowl of an electric mixer. Bring about 2 quarts of water to the boil in a casserole to hold the mixing bowl. Set the bowl in the water and beat vigorously while adding the sugar. Beat constantly for about 5 minutes, or until the eggs are lukewarm.

4. Return the bowl to the electric mixer and continue beating on high speed until the mixture is thick, mousselike, and at room temperature. To test, run a spatula through the mass. If it is ready, the spatula will leave a track.

5. Meanwhile, combine the flour, cornstarch, and cocoa. Sift together two or three times. Fold the mixture into the batter, using a wooden spoon or spatula. Fold in the butter and pour the mixture into the prepared pan. Bake for 25 to 30 minutes, or until the cake pulls away from the pan. Turn out the cake onto a rack to cool.

Yield: 1 spongecake.

CHOCOLATE SPONGECAKE

6 eggs

1 cup sugar

½ cup plus 3 tablespoons flour

4 tablespoons cornstarch

6 tablespoons cocoa

3 tablespoons butter, melted

CHOCOLATE CAKE

1. Preheat the oven to 350 degrees.

2. Beat the egg yolks and sugar until very thick and lemon-colored. Stir in the chocolate. Fold in the nuts.

3. Beat the egg whites until stiff but not dry and fold into the chocolate-nut mixture. Turn into a greased 10-inch springform pan and bake for 1 hour, or until the center springs back when lightly touched with the fingertips. Cool in the pan. Serve, if desired, with whipped cream.

Yield: 8 to 12 servings.

10 eggs, separated and at room temperature or slightly warmer

14 tablespoons (about 1 cup) sugar

6 ounces bittersweet or semisweet chocolate, melted slowly over hot water and cooled

2 cups finely chopped (not ground) walnuts

HONEY-CHOCOLATE CAKE

11 tablespoons butter

1¾ cups honey

½ cup cocoa

2 eggs

1 teaspoon vanilla extract

2½ cups sifted cake flour

1½ teaspoons baking soda

½ teaspoon salt

1 cup milk

Honey frosting (see following recipe)

1. Preheat the oven to 325 degrees.

2. Grease and flour three round 9-inch cake tins.

3. Cream the butter until soft. Beat the honey in gradually. Add the cocoa and mix well. Beat in the eggs one at a time. Add the vanilla.

4. Sift together the dry ingredients. Add dry ingredients alternately with milk, beating constantly. Pour the batter into the prepared pans and bake for 50 minutes, or until the cakes test done.

5. Turn the cake rounds onto racks to cool. Spread a little frosting between each layer and stack them. Frost the top and sides of the cake and serve cut into wedges.

Yield: 16 to 24 servings.

HONEY FROSTING

1½ cups honey

2 egg whites

⅛ teaspoon salt

½ teaspoon vanilla extract

1 tablespoon Cognac

1. Boil the honey over medium heat to the soft-ball stage, 238 degrees on a candy thermometer.

2. Beat the egg whites and salt until stiff. Pour the hot honey into the egg whites in a thin stream, beating constantly. Add the vanilla and Cognac. Beat the frosting until it is thick enough to spread.

Yield: Enough for one 9-inch 3-layer cake.

ROSACE À L'ORANGE (GENOISE WITH ORANGES)

1 genoise (see following recipe)

4 oranges

4 cups water

2¾ cups granulated sugar

⅔ cup dessert syrup (see following recipe), using Grand Marnier where indicated

Juice of ½ orange

1¼ cups crème patissière (see following recipe)

1¼ cups whipped cream

Butter for greasing the mold

Sugar to dust a mold

When Gaston Lenotre came to our kitchen to demonstrate his incredible skills, he talked of the pitfalls of pastrymaking. "Chefs de cuisine can cover up their mistakes because their cooking is imprecise," Mr. Lenotre told us. "You simply add more of this or more of that and the public never knows. Drop a platter of roast birds and they won't shatter. Drop a wedding cake and you start from scratch. In pastrymaking, everything must be precise or it's a failure. If the butter is too soft or not chilled enough in making puff pastry, if you overbeat or overheat your eggs, they cook or fall. If you overbeat your whites they start to weep."

Mr. Lenotre, generally considered to be the greatest pastry chef in France, prepared two classic French cakes for us, this rosace à l'orange and the following ambassadeur, both based on the genoise, one of the foundation cakes of French pastrymaking. He also made a very Gallic and delicious lemon meringue pie, which appears on page 894.

1. Prepare the genoise as much as a day in advance.

2. Trim off and discard the ends of the oranges. Cut the oranges into very thin slices.

3. Combine the water and sugar and bring to the boil. When the sugar dissolves, add the orange slices and simmer over very gentle heat for 2 hours. Pour the orange slices and syrup into a bowl and let stand overnight.

4. Prepare the dessert syrup and add the orange juice. Set aside.

5. Drain the orange slices. Set aside half of them for decorating. Cut the remaining slices into small pieces. The drained syrup may be used as a side dish for this dessert, flavored perhaps with a little rum. Fold the small pieces into the crème patissière. Fold this mixture into the whipped cream.

6. Select a round mold slightly larger and deeper than the genoise. Butter the bottom and sides and sprinkle with sugar. Line the bottom and sides of the mold with the reserved orange slices, edges overlapping so that both bottom and sides are completely covered.

7. Spoon half the crème patissière over the bottom layer of orange slices, smoothing it over.

8. Slice the genoise in half horizontally. Brush both halves with the orange-flavored dessert syrup. Place one layer on top of the crème patissière. Trim the sides of the genoise if necessary to make it fit. Top with the remaining crème patissière. Add the second layer of

genoise. Top with a small plate that fits snugly inside the mold. Cover with a weight. Refrigerate for 2 hours.

9. To unmold, remove the plate and weight. Dip the mold in hot water and invert it onto a serving dish. Keep refrigerated until ready to serve.

Yield: 8 or more servings.

GENOISE

Butter for greasing cake pans

Flour for coating

5 large eggs, slightly less than 1¼ cups

1 cup granulated sugar

1¼ cups flour

4 tablespoons clarified butter, melted

1 vanilla bean, or ½ teaspoon vanilla extract

1. Preheat the oven to 350 degrees.

2. Butter generously the bottom and sides of two 8-inch cake pans. Sprinkle with flour, shaking to coat evenly. Shake out excess. Refrigerate the pans.

3. Select a 2-quart metal mixing bowl that will fit snugly inside a slightly larger saucepan. Add enough water in the saucepan to almost touch the bottom of the bowl when it is added. Bring the water to the boil.

4. Put the eggs and sugar in the mixing bowl and beat vigorously using a heavy wire whisk. Set the bowl over the water, which should simmer constantly. The essential thing is to avoid overheating the egg mixture. At this point you may switch from the whisk to a portable electric beater. Use high speed initially.

5. Beat the mixture without stopping until it is thick and glossy and falls from the whisk or beater in a soft ribbon.

6. Transfer the bowl, beating constantly, to a flat surface. If an electric mixer is used, the total beating time on high speed is about 5 minutes. Then reduce to low speed for 10 minutes.

7. Using a rubber spatula or a large kitchen spoon, start folding in the flour, holding the flour sifter over the mixture and adding it fairly rapidly. It is best if you have an assistant as you fold.

8. After all the flour has been incorporated, start adding the butter, about a tablespoon or slightly less at a time, folding it in rapidly.

9. Split the vanilla bean in half lengthwise and scrape the seeds into the cake. Or use vanilla extract. Stir quickly. Pour the mixture into the two prepared pans.

10. Place in the oven and bake for 30 minutes, or until golden brown. Let the cake cool for about 10 minutes. Turn onto racks while still warm. Let cool completely before use.

Yield: 2 cakes.

Note: It is almost as easy to prepare two cakes as one. This recipe is for two. Genoise keeps for a week in the refrigerator wrapped in aluminum foil. It freezes well.

Combine ⅔ cup water with ½ cup sugar in a saucepan. Bring to the boil and simmer until the sugar dissolves. Let cool. Stir in 3 tablespoons of a liqueur such as Grand Marnier, kirsch, or rum.

Yield: About 1 cup.

DESSERT SYRUP

CRÈME PATISSIÈRE (PASTRY CREAM)

1. Place the milk and split vanilla bean, if used, in a saucepan and bring to the boil. Cover and keep hot.
2. Put the sugar and egg yolks in a mixing bowl and beat with a wire whisk or electric mixer until the mixture is golden yellow and forms a ribbon. Using the whisk, stir in the cornstarch.
3. Strain the hot milk into the egg and sugar mixture, beating constantly with the whisk. The vanilla bean may be rinsed off and stored in sugar.
4. Pour the mixture back into the saucepan and bring to the boil, stirring constantly with the whisk. Cook for 1 minute, stirring vigorously. Add the vanilla extract if used. If the pastry cream is not to be used immediately, rub the surface with butter to prevent a skin from forming as it cools.

Yield: About 1¼ cups.

1 cup milk
¼ vanilla bean, or ½ teaspoon vanilla extract
⅓ cup granulated sugar
3 egg yolks
2 tablespoons cornstarch
1 tablespoon soft butter, optional

Ambassadeur
(Genoise with candied fruit)

1 genoise (see preceding recipe)

3½ tablespoons chopped candied fruit mix

3 tablespoons Grand Marnier

1¼ cups crème patissière (see preceding recipe)

1 cup dessert syrup (see preceding recipe)

1 cup almond paste, homemade(see following recipe) or purchased

Confectioners' sugar

Chocolate icing (see following recipe), optional

1. Prepare the genoise a day in advance. Similarly, soak the candied fruit in the Grand Marnier.

2. Prepare the crème patissière and let it cool. Divide it in half. Place one half in the refrigerator. Drain the candied fruit and add it to the other half. Stir to blend.

3. Using a long, sharp knife, cut the genoise horizontally into three layers of equal thickness.

4. Brush the bottom layer generously with about one third of the dessert syrup. Spread this neatly with half the blended crème patissière and candied fruit. Place the center cake layer on top. Brush with a third of the dessert syrup. Add the remaining crème patissière and candied fruit mixture, spreading it neatly. Top with the final cake layer and brush with the remainder of the dessert syrup.

5. Spread the entire cake with the refrigerated crème patissière. Chill in the refrigerator for 1 hour.

6. Roll out the almond paste to use as a covering for the cake. Roll out like dough, using confectioners' sugar rather than flour to roll it on and keep it from sticking. Cover a cold surface with a light layer of confectioners' sugar. Shape the paste into a ball and flatten it. Cover the top lightly with confectioners' sugar and roll with a rolling pin. Add more sugar as necessary to prevent sticking. Roll the paste into a circle large enough to completely cover the top and sides of the cake. Pick up the dough like pastry. Cover the cake, pressing the dough and shaping it with the hands and fingers. Chill.

7. Using the chocolate icing and a pastry bag, squeeze out decorations on the surface of the cake. The traditional icing garnish is in script. The word *Ambassadeur* is piped out over the almond paste covering.

Yield: 8 or more servings.

In a mixing bowl, combine the almond powder and confectioners' sugar. Add the egg white and blend quickly until smooth.

Yield: About 1 cup.

ALMOND PASTE

⅔ cup plus 2 tablespoons powdered almonds

1¾ cups plus 2 tablespoons sifted confectioners' sugar

1 egg white from a small egg

CHOCOLATE ICING

3½ ounces (3½ squares) semisweet chocolate

½ cup confectioners' sugar

2½ tablespoons butter, cut into pieces

2 tablespoons cold water

1. Melt the chocolate in the top of a double boiler over hot, not boiling, water.

2. Sift the sugar. Add the sugar and butter to the chocolate, stirring until smooth. Remove the saucepan from the heat and add the water, 1 tablespoon at a time. This cools the mixture a bit.

3. The mixture must be lukewarm when it is used or it will not spread or ooze from a tube properly.

4. Spread the icing on a cake or use it for decoration.

Yield: About ¾ cup.

HUGUENOT TORTE

6 ounces pecan meats
(about 1½ cups)

½ cup flour
Salt to taste

2 teaspoons baking
powder

2 apples (about
¾ pound)

3 large eggs

1 cup plus 1 tablespoon
sugar

1 teaspoon vanilla
extract

⅔ cup heavy cream

8 crisp, toasted, browned
pecans

I am persuaded that this is one of the finest desserts of Southern origin.
I am also persuaded that it has been perpetuated with greatest emphasis
because it is included in a soft-cover volume titled *Charleston Receipts*,
first published in 1950 by The Junior League of Charleston, South Carolina. The following version of the dessert was adapted from the book by
a young master chef, Bill Neal of Chapel Hill, North Carolina.

1. Preheat the oven to 325 degrees.

2. Butter the bottom and sides of two 9-inch cake pans. Cut two
   rounds of wax paper to fit inside the bottom of the pans. Place
   rounds in the pans and butter lightly. Sprinkle the paper with
   flour; shake out the excess.

3. Process the pecan meats in a food processor or blender until fine
   but not a paste.

4. Put the processed pecans in a mixing bowl and add the ½ cup of
   flour, the salt, and baking powder. Blend well.

5. Peel the apples and cut them into quarters. Cut away the cores.
   Cut each quarter into thin slices, and the slices into thin strips.
   Cut the strips into very small cubes. There should be about 2
   cups. Add the apples to the pecan mixture and stir to blend well.

6. Beat the eggs with a whisk or electric mixer, about 2 minutes.
   Continue beating while gradually adding 1 cup of the sugar, a
   little at a time, for about 5 minutes. Beat in the vanilla. Gradually
   fold in the apple mixture.

7. Pour an equal portion of the batter into each of the prepared pans
   and smooth over the tops. Place the pans on the center shelf of
   the oven and bake for 35 minutes.

8. Transfer the cake pans to a rack and let stand for 10 minutes.

9. Run a knife around the rim of each cake and unmold. Let stand
   on a rack until the layers are cool.

10. Put the cream in a mixing bowl and start beating. Gradually add
    the remaining 1 tablespoon of sugar and continue beating until
    the cream is stiff.

11. Spread 1 cake layer with slightly more than half the whipped
    cream. Top with the second layer.

12. Spoon the remaining whipped cream into a pastry bag outfitted
    with a No. 5 star tube. Pipe 8 rosettes of whipped cream on top of
    the cake.

13. Chill the cake briefly. Top each rosette with a pecan.

Yield: 8 servings.

Walnut and Almond Torte

1. Preheat the oven to 350 degrees.
2. Blend the nuts, zwieback, orange rind, cinnamon, and cloves in a mixing bowl.
3. Beat the egg yolks with the 1½ cups of sugar until light and lemon-colored, about 15 minutes. Add the vanilla and fold into the nut mixture.
4. Beat the egg whites until stiff but not dry and gently fold into the batter.
5. Butter a 12 × 15 × 3-inch pan and pour in the batter. Bake for exactly 1 hour without opening the oven door.
6. While the torte is baking, make the syrup. Combine the water, 3 cups sugar, and lemon slice in a saucepan and simmer for about 20 minutes.
7. Pour the warm syrup over the torte immediately upon removing the torte from the oven. Let the torte stand for 24 hours. Cut into 3-inch squares and serve topped with whipped cream.

Yield: 20 pieces.

3 cups ground walnuts
3 cups ground almonds
16 pieces of zwieback, ground
Grated rind of 1 orange
½ teaspoon cinnamon
¼ teaspoon ground cloves
12 eggs, separated
1½ cups sugar
1 teaspoon vanilla extract
4 cups water
3 cups sugar
1 slice of lemon
Whipped cream

Tourte Landaise (An egg cake from the Landes region of France)

1. Place the butter in a heavy saucepan and let stand over gentle heat until melted. Let cool, but the butter should remain liquid.
2. Preheat the oven to 325 degrees.
3. Put the flour in a mixing bowl and add the baking powder and salt. Add the sugar and blend well. Make a well in the center of the flour and add the yolks, stirring and mixing. Add the milk alternately with the melted butter and, when blended, beat the batter with the hands. Combine the lemon juice and Pernod and add.
4. Beat the egg whites until stiff and fold them in.
5. Butter two 6-cup charlotte molds and add half the batter to each. Bake for 1 hour and increase the heat to 350 degrees. Bake for 10 minutes longer. Let stand briefly and then unmold the cakes. Let cool to room temperature. Serve sliced with crème patissière.

Yield: 8 to 12 servings.

½ pound sweet butter
4¼ cups cake flour
1 tablespoon baking powder
½ teaspoon salt
1 cup plus 2 tablespoons sugar
4 eggs, separated
1 cup milk
2 tablespoons lemon juice
3 tablespoons Pernod, Ricard, or other anise-flavored liqueur
Crème patissière (see recipe page 871)

HAZELNUT CHEESECAKE

1½ cups shelled, toasted, hulled hazelnuts, or blanched, toasted almonds

Butter

⅓ cup graham cracker crumbs, approximately

2 pounds cream cheese, at room temperature

½ cup heavy cream

4 eggs

1¾ cups sugar

1 teaspoon vanilla extract

It is fascinating to discover the extent to which one ingredient can alter, even glorify, the nature of a dish. Some years ago we came into possession of a cheesecake recipe that seemed to be the essence of all great cheesecakes. It was delicate, rich, and subtly flavored. Moreover, it was ultimately refined in texture. Sometime later we purchased a pound of toasted hazelnuts. These we ground and blended into the cake's batter. The result is to our minds a paradigm of cheesecakes. We hasten to add that hazelnuts are a luxury. Many supermarkets carry untoasted hazelnuts that may be roasted at home.

1. Because of the importance of oven temperature, the nuts must be toasted well in advance of proceeding with the recipe. If your hazelnuts are untoasted, preheat the oven to 400 degrees. Place the nuts on a baking sheet or in a skillet and bake them, stirring them often so that they brown evenly. When nicely browned, remove them and let cool.

2. When ready to make the cheesecake, preheat the oven to 300 degrees.

3. Place the nuts in the container of a blender or food processor and blend. If you want a crunchy texture, blend them until coarse-fine. If you want a smooth texture, blend them until they are almost pastelike.

4. Butter the inside of a metal cake pan 8 inches wide and 3 inches deep. Do not use a springform pan.

5. Sprinkle the inside with graham cracker crumbs and shake the crumbs around the bottom and sides until coated. Shake out the excess crumbs and set the pan aside.

6. Place the cream cheese, cream, eggs, sugar, and vanilla in the bowl of an electric mixer. Start beating at low speed and, as the ingredients blend, increase the speed to high. Continue beating until thoroughly blended and smooth. Add the nuts and continue beating until thoroughly blended.

7. Pour and scrape the batter into the prepared pan and shake gently to level the mixture.

8. Set the pan inside a slightly wider pan and pour boiling water into the large pan to a depth of about ½ inch. Do not let the edge of the cheesecake pan touch the other larger pan. Set the pans thus arranged inside the oven and bake for 2 hours. At the end of that time, turn off the oven heat and let the cake sit in the oven for 1 hour longer.

9. Lift the cake out of its water bath and place it on a rack. Let the cake stand for at least 2 hours.

10. Place a round cake plate over the cake and carefully turn both upside down to unmold the cake. Serve lukewarm or at room temperature.

Yield: 12 or more servings.

Note: The consistency of this cake is softer than most cheesecakes.

GINGERBREAD

1. Preheat the oven to 350 degrees.

2. Combine the molasses and butter in a saucepan and bring just to the boil, stirring. Let cool.

3. Combine in the bowl of an electric mixer the egg and sugar. Beat to blend.

4. Sift together the flour, baking soda, ginger, cinnamon, cloves, and nutmeg. Add the orange peel and salt.

5. Gradually add the dry ingredients to the egg mixture. Spoon and scrape in the molasses mixture while beating. Add the boiling water and sour cream. Blend well.

6. Pour the mixture into a buttered 9 × 13-inch pan. Bake for 50 minutes. The center of the gingerbread will sink when it cools. Serve, if desired, with applesauce or sweetened whipped cream.

Yield: 8 to 12 servings.

1 cup molasses (do not use blackstrap molasses)

½ pound butter

1 egg

1 cup sugar

2¼ cups flour

1½ teaspoons baking soda

1½ teaspoons ground ginger

1 teaspoon ground cinnamon

½ teaspoon ground cloves

¼ teaspoon grated nutmeg

Grated peel of 1 orange

Salt to taste

½ cup boiling water

3 tablespoons sour cream

DATE-NUT CAKE

1 cup pitted diced dates

¾ cup dark seedless raisins

¼ cup golden seedless raisins

1 teaspoon baking soda

1 cup boiling water

1 cup sugar

¼ pound butter

1 teaspoon vanilla extract

1 egg

1⅓ cups sifted flour

¾ cup walnuts broken into small pieces

1. Preheat the oven to 350 degrees.

2. Butter a standard loaf pan (9½ × 5½ × 2¾ inches). Line the bottom with a rectangle of wax paper. Butter this rectangle and sprinkle with flour. Shake out the excess flour.

3. Put the dates and raisins in a mixing bowl. Dissolve the baking soda with the boiling water and pour it over the date mixture.

4. Cream together the sugar and ¼ pound butter. Beat in the vanilla and egg. Add the flour and mix well. Add the date mixture, including the liquid. Add the walnuts. Please note that this will be a quite liquid batter.

5. Pour the mixture into the prepared pan and smooth over the top. Place in the oven and bake from 1 hour to 1 hour and 10 minutes, or until the top of the cake is dark brown and a knife inserted in the center comes out clean.

6. Let cool for about 5 minutes. Unmold onto a rack. Remove the paper.

Yield: 1 loaf.

BOURBON-PECAN CAKE

1. Preheat the oven to 350 degrees.
2. Put the butter in the bowl of an electric mixer. Start beating and gradually add the sugar, beating on high. Add the eggs, one at a time, beating well after each addition.
3. Sift together the baking powder, flour, and salt. Beat the flour mixture, maple syrup, and bourbon into the creamed butter, adding the ingredients alternately. Stir in the pecans.
4. Butter a small tube pan (one that measures 9½ inches in diameter, 6 cups, is suitable), loaf, or Bundt pan and spoon in the mixture, smoothing it over on top.
5. Bake for 45 to 50 minutes. Let cool for 10 minutes. Remove from the pan and let cool. Serve sprinkled with confectioners' sugar.

Yield: 8 or more servings.

¼ pound butter, at room temperature
½ cup dark brown sugar
2 large eggs
2½ teaspoons baking powder
2 cups flour
Salt to taste
½ cup maple syrup
½ cup bourbon, rum, or Cognac
1½ cups coarsely chopped pecans
Confectioners' sugar for garnish

CARROT LAYER CAKE

1 pound carrots, approximately

2 cups sugar

1½ cups corn or peanut oil

4 eggs

2 cups flour

2 teaspoons baking powder

2 teaspoons baking soda

1 teaspoon salt

½ cup coarsely chopped pecans

Cream cheese frosting (see following recipe)

1. Preheat the oven to 325 degrees.
2. Trim, scrape, and grate the carrots, then measure them; there should be about 3 cups. Set aside.
3. Combine the sugar and oil in the bowl of an electric mixer. Start beating. Add the eggs, 1 at a time, beating well after each addition.
4. Sift together the flour, baking powder, baking soda, and salt. Add this to the oil mixture while beating. Add the grated carrots and nuts and blend well.
5. Lightly oil three 9-inch cake pans. Line the bottoms with circles of wax paper; oil the paper. Pour the batter into the pans and bake for 45 minutes.
6. Turn the cakes onto wire racks and let cool. Remove the paper liners. Frost with cream cheese frosting.

Yield: 8 or more servings.

CREAM CHEESE FROSTING

2 cups confectioners' sugar

1 package (8 ounces) cream cheese

4 tablespoons butter, at room temperature

2 teaspoons vanilla extract

1. Sift the sugar into the bowl of an electric mixer.
2. Add the cream cheese, butter, and vanilla. Beat until smooth and creamy.

Yield: Enough frosting for a 3-layer cake.

MARY ANN'S FRUITCAKE

1. Preheat the oven to 250 degrees. Butter the inside of a 10-inch, 12-cup tube pan. Sprinkle liberally with flour and shake out the excess. Set the pan aside.

2. In a large mixing bowl, combine the raisins and pecan meats. Sprinkle the flour and salt over all and toss with the hands until thoroughly blended. Set aside.

3. Place the butter in the bowl of an electric beater. Start beating and gradually add the sugar. Cream the mixture well and add the egg yolks one at a time, beating constantly. Blend the baking soda and water and add it, beating. Beat in the Grand Marnier. Pour this mixture into the nut mixture and blend together with the hands.

4. Beat the whites until stiff and fold them in with the hands. Continue folding until the whites are not apparent.

5. Spoon and scrape the mixture into the prepared pan, smoothing the top with a spatula. Bake for 2 to 2¼ hours, or until the cake is puffed above the pan and nicely browned on top. If the cake starts to brown too soon, cover with aluminum foil. Remove the cake from the pan shortly after it is baked. Tapping the bottom of the cake pan with a heavy knife will help loosen it. Store the cake for at least 10 days. If desired, add an occasional touch of Cognac or rum to the cake as it stands. Keep it closely covered and refrigerated until ready to use.

Yield: One 10-inch cake.

---

1 pound golden seedless raisins

1 pound pecan meats, broken

3 cups sifted flour

1 teaspoon salt

1 pound butter, at room temperature

2 cups sugar

6 eggs, separated

1 teaspoon baking soda

1 tablespoon warm water

¼ cup Grand Marnier

No-Bake Fruitcake

1 pound seedless raisins
1 pound pitted dates
1 pound dried figs
1 pound shredded coconut
1 pound shelled walnuts
¼ teaspoon salt
1 teaspoon vanilla extract
¼ cup rum or Cognac, optional

1. Put the raisins, dates, figs, coconut, and walnuts through a food chopper, using the medium knife. Or coarsely chop, using a food processor. Do not overblend, however.

2. Empty the mixture into a large mixing bowl and add the salt and vanilla and, if desired, the rum or Cognac. Blend well.

3. Spoon and pack the mixture into a mold. Two 6-cup loaf pans are suitable. Cover and place a weight on top. Refrigerate for 3 days, or keep in a cold place to age. Serve thinly sliced.

Yield: 5 pounds.

GENEVIEVE RIORDAN'S APPLE PIE

The one dessert that best distinguishes the differences between the cuisines of France and America is apple pie. The most obvious difference has to do with the presentation. An American apple pie is almost invariably a two-crust affair, one on top and one on the bottom. A French apple tart is just as invariably an open, single-crust creation. And, whereas the American dough for a pastry crust may be made with white shortening or lard or butter—and often a combination of two—a French pastry crust is almost always made with butter.

1. Cut the pastry in half. Roll out one half of it on a lightly floured surface and line a 9-inch pie plate with the dough. Set the other half of the dough aside.

2. Preheat the oven to 450 degrees.

3. Peel the apples and cut them into quarters. Cut away the core. Cut the quarters lengthwise into pieces about ⅛ inch thick. There should be 6 or 7 cups.

4. Put the slices in a mixing bowl. Add ½ to ⅔ cup of the sugar and the cinnamon and nutmeg. Blend well with the hands.

5. Blend the flour with the remaining 1½ tablespoons sugar. Sprinkle this over the bottom pastry in the pie plate.

6. Pour the apples into the prepared pie plate. There should be a goodly mountain of apple slices. Dot with butter and sprinkle lemon juice over all.

7. Roll out the second half of the dough.

8. Moisten the rim of the bottom pie crust with a little water. Cover the apple slices with the second crust. Press the rim of the second crust down onto the first. Cut around the pie plate to trim off any excess dough. Press around the edges to seal.

9. Cut small slits in the top of the pie to allow steam to escape. Brush the top with milk, cream, or beaten egg.

10. Place the pie in the oven and bake for 10 minutes. Reduce the oven temperature to 400 degrees. Continue baking for 35 to 40 minutes longer. Let cool on a rack or serve hot.

Yield: 6 to 8 servings.

Pie pastry (see following recipe)

5 or 6 firm, tart-sweet, unblemished cooking apples, such as Granny Smith, Rhode Island Greenings, or McIntosh, about 1¾ pounds

½ to ⅔ cup plus 1½ tablespoons sugar

1 teaspoon ground cinnamon

1 teaspoon grated nutmeg

1½ tablespoons flour

2 tablespoons butter

Juice of ½ lemon

1 tablespoon milk, cream, or beaten egg

PIE PASTRY

2 cups flour
½ teaspoon salt
⅔ cup solid white
   shortening
1½ to 3 tablespoons ice
   water

1. Pour the flour into the container of a food processor and add the salt.
2. Add the shortening in small spoonfuls.
3. Start processing, adding the water gradually. Add only enough water so that the dough can be gathered into a ball and rolled out. One and one half tablespoons of water should be sufficient.
4. Gather the dough, wrap it in wax paper, and refrigerate it for at least ½ hour before rolling.

Yield: Pastry for a 1- or 2-crust pie.

FRENCH APPLE TART

1. Preheat the oven to 400 degrees.

2. Roll out the pastry and line an 11-inch pie tin, preferably a quiche pan with removable bottom.

3. Peel the apples and cut them into quarters. Cut away and discard the cores. Trim off and reserve the ends of the apple quarters. Chop these pieces. There should be about ½ cup.

4. Cut the quarters lengthwise into slices. There should be 5 cups of sliced apples.

5. Scatter the chopped apple ends over the pie shell.

6. Arrange the apple slices overlapping in concentric circles starting with the outer layer and working to the center.

7. Sprinkle the apples with the sugar and dot with the butter.

8. Place the tart in the oven and bake for 15 minutes. Reduce the oven temperature to 375 degrees and continue baking for 25 minutes longer.

9. Heat the apple jelly over low heat, stirring, until melted. Brush the top of the hot apple tart with the jelly. Serve hot or cold.

Yield: 6 to 8 servings.

Tart pastry (see following recipe)

5 firm, tart-sweet, unblemished cooking apples, such as McIntosh or Granny Smith

½ cup sugar

2 tablespoons butter

⅓ cup clear apple jelly

1. Cut the butter into small cubes and put them in the container of a food processor. Add the flour and sugar.

2. Start processing while gradually adding the water. Add only enough water so that the dough holds together and can be shaped into a ball.

3. Gather the dough into a ball. Wrap it in wax paper and refrigerate for 30 minutes or longer before rolling.

Yield: Pastry for an 11-inch tart.

TART PASTRY

12 tablespoons cold butter

1½ cups flour

2 tablespoons sugar

2 to 3 tablespoons ice water

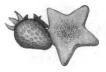

Tarte au Citron (French Lemon Tart)

Tart pastry (see preceding recipe)
5 egg yolks
½ cup sugar
½ cup heavy cream
6 tablespoons fresh lemon juice
1 tablespoon grated lemon rind
½ cup finely chopped peeled apple

In the world of food, one of the most quoted of writers is an English clergyman named Sydney Smith, who lived from 1771 to 1845. He wrote about tea and how to make salads and how he managed to pursue his gourmet concerns in spite of difficulties such as isolation: "My living in Yorkshire was so far out of the way," he wrote, "that it was actually 12 miles from a lemon."

A dozen miles from the nearest lemon would be a sorry plight indeed, for without the lemon there would not be such great dishes as the Greek soup avgolemono, the French maquereau au vin blanc, and the very American lemon meringue pie. Best of all is a French lemon tart.

1. Preheat the oven to 400 degrees.
2. Roll out the dough on a lightly floured board to a thickness of ⅛ inch. Fit it into a 10-inch metal quiche or flan pan with removable bottom. Trim off the edges.
3. Line the pastry with wax paper and add dried beans to cover the bottom.
4. Place the pastry in the oven and bake for 10 minutes.
5. Remove the beans and wax paper. Reduce the oven temperature to 350 degrees.
6. Combine the yolks and sugar in a mixing bowl. Beat vigorously with a wire whisk until the mixture is thick and light lemon in color.
7. Beat in the cream, lemon juice, lemon rind, and chopped apple.
8. Pour the mixture into the prepared pastry and place the pie on the bottom rack of the oven. Bake for 30 minutes. Let cool before serving.

Yield: 4 servings.

STRAWBERRY TART

1. Preheat the oven to 425 degrees. Roll out the dough to a thickness of ⅛ inch. Fit it into a 10-inch metal quiche pan with a removable bottom. Trim the edges. Line the pastry with wax paper and add dried beans to cover the bottom. Bake for 10 minutes, remove the wax paper and beans, and bake for 3 to 5 minutes longer. Let cool before filling.

2. Spoon the crème patissière into the pie shell and smooth it over. Arrange the strawberries bottom side down, close together, and symmetrically over the crème patissière.

3. Spoon the marmalade into a saucepan and add the water. Cook, stirring, until the marmalade is thinned. Put it through a strainer.

4. When the marmalade is cooled but still liquid, brush the berries with it. Sprinkle the almonds over all. Cut into wedges to serve.

Yield: 8 to 10 servings.

Note: To toast the almond slivers, put them in one layer in a heatproof dish and bake at 350 degrees, stirring occasionally, until nicely browned.

Tart pastry (see recipe page 885)

Crème patissière (see recipe page 871)

3 pints firm, fresh, red, ripe strawberries, hulled, rinsed, and drained

1 cup orange marmalade

1 tablespoon water

⅓ cup toasted almond slivers (see note)

VISIDANTINE (AN ALMOND TART)

1. Roll the dough into a circle on a lightly floured board. Line a 9-inch quiche tin with a removable bottom with the mixture. Build up the sides slightly. Prick the bottom. Refrigerate. There will be leftover dough, which may be used to make an assortment of cookies.

2. Preheat the oven to 400 degrees.

3. To prepare the filling, cream the butter in the bowl of an electric mixer.

4. Separately, blend the sugar and ground almonds. Add about a third of the mixture and 1 egg to the butter. Beat well. Add another third of the mixture and 1 more egg and beat well. Add the final third of almond mixture and the last egg and blend well. Beat in the rum.

5. Spoon and scrape this mixture into the prepared pan and sprinkle with the almonds. Place in the oven and bake for 35 minutes. Remove the tart from the ring.

6. Melt the apricot preserves with a little water over low heat, stirring. Spread this over the top of the tart.

Yield: 6 to 8 servings.

Tart pastry (see recipe page 885)

¼ pound butter, at room temperature

⅔ cup sugar

1⅓ cups ground, blanched almonds

3 large eggs

1 tablespoon dark rum

1 cup thinly sliced blanched almonds

¼ cup apricot preserves

PEAR AND GINGER TART

Tart pastry (see recipe
page 885)

8 ripe but firm Comice
or Anjou pears, about
3 pounds

⅔ cup sugar

¾ teaspoon ground
ginger

½ cup water

6 tablespoons apricot
preserves

Whipped cream,
optional

1. Preheat the oven to 425 degrees. Roll out the dough to a thickness of ⅛ inch. Fit it into a 10-inch metal quiche pan with a removable bottom. Trim the edges. Line the pastry with wax paper and add dried beans to cover the bottom. Bake for 10 minutes, remove wax paper and beans, and bake for 2 minutes longer. Let cool before filling.

2. Reheat the oven to 425 degrees.

3. Peel six of the pears and cut each of them into eighths. Cut away and discard the cores.

4. Place the pear wedges in a saucepan and add the sugar, ginger, and water. Cover and cook until tender but still firm, 8 to 10 minutes. They must not be mushy. Turn the pear wedges as they cook so that the pieces cook evenly. Chill thoroughly. Drain but reserve 4 tablespoons of the pear liquid.

5. Arrange the pear wedges close together in the pastry shell.

6. Peel and quarter the remaining 2 pears. Scoop out and discard the cores. Cut the quarters into thin slices. Arrange the slices symmetrically over the cooked pears.

7. Combine the apricot preserves with the reserved pear liquid. Bring to the boil and strain. Brush tart with half of the apricot mixture. Bake for 30 minutes.

8. Remove from the oven and brush with remaining sauce. Let stand until warm. Serve with whipped cream, if desired.

Yield: 8 to 10 servings.

RHUBARB AND STRAWBERRY PIE

1. Preheat the oven to 400 degrees.

2. Prepare the pastry and use it to line a 9- or 10-inch pie plate, preferably a quiche pan with a removable bottom.

3. Put the rhubarb and strawberries in a mixing bowl and add the sugar and cardamom blended with the flour. Toss. Add the eggs and blend thoroughly. Pour this mixture into the prepared pie shell and place on a baking sheet. Bake for 40 minutes, or until set. Remove and let cool.

4. Heat the marmalade with the water, stirring, until melted. Spoon this over the pie and smooth it over. Remove the pie from the quiche pan, if used, or cut it directly into wedges from the pie plate.

Yield: 8 or more servings.

Sweet pastry for a 1-crust pie (see following recipe)

2 cups fresh young rhubarb cut into ½-inch cubes (do not use the leaves)

2 cups fresh strawberries, halved if small, quartered if large

1 cup sugar

½ teaspoon ground cardamom

3 tablespoons flour

2 eggs, lightly beaten

½ cup orange marmalade

1 tablespoon water

1. Combine the flour, yolks, sugar, and salt in the container of a food processor. Cut the butter into fine pieces and add it. Process, adding just enough water to make the pastry hold together.

2. Remove the dough and shape it into a ball or rectangle. Wrap in wax paper and chill for 30 minutes or longer.

3. Roll the dough out on a floured board, turning as necessary and using a little more flour as necessary to prevent sticking as it is rolled.

4. Line a pie plate with the pastry and trim off the excess around the edge.

Yield: Pastry for a 1-crust pie.

SWEET PASTRY FOR A ONE-CRUST PIE

1½ cups flour

2 egg yolks

2 tablespoons confectioners' sugar

Salt to taste

8 tablespoons cold butter

3 tablespoons water, approximately

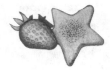

CHESS PIE

Sweet pastry for a 9-inch pie (see preceding recipe)

¼ pound butter, at room temperature

2 cups sugar

1 tablespoon flour

2 tablespoons white cornmeal

Salt to taste

4 eggs

¼ cup milk

¼ cup freshly squeezed lemon juice

2 teaspoons grated fresh lemon rind

Sweetened whipped cream for garnish, optional

Freshly grated nutmeg for garnish

The origin of the name "chess pie" was explained to me on a visit to Kentucky as follows: A visitor to the South went to a dining establishment. At the time for dessert, the waitress told him that pie was included. He said he would like apple pie and she replied that it was not served. "Then I'll take peach," he said. No peach either. "What kind of pie do you serve?" he asked. "Jes' pie," she told him.

1. Preheat the oven to 350 degrees.

2. Line a 9-inch pie plate with the pastry and flute the rim.

3. Put the butter and sugar into the bowl of an electric mixer and beat until creamy. Beat in the flour, cornmeal, and salt. Add the eggs, one at a time, and beat well after each addition. Beat in the milk, lemon juice, and lemon rind.

4. Pour and scrape the mixture into the pastry-lined pie plate and place on the lowest shelf of the oven. Bake for 45 minutes, or until the filling is golden and firm. Let cool to room temperature.

5. Serve cut into very small wedges with, if desired, a dollop of sweetened whipped cream on each serving. Before serving, sprinkle each portion with a small amount of freshly grated nutmeg.

Yield: 8 or more servings.

MISSISSIPPI PECAN PIE

Pastry for a 10-inch pie (see recipe page 884)

1¼ cups dark corn syrup

1 cup sugar

4 whole eggs

4 tablespoons butter, melted

1½ cups chopped pecan meats

1 teaspoon pure vanilla extract

2 tablespoons dark rum

1. Preheat the oven to 350 degrees.

2. Roll out the pastry and line a 10-inch pie tin.

3. Combine the corn syrup and sugar in a saucepan and bring to the boil. Cook, stirring, just until the sugar is dissolved.

4. Beat the eggs in a mixing bowl and gradually add the sugar mixture, beating. Add the remaining ingredients and pour the mixture into the pie shell. Bake for 50 minutes to 1 hour, or until the pie is set.

Yield: 8 servings.

PUMPKIN CREAM PIE

One of the curious things about holiday customs in America is the general inability to relate holiday ornaments to the stove. The vast majority of Easter eggs go for naught once the day is done. And so with pumpkins. Hundreds of thousands of pounds of these joyous delights never see the inside of a saucepan. Whereas most recipes for pumpkin pie call for canned pumpkin, a pie made with the fresh pulp is infinitely more delicate and delicious. Please note that we are not recommending the use of a carved pumpkin with a funny face several days old. But the use of a fresh pumpkin and, preferably, a small, young one newly picked.

1. Preheat the oven to 425 degrees.

2. Line a pie dish with the pastry and build up a fluted edge. Chill.

3. Combine the remaining ingredients in a mixing bowl. Blend well. Pour the mixture into the prepared shell and place in the oven.

4. Bake for 15 minutes. Reduce the heat to 350 degrees. Bake for 30 to 40 minutes longer, or until the filling is set. Serve, if desired, with sweetened and/or rum-flavored whipped cream.

Yield: 6 to 8 servings.

Pastry for a 9-inch pie (see recipe page 884)

3 cups fresh pumpkin purée (see following instructions) or use canned pumpkin

¾ cup sugar

½ teaspoon salt

½ teaspoon grated nutmeg

¼ teaspoon ground cinnamon

1 teaspoon grated fresh ginger, or ½ teaspoon ground ginger

3 large eggs, lightly beaten

1 cup heavy cream

FRESH PUMPKIN PURÉE

One 3- to 4-pound pumpkin

1. Cut around and discard the stem of the pumpkin.

2. Cut the pumpkin into eighths. Scoop away and discard the seeds and fibers from the pumpkin pieces. Place the unpeeled pumpkin pieces in the top of a steamer large enough to hold them. Cover and steam over boiling water for about 15 minutes, or until the pumpkin flesh is tender.

3. Remove and let cool. When cool enough to handle, scrape the flesh from the outer peel. Discard the peel. Blend the flesh, using a food processor or blender, or put it through a ricer.

Yield: About 3½ cups.

Note: This purée can be kept indefinitely in the freezer.

MINCEMEAT PIE

½ pound cooked beef

½ pound cooked beef tongue

1 pound black currants

1½ pounds black raisins

2 ounces chopped candied lemon peel

2 ounces chopped candied orange peel

½ cup chopped diced candied citron

½ cup chopped glacéed cherries

½ cup chopped glacéed pineapple

¾ pound finely chopped or ground suet

2 cups brown sugar

2 cups peeled, cored, finely diced apple

Grated rind of 1 lemon

Grated rind of 1 orange

¼ cup lemon juice

1 teaspoon grated nutmeg

½ teaspoon ground cloves

½ teaspoon ground allspice

1 teaspoon ground cinnamon

2 cups Cognac or other brandy

½ cup dry sherry

½ teaspoon salt, or to taste

Pastry for a 9-inch pie (see recipe page 884)

The texture of mincemeat is a question of personal taste. Some like it fine, some medium, and some coarse. If you want it coarse, the various fruits and meats should be chopped or cubed by hand. If you want it medium or fine, use a food processor and process to the desired texture. Some sources recommend grinding the mincemeat; others recommend grinding half the ingredients and chopping the rest. Take your choice.

1. Cube or chop the beef, tongue, currants, raisins, lemon peel, orange peel, candied citron, cherries, pineapple, and suet. Pour this mixture into a bowl.

2. Add the remaining ingredients and mix well with the hands. There should be about 12 cups. Spoon the mixture into fruit jars and seal tightly. Let it age for at least 3 weeks, and preferably a month, before using. Store in a cool place to age.

3. When ready to bake, preheat oven to 450 degrees.

4. Roll out pie pastry and line a 9-inch pie plate. Fill with 3 to 4 cups mincemeat. Cover the pie with the upper crust. Bake for about 30 minutes.

Yield: 3 to 4 pies.

CHOCOLATE SABAYON PIE

1. Preheat the oven to 425 degrees. Line a 10-inch pie plate with the pastry. Prick the bottom and sides of the pastry with the tines of a fork. Place the pie shell on a baking sheet and bake for 12 to 15 minutes. Let cool before filling.

2. Combine the chocolate and water in a saucepan. Place the pan in a basin of barely simmering water and let stand, stirring as necessary, until the chocolate melts.

3. As the chocolate melts, put the egg yolks and sugar in the bowl of an electric mixer. Add the crème de cacao and set the bowl in a basin of barely simmering water. Beat vigorously with a wire whisk until the sauce becomes rich and thick, like a stiff custard.

4. Let the melted chocolate cool slightly (if it is too hot when added to the sauce, it will tend to cook the eggs). Add the chocolate to the sauce and fold it in with a plastic spatula. Beat in the rum.

5. Whip the 1½ cups of cream until stiff. Fold this into the chocolate mixture. Spoon into the baked pastry shell and chill. Serve cold. Garnish with additional whipped cream, if desired.

Yield: 8 or more servings.

Pastry for a 10-inch pie (see recipe page 884)

10 ounces (squares) sweet or bittersweet chocolate

¼ cup plus 2 tablespoons water

2 egg yolks

1 tablespoon sugar

3 tablespoons crème de cacao, or any other chocolate-flavored liqueur

2 tablespoons dark rum

1½ cups heavy cream

Whipped cream for garnish, optional

LEMON MERINGUE PIE

Sweet pie pastry (see recipe page 889)

1 cup milk

¼ vanilla bean, split lengthwise, or ½ teaspoon vanilla extract

2 tablespoons sugar

3 egg yolks

3 tablespoons cornstarch

Juice of ½ lemon, or more if a stronger lemon flavor is desired

Finely grated rind of ½ lemon

French meringue (see following recipe)

1 or 2 tablespoons confectioners' sugar

1. Preheat the oven to 425 degrees.

2. Line a quiche tin with a removable bottom with the rolled out dough.

3. Cover the bottom of the pan with wax paper and add dried beans to weight the dough down. This will prevent the dough from buckling. Bake the pastry for 25 minutes, or until nicely golden and cooked. Remove the pastry and allow to cool. Remove the beans and wax paper.

4. Place the milk and split vanilla bean, if used, in a saucepan and bring to the boil. Cover and keep hot.

5. Put the sugar and egg yolks in a mixing bowl (this may be done in a mixer) and beat with a wire whisk until the mixture is golden yellow and forms a ribbon. Using the whisk, beat in the cornstarch.

6. Strain the hot milk into the egg and sugar mixture, beating constantly with the whisk. The vanilla bean may be rinsed off and stored in sugar.

7. Pour the mixture back into the saucepan and bring to the boil, stirring constantly with the whisk. Cook for 1 minute, stirring vigorously. If vanilla extract is used, add it. Add the lemon juice and grated rind. Pour the mixture into the baked pastry shell.

8. Spoon half the meringue onto the filling and smooth it over with a spatula. Fit a pastry bag with a star tube and spoon in the remaining meringue. Pipe the meringue out in star-shaped peaks to cover the pie.

9. Return the pie to the oven and bake for about 5 minutes, or until the meringue is lightly browned. Watch carefully that the meringue does not burn.

10. Sift confectioners' sugar over the top and run the pie briefly under the broiler to give it a further light glaze.

Yield: 6 or more servings.

1. Do not make this meringue until you are ready to use it. Beat the egg whites in the bowl of an electric mixer or by hand, using a wire whisk. When they stand in peaks, beat in the 2 teaspoons of granulated sugar.

2. Continue beating the meringue until quite stiff. Blend remaining ⅓ cup of granulated sugar with the confectioners' sugar and sift this over the whites, folding the mixture in with a rubber spatula.

Yield: Meringue for a 9- or 10-inch pie.

FRENCH MERINGUE

2 egg whites

⅓ cup plus 2 teaspoons granulated sugar

½ cup confectioners' sugar

SOUR CREAM LIME PIE

Ann Seranne, who brought us into the "food world" more than four decades ago as a receptionist and sometime writer for *Gourmet* magazine, made some of the best pies in the world, kneading the dough and rolling it out with a speed and dexterity that was a marvel to behold. This is one of her best.

1. Preheat the oven to 425 degrees. Line a 9-inch pie plate with the pastry. Prick the bottom and sides of the pastry with the tines of a fork. Place the pie shell on a baking sheet and bake for 12 to 15 minutes. Let cool before filling.

2. Combine the sugar, cornstarch, butter, lime rind, lime juice, and light cream in a saucepan. Bring slowly to the boil, stirring constantly. Cook until thickened and smooth.

3. Remove from the heat and let cool. Fold in the sour cream.

4. Pour the mixture into the baked pie shell. Spoon and smooth over the sour cream topping or sweetened whipped cream. Sprinkle with grated rind, if desired.

Yield: 6 to 8 servings.

Pastry for a 9-inch pie (see recipe page 884)

1 cup sugar

3 tablespoons cornstarch

4 tablespoons butter

1 tablespoon grated lime rind

⅓ cup lime juice

1 cup light cream

1 cup sour cream

Whipped sour cream for topping (see following recipe), or sweetened whipped cream

Grated lime rind for garnish, optional

Whip the heavy cream and fold in the sugar. Fold in the sour cream and use as a topping for sweet custard pies.

Yield: 2 cups.

WHIPPED SOUR CREAM TOPPING

1 cup heavy cream

1 tablespoon confectioners' sugar

1 cup sour cream

BLUEBERRY PIE

Pastry for a 9-inch pie
(see recipe page 884)
¾ cup sugar
3 tablespoons quick-
cooking tapioca
¼ teaspoon salt
Dash of ground
cinnamon
4 cups blueberries
1 tablespoon lemon juice
1 tablespoon butter

1. Preheat the oven to 425 degrees.
2. Line a 9-inch pie plate with half the pastry.
3. Mix the sugar, tapioca, salt, and cinnamon. Sprinkle the mixture over the berries. Add lemon juice. Spoon the berries into the prepared pie plate and dot with the butter.
4. Cut the remaining pastry into strips and make a lattice top for the pie. Trim edges, moisten, and border with a strip of pastry.
5. Bake for about 50 minutes.

Yield: 6 to 8 servings.

PAPAYA COCONUT PIE

Pastry for a 9-inch pie
(see recipe page 884)
1½ cups cubed papaya or
mango out of the shell
1 cup sugar
Salt to taste
½ teaspoon ground
cinnamon
¼ teaspoon ground cloves
2 large eggs, lightly
beaten
1 cup milk
¾ cup finely grated fresh
coconut (see instruc-
tions page 864)
2 tablespoons honey,
warmed

1. Preheat the oven to 425 degrees.
2. Line a 9-inch pie plate with pastry. Refrigerate.
3. Combine the papaya and ½ cup of the sugar in a saucepan and cook over moderate heat, stirring often, until the sugar has dissolved. Cover and cook for about 5 minutes.
4. Put the remaining ½ cup of sugar in a mixing bowl. Add the salt, cinnamon, cloves, eggs, and milk. Stir in ¼ cup of the coconut. Pour the mixture into the unbaked pie shell.
5. Place in the oven and bake for 15 minutes. Reduce the oven heat to 350 degrees and continue baking for 30 minutes longer. During the last 15 minutes of baking, remove the pie and sprinkle the top with the remaining coconut. Drizzle warmed honey over the top and return to the oven to complete baking.

Yield: 6 to 8 servings.

KEY LIME PIE

Key limes, which are grown in Florida and throughout the Caribbean, are smaller and have a more pronounced flavor than the more common Persian limes.

1. Preheat the oven to 375 degrees.

2. Combine the crumbs, sugar, almonds, and butter in a bowl. Blend well.

3. Use the mixture to line the bottom and sides of a 10-inch pie plate. Bake for 8 to 10 minutes. Remove the crust to a rack and let cool.

4. Reduce the oven temperature to 350 degrees.

5. Beat the yolks in a mixing bowl. Pour in the condensed milk, stirring constantly. Add the lime juice and rind.

6. Pour the mixture into the crumb crust. Place the pie in the oven and bake for 15 minutes. Transfer to a rack and let cool.

7. In a mixing bowl, beat the egg whites until frothy.

8. Gradually add the sugar and cream of tartar, beating constantly until peaks form. Continue beating until stiff.

9. Spread the meringue over the pie, being sure to cover all the way to the edge of the crust. Bake for 5 to 6 minutes, or until the meringue is nicely browned. Remove to a rack to cool. Serve chilled.

Yield: 6 to 8 servings.

Note: If you prefer, you may ignore the meringue and spread the pie, once baked and cooled, with a layer of sweetened whipped cream.

THE GRAHAM CRACKER CRUST:

1½ cups graham cracker crumbs

¼ cup sugar

¼ cup finely chopped almonds

4 tablespoons butter, melted

THE PIE FILLING:

6 egg yolks

One 14-ounce can sweetened condensed milk, about 1¼ cups

¾ cup fresh lime juice, preferably Key limes

2 teaspoons grated lime rind

THE MERINGUE (SEE NOTE):

6 egg whites

1 cup sugar

½ teaspoon cream of tartar

VANILLA ICE CREAM

6 egg yolks
1 cup sugar
4 cups milk
1 cup heavy cream
1 vanilla bean, or
   2 teaspoons vanilla
   extract

1. Put the yolks and sugar in a heavy casserole. Beat with a wire whisk until pale yellow.

2. In another saucepan, combine the milk and cream. If the vanilla bean is used, split it down one side and add it. Bring just to the boil.

3. Add about ½ cup of the hot mixture to the egg yolk mixture and beat rapidly. Add the remaining hot mixture, stirring rapidly. Scrape the tiny black seeds from the center of the vanilla bean into the custard. Heat slowly, stirring and scraping all around the bottom with a wooden spoon. Bring the mixture almost, but not quite, to the boil. The correct temperature is 180 degrees. This cooking will rid the custard of the raw taste of the yolks.

4. Pour the mixture into a cold mixing bowl, which will prevent it from cooking further. Let stand until cool or at room temperature. If the vanilla bean is not used, add the vanilla extract at this point.

5. Pour the mixture into the container of an electric or hand-cranked ice cream freezer. Freeze according to the manufacturer's instructions.

Yield: 8 to 12 servings.

CHOCOLATE ICE CREAM

Prepare the recipe for vanilla ice cream but use only ¾ cup of sugar.

Put 8 ounces (8 squares) of chocolate in a small heavy saucepan. You can vary the chocolate to your own taste, using sweet, semi-sweet, or bitter. Or you can use a combination of two. Set the saucepan in a larger pan containing boiling water. Let the chocolate stand over its hot water bath until softened. Stir with a rubber spatula until smooth.

Add the melted chocolate to the hot vanilla custard. Pour a little of the custard into the saucepan to retrieve the chocolate that clings to the bottom and sides of the saucepan. Scrape this into the custard.

Proceed to freeze the custard as for vanilla ice cream.

LEMON LOTUS ICE CREAM

1. Trim off and discard the ends of 1 lemon. Cut the lemon into thin slices. Remove the seeds from the slices and cut the slices in half.

2. Squeeze the remaining 3 lemons and combine the juice with the sugar in a mixing bowl. Add the lemon slices and refrigerate, preferably overnight. Stir until all the sugar has dissolved.

3. Combine the half-and-half and milk in the canister of an ice cream freezer. Chill thoroughly, preferably in the freezer, for 10 to 25 minutes. Do not allow the mixture to freeze.

4. Add the lemon and sugar mixture to the cream mixture and install the canister in the ice cream freezer. Freeze according to the manufacturer's directions. Keep frozen until ready to serve.

Yield: 6 servings.

4 lemons
2 cups sugar
4 cups (1 quart) half-and-half
2 cups milk

FRESH MANGO ICE CREAM

1. In a saucepan with a heavy bottom, combine the cream, milk, egg yolks, ½ cup of the sugar, salt, and vanilla extract. Cook over low heat or in a double boiler, stirring constantly with a wooden spoon all around the bottom to make sure the custard does not stick.

2. Continue cooking and stirring until the custard is as thick as heavy cream (180 degrees). Remove the custard from the heat immediately, stirring constantly for a minute or so. Let cool.

3. Run a knife around the circumference of each mango, cutting through to the large seed in the center. Using a heavy kitchen spoon, run it inside each mango and around the seed. Scrape the flesh from the seed into a mixing bowl. Scoop out the flesh in each half. Chop the flesh and add the remaining ½ cup of sugar. Stir to dissolve. Add this to the custard and add the rum.

4. Pour the mixture into the container of an electric or hand-cranked ice cream freezer and freeze according to the manufacturer's instructions.

Yield: 8 to 10 servings.

1 cup heavy cream
2 cups milk
5 egg yolks
1 cup sugar
Salt to taste
1 teaspoon pure vanilla extract
2 fresh, ripe, unblemished mangoes
¼ cup dark rum

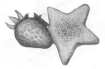

STRAWBERRY-YOGURT ICE CREAM

1 quart plain yogurt
1 pint strawberries, hulled and cut in half
1 cup sugar
6 egg yolks
1 quart milk
¼ cup heavy cream

1. Line a colander with cheesecloth and spoon and scrape the yogurt into it. Bring up the edges of the cheesecloth and tie the ends with string. Hang the cheesecloth bag in the refrigerator, letting the yogurt drip into a bowl. Let stand overnight.

2. Put the strawberries in a saucepan and add ¼ cup of the sugar. Cook over low heat, stirring often, until the sugar has dissolved. Do not cook until the berries soften.

3. Beat the egg yolks and remaining sugar in a large mixing bowl until light and lemon-colored.

4. Combine the milk and cream in a saucepan and bring to the boil. Add this gradually to the yolk mixture, beating rapidly with a wire whisk. Pour this into the saucepan and return to the boil. Cook, stirring, until the mixture coats a wooden spoon. On a thermometer, cook to 180 degrees. Do not boil or it will curdle.

5. Open the cheesecloth bag and remove the yogurt. There should be about 1½ cups. Add this to the hot custard, beating it in. Let the custard cool.

6. Partly freeze the custard in an electric or hand-cranked ice cream freezer. Add the strawberry mixture. Continue freezing until frozen.

Yield: 8 to 10 servings.

PEAR SORBET

1. Remove the core and stem from each of the pears. Peel the pears. Cut the pears in half lengthwise. Using a melon ball cutter, remove the center core. Cut away the bottom center line leading from the core to the stem end.

2. Combine the sugar and water in a saucepan. Bring to the boil and simmer for 5 minutes. Add the pears and simmer, uncovered, until the pears are tender, about 15 minutes.

3. Remove from the heat and let the pears cool in the syrup. Refrigerate until thoroughly chilled.

4. Drain the pears, but save the liquid. There should be about 1⅓ cups of liquid. Put the pears into the container of a food processor and process as fine as possible. There should be about 3 cups of purée.

5. Combine the purée, cooking liquid, and lemon juice in the container of an electric or hand-cranked ice cream freezer. Freeze according to manufacturer's instructions. Serve with strawberry sauce, if desired.

Yield: 8 to 12 servings.

4 ripe, not too firm, unblemished pears, preferably Bosc pears, about 2½ pounds

2½ cups sugar

2¼ cups water

1 tablespoon fresh lemon juice

Strawberry sauce, optional (see following recipe)

STRAWBERRY SAUCE

1. Place the strawberries in the container of a food processor or blender.

2. If fresh strawberries are used, add the sugar, or even more to taste. If frozen berries are used, remember that they are already sweetened. Purée as fine as possible.

3. Place a fine sieve inside a mixing bowl. Pour in the strawberry purée.

4. Strain the pulp through the sieve, pressing the sides with a rubber or plastic spatula. Discard the seeds.

5. Add the pear liqueur or kirsch. Chill thoroughly.

6. Serve over ice cream or sorbet.

Yield: 1½ to 2 cups.

Two ½-pint containers of fresh strawberries, or two 10-ounce packages of frozen strawberries

½ cup sugar, approximately

¼ cup white pear liqueur (eau de vie de poire) or kirsch

CANTALOUPE SORBET

2 ripe, unblemished
  cantaloupes, about
  2 pounds each
1 cup water
1 cup sugar
2 tablespoons lemon
  juice

1. Cut the cantaloupe in half and scrape out the seeds. Cut the cantaloupe halves into wedges. Using a sharp knife, cut away the skin from the flesh of each wedge. Cut the flesh into cubes. Discard the skins.

2. Put the cantaloupe flesh into the container of a food processor. Process to a fine purée. There should be 4½ to 5 cups. Chill.

3. Combine the water and sugar in a saucepan. Bring to the boil and cook for about 5 minutes. Let cool. Chill.

4. Combine the melon purée, syrup, and lemon juice.

5. Pour the mixture into the container of an electric or hand-cranked ice cream freezer. Freeze according to the manufacturer's instructions.

Yield: About 6 servings.

GRAPEFRUIT AND LEMON ICE

2 cups sugar
2 cups water
  Grated rind of
  1 grapefruit
4 cups fresh,
  unsweetened
  grapefruit juice (4 or
  5 grapefruits)
⅓ cup lemon juice

1. Combine the sugar and water in a saucepan and bring to the boil, stirring until the sugar has dissolved. Boil for 5 minutes and add the grated rind. Remove from the heat and let cool.

2. Combine the syrup, grapefruit juice, and lemon juice in the container of an electric or hand-cranked ice cream freezer. Freeze according to the manufacturer's instructions. Scoop out the grapefruit ice into a mixing bowl, packing it down. Cover with plastic wrap and place in the freezer until ready to use.

Yield: 2 quarts, or 12 to 14 servings.

Note: This ice is delectable when served with sweetened grapefruit sections steeped in a little vodka as a garnish.

ACKNOWLEDGMENTS

Many amateur cooks and professional chefs have been generous with their time and in sharing techniques and recipes that are included in this book. To all we are grateful.

Rita Alexander
Date-nut cake
Pine nut cookies

Sybil Arant
Catfish baked with cheese

Manina Anagnostou
Spanakopetes

Barefoot Caterers of Malibu (Heidi Hagman and Jonine Bernstein)
Gravlax
Spanakopitta (attributed to Eva Zane)
Mushroom-and-cheese-stuffed zucchini

Jo Bastis
Meat-filled phyllo rolls

Laura Benson
Steamed rutabaga
Gingerbread
Trifle

Jo and Angelo Bettoja
Tozzetti or biscotti

Stephen Bierman
Chicken au poivre
Chicken breasts stuffed with spinach and ricotta

Paul Bocuse
Sautéed chicken with two vinegars
Baked lobsters with vegetables

Alison Boteler
Spinach pie

Ann Bolderson
Gazpacho
Chicken Parmesan
Banana bread
Mango chutney

Clyde Brooks
French bread

Paschall Campbell
Lemon lotus ice cream

Teresa Candler
Bagna caôda

Penelope Casas
White gazpacho, Estremadura style
Polvorones, Seville style

Alain Chapel
Lime mousse

Alexa, Lygia, and Molly Chappellet
Nut and seed bread

Nancy and Robert Charles
Asparagus salad with Thai dressing
Kay Ahuja's Indian okra and onions

Charles Chevillot of La Petite Ferme
Mussels vinaigrette
Beef brochettes

Pramoda Chitrabhanu
Zucchini and tomatoes, Gujarati style
Vegetable koorma
Spiced potatoes
Pooris

Bernard Clayton
California sourdough whole wheat bread
Old Milwaukee rye bread
Cottage cheese or clabber bread
Kugelhopf

Pier Angelo Cornaro of Dell'Angelo Antico in Bergamo
Veal and artichokes
Polenta with Gorgonzola cheese

Paul Damaz
  Caldo verde

Marcel Dragon of the Stanford Court in San Francisco
  Caviar and potatoes

Sarah Elmaleh
  Spicy orange salad, Moroccan style

Neset Eren
  Shish kebab

Ann and Edward Faicco
  Pork and potato stew
  Pasta with sausages and pork

Joseph Famularo
  Pasta with ginger and garlic

Margaret Field
  Chili con carne with cubed meat

Blanche Finley
  Oven-baked chicken wings with honey

Daniel Fuchs of Maxwell's Plum in Manhattan
  Duck and string bean salad

Gail Garraty
  Broiled snappers with herbs
  Beet and yogurt soup

Ed Giobbi
  Pasta with asparagus
  Pasta with broccoli
  Penne modo mio
  Cold pasta and broccoli with pesto
  Spaghetti carbonara

Freddy Girardet
  Striped bass fillet with oysters

Eduardo Giurici of Casa Albona in Amagansett, New York
  Scungilli with diavolo sauce and linguine
  Chicken cacciatore

Arthur Gloka
  Bluefish cooked in foil

Ed Gorman
  Wash-boiler clambake

Jacques Grimaud
  Roast chicken with mustard sauce
  Tourte landaise

Sue Gross
  Sourdough French bread
  Water bagels
  Honey-chocolate cake
  Honey brownies

Montse Guillen of Montse Guillen in Barcelona
  Baked vegetables, Catalan style

Dorothy Guth
  Bourbon-pecan cake
  Creole pralines

Kathleen Haven and Marie Zazzi
  Striped bass with onions, tomatoes, and peppers
  Frijoles de olla

Marcella Hazan
  Fish steaks with oil and lemon sauce
  Homemade pasta
  Pasta with scallops
  Penne with ham and asparagus
  Pesto genovese
  Pasta with funghi trifolati
  Fried fennel

Eleanor Hempstead
  Mint surprise cookies

Eleanor Hutflas
  Clam fritters

Madhur Jaffrey
  Grilled boneless leg of lamb, Indian style
  Bengalese cabbage with mustard seeds and coconut
  Fresh green chutney

Steve Johnides
  Moussaka à la grecque

Danny Kaye
  Stir-fried oysters and shrimp
  Batter-fried scallops
  Lion's head

Diana Kennedy
  Mushroom tacos
  Green chili gordas
  Swiss walnut fingers

Sean Kinsella
  Irish stew

Chico Kobashi
Japanese skewered beef and shrimp

Gunter Kraftner of the Swedish Embassy
Matjes herring with dill and sour cream
Herring tidbits with leeks and onion

Albert Kumin
Black forest cake
Dacquoise

Aline Landais
Blanquette de veau

Suzy Larochette of Maison Arabe in Marrakesh
Striped bass with spices
Moroccan tomato salad
Bananas in ginger syrup

Pierre Larré
Pan-fried trout

Virginia Lee
Bean sauce hot fish
Stir-fried fish with tree ears
Braised ducks with leeks
Snow peas and abalone mushrooms
Chinese New Year bean sprouts
Steamed Chinese bread

Calvin Lee
Chicken wings with oyster sauce

Gaston Lenotre
Rosace à l'orange
Ambassadeur
Lemon meringue pie

Edna Lewis
Sautéed fresh roe
Lentil and scallion salad
Coconut layer cake

Aphrodite and Leon Lianides
Avgolemono soup with orzo
Roast leg of lamb with orzo
Greek salad
Seafood and orzo salad
Greek Easter bread
Walnut and almond torte
Greek Easter cookies

David Liederman
Baked lobster with herb butter (attributed to Paul Bocuse)

Marianne Lipsky
Chesa Grischuna shrimp

Joseph Luppi
Smoked chicken

Egi Maccioni
Squab with mushrooms and tomatoes
Gorgonzola-Mascarpone cheese with polenta
Spinach ravioli

Rosemary Manell
Salmon pâté
Food processor mayonnaise
Almond macaroons

Sara Mann
Chicken paprikash

Jennifer Manocherian
Leg of lamb, Persian style
Rice with dill, Persian style

Isabelle Marique
Carbonnade flamande

Barbara McGinnis
Leg of lamb with flageolets

Ismail Merchant
Pan-roasted lamb
Green beans with mustard sauce
Sheer khorma

Migliucci family of Mario's restaurant
Fried zucchini
Eggplant stuffed with prosciutto and cheese
Gnocchi di patate

Jean Mincielli of Le Duc restaurant
Raw fish with green peppercorns
Cold shrimp salad with feta cheese

Dorothy Moore
High-temperature roast leg of lamb

Pat Moore of Charles Dickens Pub
Roast ribs of beef
Fish and chips

Luigi Nanni of Nanni's and II Valetto in Manhattan
Baked stuffed clams
Clam soup
Chicken with prosciutto and mushrooms
Calamari alla Nanni
Pasta with field mushrooms
Pasta with tomatoes, basil, and hot peppers
Ragu abruzzese

Bill Neal
Charcoal-grilled stuffed quail
Huguenot torte

Amnuay Nethongkome of Bangkok Cuisine
Cucumber salad
Thai shrimp soup
Masman beef curry

Leslie Newman
Lotos salad for a crowd
Braised Chinese mushrooms
Red-cooked duck
Many flavor duck salad
Bean curd in spicy meat sauce
Noodles with hot meat sauce
Chinese roast pork
New Year's Eve fruit compote

Guy Pascal of La Côte Basque
Tuiles d'amande
Eugénie
Visidantine

Jacques Pepin
Cold zucchini soup

Jane Phalen
French bread dough

Josephine Premice
Haitian-style chicken

Paul Prudhomme of K-Paul's Louisiana Kitchen in New Orleans
Cajun popcorn
Blackened redfish
Seafood gumbo
Red beans with rice
Dirty rice

Deborah Davis Rabinowitz
Chess pie

Joseph Renggli of the Four Seasons
Striped bass in phyllo pastry
Sautéed sweet peppers
Pears stuffed with gorgonzola

Irma Rhode
Sweet potato salad

Raymond Richez
India House lamb curry
Chocolate mousse cake

Genevieve Riordan
Apple pie

Cecile Rivel
Indonesian-style chicken
Whole wheat orange bread

Maria Robbins
Shchi
Piroshki
Fau

Petita Robles
Paella

Margarita de Rosenzweig-Diaz
Pozole
Torta de masa

Rita Rosner
No-bake fruitcake

Julie Sahni
Sookha keema

Sarah Schecht
Challah

Alain Senderens of L'Archestrate in Paris
Squab with endives

Ann Seranne
Mexican quiche with chilies and cheese
High-temperature rib roast of beef
Pita bread
Sour cream lime pie

Daulat Ram Sharma of Gaylord's restaurant
Murghi massala
Spiced eggplant
Gaylord's tandoori chicken

Dinah Shore
Cioppino

Ayesha Singh
Chicken and rice casserole, Indian style

Jeri Sipe
Sesame chicken wings
Sesame chicken with garlic sauce
Spicy cucumber salad

Metita Soeharjo (and Copeland Marks)
Shrimp in coconut milk

Tjasa Sprague
Whole wheat bread

Karen Sriuttamayotin
Thai beef with Chinese vegetables

Paul Steindler
Eggs with caviar
Lobster salad à l'Aja

Wen dah Tai, formerly of Uncle Tai's Hunan Yuan restaurant
Hot and sour fish soup
Hunan beef
Chinese lamb with scallions
Shredded chicken with bean sprouts
Hunan shrimp
Sliced duck with young gingerroot

May Wong Trent
Vietnamese grilled pork patties in lettuce leaves
Sesame chicken with asparagus ring
Vietnamese grilled lemon duck

Jean Troisgros
Veal scaloppine with mustard seeds
Panaché de poisson
Salade de poulet Troisgros

Barbara Tropp
Strange flavor eggplant
Tangy noodles

Roger Vergé of Moulin de Mougins above Cannes
Roast rack of lamb with green peppercorns
Zucchini and tomato casserole
Bitter chocolate mousse

Jean Vergnes
Trout meunière with pecans
Spaghetti primavera (with Sirio Maccioni of Le Cirque)

Alfredo Viazzi of Alfredo's restaurants
Fresh mozzarella with tomatoes and anchovies
Fettucelle with tuna and anchovies
Green tagliarini with chicken livers and prosciutto
Green tagliarini with four cheeses

Jesús Villalba
Cold avocado soup
Roast suckling pig
Rice with pigeon peas
Codfish fritters

Alice Walters of Chez Panisse in Berkeley
Grilled salmon and tuna with anchovy butter
Baked goat cheese with lettuce salad
Buckwheat crêpes with glazed fruits
Calzoni

Tsung Ting Wang of the Shun Lee Palace and Shun Lee Dynasty
Hunan lamb
Pon pon chicken
Chicken soong

Eckart Witzigmann of the Aubergine in Munich
Gingerbread pudding with dark beer sabayon

Paula Wolfert
Moroccan chicken with lemon and olives
Couscous

Shirley and Peter Wood
Zucchini and nut bread

Cynthia Zeger
Chocolate cake

Index